T0369734

Red Sea Citizens

Red Sea Citizens

Cosmopolitan Society and Cultural Change in Massawa

Jonathan Miran

Indiana University Press
Bloomington & Indianapolis

This book is a publication of

Indiana University Press
601 North Morton Street
Bloomington, IN 47404-3797 USA

http://iupress.indiana.edu

Telephone orders 800-842-6796
Fax orders 812-855-7931
Orders by e-mail iuporder@indiana.edu

The paper used in this publication meets the minimum requirements of American National Standard for Information Sciences—Permanence of Paper for Printed Library Materials, ANSI Z39.48-1984.

Manufactured in the United States of America

Library of Congress Cataloging-in-Publication Data

Miran, Jonathan.
Red Sea citizens : cosmopolitan society and cultural change in Massawa / Jonathan Miran.
p. cm.
Includes bibliographical references and index.
ISBN 978-0-253-35312-2 (cloth : alk. paper) — ISBN 978-0-253-22079-0 (pbk. : alk. paper) 1. Mits'iwa (Eritrea)—History. 2. Mits'iwa (Eritrea)—Commerce—History. I. Title.
DT398.M3M57 2008
963.5—dc22

2008049093

1 2 3 4 5 14 13 12 11 10 09

To my sons, Ethan and Noam

To my sons Elliot and Noam

Contents

Acknowledgments

I am indebted to numerous individuals and institutions that assisted me in different ways throughout the years of research for this book. Field research in Eritrea in 1999–2000 was supported by an International Dissertation Research Fellowship (IDRF) provided by the Social Science Research Council and the American Council of Learned Societies, as well as by a grant from the College of Arts and Letters at Michigan State University. Funds for further archival research in Italy (2004) and a research trip to Eritrea (2006) were provided by grants from what was then the Bureau for Faculty Research at Western Washington University. Special thanks go to Geri Walker at BFR and also to Rob Stoops and David Curley in the Liberal Studies Department. The Centre Français d'Archéologie et de Sciences Sociales de Sanaa (CEFAS, Yemen) and the Centre Français des Études Éthiopiennes in Addis Ababa (CFEE, Ethiopia) assisted in funding research trips to Eritrea in 2001 and 2007. More recently, generous financial support was provided by the Alexander von Humboldt Foundation in the form of a research fellowship at the Ethiopian Studies Research Unit, Asia-Africa Institute, University of Hamburg. I am deeply grateful to Professor Siegbert Uhlig, who supported my application and made this possible. The final revisions and preparations of the book were done in Hamburg in the best working conditions one could wish for.

A draft of this book was written under the guidance of the late Harold Marcus. Harold put his confidence in me but, sadly, was not able to see the completion of this work. I owe immeasurable gratitude to David Robinson, who took over the direction of my work. I feel privileged to have studied under him, and I will always aspire to his excellence and commitment as a scholar and as a teacher. James McCann's guidance and advice as I wrote this manuscript is unequalled. His critical comments have been crucial in making this a better work. I thank both in a very special way for all their support and for teaching me the craft of history. I would also like to thank, at Michigan State, Alan Fisher, from whom I learned much.

In Eritrea I am grateful to several scholars at the University of Asmara (some formerly) who supported my research, especially in its early stages. Thanks go to Uoldelul Chelati Dirar, Abebe Kifleyesus, Richard Reid, Abdulkader Saleh, and Adhana Mengisteab. I owe a special debt of gratitude to Fr. Ezio Tonini, who directs the unique and inestimable library at the Pavoni Social Centre in Asmara. Fr. Ezio's devotion to and passion for Northeast African studies is exemplary and admirable. Certain institutions and individuals in the Muslim community in Asmara have extended pivotal assistance with my research. I would like to thank the Honorable Mufti of Eritrea, Shaykh Alamin Osman Alamin, and Shaykh Salem Ibrahim al-Mukhtar at the Dar al-Iftaʾ for their confidence and help. My appreciation goes also to the members of the Asmara Awqaf Council (in 1999–2000), who enabled me to consult the Massawa court registers, and especially its secretaries at the time, Ustadh Muhammad ʿUmar and Shaykh Ibrahim, as well as the late ʿAbdalqadir Zakariya, who at the time sat on the council as a member. At the Research and Documentation Centre in Asmara, Iyob, Aster, John, and Yusuf proved always helpful.

Very special thanks to Sayyid Hassan Muhammad ʿUthman Hayuti in Asmara. Hassan's insights offered exceptional access into some of the nuances of my subject of study. My warmest sense of gratitude goes to all those in Massawa who made me feel at home and who answered my questions with a passion for the history of their town. Many deserve appreciation and gratitude. Over the years several have become dear friends. In many ways this study is dedicated to the people of Massawa, the *Maṣawwiʿīn*, in its most inclusive sense, I should add. My deepest gratitude goes to Sayyid Sadeq al-Safi, whose kindness and generosity moved me time and again. I am also extremely indebted to Muhammad Saleh Afandi, whose assistance was always singular. Thanks also to Osman Hajji Mahmud, Hamed ʿAbd al-Baqi ʿAbbasi, Muhammad Ahmad ʿAbbasi, ʿUmar Wahhab al-Barri and Muhammad Nur Saʿid, director of the Massawa Municipal Library. I also extend thanks to Mesghenna Gebreghziabehr and his wife, Hirut, for their friendship, as well as to my former neighbors in Tewalet, Zekeria ʿAbdelkerim and Mebrahtu Ateweberhan, who conducted their dissertation research in marine biology in Massawa at the same time as I did. We shared the different pains and pleasures of doctoral field research. I must, however, confess that on particularly hot days I was ready to switch from history to marine biology. Seeing them in the morning take off on their small motor boat to "collect data" in the Red Sea waters was often more than tempting . . .

In Italy I would like to thank the staff of the Italian Archivio Storico del Ministero degli Affari Esteri, especially Stefania Ruggeri and Cinzia Maria Aicardi, and the staff of the Archivio Centrale dello Stato, also in Rome. For the consultation and reproduction of photographic documentation I am indebted to the very kind assistance of Clara Vitulo of the Biblioteca Reale in Turin, Antonella Martellucci at the Istituto Italiano per l'Africa e l'Oriente in Rome, Roberto Roda at the Centro di Documentazione Storica (Centro Etnografico Ferrarese) in Ferrara, and the staff at the Bibliothèque Nationale de France in Paris.

I am thankful to Imam Bachir Ouattara, who helped me to begin reading the Massawa court records. Thanks to the intensive sessions with Bachir in Abidjan in September 2001, I was able to build up enough confidence to continue to work with the records on my own. Several scholars have been extremely generous in providing advice or sharing information about sources. I should especially mention and thank Federico Cresti, Tom Killion, R. S. O'Fahey, and Wolbert Smidt. Special thanks to Massimo Zaccaria for his collegiality and friendship. Maria Bulakh, Saleh Mahmud Idris, and Alaa Fouda have been most kind and helpful in assisting me with various linguistic issues. Didier Morin read several chapters and offered comments. I am also grateful to Alessandro Gori for his erudite assistance on many occasions. I am greatly indebted to Fouad Makki, who read an early version of the study and provided judicious comments and suggestions. Thanks also to William Gervase Clarence-Smith, who kindly took the time to read an early draft of the study.

Other scholars who have expressed interest in my research and provided support and advice in various ways and stages over the years are Lee Cassanelli, Jay Spaulding, Irma Taddia, and Alessandro Triulzi. Beyond their encouragement, their work has been a source of inspiration to me. Immense gratitude to Bairu Tafla, whose erudition in Eritrean and Ethiopian history is unique in those fields. Special thanks go to Terry Walz, whose encouragement and help has meant a great deal to me. I thank Nancy Um for regular exchanges and advice on our various common Red Sea points of interest. Thanks also to Matt Hopper. I would also like to acknowledge my former teachers at the Institut National des Langues et Civilisations Orientales (Inalco) in Paris, where I first ventured into the

Ethiopian and Northeast African Studies. Michel Perret, Alain Rouaud, and the late Joseph Tubiana have been a source of support and inspiration over the years.

In Hamburg, Mussie Tesfagiorgis, my former student at the University of Asmara, became a close friend and helped me in many ways. Thanks to the wonderful *Encyclopaedia Aethiopica* team, to the members of the African and Ethiopian Studies Department at the Asia-Africa Institute, and to Mersha Alehegne, Getie Gelaye, and Carmen Geisenheyner. Many thanks to Matthias Schulz for preparing the maps.

For their unwavering friendship I thank Semhar Amaha and Aron Berhane in Asmara, as well as Andrea Gogröf-Voorhees, Kimberly Lynn Hossain, and Milt Krieger at WWU.

Finally, I owe the greatest debt of gratitude to my parents for their unfailing love and support over the years.

Note on Language

Since the text includes names and words in a variety of languages spoken by the peoples inhabiting the region under study, the question of transliteration is a challenging one. For Arabic names, terms, and words I tend to follow the transliteration used by the *International Journal of Middle East Studies,* but some names, such as Hijaz and Mecca, are rendered according to common usage. With words in the relevant Semitic languages of Ethiopia and Eritrea, such as Amharic, Tigrinya, and Tigre, I have chosen to spell them in a simplified form, avoiding special symbols for vowels and consonants that are not used in English. The same is true for proper names in Afar and Saho. I have judged that a scientific transliteration as practiced by philologists and linguists would render the text much less accessible. For example—somewhat inelegantly—the first, fifth, and sixth orders in the Ethiopic syllabary have become a simple "e." Nevertheless, I have in most cases maintained the *ayn* in names such as ᶜAd Temaryam or Beni ᶜAmer. With some well-known proper names, such as Massawa, I followed the standard English spelling.

Place names have presented a particular difficulty since they have sometimes been pronounced and spelled in different ways by different people, in different languages, and in various historical contexts. I have tended to choose the variant mostly used in other studies, and in some cases I have followed the common vernacular pronunciation. I have spelled places as Hergigo (and not Ḥarqīqū, Hirghigho, Archico, Arkiko [or Dohono] etc.), Emkullo (and not Moncullo, Monkulu, Um Kullū, etc.), Hetumlo (and not Hotumlo, Otumlo, Ḥuṭumlū, etc), Semhar, Zula, Sahel, Keren, and so on. The same is usually true for the Tigre and Saho-speaking groups: ᶜAd Tekles, Minifire, Bet Asgede, Asaorta, etc. In cases where I was unable to identify a place name I have followed my source and added a question mark (?) after it. However—and this lies at the heart of the difficulty of the task—I did use an Arabized version when writing the names of Tigre and Saho-speaking groups whose names (sometimes ethnogenesis) specifically derive from or are rooted in Arab-Islamic culture. Examples include the Bayt Shaykh Maḥmūd and the ʿAd Muʿallim. This is also true for the names of informants, most of whom I interviewed in Arabic.

Similarly, I have very often used an Arabic transliteration for names that appear in the records of Massawa's *sharīʿa* court in Arabic, even though the primary language spoken by some of the persons mentioned was often Tigre or Saho. I have thus followed my source, which has Arabized the names of persons appearing in court.

By adopting such an approach, I may have employed my own sort of social engineering, which does not always do justice to a far more complex reality of the instrumentality of language usage in a multi-cultural and multi-lingual zone that has been exposed to different processes of linguistic and cultural dynamics to one degree or another and in different intensities. I am fully aware that the method that I have chosen to employ is not optimal and might lead to an Arabo-centric bias, reflecting my use of certain Arabic sources as well as Eritrean Muslim elites' own relationship to an Arabic literary tradition. I hope that the text itself will clarify and offer a more nuanced appreciation of such issues.

Red Sea Citizens

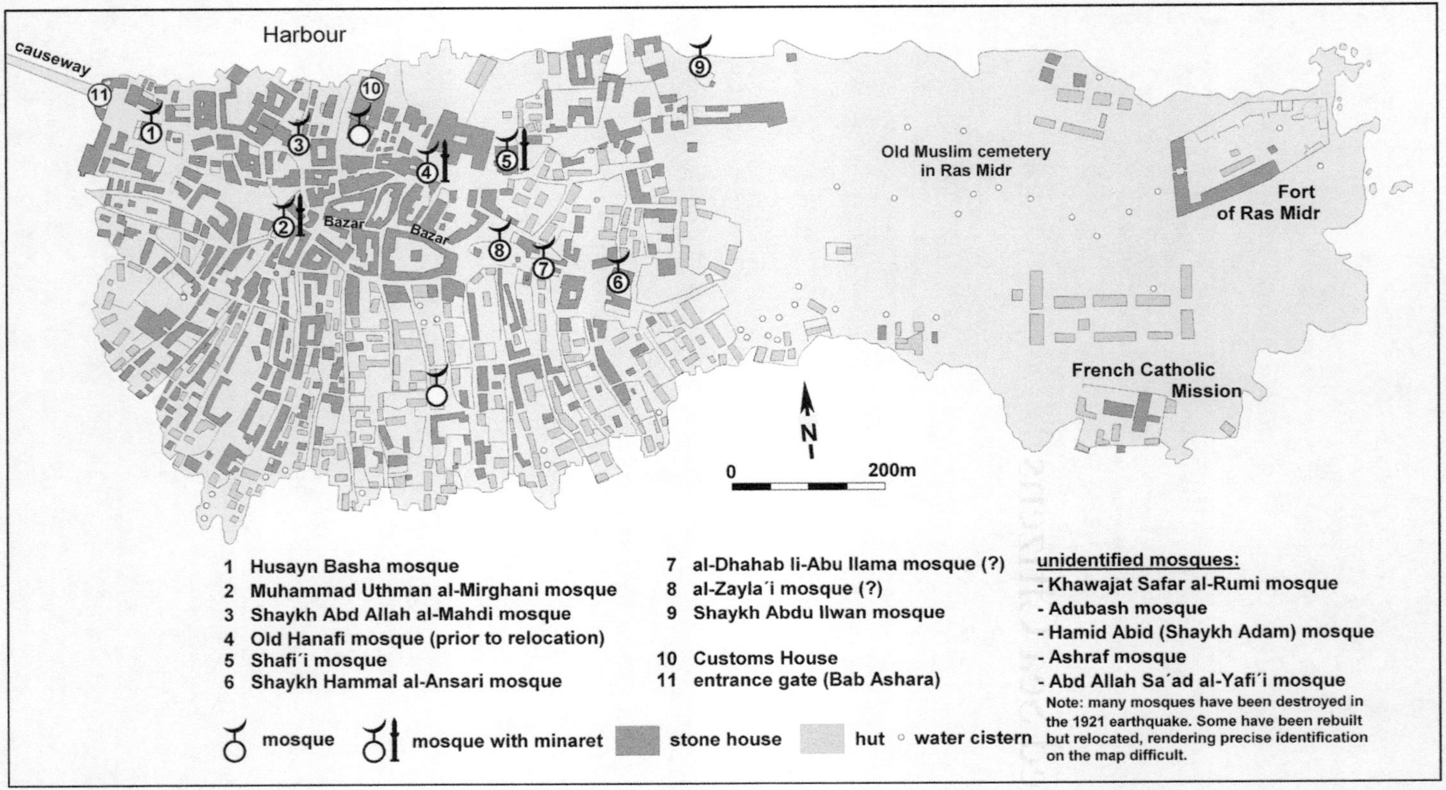

Map 1. Massawa Old Town (1885). Map by Matthias Schulz. Based on 2nd Lt. Giuseppe Brengola, Pianta di Massaua (1:2000), 24 settembre 1885, Istituto Geografico Militare.

Introduction

Facing the Land, Facing the Sea

> Massowah is a very peculiar place, both as regards its situation and the manners and customs of its inhabitants. Although geographically pertaining to Africa, the natives are more Arab than Abyssinian or Negro in character. In dress, food and domestic habits, they resemble the people of Jiddah; and I imagine there is as much African blood mixed with that of the Arabs of the seaboard of the Hijaz, as there is Arab blood in the veins of the Africans at Massowah.
> —Hormuzd Rassam, 1869[1]

> The Massowah race is far from pure; being a mixture of Turkish, Arab, and African blood.
> —Henry Blanc, 1868[2]

> The mixture of races at Massowah renders it hopeless to give its inhabitants a distinct name.
> —Walter Plowden, 1868[3]

The paradoxical character of the Red Sea port of Massawa and the identity of its inhabitants as expressed in the above somewhat puzzled statements unquestionably convey European stereotypical orientalist conceptions and discourses about peoples and places beyond "orderly" Europe. The observations also inevitably disclose an ingrained and intricate state of hybridity and sociocultural *métissage* emblematic of port-towns in the Red Sea area and beyond, at least at the time of writing. This book historicizes this process by reconstructing the economic, social, and cultural dynamics involved in the making of a complex commerce and brokerage-oriented urban society in Massawa in a period of profound change in the greater part of the nineteenth century.

Massawa is located on the African shores of the southern part of the Red Sea in what is today modern Eritrea. Cutting across the world's most arid region, the Red Sea is the saltiest and one of the hottest open seas on the globe. Massawa lies on the coast, opposite the Dahlak Archipelago, at a point where the escarpment of the highland plateau and the Red Sea are dramatically closest to each other. Massawa's infamous hot and dry climate, never failing to strike both those reaching it from the pleasantly cool highlands and those coming ashore from the breezy sea, is characteristic of most of the Red Sea littoral, on both African and Arabian shores. Today, Massawa is Eritrea's chief port and a somewhat placid and laid-back town of some forty thousand inhabitants. After having seen Ottoman, Egyptian, Italian, British, and Ethiopian occupiers in the past five centuries, it seems somehow unperturbed, serene, and fatalistic since its most recent "liberation" by the "Fighters" of the Eritrean Popular Liberation Front (EPLF) in February 1990 and the establishment of the State of Eritrea. History is ubiquitous in Massawa, or as my Sudanese friend Hishām put it so aptly after a brief visit recently, "When walking its streets one can *smell* its history." It is also true that when wandering today through the town's narrow alleys, one has to sometimes stretch the imagination in order to visualize the Massawa that this book is about—Massawa's days of greater fortune, at least for some! The sorry scenes of the ruins left by the 1990 Ethiopian Air Force bombing campaign, dingy bars with sad and sweaty prostitutes, and the decrepitude of the town's feeble population mask a vibrant Massawa of the past, often leaving in one's mind a general impression of decay and disintegration. The spiritual Qurʾānic inscriptions carved in wood or stone ornamenting numerous door lintels throughout the old town seem to belong to another world from the one inhabited by the majority of its contemporary residents.

The date of Massawa's foundation is shrouded in scholarly controversy and is impossible to establish at this stage. Scholars are still divided on the question whether the medieval Islamic Red Sea port identified by Arab geographers such as al-Yaʿqūbī, al-Ḥamdānī, al-Masʿūdī, al-Maqrīzī, and Ibn Hawqal, among others, as Bāḍiʿ, should or should not be identified as Massawa in its earlier days. The confusion is undoubtedly also rooted in linguistics since the name of Massawa in Beja is Báde and in Tigre and Tigrinya, Bāṣeʿ.[4] Those whose interpretation of the evidence

Figure Intro.1. Massawa Island, 1884. *Illustrated London News,* author's collection.

does not lead them to believe that Bāḍiᶜ refers to Massawa argue that it has been situated further north, some three hundred kilometers to the north of present-day Massawa, in the island of al-Rīḥ (or Ayrī, near the gulf of ᶜAqīq). They also argue that the foundation of Massawa possibly followed the decline of Dahlak, which had served until then as the major gateway and entrepôt serving the adjacent inlands. Be that as it may, Massawa's appearance in medieval European cartography dates to around the fourteenth or fifteenth century. It may well be the case that its first identification in medieval European cartography is in Marino Sanuto's 1321 map after Pietro Vesconte (1311) as "Nece," with a possible confusion between *n* and *b* derived from the Arabic sources. Another possible early appearance of Massawa in the sources is the planisphere of "Presbyter Johannes" attributed to Giovanni di Carignano (d. 1344) identifying "Betea."[5]

Historically, the port-town's raison d'être was to mediate between multiple commercial spheres and circuits connecting regions of the northeast African interior and beyond it with regions of the Middle East and South Asia. Historically, it replaced in that function the Axumite port of Adulis and later, after the rise of Islam, port sites such as Dahlak al-Kabīr in the Dahlak Archipelago. Massawa's ever fluctuating mercantile-oriented inhabitants operated as a Janus-faced middleman society of commercial intermediaries and cross-cultural brokers. In the sixteenth century, the port-town emerged as a focal point of contestation between Portugal and the Ottoman Empire, rooted in regional imperialist struggles for dominance in the Red Sea area and the northwestern Indian Ocean. Since then, it has continuously held a central position in the political, military, and diplomatic aspirations and schemes of the various powers who attempted to establish contact—forcefully or not—with this part of the Horn of Africa. Correctly identifying the port-town as a fitting steppingstone for making inroads into the propitious Ethiopian highlands, these powers either struggled to control Massawa, controlled it, or attempted to prevent others from controlling it.

The Ottoman Empire maintained its sovereignty over the port from the sixteenth century until 1813, when Muḥammad ʿAlī of Egypt defeated the Wahhābīs in the Hijaz. From that date until 1841 the port was under Egyptian domination but not sovereignty, which remained with the Ottoman Porte. In 1841 the Egyptians evacuated most of their acquisitions, and the Red Sea territories—including Massawa—nominally returned to the Ottomans. The Ottomans were unable to exercise effective control, and Massawa remained practically in the hands of the Balaw *nāʾibs*, a local dynasty of power brokers. In 1846 the Ottoman sultan leased Massawa and Sawākin to Muḥammad ʿAlī against payment of an annual tribute of five thousand purses, but this arrangement lasted only until 1849, when the ports again reverted to the Ottomans and were placed under the administration of Jiddah. The period during which notions of sovereignty and autonomy were radically transformed in the area culminated in 1865, when both ports were transferred to the Egyptians under Khedive Ismāʿīl, who administered Massawa and Sawākin for twenty years. The heyday of European "high imperialism" and the "Scramble for Africa" conducted Italy into the arena; in 1885 it occupied Massawa, heralding the advent of Italian colonial rule in northeastern Africa (1885–1941). In 1890 the colony of Eritrea was established, with Massawa serving as its capital until 1899, when it transferred to Asmara in the highlands.[6]

This book does not aim to provide a comprehensive treatment of Massawa's history and evolution as a coastal urban site. It examines how a particular new conjuncture (in Braudel's sense) of technological, political, economic, and migratory factors in the wider Red Sea and northwestern Indian Ocean area in the middle decades of the nineteenth century transformed Massawa. The conjuncture, or transition, witnessed the replacement of one order by a new one with particular economic, political, social, cultural, and religious characteristics and orientations that constitute the very backbone of this book. From a somnolent little port-town with no more than a handful of coral stone houses and a multitude of disorderly thatched huts in the first decades of the nineteenth century, Massawa metamorphosed into a thriving, animated, and vivacious multiethnic and cosmopolitan Red Sea hub in command of long-distance and regional trading networks spanning northeast Africa, the Red Sea area, and beyond in the final decades of the century. It also developed extended urban spaces on the mainland, a vibrant class of merchants that included some ultra-wealthy and powerful citizens who articulated—somewhat paradoxically—a strong sense of local urban yet worldly identity. The interrelated processes of what has been sometimes referred to as the "transportation revolution," specifically in this context the introduction of steamship navigation and spectacular commercial expansion, prompted heightened imperialist vying in the Red Sea and northwestern Indian Ocean areas. The opening of the Suez Canal in 1869 accelerated connections between the Indian Ocean and the Mediterranean—between Europe and its colonies or colonies to be. As one writer put it, from a "side street for maritime commerce" the Red Sea became quickly the "highway to the East."[7] The circulation of Muslim pilgrims to Mecca also expanded in spectacular ways, making a significant impact in boosting shipping and commerce in the Red Sea area. This process, referred to by one historian as the Red Sea "shipping bonanza," was characterized mainly by the amplified transregional flow of capital, labor, commercial expertise, and services, which gradually led to the reconfiguration of port hierarchies and trading circuits in the Red Sea area.[8] Intensified interconnections subsequently reorganized the structure of Massawa's commercial relationships, which, as a result, shaped the particular social and cultural makeup of the port-town's inhabitants. Massawa's excellent natural deep-water harbor accounted for and sustained its viability as a port-town, since it could easily service larger vessels following their introduction to the area.

One result of the rearrangement of the Red Sea trade system and the creation of new centers of distribution and redistribution was intensified migratory waves and patterns of circulation across the Red Sea and the western Indian Ocean expanse. Massawa rapidly became a propitious and lucrative destination for merchants, financiers, entrepreneurs, commercial agents, brokers, porters, pearlers, fishermen, and also slave traders from overseas, from places such as Egypt, the Hijaz, Hadramawt, and the Tihāma plain in the Arabian Peninsula, and from Gujarat in northwestern India. At the same time it drew a growing number of Afar-, Saho-, and Tigre-speaking pastoralists from the coastlands and interior, who migrated into the burgeoning port-town and provided it with a variety of brokering, peddling, and labor services. Migrants eventually connected and reconnected to systems of family, business, transportation, and labor networks ranging from the Indian subcontinent to the Arabian Peninsula and the eastern Mediterranean and into the African hinterlands.

Overseas and inland migrants who settled in Massawa and made it their home gradually developed notions of culture that both made them distinctly *Massawan* and at the same time epitomized what I call a "Red Sea society." If on one level Massawans shared social and cultural affinities (and business interests) with the inhabitants of other Red Sea ports such as Sawākin, Jiddah, Ḥudayda, and Luḥayya, they also preserved and cultivated their own specificity, stemming from the particular geographical context and the historical development of their town. The local/universal dialectic in this context mirrored the discursive breadth and possibilities that provided Massawans the means to negotiate their identity(ies) in different contexts. In reconstructing these complex notions of society and culture I refute essentialist perceptions that see Massawa as either somehow alien to its "African" environment (e.g., "Arab," "Turkish," "Ottoman"), or, on the other hand, "Eritrean" from times immemorial. Ideological and cultural influences and orientations (conveyed and articulated by migrants, imperial states, or nations) were struggled over, appropriated, and localized by Massawans, who refashioned them to create new notions of identity and culture.

The new historical conjuncture not only *made* a new town in the physical sense, but also generated among Massawans the development of new—one could say "modern" and "cosmopolitan"—self-perceptions/designations, ideas, and ideals about identity and a sense of self-awareness of their place in multiple frames of reference. While the application of the term as an analytical category is often fuzzy, I follow a fairly standard understanding of "cosmopolitanism" as a broadly defined "social project that exists outside the confines of kinship, ethnicity or nationality," which implies a consciousness of human diversity and usually refers to a trans-communal society. Yet "cosmopolitanism" can also refer to the challenge or aspiration to create unity in a context of social diversity.[9] This fits well in the context of Massawa, where in response to a rapidly changing social and cultural environment, and in trying to project some sense of unity within a social environment of diversity, the town's leading inhabitants defined their community through commercial, social, religious, and cultural strategies, negotiated on a continuum spanning the "local" and the "global," and promoting a distinct idealized sense of citizenship, of "being Massawan." Urban dwellers perceived their town as a socially and culturally bounded corporate entity that gradually, and on one level, had transcended particularistic and sectarian identities to become what could be understood as "cosmopolitan."[10] In more material terms, belonging to this cultural, or moral, community, as anthropologist Abner Cohen put it, usually indicated some type of mediating occupation connected with the town's commercial operations, especially as a merchant or agent.[11] A sense of historical permanence and a strong identification with the physical setting of the town were also central manifestations of the corporate ethos. It also meant possessing a strong awareness of one's Muslim identity as a basis of solidarity and ethics, a sense of attachment to the wider *umma*, and a sense of connectedness to Arab history and Arab culture. Another crucial marker of the Massawa esprit de corps was manifested in expressions of urban identity, which translated first and foremost into being part of a locally renowned family with a patronym, and usually living in a residential complex built in coral stone. In some senses these characteristics remind one of comparable sociocultural dynamics in towns of the East African coast, where the Swahili proudly refer to their own sense of *utamaduni*, "urbanity, being urban," but also "being civilized."

I devote significant discussion to the institution of the family, which was fundamental to the town's merchant elites and the articulation of its social and cultural disposition. These central themes are complemented by analyses of the material and non-material strategies of integration, sources of urban authority (different forms of capital) and the access that they enabled into transregional networks, the role of Islam in town and countryside, the relationships between urban space and religious symbolism, and the different arenas of struggle over the establishment of a new communal moral order in a period of rapid economic and social change. The book unveils first and foremost complex processes of formation of society and culture in a northeast African Red Sea port. It imagines social spaces through the reconstruction of social, cultural, material, and religious networks and webs of connections. At the same time it reveals the inner workings of a community of intermediaries and brokers by reconstructing the commercial and social webs of networks and relationships that connected land and sea, that linked inland producers and consumers with overseas importers and exporters in long-distance trade. In many ways Massawan brokers tied these fields and spheres together.

Horizons Multiplied: Spaces, Connections, and Circuits in the Red Sea Area

In recent years, historians and other social scientists have questioned the usefulness of the traditional area-studies paradigm. They argue that the

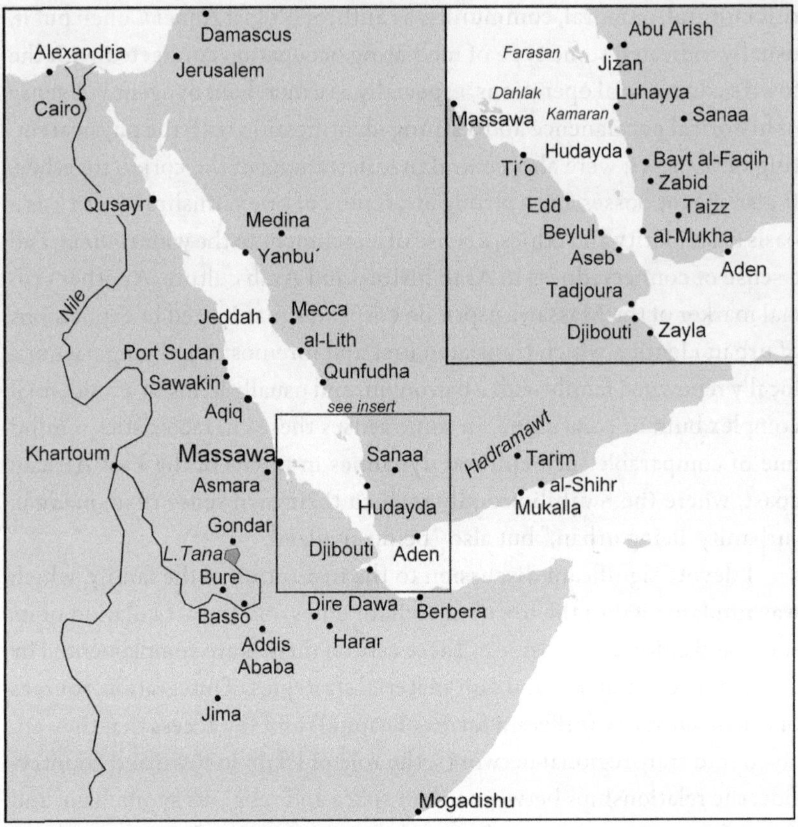

Map 2. The Red Sea Area. Map by Matthias Schulz.

arbitrary erection of boundaries between continents, geographical areas, and civilizations limits our understanding of the flexible and complex connections and cross-cultural contacts that may create more useful spaces of analysis. Accordingly, scholars understand the Indian Ocean as a cultural complex that should be analyzed from within a framework that transgresses the rigid geographical divisions of Africa, the Middle East, the Indian subcontinent, and Southeast Asia. New scholarship therefore devotes greater attention to the movement of people, commodities, and ideas across the ocean and the ways in which these interactions contributed to shaping societies and cultures in the regions bordering it. Few areas epitomize so strikingly the artificiality of traditional area-studies boundaries such as the Red Sea and Gulf of Aden region, where "Africa" and "Asia" are separated by a body of water that has never precluded extensive human contact between both shores—sometimes, and in some places, on a quasi-daily basis.[12] Indeed, I argue for a more subtle and useful understanding of the Red Sea area—one that perceives this arena as a cultural corridor that historically could serve as both an interface and—before the introduction of steamship navigation and due to a particular wind regime—a barrier between the Indian Ocean and the Mediterranean Sea, and whose coastal inhabitants share distinct cultural affinities.[13]

One of the consequences of the recent rising academic interest in world and global history is the growing attention devoted to history from the perspective of seas and oceans, or what two scholars have coined "the new thalassology."[14] No one would claim that the interest is new. Fernand Braudel's magisterial study of the Mediterranean has inspired (and intimidated) historians who have come to see it as the prototype sea history. If studies of the Indian Ocean have relatively recently stimulated a handful of undaunted historians to attempt overarching analyses of this body of water in seeking interregional arenas, interconnections, continuities, and discontinuities, smaller seas such as the Red Sea still await to be studied as historical spaces.[15] Nevertheless, recent years have witnessed several attempts to address this lacuna in the form of conferences, specialized panels, doctoral dissertations, and several publications on various Red Sea–related subjects. Some have attempted—still quite timidly—to cross the Red Sea, so to speak, transgress conventional geo-cultural and area-studies boundaries, and address the more conceptual questions of interactions between both shores of this body of water.[16] One can hope that more research in this direction will be conducted in coming years, as well as comparative studies of Red Sea port cities and towns such as Jiddah, Sawākin, and various ports of the Tihāma plain, where multicultural, or cosmopolitan, communities unveil conspicuous transregional connections.[17] Interestingly, recent historical studies on transregional connections and interactions in the Arab/Persian Gulf are tackling some of these questions in promising ways.[18]

New approaches to area studies or regional history should, however, have the global in mind, or as historian Frederick Cooper aptly wrote, such studies should target "more than local and less than global."[19] In this book I weave the local with the supralocal, the regional, and the cross-regional—I link Massawa and its hinterlands with the sea and the port's forelands in a way that may help us imagine new historical spaces, irrespectively of both geographical and political borders. Indeed, the story of Massawa bears implications that reach further than the local urban history of a Red Sea

Figure Intro.2. Panorama of Massawa, ca. 1895.
Photographer: Luigi Naretti. Biblioteca Reale, Torino.

town. It is a story of a town and the dynamic political, economic, social, and cultural relationships and connections to its hinterlands and, across the seas, to its forelands. These connections reveal the fluidity and flexibility of boundaries, both in time and in space, and help us to creatively imagine new sociospatial arenas, especially in those interstitial areas—such as the Red Sea—that fall between larger traditional geographical and political units, corroborating what Lewis and Wigen had called the "myth of continents."[20]

More concretely, one can clearly imagine Massawa within a spatial contour of several transregional political spheres of influence, commercial circuits, and religious webs of networks that connected in variegated ways spaces between northeast Africa, Arabia, and South Asia. For example, Ottoman and Egyptian regional dominance from the sixteenth to the nineteenth centuries created spaces connecting Egypt, the Sudan, the Hijaz, the Yemen, the Eritrean coasts, and beyond. Soldiers and governors, but also languages, modes of administration, and traditions of authority moved across the area. The hegemony of the *nāʾibs*, who dominated the Eritrean coastlands between the early eighteenth and mid nineteenth centuries, and the intermixing of Ottoman soldiers with coastal Balaw lineages, reveal conspicuous ways in which Ottoman indirect rule made an impact on shaping regions in the Red Sea area's inlands. Long-distance cross-Saharan trade circuits and networks culminating on the African shores of the Sudanese and Eritrean coasts, tied to maritime trade in the Red Sea and the northwestern Indian ocean, moved around commodities (using comparable brokerage institutions), slaves, and capital but also merchants, entrepreneurs, and agents across the spaces spanning Africa, Arabia, and South Asia.

An excellent example of how capital, commodities, and labor came together in the Red Sea space is the pearling economy in the Dahlak Archipelago, connecting South Asian financiers with Persian Gulf, Hijazi, Yemeni, and "African" pearl-divers, brokers, boat owners, and captains. The pearling economy produced one of Massawa's wealthiest merchants, ᶜAlī al-Nahārī (d. 1930/31), who had traded directly with Europe and India and had invested his earnings in real estate in Paris in the early decades of the twentieth century. Henry de Monfreid (1879–1974), the eccentric French adventurer, commercial entrepreneur, arms and drug smuggler and author of dozens of books, immortalized ᶜAlī al-Nahārī (referred to as "Saïd Ali") as one of the principal characters in his first book, and one of his most known, *Les secrets de la mer Rouge*.[21] The type of "micro-history" illustrated in the case of the Dahlak pearling economy proves especially useful in capturing interregional connections and reveals clearly its global dimensions.[22] From a religious perspective, several Sufi webs of networks growing out of the so-called Islamic Revival in the long nineteenth century (such as the Khatmiyya *ṭarīqa*), tied the Hijaz, the Sudan, the Eritrean region, and the Yemen together in several types of scholarly and "missionary" circuits. Political, economic, and religious interconnections and networks became significantly more conspicuous in the Red Sea area as the interrelated succession of technological, economic, and political change beginning in the second third of the nineteenth century intensified and amplified the flow of capital and manpower (labor and specialized services), but also ideas and culture.

Capturing the Edge: Writing Massawa into the Historical Record

A crucial question that such a multi-angled vantage point poses is how should one organize a study of Massawa in terms of time and space? In considering a port-town that lies at a geographical and historical meeting point of several "frontiers" between the Red Sea and the facing Arabian Peninsula, the Sudanese Nile valley, and the northern Ethio-Eritrean highland plateau, and whose interaction with all these spheres has shaped its historical evolution, how does one amalgamate these multiple historical frames of reference into a more or less coherent narrative? Clearly, the history of Massawa in my time concern cannot be written within the framework of "national" or "imperial" histories. Massawa has been on the periphery of both the Ottoman Empire and khedival Egypt's African empire; it has also been on the "margins" of the historic Ethiopian state. How does one tackle peripheries and margins in historical writing? In this book I adopt an approach that writes Massawa into a historical narrative that emerges from a multi-layered dynamic perspective that brings to the fore the local, the regional, the transregional, and the interactions and spatial connections between all these spheres. Transgressing analytical categories such as states, nations, ethnic groups, and political boundaries, I emphasize a more regional perspective by focusing on the history of Massawa as shaped by economic, social, cultural, and religious dynamics at work in its urban environment, its close and more distant hinterlands, and its forelands and in the interplay between these spheres.[23] This approach blurs conventional borders and cuts across both spatial and temporal boundaries as they have been conceptualized in the past and promotes a more flexible understanding of the history of a Red Sea port-town as shaped by its interaction with both land and sea. It also attempts to cut through the particular traditions and epistemologies (e.g., "orientalist," "imperialist," "colonialist," "Islamic," "nationalist") that have characterized the production of knowledge on the Horn of Africa at large.

I believe that an approach emphasizing continuities, but also discontinuities, in structures and processes carries the analysis beyond historical narratives that see sharp breaks and divides between historical periods such as the Ottoman period (16th century to 1865), the Egyptian period (1865–85), and the Italian period (1885–1941). The temporal scope of the study subverts the chronological divisions based on traditional views of the area's political history. Instead, it perceives the commercial transformation of the Red Sea region, beginning in the 1840s as a threshold and a pivotal motor for change in multiple fields, including the social, the cultural, and also the political itself. Commercial change gave rise to competition and conflict between Ottomans, Egyptians, northern Ethiopians, and the coastland-based *nāʾibs*, eventually leading to major changes in notions of imperial control and sovereignty in the region. My time frame thus spans the transition between different occupiers (or colonial powers) and exposes how Massawans managed to create niches and exploit opportunities as well as overcome the challenges offered by the change that culminated with a European colonial–dominated economy by the early twentieth century.

Past historiography has exclusively tended to attach Massawa to politically dominant forces in the region and ignored the multifaceted dynamics of its historical experience. In northeastern Africa, this tendency has placed the centralized highland Ethiopian polity, in its historically varied configurations, as the central organizing theme of the history of the area. Writing from the "center" (and from the highlands)—physically or mentally—has produced an often biased, limited, and rather rigid understanding of the fluid political, social, economic, and cultural dynamics at play among the various societies that inhabit the wider region, especially in the peripheries.[24] Such approaches have also contributed to the writing of history "backward," from present to past, in a teleological perspective. This approach has promoted inflexible and static understandings of the historical trajectories of Massawa, the northern lowlands, and the Red Sea coasts, viewed as a marginal periphery, having a unique and exclusive role: Ethiopia's access to the sea.[25] Rigid perceptions understand the port of Massawa as Ethiopia's port, the "Gateway to Ethiopia" or the outlet of the Ethiopian long-distance trade, without taking into consideration other political, economic, and social factors shaping its evolution.[26] Contemporary politically motivated *claims* to historical sovereignty over the port should not be confused with actual connections and relationships in the past. Notwithstanding its important historical role in the political and commercial relations between highland Abyssinian polities and the outside world, Massawa's history as a trade emporium and an entrepôt has not always been exclusively dependent on its relationship with Ethiopian highland polities. To say it in other words, the sea, not only the dominant polities in the port's inland, has had a significant impact in shaping Massawa's historical orientation.

In the nineteenth century, the development of steam navigation, the redeployment of new port hierarchies, and the reconfiguration of the Red Sea seascape strongly influenced the evolution of Massawa as a port and as a town. Similarly, the new regional dynamics generated by the ascending aspirations and effectiveness of Egyptian dominance in the Red Sea area made a direct impact on the development of Massawa—the composition of its population, new patterns of migration, and its innate mercantile disposition. Egyptian efforts to link its economy more closely to its surroundings from the 1860s onward resulted in the redefinition of its closer hinterlands, involving new patterns of production, exchange, and trade. In political terms, Massawa's long-term association with the Ottoman Empire and Egypt has attached its administrative and political, but also institutional, social, cultural, and even architectural, orientation to other Red Sea ports such as Jiddah, Sawākin, Ḥudayda and Luḥayya, to take only a few examples.[27]

In this context it is worth noting that, although Massawa was situated in the Ottoman periphery, the reconstruction of its history adjoins other studies on the urban history of the late Ottoman Empire. These studies reassess the economic, social, and cultural transformation of Ottoman cities and port-towns resulting from the structural transformations of the global economy in the nineteenth century. Such work makes an effort to move away from previous historically deterministic paradigms that tended to place the "West" as the only referent of social change in Ottoman urban settings in that period. Exemplifying this new research is the volume *The Empire in the City,* which establishes the historical agency of the Ottoman state in the process of modernization, emphasizes the cultural dimensions of urban change, and explores the changing functions of cities and towns from the perspective of center-periphery relations in the late Ottoman Empire.[28] In this context one of the aspects of my study shows how since 1865 khedival Egypt's promotion of its own *mission civilisatrice* in Massawa (but also in Sawākin) had an important impact on the development of the town's urban spaces and administrative institutions and its practices, social composition, and cultural orientations. Although some Egyptian and Ottoman ideas about "modernity" were strongly inspired by Europe, this indirectly disproves those still widely held views that see the advent of Italian colonial rule in 1885 as the sole significant break between a pre-colonial order and a colonial order that was responsible for bringing the modern to "dark Africa."

Thanks to its strategic location, Massawa was occupied by Ottomans, Egyptians, Italians, British, and Ethiopians before the State of Eritrea gained its independence in 1993. This historical trajectory has also subjected the port-town to multiple, and often competing, ideological representations and discourses, at times utterly opposed to each other. Since the 1940s Eritrean representations of Massawa have played a role in the construction of nationalist ideologies and conceptions of identity in Eritrea and thus displayed discursive dichotomies (real or imagined) between highlanders and lowlanders, Christians and Muslims, and also pro- and anti-independence aspirations. During this period the cultural orientation of Eritrean nationalism was still not well defined, and different kinds of historical and popular representations reflected the dynamics of cultural competition.[29] For example, in their attempt to rally Eritrean Muslims and define the specificity of their identity, pro-independence Muslim community leaders, nationalists, and intellectuals discussed and wrote about Massawa's unique and symbolic position in Eritrea's Islamic past. In their writings, they perceived Massawa, Hergigo, and the Dahlak Archipelago as important historical centers of religion and culture, intimately related to the Islamic world and the Middle East. These writings portrayed Massawa and Hergigo as the first important "civilized" settlements and urban political and administrative centers in the country.[30] Arab and Islamic-centered perceptions of Eritrea, placing Massawa and its area at the center of a rich and glorious Islamic past in the region, were grafted onto the 1960s and 1970s by the sectarian Arab and Muslim-oriented liberation movements.[31] Indeed, some of the most prominent leaders and ideologues of these movements, such as ʿUthmān Ṣāliḥ Sabī, were themselves from Hergigo.[32]

Throughout the thirty-year Eritrean struggle for independence and up to this day, a critical ideological cleavage has existed between so-called Ethio-centric and Eritrean nationalist views. These two conflicting views show how the histories of Massawa and the coast have been instrumental in furthering politically oriented ideological agendas. Rigid Ethio-centric views still claim Massawa and the Red Sea coast as forming part of a historical "Greater Ethiopia" that had traditionally maintained some type of sovereignty over the rulers of the coast. Eritrean nationalists, in contrast, claim the "Eritrean-ness" of Massawa and the coast since time immemorial. Following the independence of Eritrea in 1993, voices called for the setting in motion of a process of the "liberation of its historiography."[33] Interestingly, and ironically reminding one in some sense the atmosphere of the 1940s, these early years generated a host of nationalist and cultural discourses expressed by Massawans and Eritreans about Massawa's history and particular cultural features. These expressions appeared in the nascent Eritrean press and in local publications. Their importance for me as a historian was that they opened windows onto particular constructions of identity that somewhat paradoxically—and very interestingly—portrayed Massawa as having a specifically distinct historical trajectory—and hence culture and identity—but at the same time was naturally "Eritrean" from times immemorial. Particularistic and collectivist-nationalist discourses seemed to somehow merge at that moment.[34] The approach adopted in this study does not revert to rewrite history from present to past, this time from the perspective of an Eritrean nationalist meta-narrative. Somewhat against the grain, the study attempts to, once again, "rescue history from the nation," as Prasenjit Duara put it (and from "empire," I would add), and grows from and focuses on the peoples and societies of a particular region in the nineteenth century—societies that today form part of the Eritrean nation. Having said that, I should add that it is the success of the Eritrean nationalist movement and the establishment of the State of Eritrea that indirectly enabled historians to focus the historical enquiry on that region and practically gain access to an area in northeast Africa that was closed to researchers for long decades. But, as we know from other cases, and as might be "natural" and understandable from the perspective of the phenomenon of nationalism, young nations seldom engage in critical, complex, or self-doubting historical enquiry before passing through a myth-making stage.

The adoption of such an approach joins a revisionist effort in the historiography of northeast Africa aiming to inscribe the societies and regions peripheral to the traditionally (and historiographically) dominant Ethiopian polity into the historical record. The lack of attention to the peripheries stems also from the particular epistemological orientation in the context of the field of Ethiopian studies, which follows a long-standing and rich philological approach (as a branch of the field of Semitic studies) mainly focusing on the study of Geʿez-language manuscripts. The production of knowledge in this context has thus tended to almost exclusively focus on Christian, Semitic-speaking highlanders. This book attempts to shed greater light on a so-called peripheral area and link it to a broader scholarly environment that engages more actively with the concerns and problems addressed in the fields of African, Middle Eastern, Indian Ocean, and world history.[35] It is in many ways a bridge linking the Horn—geographically, conceptually, and comparatively—with its wider region and promotes an approach that seeks to dynamically link the Ethiopian *orbis* with its broader environment.

A last set of remarks—and, indirectly, somewhat of a caveat—concerns the perception of Massawa in the "scholarly imagination" in regard to its role and position in the slave trade. In the course of my years of research I have encountered many a scholar who instinctively and primarily associated the town and its history with the slave trade. While it is known that slaves—approximately 111,000 for the entire nineteenth century, according to Ralph Austen's cautious estimate—were exported through the port of Massawa, one would be surprised to learn how little we actually know about that facet of Massawa's history and how flimsy is the evidence (mostly anecdotal travelers' observations and estimates).[36] By this remark

I in no way intend to minimize Massawa's role as one of the important ports in northeast Africa through which slaves, chiefly from southern and western Ethiopia and the Nile Valley area, had been exported across the Red Sea to the Arabian Peninsula. There is no doubt that the process of commercialization and its consequences, which constitutes the broader structural contextual framework of my story, has fueled slavery in the area. Yet, while slaves and slavery inevitably and intermittently appear (and disappear) in the narrative that follows, with the exception of an analysis of manumission acts registered in the Islamic court of Massawa between 1873 and 1885, this study does not offer new data or interpretation about the role of Massawa as a slave-exporting port. We are still in the dark as to many questions, among which are the identity of the slave traders, the proportion between free and unfree labor in Massawa, the role played by slaves and later freed slaves in the urban economy and in the Dahlak pearling industry, and the impact that such individuals or groups may have had on local culture and society. The title of Ehud Toledano's recent book on slavery in the Middle East, *As If Silent and Absent,* captures aptly the historian's frustration when approaching the sources. Unsurprisingly, beyond the odd "we are not proud of that part of our history," the collection of oral data does not reach far in that respect.[37]

Coastal Cosmopolitans: Between Local and Global

> To be truly cosmopolitan, a man must be
> at home even in his own country.
> —Thomas Wentworth Higginson

Massawa's urban dwellers have historically performed the role of commercial mediators and cultural brokers between partners situated in multiple commercial settings in transregional systems of long-distance trade. It is therefore inherently a place where people and culture mix; a perfect *lieu de métissage,* a locus of intermixing *par excellence.* Studying Massawa's mercantile community inescapably relates to wider questions and debates about the social and cultural formation and transformation of coastal mercantile communities at large. In eastern Africa, scholarship and debates revolving around the history, culture, and competing notions of identity of the Swahili-speaking peoples have produced sophisticated and contentious results over the years. By analyzing archaeological, linguistic, and historical evidence historians and anthropologists of East Africa have convincingly refuted the "alien origin" theory of coastal societies and have proposed interpretive frameworks for understanding the dynamics of Swahili history and identity formation in terms of internal forces and negotiated discourses.[38] East African coastal communities have developed in close relation to their hinterlands and increasingly differentiated from them due to their role in cross-cultural brokerage mediating between economic spheres of production, exchange, and commerce in both hinterlands and forelands. Balanced views of Swahili history assume the African roots of the Swahili, interpreting their origins and civilization in a cultural, rather than a racial or ethnic sense.[39]

Reminding the spirit of outdated historical writing on East African "Swahili" towns, historian Ghada Hashim Talhami observed that "although greatly dependent on the caravan trade of the African interior, Massawa and Suakin remained, for most of their history, alien enclaves on the Sudanese and Ethiopian coastlines." She added, "Although they included some indigenous elements, the people of Suakin and Massawa were basically different from the tribes of Kassala and the Semhar."[40] Echoing this idea, Gabriel Warburg wrote that "both Suakin and Massawa had the characteristics of Red Sea towns, rather than African ones, as was evident in their mixed populations, architecture and modes of dressing and living. Only after they were ceded to the khedive Ismaʿil in 1865 were they forced to rely on their African hinterland for their economic development."[41] Similarly, M. C. Jedrej noted that "not only were Suakin and Massawa political dependencies of the Ottoman *vilayet* of Jedda, these towns were also Arabian rather than African in a cultural sense and therefore resembled Jedda, Hodeida and Mocha rather than the settlements of the Nile Valley in the interior of Africa."[42] Although the first part of Warburg's observation correctly points to the cultural distinctiveness of Red Sea port-towns—a phenomenon that I propose to deconstruct and historically contextualize—this book directly challenges perceptions viewing Massawa as an alien element in its environment. The coastal urban settlements of Massawa and Hergigo were, from their inception, intimately linked to their hinterland and interior in a dense web of relationships and networks, and were thus very "African" (today some would say "Eritrean") settlements from their grass roots. Moreover, since at least the eighteenth century, the Ottoman imperial framework of decentralized rule placed the *nāʾibs*, a local dynasty of power holders, in a position of autonomy and dominance in Massawa and its hinterlands. This process contributed significantly to the formation of the political, economic, and even cultural foundations of a *region* gravitating toward Massawa, which can also be perceived as a "regional capital." Indeed, one of my principal arguments is that scholarly and popular accounts—both external and internal—have overemphasized Massawa's outgoing and "foreign" character by focusing on cultural discourses and representations without contextualizing their instrumentality and without tracing their historical evolution. It seems to me important to contextualize historically Massawa's specificity and analyze the development of its culturally outgoing dispositions, but at the same time locally rooted social realities.

Several models have attempted to explain the structure and operation of cross-cultural brokers. The anthropologist Abner Cohen was among the first to articulate the idea of a trade diaspora as a community whose constitutional strategy was to monopolize a certain commodity, a trade route or a particular stage in the process of long-distance trade. In order to accomplish this, Cohen wrote that "a diaspora of this kind is distinct as a type of social grouping in its culture and structure. Its members are culturally distinct from both their society of origin and from the societies among which they live."[43] Cohen suggested that trade diasporas tended to develop autonomous informal political and judicial organizations in order to provide stability and order and thus respond successfully to external pressures. While I do not find the concept of "trade diaspora" particularly useful in the context of Massawa, Cohen's model corroborates the existence of certain urban institutions in the port-town that were dominated by local merchant families, institutions such as the *sharīʿa* court, the "Local Council" and the professional offices, all controlling and regulating local commercial interests, communal affairs, and social practices.[44] The members of such a community, Cohen suggests, "form a moral community which constrains the behavior of the individual and ensures a large measure of conformity with common values and principles."[45] Such insights are, in principle, useful in thinking about the evolution of the history of Massawa's mercantile-oriented society. The case of Massawa suggests that, among other factors, the monopolization of commercial mediation by the town's merchants gradually led to the development of expressions of a distinct sense of solidarity or feeling of belonging together—what Max Weber called a *Zusammengehörigkeitsgefühl*—serving to define the social borders of the community and maintain its role in brokerage operations.[46]

In periods of intensified commercial vitality and opportunities—such as the middle decades of the nineteenth century—local mercantile individuals and families originally from the Semhar, Sahel, Barka, Dahlak islands, and Tigray regions, on the one hand, and Egyptian, Hijazi, Ye-

Figure Intro.3. The French consulate in Massawa (Bayt Bā Ḥamdūn), 1886. Photographer: Firmin André Salles. Bibliothèque Nationale de France, Paris.

meni, Hadrami, and Indian merchants and entrepreneurs, but also Ottoman soldiers and officials, on the other, settled in Massawa. Some gradually intermixed and made a community that developed certain notions about themselves as a group, based on idealized cultural, religious, and social affinities. This cosmopolitan urban culture was characterized by specific notions of prestige, status, authority, and power, involving complex mechanisms of translating material capital to social and symbolic forms of capital and vice versa. The distinct social structure of Massawa's urban community placed the institution of the family as a tightly knit corporation at the center of social and economic life. Most high-status families, including the *ashrāf* and the *sayyid*s, maintained their sociocultural distinction by intermarrying among themselves, by taking women in Arabia, Yemen, and in Red Sea ports, and by marrying into established families in Massawa. However, they also married into locally prestigious Muslim families among the Tigre- and Saho-speaking clans such as the Balaw, the Bayt Shaykh Maḥmūd, the ʿAd Shaykh and the ʿAd Muʿallim. These alliances enabled them to reproduce their high status and deal with family relatives, who were also business associates, in other Red Sea ports such as Jiddah, Sawākin, Luḥayya, Ḥudayda, and Qunfudha and at the same time with kin-related groups of the African interior. It is also through such marriage links that they established themselves locally, that they and their offspring "became native," or as one scholar put it when discussing Hadrami *muwalladīn,* "local cosmopolitans."[47] Massawa families constituted the link between these worlds. In cultural terms, these processes resulted in a competition over religious and cultural prestige involving mainly their association to prestigious origins and descent. Designation and self-designation as "Arabs" could be functional in such a locality but did not always reflect locally grounded social realities.

In such a setting, it is not surprising that conceptions of identity and self-designation have always preoccupied Massawans. Several informants in Massawa told me the following revealing anecdote. After the independence of Eritrea in 1993, the government had asked all the country's residents to fill out an application form for the issuance of an Eritrean identity card. Applicants were asked to fill in their "Ethnic Group" (Ar. *qawmiyya*) and their "Tribe" (Ar. *qabīla*). According to one informant, the town dwellers filled "Tigre," the region's ethnic majority, under "Ethnic Group," but entered "Massawan" (Maṣawwiʿī) under "Tribe." According to another informant, the application form distributed by the government generated a sense of uneasiness among town's inhabitants since they did not belong to any ethnic group but were organized in families. According to that version, they refused to note their ethnic belonging as "Tigre." The authorities finally accepted the claim and permitted the town dwellers to inscribe their family name as their ethnic affiliation. Yet another version of the story suggests that indeed, Massawans entered "Tigre" as their ethnicity, but left the space under "Tribe" blank, or inscribed "none." I would assume that there were different responses to the form—a phenomenon that is in itself revealing and enlightening as to the fluidity, diversity, subjectivity, vagueness, and, more than anything, potentially paradoxical nature of notions of identity in such a setting.[48] Indeed, questions such as who founded Massawa? who is a "true" Massawan? and what does it mean to be Massawan? are all open issues that are still debated and struggled over in friendly, yet passionate, arguments in Massawa's cafés, still nowadays. Especially, I should add, following the meddling of the odd historian, posing intentionally provocative questions!

Massawans today convey in interviews a strong sense of group identity—even if partly anecdotal and without a doubt invoking more recent constructions of identity and culture conditioned throughout Eritrea's turbulent history in the second half of the twentieth century. Self-designations suggesting a community sui generis, such as *ahl Maṣawwa*ᶜ (Ar., the Massawa family), or expressions such as *nazionalità di Massawa* (It., Massawa nationality, or citizenship), constantly come up in conversations.[49] Attempting to explain this sense of tight-knit yet cosmopolitan identity, one informant who traces the arrival of the first member of his family to Massawa from Egypt in the mid-nineteenth century said that "the townspeople identified with Massawa. They were *shaᶜab Maṣawwa*ᶜ [Ar., "the people, nation of Massawa"]. This was their identity. Everyone came from abroad. They were all foreigners and they lived their life and intermarried here."[50] Another informant from a family of *sayyids*, whose ancestors came from Wādī Fāṭma on the outskirts of Mecca, characterized Massawa as a "big chain" whose families are all related to one another.[51] Yet the paradoxical character of this sense of identity emerges when considering the insistence on traditions of foreign origins and a sense of cosmopolitanism that have also taken a central position in the ways by which Massawans express their distinctiveness. Locally perceived prestigious origins from the Arab Middle East and the Muslim world have been fundamental in cultivating and maintaining the special sense of belonging of those who perceived themselves as Massawans. "Here everybody is of Arab origins; we all came from outside; there are people here from Yemen, Saudi Arabia, Turkey [*sic*], etc.," exemplifies the message that I heard on many occasions during interviews.[52] Reminding one to some extent of the situation on the East African coasts, Massawans who speak Tigre and physically resemble each other and many of the lowland peoples of the Eritrean region still insist on pointing to distant origins in Pakistan, Morocco, Iran, or Iraq, to take several unusual examples (as opposed to the more common and frequent Yemeni, Hadrami, Hijazi, and Egyptian origins). It is, however, clear that many of those who insist on distant origins are the descendants of peoples who have been in the Ethio-Eritrean region for several centuries at least and who have no memory of migrations such as that of the more recent nineteenth-century migrants from the Arabian Peninsula and Egypt.

One expression of the urban merchant elite used to distinguish between urban and non-urban and express the urban-mercantile versus the nomadic-rural dichotomy, is *seb bar* in the Tigre language, signifying "country folk," "villagers," but in our context can also mean "people from outside," in a somewhat demeaning way. The self-designated *seb medinat* (townspeople) perceived themselves as the extreme opposite of what they believed were the "disorganized" and "backward" *seb bar*. In its most radical usage the expression *al-barrānī barra* (Ar., outsiders outside) referred to the restriction placed on "outsiders" to pass the night on Massawa Island.[53] Informants have also mentioned the term *mutaḥaḍḍir* (Ar., "civilized," but also "settled," "urban," as opposed to "nomad"). One in particular proudly said that "Massawans are *mutaḥaḍḍirīn*. . . . [C]ivilization came [to Eritrea] from the Red Sea through Massawans. Beforehand, the people of the inland did not know how to behave in a civilized way . . . they gradually learned from us the Massawans." Very much like in different localities on the East African coasts, informants in Massawa mirror a wide arc of inclusivist and exclusivist notions of Massawan identity shaped by a host of complex factors, ranging from the personal-psychological to the political. Some exclusivist ideas are expressed rather with a kind of mischievous self-satisfied, self-incredulous smile ("we the *aṣliīn* [Ar., original, real] Massawans") but convey deeper sentiments about the issue. Most interesting and revealing are the gaps and paradoxes between self- or socially perceived prestige and current realities. The slight unease of individuals whose family names projected local prestige but whose current situation was weak was noticeable when I sat in the company of middle-aged and elderly Massawans in the town's cafés, especially so when in the company of other Massawans who had origins "from the tribes" and whose fortunes in the present fared better.

Yet, as in other places in East Africa and elsewhere, such designations could somewhat paradoxically work both ways, depending on the instrumentality of such discourses in different historical contexts.[54] For example, in the context of mid-twentieth-century Eritrean nationalism, some Tigre-speaking Muslim inlanders had, so to speak, gotten even with the self-claimed "superior" Massawans, by referring to them as the "*ṭarashat al-baḥr*" (Ar., the spew of the sea), those whom the sea has spat out onto the Eritrean shores, and who were somehow "foreign" to the land—therefore less legitimate in making claims to leadership as nationalists and setting the nationalist political agenda.[55] It is therefore important to note that when I refer to or highlight different claims of origin throughout my account, I use it for heuristic purposes, and not as an assertion of any rigid or objective "truth" about the relevant protagonists.[56]

The Sources

With respect to sources, embarking on the study leading to this book presented both excitement and concern. The independence of Eritrea in

1993 marked the opening up of the country to scholars after decades during which it was impossible to conduct research there. Discovering new sources was therefore a potentially rewarding possibility. On the other hand, the paucity of secondary literature about Eritrea meant that there was almost no solid ground to rely on, even when discussing the most basic "facts" about the history and peoples of the region. Both hopes and challenges are reflected in the final result. This study is based on a variety of published and unpublished primary and secondary sources. With respect to the broad temporal framework of the book, valuable European sources on Massawa begin with the account of the Scottish traveler James Bruce published in 1790.[57] From the 1830s we have numerous accounts by German, French, British, and other Europeans who either landed in Massawa on their way inland to the highland plateau or transited in the port before heading toward other Red Sea and Indian Ocean destinations. One source that was extremely useful for mid-nineteenth-century ethnographic data and information about coastal and lowland societies is Werner Munzinger's *Ostafrikanische Studien,* published in 1864. Munzinger (1832–75), son of a former president of the Swiss Confederation, Josef Munzinger, was an "adventurer" who lived in northeastern Africa for more than two decades, including eight years in Massawa and Keren. In the 1860s and 1870s he became involved in regional politics while serving in various capacities the French and Egyptian governments, including the governor of Massawa under Khedive Ismāʿīl.[58]

Following the acquisition of the Bay of Assab by the Italian Rubattino shipping company in 1869, the increasing number of Italian travelers and a variety of commercial prospectors visiting Massawa and the region—culminating in 1885 with the Italian takeover of the town—revealed the steadfast growth of Italian imperial aspirations. From 1885 to the early 1900s, there are numerous accounts in Italian—of every sort and quality, some extremely revealing of early Italian colonial perceptions and prejudice—on the *colonia primogenita* (the first-born colony) and its capital Massawa (until 1900). Some accounts from the 1880s—especially those of the Eldorado seekers—expressed little enthusiasm and more disappointment about the small, barren, unbearably hot and dry port and its region, deeming it unworthy of an aspiring imperial power such as Italy. Reaching Massawa in the beginning of the hot season in May 1880, L. Pennazzi could not have expressed his point with greater poignancy: "Had Dante known Massawa, his Inferno would have surely included one more pit into which the great poet would have sent the guiltiest of his damned."[59]

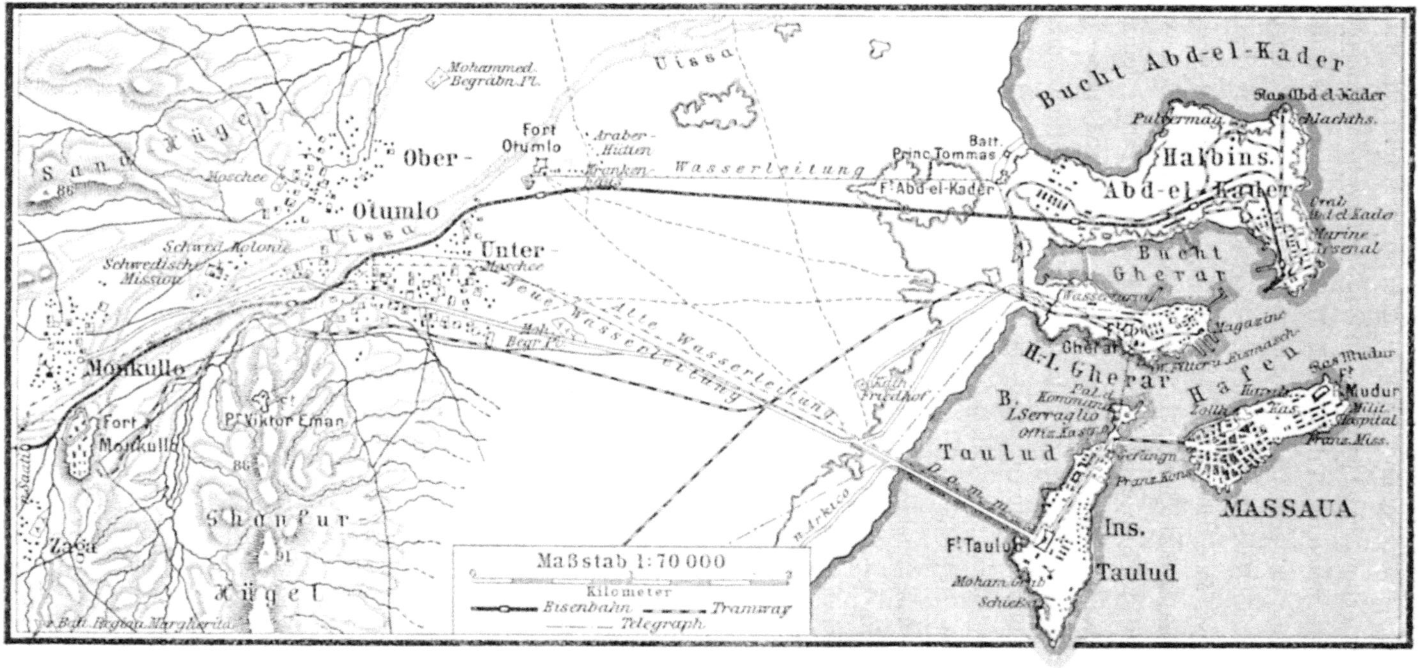

Figure Intro.4. The Massawa conurbation.
Brockhaus Konversations-Lexikon, 1890s.

Imperialist fantasizing was boundless, and passionate first impressions of this type were common among Italian travelers during the period. They usually mellowed a bit with time. In 1899 Saint Yves—a Francophone observer—attempted to set the picture straight by replying perceptively to all those who attacked Massawa in their writings: "One should not condemn the ancient town and talk about it so mercilessly. If Massawa has had such a long existence, if its port is—after the Graeco-Phoenician Adulis—the most prominent of ports on the African coasts of the Red Sea, its position must really be favorable."[60] Nevertheless, several early colonial official and private accounts, ethnographic descriptions, and studies have been fundamental in opening windows on social, cultural, and religious dynamics at play in the town and among its inhabitants. Dante Odorizzi's colonial handbook detailing the political, economic, geographic, and ethnographic aspects of the lands and peoples of the Commissariato of Massawa is one such valuable source. It appears that Odorizzi based much of the information included in his survey on a 1898 report written by Teobaldo Folchi, Massawa's first *commissario regionale,* and recently discovered by researcher Massimo Zaccaria.[61] Most colonial archival material consulted in Rome revolved around the Khatmiyya family, the administration of law, and the chiefs and notables of the Tigre-, Saho-, and Afar-speaking groups of Massawa's hinterlands between 1885 and 1910.

As for Massawans themselves, unfortunately, due to the troubled decades that the town has gone through since the 1960s and the resulting experience of exile from Eritrea, we have but scanty evidence of local historical writing. There are reports that prominent members of the community such as Sayyid Muḥammad ʿUthmān Ḥayūtī (1901–96) and Yāsīn Maḥmūd Bā Ṭūq (1914–67), both of solidly established Massawa families of Hadrami origins, have written texts on the history of Massawa and Eritrea. Interestingly, Ḥayūtī, a descendant of the scholarly minded Ḥibshī family and a prominent intellectual of twentieth-century Massawa, who was known to possess an exceptional knowledge of the town's family histories, had also translated into Arabic Odorizzi's survey of the populations of the Semhar coastland. In one incomplete manuscript written in the 1970s or 1980s, Ḥayūtī argues passionately for the writing of Eritrean history *by* Eritreans and *for* Eritreans. He uses both Italian and German sources (Odorizzi, Conti Rossini, Martini's diaries, Dillman) and oral data in trying to reconstruct the Eritrean past, dividing it to five distinct periods. The manuscript includes an introduction, a section on the geography of Eritrea, and a chapter on pre-Islamic Eritrea.[62] According to another source, Yāsīn

Maḥmūd Bā Ṭūq, who became Massawa's deputy-mayor in 1958, has written a text titled *Fuṣūl ᶜan māḍī shuᶜūb Iritrīyā wa-ḥāḍiriha* (Chapters on the past and present of Eritrea's peoples). Unfortunately, most of these manuscripts were lost, and only further research among the exiled community of Massawans, especially in Jiddah, might, in the future, prove useful in locating such writings.[63]

An important local source—although not from Massawa—is the scholarship of Eritrea's first Grand Muftī, Shaykh Ibrāhīm al-Mukhtār Aḥmad ᶜUmar (1909–69). In his intellectual quest for Eritrea's Islamic past, Shaykh Ibrāhīm devoted a substantial unpublished manuscript to Massawa, its history, its population and its importance in the history of Islam in Eritrea. In another text on the history of Eritrea's towns, forty additional pages discuss Massawa's specific religious and historical features.[64] Since the independence of the State of Eritrea in 1993 several historical studies in Arabic have been published. One useful volume that deserves mention is Muḥammad ᶜUthmān Abū Bakr's survey of Eritrean history which includes a copious chapter on the Semhar with useful ethnographic information on local societies and families.[65] It should, after all, be noted that the works of Munzinger (1858, 1864), Folchi (1898), Salvadei (1902), Odorizzi (1910), Ibrāhīm al-Mukhtār (1958) and Muḥammad ᶜUthmān Abū Bakr (1994) had all involved the extensive collection of oral data, which has been crucial in contributing to the reconstruction of Massawa's history.

An important local source that this study makes use of is a collection of records from Massawa's Islamic court (Ar. *al-maḥkama al-sharᶜiyya*) covering the period between the 1860s and the early 1900s.[66] The *maḥkama* records open a window onto the Massawan social scene and enable one to move beyond images of the exotic, or the invisible *tout court,* characteristic of most European sources. The court record collection comprises twenty-nine registers, of which nineteen correspond to the period under direct Egyptian administration (1865–85), five cover years under Italian administration (1885–1902), and five additional volumes relate to periods of transition between Egyptians and Italians. I have mostly made use of registrations of real estate and moveable property transactions, marriage, divorce, power of attorney, inheritance, child custody, death acts, conversion to Islam, religious endowments (*waqf*), and slave manumission. Real estate property transactions are particularly abundant in the final decades of the nineteenth century. Houses, coffee shops, stores and shops, water cisterns were all properly registered in detail when bought and sold, and title deeds were issued to individuals by the court. The methodological approach of using court records as a historical source adopted here is mostly a quantitative approach used in a framework of prosopographical analysis. By isolating specific social, economic, religious, and ethnic attributes I could identify certain trends, patterns, and dynamics that characterize status, ethnic, and other types of groups sharing specific common attributes. With regard to Islamic court records as a source for social history in the Horn of Africa, it should be noted that a rich corpus of source materials from late-nineteenth-century Brava, on the Benaadir coast in southern Somalia, has been published recently. It is a fascinating and highly promising source for studying various issues in social and economic history, including the sociocultural construction of coastal identities in northeastern Africa.[67]

A last category of sources is the gathering of oral data through interviews. Unfortunately, since the 1960s Massawa's population has suffered multiple demographic and social upheavals resulting in the breakdown of communal structures and forced outward migration. Many Massawans left their town and settled in the diaspora, mostly in the Middle East, while many newcomers from the highlands and from Massawa's vicinities came to settle in the port-town. Notwithstanding these basic difficulties I have conducted interviews with more than fifty informants in Massawa, Asmara, Ghinda, Hergigo, Emberemi, and Hetumlo. Interviews revolved around family histories, individual migratory and professional trajectories, commercial and economic activities, and religious practices. Interviews provided basic data and complemented documentary evidence on social structures, communal dynamics, cultural characteristics, self-perceptions, and the perception of other groups in the region under study. Interviews were instrumental in revealing the complexities and subtleties of an urban coastal society such as Massawa. It was not rare, for example, that my questioning stimulated informants to eagerly debate about Massawa's history, and sometimes amplify the role of their own "tribe" of origin in the foundation of Massawa.

A Note on the Geographical Setting: Climate, Seasonality, Peoples

A final introductory note is devoted to the physical and human setting of Massawa's region. Eritrea is known for its varying climates and seasons, ranging from the cold of the rugged mountain peaks to the terrible heat of the arid desert of the Danakil depression. Indeed, one of the most striking geographical features in the Horn of Africa is the dramatic and spectacular geography of the landscape, extending from Massawa and the Red Sea coasts to the highland plateau, rising abruptly above the narrow lowland plain only some three dozen kilometers from the sea. Any traveler who has descended the serpentine road from Asmara (2340 meters) in the highlands down to Massawa on the coast has witnessed the breathtaking and sharp transition from one geographic, climatic, and human environment to another in less than three hours and about 120 kilometers of road. Anyone who has taken the minibus on that spectacular road has experienced the gradual peeling off of one's clothes as the vehicle advances nauseatingly down the highlands and into the lowlands. Depending on the season, Ghinda is usually still warm and pleasant; by the time you get to Gahtelay on the plain, Asmara feels days and seasons away. "Three seasons in two hours," they famously call it in travel guides, posters, and other official tourist publications.

The Eritrean region's geography is dominated by its division between the hot and dry lowlands of the coastal and western plains (*metahit* in Tigrinya), and the cooler and better-watered highlands of the central plateau (*kebessa* in Tigrinya) and northern highlands.[68] While in the dry lowlands annual average temperatures rise to around thirty degrees centigrade with average annual precipitations of less than ten centimeters, the highlands have an average temperature of seventeen degrees with average annual precipitation of over sixty centimeters. These topographic, climatic, and variations in seasonality form different ecological regions that are also displayed in the economy, cultures, and languages of the region's peoples.

A particularly striking aspect of climate in the region is that while the highlands have a bimodal rainfall regime (small rains between March and May and big rains between June and September), the coastal lowlands have only limited rains, principally in December and January. In other words, while Asmara, on the highland plateau, for example, experiences the most torrential rains in the summer months, Massawa and the coastal plain live through the driest season. Such conditions lead to significant social consequences regarding seasonality and migration. Lowland nomadic groups move in a seasonal cycle up the hills and the slopes of the plateau for grazing and cultivation. In turn, some semi-highlander nomadic groups and farmers migrate down the escarpments to the foothills and the plains during the winter in search of pastures and a second harvest. The Sahos, for example, move to the coast between December and February to benefit from the *dada*ᶜ rains. This pattern of migration and seasonality is typical of the central coastal region, called the Semhar plain, where the mountains come closest to the sea. Even if still relatively dry, the Semhar region, which extends from Massawa to Ghinda (962 meters), enjoys far better conditions than the sparsely inhabited coastal plain extending from the Sudan down to Massawa as well as the barren coast extending south of Massawa toward Assab and Djibouti. Semhar is the region par excellence, where Tigre- and Saho-speaking pastoralists migrate up and down the escarpment. It is in the region straddling the plain, the foothills, and the hills, in localities such as ᶜAylet, ᶜAsus, Gumhod, and Ghinda, that the abrupt human variation in language, religion, and culture is most manifest.

The segments of this book relating to the interaction between Massawa and its hinterlands are mostly concerned with Tigre- and Saho-speaking pastoralists and agro-pastoralists inhabiting Massawa's interior regions. Tigre-speaking groups inhabit a large arc around the highlands and northeastern lowlands. Like Tigrinya, the language of the predominantly Christian sedentary agriculturalists of the highlands, Tigre is a Semitic language. By the nineteenth century virtually all Tigre-speaking groups adopted Islam. The Tigre-speaking groups are divided into a number of tribes and tribal confederations and include the Beni ᶜAmer of the western lowlands; the Marya, Bet Juk, and a large part of the Mensaᶜ, all inhabiting the area around Keren; the Habab, ᶜAd Tekles, ᶜAd Temaryam, the ᶜAd Muᶜallim of the northern highlands, and segments of the ᶜAd Shaykh, the ᶜAd Shuma, Meshalit, ᶜAd Tsaura, Bet Mala, and other smaller groups inhabiting the region of Semhar of Massawa's close interior. With the exception of the Irob, who inhabit northeastern Tigray, the Saho-speaking groups are Muslim agro-pastoralists speaking an Eastern Cushitic language and inhabiting parts of the coast, the eastern escarpment of the highland plateau south of Massawa, and the foothills of Akkele Guzay. The main Saho-speaking clans are the Asaorta, Minifire, Hazu, Dabrimela, and the Taroᶜa. Another important coastal group is the Afar-speaking people inhabiting the Danakil (or Afar) coast south of Massawa and the Buri peninsula. The Afar are mostly pastoralists but include many fishermen and some merchants. Afar is another Cushitic language—linguistically very close to Saho—and the Afar people are all Muslims. One other interesting small coastal group is the Arabic-speaking Rashayda, who migrated to the Sudanese and Eritrean coasts from the Arabian Peninsula some time in the early nineteenth century. The Rashayda are traditionally pastoralists and have not assimilated into local Tigre- or Saho-speaking societies.[69]

In contrast to interior pastoralist and agro-pastoralist societies, the population of the town of Massawa was sedentary, cosmopolitan, and polyglot. As in other settings across the Red Sea and Indian Ocean zone, languages flowed with great ease in greater Massawa. Ottoman Turkish and Arabic were the languages of administration for the greater part of the nineteenth century, until Italy occupied Massawa in 1885. The predominant languages of the local population in the nineteenth century were Tigre, Arabic, and to a lesser extent Saho. Arabic was the literary and religious language, but was also employed with Arabic-speaking merchants who visited from across the sea. Tigre was mostly the everyday language of the home, the streets, and the markets. As in many other settings where commercial mediation is the primary occupation, urban Massawans usually had to use more than one of these languages, at times shifting from one language to another even in the course of one business transaction. Massawa was not only the town of its inhabitants; it regularly hosted a variety of people—traders, peddlers, laborers, fishermen, caravaneers—who came to the port to buy or sell goods, provide their labor and services. Many a traveler in the nineteenth century noted the numerous languages heard in town. Languages such as Amharic, Tigrinya, Oromo, Somali, Afar, Swahili, Farsi, and several Indian languages were the music of its markets. In addition Greek, Italian, Armenian, Albanian, and French were used by European merchants conducting business in the port. Wider political and migratory developments shifted general patterns of language usage in the port throughout the century. In the second half of the century the use of Arabic was strengthened, especially due to the intensified migration of merchants and commercial entrepreneurs from Arabic-speaking lands, as well as the result of the two-decade-long Egyptian occupation. Similarly, the Italian creation of the Colony of Eritrea in 1890, with Massawa as its capital, also triggered a gradual process of migration of Tigrinya-speaking highlanders to the Massawa conurbation.

Finally, it is important to stress the critical role of the yearly seasonal cycles in determining the rhythm of life of Massawa as a trading town and port. Seasonal shifts greatly determined all aspects of commercial and social life—including patterns of linguistic usage. Seasonal patterns determined the regime of winds and affected sail-powered vessels bound to or from Massawa. On the other hand seasonal variations in the port's hinterlands affected the rhythms of the caravan trade and the arrival of merchandise, caravan traders, and transporters, as well as the activities of the host of peddlers, laborers, and service providers essential to the complex operation of caravans. The slightest change of climatic conditions could have far-reaching consequences in the port's complex commercial operation requiring a maximal degree of synchronization. It was not rare that camel and boat did not meet and that one had to wait for the other. Goods deteriorated, boat crews or caravaneers wandered around the town's narrow alleys, sipping coffee and exchanging information in its numerous coffee houses. Massawan brokers had to keep all ends under control, with patience, savvy, and sagacious social skills.

1

Making a Region between the Sea and the Mountain

Nāʾib *Autonomy and Dominance, to the 1850s*

I am the gate of Abyssinia.
—Nāʾib Idrīs, 1805[1]

The Sultan rules in Istanbul, the Pasha
in Egypt, and Nāʾib Ḥasan in Massawa!
—Nāʾib Ḥasan, 1840s[2]

About a century following Özdemir Pasha's conquest of the ports of Massawa and Hergigo in 1557, the Ottoman authorities devolved power to a locally potent family of the Beja-descended Balaws and appointed its chief as their *nāʾib,* or deputy. By the middle of the eighteenth century, the *nāʾibs* were able to develop their political power, impose their authority—perhaps hegemony—and practically become the most powerful rulers in a vast area extending between the Red Sea coast and the highland plateau. Past historical accounts have often tended to portray the lowland-based and Muslim *nāʾibs* in a negative light, describing them as naturally inclined "warmongers," "greedy," "uncooperative," and "unruly" elements, who were the primary cause of the incessant state of disorder and chaos between the northern borderlands of the historic Christian Ethiopian state and the Red Sea coast. Essentialist attitudes were partly rooted in European travelers' and missionaries' accounts since the so-called religious wars of the sixteenth century—views that perceived the Ethiopian polity as an isolated and threatened bastion of "civilization" in a hostile Muslim environment.[3] This tendency persisted and was prevalent among nineteenth-century European observers who traveled in the area as the power of the *nāʾib*s was already in a process of decline.[4]

Some modern writers too denigrated the *nāʾib*s, attributing to them an innate hostile nature and portraying them as the main factor for withholding the seemingly natural and inevitable progression of an equally seemingly monolithic Ethiopian state. In these writings the chafing *nāʾib*s "attack travelers," they use "extortion," and they "encroach" upon territories. State- and empire-centric perspectives promote a static and historically deterministic character to the evolution of the region, whereby struggles are only normal between large historic polities, each having its natural place and "reasonable" aspirations within these conflicts. Interestingly, today too, some who are sympathetic to the idea of a historically and inescapably predominant "Greater Ethiopia" in the region see the independence of an Eritrean state, as something of an anomaly, an unnatural and therefore unviable development in the recent history of the Horn of Africa.[5]

In this chapter I seek to inscribe local historical agents in the shaping and making of regional histories. Implicit in this approach is an effort to transcend, or emphatically maneuver away from, the limiting boundaries to the historical imagination characteristic of politically and ideologically oriented historiographical projects. Historian Frederick Cooper has called for a writing of history "forward" in order to avoid the traps of the manipulation of history that project present collectivities—such as states, nations, and ethnic groups—into the past.[6] Accordingly, various claims to the "Eritrean-ness" of this region from times immemorial, or to the area's eternal belonging to a historic Ethiopian state, or even claims, such as those advanced by the British in the 1940s, that the broader Muslim-majority lowland regions are somehow organically associated to the Sudan, teach us more about the political objectives and ideological agendas of those advancing them than about any dispassionate aspiration to imagine and evaluate those historical trajectories that have *seemingly* less tangible use for the present.

The chapter examines a region—a loosely defined borderland territory, or frontier space—situated both on the margins of the Ottoman Empire on the one hand, and on the periphery of the different configurations of Christian highland political formations (or the historic Ethiopian state) on the other, from the 1600s to the 1850s. I suggest that it may well be useful to think about the area extending from Massawa and the Red Sea coasts to the northern parts of the highland plateau, situated in the eastern parts of the modern Eritrean state, as a frontier space. This area was a meeting place of peoples in which geographic, economic, political, and cultural borders were not clearly defined, but which in certain periods did indeed develop patterns of cohesiveness but also fragmentation. Between the late eighteenth century and the early twentieth, a conjuncture of political, economic, and religious global and regional processes has promoted regional integration, incorporation, and cohesiveness in this area or in parts thereof, while other historical factors have generated fragmentation and division. I identify two macro-level processes in the nineteenth century that in some senses were causal and interconnected but in other cases not. The first level involved the expansion and amplification of interregional interactions and connections across the mostly Tigre-speaking area with the Nilotic Sudan and Egypt, as well as with the Arabian Peninsula and the western Indian Ocean at large. The second level of processes is one of regional integration through the weaving of intraregional political, commercial, religious, and social networks and alliances within and across the areas inhabited by Tigre-speaking communities.[7]

Writing the *nāʾib*s and the region that they dominated into the historical narrative, the chapter tells the story of the rise and fall of the *nāʾib*s against that backdrop. It propounds that as a regional dynasty of power brokers in control of a strategically important region in between larger rivaling political entities, the Nāʾib family struggled to promote its own interests, maneuvering between diplomacy and force, and constantly tested the limits of their power. The narrative places the *nāʾib*s at the center of the account, examines their political, economic, social, and religious bases of power in the region, and explores the methods, meanings, and limitations of their autonomy, authority, and dominance until the middle of the nineteenth century, when a renewed wave of imperialism and the changing political economy of commerce in northeast Africa and the Red Sea region diminished and transformed their political power. Among several outcomes, the ways in which the *nāʾib*s have established and developed their control have laid down the infrastructure of networks, alliances, and spheres of influence that gravitated toward Massawa as the chief urban center in that region. The legacy of a decentralized and indirect mode of Ottoman imperial control and the role of the *nāʾib*s in the region molded political, commercial, social, and religious networks and fields of action that contributed directly to the shaping of an interconnected and interrelated *region* in the predominantly Muslim areas of eastern and northern Eritrea. Processes of a similar character have occurred in other provinces of the progressively decentralized Ottoman Empire where local regional power holders and magnate families contributed to the formation of regions through tax collection and through the establishment and cementing of political and economic networks.[8]

Before the "Turks": The Balaw in Semhar

The origin of the Balaw may be traced to the region of Sawākin in eastern Sudan, where a gradual fusion between Beja-speaking nomads and Arabs gave birth to a ruling stratum called "Balaw" (also "Belew" and "Bäläw"). Evidence suggests that following a long period of famine in the eastern Sudan at the end of the fourteenth century, the Balaw began migrating southward through the Tigre-speaking regions of present-day western and northern Eritrea. Some groups continued to the Semhar region in eastern Eritrea and further south along the Afar coast down to Zaylaᶜ. The Balaw fused into local groups in all these regions, adopted local languages, and influenced—to varying degrees—social and political configurations. In some societies they attained positions of political preeminence and leadership.[9]

Balaw historical traditions collected by Werner Munzinger in the middle of the nineteenth century locate the gradual arrival of Balaw families to the coastal strip of Semhar in the fifteenth century. According to these traditions the Balaw Bayt Yūsuf was among the first notable families to move from the Barka to the Semhar region following its expulsion by the Jaᶜliīn. The family established its political ascendancy in the village of Zaga as vassals of the *bahr negash,* the highland-based ruler of the maritime province.[10] Traditions further record that Ḥummād, the son of Sayyid ᶜĀmir Qunnu, who was Yūsuf's servant in Zaga, overthrew Yūsuf with the assistance of Shaykh Maḥmūd and became the leader of the Balaw in Semhar. Ḥummād then moved to Hergigo (in Saho, Dakano [elephant]), situated several kilometers south of Massawa on the coast.[11] There, he established the supremacy of his family and founded the dynasty that would carry the title of *nāᵓib* up to the twentieth century.[12]

The town of Hergigo predated the arrival of the Balaw to the region and was the most important port on that part of the coast. Historically and in function, it had replaced the ancient Axumite port of Adulis, and later Zula, situated some fifty kilometers to the south. As the Red Sea port closest to the highland plateau, Hergigo offered convenient access to coast-bound caravans coming from the highlands and served as a gate at the

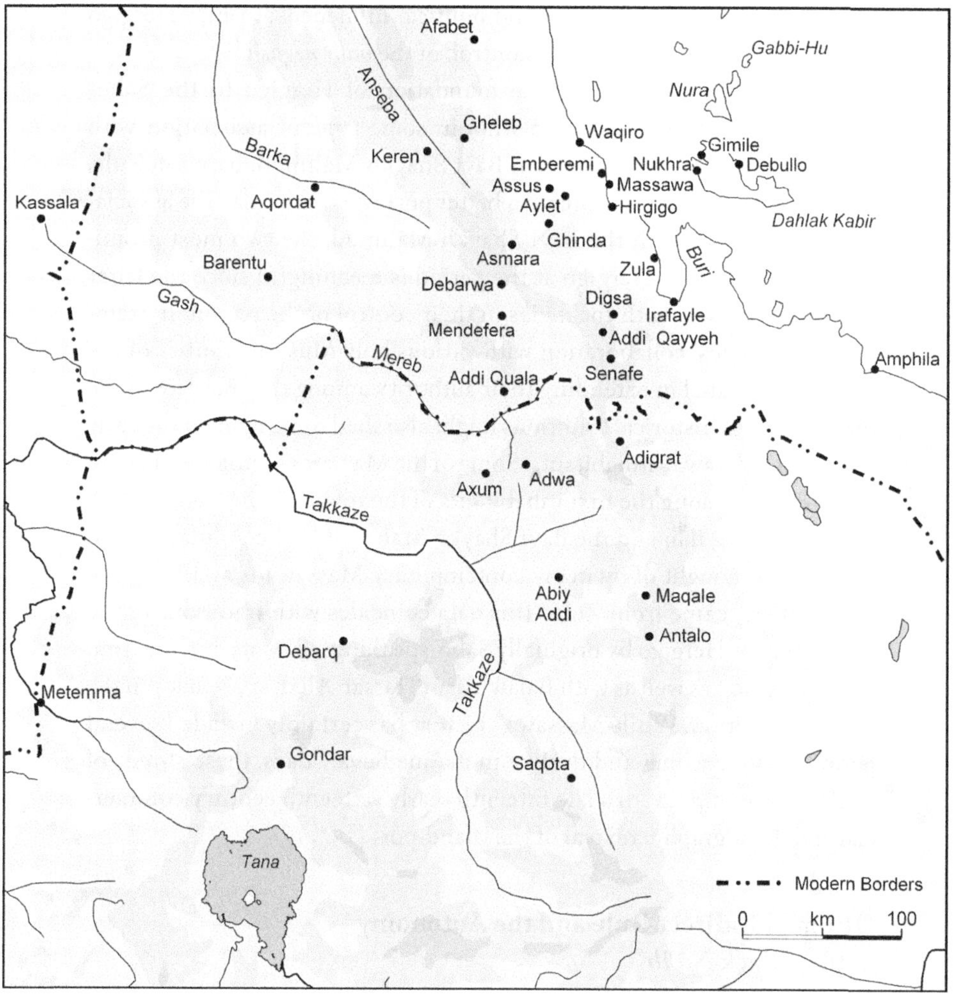

Map 3. Massawa's Inlands: Eritrea and northern Ethiopia. Map by Matthias Schulz.

entrance to the inland. Hergigo's other advantages were both its position facing the island-port of Massawa, whose deep-water harbor suited larger seafaring vessels (hence access to long-distance waterborne shipping networks), and its relatively good provision of water in an utterly arid area. An early-seventeenth-century Portuguese observer reported that Hergigo was a rather flourishing port consisting of four hundred houses constructed of clay and coarse grass, and essential to anyone in possession of Massawa Island. The island-port was indeed dependent on Hergigo for supplying it with water and foodstuffs on a daily basis. Unlike Massawa, which remained independent of highland political influence, at times Hergigo came under the attack, and also control, of the *bahr negash*.[13]

Oral traditions attribute the foundation of Hergigo to the Saho-speaking nomad group of Idda who, in some type of association with elements of the holy Muslim clan Bayt Shaykh Maḥmūd, based in Zula, settled in Hergigo, which offered a better port site than Zula. The association of the Balaw with the Bayt Shaykh Maḥmūd, the two most prominent family-clans in Hergigo at the period is meaningful since the latter cooperated closely with the *nāʾib*s in their control of the region. It exemplified the *nāʾib*s' collaboration with various holy Muslim families of the Semhar and Sahel in extending their authority among the societies of the region.[14] These historical traditions might also shed some light on the early history of Massawa's inhabitants. Some of the Massawa families that claim to have been among the first inhabitants of the town belong to the Balaw Yūsuf Ḥassab Allāh and the Bayt Shaykh Maḥmūd.[15] The ʿAdūlāy family, who is also thought of by many contemporary Massawans as among the early settlers, came from Zula. This data coincides with traditions of the foundation of Hergigo by originally Saho-speaking elements moving from the Zula region as well as with Balaw Yūsuf Ḥassab Allāh supremacy in the sixteenth century. While Massawa's history has certainly included several periods of flourishing and decline in its "medieval" days, these shreds of evidence might point to a late fifteenth–early sixteenth century commercial and demographic revival of the island-port.[16]

Ottoman Indirect Rule and the Autonomy of the "Black *Nāʾib*"

In 1557 Özdemir Pasha conquered Massawa Island and the port of Hergigo and made them one of the *sanjak*s of the Ottoman province of Habesh (*Habeş eyaleti*), which had been established two years earlier with its center in Sawākin.[17] The broader background to this event should be viewed through the prism of Ottoman-Portuguese power struggles in the Red Sea basin, which followed the Ottoman occupation of Egypt and western Arabia in 1516–17. After having established their control over the two southern Red Sea ports and a stretch of the coast, in 1559 the Ottomans turned inland and took Debarwa, the capital of Bahr Negash Yeshaq, who ruled the maritime province for the king of Ethiopia. In Debarwa they constructed a large Friday mosque and several other smaller ones. Encountering resistance and pushed back by the *bahr negash* and highland forces, the Turks remained relatively briefly in the highlands. They did not, however, give up their ambitions to establish their foothold on the plateau, and in 1578, under the governorship of Ahmet Pasha, they allied their forces with those of Bahr Negash Yeshaq—who had switched alliances due to power struggles with his master, *negus* Sarsa Dengel (r. 1563–97)—and launched an attack against the Ethiopian king.[18] The Ottomans were only partly successful, and in 1589 they were apparently compelled to withdraw their forces to the coast. Having lost either the political interest or the military ability to pursue these efforts, the Ottomans seem to have abandoned their ambitions to establish themselves on the plateau.

Ottoman authority in the region dwindled well into the first decades of the seventeenth century. Within the broader framework of Ottoman imperialism in that period it was not uncommon that after initial conquests, different systems of administration and governance developed, with varying balances between central and regional-local authority. The high level of centralization characterizing the empire in the sixteenth century was brief. In many localities, especially beyond the commercially important urban centers, the Ottoman government gave recognition to local families of chiefs or power magnates who collected revenues for the Ottoman government and secured commercially or strategically important routes.[19] Accordingly, the Ottomans left but a small garrison in Massawa and handed Hergigo to the local Balaw chieftain, whom they appointed their *nāʾib.* At this point the available sources do not establish the exact date of the devolution of power. It is also not clear how formal or informal the actual transfer of power might have been. The lack of clarity might be, at least in part, rooted in a gradual process of power transfer, both in time and in space. According to the evidence the *qāʾim maqām* of the pasha of Sawākin still ruled Massawa in 1633. When Evliya Çelebi visited the port in 1673 he reported that it was ruled by a *nāʾib* of the Balaw, who was assisted by an Agha and a Turkish garrison. Çelebi portrayed the ruler of Hergigo as the "black *nāʾib*" (Tur. *kara nāʾib*), who spoke Turkish correctly even if with a marked Levantine accent![20] Until new evidence comes to light (for example, in the Ottoman archives in Istanbul), it would be reasonable to assume that the Ottomans had transferred power, de jure or de facto, to the *nāʾib*s some time in the middle decades of the seventeenth century. The chronicle of Iyasu I (1682–1706) confirms the *nāʾib*s' position of power in the late-seventeenth century, when reporting that in 1693 Nāʾib Mūsā b. ʿUmar Qunnu attempted to use extortion against the Armenian merchant Khodja Murad, who was on his way to Emperor Iyasu I with gifts. Following Iyasu's threats to attack the *nāʾibs*, the chronicle reports, the latter finally submitted to the emperor's pressures.[21] It would also be useful to examine the effects of the 1701 Ottoman administrative reform, which resulted in the merging of the *sanjaks* of Massawa and Sawākin with the Ottoman Hijazi province, with its base in Jiddah, on the question of authority in Massawa and its region and the role of the *nāʾibs* within that new provincial structural framework.

According to *nāʾib* historical traditions, by the time of the Ottoman conquest in the sixteenth century, the family had already acquired wealth and attained a position of considerable influence in Hergigo and the Semhar at large. Again, in accordance with a tradition of Ottoman provincial practice, which oscillated between the need for cooperation to maintain order and the awareness of the flimsy character of their relations with local power holders, officials manipulated internal *nāʾib* family struggles over authority, generating and exploiting divisions within the family. One should not, however, forget that this kind of manipulation was two-directional. The *nāʾibs* too could turn such dynamics to their benefit. In the words of historian Dina Rizk Khoury: "The ambiguous and fluid nature of relations between the local and the imperial meant that local elites were at all times keenly aware of their power to negotiate a position for themselves within the Ottoman provincial order."[22] Intra-family struggles may explain the divergence of traditions in respect to the appointment of the first *nāʾib* and reflect the viewpoints of different family factions. According to one version, Ḥummād ʿĀmir Qunnu, who is designated as the most prominent Balaw chief at the time, fled with his family, wives, slaves, and servants from Hergigo to the nearby Buri peninsula following an Ottoman advance from Massawa to the mainland, possibly in the mid-seventeenth century.[23] Ḥummād was chief in Hergigo and opposed the Ottomans, who had curbed his authority on the coast. While fleeing to Buri, Ḥummād killed his younger brother's son, ʿAlī b. Mūsā, whom he suspected of siding with the Ottomans. Years later, the story continues, ʿĀmir, ʿAlī's son, sought the assistance of the Ottomans, came to Massawa, and was appointed as the first *nāʾib*. In return for his submitting to the Sultan's authority, supplying Massawa with water, and maintaining order and stability on the mainland, the Ottoman authorities presented him with the paraphernalia symbolizing their power and authority (a silk robe and a golden-handled sword) and a monthly payment from the customs of Massawa for maintaining a garrison of troops.[24] Struggles and divisions within the family were commonplace during the first decades of the *nāʾib*'s tenure in office. Most quarrels revolved around the contestation for the office of *nāʾib,* with its privileges, and involved maneuvers aimed at gaining Ottoman recognition of one faction over the other. The most significant division within the family confronted the two sons of ʿĀmir, the first *nāʾib* in office. The rivalry between the two brothers, Ḥasan ʿĀmir (r. 1720–37) and ʿUthmān ʿĀmir (r. 1741–81) gave birth to a family division that split it into two distinct lineages and that extended into the twentieth century in the Italian colonial period.[25]

Relations between the Ottoman authorities and their representatives on the one hand and the centralized highland Ethiopian polity on the other remained strained throughout the seventeenth and eighteenth centuries. Since Massawa handled the bulk of highland foreign trade, the crucial points at issue were access to the sea and the tax duties imposed on merchandise-laden caravans heading from the coast to the highlands or vice versa. However, in between intermittent incidents, a state of coexistence prevailed between the ports and the highland rulers, who did not shy away from continuously threatening to take over the ports while never showing any real intention or capability of incorporating them into their dominions.[26] The *nāʾib*s found themselves at the center of these trials of strength. In congruence with trends in the broader Ottoman imperial framework, *nāʾib* authority and autonomy grew significantly beginning in the middle decades of the eighteenth century. Ottomanist historian Suraiya Faroqhi, noted that in this period the Ottoman dominions at large appeared as "a congeries of domains controlled by different local power holders."[27]

Following the death of the *abuna* in 1738, Emperor Iyasu II sent an embassy to Cairo in 1745 to have a new *abuna* ordained. The *nāʾib* detained the emperor's envoys in Hergigo for six months and took most of their gold. Eventually, when the new *abuna* arrived the following year, the *nāʾib* detained him again on the coast until he had paid the required fee.[28] This incident coincided with the beginning of the process of the weakening of the centralized Christian highland polity in the middle of the eighteenth century, a period known as the *Zemene Mesefint.* The collapse of central authority in favor of the growingly autonomous regional rulers created a power vacuum which benefited the *nāʾib* whose control of Massawa, Hergigo and the lowland areas between the sea and the mountains was seldom seriously challenged. When James Bruce arrived in Massawa in 1768 he reported that the *nāʾib* did not pay tribute either to the pasha of Jiddah, to which the Ottomans affixed the port's authorities, or to the Ethiopian king.[29] In the absence of modern, rigid notions of borders and unitary sovereignty, the question of tribute payment, as will be argued below, was a central issue in claiming and legitimizing authority in the region and a source of ardent contestation.

Now more than ever, the *nāʾib*s needed to maneuver their way and carefully preserve a viable balance in their relations with the rulers of the northern highland provinces, who, while promoting their own autonomy and hegemony, engaged in power politics vis-à-vis the *nāʾib,* usually vacillating between various degrees of forceful intimidation and interested collaboration. All in all, the conjunction of the state of political instability in the central and northern highlands and the decline of Ottoman direct control over their province of Habesh provided a fertile ground for the expansion and consolidation of *nāʾib* dominance in the wider region.

Power without Pashas: The Anatomy of *Nāʾib* Authority and Dominance

In the second half of the eighteenth century the *nāʾib*s were the most powerful rulers of the region between the sea and the highlands. The success of the *nāʾib*s in extending their influence and authority over the diverse societies inhabiting this area depended first and foremost on their ability to exercise effective control by coercion and a measured application of force. It also depended on their ability to provide security to the pastoralist societies that found themselves on the fringes of the northerly highland provinces and the Sudanese region, vulnerable to attempts at expansion, and subject to raids and attacks by more powerful forces. In the later years of the *Zemene Mesefint,* Walter Plowden illustrated this point by referring to the lowland nomad populations as those "flying-fish" who "are preyed on by all."[30] Werner Munzinger also recognized the innate exposedness of these societies when observing that "the inhabitants of Semhar depend on Abyssinia for its pastures, on Massawa for its market, on both for security."[31] In a borderland region that lay outside any coherent and effective state control, the *nāʾib*s performed certain functions that are normally accomplished by a centralized state. Securing a viable regional economic system through the control of the main trading routes and of grazing and agricultural lands and providing security for herds, flocks, and camels were central aspects of this process. Tribute payment, the recognition of *nāʾib* authority, and, not less importantly, the weaving of convoluted social, family, and economic alliances and networks of patron-client relations provided security to the relatively small-scale communities of the region.

The exact geographic limitations of *nāʾib* influence fluctuated over time, reflecting expansion and contraction, in terms of both space and political influence. At the peak of their power the *nāʾibs* extended their authority over the totality of Tigre-speaking pastoralist and agro-pastoralist populations in the regions of Semhar, Sahel, and the northern coasts as far as ʿAqīq, approximately three hundred kilometers north of Massawa. Early-nineteenth-century sources observed that Massawans traded with tribes in the Sawākin area and that the *nāʾib* maintained relations with "his fellow-countrymen" in Sawākin.[32] The most important groups (numerically) coming under *nāʾib* control were the Habab, the Mensaʿ, and segments of the Bet Taqwe (Bilin).[33] The *nāʾibs* also spread their influence over Saho-speaking pastoralists in the foothills of Tigray, Akkele Guzay, and Hamasen, of which the Asaorta and the Taroʿa were the most dominant groups. Other Afar-, Saho-, and Tigre-speaking societies under *nāʾib* influence inhabited the Buri peninsula, the Zula area, and regions on the Afar coast as south as ʿEdd, about five hundred kilometers south of Massawa, as well as the Dahlak islands.[34]

In what follows I examine the political, economic, social, and religious bases of *nāʾib* authority and supremacy. The treatment follows an analytical-thematic approach that is not always chronological. Examples are drawn from the period between the 1700s and the 1850s.

Developing Power, Applying Force, and the Formation of Military Households

The most important source of power and authority that *nāʾib* supremacy rested upon was control of an organized military apparatus in the coastlands. The Ottomans withdrew most of their forces from Massawa in the late sixteenth century, leaving only a small policing force and the customs house personnel on the island. A militia, composed of two forces, one made up of what the sources refer to as "Arabs" and the other of "Turks," and placed under the authority of the *nāʾib*, replaced the Ottoman military troops.[35] The commander of the so-called Turkish semi-regular militia held the Ottoman title *sirdār*, and was often kin-related to the *nāʾib*. In the first decade of the nineteenth century, for example, Lord Valentia reported that the *sirdār* was Nāʾib Idrīs's own brother.[36] According to Folchi, the *sirdār* was the commander of the Balaw patrician guard (It. *guardie no-*

bili [Bellou]).[37] On the other hand, the "Arab" irregular militia was composed of servants, slaves, and poor relatives of the *nāʾib,* and was headed by a *kāhia.* Both positions became hereditary within the families that controlled them. This process also comprised a gradual mixing of soldiers of the Ottoman garrison (mostly Albanians, but also Turks and Bosnians) who married into local Balaw families.[38] Such practice was not uncommon on a wider scale in other regions of the Ottoman Empire (even closer to the imperial center), reminiscent of the processes leading to the development of the military households in seventeenth-century Egypt.[39]

With time, several families who controlled troops and monopolized certain ranks emerged from this nucleus of forces as independent and potent families. Hence, the Bayt ʿAsker and the Bayt Shāwish were both descended from the troops of the *kāhia,* and the Bayt Sardāl, Bayt Kekiyā (Kāhia), and Bayt Agha also became family-clans on their own. These families wielded much power in the region and were able, consequently, to convert their symbolic power and prestige into advantageous positions in commerce and local politics. Some, like the Kekiyā family, have been especially active in Eritrea's twentieth-century history and have preserved political and economic prominence and prestige in the country to this very day.[40] But the *nāʾib*'s forces also recruited among other Saho- and Tigre-speaking populations of Semhar for their military expeditions. Together with the nucleus of Balaw soldiers, their forces could often attain several thousand men.

Nāʾib military supremacy in the region depended on access to firearms and gunpowder via the coast. Their relationship with the Ottomans, who supplied them with rifles and gunpowder, secured this position of superiority.[41] When diplomacy and political accords failed to serve their interests, the *nāʾib*s, supported by their military potency, turned to the employment of outright force. At the height of their power they attempted to challenge the authority of larger entities such as the Ottomans, the Egyptians, and the rulers of the northern highland provinces (usually Tigray) by recourse to force. Yet more often they utilized their coercive powers to open up or secure trade routes or strategic territories, or to subjugate rebellious elements. Nāʾib Muḥammad ʿĀmir (r. 1737–41), for example, conducted expeditions against the Afar Dammohoyta clan of the Buri peninsula, who had been raiding Zula. Nāʾib Aḥmad Ḥasan (r. 1781–1801) was engaged in a long war with the inhabitants of Debarwa, in the highlands, who had supported several villages in Serae that refused to pay tribute to the *nāʾib*.[42] At the turn of the nineteenth century, the *nāʾib*s had conducted an expedition against the port of ᶜEdd on the Afar coast. ᶜEdd had been providing an outlet for highland caravans, to the great annoyance of the *nāʾib*s, whose interest was to have all highland trade pass through their dominions, use Massawa as an outlet, and pay them passage dues. The *nāʾib*'s forces attacked ᶜEdd, burnt the village, and forced the village chief to submit to their authority and swear on the Qurʾān that he would not allow highland caravans to pass through that port.[43] As the Ottoman-designated rulers of the region, the *nāʾib*s also utilized their symbolic power in legitimizing their authority. Appointment by the Ottoman authorities in Jiddah, Mecca, or Istanbul added to the *nāʾib*s' prestige.

Controlling Space: Routes, Land, Villages, and Regional Markets

The control of valuable grazing and agricultural lands, caravan trading routes, the means of transportation, and strategic market villages in Massawa's orbit were all central in establishing and securing *nāʾib* power between the mountain and the sea. Spatial dominance involved forceful imposition, political agreements with highland and lowland rulers, and calculated marriage alliances with prominent chiefs, land-based merchants, and commercial brokers. It also involved the settlement of originally Hergigo-based (Balaw) families in key strategic locations, which oftentimes led to the establishment of new market-villages on the trading routes in the vicinities of Massawa and Hergigo. This illustrates the ways by which the *nāʾib*s secured the essential material bases of their power.

As a result of the prevailing state of political instability in the northern highland provinces, the *nāʾib*s were also able to extend their authority over the Saho-speaking pastoralist groups who moved their livestock between the lowlands and the foothills and into Akkele Guzay, Hamasen, and Tigray alternately between seasons.[44] At some point they also controlled several Tigrinya-speaking, mostly farming, populations in the highlands. According to the traditions collected by Odorizzi, Nāʾib ᶜUthmān ᶜĀmir (r. 1741–81) received from the highland rulers forty-four *gult* lands in exchange for firearms.[45] Odorizzi assumed that the number was exaggerated and located the territories at Zeban Zegeb near ᶜAddi Qeyyeh, Maᶜreba west of Halay, Emba Derho, Belesa and Quazen north of Asmara, and Bet Mekae in the western part of Asmara, as well as other lands in Serae and near ʿAdwa.[46] The traditions collected by Kolmodin in Hamasen also suggest that Bahr Negash Solomon (ruled until ca. 1743) had given the *nāʾib* some lands. Bahr Negash Bokru (r. ca. 1770–76), Solomon's son, who had sustained antagonistic relations with the *nāʾib* in power, culminating in violent conflict, eventually took these lands back.[47] Guillaume Lejean also reported that the *nāʾib* controlled sixteen villages in the region of Halay, and Alberto Pollera noted that the *nāʾibs* possessed *gult* lands on the edge of the plateau at Halhale in Tselema, and Mezber in Tigray.[48]

In return for *gult* land and grazing rights on the plateau, the *nāʾibs* were expected to pay the northern highland rulers regular tribute. This would become a critical point of contention when in the mid-nineteenth century, as the scramble for the coast gained momentum, the northern highland chiefs would claim authority over the *nāʾibs*—and therefore legitimate rights of sovereignty on the coast—on the basis of past localized tribute payment in the highlands. This process was not uncommon in other settings at that period—for example in Southeast Asia—where creeping imperialism led local rulers to claim tributary relations with territories sought after by European colonial or paracolonial powers.[49] The possession of *gult* land by the *nāʾib* and his vassals in the highland regions, relatively far from the coast, points to the extent of his power at the period and also illustrates how *nāʾibs* and highland chiefs could collaborate and serve their mutual interests. Nevertheless, by the 1870s, as a result of the increasing aspirations of northern highland rulers, the restoration of the centralized highland polity, and the ensuing decline of the position of the *nāʾibs*, all *gult* land had been returned to highland rulers.

Alongside their actual settlement in Massawa's close environment in localities such as Emkullo, Hetumlo, Zaga, and Emberemi, the *nāʾibs* controlled all the trading routes from Massawa to the interior. They levied taxes on the lucrative caravans making their way via these routes from the interior to the coast. Two important routes linked the coast to ʿAdwa in Tigray: one leaving Massawa through Emkullo and passing through Guraʿ and ʿAddi Kwala; the other leaving Hergigo and passing via Wiʿa, Halay, and Tserona. Both routes had checkposts where caravans and travelers were obliged to pay a passing fee. The *nāʾibs* directly controlled passage stations such as Halay.[50] They also controlled the two mainland caravan-departure villages in Massawa's suburbs: Hergigo, as their chief village and seat of residence, and Emkullo, founded by a group of Hergigo-based families under Nāʾib ʿUthmān ʿĀmir (r. 1741–81).[51] Furthermore, the *nāʾibs* often controlled the means of transportation, and highland-bound travelers had to secure their services in order to be provided with camels and guides for travel toward ᶜAdwa.[52] The documentary evidence abounds with the testimonies of European travelers who had experienced the stressful dependence on the *nāʾib*'s good will and permission to travel inland.

A second system of westerly trading routes left Emkullo and bifurcated at ᶜAylet, a relatively large village, market center, and caravan station situated roughly thirty kilometers to the west of Massawa. Four main routes lying within *nāʾib*-controlled territories left ᶜAylet toward Senhit, Bet Eshaqan (Mensaᶜ), Karxum (?), and Hamasen.[53] ᶜAylet was the most important *nāʾib*-dominated village in the inland. Like Emkullo, ᶜAylet too was founded by Balaws of Hergigo, specifically by the descendants of the sons of Nāʾib ᶜĀmir ᶜAlī (r. 1690–1720), ᶜAbd al-Rasūl, and Osman Shagarai, who had migrated to the site and ended up settling there.[54] But ᶜAylet gradually attracted other settlers, most importantly the Bayt Shaykh Maḥmūd (from Zula) and the ᶜAd Tsaura, both originally Saho-speaking groups who had gradually adopted the Tigre language. ᶜAylet 's position at the foothills of the plateau had made it the most important market village between the coast and the highlands in the middle decades of the nineteenth century. Surrounding pastoralist groups brought livestock and produce to ᶜAylet before the goods were dispatched to Massawa through the coast-controlled networks handled by Balaw merchants. The strong association of the *nāʾibs* with the region is further attested by the settlement of the ᶜAd ᶜAsker near ᶜAylet, on the plains toward Sabarguma. The ᶜAd ᶜAsker were a mixed Saho clan who had gradually adopted the Tigre language and who, prior to their settlement in this region, served those soldiers from Hergigo who had moved to this area following their release from duty.[55]

Finally, although the settlements of ᶜAsus and Gumhod were slightly smaller than ᶜAylet , their economic role as market centers at the foothills of the escarpment and as points of encounter and exchange between coast-based merchants and pastoralists, all of whom were tributary to the *nāʾibs*, was fairly similar. Both Gumhod and ᶜAsus were settled by members of originally Hergigo-based households and family relatives of the *nāʾibs* who developed patron-client relations with local pastoralist clans.[56] The importance of this lies in demonstrating the closely knit social, political, and economic webs that linked the people of the region within the framework of Ottoman indirect control, and the pivotal role of the *nāʾibs* in the process.

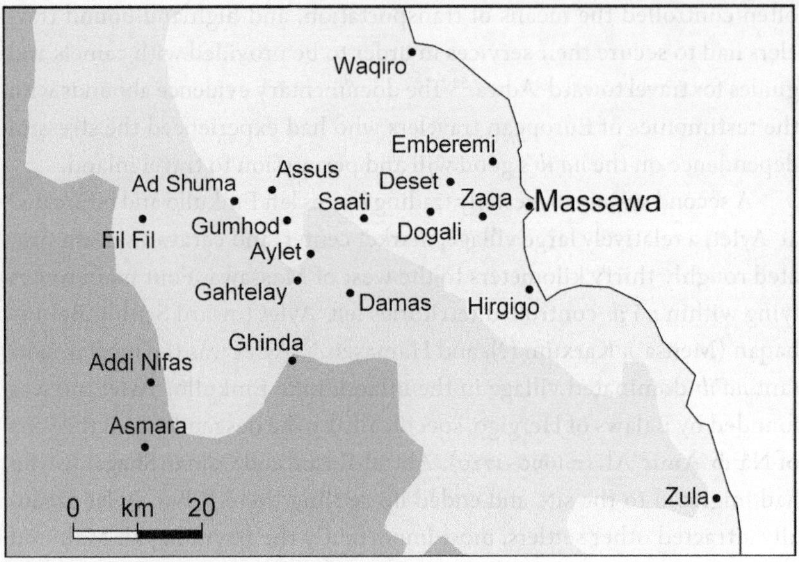

Map 4. Massawa's Close Inlands. Map: Matthias Schulz.

Collecting Revenues: Ottoman Stipends, Taxes, and Tribute

The control of grazing and agricultural lands, trade routes, and centers of commercial exchange provided the *nāʾibs* with economic revenue as privileged participants in the regional economic system. Traveling and settled merchants from Hergigo and pastoralist and agro-pastoralist producers throughout the region exchanged livestock (mostly camels and goats) and agricultural products for manufactured goods imported at Massawa. However, their position as power holders in the region enabled the *nāʾibs* to derive considerable revenue from Ottoman stipends, tax levying on caravans and travelers, and collection of tribute—mostly in kind—from the societies subject to them.[57] The *nāʾibs* received a sum of 1,005 thalers per month from the Massawa customs administration under Nāʾib Idrīs ʿUthmān (r. 1801–31). This sum was supposed to enable the *nāʾib* to keep a force of approximately four hundred soldiers and provide for his militias.[58] The *nāʾib,* according to this arrangement, kept one-fifteenth of the sum for himself, while the soldiers and the militias at Hergigo shared the remaining cash. The *nāʾib,* for his part, paid the government 1,000 thalers per year as recognition of its sovereignty over the province. The Massawa administration paid the *nāʾib*s an additional sum of 90 thalers per month in exchange for the supply of wood from Hergigo.[59]

Between roughly 1750 and 1850 most foreign travelers, missionaries, official envoys, pilgrims, and caravan merchants passing through *nāʾib*-dominated territories had complained of the high taxes that the *nāʾib* forced them to pay. The basic duty that the *nāʾib*s collected on entrance to Massawa was called the *avaït*. Caravan merchants paid the *avaït* awarding their caravans the right of entry to the port. The *avaït* was divided among the branches of the Balaw family. The *nāʾib*s also collected the *fascès,* or exit rights, but handed these funds over to the Ottoman authorities, possibly the customs administration, which had always depended on the provincial central administration in Jiddah.[60] In addition to the *avaït* the *nāʾib*s levied taxes on commodities carried into Massawa by caravans or boats. In the first decade of the nineteenth century Valentia reported that the *nāʾib* received 10 percent of the value of all goods exported and imported at Massawa and one thaler for each person entering the country to trade.[61] A report dating from the 1830s stated that the *nāʾib*s levied one thaler per slave, one thaler per horn of musk (the government taking one-tenth of all musk), and one thaler on every ivory tooth weighing forty pounds (equal to approximately 5% of its contemporary value).[62] South of Massawa, the *nāʾib*s established a post at Giumbedli, near Irafalo, on the road to the Buri peninsula, where they collected one *rohoia* (between three and four liters) for every animal laden with salt arriving from the salt fields of Mekaʿenile. On every butter-laden camel arriving at Gherar, opposite Massawa, the *nāʾib*s could draw one *kubba* (a little less than a *rohoia,* hence, less than 3–4 liters).[63] Although the sum was negotiable, the *nāʾib* also required travelers, envoys, and pilgrims to pay passage duties—a straining and nerve-wracking experience as reported by most European travelers. Henry Salt, for example, was asked by the *nāʾib* to pay 1,000 thalers, and a group of Catholic missionaries were invited to pay 1,000 *écu*s for travel into the interior.[64] In the 1830s the *nāʾib* required a group of Christian Habesha pilgrims on their way to Jerusalem to pay him and leave all their animals with him at Hergigo.[65]

The question of tribute collected from the populations under the *nāʾib*s passed through different phases between the late eighteenth century and the 1850s. At the beginning of the nineteenth century, Lord Valentia reported that the *nāʾib* received 60 thalers in money and camels, goats, and asses from the chief of the Dahlak islands.[66] Tribute collection in the

Figure 1.1. Habab chiefs, early twentieth century? Postcard, author's collection.

early period was rather irregular, erratic, and specifically targeted. Only later, after relatively wealthy groups, in particular the Habab, came under the *nāʾib,* the payment of tribute had become a more important political tool for establishing authority and enforcing recognition, and possibly the main source of income for maintaining the *nāʾib*'s militias and dependents. As such, tribute was also collected following the investiture of chiefs and the mediation of disputes, both performed by the *nāʾib.* Thus, following the investiture of a *kantebay* of the Habab by the *nāʾib,* the newly elected *kantebay* gave the *nāʾib* one hundred camels, one hundred cows, one hundred goats, and one hundred wool blankets in exchange for confirmation.[67] According to Captain Boari's analysis of the tributes in Semhar, the *nāʾibs* maintained a cautious balance in the collection of tribute and avoided heavy taxing that would disturb the regular vivacity of regional commerce.[68]

Beginning in the early 1850s, the gradual transition from indirect to direct control radically transformed the structure of tribute relations. It curtailed the *nāʾibs*' political power and ended their state of autonomy and quasi independence in conducting their regional affairs. The aspiring-to-modernize administration in Massawa introduced a well-regulated annual cash tribute on groups of the Semhar and Sahel areas. The Habab were to pay 3,000 thalers, the ʿAd Tekles, the ʿAd Temaryam, and the Semhar groups 1,000 thalers each. Exempted from the new tribute regime were the town of Massawa and the settled centers of Hergigo, Hetumlo, Emkullo, and Emberemi, which were commercial centers with little property in livestock or agricultural produce. Enfeebled politically, but still useful to the government, the *nāʾibs* were given the role of collecting tribute from the region's various populations for the administration.[69]

Doing Politics: Marriage Alliances, Chief Investiture, and the Administration of Justice

Writing in the 1850s, Werner Munzinger exposed his views on the political strategies devised by the *nāʾibs* in imposing their command over their subjects:

> In a strict sense, the subjects [of the *nāʾib*] included the Beduins of Semhar and the Chohos [Saho]. Nevertheless, in their astuteness, the *nāʾibs* were able to impose their right of arbitration on the entire coast up to the Abyssinian borders by establishing their influence through marriage and by creating divisions and dissent [among these other societies], which they fully used to their advantage. After some time they were proclaimed, without any opposition, the princes of the land where the Tigre language is spoken. The aim of their efforts was to have all caravans from Abyssinia pass via Massawa, securing them significant revenues.[70]

Many examples illustrate the extent to which marriage alliances between members of the *nāʾib* family and important local chiefs or wealthy merchants was a common strategic tool used by *nāʾibs* in the process of establishing their ascendancy in the region. The ʿAd Shuma, for example, tell of Shuma, the daughter of ʿOmar Malaze, who had crossed the Red Sea and landed in the Sawākin area, becoming a leading member in the ʿAd Tsaura group. Shuma, tradition tells, was the founding female ancestor of the ʿAd Shuma, and married a member of the *nāʾib* family from Hergigo. Her sister, Fāṭma, also married into the *nāʾib* family.[71] This practice was even more commonplace between the Balaw and high-status Saho-speaking groups from the area between Hergigo and Zula. One such group, the Muslim holy clan of Bayt Shaykh Maḥmūd, was closely allied through marriage connections with the *nāʾibs*. Another example is the Bet Lelish (or Lelish Are) clan of the Asaorta.[72] The history of the foundation of Emkullo (located several kilometers inland from Massawa) in the second half of the eighteenth century is also rooted in a marriage alliance between the *nāʾib* family and a family of Hadrami *sādah* and prominent merchants in Massawa.[73] Traditions relate that Nāʾib ʿUthmān ʿĀmir's (r. 1741–81) daughter, Settel, married a member of the Bā ʿAlawī family. Settel was pregnant and suffered from poor health, so they both settled in the less oppressively hot site of Emkullo, where Settel could have better provisions of milk for curing her illness. From that point onward both Massawa families and Beduin families from the Sahel and Semhar began settling there.[74]

Throughout their area of influence the *nāʾib*s also invested chiefs, mediated between contestant parties, and arbitrated in legal disputes. Munzinger, again, described the mechanisms through which the *nāʾib* built and exercised his political power:

> The *na'ib* traveled most of the year and was accompanied by a large party. To one site he came to pronounce arbitration, at another place he settled disputes concerning borders, repress brigandage and recover stolen goods. He also toured the region and collected the annual tribute. He seldom intervened in internal matters, except among the Beduins and the Chohos [Saho] in order to confirm the schum [*shum*]. His supremacy was not that of a regular monarch, but was limited to arbitration among societies living in regular interaction and who were incessantly in conflict with each other. The only thing common to them all was their dependence on the *na'ib*.[75]

As a symbol of their formal investiture, the chiefs of ʿAylet received several meters of silk or cotton cloth from the *nāʾib*.[76] The *nāʾib* judged cases in the *kassamet,* his court of justice, an institution that all recognized and about which we have little knowledge. Munzinger observed that arbitrating between litigants could be profitable for the *nāʾib*s, since they required the wrongful party to pay them the objects—slaves, cows, or money—that were the subject of dispute.[77]

Mensaʿ local traditions provide a relatively detailed example of the *nāʾib*'s role in internal politics. The Mensaʿ were cultivators and pastoralists inhabiting a region approximately fifty kilometers northwest of Massawa. They were divided into two groups: the Mensaʿ Bet Eshaqan and the Mensaʿ Bet Abrehe.[78] Alliance with (often through marriage) or opposition to the *nāʾib*s was a central issue in Mensaʿ internal power politics and contestations. Mensaᶜ chiefs manipulated regional politics by allying with one another, a strategy aimed at undermining the rivalry between the *nāʾibs* and the Tigrinya-speaking highland rulers for influence and authority over the Mensaᶜ.[79]

Mensaᶜ Bet Abrehe historical traditions tell of the story of the investiture of Tedros by Nāʾib Ḥasan Idrīs (r. 1845–49).[80] The account is revealing of the political dynamics characteristic of a small inland society and of the tortuous and intricate—yet critical—relationship between the *nāʾibs* and their subjects. Following the death of Kantebay Tesfamikael, his grandson Tedros expected to be invested as *kantebay* of the Mensaᶜ Bet Abrehe.[81] While Nāʾib Ḥasan Idrīs was collecting tribute from the ᶜAd Temaryam in Afᶜabet, the two brothers Jahad and ᶜAdala, from the ᶜAd ᶜAlay clan of the Mensaᶜ Bet Abrehe, approached the *nāʾib* and asked him to appoint Jahad as *kantebay* in return for five hundred head of cattle. Fully aware of Tedros's expectation to be appointed to office, the *nāʾib* sent for him to give him the opportunity to confront the brothers and claim his rights before them. Subsequently, Tedros's representative offered the *nāʾib* 1,500 head of cattle in return for Tedros's investiture as *kantebay.* The *nāʾib* asked the brothers if they were able to match this offer or raise it. They eventually backed off. Tedros was invested as *kantebay* and was handed the symbolic tribal drum, a European sword, a robe, a cap, and a golden bracelet.[82] Some time later, Nāʾib Ḥasan was displeased with Kantebay Tedros, who failed to send him tribute in gifts of livestock. The *nāʾib* launched an expedition against the *kantebay,* but the latter had already fled from his camp. Tradition relates that a man approached the *nāʾib* and informed him that Tedros was frightened but not rebellious. If the *nāʾib* promised not to arrest him, the man would bring Tedros to the *nāʾib.* Nāʾib Ḥasan promised but failed to keep his word. Tedros was taken to the *medún,* to Hergigo, where he was imprisoned for two years.[83] He was released and re-invested *kantebay* only after Nāʾib Muḥammad ᶜAbd al-Raḥīm overthrew Nāʾib Ḥasan from power. Kantebay Tedros offered the new *nāʾib* a daughter in marriage and some cattle.[84]

Spreading Islam: Nāʾibs *and Holy Families*

The extension and consolidation of *nāʾib* supremacy accompanied a spectacular process of Islamic diffusion among Tigre-speaking societies, namely the Bet Asgede confederation (Habab, ᶜAd Tekles, ᶜAd Temaryam), Mensaᶜ, Marya, Bet Juk, and segments of the Bilin. Several extra- and cross-regional factors account for the context of this process, which is located in the first half of the nineteenth century, especially between the 1820s and 1850s. The energetic activities of several Muslim holy families and Sufi brotherhoods (Ar. sing. *ṭarīqa,* pl. *ṭuruq*) such as the Qādiriyya, but much more notably the Khatmiyya, reflected this reawakening in the wider area. In the lowland plains between Massawa and the highlands the atmosphere of Islamic revival inspired and fueled intense and widespread propagating activities by Muslim holy clans and families such as the ᶜAd Shaykh, the Bayt Shaykh Maḥmūd, the ᶜAd Muᶜallim, and the ᶜAd Darqī.[85]

From the 1820s onward the *conjoncture* in the Braudelian sense of Egyptian expansion into the Sudan under Muḥammad ᶜAlī (r. 1805–49), together with the revitalization of the commercial axes connecting the Red Sea and the Nile Valley, both fueled and catalyzed the spectacular process of Islamic diffusion among the largely Tigre-speaking societies of the Eritrean region. Some groups such as the Bet Asgede confederation, the Marya, the Mensaᶜ, and the Bilin had practiced, in different forms and to varying degrees, forms of Orthodox Christianity until then. The political decentralization of the Christian Ethiopian state and the vulnerability of predominantly pastoralist societies on its northern fringes were also conducive to the success of the spread of Islam in the area. Northern highland Christian chiefs tended to raid these societies intermittently but persistently in an effort to extend their rule over them and impose tribute payment. The struggle between Egyptians and Tigrinya-speaking highlanders for the control of the northern territories and eventual Egyptian military superiority provided a fertile ground for the activities of Muslim preachers and traders, but also Egyptian official "persuasion" to adopt Islam.[86] Furthermore, the revival of Red Sea trade directly influenced the intensity and character of inland trade, and an increasing number of Muslim traders, both from the Sudanese region and from across the Red Sea, participated actively in preaching and propagating Islam along trade routes and in market villages.[87] Conversion to Islam in this context vested Tigre-speaking communities with a new identity and a powerful counter-hegemonic force and ideology, endowing them with a source of authority and political legitimacy.

The *nāʾib*s and other *nāʾib*-related families from Semhar were active participants in the process of extending their influence hand in hand with the diffusion of Islam. The *nāʾib*s developed an increasing position of prestige and religious sanction as Muslims, mainly by their association with the Islamic institutions at Massawa and with a number of holy clans and families in the Semhar and Sahel. One such clan was the Bayt Shaykh Maḥmūd, who propagated Islam throughout the region as far as the Sahel, the Keren area, and the Barka. The *nāʾibs* were closely associated with the Bayt Shaykh Maḥmūd, with whom they shared the control of important mainland suburbs of Massawa (Hergigo and Emkullo) and important inland villages (ʿAylet and Gumhod).[88] In Hergigo, the Bayt Shaykh Maḥmūd was the most prominent group after the cluster of originally Balaw families, with whom many were linked in marriage. Several in particular were connected to the Kekiyā family.[89] The *nāʾibs* cooperated with the Bayt Shaykh Maḥmūd by sending families of this clan to provide religious services among groups such as the Ghedem Sikta, ʿAd Ha, and ʿAd ʿAsker.[90] The same pattern of cooperation, perhaps to a more limited extent than with the Bayt Shaykh Maḥmūd, may have occurred with the ʿAd Muʿallim, serving especially the ʿAd Temaryam, and the ʿAd Darqī active among the Habab.[91]

Of equal, if not surpassing, importance, a pattern of cooperation existed between the *nāʾibs* and the potent ʿAd Shaykh holy family, the most influential in the region before its prominence was surpassed by the Khatmiyya *ṭarīqa* under Italian colonial rule. In the early nineteenth century, the family was especially active in the Sahel region. It was led by Shaykh al-Amīn b. Ḥāmid b. Nafʿūtāy, who gradually gained widespread reputation through his preaching and miracle working among the Muslim *tigre* serf classes of the Bet Asgede, who approached him to seek his *baraka*. Thus began a process of marriages with that group, eventually resulting in the conversion of the *tigre* class of the Bet Asgede to Islam, and marking their social liberation and emancipation.[92] The ʿAd Shaykh undermined the prevailing social structure and manipulated the social distinction between Bet Asgede "nobles" and *tigre* "serfs" to their own advantage. They allied themselves with the latter and provided them with a new counter-hegemonic ideology that challenged their state of subservience.[93] Subsequently, Shaykh al-Amīn married the daughter of the *kantebay* of the Bet Asgede, marking the conversion of the upper class as well. Many of the newly converted joined the ʿAd Shaykh holy family, which enlarged itself relatively rapidly and gradually became an independent group. In the process the family accumulated considerable wealth from gifts and offerings in return for *baraka*.[94]

In the course of the century, sections of the family split off from the main group and moved westward to Barka and ʿAnseba. One group, led by Shaykh Muḥammad b. ʿAlī b. al-Amīn (ca. 1795–1877) settled in Semhar.

Shaykh Muḥammad was undoubtedly one of the more influential religious figures of the coastlands and the interior from the 1840s to his death in 1877. His *baraka* attracted scores of pilgrims to Emberemi, which one mid-nineteenth-century observer qualified as a "little Mecca."[95] The ʿAd Shaykh operated in tandem with the *nāʾibs* in the process of diffusing Islam and attracted adepts into the Qādiriyya *ṭarīqa,* mostly from among the Marya and the Mensaʿ.[96] Later in the nineteenth century, and concomitantly with the transformation of *nāʾib* power, the influence of the ʿAd Shaykh waned in favor of the Khatmiyya *ṭarīqa,* which flourished under Egyptian and Italian colonial rule.

The *nāʾibs* may have also exercised a certain degree of influence and authority in the administration of Islamic law. Even though local *qāḍīs* judged within their societies, they tended to approach either the *nāʾib,* knowledgeable *shaykhs* in the region, or the *qāḍīs* and *muftīs* of Massawa for further advice in complex matters.[97] The identification of the legal rites (Ar. sing. *madhhab*) of the societies subject to the *nāʾibs* reveals that a sweeping majority were Ḥanafī, the official *madhhab* of the Ottoman Empire and the Egyptians.[98]

Return of the Pashas: The Scramble for the Coast and the Transformation of *Nāʾib* Political Agency (1840s and 1850s)

A sea change in the geopolitical position of the Red Sea area and northeast Africa marked the beginning of the nineteenth century. The slow but steady revival of Red Sea trade, the mounting regional imperialist ambitions of Muḥammad ʿAlī's Egypt, the renewed Ottoman centralizing impulse and their renewed ambitions on both sides of the southern Red Sea coasts, and the gradual consolidation of political power in the northern highland province of Tigray transformed the regional power balance and presented the *nāʾibs* with new pressures and challenges. The rulers of Tigray were increasingly interested in securing their access to the sea, through which they could procure arms and strengthen their position vis-à-vis other central highland political formations. The revitalization of trade in the Red Sea area also triggered interest in commerce and politics in the region from Europeans, who from the 1830s attempted to establish direct relations with highland rulers. The *nāʾibs* found themselves at the heart of imperialist power politics and diplomatic competition and saw their power progressively erode.[99]

Past historiography privileging almost exclusively political and diplomatic dimensions has tended all too lightly to mark the end of *nāʾib* power as a result of various skirmishes or incidents initiated by the larger contenders for power in the region. These perceptions might have reflected the wishful thinking of European semi-official and official envoys writing reports to their governments in London and Paris. Historians have advanced various dates—among them 1808–1809, 1813–14, 1847–49, 1865–66—as marking the supposed end of the power of the *nāʾibs*.[100] Clearly, the power of the *nāʾibs* had begun a process of gradual erosion since the first decade of the nineteenth century and throughout the checkered, albeit overall progressive, transition from Ottoman indirect control to Egyptian direct administration. However, their power was still several decades away from being totally eclipsed.

The first significant change in the *nāʾib*'s position may be traced to the end of 1808, when the *sharīf* Ghālib of Mecca sent troops to Massawa to establish his authority in the port.[101] Sources based on *nāʾib* traditions suggest that the action was triggered by growing internal struggles within the family following Nāʾib Idrīs ʿUthmān's (r. 1801–31) appeal for the *sharīf*'s assistance to suppress a local revolt, possibly instigated by a family rival.[102] Three years later, following the Egyptian conquest of the Hijaz, a Wahhābī fleet attempted unsuccessfully to seize Massawa.[103] In 1814, the newly appointed Egyptian governor of the *Wilāya* of Jiddah, Aḥmad Ṭūsūn, sent a force of sixty soldiers and a *qāʾim maqām* to Massawa. Ottoman-Egyptian trials of power, as they played out in the southern coasts of the Red Sea, did not—at least at this point—alter the position of the *nāʾib*, who retained his authority and his monthly stipend.[104]

Muḥammad Alī's invasion of Arabia in 1811–18 and his campaign in the Sudan in 1820–21 prompted increasing Egyptian efforts to tighten their control over Massawa and, in effect, set in motion a gradual process of the establishment of direct control. The Egyptians incessantly put to the test the limits of their power both vis-à-vis the Ottoman Porte and locally, in their newly occupied dominions. In 1826 the *qāʾim maqām* at Massawa suspended the monthly pay of the *nāʾib*'s militias, inducing the rebellion of the *nāʾib*, who sent his soldiers to attack Massawa and cut the island-port's water supply. The *qāʾim maqām* fled from Massawa, taking as hostages three of the *nāʾib*'s officials, who were eventually left on the Dahlak islands.[105] In the wake of this trial of power, and upon the request of the inhabitants of Massawa, a new Egyptian *qāʾim maqām* returned to the port with a new modest garrison. Nevertheless, real power still remained in the hands of the *nāʾib*.[106]

In the 1830s, political developments in the northern areas of the highland plateau, European ventures to establish relations with highland rulers, and Egyptian advances on the western fringes of the plateau and in the Red Sea greatly affected the situation on the coast. The new regional order that began taking shape brushed aside the *nāʾib*s. By 1831, Dejazmatch Webe Haile Mariam (1799–1867) had succeeded in placing himself as the most powerful ruler in the northern highlands, where he controlled a vast territory that included Tigray, Semen, Walqayt, and Wegera.[107] Webe's precise relationship with the *nāʾib* is not very clear, but the northern highlanders were increasingly disposed to claim sovereignty over the coast without the actual means, and/or desire, to enforce it in practice and translate it into effective presence.[108] Between 1832 and 1837 pressure escalated on the western marches of the plateau as a result of Khurshīd Pasha's methodical extension toward and into the highlands.[109] The Egyptian takeover of Kassala in 1840 and the fear of imminent Egyptian ambitions to secure territorial continuity between the Nile and the Red Sea impelled a decade of triangular confrontations between Webe, the *nāʾib*s, and the Egyptians, out of which the *nāʾib*s emerged considerably diminished politically. Tensions heightened as Europeans manipulated all sides, seeking to promote their own agenda and drag their governments into greater involvement in the region.

Massawa remained under Egyptian domination (but not sovereignty, which remained with Istanbul) from 1813 until in early 1841 an agreement between the Ottoman Porte and Muḥammad ʿAlī led to the evacuation of the Egyptian troops from the port-town. The Ottomans garrisoned Massawa under a *qāʾim maqām* with a handful of soldiers, but were unable to exercise effective control. The Egyptians returned only five years later, in 1846, after the Ottoman Sultan leased both Massawa and Sawākin to Muḥammad ʿAlī against payment of an annual tribute of 5,000 *kīs* (purses), or 25,000 Egyptian pounds.[110] In the interval, the *nāʾib*s once again held effective power in Semhar and challenged Webe's aspirations to impose his authority over the areas between the highland and the sea. Conflict mounted during the second half of the year 1843. After Nāʾib Yaḥyā Aḥmad's (r. 1841–44) son raided Hamasen, took three thousand head of cattle, and burnt a village, Webe threatened to reciprocate and raid Hergigo if the cattle and a sum of 4,000 francs (about 600 thalers) of caravan taxes were not returned. The issue was brought before the *majlis* at Massawa and, fearing a destructive raid, the *nāʾib* accepted Webe's demands.[111] Notwithstanding, Webe eventually conducted a furtive raid in the *nāʾib*'s lands in December 1843, but returned rapidly back to the highlands. In September 1844 hostilities resumed but not for long. As a result of increased Egyptian military pressure on Webe's northern borders, his armies had their hands full as they raided the Bogos and Habab areas.[112]

As the struggle over the coast mounted, Webe made some efforts to establish his authority in Semhar by applying pressure over the *nāʾib*s and—as all external powers have done—by playing on the historical division and rivalry within the Balaw dynasty. Following Nāʾib Yaḥyā Aḥmad's death in 1844, Nāʾib Ḥasan Idrīs replaced him in office.[113] Webe calculatingly exploited the divisions in the family by recognizing and trying to co-opt the late Nāʾib Yaḥyā's son, Muḥammad Yaḥyā, as the only *nāʾib* but to no avail at that stage. Webe also sought the French government's protection in return for an eventual territorial foothold in the bay of Hergigo. Approaching Consul Degoutin, Webe justified and claimed his rights on the coast since the *nāʾib*s had paid him tribute—an assertion that was only partly accurate since it applied only to land and grazing rights in the highlands and on the northeastern rims of the plateau. The French, who were unwilling to put their delicate relationship with the Ottoman sultan in Istanbul at risk, refused to venture themselves in the affair.[114] In December 1845, Rustum Agha, the Ottoman governor of Massawa, appointed Muḥammad Yaḥyā as *nāʾib,* and thus satisfied Webe's political speculation. Soon after, following the withholding of their payment, the *nāʾib*s once again rebelled against Ottoman authority. Rustum Agha attacked Hergigo, where he encountered resolute resistance by a united front of both branches of the *nāʾib* family, compelling the Ottoman forces to withdraw back to the island, which the *nāʾib*s blockaded again.[115]

All in all, the return of Massawa and the coast to the Egyptian government in 1846 signaled a further blow to *nāʾib* authority. The Egyptians, who perceived the connection of their Sudanese possessions—especially the province of Taka—with the Red Sea coast as vital to their imperialist hegemonic aspirations, pursued a more aggressive policy of direct control in the ports and their surroundings. This attitude built up toward a head-to-head confrontation with the *nāʾib*s, and in March 1847, a resolute new Egyptian governor, Ismāʿīl Ḥaqqī, arrived at Massawa with a relatively important infantry force. Determined to eliminate the *nāʾib*s, his forces landed in Hergigo on 16 June 1847. They burnt down the village, destroyed the houses of the *nāʾib* and those of other important Balaw dignitaries, ordered the construction of a fortress, and placed a battalion to guard the wells that provided Massawa with water. Many of Hergigo's dwellers left the area and sought refuge on the mountain slopes. Emkullo, another important *nāʾib* stronghold, was also garrisoned by one hundred soldiers.[116]

Grasping the geopolitical significance of the resolute Egyptian encroachment on the coast, Webe sent his own forces to raid the Semhar and attempt to capture Hergigo. His forces raided Emkullo and destroyed it on 6 January 1849, before pillaging Hergigo and other coastal villages and leaving five hundred dead, capturing five hundred prisoners, and taking ten thousand head of cattle. Observers reported that about fifteen thousand of the mainland inhabitants opposite Massawa and the surrounding villages sought refuge on the island-port.[117] Webe continued to demand tribute payment and threatened to pillage the coast if it was not made. In the wake of Webe's devastating raid in Semhar and as a result of internal Egyptian political developments in the aftermath of Muḥammad ʿAlī's death in 1849, Massawa and Sawākin returned to the Porte in that same year. The ports would stay in Ottoman hands until 1865.

During the ups and downs of the 1840s, sovereignty over the port was transferred between Ottomans and Egyptians three times. The *nāʾib*s continued to enjoy a high degree of autonomy especially in the period of Ottoman sovereignty (1841–46). In 1847 Plowden noted that "within the last eight years it is evident also that the *nāʾib* has been considered in all respects (. . .) as an independent Sovereign on the mainland." The *nāʾib,* the British consul's memorandum continued, "makes war or peace at pleasure, receives tribute from all the native tribes and sells land to individuals."[118] But the increasing involvement of Egypt in the second half of the decade changed this state of affairs and, again, further impeded the *nāʾib*'s political power. Nevertheless, even following the return of Massawa to the Porte the gradual erosion of their power continued.

The transformation of the structure of relations between the *nāʾib*s and the Egyptians (and the Ottomans) was a direct result of the Egyptians' growing military presence and interventionist approach in Massawa and the mainland. The interference and manipulation of local family politics and the transition to a direct mode of tribute collection in the interior undermined the authority of the *nāʾib,* cut off part of his direct revenues, and, overall, contributed to the wearing away of his pervasive influence. As their interest in regaining a foothold on the Red Sea coasts mounted, the Ottoman authorities sought to find a way to somehow curtail and neutralize the now-redundant influence of the *nāʾib*s.[119] As in the past, the cooption by Ottoman governors of one *nāʾib* over a rival pretender to the office was highly characteristic of this transitional period and resulted in vesting governors with more practical power. As governors changed, alliances also tended to switch. A good example illustrating this pattern was the rivalry between Nāʾib Ḥasan Idrīs (Bayt ʿUthmān, r. 1843–47 and r. 1849–51) and Nāʾib Muḥammad Yaḥyā (Bayt Ḥasan, r. 1847–49) and their descendants throughout the 1850s and 1860s.[120] The typical pattern involved the deportation of the deposed or un-appointed *nāʾib* to Mecca, the seat of the *mushīr*. He stayed there until either the authorities reinstated him and sent him back to Hergigo or he was sent back to Hergigo in the company of a new governor with whom he was to exercise control in tandem.[121]

Nāʾib Ḥasan Idrīs's reappointment in 1849 changed his position considerably in comparison with his first term in office in the middle of the same decade. While in the past the *nāʾibs* had received an annual pay from the Ottoman authorities, they were now required to pay tribute to the governor. To such request the *nāʾibs* are reported to have replied: "We are accustomed to receive tribute, not pay it."[122] Nāʾib Ḥasan's position, the sources continue, resembled that of a "civil servant" who received a pay of 30 thalers per month and who was charged to collect tribute for the Ottoman government from the pastoralist populations of Semhar. "The governors from Constantinople," Consul Plowden remarked in his long report of 1854, "(. . .) have but one thought, the extraction of money."[123] The combination of these changes upset the relative state of stability in Semhar and unsettled the control of coastal authority over the inland populations. Plowden remarked again that "having destroyed the power of the *nāʾibs*, the whole land is without law or security."[124]

Indeed, the interior groups—especially the Saho-speaking and the Habab—rebelled against Ottoman efforts to extract the tribute by force. At the end of June 1850 a force of 250 Ottoman soldiers, together with segments of the *nāʾib*'s militias, attacked Habab territory, where they were met with firm resistance. Similarly, in February 1853 the pasha in Massawa prepared a joint land and seaborne expedition against the small port of Amphila, south of Massawa, to confirm there the Ottoman sultan's authority and collect tribute. There too, the Saho-speaking groups assembled 3,000 men and threatened to pillage the territory to their north. The *nāʾib* succeeded in "pacifying" them and eventually called off the expedition.[125] However, the tensions between Saho-speaking groups of the area and the Ottoman authorities in Massawa continued to destabilize communications between the coast and the highlands since the Saho controlled the principal routes and the means of transportation, namely camels. Munzinger remarked that following the clashes of 1853–54 the Saho "had lost all respect to these authorities and security was never totally re-established."[126] As had been the case on several occasions in the past, *nāʾib*s who were either removed from office or out of official power allied themselves with mainland "rebellious" groups and attempted to challenge coastal authority and rival acting *nāʾib*s. Thus, Nāʾib Idrīs allied himself with the Saho-speaking groups against the Ottomans and Nāʾib Muḥammad Yaḥyā. Together, they attacked the villages of ʿAylet , Zaga, and Emkullo and ravaged the suburbs of Massawa in December 1854. Idrīs demanded that the Ottomans withdraw from Hergigo, but an Egyptian force of 360 soldiers coming from Taka assisted them in reestablishing a state of relative order only in 1856.[127]

The *nāʾib*s' new capacity as tribute collectors for the Ottoman governor placed them under substantial pressure. They were able to preserve their wavering powers over societies between the coast and the mountains only through force-induced tribute collection and subordination. Both the need for income from tribute and the redefinition of their position under a reinvigorated Ottoman administration on the coast and on the mainland put the *nāʾib*s in a difficult position. They were caught in an uneasy spot between the authorities, to whom they owed the survival—even if diminished—of their authority and the inland populations, who could not ignore the new situation as they were put under growing pressure by both the authorities in Massawa and the *nāʾib*s. The transformation in the structure of relations between the *nāʾib*s and inland populations was abrupt in relation to past, more flexible relations permitting various degrees of political and economic cooperation and founded on an intricate web of regionally based economic and social ties. The "modern" Ottoman-Egyptian regime of tribute collection ended this order. During the 1850s and 1860s the *nāʾib*s conducted forceful expeditions—often in tandem with Ottoman forces—against populations in the Hamasen, Mensaʿ, and Bogos areas.[128]

Although the political power of the *nāʾib*s declined considerably, they were able to capitalize on their pivotal position in regional commercial networks and on their position of prestige among lowland societies, established over time. They thus converted their political capital into economic capital. As a result of the trials of power of the 1840s and 1850s that culminated in their enfeeblement (and the destruction of their centers of power in Hergigo) many *nāʾib*-associated families and individuals left the area and devoted themselves to trade between the coast and the White Nile.

They dispersed among all the lowland groups, where they often settled and married into local families.[129] Dominating the commerce with the coast, they brought ivory from the Nile region and wax and coffee from Metemma and dispatched those commodities via Keren to Massawa. Munzinger remarked that these new commercial entrepreneurs "are known everywhere by the name *ʿaskar* (soldiers) and are in general highly esteemed"; thus, he added, "the ex-inhabitants of Hergigo flourish among strangers."[130]

The conjuncture of a decentralized and indirect mode of Ottoman control, the unwillingness or inability of highland rulers to take control over the Red Sea coastlands, and the political instability in the central and northern highlands during the so-called *Zemene Mesefint* (1769–1855) denoted the absence of a strong state in the region between the coast and the mountain between the early 1600s and the middle of the nineteenth century. This state of affairs enabled the *nāʾib*s to acquire power, impose their authority, and extend their influence over societies of the region. The hegemonic order established by the *nāʾib*s provided relative security and stability in the area through political, economic, social, and religious means. These networks and fields of action linked the coast-based *nāʾib*s with interior societies and contributed to shape the mostly lowland region of present-day eastern Eritrea. The laying out of a regional infrastructure of social, political, commercial, and religious networks and alliances connected and gravitated toward Massawa was one of the outcomes of these processes.

From around the 1830s onward the reinvigoration of Red Sea area sparked off a truculent struggle between large rivaling polities over control of the coastlands. From the mid-1840s the clash of sovereignties resulted in the transition from indirect to direct Ottoman and Egyptian control, which significantly eroded the power of the *nāʾib*s. The diminution of *nāʾib* political power reflected the transformation in the meanings of sovereignty typical of other localities in Asia and Africa at that time. From mid-century, with the wave of reinvigorated imperialism, the notion of indivisible and unitary sovereignty was increasingly imposed, representing a break from methods of governance and legitimacy that had been common in the past.[131] An intimately related consequence of creeping imperialism was a gradual shift in the conception and meaning of borders. Effective military occupation and control, together with a centralized and modernized imperial administration, translated into a more rigidified notion of frontiers—one that was not there beforehand, when boundaries were nebulous and undefined. Egypt's expansionist enterprise in northeast Africa under Muḥammad ʿAlī and the *khedives* aspired to create territorial continuities between possessions in the Nile Valley and the Red Sea coasts—a process that led to a more pronounced definition of territorial boundaries. The rigidification of frontiers culminated in the late nineteenth century with the creation and consolidation of the Italian colony of Eritrea.

Following a period of instability in mid-century, the scramble for the Red Sea coast culminated with the Egyptian occupation (1865–85) of parts of the coastlands controlled by the *nāʾib*s until then.[132] The rise of Massawa to its position as a major Red Sea hub crystallized and cemented even further the region between the mountain and the sea. The port's role as the focal point for economic and political, but also social, religious, and cultural activities and influence throughout the region was further enhanced. The growing new class of merchants and brokers who made their fortunes as result of the transforming political economy of commerce in the area in the middle decades of the century also contributed to erode the power of the *nāʾib*s. Tensions between the *nāʾib*s and Massawa's merchant community have been recorded on various occasions, in which the latter had complained about the *nāʾib*s' abuse of power and their disruption of regular and safe commercial activities.[133]

By all means, the story of the *nāʾib*s does not end here. The *nāʾib* family continued to wield power, first and foremost through the domination of a widespread web of commercial networks connecting Massawa with the Nile Valley. To some extent it also maintained the bases of its regional authority. The Egyptians and later the Italians developed relations of accommodation with the *nāʾib* family, assisting them in administering their territories and in maintaining stability. The *nāʾib*s continued to convert and reconvert the political, economic, and social capital acquired in past centuries in adjusting and accommodating to rapidly changing times—and new opportunities.

2

On Camels and Boats

Spaces, Structures, and Circuits of Production and Exchange

At the peak of its boom years in the 1870s and 1880s, observers who witnessed the impressive inflow of caravan traffic into and out of Massawa, its colorful and vivacious markets, and its vigorous multi-ethnic class of merchants, brokers, and commercial financiers referred to the port-town as the "Zanzibar of the Red Sea." This chapter explores the economic connections and relationships that linked Massawa to its hinterlands and to its forelands in the Red Sea and northwestern Indian Ocean area. I analyze the port's articulation to spheres of production and exchange and the ways by which the impact of the structural transformations of the global economy on the western Indian Ocean area transformed Massawa's economic roles and functions. Beginning in the early middle decades of the nineteenth century, the conjuncture, in Braudel's sense, of the transportation revolution, remarkable commercial amplification, and heightened imperialist activities in the Red Sea area, reconfigured Massawa's relationships with both its forelands and its hinterlands.[1]

The examination of Massawa's overland long-distance caravan trade with the Ethiopian and Sudanese regions reveals that the port was linked to distant producing inlands through two distinct overland caravan routes, each shaped by different historical, geographical, and political dynamics. Each route connected to the commercial structures of the port through different mechanisms, influencing the structure of inland trading patterns and networks. The chapter also examines the ramifications of northeastern Africa's integration into the world economy on the development of Massawa's regional fields of production and exchange in its immediate interior and in the Dahlak Archipelago. Since the 1860s the balance between long-distance trade and regional trade at Massawa significantly shifted in favor of the latter. A number of political and economic factors accounted for the gradual decline of long-distance trade and the marked development of regional production and commerce. Massawa became more tightly connected to its close inlands, and islands, which came to take the role of its primary economic hinterlands. This process made a considerable impact on the lowland pastoralist societies of the region, some of whom were led to modify their modes of production and ways of life, increasingly integrating cultivation with herding and settling in villages. Others interacted with developing regional markets along the caravan routes where they traded their products and offered transportation and brokerage services. The pearling economy in the Dahlak Archipelago also epitomized this pattern; by the early decades of the twentieth century, the exportation of mother-of-pearl from Massawa represented one of the more lucrative economic enterprises of Italian Eritrea's economy. The broad-ranging process drew the region and its inhabitants closer to urban coastal economic and social spheres of influence and consequently shaped Massawa's landward disposition.

Following the overarching conceptual approach of this study, I have chosen to work from within a broad temporal framework, which avoids automatically equating political transitions with economic transformations. More than fashion economic enterprise as neatly wrapped projects, in the case of Massawa the occupying and colonial powers (Egypt and Italy) adapted to economic developments that were initiated by larger international economic forces holding sway on this part of the world prior to political transitions (1865 and 1885). They identified opportunities (e.g., agriculture, pearling) and made efforts to capitalize on them to advance colonial objectives. In many cases they relied on and promoted commercial enterprise that was operated by local, regional, and transregional networks that were already in place before transformations in political sovereignty. One could argue that in general, Massawa was first and foremost the town of its merchants. Imperial administrations, which did not invest in significant economic development until the 1920s, were sometimes dependent on and poorer than local prominent merchants. On at least two occasions—one in the 1830s under Egyptian dominance and the other in the 1920s under the Italians—sources note how the administrations in place had borrowed cash from the town's leading merchants.

Commercial Revival and Transformation in the Red Sea

At the opening of the nineteenth century, international commerce in the Red Sea basin was relatively stagnant. The Red Sea was on the margins of the great international waterways, and the only European vessels that ventured into the area seldom went beyond the port of Mukhā, where merchants purchased coffee. Up until the beginning of the nineteenth century, the Red Sea was, in the words of the historian André Raymond, a "divided sea" comprising a northern Egyptian-dominated sphere and a southern sector where Yemeni, Indian, and European vessels operated.[2] Already alluded to by Arab mariners such as Aḥmad ibn al-Majīd in his famous *Kitāb al-Fawāʾid* (AH 895/AD 1490), this division was based on a different wind regime governing navigation in the basin—from the Bāb al-Mandab strait to some point between al-Qufundha and Jiddah, and from there to Suez. In the northern part of the Red Sea, the prevailing wind blows from the north all year long, making it difficult and slow to sail from south to north. On the other hand, in the southern half of the sea, while the wind blows from the north most of the year, between October and April the northeast monsoon winds of the Arabian Sea produce a strong southerly wind in the southern sector of the Red Sea.[3] Between the last quarter of the eighteenth century and Muḥammad ʿAlī's final suppression of the Wahhābī revolt in 1818, the political troubles with the Mamluks in Egypt and the Wahhābīs and their allies in the Hijaz and the Yemen also negatively affected regional commerce in the basin.

Beginning in the second and third decades of the nineteenth century several factors contributed toward the transformation of Red Sea commercial structures, relationships, and dynamics, ultimately generating accelerated European penetration. From that point on the Red Sea regained its importance as a waterway in the global system connecting the Mediterranean and Indian Ocean and gained a crucial position in the vast commercial triangle Zanzibar–Cairo (Suez)–Bombay. The rise of Muḥammad ʿAlī in Egypt, his suppression of the Wahhābī revolt in the Hijaz, and his policies of expansionism in northeast Africa marked a renewed period of Ottoman-Egyptian dominance in the basin, bringing more security and stability for trade. The introduction of steamship navigation in the early 1830s, with the opening of several British lines connecting Bombay with Suez, transformed navigational and commercial patterns, having a direct impact on the configuration of port hierarchies and subsequently on interport competition.[4] Clearly, perhaps for the first time in the history of the Red Sea, modern technology had bridged the "divided sea." The advent of Egyptian hegemony transformed the Red Sea area as a socioeconomic space generating new patterns of mobility and settlement in the basin's ports. Egypt was itself drawn into the European economic system, a process that deeply marked the expanding economic and commercial dynamics in the territories and waterways under its control. From the 1840s onward the Red Sea increasingly served as a conduit between the Indian Ocean and the Mediterranean. The steamship-led transportation revolution connected Europe to Africa and Asia more dynamically, but it also transformed Africa-Asia trade structures, rendering the Red Sea area an auxiliary zone serving the new European-centered system, and "regionalizing" it.

The port of Mukhā, previously the most important international entrepôt in the area, declined in favor of Aden and Jiddah, which replaced Mukhā's role in the Red Sea and northwestern Indian Ocean systems.[5] In order to provide its vessels with a port of transit between Bombay and Suez, the British occupied Aden in January 1839, before turning it to a free port in 1850. Following the removal of the Wahhābīs, the port of Jiddah regained importance as the port for pilgrims to Mecca, a development that closely affected trade since pilgrims often engaged in business while on the *ḥājj*. Jiddah became the regional port serving Arabia, and an international entrepôt linking long-distance with regional navigation networks and redistributing European, Egyptian, Indian, Javanese merchandise as well as goods from the Arabian Gulf reaching it either directly or via the smaller cabotage networks from Ḥudayda, Luḥayya, Massawa, or Sawākin.[6] Vessels from India increasingly arrived directly to Jiddah, where new navigation lines connected to traditional regional Red Sea navigation networks, thus also making Jiddah the chief Red Sea entrepôt. If 38 steamships visited Jiddah in 1864, the number was multiplied by more than five, to reach 205 in 1875.[7] In the late 1860s, about 50 large sailing ships, with mainly cottons, rice, and spices, reached Jiddah from India every year.[8] Jiddah's merchants participated in a web of trading networks extending from Turkey, Syria, and Egypt through the southern Red Sea area to India. In such an expansive commercial system, merchants, financiers, sailors, laborers, career officers, pilgrims, slaves, and a variety of commodities crossed the seas from port to port more dynamically. Commercialization unquestionably also fueled the slave trade and slave traffic across northeastern Africa and the northwestern Indian Ocean area. The Muslim pilgrimage to Mecca was not a negligible factor in this system, and shipping commodities and pilgrims could bring both piety and profit. Many entrepreneurs settled in Red Sea ports—some staying only temporarily, until running out of luck; others making these ports their new homes. Indeed, when one looks at the composition of the mercantile, labor, and service-oriented populations of burgeoning Red Sea and Gulf of Aden ports (for example, Jiddah,

Sawākin, Ḥudayda, and Aden) in the second half of the nineteenth century, it almost seems as if these ports have been subject to a takeover by Hadrami, Egyptian, and Indian entrepreneurs. For example, at the height of its boom years, in 1870, one observer noted that Jiddah's merchants numbered 200, of whom 150 were Hadramis.[9] In Massawa too, a large majority of the town's "big merchants" as well as those controlling its commercial, religious, and juridical institutions from the 1870s at least, were recently settled entrepreneurs.

Trading and Shipping Networks: Between Interdependence and Competition

Political, navigational, and commercial change had a critical impact on the relationships between European, Arab, and Indian commercial systems operating in the Red Sea in the middle decades of the century. Contrary to the received wisdom of a sharp break as a result of European economic penetration, Arab and Indian commercial networks proved resilient and capable of adjustment to both political and economic change. Such networks established new business enterprises and restructured existing ones in ports ranging from the Indian subcontinent to the eastern Mediterranean; they also continued to dominate the trade of specific commodities or monopolize navigation routes between ports. But "adjustment" and "adaptation" did not mean "independence." Indeed, as much as these networks were able to preserve their operational autonomy and find lucrative niches in regional trade, trading networks in the Red Sea area became increasingly subordinated to a more extensive European-dominated structure and system of industry, markets, and national and imperial polities.[10]

It is significant to dwell upon several aspects of the modus operandi of these networks in order to provide the context for understanding the development of Massawa's seaward mercantile connections and relationships. The northern Red Sea "Arab" system was a network of Egyptian, Hadrami, and Hijazi traders and agents extending along the basin and having main commercial house offices in Cairo and Jiddah and agents, or brokers, in Suez, Qusayr, Sawākin, and Massawa. Merchants and agents in these ports were linked to one another in networks and organized in tightly knit corporations with well-regulated operating practices and exclusive channels for gathering and exchanging business information. They were able to reduce the cost of trade by coordinating navigation rigorously in order to maximize efficiency and minimize transportation costs.

In 1840, for example, the rotation of vessels on the Jiddah-Suez line was of one leaving for Jiddah every three years so that other vessels would have the possibility to accomplish their tour. Twenty-five years later, in 1865, each vessel performed the rotation seven times a year. This spectacular change reflects clearly the ramifications of the transportation revolution in the Red Sea but particularly the linking of Arab with European navigation networks.[11] The historian Jean-Louis Miège described the exchange system of Arab Red Sea networks before the expansion of monetization:

> It is mainly a barter commerce, of product to product. This explains that sometimes, paradoxically, products are sold very cheaply below the usual rates because they were simply taken in order to exchange or purchase a complementary product. Pricing rules do not play as a function of the demand of the buyer. They are dependent on the seller's offer. He is the one who determines the price of exchange of the additional product that serves as a compensation. Money is very little utilized. There is a balance between imports and exports, a balance that is sought after and that tends to increase the turnover.[12]

The announcement of the Suez Canal project in 1854 led to an augmentation of European navigational and commercial operation in the Red Sea, culminating with the opening of the canal in 1869. Both the number and size of ships grew spectacularly. The total transits in 1870 amounted to 486 ships, and the figure grew in 1880 to 2,026 ships, in 1890 to 3,389, and in 1910 to 4,533.[13] Massively growing European presence and operations in the area led to the heightening of competition between traditional Arab sailing boats—dhows, baggalas, booms, *sanbūqs*[14]—and European steamships. But European steamships did not eliminate local Arab and African shipping. As in other arenas of the Indian Ocean, such as East Africa, the Gulf, or Indonesia, a parallel system operated, characterized by dualism. Sailing ships continued to operate on short to mid-range routes, carrying goods to regional ports as well as to international entrepôts, where they were subsequently loaded onto steamships for long-distance shipping.[15] In the late nineteenth century, for example, pearls extracted in the Dahlak Archipelago off the Massawa coast were sometimes taken by *nakhūdas* to Aden on a *sanbūq*, and from there, they were shipped directly by steamship to the Bombay markets. The *sanbūq* transported other goods to Aden.[16] As will be described below, in the case of Massawa, dualism meant that a lively traffic of sailing vessels with Luḥayya, Ḥudayda, and Sawākin, but also Jiddah and Aden, continued to operate deep into the Italian colonial period and beyond. To get a sense of scale, in 1898, for example, 120 steamships entered the port of Massawa (15 from Italy, 51 from Aden, 11 from Trieste, 2 from Cardiff, and the remaining vessels from various destinations and carrying British, Egyptian, and Austro-Hungarian flags). In the same year 3,644 sailing vessels, of which 2,620 came from other Eritrean ports and 1,024 from the Red Sea basin at large (2,501 carrying Italian flags and 1,143 Ottoman flags) entered Massawa harbor.[17]

Thanks to their liquidity, methods of credit, the solid relations of trust, and their role in regional trade and cabotage, Arab trading and shipping networks proved resistant and flexible enough to maintain their position and keep most European competition away, at least until the 1880s. Working on low margins, in some instances they were also able to undercut European business operations by, for example, supplying Jiddah with European goods at lower costs via Hadrami traders in Cairo.[18] Egyptian hegemony in the basin in the 1860s and the launching of the Khedival Azizieh Navigation company (est. 1863), setting up a steamer service linking with regularity Suez with Sawākin, and from 1867, Massawa, was another way of responding to direct European penetration, even though Egypt's westernizing tendencies in that period makes this statement more complex than it seems.[19] The introduction of regular modern navigation lines between India and the Red Sea and the growth in importance of Aden and Jiddah in the 1840s and 1850s contributed to the strengthening of established Indian networks in the area. Banyan and Parsis from Bombay had been present in the region for several centuries, but they gradually settled in greater numbers in both ports, as well as in other ports such as Massawa, Sawākin, Luḥayya, and Ḥudayda, and constituted a critical challenge to Arab trade networks.[20] Yet on another level, Arab and Indian trading networks must also be contextualized and differentiated, even if they usually oscillated between complementarity and competition. Historian Janet Ewald has argued that Arab traders benefited from the policies of the Ottoman and Arab authorities, who favored and supported local traders over Indian counterparts by offering monopolies to local traders, prohibiting the importation of certain Indian goods, and, in general, favoring Arab traders.[21] The same patterns are true as viewed from Massawa under both the Egyptian and Italian authorities, as I will discuss in the next chapter.

The paramount role of Indian financiers and creditors, their backing by big merchant houses in India, their organization as a culturally distinct

Figure 2.1. Causeway, colonial edifices, and governor's *palazzo*, Massawa, ca. 1890. Photographer: Luigi Naretti. Biblioteca Reale, Torino.

trade diaspora, and their status as British subjects all benefited Indian networks, reported as dominating the commerce of key Red Sea ports in the last decades of the century.[22] The reconfiguration of Red Sea navigation, commerce, and trading networks greatly affected the traditional system of Arab networks, and Indian, Greek, Jewish, Armenian, Syrian, and European merchants present in the southern Red Sea and Gulf of Aden area were now able to compete over—sometimes control—large shares of the trade in one commodity or another.

Yet the resilience and dominance of Arab and Indian trade networks vis-à-vis European commercial entrepreneurs in the 1870s and 1880s is sharply displayed in the southern Red Sea area. Following the purchase of the Bay of Assab in 1869 by the Italian Rubattino shipping company, several Italian business entrepreneurs—mostly, but not exclusively, from northern Italy—had launched commercial exploratory ventures in the Red Sea area. Many were undertaken under the aegis of various "commercial geographical" and "commercial exploration" societies that had been set up for that objective and that had worked hard at promoting the link between promising overseas economic opportunities and the need for overseas expansion. Examples of such organizations include the Società Geografica Italiana (est. in Florence in 1867), the Società di Esplorazione Commerciale in Africa (est. in Milan in 1879), and the Società Africana d'Italia (est. in Naples in 1882, replacing the Club Africano). Yet once the expeditions reached the area, they soon discovered that Italian products had a hard time competing, both in price and in quality, with English goods marketed by Indian entrepreneurs. For example, the short-lived Società Italiana per il Commercio coll'Africa, which had engaged in commercial transactions, buying and selling goods, experienced immense difficulty in breaking into the highly competitive Red Sea market and, ultimately, was unable to make profit from its operations.

In the 1880s several other societies and independent entrepreneurs met with similar failure in their commercial ventures in the area.[23] On the other hand, some European commercial entrepreneurs, such as the Trieste-based Jewish Bienenfeld brothers, Giuseppe (d. 1913) and Vittorio (d. 1933), were able to compete to some extent by modeling their commercial brokerage operations and spatial organization and layout on other regional networks in the Red Sea and Indian Ocean areas. The Bienenfeld brothers traded in a variety of commodities (among which were pearls, but also other Indian and English goods), connecting Asia, the Red Sea, Eastern Africa, and Europe, and opened branches in ports such as Massawa, Jiddah, Aden, Mombasa, and Rangoon.[24] Together with other entrepreneurs, such as Enrico Tagliabue and Giuseppe Guasconi, they were among those who spearheaded the promotion of European trade with the area and were closely associated with political power. With other entrepreneurs they founded the first Società Commerciale Eritrea (later bought by the Società Coloniale Italiana), which did not meet much success. At some point in the 1880s Giuseppe served as Italian consul at Aden, a position from which he assisted in practice various commercial entrepreneurs in the southern Red Sea area.[25] All in all, the sweeping inability of Italian commercial operators to penetrate the Red Sea commercial system and successfully compete with its flexible networks is one factor accounting for the spectacular success of Massawan merchants, as well as Arab and Indian migrant entrepreneurs in the port-town under Italian colonial rule. Furthermore, since before the second decade of the twentieth century Italian economic investment and enterprise in Eritrea were so limited, the colonial authorities worked together with local merchant-entrepreneurs in various sectors such as salt production and commercialization, commercial agriculture, and transportation services—also accounting for the success of Massawa's businessmen in the colonial era.

Massawa in the Red Sea System: From International Entrepôt to Regional Emporium

The port of Massawa was connected to several maritime spheres of commerce, all highly complex systems and at times overlapping and intertwined. On a large-scale commercial level, Massawa served as a service center for shipping and trade in the western Indian Ocean, exporting and importing commodities to and from Europe, Egypt, and Arabia on the one hand, and to and from India and as far as Aceh in northern Sumatra on the other.[26] A French report from 1841 noted that products from Aceh (cotton, silk, wood), with a value of 167,250 thalers, represented 20 percent of the total value of commodities that reached Massawa in that year. Products from Bombay (cottons, silk, calico, lead, tin) totaled 118,130 thalers (15%); from Jiddah (mirrors, swords, Persian carpets, razors, calico from Cairo) totaled 96,400 thalers (12%); from Abyssinia and the Galla regions (wheat, butter, coffee, wax, wool blankets, ivory, tortoise shells, one thousand slaves, gum, honey, mules, gold, ostrich feathers, etc.) totaled 281,275 thalers (36%); from Mukhā and Yemen (rice, corn, dates, tombac) totaled 68,500 thalers (8%), and from Sawākin (corn, ivory, palm leaf mats, water) totaled 40,750 thalers (5%). As these data make clear, at that point Massawa was mainly connected to ports serving as international entrepôts, such as Jiddah for its northern outlets and Bombay for the handling of commerce with India and beyond. Mid-range maritime links with Jiddah and other Red Sea ports were regular and intensive. In 1841 the same French report observed that every year about 250 Arab boats of about 40 to 200 tons visited Massawa.[27] However, very few ship owners in Massawa were able to organize direct shipments as far as Bombay. Around 1840 Théophile Lefebvre saw in Massawa harbor two vessels that made yearly trips to and from India and a vessel that came from Ile Maurice to buy mules from Ethiopia.[28] At this point, ships circulating between India and the Red Sea were mostly owned by merchants and shippers of Gujarat. Corroborating this information, the French report referred to above noted that every year only one or two "European" ships of 300–400 tons come to the port. Sources report that in 1841 Mussa Mufarrah, a rich merchant and, apparently, one of the four principal ship owners in Massawa, expected his ship's return from Bombay, laden with merchandise and a peculiar white slave destined for Istanbul.[29] In 1848 another French document noted that twenty vessels of 100

Figure 2.2. The Massawa customs house, 1885–86.
Photographer: unknown. Centro etnografico ferrarese, Ferrara, Italy.

tons reached Massawa from Sawākin, twenty from Jiddah, twenty from Luḥayya and Ḥudayda, ten from Mukhā, and three large vessels from India and Europe.[30]

In the early 1860s a British report observed that no English merchant vessels visited Massawa, that two Indian vessels belonging to the Banyans at Massawa visited it each year, and that about thirty Arab "*bugalows*" (*baggalas*) rotated between Massawa and Jiddah, Suez, Ḥudayda, Mukhā, and Aden throughout the year.[31] With the gradual rise of Aden as an international entrepôt in the 1840s and 1850s, Massawa's trade with India tended to pass through that port, via the mediation of Indian merchants and agents established in growing numbers in the British port-colony. Furthermore, Aden's location beyond the Bāb al-Mandab straits, led to the development of the Tihāma plain ports of Luḥayya and Ḥudayda, which were both dependent on Jiddah within the southern Red Sea trading system. Both were important points for the exportation of Yemeni highland commodities such as coffee and grains and were growing regional entrepôts and markets. Both ports interacted with Massawa, which provided them mostly with butter and in turn could export to Massawa grains and dates in years of food shortage in the African inland.[32] Much like Massawa, Luḥayya and Ḥudayda hosted important communities of Arab and Indian merchants who were strongly tied into Red Sea and Indian Ocean networks.

A report filed by the Egyptians following their takeover of the port reveals the rearrangement of port hierarchies and the redeployment of Massawa's seaward connections. According to the report, Massawa's exportations for the year 1864–65 were directed toward Jiddah (789,338 Fr.), Aden (489,748 Fr.), Ḥudayda (232,937 Fr.), Luḥayya (82, 236 Fr.), and Sawākin (6,444 Fr.). Its imports were largest from Aden (1,663,656 Fr.), followed by Jiddah (888,517 Fr.), Sawākin (97,440 Fr.), Ḥudayda (55,246 Fr.), and finally Luḥayya (49,859 Fr.).[33] The data is significant in illustrating the port hierarchy that took shape vis-à-vis Massawa following the transformation and rearrangement of Red Sea commercial activities since the 1830s. Jiddah and Aden served as entrepôts for luxury products in international trade, such as ivory, mother-of-pearl, gold, and wax, leaving Massawa on their way to the Middle East, Europe, and India. A second set of regional emporia and entrepôts—Ḥudayda, Luḥayya, and Sawākin—increasingly received from other ports on both shores of the Red Sea products such as butter, honey, civet, and gum for local consumption and further regional marketing. This constituted another exchange sphere—an intermediate system, more regional in character—involving an intensive traffic of boats regularly crossing the Red Sea and navigating between its islands.[34] This process epitomized the dualism of maritime transportation following the introduction of steamship navigation to the Red Sea.

The revival of Red Sea commerce also affected the traffic of small-scale sailing between Massawa, minor ports along the African coasts such as ᶜAqīq, Hergigo, Zula, Meder, ᶜEdd, and the multitude of islands of the Dahlak Archipelago. Prior to the physical linking of Massawa and Tewalet (also Ṭawlūd) islands with the mainland by two causeways in the 1870s, small boats transported people, goods, and fresh water from Hergigo and the mainland opposite the port on a daily basis. Commercial expansion had a significant impact on the extraction, exploitation, and distribution of local resources on and off the Massawa coasts. In a period of increased demand and pressure for exportable commodities and the provisioning of a growing port, the means of transportation were crucial. In the mid-1830s a number of European observers in the Red Sea area reported a growing

Figure 2.3. Boat repair area in ʿEdaga Beʿray, ca. 1890. Photographer: Luigi Naretti. Biblioteca Reale, Torino.

vitality in marine activities in Massawa's environment. The two French members of a Saint-Simonian mission to Ethiopia, Edmond Combes and Maurice Tamisier, estimated the number of boats sailing in the port's surroundings at approximately sixty, while Lefebvre counted thirty-five boats docked in the harbor. Furthermore, according to these travelers, boat builders in Massawa constructed dhows and rowing boats, which were destined to transport slaves to Jiddah but also coral stone and marine products from the islands to Massawa.[35] According to Ferret and Galinier most of the town's craftsmen were boat builders, almost all of "non-African" origins.[36] In the 1850s, Werner Munzinger qualified the boats built in Massawa as "very elegant and solid."[37]

To the Sea on Camel and Mule: Transregional Overland Caravan Systems

Moving on to Massawa's inland connections, the port-town's century-long economic raison d'être was its role as the Red Sea outlet of two main routes of the overland caravan trade: the "Ethiopian" trade route and the final stretch of the West–East trans-Saharan trade network connecting Kassala to the port.[38] Massawa's geographic position at a point on the coast closest to the highland plateau (about 50–60 kilometers) made it an ideal point of access for caravans coming to the coast to sell their commodities for exportation and purchase imported items to be taken back to inland markets. The Ethiopian long-distance trade route originated in the rich Oromo southern and western peripheries of Ethiopia and passed through a web of cross-regional and regional trade networks in the Ethiopian highlands before ending on the coast in Massawa. The port's position on the Red Sea as the terminal of the trans-Saharan routes reached even further. It connected Massawa to a complex web of trade routes that had their origins in northern and western Africa, extending as far as the port of Essaouira on the Moroccan Atlantic coasts.[39] Past historiography has tended to focus more often on the Ethiopian trade route connecting the southern, western, and central highlands with the coast, while the westerly routes from Kassala and the Sudan have been mentioned less in the literature.[40] These two long-distance trade routes connected Massawa with distant inlands and areas of production and exchange. Yet they were tied to coastal commercial structures in different ways and thus affected the political economy of trading networks in distinct ways. These variations had an impact on the mercantile disposition of the Massawa conurbation.

Commercial expansion in the nineteenth century and the framework created by new international market forces had an important effect on long-distance trade and far-reaching ramifications on interior, littoral, and coastal communities. Growing pressure to extract goods and slaves for exportation linked inland regions to the international market and generated a series of processes that made a considerable economic, political, and social impact on the societies of the wider region.[41]

The Organization and Economics of Caravan Trade across the Highland Ethiopian Route

Most luxury commodities reaching Massawa via the Ethiopian highlands, such as slaves, gold, and ivory, originated in the Oromo regions of southern and western Ethiopia, often beyond the control of the highland Ethiopian state in its various historical manifestations. Notwithstanding the largely agriculture-oriented highland polity's position on the trade routes between producing areas and the sea, its tradition of strong centralized polities with armies and taxation institutions and the large markets in its towns all accounted for the ability to exploit economically and benefit from long-distance commercial activities and to exercise enough purchasing power to consume imports.[42] Indeed, highlanders were those who purchased and consumed almost the totality of imported manufactured goods—especially a wide variety of textiles and cloths imported from India and Egypt through Massawa.

Caravan trade on the Ethiopia route linked the port with distant inland areas. The road distance between, for example, Enarea in the southwest and Massawa is approximately 1,200 kilometers. But the connection was not direct. Caravan merchants moved commodities progressively through a series of interrelated regional trading circuits and networks that moved in a northeasterly direction from one regional market to another before culminating on the coast, in Massawa. In practice, the length of the journey depended on the route taken, the type of animals engaged, the size of the caravan, the trade carried out en route, and the problems and obstacles encountered during the journey. Starting with the products of the west and southwest—slaves, ivory, gold, wax, civet, and coffee—caravans swelled by smaller parties and traders as they made their way to the coast. The face and shape of a caravan, in terms of its commodities, porters, guides, merchants, and pack animals, changed throughout its long journey. Some merchants made only part of the route, working and "specializing" on one stretch of the route such as Basso–Bure–Gondar for example; others made it all the way, most often from Gojjam to the coast.

The operation of large-scale caravans was not haphazard; it involved an elaborate organization and a disciplinary regime that had to balance factors relating to climatic conditions, the topography, security, the organization of markets, and sailing conditions from and to Massawa. The arduous conditions of transportation in a difficult mountainous terrain governed the progress of caravans toward Massawa, and caravaneers had to take into account the seasonal rhythms of the climate, which left most areas impossible to pass through during the rainy seasons. Hence, between June and October trade in highland Ethiopia came to a practical standstill.[43] "Big" highland Muslim Jeberti merchants usually organized and assembled large-scale caravans (Ar. *qāfilah*) at the furthest regional market of Basso in the Ethiopian province of Gojjam, to the north of the Oromo regions of the southwest (also the Gibe region).[44] Sometimes Ethiopian traders went further south, as far as Saqqa in Limma Ennarya, where they could purchase commodities at even lower prices, since they were closer to areas of production.[45] Big merchants announced the organization of a caravan leaving to the north and attracted smaller merchants who joined it, thus benefiting from the protection that a large and organized caravan could provide.[46] A hierarchical arrangement ordered the organization of merchants and commodities on the caravan. Munzinger noted that "the kind of merchandise that a trader takes to Massawa is regulated by custom. A small trader would be perceived very negatively if he showed up in the port with ivory and gold, which is only permitted to the big merchants."[47]

The leader and initiator of the caravan was the *neggadras,* who was responsible for the caravan's security and for paying the duties and fees for the entire party in the numerous checkpoint stations in the highlands along the route.[48] In most centers requiring passage fees caravan leaders dealt with the local *neggadras,* who was also a Muslim Jeberti and with whom many of the big merchants cultivated good relations over time. In these stations caravan leaders paid fees in proportion to the goods carried by each party, while at other locations the caravan's *neggadras* may have had to rely on his bargaining powers or on his good relationship with men of influence on the spot.[49] From Basso caravans traveled northward in Gojjam and into Begemder, where they often stopped in Derita, before reaching Gondar, the largest commercial center of northern Ethiopia.[50] In Gondar caravans swelled with rich products such as ivory and gold, expedited with the itinerant *jallāba* from the Sudanese regions through Metemma. In the rich Gondari markets caravans also absorbed Ethiopian goods that reached it from Walqayt (e.g., rhinoceros and antelope horns) and from other regional markets in Begemder (e.g., hippopotamus teeth, wax, mules, and cardamom from Gojjam). Some caravans left Gondar toward Sinnār and the Nile Valley—the other historical south–north continental commercial route linking East Africa and the Horn with Egypt.

Caravans moved from one place to another rather slowly. Mules, the main mode of transportation in the highlands, could make but a limited distance every day. Slaves usually performed a double role on caravans; that is, beyond their being themselves a commodity to be exported, they served as porters and as servants to the wealthier merchants on the journey.[51] At halts, the caravan established a temporary camp outside the town or village, where enough shade was available, or near a water well, a spring, or a river. Plowden provides a visually vivid description of one such caravan at halt:

> The packages are piled up to the height of four or five feet, with spaces left at intervals; the long sticks with which they drive the mules are thrown across these to form a roof, and soft hides are laid over all, making a series of waterproof cabins, in which the

> wealthy nestle among their goods; the followers erect temporary huts all round, and in the center the mules are tied at night. Numbers of young men are sent to cut grass; others to trade with the nearest villagers for supplies. Strict watch is kept all night by the light of large wood fires. At daylight they resume their journey, and a caravan of 200–300 mules will be on in less than a half an hour. The small traders who carry goods from market to market, disperse themselves at night in the villages amongst their friends.[52]

After the rainy seasons around the month of October, when the river waters began to decline, caravans in the northern highlands began to organize to continue toward Massawa. From Gondar, caravans advanced to Debarq, before crossing the Tekkeze and reaching ᶜAdwa, an important commercial center in the north, second only to Gondar.[53] In ᶜAdwa caravans adjoined other caravans coming from Massawa and the Afar coast—an opportunity to exchange information and news about business and politics in Massawa and Gondar. Before descending to the lowlands toward Massawa, caravans provisioned themselves with grain (cereals) to be consumed during their stay in Massawa since prices on the island were high.[54] Antoine d'Abbadie provided a detailed itinerary of the two routes that connected ᶜAdwa to Massawa in the early 1840s. The first continued north, passing through Hamasen via ᶜAddi Kwala, and finished at Emkullo in Massawa's outskirts. The second took a more easterly route and descended the slopes of Akkele Guzay via Halay and Digsa, ending its journey at Hergigo on the coast.[55] When descending the slopes of the plateau caravans usually changed their means of transportation from mules or oxen to camels, eventually leaving them at Hergigo where, according to the French travelers Combes and Tamisier, "a local shaikh would take care of them for one thaler per month."[56] In the final lowland stretch before reaching the coast, both routes passed through territories that were traditionally controlled directly or indirectly by the Balaw *nāʾib*s or their dependents. There, before reaching Massawa, they halted in regional market villages such as ᶜAylet and Zaga, where they were connected with coastal commercial structures, usually through the members of Balaw families. In the early 1860s Walker observed that caravans employed porters from ᶜAdwa to ᶜAylet, where they were discharged and paid a dollar a head for their service.[57] This reinforces the idea that caravans were linked to coastal structures of porterage and commerce immediately following their descent from the plateau.

Figure 2.4. Preparation of a caravan at Massawa, 1885–86.
Photographer: E. B. Centro etnografico ferrarese, Ferrara, Italy.

Much evidence attests to the fact that in the middle decades of the century only one or two very large caravans reached Massawa every year, often in June or July.[58] Caravan merchants were under pressure to make it to Massawa in time for the Indian merchants to expedite goods on vessels before the monsoon made it practically impossible to go beyond the Bāb al-Mandab. They were sometimes withheld in the highlands due to a particularly long rainy season or due to continued periods of insecurity in northern Ethiopia. Nevertheless, there were many other medium-sized caravans carrying either regional products or merchandise that had been intercepted at inland markets and moved from the regions that lie beyond the Tekkeze River—in Tigray and Hamasen—to Massawa all year around.[59] Markets such as ʿAdigrat, Antalo, Maqale, ʿAddi Kwala, and Abiy Addi engaged in a continuous flow of traffic with the port, and small caravans circulated between them and Massawa all year long, but especially during the summer months, before vessels set out from Massawa overseas.[60]

At least until the 1850s and 1860s slaves, ivory, and gold were the main luxury commodities around which long-distance caravan trade was organized. A poem composed by Wad Keray in Hergigo following the devastating events of 1848 noted that "the girls of the village wear the gold of Sennar," which was of the best quality.[61] But slaves were by far the most lucrative export item and the most in demand overseas. The centrality of slave exportation to the economics of long-distance caravan trade from the 1830s to the 1850s is unquestionable. It would not be completely far-fetched to judge that moving slaves for exportation was often the very motor behind the dynamics of the long-distance caravan trade. In 1838 slaves were estimated as constituting 57 percent of Massawa's total exports, 21 percent in 1840, 37 percent in 1842, 15 percent in 1852 and 12 percent in 1861.[62] The revival of Red Sea commerce led to a renewed demand for slaves captured mainly in the Oromo, Omotic, and Nilotic regions of the west and the southwest and exported to Jiddah, Egypt, and to other Middle Eastern destinations, where they were exploited mostly as domestic servants. Other slaves found their way to the Tihāma coasts, where they were used in all sorts of labor, at time related to marine activities, probably in the pearling economy. Even if inherently problematic, estimates for the exportation of slaves from Massawa put the figure at around 111,000 slaves for the entire nineteenth century. Estimates put at roughly 1,500 the number of slaves exported from Massawa every year between 1811 and 1875. All estimates are problematic since much of this trade was carried out clandestinely, at least from the 1850s, when the British mounted their pressure on the Ottomans and Egyptians to suppress it.[63] Ivory and gold were the two other most important commodities that caravans brought to the coast, accounting for roughly 20 percent of Massawa's exportations in the 1840s and 1850s. Estimates vary between 15,000 and 30,000 kilos of ivory, with a value of 20,000 to 50,000 Maria Theresa dollars, exported from Massawa in different years in the 1840s and 1850s. Most ivory was exported to India and handled by the Indian merchants almost exclusively, while gold was exported to both India and Egypt.[64]

Unlike the situation in some locations in eastern Africa and the Somali region, it seems fairly clear that coastal urban merchants were not the initiators, organizers, or principal financiers of the large caravan trade originating in the southwest and passing through highland Ethiopia to the coast. Caravan trade was almost exclusively in the hands of the Jeberti traders, who maintained their own networks on the highlands, navigating between one region and the other with relative convenience. The centuries-long traditional role of the Muslim Jebertis as merchants and traders among predominantly Christian societies and polities led to their organization in trade networks that monopolized and dominated markets, the movement of commodities, and the organization of caravans across the highlands. The chiefs of trade (*neggadras*es) in Ayubai, Derita, Gondar, Saqota, Debarq, and ᶜAdwa were usually Muslim Jebertis who served at the same time the interests of the administrations of their provinces and towns, and those of the merchants involved in the highland caravan trade. In addition to the constraints of geography, this modus operandi made it difficult for coastal merchants to easily penetrate highland Jeberti trading structures. Notwithstanding, this did not mean that Massawa merchants did not tie links with inland traders or order commodities from the interior, even if discretely and with considerable caution. In the 1840s Théophile Lefebvre noted that some of Massawa's rich merchants "extend their speculations as far as the most remote Galla [Oromo] lands, but they keep the secret of their commercial relationships in these areas with the utmost discretion."[65] Massawa merchants operated as brokers and wholesale merchants in their commercial ventures connected with this route. Brokers and the institution of brokerage at Massawa were a way for coastal merchants to dominate trade in the port without being involved in the process of moving commodities from their sources in long-distance trade. The infrastructure of merchant capital was somewhat different on the route connecting Kassala and beyond it to Massawa. Coastal commercial structures connected to this route in a very different manner.

Caravan Networks and the Political Economy of the Massawa–Kassala Trade Route

The character of caravan trade on Massawa's westerly route was structurally different from that of the highland Ethiopian route. From the early decades of the nineteenth century the effects of the commercial revival, Egyptian imperialism in the Sudan, and what is known as the "Islamic revival" had all contributed to territorial incorporation and continuity across the regions around the route connecting the Nile Valley with the Red Sea coast. Consequently, the Sudanese regions connected to coastal commercial structures in Massawa in particular ways involving discrete organizational and operational patterns. The caravan trade network along the Kassala–Massawa route constituted the final stage of a far-reaching and wide system of trans-Saharan trading networks and caravan routes having their easterly Red Sea outlets at Sawākin and Massawa. Originating in northern and western Africa, Saharan and central African networks of exchange crossed regions and towns such as Bornou, Bagirmi, Darfur, Kordofan, and Sinnār—before reaching Kassala and the Red Sea ports. Pilgrimage to Mecca was closely associated with the movement of caravans in this direction. This phenomenon has a historical reflection in the communities of West Africans called Takrūrīs, some of whom "got stuck" on the way to Mecca and remained over time in the eastern Sudan and in Eritrea.[66] Similarly to other large-scale and long-distance exchange systems, trans-Saharan commercial webs operated simultaneously on regional, cross-regional, and transregional levels, moving commodities and pilgrims across Africa and connecting to global economic structures.[67] On that scale, Kassala, the last commercial center of importance before the coast, connected to other Sudanese regional markets at Shendi, Khartoum, Sinnār, Gedaref, Metemma—and then Gondar in the Ethiopian highlands, before expediting merchandise to the ports of Sawākin and Massawa.[68]

The westerly trade routes from Massawa to Kassala passed across the lowland regions of Semhar, the northern appendages of the plateau, inhabited by the Mensaᶜ, Habab, ᶜAd Temaryam, Meshalit, Bet Juk, Bilin, and Marya, and again the lowlands of Barka, where the Beni ᶜAmer live.[69] This route was much more convenient than the one crossing the Ethiopian highlands and could be carried out in a fortnight with camels alone. Another advantage was that it surrounded, and thus avoided, the central and northern highlands, where security was oftentimes precarious and where caravan passage fees were high. Different trade networks operated caravans reaching Kassala, either from Metemma, Gallabat, Gedaref, or Sinnār—particularly those of the Sudanese *jallāba*. In *La Colonia Eritrea e i suoi commerci,* Ennio Alamanni provided detailed descriptions of the itineraries taken by caravans, merchants, and travelers from Massawa to Kassala and vice versa. The average duration of the entire journey with camels was about fifteen days.[70]

In the 1850s Munzinger reported that elements of the Ghengheren (Jangeren) living with the ᶜAd Temaryam provided commercial transportation services between Keren and Massawa.[71] The cameleers engaged by the Massawa/ Hergigo traders were almost exclusively of the Habab group, who settled in greater numbers in Massawa's mainland outskirts from the 1850s and 1860s onward. They grew to dominate camel caravan transportation well into the twentieth century and often provided their services in this capacity to the Italian colonial authorities in Massawa.[72] Their camels were the best suited for the first part of the journey to Keren, crossing through the mountains and the Habab regions to the northwest of the port.[73] However, most caravans attempted to avoid as much as possible traveling through difficult mountainous terrain and preferred the valley routes—even if longer—that were suited for camel transportation. From Massawa to Keren the caravan route was divided into three stages: (1) from the coast through Semhar to ʿAyn, (2) from ʿAyn through the Lebka valley to Meshalit, and (3) from there to Keren through the ʿAnseba valley.[74] The journey took approximately seven days. Keren was an important regional market and center of redistribution where traders exchanged Barka and Bogos goods. Already in the 1850s the Italian Lazarist missionary Giuseppe Sapeto noted that it was the meeting place of traders from Gash, Saqala (?), Shendi, and Damer, capital of the ancient Meroe. They all came to Keren to sell cotton from Sinnār and Egypt. Traders from Massawa came there to exchange various Indian textiles for butter, ivory, hides, ostrich feathers, and other goods that were taken back to the port for exportation.[75] Keren was the Gash region's dhurra market for the entire ʿAnseba valley area. After arriving to Keren, according to Douin, the Habab camels were changed to Barka camels, more suited for dry lowland travel.[76] From Keren to Kassala the route was more straightforward through the flat lowlands, and the journey could take some ten days to accomplish.[77]

Three principal factors accounted for the development of a regional territorial integrity and continuity along this route throughout the nineteenth century: the impact of Balaw *nāʾib* hegemony, the spread of Islam, and Egyptian expansionism. The human geography and modes of production of lowland nomadic pastoralist societies between Massawa and the ʿAnseba valley and Keren defined their relationship to and dependence on the rulers of the littoral and the coast—the Balaw *nāʾib*s and their associates. Tigre-speaking pastoralists moved seasonally with their flocks, alternating between grazing in the littoral region in winter and on the slopes and hills to the west and northwest in the summer months. Access to grazing lands, therefore, subordinated them to the *nāʾib*s in control of the coastlands. The spread of Islam in the region also catalyzed the vitality of the Kassala–Massawa trade network. Holy men and traders were able to circulate with greater ease and in greater numbers between the province of Taka and the coast and connect Sudanese and coastal trading networks and transportation arrangements. In contrast to the highland network, where Jeberti and Christian interlocutors dominated, the growing influence of the ʿAd Shaykh holy family and the Khatmiyya Sufi order facilitated and enhanced the consolidation of trading networks and commercial relations between the Nile and the Red Sea.

Egyptian expansion in the Sudan since the second decade of the century had a significant impact on the development of the Massawa–Kassala trade route. Against a background of Red Sea commercial revival and seeking to provide a sea outlet to their recently conquered rich Sudanese territories, the Egyptians took Kassala in 1840 with the aim of eventually linking it to Sawākin and Massawa. Their headway from the west was temporarily halted after the death of Muḥammad ʿAlī in 1849, and renewed Ottoman forays slowed down the Egyptian imperialist drive. Only with Khedive Ismāʿīl's access to power in 1863 was Egyptian expansionism relaunched with increased vigor, culminating in the handover of Massawa to the *khedive* in 1865 and the occupation of Keren in June 1872.[78] With the placing of ʿAylet under Egyptian protection and the new occupied territories around Keren, the Egyptians had succeeded in practically creating a bridge between Kassala and Massawa. Yet subsequent struggles between Ethiopians, Egyptians, and Italians culminated in the middle years of the 1880s—promoting insecurity and instability, and undermining regular commercial activities in the region.

Caravan trade on Massawa's westerly route involved the circulation of large-scale caravans similar to those of the Ethiopian caravan network, even if in smaller numbers. Merchants moved goods originating in the Sudan and beyond such as slaves, ivory, hippopotamus teeth, gold, wax, gum, honey, tamarinds, dates, and ostrich feathers from Sinnār and Kassala to Massawa. Caravans brought ostrich feathers, ivory, and butter from the Hadendoa regions in the Sudan and butter and mats from the Barka region.[79] Indian merchants much favored the vitality of this route since they could procure ivory directly at Massawa, which is much closer than Sawākin for eastbound shipping.[80] Numerous manumission acts recorded in Massawa's Islamic court between 1865 and 1885 attest the presence of a great number of Sudanese slaves in Massawa (or passing through the port). The records often identified manumitted slaves with reference to their ethnic origin, for example al-Sūdānī, al-Shanqala, or al-Dinkāwī.[81] In the opposite direction, long-distance caravans from Massawa to Kassala carried mostly a variety of Indian cloths and manufactured products.[82] In contrast with the situation on the highland trade route, where Jeberti networks dominated most highland trade and caravan movement, traders from Massawa and Hergigo were able to penetrate deep into the western trade route and exercise their business operations on the ground at Kassala and in markets along it. Locally organized caravans laden with a variety of imported cloth left Hergigo toward Taka, where they exchanged cloth for ivory. Munzinger noted that some of the Hergigo traders could finish their business already in the Habab and Bogos areas.[83] He also observed that the "Taaura" (ʿAd Tsaura), who grazed with the ʿAd Temaryam, provided the transportation of goods from Keren to Massawa.[84]

Since the political diminishing of the Balaw *nāʾib* dynasty and the growth of Egyptian hegemony, traders from Hergigo were extremely active along the route, dominating the trade in ivory, wax, and coffee brought from the Nile region and from Metemma.[85] The Hergigo traders capitalized on the former power but everlasting prestige of the *nāi'b*s and were able to build their commercial enterprises on patronage relations and local alliances established over past decades.[86] Throughout the 1860s and 1870s merchants from Massawa and Hergigo settled in key towns and market villages along the route—most importantly in Keren, but also further to the west.[87] Munzinger reported that following the destruction of Hergigo by the Ottomans, approximately eighty Hergigo traders settled among the Marya.[88] Hergigo merchants ventured considerably deeper, as far as Kassala and probably beyond.[89] In the early 1880s, Sayyid Muḥammad al-Ṣāfī, one of Massawa's wealthier Hadrami merchants, sent his son and a slave (Maḥbūb al-Ṣāfī) to Taka province and Kassala to establish business relations for the account of the Ṣāfī trading house. They carried on them a considerable sum of approximately 150,000 Egyptian piasters.[90] The establishment of a strong Muslim power, providing relative stability—even if intermittent—and seeking to develop trade relations between the Sudanese interior and the Red Sea ports was an opportunity for coastal traders to expand their activities in this direction.

Beyond its position in relation to long-distance caravan trade, the Kassala–Massawa route animated a regional trade and exchange system that grew to be active with the general trends of commercialization in the wider area. Commercial economic relations intensified along the caravan trade routes, drawing to them producers, porters, and small-scale traders. Pastoralists and agro-pastoralists traded hides, butter, milk, camels, cows, and agricultural products in return for a wide variety of cloths and manufactured products imported at Massawa. Products for local consumption or for exportation were either brought to regional markets along the trade route or brought to littoral market villages in small caravans, or, in the case

Figure 2.5. Caravaneers, ca. 1890–1900. Photographer: Roberto Gentile. Biblioteca Reale, Torino.

of groups living in proximity to the port, brought directly to Massawa. The Habab brought camels, goat and cow hides, butter, animal fat (Ar. *shaḥm*) and other provisions required at Massawa; many of these goods—especially butter—were then exported to Arabia.[91] D'Abbadie noted as early as in the 1840s that the Bilin traded almost exclusively with Massawa, buying cloth, drapes, and rugs in exchange for oxen.[92]

Groups such as the Mensaᶜ, the Bet Juk, the Bilin, and the Marya practiced agriculture in the ᶜAnseba valley area. They cultivated cereals and other agricultural produce, which they marketed along the trade route in places such as the Meshalit region, the Shiᶜib plain (Mensaᶜ), ᶜAyn (Habab), Wasentat (Bet Juk), and the larger regional market in Keren. The Mensaᶜ were reported to produce excellent wheat and barley, and the Bilin (Bogos) cultivated corn and tobacco.[93] Mid-nineteenth-century commercialization in the wider region had a significant impact on pastoralist and agro-pastoralist societies of the region, who produced more for exportation and for provisioning the growing urban centers of Massawa and Keren. Referring to the region around Keren in the mid-1860s, Werner Munzinger, acting as French consular agent at Massawa, noted that "Bogos is the centre of the large province of Ainseba. Possession of it is important if only for its fertility. But it is also the only camel route from Massawa to the Sudan. Possession of it means the control over the provinces of Barka, Marea,

Bedjouk (Christians) whose resources are large and are capable of increasing a hundredfold in a short time. This province, if well administered, would be the flower of all the Egyptian Sudan."[94]

In large market villages in Massawa's proximity, as far as Keren, transactions between regional caravaneers and traders involved the mediation of traders, brokers, or service suppliers connected with coastal commercial networks. In the 1850s Munzinger noted that "the Habab caravans have their brokers at Zaga, near Massawa."[95] According to Douin, the Beduin residents of Zaga provided traders with water, wood, and the means of transportation.[96] Since mid-century the advent of Egyptian hegemony, increased commercialization and taxation, and the dwindling of the slave trade had all contributed toward making the regions along the Massawa–Keren route increasingly important economic hinterlands in relation to the port. This process drew pastoralist and agro-pastoralist societies closer to Massawa's economic and social spheres through migration to the port and the consolidation of clientship relationships in regional commercial and transportation structures.

Growth in Regional Production and Trade

Mirroring in a way Massawa's changing position vis-à-vis its forelands, from a trade emporium serving almost exclusively distant inland centers of production and consumption the port became more closely integrated to the dynamically growing region in its closer hinterlands. Long-distance trade, especially on the Ethiopian route, declined and transformed progressively from mid-century as a result of attempts to suppress the slave trade and because of the reigning state of political instability in northern Ethiopia and on its borders. The erratic trajectories governing the administration of the Egyptian Sudan, and Massawa in particular, were characterized by the constant vacillation and experimentation between centralized and decentralized modes of administration, which also accounted for the port's growing integration to its hinterlands. Since the Egyptian takeover of Massawa and Sawākin in 1865–66, both ports and their surroundings were not governed by the central governorate of the Sudan in Khartoum. Khedive Ismāʿīl's grand plans for the development and modernization of the Red Sea ports placed them in a privileged position by their separation from the usual lingering bureaucracy, hierarchical rituals, and power politics in Khartoum.[97] For Ismāʿīl, the Red Sea ports were too important to leave in the hands of the Khartoum officialdom; Cairo could therefore choose to directly rule strategically pivotal provinces and, in this case, ports. From 1866 to 1871 a *ḥukmdār* governed Massawa. In 1871 the Egyptians created a new administrative division including Massawa, Sawākin, Kassala, and the Somali coast under a separate administrative unit called the "Eastern Sudan and the Red Sea Littoral," once again placing the ports in a distinct position and creating—after the occupation of Keren—territorial continuity between Massawa and Kassala. In 1872 Massawa was an autonomous governorate under Werner Munzinger, before the Egyptian army took over its administration in the middle of the decade. From 1877, under the overlordship of Gordon in Khartoum, Sawākin and Massawa formed a single *muḥāfiẓa*.[98] All in all, the establishment of a centralized administration in the Massawa area, which was justified by adamant Egyptian efforts at economic exploitation, resulted in drawing the port more substantially and firmly to its close hinterlands.

East African economic history suggests that trade in precolonial East Africa occurred within two discrete spheres of exchange: one involving luxury goods and another, subsistence goods. Prestige goods were exchanged for goods in the same category and subsistence goods for other subsistence goods, thus constituting multi-centric economies. With the expansion of global, interregional, and regional trade in the nineteenth century, the borders between the two spheres of exchange broke down and an increasing shift toward market trade took place. This came about largely through the process of growing monetization and the appearance of new regional and local markets where subsistence goods could be exchanged in return for prestige goods.[99] This model fits well the case of Massawa and its hinterlands, where the gradual penetration of money relations from the port to the inland and the development of regional and local markets in its surroundings are emblematic of the transition to a more market-oriented economy. In other words, commercial expansion prompted the diversification and intensification of modes of production and exchange, leading to the *commodification* of the regional economy, which subsequently also transformed social relations among the inhabitants of the area.

In the first half of the century luxury items from southwestern Ethiopia and the Sudanese regions constituted Massawa's bulk of exports; beginning in the 1850s, the transformation of Massawa and its region's commercial configuration and political economy set in motion far-reaching socioeconomic effects. Slaves, formerly Massawa's most important single export item and an important motor fostering long-distance trade, significantly decreased in number, principally as a result of British pressure on the Ottoman Empire to suppress the slave trade in the late 1850s and 1860s. Egyptian measures eventually went a step further in the 1877 Anglo-Egyptian treaty for the suppression of the slave trade.[100] As noted, it is difficult to evaluate the clandestine operations involved in transporting slaves after measures for tighter control were put in place. Three other "luxury" products brought to the coast from afar whose exports declined or remained stable after mid-century were ivory, gold, and civet.

In terms of economic viability and productivity, the lowlands between the coast and the mountains, as well as the Massawa region, have always been portrayed with rather negative overtones in the historical literature, not entirely unjustifiably. Compared to the rich distant inlands, European travelers, official envoys, and Habesha highlanders described the mostly dry and excessively hot Semhar region as a barren area with little, if at all, economic potential, barely providing its poor nomadic inhabitants with the necessities of existence. Notwithstanding, in the second half of the nineteenth century, commercial expansion in the wider area and Egyptian economic initiatives led to the development, diversification, and intensification of economic enterprise and exchange in Semhar, transforming the political economy of production and commercialization. The most spectacular change in the structure of Massawa's exports was the rise of regionally and locally produced pastoralist commodities such as hides, skins, butter (ghee), and the marine products from the Dahlak Archipelago. Even if more difficult to assess with precision—due to the discrete practice of the transactions—high-value marine products such as pearls, mother-of-pearl, and tortoise shells came to hold a most significant place in Massawa's exports, involving impressively large sums of money in transactions.[101] By the penultimate decade of the nineteenth century a table of twenty items exported from Massawa included eleven produced in Massawa's close hinterlands and in the islands off the coast: gum, wax, ostrich feathers, tallow, hides, skins, pearls, mother-of-pearl, tortoise shells, butter, and gold dust.[102] Added to these processes, growing Ottoman and Egyptian direct involvement in the administration and economy of Massawa and its region since mid-century translated into a more organized, modern, and direct system of tribute and tax collection, which constituted an additional factor toward monetizing socioeconomic relations in the region.[103]

The expansion of Red Sea commerce made an impact on inland, littoral, coastal, and insular societies by gradually integrating them into a market-oriented regional economy. Commercial expansion increasingly transformed trade relations from reciprocity and redistribution to market trade. The development of a new economic order changed the lives of pastoralists by diversifying their modes of production and intensifying them. New commercial relations translated into pressure on the region's inhabitants to supply products for exportation and consumption, labor, and other services to new market places, but especially to Massawa and its growing population. This process involved two important features: the development of regional and local market villages functioning as mediating links or centers for trade networks and the development of modest but dynamic small- and medium-scale agricultural cultivation wherever land and climatic conditions permitted. The development and growth of intermediate Red Sea trading activities—for example between the Eritrean and Tihāma coasts—led to the growth of transregional exchange, reflecting the growing function of Massawa as a regional port beyond its role as a transit point for international commerce. This meant that non-"prestige" pastoralist products, such as butter, gained new value as exportable goods for consumption in Massawa's forelands. Accordingly, butter exports were mostly oriented toward regional Red Sea emporia such as Sawākin, Ḥudayda, Luḥayya, and Jiddah.

Pastoralist and Agricultural Production and Exchange

Evidence from the middle decades of the century defines the basic economic patterns of port-hinterland exchanges: Saho- and Tigre-speaking pastoralists, principally the wealthier and larger Asaorta and the Habab, came to regional markets or directly to Massawa to sell their products in the markets of the port and its outskirts. Observers noted that the Beduins provided the port with meat, fish, watermelons, and milk on a daily basis and that the Saho, especially rich in herds, sold goats, sheep, milk, and butter in the Massawa market, where they purchased tobacco, cloth, and other imported objects. The Habab, another observer noted, come to Emkullo, near Massawa, to sell their butter.[104] As early as in the 1850s Munzinger judged that the products of Semhar, namely gum, wax, fat (*shaḥm*), butter, and hides, were *important* items of commerce in the region. "Commerce with the Beduins is considerable. Since all the Chohos [Sahos] and Beduins are shepherds who seldom practice agriculture and produce nothing else, the main objects of exportation and importation are [the pastoralist products] that they produce and extract."[105] In response to the intensification of trade and the growing demand of the market economy beginning in the 1840s, the *nāʾibs* and their associates—and later the Egyptians—vigorously encouraged pastoralists to increase production and exploit more fully the region's resources. Munzinger made a revealing observation by noting that brokers and traders from Hergigo and Zula ordered specific products from the plain extending between these two villages—a process that modified, to some extent, the modes of production of Saho-speaking pastoralists.

> The plain . . . between Hergigo and Zula . . . produces only thorny gum. Since this region is considered to be Choho [Saho] territory, they are those who have the exploitation rights that occurs during the hottest months on the order of Hergigo's and Zula's inhabitants. The product is taken to Massawa. Considering the large number of gum bushes (trees) in Semhar, the exploitation can be considerably augmented. Today it is done only in response to the orders.[106]

The Sahos brought to Massawa cow hides worked in milk (*felem*), sizable goat skins, and butter, while the Beduins and the Habab brought the same articles but especially cow and ox hides, butter, fat, dhurra, mats, nets, and all the day-to-day provisions needed on the island for local consumption. An estimate from the 1880s put at three thousand cow hides and six thousand goat and sheep skins originating in the Habab areas and sold at Massawa annually. Merchants from Massawa maintained a lively commerce with the Habab, and some of them traveled personally to their region, exchanging local products for imported manufactured objects and cloths.[107] Afar-speaking groups who inhabited the coast and littoral south of Massawa and practiced mostly herding and fishing bred camels that were in great demand in Massawa, where their prices rose considerably in the 1860s. Some of the coastal Afar, especially the Dammohoyta in the Buri peninsula area, exported butter and *jarīd* (Ar., palm branches stripped of their leaves) using their boats—returning with grain, dates, and other goods for local consumption.[108] It is possible that this signified a change from the 1850s when Plowden reported that neither camels nor sheep and goats appear on the Massawa market.[109] The Egyptian takeover of Massawa in 1865 propelled, more than ever before, the coastlands' integration to a market economy that gravitated toward the port. The process was not only economic in nature—it also had cultural and ideological ramifications. Munzinger reported that coastal Afaris took pride in their links with Arabia and Massawa, wore colored silk dress, and practiced Islam more strictly.[110] In the southern parts of the coast, in places such as ʿEdd, commerce with the Yemeni coast was handled directly. There, Afari traders exchanged butter, skins, and straw for tobacco and maize coming from Ḥudayda or Aden.[111]

The development of agricultural cultivation also reflected the changing political economy of the Semhar and the diversification of its inhabitants' modes of production. Even if limited and initially principally confined to the surroundings of villages, some pastoralist societies cultivated during the winter months, when sufficient precipitation enabled them to do so. In the early 1860s Munzinger noted that the most cultivated areas were at Ueddubo, Emberemi, Hergigo, and the Motad plain; Lejean observed that the Beduins planted dhurra between Emkullo and Deset, and he provided a detailed map showing all cultivated areas in Semhar between the coast and the mountains.[112]

After the Egyptians took over the direct administration of Massawa in 1866 they constantly acted to develop and intensify agricultural enterprise in Massawa's hinterlands.[113] The development of agriculture in newly acquired territories had always been highly placed on the Egyptian imperialist agenda. Werner Munzinger, who was appointed as governor of Massawa in the service of khedival Egypt in 1871, made energetic efforts in developing irrigation for cultivation in the Zula area.[114] Munzinger's superior, Aḥmad Mumtāz Pasha, who was appointed by Khedive Ismāᶜīl as governor of the eastern Sudan in 1870, made every effort to encourage cotton cultivation and agricultural enterprise in selected spots along the coast and in the two Red Sea ports' hinterlands. He toured the Red Sea littoral in 1871 and identified the most suitable areas for developing agriculture. In his report he noted that out of a total of about 22,000 square kilometers—the area of the Massawa *muḥāfiẓa*—just over 2,600 square kilometers were suitable for agriculture. He argued that if local pastoralist and agro-pastoralist groups would be encouraged to grow millet and cotton, the need to purchase millet would be eliminated and it would be possible to export cotton via Massawa.[115] Even if, in hindsight, these plans and projects appear to be overambitious and difficult to realize in the short period of Egyptian rule, agricultural activities expanded in the region. By the early years of Italian colonial rule Salvadei noted that during the rainy seasons cultivation in Semhar was intensive "near Shiᶜib, in ᶜAylet, on the Agametta and Agambusa terraces, in the plain of Sabarguma, near Saᶜati, in the environs of Emkullo and Hergigo and in the valley of Katra. Dhurra, maize, dagussa (finger millet), *teff*, panico, sesame and cotton are planted everywhere."[116]

Early-twentieth-century colonial surveys on the possession and exploitation of land in the Semhar region further illuminate the general intensification of cultivation. They noted that from December to April the inhabitants of Semhar returned from the escarpments and the highlands to the lowlands, where many engaged in cultivation. With the exception of limited private land and concessions of land made by the colonial authorities, most cultivable land was exploited. Land granted by the colonial administration as private property or as perpetual concessions was allotted almost exclusively for construction purposes; the authorities seldom granted private land for cultivation per se. Every year, in the first days of November, the Commissariato Regionale announced the opening of the cultivation season, inviting prospective entrepreneurs to present their requests for official permits. In addition, the authorities recognized permanent rights on land in the vicinities of established settled centers, where notable families claimed to have cultivated land for more than three decades. Such places were located near Hergigo, Emkullo, and Emberemi.[117] The "notable families" were usually Balaw or *nāʾib*-associated families who controlled land. As early as 1844, for example, the *nāʾib* allotted a small plot of land to the French consul Degoutin in Emkullo.[118]

In the Sahel region the reports make special mention of the ᶜAd Temaryam and the Rashayda, who both engaged in cultivation some time before the colonial period and practiced their particular customs of land tenure. The Rashayda cultivated mostly millet, dhurra, and watermelons on the coasts north of Massawa between the Weqiro and Lebka rivers. Although they had been cultivators in the past (two–three centuries before), Habab pastoralists were reported to have lost all memory of customs of land tenure. Early-twentieth-century Italian colonial reports noted that the Habab, ᶜAd Shaykh, ᶜAd Muᶜallim, Bet Mala, and ᶜAd Taura had all begun to cultivate lands in an organized manner in very recent times.[119] Toward Keren, as one climbed to higher terrain, cultivation was less recent and more established socially and legally among traditionally agro-pastoralist groups such as the Mensaᶜ, Marya, Bet Juk, and ᶜAd Tekles.[120]

Agriculture in the lowlands expanded significantly under Italian colonial rule. In the first decade of the twentieth century several commercial agricultural enterprises and "experiments" were initiated in the Weqiro, Zula, and Dogᶜali regions by several of Massawa's leading merchant-business families. Thus, in 1908 Muḥammad Sālim Bā Ṭūq received a land concession of 906 hectares near Weqiro, north of Massawa; Ḥasan b. Muḥammad Ṣāfī received a concession of 300 hectares for the cultivation of cotton in Weqiro as well; and Aḥmad Afandī al-Ghūl received 20 hectares for the same purpose.[121]

Another commodity that was produced in the Eritrean coastlands and islands was salt. Centers of salt production in the broader coastland area extended from Lake Assal in present-day Djibouti to Mersa Teklay in the northern parts of the Eritrean coasts. Salt from Mersa Teklay was sent to the adjacent Sahel region and further west, as far as the Barka and Gedaref in Sudan. Closer to Massawa, there were three major centers of salt production. The first was at Weqiro, north of Massawa, producing salt that was expedited to the Sahel, Barka, and the Sudan as well as the highland plateau. A second salt-producing location was on the island of Ghabbi-hu in the Dahlak Archipelago, while the third setting was at Bardeli in the south-central part of the Buri peninsula south of Massawa. The salt pans of Buri were already exploited during the Egyptian period under concessions granted by the administration to selected entrepreneurs. Later, the Italian administration also granted concessions for the exploitation of salt in the area. In 1892 ᶜAlī ᶜAbd Allāh Dossal, a prominent Massawa merchant of Indian origins, received a concession by the governor of the colony and the Massawa customs for the exportation of 3,000 tons of salt to India. The salt, extracted in the island of Ghabbi-hu, was to be first moved to ᶜAbd al-Qādir peninsula near Massawa before its shipment across the sea to the subcontinent.[122] A year later, in 1893, the authorities granted the Del Mar-al-Ghūl Brothers company, an Italian-Massawan joint venture, the concession for all salt production and trading in Weqiro, Ghabbi-hu, and Bardeli in return for 7,000 lire per year. The Ghūl family, which came to Massawa with the Egyptians, was also one of the wealthiest and most prominent families of the port-town, and was involved in several economic projects with the Italian authorities and independent business entrepreneurs. Nevertheless, salt production was not profitable until the Società Italiana per le Saline Eritree was established in 1904, after which it was exported mainly to India and Ethiopia. Salt production and exportation was indeed one of the only economic initiatives yielding profits for investors, especially between 1915 and 1929.[123]

Massawa's Satellites: Regional Market Villages

One of the most significant developments that the changing regional economy evoked was the creation and growth of regional market villages that functioned as points of reception for goods, transit stations along regional and transregional trade routes, and centers for regional trading and transportation networks. Such villages were closely connected with Massawa's commercial structures. The historian Jonathon Glassman dubbed the process by which wealth moved from villages to towns through commerce the "urbanization of the countryside."[124] Settlements in Semhar owed their origins to the regional trade with Massawa and were originally established as caravan camps, thanks to their location near water sources and grazing lands. With the intensification of commercial relations with the port, camps gradually developed into small villages. These included ᶜAylet, Zaga, Gumhod, ᶜAsus, Deset, Emberemi, Zula[125]—all sitting on regional trade routes conducting to and from Massawa, and all connected with coastal political, economic, and social structures through the agency of the Balaws (as shown in the previous chapter).[126] Captain Gatta, for example, noted that Zaga consisted of approximately one hundred huts "inhabited by many Massawans."[127] People who came from Hergigo, Zula, and Arabia inhabited the village of Gumhod, while ᶜAsus's population included people from the ᶜAd Muᶜallim group, who are believed to have founded the village, as well as from the Hergigo Balaws, Beni ᶜAmer, ᶜAd Temaryam, and groups from Arabia.[128] Some of the ᶜAd Muᶜallim inhabitants of Zaga and ᶜAsus were caravaneers serving on the Massawa–Keren and Massawa–Asmara routes.[129] These villages constituted a set of strategically located settlements in Massawa's inlands—all connected to Massawa through the outer localities of the conurbation: Hergigo, Emkullo, Hetumlo.

The most important of the inland Semhar villages was ᶜAylet. Situated ideally on the first terrace of the highland slopes (altitude about 250 meters) on the way to the rich Mensaᶜ lands, ᶜAylet's position placed it at the center of a regional system of trade routes leading to and from these areas.[130] Already in the early 1850s Sapeto remarked that it was a "populous village," before it became a somewhat important regional hub in the 1860s and 1870s.[131] Recognizing its strategic importance, in 1872 the Swedish Evangelical Mission opened a clinic and a small school in ᶜAylet.[132] Parkyns noted that many Beduin and Saho petty merchants passed through ᶜAylet with their goods to and from Massawa—often spending the night in the village. Caravans coming from Massawa before climbing up the plateau into Hamasen often changed their means of transportation from camels to oxen or mules in ᶜAylet's surroundings.[133] Echoing the concept of the "urbanization of the countryside," some observers noted how the dwellers of ᶜAylet developed, to some degree, "urban and mercantile ways" and were devout Muslims. Suggesting a departure from their former pastoralist lifestyle, Parkyns noted that they "appear to be very sociably inclined. In the evening, parties of the men might be seen congregated about the doors of each other's houses to chat."[134] The village was also situated near a valley where large numbers of camel herds grazed. In addition its hot springs attracted people from the broader region—according to Parkyns, "from the most distant parts of Abyssinia, from the islands about the Red Sea, even from Jiddah and other towns on the Arabian coast."[135]

Sections of the Hergigo-based Balaw clan and the *nāʾib*s founded, inhabited, and controlled the important village of ʿAylet. Indeed, after Hergigo was burned down in 1847, the acting *nāʾib* moved his residence—or was forced by the Egyptians to move—to ʿAylet, where under the protection of an Egyptian garrison he continued to conduct his affairs.[136] On the basis of oral accounts, several patterns of regional migration may be identified. Saho-speaking groups, especially from the Bayt Shaykh Maḥmūd, moved from the littoral plain south of Massawa to ʿAylet in the middle decades of the century. The grandfather of Ismāʿīl and ʿUthmān Ḥājj Maḥmūd moved from Zula to ʿAylet, where he joined other members of the family who had previously settled there. There, he grew crops such as maize and grain and owned camels, sheep, and cows.[137] Observers in the 1880s estimated the number of huts in ʿAylet at five hundred, with a population of two thousand.[138]

THE PEARLING ECONOMY IN THE DAHLAK ARCHIPELAGO

> There is a widespread belief among the pearl and mother-of-pearl fishers in the Dahlak islands. A long time ago, during a famine, a mysterious genie dropped a magnificent large pearl in these waters, which if found, would provide great fortune to the inhabitants of the archipelago. It is for this reason that they have dedicated themselves so devotedly to the fishing of those precious oysters, in the hopes of finding that extraordinary gem.
> —Giovanni Salvadei, 1913[139]

The lucrative economic system consisting of the extraction and commercialization of marine products in the Dahlak Archipelago constituted another dynamic sphere of economic activities in Massawa's region. The pearling economy serves as an excellent example displaying the ways by which mid-nineteenth-century commercial transformation in the wider area, but also globally, intensified the chain of production, trade, and consumption of marine products. It involved a distinct infrastructure of financing, labor, and commercialization that married an assortment of Red Sea and Indian Ocean actors. Pearl divers who were either African slaves or freed slaves and Arabs provided the labor; Persian Gulf, Hijazi, Yemeni, Dahlaki, or Massawan boat owners handled fishing crews and provided for transportation;[140] Indian and Arab merchants financed pearl-fishing enterprises and purchased the luxurious marine products that found their way first to Bombay and then to consumers in the capitals of Europe, especially London, Paris, and Vienna.[141] The pearling economy epitomizes interregional connections across the northwestern Indian Ocean in a period that saw its accelerated incorporation into global economic structures that reconfigured patterns of production, labor, commercialization, and consumption in Europe, Africa, and Asia. It also reveals how Italian colonial intervention in the late nineteenth and early twentieth centuries made efforts to "modernize" this economic sector in their colony and render it more economically efficient.

The Dahlak Archipelago comprises approximately 125 islands, islets, rocks, and reefs with deeply indented coasts off the Red Sea coasts opposite the port of Massawa. The most important islands are Dahlak al-Kabīr, Nukhra, Nura, Dohol, Raka (Baka), Daraka, and Hawatib. The islands are flat, and rainfall and vegetation are scanty, making living conditions especially harsh for a small population of between 1,500 and 2,500, depending on historical periods. Occupied by the Umayyad Muslims in the early eighth century, the Dahlak islands served initially as a prison and a place of refuge. According to some oral traditions, the name Dahlak is a distortion of the Arabic *hadha ḥalak,* ("this one is darkened, damned"), meaning that he who has gone there is lost, "he will not return, he has gone to hell, to Gehenem."[142] In the twelfth and thirteen centuries the islands were the seat of an independent emirate ruled by a line of sultans and served as an important transit station in the trade between Egypt and India, but also in the Persian/Arabian Gulf and in cross–Red Sea trade between Ethiopia and Yemen. Numerous tombstones with Arabic inscriptions dating about the ninth to the thirteenth centuries are still found today in a vast necropolis near the village Dahlak al-Kabīr on the island bearing the same name.[143] The Dahlak Archipelago was also a gateway in the process of Islamization in northeast Africa.

The economy of the Dahlak islands involved chiefly the extraction of marine products such as pearls (*Meleagrina muricata,* Ar. *bulbul*), mother-of-pearl (*Meleagrina margaritifera,* Ar. *ṣadof*), and tortoise shells (Ar. *dobel, baie*). As early as the twelfth century the historian ᶜUmāra al-Yamanī (d. 1174) alluded to pearl-fishing activities in the islands, and in the fifteenth century further accounts made note of the vitality of the pearl trade in the area.[144] In the late seventeenth century the Ottoman traveler Evliya Çelebi observed that the village of Dahlak al-Kabīr contained six hundred houses and forty to fifty well-provisioned stores. He noted that taxes from pearl fishing constituted part of the revenues of the Ottoman pasha of Massawa.[145] A century later, according to Bruce, the islands once again fell into a state of disrepair. However, at the turn of the nineteenth century, Lord Valentia noted that Massawa merchants continued to export pearls, pearl shells, and tortoise shells to the East Indies and China.[146]

Seeking the "Sky's Tears": Divers, Nakhūdas, *and Pearl Merchants*

Around the middle of the nineteenth century, Werner Munzinger observed that the two main islands in the archipelago were Dahlak and Nura—both covered by some vegetation and having inhabitants who possessed many goats, camels, and mules. The division of labor among the inhabitants represented a system by which men acted as boat owners and captains, fishermen, and pearl divers while women and children bred animals and took care of the household. Every village had a hereditary chief, dependent of the Ottoman pasha of Massawa, who paid an annual tribute of approximately 1,000 thalers collected yearly by the pasha's soldiers. Following the Egyptian occupation in 1866 the office of *shaykh al-mashāʾikh*—a supreme chief for all the Dahlak chiefs—was established and based at Debᶜullo, on the eastern shores of Dahlak island.[147] Debᶜullo was the big pearl market in the archipelago, where Massawan, Indian, Arab, and Persian merchants purchased pearls, mother-of-pearl, tortoise shells, and other marine products in an annually held fair. Indian traders, who dominated the market, connected directly with their own networks in Luḥayya, Ḥudayda, and Aden on the Yemeni coasts before expediting pearls to Bombay. The yellowish and finely formed pearls were sent to Bombay, the white ones went to Baghdad, and the imperfect pearls could find a market in other Arabian Red Sea ports.[148] Tortoise shells were available for purchase in all the ports of the archipelago, in Massawa, in ᶜAqīq up north still on the African shores, and in the Yemeni ports on the other side of the Red Sea. Involving elaborate techniques, catching tortoise required a boat crew of approximately twenty men. The shells were made of thirteen pieces, of which the heaviest were the best-valued and thus sent to India. After the boat owner got his share, the fishermen divided the remaining pieces, and the one who caught the tortoise usually received the hexagonal part in recompense. Fishing of mother-of-pearl took place between Suez and Berbera; the fishing was carried out with 5–12-ton vessels (Ar. *sanbūq*) and small rowing canoes (Ar. *hūrī*). In mid-century the principal market for mother-of-pearl was still in Jiddah.[149]

The Italian geologist and mineralogist Arturo Issel (1842–1922) provided valuable information on economic aspects of the Dahlak archipelago in his book *Viaggio nel Mar Rosso e tra i Bogos* published in 1872.[150] Issel described in great detail his tour in the Dahlak islands conducted in 1870. The *sanbūq* on which Issel sailed from island to island in search of the pearl divers had a typically heterogeneous crew: the *nakhūda* was a native of Hijaz, three sailors were Yemeni, and two "Abyssinians" were at Issel's service.[151] Optimal conditions of clear and calm waters enabling and facilitating pearl diving prevailed twice a year, between late March and May and between September and November. Diving operations usually began after the rains; local traditions attributed the formation of the pearly secretion to the mixing of fresh and salty water, suggesting why pearlers sometimes referred to the precious gems as "the sky's tears."[152] After several days Issel and his *nakhūda* finally identified some action near the island of Sarato. Issel noted that there were thirteen boats of many types; one was from the Farasān islands with a crew of about forty, of which two-thirds were divers. Pearl divers, predominantly Muslim, came from various Red Sea islands such as Farasān, Nukhra, Dohol, Dahlak, Kamarān and from the Afar coast, but many were also either slaves or freed slaves, mainly from the Sudanese area: "they wear a special square turban with yellowish metallic threads," a Swiss traveler noted at the end of the 1880s.[153] Luigi Naretti's collective portrait from the 1890s makes the multi-ethnic character of pearl fishermen in Massawa clearly apparent (see Figure 2.7). During the pearl-fishing season, a diver's working day started at nine or ten in the morning and lasted until three in the afternoon. They were taken in *sanbūqs* to the diving area, where they launched small boats (*hūrī*) and dived into depths of 5–7 meters. They collected the oysters in a straw bag called a *zambīl*. After the day's diving, on the boat's way back from the fishing waters, the boat crew opened the oyster shells and searched for pearls. In average, a pearl was found in every forty to fifty oyster shells. Henry de Monfreid wrote that in order to prevent cheating (i.e., divers finding pearls and concealing them for themselves), and perhaps also to increase good

Figure 2.6. Pearlers in the Dahlak Archipelago, ca. 1890–1900. Photographer: Roberto Gentile. Biblioteca Reale, Torino.

fortune, each oyster-shell-opening session was preceded by a recitation of the Fātiḥa, the opening chapter of the Qurʾān.[154] According to Issel, the daily production of a well-equipped boat might have been approximately 3,500 pearl oysters and 500 mother-of-pearl.

The marine economy around the Dahlak Archipelago intensified in the closing two decades of the nineteenth century. Estimates put the number of boats engaged in pearl-fishing activities at between 300 and 350, employing an estimated 10,000 men as fishermen and divers.[155] Alamanni gave the larger figure of 450 boats, of which only a minority were from Massawa. More detailed estimates put at 32 Dahlaki boats, employing 600–700 fishermen, and at 70–80 Yemeni boats, employing approximately 65 men on each (totaling roughly 5,000 men). Added to these were about 200 boats belonging to the Hijazi Beduin tribe of Zubayd, who inhabited the coast between Yanbuᶜ and Jiddah and whose port was at Rābigh. Almost all Zubaydis, the Italian report added, were mother-of-pearl divers.[156] About a decade and a half into Italian rule, at the turn of the century, a survey report noted that a large number of sailing boats came from

Jiddah, Luḥayya, and Ḥudayda, as well as large galleys from the Persian Gulf with 50–80 pearl divers on each vessel. Most boats operating in the Dahlak Archipelago belonged either to merchants based in ports on the Arabian shores of the Red Sea or to Massawa merchants, or belonged to private *nakhūda*s who organized pearl-fishing trips and were independent to sell their proceeds to whoever would pay most. Independent *nakhūda*s needed enough capital to finance their expeditions and equip their boat crews. In many cases, *nakhūda*s were contracted to pearl merchants in the ports, many of whom were Indian. As in the Persian Gulf region, Indian finance was pivotal to the Red Sea pearl economy. Merchants financed pearl-fishing operations by providing advances either in cash or in provisions (e.g., rice, dhurra, oil, butter, and tobacco for chewing) to *nakhūda*s and pearling crews prior to the fishing expeditions. In return, the *nakhūda* was committed to return to his merchant with the proceeds of the dive at the end of the fishing season and sell it to him.[157]

In the case of *nakhūda*-owned boats, there were distinct and elaborate systems of labor, the division of gains from production and the advancing of credit. Under one regime, pearl divers worked alternately four days for their own profit and one day for the owner. In most cases, the oysters were opened on the boat under the close supervision of the *nakhūda*. Often, divers were paid in nature with the products that they caught; the owner of the boat took one-third of the catch and divided the remaining two-thirds with the sailors and divers, less the cost of food consumed by them.[158] This system of credit, debt, and dependency epitomized the configuration of labor relations in the Dahlak pearl economy and in turn fueled it. Debt tied pearl divers to *nakhūda*s, boat owners, and financiers. In some instances pearlers were heavily indebted to boat owners, spurring them to work long hours and days, maximizing their labor and also the risk of wearing out their health.[159]

Some of the divers were local Dahlakis whose craft passed from generation to generation in pearl-fishing families and who jealously preserved their fishing methods and techniques in order to protect their livelihood. In 1889 and in 1895, for example, attempts by entrepreneurs from Torre del Greco, near Naples, to directly operate pearl-fishing enterprises in the archipelago were doomed to fail. As soon as the Italian vessels appeared in the Dahlaki waters, the local pearl fishers abandoned the pearl banks to avoid disclosing location or methods. They also attempted to resist European pressures and incitement to overexploit pearl banks.[160] The particular seasonal character and dangers of the pearl-diving occupation also account for the development of a lively culture among pearl divers, manifested through song and spiritual religious expressions. Alas, our sources do not reveal more than flimsy remarks on those aspects. But the pearl-diver population also included non-locals. In the 1880s Alamanni noted that most divers were liberated slaves.[161] The known sources make this claim impossible to verify at this point. The ever-passionate Italian journalist Vico Mantegazza, writing from Massawa, noted that "one should see how these blacks are embarked on the sailing boats going out for pearl-fishing, not far from here. They are slaves in the strict sense of the word, receiving from their owner, who is the master of the boat, barely enough to keep them from dying of hunger. And they are forced to work like animals/beasts."[162] In his experience-based yet fictionalized accounts, Henry de Monfreid also mentioned the existence of slaves and freed slaves on pearl-diving crews (many carrying Sudanese names) in the early twentieth century.[163] While it has been argued that significant proportions of pearling crews in the Persian Gulf had employed African slaves, at the moment the available evidence does not provide solid insight as to the extent and proportion between skilled and unskilled, free and unfree, labor or the precise terms of employment of freed slaves in the Dahlak pearl-fishing economy.[164]

The commercialization of the season's catch was conducted in several ways. In certain cases, itinerant merchants and entrepreneurs came directly to fishing waters and bought pearls and other products on fishing boats at sea. Such merchants, but also independent *nakhūdas*, then continued to Massawa, Jiddah, Ḥudayda, or Aden, where they could obtain the best prices for their goods. Independent *nakhūdas* from the Persian Gulf sometimes went as far as Bombay. Whereas in 1870 Issel reported that white pearls were exported to Baghdad, early-twentieth-century reports noted that they were sent to Europe by itinerant agents of European firms (e.g., French, Armenian) who bought the pearls in Massawa, or by merchants in Jiddah, which was the chief market for pearls in the area after Massawa and Aden. On the other hand, the yellowish pearls were regularly expedited by Indian merchants to Bombay.[165] In the late nineteenth and early twentieth centuries Massawa-based pearl and mother-of-pearl merchants and entrepreneurs included members of the Bā Ḥamdūn, Ṣāfī, Bā Ṭūq, al-Ghūl, and Bā Junayd families as well as Indians (from Bombay) such as ʿAlī ʿAbd Allāh Dossal, Dremshi Nangi, Minahim Missa, and others.[166]

Figures for the exportation of pearls are unreliable due to the semi-clandestine nature of transactions and the high occurrences of smuggling and frequent evasion from the customs authorities. Fascinated by the "mysterious" pearl trade at Massawa, the Swiss traveler Victor Buchs noted that one could spend months in Massawa without suspecting the trade's existence since local fishermen carried it out secretly, away from the eyes of customs officials. He nevertheless evaluated the annual exportation at 1,500,000 thalers.[167] Comments in the same spirit were voiced by the Italian Parazzoli, who reported having seen in Bombay an impressive amount of sealed boxes coming from Massawa, containing pearls of a value of 20,000 to 100,000 lire each. The Italian consul in Bombay told Parazzoli that he was aware of great quantities of pearls coming from Eritrea to Bombay and in response to his astonishment was mockingly told by a local trader: "You do not even know the products of your own country!"[168] In the same spirit and mirroring the idea of the lack of effectiveness in exploiting the pearling industry's potential, Giovanni Salvadei (commissario of Massawa, 1901–1905) cited a metaphor that he had heard from Mohammed Ali Chefar, chief of the Afar-speaking Dahimmela, and that was in fact addressed in relation to the colony's salt mines: "You Italians are like a camel, who carries forages on his back, but languishes of hunger."[169] At the beginning of the twentieth century Salvadei gave a much higher figure for the total value of pearl exports, putting it at 4,000,000 lire.[170] Estimates for mother-of-pearl exports, on the other hand, are much more reliable since they passed through well-regulated channels of trade and were taxed. Figures between 1887 and 1892 put at roughly 500,000 kilograms the mother-of-pearl exported annually from Massawa. The total value of mother-of-pearl fished in 1889, for example, amounted to 652,331 lire.[171]

Colonial Intervention and Pearlers' Resistance

Seeking to control more closely the furtive marine products and divert the Dahlak trade toward Massawa, the Italian colonial authorities abolished an 8 percent customs tax on mother-of-pearl in May 1892. This measure caused exportations to double to nearly one million kilograms in 1893. It placed Massawa as the chief market for mother-of-pearl in the Red Sea, providing merchants with better conditions than in Sawākin, Ḥudayda, or Luḥayya, where taxes remained in place, and attracted an increasing volume of transactions at the port. This exemplifies the flexibility of the Red

Sea market and its trade networks, which were able to adjust to new conditions created by a beneficial taxing regime and swiftly rearrange commercial operations fixed on Massawa. It also illustrates the dynamics of interport competition in the Red Sea basin in the period. A few years later it was estimated that between 300 and 400 tons of mother-of-pearl, with a value between 350,000 and 450,000 lire reached Massawa annually. Most was extracted in Eritrean waters, but some also came from Jiddah, ʿAqīq, and the Farasān islands. From Massawa, locally based agencies shipped it to Trieste (Austro-Hungary), Genoa, Venice, London, Bombay, and also New York. At the turn of the century most mother-of-pearl (about 75%) was exported to Trieste, before being expedited overland to the button factories in Bohemia. An agency of the Trieste-based Bienenfeld firm operated in Massawa. Similarly, the goods reaching the Italian ports made their way to the loci of button production in Lombardy, chiefly in Brescia and Bergamo.[172]

Throughout the 1890s Italian attempts to systematize and control the remunerative marine industry were constant but not always coherent. More and more voices in commercial circles in Italy expressed the absurdity of allowing the semi-clandestine and "informal" yet profitable marine economy to evade colonial control and regulation. Instead of making profits for Italy and promoting its economic interests, these voices complained, the situation allowed the foreign, Indian merchants—who were also British subjects—to carry out their trade for their own benefit by making huge profits from the colony's natural resources. But requests to grant exclusive fishing rights presented by commercial entrepreneurs such as Luigi Pennazzi, Luigi Stefanoni, and Alberto Cané did not always fall on open ears in government and colonial offices, at least until the appointment of Oreste Baratieri as governor of Eritrea in February 1892 and the subsequent abolition of the customs tax in May 1892. Baratieri made efforts toward the promotion of collaboration with the Venetian Society for Fishing and Aquiculture in making the Italian port city a center where the mother-of-pearl industry could flourish.[173] Several other initiatives and studies were undertaken by Italian economic entrepreneurs in the mid to late 1890s.

In 1898, under Ferdinando Martini's vigorous and enterprising governorship, the colonial authorities approved a proposal submitted by the Milan-based businessman Ambrogio Parazzoli, involving the establishment of a company having exclusive rights to fish pearls and mother-of-pearl in Italian waters. The company was to maintain a privileged relationship with the colonial authorities and direct all marine products to Massawa en route for exportation to Europe. It would also exclusively employ divers and laborers who were Italian subjects and would initiate and establish a laboratory-school for at least fifty students for developing an industry for mother-of-pearl products.[174] An agreement between Governor Martini and the Milan-based Società A. Parazzoli (to become at some point later Società Perlifera Italiana [the Italian Pearling Society]) granted the company a concession for pearl fishing and the harvesting of oysters in Eritrea's waters.[175] The company's role was limited to the regulation, control, and surveillance of pearling activities, in return for no less than 50 percent of the total proceeds, later commuted to a still shameless 33 percent. The reaction of local pearlers and merchants was not long in coming, and in August 1899 they had deserted the three main islands of the archipelago, as well as other smaller ones. The Società Perlifera Italiana had no choice but to compromise and reduce the charge to 20 percent, a rate that was still disputed by the divers but that they were finally compelled to accept. Overall, the concession in this case was a total failure; the operation of the Società Perlifera Italiana had a devastating effect on the pearling economy in the region. Revenues from the pearling sector nose-dived from 906,000 lire in 1898 to 201,000 lire in 1902. Consequently, in 1903 the colonial authorities revoked the company's monopoly, and the pearling sector was liberalized.[176]

From the early twentieth century on, mother-of-pearl fishing in Eritrea was regulated by a maritime code and other colonial regulations relating to indigenous shipping and to fishing in general. The basic principle required anyone—colonial subject or alien—desiring to conduct fishing activities in Italian waters to obtain a permit from the Massawa port authorities. Mother-of-pearl fishing activities was permitted between Ras Kassar and ᶜEdd, including the Dahlak Archipelago, between 1 February and 31 May and between 15 August and 31 October. Once the product reached Massawa it had to be deposited at the customs within twenty-four hours, and the customs tax of 3 percent of value was to be paid. As to pearl fishing, a private company was to supervise all pearling activities in return for a tax.[177]

Both external market demands for the marine products and colonial regulation and control over the economic activities in the Dahlak islands seem to have transformed the less centralized system that characterized the older economic order centered on the archipelago's natural resources. From the 1890s onward, Massawa drew the islands closer to the port, gen-

Figure 2.7. Pearl fishermen in Massawa, ca. 1890. Photographer: Luigi Naretti. Biblioteca Reale, Torino.

erating several patterns of change. Odorizzi noted that the new economic order had a negative and disruptive effect on the pearl divers and sailors inhabiting the islands. Since the 1890s the islands had witnessed a demographic decline due to illness, a very limited birth rate, and migration to Massawa. On the other hand, Odorizzi had identified several groups—originally from the coastal areas of ʿAqīq, the Afar littoral, and Arabia—who had settled in various locations in the islands since the 1880s and 1890s. It is also interesting and revealing to note a change in the settlement pattern on the island. While in the middle decades of the century observers recognized the village of Debʿullo on the eastern, sea-facing, shores of Dahlak island as the largest market and settlement in the archipelago, in the first years of the century, of the one hundred stone houses only half were inhabited. The shift in importance turned to settlements on the western shores, facing Massawa. While Salait and Dassoho close to the eastern shores recorded a trend of depopulation, Dahlak Kabīr, Jumʿelle, and Kumebah on the western shores either remained stable or received new groups of pastoralist migrants from the Eritrean coasts. In 1898–99 one report noted that there were 142 officially registered *sanbūqs* for the fishing season and 2,827 pearl fishers.[178]

In the second half of the nineteenth century, the political economy of the Dahlak Archipelago had been transformed. The marine economy that had been part of a western Indian Ocean interregional economy, largely dominated by a host of Red Sea and Indian Ocean actors predominantly from India, the Arabian coasts, and adjacent islands, was gradually drawn closer to Massawa and the Eritrean coasts by Egyptian and Italian control, regulation, and systematization. By controlling commercialization, the Italian colonial authorities made efforts to direct the mother-of-pearl trade to Europe, especially to Italy. However, informal commercial patterns continued alongside the new colonial order. At the end of the century, more than ever before, the Dahlak Archipelago came to constitute an important part of Massawa's economic "hinterlands."

The natural-pearl economy in the northwestern Indian Ocean declined in the 1930s on account of the worldwide depression's effect on demand and also competition from Japanese freshwater cultured pearls since the early twentieth century.[179] Mother-of-pearl exportations remained an important colonial economic enterprise throughout most of the Italian colonial period. Most exports were destined to Italy, but some also went to the United States. The establishment of the Pescherie Italiane d'Africa Orientale (Italian Fisheries of East Africa) in 1919 boosted mother-of-pearl exports, which remained high for a decade. Indeed, the value of mother-of-pearl rose spectacularly; for example, between 1923 and 1929 alone, prices of mother-of-pearl almost doubled, to 5,551,719 lire. Yet the world financial crisis affected this sector, and by 1932 export values fell to about 1,000,000 lire. In that year the Pescherie Italiane d'Africa Orientale went bankrupt.[180] It was only in the 1950s that the world market in mother-of-pearl completely declined, as plastic replaced mother-of-pearl in buttons, cutlery handles, and other items.[181]

The conjuncture of commercial intensification and tighter political and economic control by the Egyptians, and later the Italians, also contributed to the development of informal and "illegal" commercial and smuggling activities on and off the Massawa coasts, as well as in the broader Red Sea area. As the discussions of the clandestine nature of pearl trading as well as pearl fishers' resistance to colonial measures suggest, contraband, piracy, and the illegal trafficking of slaves were phenomena that exposed the effects of the intensified external pressures by international market forces and the imposed measures of control by imperialist powers in the second half of the nineteenth century. The sites for illegal activities and secret trades were usually north and south of Massawa's coasts and around the islands, where smugglers found an ideal—even if dangerous—labyrinthine space for evading the reach of the long arm of the authorities. Slave-transporting boats were usually undistinguishable from ordinary fishing, pearling, or trading boats, which made it even more difficult for the authorities. Accordingly, merchants too—the flimsy sources seem to tell us—could have their hands in both legitimate and illegal commercial activities at the same time. Clearly, this is one explanation for the difficulty historians face in reconstructing slaving activities in this area.[182] Already in the 1860s Egyptian reports associated Emberemi, some fifteen kilometers north of Massawa, with contraband and illegal slaving activities.[183] The French traveler Denis de Rivoyre also pointed to the phenomenon of slave caravans reaching the coast north of Massawa, where small boats waited for them to transport slaves to Arabia.[184] South of Massawa, around Zula and the Buri peninsula and on the northern Afar littoral, the situation was even more acute. Profit-tempted merchants in Massawa actively participated in—perhaps also initiated—such activities. They found themselves in a tight spot, on the one hand cooperating with the authorities, which legitimized their paramount position, but on the other, tempted by the lucrative profits that trade—of any kind—offered in this period. Disembarkation on the Arabian shores of the Red Sea also followed a comparable pattern, involving clandestine night landing at isolated spots mostly south of Jiddah.[185] Clearly, the very nature of such traffic, especially in the second half of the nineteenth century, makes quantitative estimates such as advanced by Austen and others (and recognized by them) quite problematic and questionable. The focus on exports from Massawa and importations at Jiddah may be misleading when attempting quantification.

Commercial transformation also had drastic ramifications on the urban geography, spatial layout, and political economy of the port and its close surroundings. Due to the spatial limitations of Massawa Island, incoming migrants, entrepreneurs, peddlers, porters, laborers, and brokers settled on the mainland opposite the port, in several villages that formed part of a larger urban complex, or a conurbation. The elements of the conurbation were the sites of multilayered economic and social processes and interactions where countryside and town linked to each other.

3

Connecting Sea and Land

Merchants, Brokers, and the Anatomy of a Red Sea Port Town

Trade and commercial brokerage have been the raison d'être of Massawa's existence as a port-town and a driving force animating its operation since its very foundation. Massawa's role in commercial intermediacy shaped the makeup and organization of its communities and urban spatial layout. Its shifting social fabric reflected its changing connections with both the African interior and the western Indian Ocean area. This chapter explores and analyzes the distinctive composition of Massawa's communities and examines the ways by which commercial expansion fashioned and transfigured the roles and orientation of its brokering and trading communities. If in the first half of the century one still found in Massawa merchants with *nisbas* denoting origins in places located beyond the Red Sea realm such as al-Izmīrī, al-ʿIrāqī, al-Qashmīrī, al-Kurdī, al-Qābūlī, al-Bunghāsī, and al-Maghribī, for example, the second half of the century witnessed their gradual fading away from the sources, as Hadrami and Indian traders and their networks established their ascendancy in the Red Sea basin, and also settled in greater numbers in Massawa. It mirrored the gradual substitution of one commercial structure by another.

New opportunities for economic enterprise and labor in the Red Sea area generated the brisk movement of people across the wider region. As one of the ports whose fortunes rose in this period, Massawa became a propitious destination for merchants, commercial agents, brokers, and pearl-fishing entrepreneurs from overseas. At the same time, Massawa attracted a growing number of people from the African interior who migrated into the burgeoning port-town and provided it with a variety of brokering, peddling, and labor services. The Egyptian-propelled modernization schemes of Massawa's urban landscape in the 1870s drew to it pastoralists, herdsmen, small-scale cultivators, and fishermen who became laborers, petty traders, cameleers, water sellers, and fruit and vegetable growers, among other occupations. Many were drawn to Massawa's markets, port docks, and construction sites, where their labor and goods could earn them cash. The visibility of these newly sedentarized individuals must have been striking to such a degree that one observer in the 1870s referred to Massawa as the "Harbour of the shepherds."[1] By the early twentieth century census data about the population of Massawa Island reveals how inward migration made Massawa a town of outlanders (see tables 1 and 2).

One of the most far-reaching consequences of urban migration and economic growth was the development and expansion of a number of villages on the mainland, opposite the island of Massawa. This process marked the formation of a wider economic and social urban space, or a conurbation, with Massawa as the key urban unit around which commercial life was organized. Scholars writing on East African Swahili port towns understand the conurbation as constituting a micro urban economic system of complementary production and exchange between different categories of settlement, which are "tied together into a single unit by various bonds of neighborhood, kinship, political and religious authority, and by some expression of shared or complementary ethnicities."[2] This insight sustains a basic idea inspired by *Annales* scholars, suggesting that a port creates in its surrounding community an environment sui generis, an interstitial milieu between land and sea.[3] The expansion of Massawa's urban spaces to the mainland settlements also had social implications. The markets, caravan stations, and residence spaces of the conurbation were the loci of multilayered social and economic interactions between locally established traders and brokers, Arab and Indian merchants and commercial entrepreneurs from abroad, and a floating population of nomads and pastoralists who constantly drifted between town and countryside.

The cyclical arrival of caravans from the interior also had a pivotal impact on the town's day-to-day operation. Earlier in the nineteenth century the arrival of particularly large caravans could double Massawa's population. These interfacial spaces were where overland and seaborne networks connected. In the outer sectors of the conurbation and on its fringes, in the markets of Hergigo, Emkullo, and Hetumlo, the social, economic, and cultural dynamics involved in the process of the integration into urban-dominated commercial networks took place and could at times offer the key to "become urban" and construct one's own circle of business, carriage, and labor networks. On the other hand, those migrants who settled in town and made a quick fortune sometimes endowed a water well or a piece of land used for a cemetery—gestures that could offer them a way to "become local" and, perhaps more importantly, local sources of authority, social legitimization, and actual access to networks of patronage on the mainland. This chapter exposes the multiple levels of mediating and brokering relationships that animated the port's operation, in both long-distance relationships and regional-local networks. It shows how these brokering relations tied the inland regions of Northeast Africa and beyond it with the wider world of the Red Sea and the northwestern Indian Ocean.

Observers estimated the population of the island-port at around 1,500 in the first decade of the century, 5,000 in the 1850s, 8,000 in the late 1870s and 1880s, and about 16,000 for the entire Massawa conurbation at the same period. A rather high estimate is offered in Teobaldo Folchi's report written in 1898: 6,100 inhabitants in Massawa Island, 3,100 in Hergigo, 14,000 in Hetumlo (of which 9,000 were females) and 600 in Emkullo, giving a total population of 23,800 in the Massawa conurbation. Estimates are at times only illustrative, and actual numbers are difficult to determine with precision. The fragmented character of the conurbation in geographically separate units, the presence of a floating population coming to the town's markets on a daily basis, and the seasonal arrival of large caravans render the evaluations of Massawa's population in this period tentative at best.[4]

Brokerage Institutions and Commercial Sponsorship as Sources of Group Solidarity

The need to mediate between peoples inhabiting different geographical and commercial spheres, belonging to a variety of cultures, practicing different religions, and speaking diverse languages has actuated various types of brokerage institutions in world history. This was all the more true in settings such as commerce-oriented city-states, where in the lack of a strong centralized and regulating bureaucratic government, brokers played the role of facilitating international commercial relationships. Particular brokerage institutions have operated in Eastern Africa and the Red Sea area, including the Ethio-Eritrean, Sudanese, and Somali regions, in the nineteenth century, both in ports and in inland market centers such as the city of Harar.[5] The organization of brokerage and commercial sponsorship institutions in western Indian Ocean ports, from the southern Red Sea area down to Mozambique, shared characteristic features. The main feature epitomizing this unity of practice was that relations between urban coastal brokers and their trading partners were personal rather than market-oriented.[6]

As a trade emporium situated between the northeast African interior and the Red Sea and the northwestern Indian Ocean area, Massawa has been at the intersection of several complex strata of intermediating relations and brokerage mechanisms: on a macro level, between the world of the sea and the port, and also between the port and the inlands; on a micro level, between the sea-oriented harbor and the outer sections of the Massawa conurbation and between these satellite villages, or neighborhoods, and the specific inlands to which they were connected. Brokerage was also commonly organized along ethnic or cultural lines; for example, Indians in Massawa served as correspondents for Indian financiers in India or in Aden, while a broker of Habab origins in Hetumlo could serve as a broker to producers in the Habab region. Between the 1830s and the early 1860s several European accounts associated the brokerage institutions of *nazīl* and *adār* with the pre-eminent occupation of Massawa's mercantile citizens.[7] It is interesting to note that the institution of *adār* was prevalent in the northeast African interior, where it had possibly originated. In mid-century, Lejean noted that *adārī*s operated among the pastoral tribes between the Red Sea and the Nile—the Beni ʿAmer, the Hadendoa, the Bogos, and the Habab. He advised any European who was planning to come to the Barka for elephant hunting to employ an *adārī,* who would provide guides, accommodation, and all the hunter's needs.[8]

In Massawa, brokers usually served as agents or correspondents to Indian merchants operating in the Red Sea area, to the Arab merchants of Jiddah, Cairo, and the Tihāma ports, and to Ethiopian merchants who came with their caravans to the port.[9] Merchants arriving from the interior to Massawa were required to have a broker, who handled all their practical and business affairs and activities during their stay in the port. The *nazīl* was also responsible for the safety and security of his guest as well as for negotiating on his behalf the *fassas,* the passage fees, to be paid to the *nāʾib* upon the merchant's return to the highlands.[10] Typically, a caravan merchant arrived to the jetty on Gherar peninsula, crossed to Massawa with his merchandise on board a boat, reached his *nazīl*'s compound consisting of a residential area and some storing shops, and unloaded his goods in the courtyard.[11] The merchant lodged with his *nazīl,* and all transactions on the island were carried through the broker, who bought part of the merchant's goods for a reduced price. It was not uncommon that the relationship between a merchant and his *nazīl* lasted a lifetime.[12] Werner Munzinger described the relationship and the broker cartel's ascendancy in these words:

> Every Abyssinian merchant (*neggade*) has in Massawa a correspondent (*nazīl*) who is his guarantor (Abyssinia having no official relationship with Turkey [*sic*]). He provides him with accommodation, fire, water and takes care of all his business during his stay. In return the *nazīl* receives a fee which is quite considerable on all sales and purchases. This commission, coming to 5–10% [on the value of the merchandise] is so profoundly rooted in the customs that it would be foolish to try to evade it. This is even more valid since the *nazīls* have all the business in their hands and conduct affairs as they wish, favoring their friends.[13]

The *adarit,* or brokerage fees, varied from 5 percent to 20 percent, and was collected by both buyer and seller according to the type of merchandise.[14] A French report of 1848 noted how local brokers made impressive profits by taking 15 percent from both buyer and seller, thus making a profit of 30 percent on business transactions.[15] Werner Munzinger also noted that following their arrival at Massawa Ethiopian merchants hesitated before selling their goods, fearing to inundate the market and bring prices down. But after a wealthy merchant made the first sale, all the provisions of the same merchandise were sold very rapidly. Barter, according to Munzinger, was not beneficial. It was much better to have cash, in Maria Theresa dollars, in order to make purchases on favorable terms. Only after they had sold all their goods did the Ethiopian merchants begin spending some of their money to buy merchandise in the port's markets. They took at least half of their cash gains with them on their return inland. As Munzinger again noted, "if the Abyssinians bring merchandise valued at 200,000 MTD, they take back with them 130,000. With the remaining 70,000 they pay for their purchases. About 60,000 are paid for Indian goods and about 10,000 remains for European goods."[16]

Massawan brokers were first and foremost related to one another by their common commercial interests as a cartel or syndicate. They worked closely with the authorities, controlled the port's markets, and regulated prices, usually by manipulating demand and offer. Lejean wrote about the Massawan merchants as forming a very compact corpus and a "curious corporation" who conducted all their business through exchange and credit.

The *adārī* was also the representative of his guest vis-à-vis the authorities and the "corporation." He added that he "would not advise any European to attempt avoiding the broker since he would be put in quarantine by the corporation."[17]

From the mid-1860s onward the institutions of *nazīl* and *adār* seem to have disappeared altogether from the accounts of observers, with the exception of those who—while writing their narratives—had relied on the earlier accounts of d'Abbadie, Munzinger, or Lejean. The lack of historical documentation leaves us with a void as to the precise evolution of this type of brokerage after 1865, when khedival Egypt took control over the port. Reading subsequent documentation—from the 1870s through the end of the century—makes it seem almost certain that they ceased to exist under this particular form. Brokers and brokerage in other forms were certainly reformulated, especially with the emerging dominant role of the mainland villages, principally Hetumlo. The appearance of an assertive and centralizing modern-type administration in Massawa, regulating duties, fees, and customs, restructuring the port's administrative bodies, and reforming its legal institutions removed large portions of the *nazīl*'s "informal" role. The creation of a local council (*majlis maḥalī*), the reinforcement of the *sharīʿa* court, the appointment of heads of professional guilds such as the *sarrtujjār*, or chief of merchants, transformed the relations between merchants/brokers and the state in Massawa from the mid-1860s onward.[18] Merchants adjusted their strategies to the new Egyptian order, which sought to promote and associate itself with any lucrative mercantile enterprise in the area. Furthermore, Egyptian building enterprise and the urban transformation of the Massawa conglomeration also had a profound effect on how the port connected to the mainland and the inlands, which signaled a departure from the functional interconnection between spatial and brokerage arrangements. The physical linking of Massawa Island to the mainland by two causeways is a case in point. Entrance to Massawa Island no longer depended on one's *nazīl*. Instead, a large stone gateway, the *Bāb ʿAshara,* regulated entrance and exit and required the payment of a fixed fee upon entrance. Brokerage institutions were at the heart of the original role played by Massawa's mercantile population. The existence of a more or less informal, tightly knit brokers' "syndicate" in Massawa in the first half of the century is significant to the economic and social roots and sources of an idealized sense of connectedness, solidarity, and a communal identity among Massawa's mercantile citizens.

"They Came from the Land, They Came from the Sea": Genealogies of an Urban Coastal Society

The identity of Massawa's founders and the origins of the port-town's old families are questions that one senses close to the surface when conducting interviews and conversations with Massawans nowadays. In a multicultural setting that since its inception has constantly absorbed both inlanders and outlanders, identity is a subject that matters. It is also the arena where different notions of local identity—inclusivist or exclusivist—were competed and struggled over through the expression of different discourses of origin and primacy. The social and cultural "nature" of Massawa is a question that Massawans themselves have constantly pondered. The paucity of historical sources and the sociocultural functionality of traditions of origin make it difficult to elucidate the flexuous history of the settlement and population structure of Hergigo and Massawa in earlier centuries. Over time, these two urban sites have been settled by peoples coming intermittently both from what are today the Ethio-Eritrean and Sudanese inlands and from overseas. The discussion that follows demonstrates the importance and complexity of various claims of primacy and origins in settings where hybridity is inherent to the historical development of a society. More importantly perhaps, and notwithstanding the intrinsic difficulty of drawing clear-cut conclusions in an effervescent discursive arena such as that of Massawa, the discussion establishes how both Hergigo's and Massawa's inceptions were deeply rooted in their particular environment on the African shores of the Red Sea.

Saho-speaking groups, originally from the Zula plain, capitalized on the proximity to the highlands and founded Hergigo. Subsequently the village became the seat of the Balaw *nāʾibs*, who established their supremacy over the coast around the fifteenth century. As the dominant port on the coast up to the nineteenth century and the chief seat of the potent *nāʾibs*, Hergigo constantly absorbed newcomers from abroad and from the inland, who settled on the coast and served principally as commercial middlemen. Two twentieth-century clan/family lists—one published by Dante Odorizzi in 1910 (almost exactly similar to and clearly based on Folchi's survey of 1898) and the other published by Muḥammad ʿUthmān Abū Bakr in 1994—provide useful and revealing trends as to the structure of the motley populations of Hergigo and Massawa.[19] Since the lists were collected through local informants, we should also be well aware of the dis-

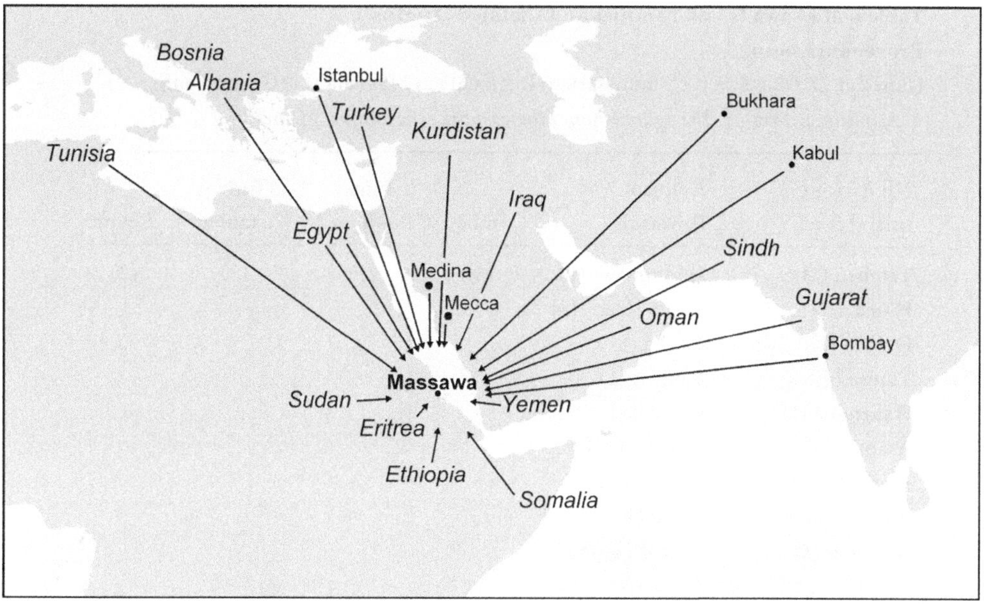

Map 5. The World of the Massawans (Claimed Places of Origin).
Map by Matthias Schulz.

cursive dimensions of this specific kind of data. Such family lists are also subject to manipulation, and Folchi's/Odorizzi's list has most probably absorbed the perspective of Massawa's elites, who emphasized their own origins from abroad. Colonial surveys—including such questionings of origins—must have set into motion a process of guessing or inventing origins. While recent migrants to Massawa could clearly indicate their places of provenance, older Massawan families—some of whom also originated from abroad centuries ago and intermixed in coastal and urban society—were asked to come forth with accurate origins. What could it mean for a poor individual from 1890s Hergigo to claim origins from Bosnia, or what did it mean for a rich and influential member of the Mentāy family to claim origins in areas of western Eritrea while forming part of the Arab and Arabized urban elite? Clearly, family names were crucial in the process of disclosing origins, for "better" or "worse."

As concerns Hergigo, both lists confirm the numeric and sociopolitical dominance of several clusters of cognatic kin in the coastal village, such as the Balaw ʿĀmir, the Balaw Yūsuf Ḥassab Allāh, the Bayt Shaykh Maḥmūd, and other ʿAd Zubayr–descended Saho-speaking clans, as well as the Bayt Tawakkal. To these are added other Saho, Tigre, and Afar-speaking groups

Table 1. Massawa Island Families and Claimed Origins/ Provenance, 1910

(Based on D. Odorizzi, Il Commissariato Regionale di Massaua al 1º Gennaio 1910, *Asmara 1911, 112–15. The figure in parentheses marks the number of families.)*

NE African Inland & Isl	Arabian Peninsula	India	Iran ("Bukhara")	Turkey ("Istanbul")	Egypt
Temben (1)	Hadramawt (9)	(5)	(2)	(3)	(2)
Hamasen (5)	Tarīm [Had] (3)				
Oromo (2)	Mecca (5)				
Tsaura (4)	Medīna (1)				
Hadendoa (1)	Jiddah (5)				
Asaorta (3)	Ḥudayda (5)				
Adulis (1)	Luḥayya (4)				
Ad Temaryam (1)	Zabīd (1)				
Rassamo (1)	Bayt al-Faqīh (1)				
Afar [Dankalia] (3)	Abū Arīsh (2)				
Mensaᶜ (1)	Ahdal (1)				
Balaw (7)					
Habab (3)					
Dehol Island (1)					
Total: **34**	**37**	**5**	**2**	**3**	**2**
Total Families: **83**					

such as the presumed founders of the settlement, the Idda, the Bayt Khalīfa, ᶜAd Shaykh, Iddefir, Ankala, Minifire, and Asaorta, among others. To these groups—all originating in the relatively close African interior in what is present-day Eritrea—the lists add several categories of groups claiming foreign origins: *ashrāf* families, several Takrūrī and Sudanese families, as well as individual families originating in Egypt, India, and the Arabian Peninsula.[20] Several families claimed descent from soldiers of the Ottoman garrison who married in the country and remained there following the end of their service. Similarly to the examples provided by the Kekiyā (Tur. Kāhya), Sardāl, and ᶜAsker families, they too have adopted names associated with their function in the capacity of the *nāʾib*'s militias. The following patronyms and their associated claims of origin make clear the point: Bashnak (from Bosnia), Kurdī (Kurdish), Shāwish Berhatu (Albanian), Salòo (Turkish), Sharafāy (Turkish), among others.[21] All in all, of the

Table 2. Population of Massawa Island (excluding Hetumlo, Emkullo, and Hergigo), 1910

(Adapted from D. Odorizzi, Il Commissariato Regionale di Massaua al 1º Gennaio 1910, *Asmara 1911, 125)*

Arabs from Jiddah, Yemen, Hadramawt, and Egypt	924	(21%)
Tigre and Saho from eastern, western, and northern Eritrea	880	(20%)
Sudanese and West African Takrūrīs	659	(15%)
Local Massawa families residing on Massawa island	495	(11%)
Italians	363	(8%)
Abyssinians of Eritrea (Hamasen)	317	(7%)
Ethiopian subjects (Tigray)	261	(6%)
Oromo and Swahili	159	(4%)
Indians	148	(3%)
Greek, Syrian, and Ottoman subjects	90	(2%)
Somalis	39	(1%)
Total	4335	

Note: Figures and ethnic designations must be taken cautiously. Figures do not include the outer elements of the Massawa conurbation, namely Hetumlo, Emkullo, and Hergigo.

sixty-seven Hergigo families listed in Odorizzi's book, twenty-two (one-third) are noted as originating from overseas, while the remaining forty-five families (two-thirds) originated in inland groups. However, the lists become knotty since the exogenous groups include those referred to as "Arab," which is a complex category in this setting, expressing (sometimes contemporary) cultural self-identifications, rather than actual family origins. The lists provide a similarly detailed breakdown for Massawa's population structure. Of the eighty-three families that Odorizzi lists, forty-nine (60%) claim exogenous descent from various parts of the Arabian Peninsula, Egypt, Turkey, Iran [*sic*], and India. The remaining thirty-four (40%) trace their origins to the Ethio-Eritrean region from places such as Temben, the Oromo-speaking areas of Ethiopia, Hamasen, the Dahlak islands, the Afar coast, and from Tigre- and Saho-speaking groups such as the Mensaʿ, the Balaw, the Asaorta, and the Hadendoa, to mention but a few examples.

Migrations often correlated with periods of commercial vitality in the Red Sea area or responded to the need for security. The politicization of Islam in the Horn of Africa in the sixteenth century, culminating with the

Figure 3.1. Ḥasan Aḥmad Ḥayūtī (ca. 1850–ca. 1939). Ḥayūtī family collection, Asmara.

jihād of Aḥmad b. Ibrāhīm al-Ghāzī (nicknamed Grañ, the "left-handed") represented a period of heightened turbulence, prompting the migration of people from both inland and overseas (from other parts of the Horn) to the port. One of the processes that accompanied the establishment of Ottoman rule in Massawa in the sixteenth century was the arrival and settlement of officials associated with the Ottoman administration. The Ottoman sultan decreed that the Ḥanafī School was the *madhhab* of the empire and that *qāḍī*s should judge according to Ḥanafī law.[22] Accordingly, one telling example is the appointment of Muḥammad Aḥmad al-ʿAbbāsī of the Bin ʿAbbās *qabīla,* originally from Medina, as the port's official *qāḍī* sometime between the end of the sixteenth century and the early seventeenth. Whether the first ʿAbbāsī came directly from the Hijaz or from Egypt is uncertain, but the ʿAbbāsīs have remained prominent in the commercial, communal, and religious realms in the port-town ever since. *Qāḍī* lists show that at least four *qāḍī*s of the ʿAbbāsī family served in office in the seventeenth and eighteenth centuries.[23] Another process that resulted from the establishment of a Muslim power on the western littoral of the Red Sea involved an enhanced wave of migration of *sayyids* and *ashrāf* from Hadramawt to Massawa from the sixteenth century onward.[24] The genealogical tree of the Ḥayūtī family, known in Massawa prior to the mid-nineteenth century as the Ḥibshī family and originally from the elite *sādah* stratum of Tarīm in Hadramawt, retraces the migration of Shaykhān b. Ḥusayn b. ʿAlī b. Aḥmad al-Ḥibshī from Zaylaʿ in the Gulf of Aden to Massawa in about 1562 (AH 970).[25] A third example of sixteenth-century presence on the island refers to Shaykh Adam b. Muḥammad Barkūy (Burkūy, Barkāwī [?]) (d. ca. 1573), originally from the province of Temben in Tigray and, according to some sources, a descendant of one of the Prophet's companions (the *ṣaḥāba*), exiled to Abyssinia in the early seventh century.[26] According to other sources he was the son of a Turkish *ʿalīm* (scholar). The first two examples refer to prominent Massawa families who, among others, have historically played a leading role in the town's economic, religious, political, and communal history well into the twentieth century.

Of Claims and Names

The inherently dichotomous character of discourses of origin in Massawa is neatly demonstrated in the case of the origin of the name "Massawa," as expressed in oral traditions. Most theories advanced seem to agree on the linguistic roots of the word, which would be a Tigre word derived from the Geʿez (Ethiopic) *meṣuwaʿ*, "cry, loud call."[27] According to one version a fisherman from Dahlak, surprised by a storm, was thrown by the winds with his boat onto an uninhabited island that was situated very close to the mainland. Following his return to Dahlak, he described it as so small that if one *shouted* strong enough he could make himself heard on the other side of the island. From that point onward, the Dahlakis who began to settle there called it "Massawa." The other version relates that before the causeways connecting Massawa to the mainland were built (1870s), when traders came to the port with their caravans, they reached Gherar on the mainland, and had to *shout* to the boatmen on Massawa Island to come and get them and their goods to the island-town.[28]

Other local traditions of foundation ascribe families coming from the Eritrean inland and the islands facing the littoral as the earliest inhabitants of the island. It seems likely that such associations correspond to several waves of migration into the port—between the fifteenth and early nineteenth centuries—prompted by conflict inland and periods of commercial revival in the Red Sea. Another theory as to the foundation of Massawa, found both in nineteenth-century literary sources and in oral traditions collected in the 1970s, argues that the Masāwa family, *sayyid*s from the Hijaz, but probably originally from Hadramawt, was the first on the island, giving the town its name. According to this tradition Muḥammad

Masāwa b. Aḥmad al-ᶜAlawī (1200/1785–1272/1855), who studied in Massawa and in the Hijaz and served as *qāḍī* in the early nineteenth century (from ca. 1230/1814), became so famous that people coming from the entire region related that "they had gone to Masāwa."[29] This theory is, unquestionably, historically erroneous since the town was referred to by different variants of the name Massawa (Maçua, Massowah, Massouah, Maṣawwaᶜ, Muṣawwaᶜ, etc.) much earlier. As suggested, such claims are more important in unveiling cultural dynamics than in affirming historical "facts." According to yet other traditions collected in the early twentieth century, a certain Shaykh Adam was the first to move his house from the Dahlak islands to Massawa. He was followed by a family from the island of Dohol, the ancestors of the Bayt Doḥul family. Subsequently, other families emigrated from the Arabian coast (Bayt ᶜAbbāsī, Bayt Bā ᶜAlawī, Bayt Khīrī) and from Semhar (Bayt Ḥilū), from Hergigo (Bayt Ḥāmidūy), from the ᶜAd Tsaura group (Bayt al-Nātī), from the Afar coast (Bayt ᶜAdūlāy), and from the Balaw groups (Bayt Mentāy and Bayt Shīnītī).[30]

These traditions concur, to some extent, with family traditions. Nowadays, the Mentāy and ᶜAdūlāy families consider their own ancestors as the first inhabitants of Massawa. The Mentāys claim to be originally of the Hedareb in western Eritrea, and the ᶜAdūlāys are from the Zula region, or in its ancient appellation, Adulis. The ᶜAdūlāys were recognized as forming part of the town elite also in the eighteenth century.[31] The example of the Mentāys and Adūlāys as prominent urban families in Massawa is significant to one of the underlying broader arguments articulated in this book. It sheds light on the conspicuous and prominent role and position, throughout the town's history, of Massawans who traced their origins to the interior. This runs counter to the perception of Massawa as an "alien" and "foreign" outpost anomalously located at its place. The Mentāys were linked in marriage to the Balaw Bayt Ḥassab Allāh (known also as Balaw Yūsuf) since at least the mid-nineteenth century.[32] In the 1830s and 1840s the Mentāy family seems to have held particular prominence in trade. In 1838 Commander Nott of the Indian navy remarked that Moosa Maffairah (Mentāy) was the principal banker and merchant at Massawa, taking in 15,000 dollars worth of gum every year, which was more than half of what was on the market.[33] He was wealthy to the point that when the dues collected at Massawa were insufficient to cover the administration's expenses, it would borrow money from him.[34] In the 1860s, Saᶜīd Muffaraḥ Mentāy and ᶜAbd Allāh Khalīl Mentāy were both noted as prominent notables of Massawa; the first served as the chief of merchants while the second was the president of the Egyptian-instituted *majlis maḥalī* and an advisor to the law court.[35] Members of the Mentāy family appear abundantly in the records of Massawa's Islamic court, both as parties in cases and as *wakīl*s or legal witnesses. In a register covering real estate transactions in the port between 1866 and 1877 the Mentāys appear in twenty-nine cases, outnumbered only by the wealthy Hadrami, Sayyid ʿAbd Allāh b. ʿUmar b. Saʿīd Bā Junayd.[36]

Notwithstanding the innate complexity of their social structures, the populations of Hergigo and Massawa were composed of families and clans originating both in the interior and from across the seas, emigrating intermittently in periods of conflict and commercial opportunities. Throughout the Ottoman period merchants, entrepreneurs, and brokers from abroad and from the inland settled in Massawa and in Hergigo, primarily from abroad in the former while in greater numbers from the land in the latter. The centuries-long dominance of the Balaw *nāʾib*s and their associates—for example the Bayt Shaykh Maḥmūd—placed them in a position of prominence in these two settlements. Balaw families connected in kinship ties with the *nāʾib*s and Bayt Shaykh Maḥmūd families were among the leading families in Hergigo and on the island (e.g., Shīnītī, Danbar, Ḥassab Allāh and Faras, Sirāj, and Khaydara families). Together with other Tigre-, Afar-, and Saho-speaking families of prominence, wealth, and prestige, they constituted what may be termed coastal urban patricians and were often interconnected in marriage ties.

Information on traders in Massawa in the early nineteenth century—before the beginning of the commercial revival—is scanty and insubstantial. Starting in the 1830s, the increasing number of European official and non-official travelers to the region provided further detail. In the late 1830s Combes and Tamisier attested to the mixed character of Massawa's population, being a blend of Beduins from the Hijaz or Yemen, some Sahos from the African continent, Ethiopian Muslims, and Oromo slaves.[37] In 1841 Théophile Lefebvre noted that the population of Massawa was divided into three separate castes: the merchants, the Arnaoutes (irregular Ottoman soldiers, mostly from the Balkans), and the Sahos, who mostly lived on the mainland. He further added that some of the merchants were quite wealthy and had extended "their speculations up to the furthest regions of the Galla."[38] According to Munzinger, the oldest families in Massawa were those owning buildings on the island. He added that he could "not find families who no longer remember their immigration." The family names mentioned by him all refer to the places of their origin: "Adulai," "Dankali," "Yemeni," "Hindi," "Mogrebi," "Bungasi," "Geddani," "Habeschi."[39]

The records of the *sharīʿa* court dating from the mid-1860s also show

how family names (Ar. *nisba*) that refer to places or ethnic origins were commonplace. The law court registers are filled with names and appellations such as Dankalī, ᶜAdūlāy, Diḥlī, Qashmīr, Yamanī, Jiddāwī, al-Maghribī, Ṭurkī, Sūmālī,[40] al-Izmīrī, ᶜIrāqī and others.[41] It is possible that some such merchants, especially those coming from beyond the Red Sea region, spent only limited periods of time in Massawa. Some might have been sent to run branch agencies before continuing to other destinations or returning back home. Such groups of merchants correspond to what historian C. A. Bayly has called "medium-term diasporic communities."[42] Scanty evidence also attests to the presence of North African traders active in the area in the 1830s. North African merchants based in Cairo were quite active in the Red Sea area in the first half of the nineteenth century, until they were overshadowed by Hadrami trade and shipping networks in mid-century.[43] Combes and Tamisier, two French observers in Massawa, claim that they were often visited in the port by a trader named Muḥammad originally from the "côtes barbaresques."[44] Munzinger too mentioned the "Bungasi" and "Mogrebi" families as old settlers in the port.[45] These pieces of information coincide with family and mosque lists that assert the presence in Hergigo of the North African *ashrāf* family, the ᶜAd Sayyid Brūj, and a private straw hut mosque bearing the same name.[46] In Massawa, the Abū ᶜIlāmā family, which had been associated with the office of *qāḍī* and *muftī* since the Ottoman era, is also noted in several sources as being of North African origins. One should handle family origins and *nisba*s with great prudence, since they have surely also played into the logic of cultural competition. On several occasions informants in present-day Massawa have either kept no memory of precise family origins or refuted the veracity of certain claims of origin concerning their own families (as they have been published, for example in the two family lists of 1910 and 1994). There is some indication that epithets designating overseas or inland regions did not always correspond to real origins but referred to the resemblance of such and such a person to the inhabitants of this or that region.

To Massawa from Across the Seas: From Peddlers to Intermediary Capitalists, 1850s–1890s

One of the outcomes of the commercial revival in the area was the redeployment of Red Sea networks. In Massawa this process was manifested by the settlement of Hadrami, Egyptian, Yemeni, Indian, and other entrepreneurs who weaved themselves into an existing structure of networks that was in the process of transformation. In the last quarter of the nineteenth century, some of these entrepreneurs were able to rise from small-time teenage peddlers to extremely wealthy merchants, owners of immovable and movable property, and leading citizens in the urban political and public arena. Despite the lack of evidence, it is more than plausible that some of them were also involved in the exportation of slaves to the Arabian Peninsula. In the early decades of the twentieth century some of them became entrepreneurs in domains other than trade (e.g., commercial agriculture, transportation services, construction); some financed social, educational, and religious institutions and were able to become leading pillars of the urban community. In what follows I sketch the stories of some such entrepreneurs, situating them in the context of Massawa and the Red Sea.

Hadrami and Egyptian Entrepreneurs: Muḥammad Sālim Bā Ṭūq, ᶜAbd Allāh Bey al-Ghūl, and Others

The "new wave" of entrepreneurs and merchants settling in Massawa mirrored the changing structure of the Red Sea commercial system.[47] Notable examples of commercial entrepreneurs include Muḥammad Sālim Bā Ṭūq (ca. 1843–1935) and ᶜAbd Allāh Bey al-Ghūl. Both became among a handful of Massawa's wealthiest merchants by the end of the century, and both headed prominent families. They were examples of merchants and entrepreneurs who were successful in capitalizing on the new political and economic order under Egyptians and Italians (ca. 1860s–1940s). They ventured in trade, they provided shipping services (owning and operating *sanbūqs*), and in the early twentieth-century they launched agricultural enterprises in the Zula–Dogᶜali–Weqiro triangle on the coastal strip adjoining Massawa. All in all, the new merchant-entrepreneurs contributed significantly to the economic development of both town and region from the 1860s and throughout the Italian colonial period in Eritrea.[48] The spectacular inward flux of overseas migrants is reflected in census data, which should be taken only illustratively, since the census does not include crucial data about the population distribution in Hetumlo, Emkullo, and Hergigo and it uses the problematic category "Arab." The data reveals that the "Arab" population of Massawa (from Egypt, the Hijaz, Hadramawt, and Yemen) almost tripled, from 358 individuals in 1886 to 924 in 1910.[49]

Muḥammad Sālim Bā Ṭūq was born in Jiddah to a Hadrami father and an Egyptian mother—in a way epitomizing the new *Homo Mare Erythraeum* of the nineteenth century. In Jiddah they were known as Bā Ṭūq al-ᶜAmūdī. Muḥammad Sālim settled in Massawa in the mid-1850s and traded in textiles and cloth from a very young age. In Massawa he married Zaynab, the daughter of ᶜAbd al-Nabī al-Qābūlī, who came from the Persian or Afghani region and settled in Massawa with his father in the 1860s. The Qābūlīs were merchants in coffee, butter, and other commodities, and ᶜAbd al-Nabī was able to accumulate much wealth and become one of the town's notables. At the end of the century he was noted as an important importer of glass beads, pottery, and chinaware.[50] With time, Muḥammad Sālim made a fortune as a textile merchant and became one of Massawa's most influential and respected notables. In the late nineteenth and early twentieth centuries the Bā Ṭūqs—together with other Massawan merchants and shippers—were involved in smuggling operations between the Eritrean and Yemeni coasts (tombac, bovine, coffee, grain, camels, etc.), fueling the already tense relationship between Italian and Ottoman authorities in the southern Red Sea area.[51] Muḥammad Sālim also traded in coffee and cereals with Ethiopia, and in 1908 he obtained an agricultural concession of 906 hectares near Weqiro, north of Massawa. Beginning in 1908, and more intensively from 1915, when he purchased twenty *sanābīq,* he provided regular transportation services for pilgrims crossing from Massawa to Jiddah on their way to Mecca. The service, operating until 1935, was recommended by the Italian and Hijazi authorities, who made efforts to thwart illegal crossings. Muḥammad Sālim also constructed approximately forty buildings in Massawa and sixty in Asmara. The Italians awarded him several honorific titles. From 1908 he was the president of the *waqf* committee for Eritrea. He died in Massawa on 2 October 1935.[52]

The other example was that of ᶜAbd Allāh Bey al-Ghūl (ᶜAbd Allāh b. Aḥmad. b. Yūsuf al-Ghūl), an Egyptian who came to Massawa probably in the late 1850s or early 1860s.[53] The al-Ghūls were originally peasants in Manshiyat al-Bakrī (in Cairo's suburbs, and President Nasser's place of residence[54]), before moving to Port Said. From there, ᶜAbd Allāh al-Ghūl moved, via Jiddah, to Massawa, where he served the Egyptian army and received the title *Bey.*[55] From 1867, when service to Massawa began, he became the khedival ᶜAzīzīyeh shipping company's (est. 1863) agent in the port. Following the withdrawal of the Egyptians in 1885, ᶜAbd Allāh stayed in Massawa and became one of the richest merchants in the port, trading in a wide variety of lucrative commodities (primarily in textiles at first), owning boats, constructing and owning residential buildings and shops, and owning land. Unsurprisingly, evidence suggests that he maintained close business links with Jiddah.[56] Together with Muḥammad Sālim Bā Ṭūq, he

Figure 3.2. Muḥammad Sālim Bā Ṭūq, ca. 1898. Postcard. Photographer: Errardo di Aichelburg, author's collection.

supplied the Italian troops in Massawa with imported bovine and colonial products. ʿAbd Allāh was perhaps the most influential member of the local urban notability and was regularly consulted by the colonial authorities on local affairs.[57] In reference to the eighteenth-century ultra-wealthy Roman family of bankers and financiers, the Italian journalist Vico Mantegazza styled him as the "Torlonia of this country," owning the largest and most luxurious house in town. ʿAbd Allāh even proposed to Mantegazza to establish and fund a bilingual Arabic-Italian newspaper in the port-town—a project that never saw the light of day.[58] The case of al-Ghūl is reminiscent of the hyper-wealthy Sawākin merchant, Muṣṭafā Shināwī Bey, who had started as a junior government employee in the Sudanese port on a salary of 150 piasters per month.[59]

Muḥammad Sālim Bā Ṭūq and ʿAbd Allāh Bey al-Ghūl were examples of entrepreneurs who came to Massawa with relatively modest means and were able to capitalize on the sweeping commercial expansion that Massawa and the southern Red Sea region was living through from the 1850s onward, but also on conducive connections with the Egyptian, and later Italian, authorities. The dominance of Hadrami networks in the Red Sea in the middle decades of the century, the political dominance of Egypt, and their cooperation with the authorities in place were pivotal factors in enabling these two individuals and their families to prosper in that context. Whether they or other comparable entrepreneurs were also involved in slave exportation is a matter open to cautious speculation. Through their accumulated wealth and a cultivated religious prestige they were able to join, and very rapidly adopt the characteristics of the upper echelons of Massawa's social structures by becoming leading and influential members of the community and its institutions. They strongly influenced the urban community's sociocultural dynamics and orientation, namely an emphasis on Arab and Islamic culture as primordial identity markers.

Their eldest sons, Maḥmūd Muḥammad Bā Ṭūq and Aḥmad Afandī al-Ghūl (b. 1854 in Jiddah (?), d. 1919) accumulated greater wealth than they did and were able to profit from their positions of influence and their commercial networks under Italian rule. Apart from their involvement in various lucrative commercial and brokerage operations, they invested much in real estate throughout the period.[60] They owned much property in buildings, shops, and boats and were influential members of the town's civic and religious institutions.[61] As with their fathers before them, part of their effort was devoted to initiate and sponsor educational enterprises in Massawa. One source suggests that in a joint initiative (probably in the 1920s), Bā Ṭūq and al-Ghūl recruited Shaykh Maḥmūd Karāmī, an Egyptian teacher, who taught Islamic subjects in town.[62]

The Egyptian authorities made considerable efforts to improve Massawa's harbor, modernize the town's urban infrastructure and foster regional and trans-regional commerce. These extensive efforts generated a wave of Egyptian and Hadrami commercial entrepreneurs who settled in the port between the 1860s and 1880s. Just as ʿAbd Allāh Bey al-Ghūl's life and business trajectory was identified with the Egyptian enterprise at Massawa, other Egyptians too settled in the port. Ibrāhīm Hilāl, served the Egyptian administration as chief scribe for contracts in Massawa before deciding to remain and settle in the port to devote himself altogether to commerce.[63] Other families of Egyptian origins, some interrelated in kinship ties, are Bayt Ḥanbūlī, Bayt Rifāʿī, Bayt Saqīra, Bayt ʿAntablī, Bayt Sanūsī, and possibly one of the two Ḥamdān households in Massawa.[64]

Hadramis have been in Massawa for centuries. They usually left Hadramawt as a result of troubled political periods, demographic pressures, and natural disasters, leading them to search for better opportunities as traders, labourers, mercenaries or religious specialists in other regions of the Indian Ocean. Their numbers in Massawa increased throughout the

Figure 3.3. Aḥmad ᶜAbd Allāh al-Ghūl, ca. 1898. Postcard. Photographer: Errardo di Aichelburg, author's collection.

nineteenth century. In 1858 an India Office report noted that there were 23 Hadrami merchants established in Massawa.[65] In 1865, an Egyptian report remarked that the wholesale (retail) trade was in the hands of several Hadrami and Indian traders.[66] One court register recording real estate transactions between 1866 and 1877 mentions the presence of several Hadramis in the port: for example Bā ᶜAlawī, Ṣāfī, Hāshim, Bā Ḥamdūn, Bā Mushmūsh, Bā Zarᶜa, ᶜAydarūs.[67] During the 1880s and increasingly after 1885 and the Italian occupation, many Yemeni laborers and entrepreneurs came to Massawa.[68] Examples of Hadrami migrants who made the port-town their home include ᶜUbayd Bā Zaḥam, who arrived to Massawa from Hadramawt in 1870. According to oral data he began very modestly as a money changer, but his sons and grandsons gradually accumulated much wealth and real estate property.[69] Another example was Shaykh Ḥasan Bā Mushmūsh, in Massawa at least since the 1860s. Real estate transactions recorded in the Islamic court show that Shaykh Ḥasan Bā Mushmūsh bought a parcel of land, a shop and a residential house in 1867–68.[70] His son ᶜAbd Allāh Ḥasan Bā Mushmūsh arranged for his family to join him in Massawa in 1889.[71] ᶜAbd Allāh Ḥasan's son, Ḥusayn ᶜAbd Allāh, born in

Figure 3.4. Yemeni porters in Massawa, ca. 1920s. Private collection, Pavoni Social Centre, Asmara.

al-Qarn in Hadramawt, crossed to Massawa with his ten brothers when he was thirteen years old.[72] This example suggests that some Hadrami traders moved to Massawa on their own and maintained close social and kinship links—and certainly commercial interests—in Hadramawt. Some, after reaching a certain degree of security in their business, may have decided to move permanently to Massawa and bring with them their family from Hadramawt.[73] A census of 1910 reveals that of the 878 individuals in Massawa Island and the close mainland suburbs that were identified as migrants from the Yemen, Hijaz and Hadramawt, 443 were men and 182 were women.[74]

Some Hadramis, on the other hand, arrived alone at a very early age, as did ᶜUbayd b. Aḥmad b. ᶜAbd Allāh Bā Ḥubayshī (1871–1934), who was born in Dawᶜan in Hadramawt and arrived to Massawa on a *sanbūq* in 1886 at the age of fifteen. ᶜUbayd Aḥmad started his business in ᶜEdaga Beᶜray, on the mainland opposite Massawa, as a modest vendor of tobacco for chewing and spices. He had a water well dug near Amatere, on the way to Gurgusum, which stands there to this day and is called after him. He married a Christian woman named Nebiyat from Mendefera in the highlands, who converted to Islam and was renamed Fāṭma Ādam.[75] ᶜUbayd Aḥmad accumulated much wealth and invested in real estate property. Informants in Massawa discussed his business career as the epitome of one who made it "from rags to riches," from peddler to real estate magnate and one of Massawa's most prominent citizens. ᶜUbayd Aḥmad's firstborn son, Aḥmad ᶜUbayd Bā Ḥubayshī (1902–59), became one of a handful of ultra-wealthy merchants and economic entrepreneurs in Eritrea, and the most important patron of the Eritrean Muslim community, initiating and generously funding religious and educational institutions in Eritrea. But wealth did not automatically translate into other forms of capital: one informant of high-status *sādah* Hadrami origins told of how at some point Aḥmad wished to marry into one of Massawa's other prominent Hadrami *sādah* families, but feared to be rejected on account of his "simple" origins. A psycho-historical analysis might argue that he tried to acquire that symbolic-religious status and prestige through the vast charitable works and financing of Eritrea's Islamic institutions for which he was known throughout his life.[76]

After the Pearl: The Nahārī Family and Entrepreneurs in the Marine Economy

The new configuration of commerce, shipping, and labor in the southern Red Sea also led to the circulation of entrepreneurs, agents, boat captains (Ar. *nakhūda*), boat builders, sailors, pearl divers, fishermen, and slaves from one shore to another and to the islands between them. Regional economic spheres overlapped through patterns of economic exploitation and labor exchange.[77] In the nineteenth century this process involved many Yemenis and other entrepreneurs from the peninsula crossing to the African coast and its islands in search of economic opportunities, mainly, but not exclusively, in the rising marine-product economy, which involved, for the most part, the extraction and commercialization of pearls and mother-of-pearl.[78] Many stayed only for the fishing season in the Dahlak waters and then returned. Family histories and early colonial sources confirm the establishment in Massawa of several such entrepreneurs from the Tihāma ports of Luḥayya and Ḥudayda in the middle decades of the nineteenth century. The ancestors of Bayt Sayyid Aḥmad Sharīf, Bayt Muḥajjab, Bayt Miḥrī, and Bayt ᶜAbd Allāh Ridèni all came from Luḥayya. The Bayt Bānibāla, Bayt Khaydara, Bayt Kḥayl, Bayt ᶜIzzī Aḥmad, and Bayt Nahārī came to Massawa from Ḥudayda.[79] In the case of the Sharīf, Nahārī, and Kḥayl families, the ancestors who moved to Massawa were mainly involved in marine activities, often owning one or more *sanbūq*s and making their wealth on this side of the Red Sea, following their migration.[80] They capitalized on connections with the Tihāma coasts and weaved new ties and networks in Massawa and the Dahlak islands through marriage with locally powerful families, the cultivation of business relationships, and the acquisition and projection of religious prestige.

The most notable example was Sayyid ᶜAbd al-Raḥīm al-Nahārī, who moved from Ḥudayda and settled in the small village of Giumᶜille on Dahlak al-Kabīr island around mid-century. He was able to accumulate wealth in the mother-of-pearl and pearl business before moving to Massawa, where he became a *qāḍī* and one of the town's most respected notables. He married Fāṭima ᶜUmar Danbar of the mainland Balaw Yūsuf group, whose family was known to be pious, respected, and of high religious status. ᶜAbd al-Raḥīm al-Nahārī's son, ᶜAbd al-Raḥmān (d. 1870), left an estate of pearls, money, boats, animals, and various goods, valued at a total of not less than 120,000 Maria Theresa dollars.[81] ᶜAbd al-Raḥmān al-Nahārī's son ᶜAlī (ca. 1850–1930/31), had attained even greater wealth.[82] He owned a large number of *sanbūq*s, was a landlord, and continued, as his father and grandfather, to prosper in the pearl business. In the early twentieth century ᶜAlī owned a large majority of the houses in the villages of Salait and Jumᶜelle in the islands.[83] ᶜAlī al-Nahārī traded directly with Europe and made a particularly large fortune under Italian colonial rule. In 1906 Governor Martini noted in his diary that [ᶜAlī] Nahārī was, together with him, on board the *Vespucci,* a ship heading toward Europe, accompanying an agent of the reputed Paris-based Rosenthal firm who had spent three months in Massawa, buying pearls for hundreds of thousands of Italian lire. ᶜAlī al-Nahārī's trips to Europe are also mentioned by the eccentric French "adventurer," writer, and sometime pearl merchant, Henry de Monfreid, who had met him in 1914 at his home in Jumᶜelle. Monfreid, who referred to Nahārī as "Saïd Ali," described him as "an ultra rich Arab who had made several trips to Paris . . . and [who] monopolizes the entire pearl market of the region."[84] In his experience-based but fictionalized account, *Les secrets de la mer Rouge,* Monfreid devotes long pages (and an entire chapter) to Saïd Ali, who clearly deeply impressed the Frenchman. Providing some information on ᶜAlī al-Nahārī, Monfreid noted, for example, that more than fifty pearling boats operated in the archipelago for his account and that in Arabia he had more than a thousand slaves cultivating his lands. Monfreid also confirms what the court records suggest—that is, Nahārī's ownership of slaves and his possible association with slaving activities. Legend, intrigue, and conspiracy all combine and abound as to the subject of the rich pearl merchant's death, and, more importantly for those concerned, the cash, pearls, and properties he had accumulated over his lifetime. In a chapter of his book that requires even greater caution as to the exact proportions between reality and fiction, Monfreid describes in detail the various scheming and machinations around Nahārī's death and his amassed capital. Monfreid openly suggests that he was murdered as a result of intentional misdosing of medicine on the part of a Greek merchant who waited to lay his hands on Nahārī's fortune through the latter's sons, who were heavily indebted to the merchant. Monfreid's depiction of those events goes on to describe how the aforementioned Greek merchant met his destiny—and his punishment. ʿAlī was thus avenged, but his fortune—which he apparently hid away from all the connivers—was never really found.[85] Speculations and stories about ʿAlī's fortunes are still with us nowadays. According to oral data collected recently, it seems that on the occasion of one of his trips to Paris, ʿAlī deposited pearls and cash in a well-known Parisian bank and purchased three buildings as investment. This sparked conflict between ʿAlī and the Italian authorities back in Eritrea, who were less than happy with large amounts of capital flowing out of the colony without their knowledge or control. In recent years, members of the now transnational Nahārī family have been engaged in various international legal procedures—especially vis-à-vis France—in their efforts to claim back the money and property of their forefather, amounting, so they claim, to millions of dollars. The story is further complicated since some of ʿAlī's financial dealings in Paris were associated with Jewish businessmen (many of the pearl dealers, such as Victor Rosenthal and the Bienenfelds, were Jews) whose properties were later confiscated or lost during the Second World War.[86] It is very possible, and in some ways ironic, that the financial and business dealings of pearl merchants, such as Nahārī, with French Jewish dealers during this period caused them to lose their invested fortunes. The story of ʿAlī al-Nahārī kept feeding the imagination of creators beyond Henry de Monfreid. In 1937 a feature film *Les secrets de la mer Rouge* was produced. ʿAlī was played by a French actor, Harry Baur, who was tortured to death by the Gestapo in Paris in 1943. Also, between 1968 and 1975 a multi-episode TV series by the same name aired in France.

Also connected to the lucrative marine commercial activities of the Dahlak islands, members of the Ṣūrī family claim origins from the Omani town of Ṣūr, where they belonged to the al-Ṭāhirī *qabīla*. ʿAlī Saʿīd (d. 1943 at about 80 years of age) came with his *sanbūq* to the Dahlak around the 1880s, settled in Debʿullo, and sailed from the islands to Oman and back, trading pearls and a variety of seashells, throughout his life. With the years, after he permanently settled in Debʿullo, he married ʿĀʾisha, the daughter of the Yemeni ʿAbdu Kḥayl, and added the *nisba* Ṣūrī, a reference to his town of origin, to his name, that becoming his family name. Following ʿAlī Saʿīd's death in 1943 the entire family moved to Massawa.[87] Descendants of the Wahhāb al-Bārrī family in Massawa relate the fascinating story of their family, reflecting the tortuous political, religious, and social history of the second half of the nineteenth century in the wider region. It also illustrates the process of "becoming Massawan." The family traces its origins to a Saho-speaking Irob clan from the region of Senʿafe in Akkele Guzay. Originally Muslim, their-great grandfather ʿAbd Allāh was forced to convert to Christianity under Emperor Yohannes (r. 1872–89).[88] ʿAbd Allāh's son, ʿAbdu Qismo Shūm Arānīsh, also converted to Christianity and was re-baptized Mesghenna Wolde Maryam. Attempting to escape from the state of disorder and oppression in northern Ethiopia, the father and his son migrated to the Dahlak islands and settled in Debʿullo, where the father worked for a Yemeni named ʿAbdu Kḥayl in the lucrative extraction and trade of marine products. Both soon reconverted to Islam, and the son adopted the name of his father's employer, ʿAbdu Kḥayl.[89] Later, he became a pious and learned Muslim, a Qurʾānic teacher, and moved to Massawa to become *imām* of the Shaykh Ḥammāl al-Anṣārī mosque and a respected Muslim notable in the community.[90]

Indian Entrepreneurs in Massawa: Merchants, Financiers, Agents, and Artisans

> In this country the Banyan is the ant;
> the European is often the cicada [grasshopper].
> —G. Saint-Yves, 1899[91]

Trade and other connections and forms of exchange between the northwestern littoral of the Indian subcontinent (in present-day India and Pakistan) and the Horn of Africa have been recorded since earliest times, attesting to interregional connections forming discrete economic spaces in parts of the Indian Ocean. Evidence of the pivotal position of both Muslim and Hindu merchants—primarily from Gujarat, but also from Sind—in the economic and commercial history of Massawa extends back to the sixteenth century, at least. The historian Richard Pankhurst has written detailed studies, based on the tapping of an extensive range of travelers' accounts and archival sources, on the history of Indian trade with the Horn of Africa and on Indian mercantile communities in the Red Sea and Gulf of Aden ports.[92]

This section aims to critically reappraise and contextualize some of the information presented by Pankhurst, as viewed from the specific angle of inquiry central to the broader framework of this study on Massawa's nineteenth-century social and economic history. My underlying suggestion is that even though the role and position of Indian traders and financiers in the large-scale international commerce of the port was paramount, their graphically "exotic" depiction in nineteenth-century literature and their quasi identification with the totality of the port's economic activities has been somewhat overstated. As a small but culturally and socially distinct trade diaspora, the "Banyans" attracted much attention.[93] In addition, the absence of any distinction between Hindu and Muslim traders, as well as between socially integrated and transient South Asians in Massawa, also overshadows the very different social situations of individuals, families, and communities from the Indian subcontinent and the ways by which they connected to Massawa.

As far back as the end of the sixteenth century, Jesuit missionaries reported the existence of a commercially preeminent, even if numerically small, mercantile community of Indians at Massawa. Throughout the seventeenth and eighteenth centuries these merchants traded Indian goods, mainly a wide variety of Indian textiles, for ivory, civet, gold, pearls, tortoise shells, myrrh, frankincense, and a host of other products from the African interior and the Dahlak Archipelago. They were also wealthy moneylenders, and thus provided the first banking services in the area. In the late seventeenth and early eighteenth century Gujarati Kapol Bania merchants from the port of Diu in Kathiawar dominated the trade of the northwestern Indian Ocean, including the Ethiopian maritime region.[94] But the fortunes of these traders fluctuated in accordance with the commercial vitality of the entire western Indian Ocean and Red Sea region and the increased competition posed by Europeans, especially the English. In the second half of the eighteenth century the role and position of the Gujaratis in the region declined considerably.[95] However, the commercial revival of the nineteenth century and increased British involvement in the region placed them back solidly in a dominant position in Red Sea and northwestern Indian Ocean trade.[96] British supremacy in the region extending from India to the Red Sea, especially following the occupation of Aden in 1839, secured and enhanced the position of Indian traders and their networks. The ports in the wider region where they were concentrated in especially large numbers were Muscat, Aden, and Zanzibar.[97] Thanks to their control of important amounts of capital, especially in Bombay (replacing the now eclipsed Surat), Indian intermediary capitalists were able to play a role within the colonial framework by mediating between local producers and merchants and British trade firms.

An elaborate Indian trading network emerged throughout the Red Sea region, and Indian traders were reported as monopolizing the exportation of gold, musk, ivory, pearls, shark fins and skins, and other lucrative African products in the most important ports of Aden, Jiddah, Massawa, Berbera, and others.[98] Ivory, pearls, musk, and other products arrived from Massawa to Ḥudayda, also to Luḥayya, on the Yemeni Tihāma littoral, before their expedition to India.[99] In the nineteenth and early twentieth centuries most Indians in Massawa came from the Gujarati region of Saurashtra in the Kathiawar peninsula, from ports such as Diu, Mangrel, and Porbandar.[100] A French report from 1841 noted that commerce in Massawa was in the hands of 7 to 8 Banyans as well as several Arab merchants from Jiddah and Mukhā. Just seven years later, in 1848, another French report noted a total of 150 merchants in Massawa, of whom 20 were Indians and some Arabs.[101] In the early 1860s Guillaume Lejean reported that Indians dominated the Red Sea, from Jiddah to the Bāb al-Mandab, without rivalry and that their headquarters was at Massawa.[102] In 1884 the number of Indians in the port was estimated at 50 to 60, in 1886, an estimate put them at between 70 and 80, and in 1910 they were 148 in Massawa Island alone.[103]

Indian entrepreneurs appear in historical sources as a highly organized, tight-knit, and highly skilled group of traders and merchants. Europeans' somewhat stereotypical images portrayed their rigorous devotion to commerce and their distinct religious and cultural identities as part and parcel of the success of their trade networks. The supremacy of Indian networks in the Red Sea in the nineteenth century rested on their ability to adapt their commercial organization on the new commercial structures and modes of exchange that developed throughout the period. The existence of ultra-wealthy mercantile houses in Bombay enabled them to purchase large quantities and sail directly to and from India. In contrast with the Arab networks, which used little financial means in their transactions,

Figure 3.5. Indians (Banyans) in Massawa, ca. 1920s. Private collection, Pavoni Social Centre, Asmara.

the Indians, who used money, maximized profits by playing on the differences in the exchange rates of the Maria Theresa dollar and the Indian rupee between ports in western India and the Red Sea.[104] Indian paramountcy in finance and commerce in Massawa was mostly founded on their access to cheap and ample credit and their domination of money-lending and banking services that called on credit networks extending back to the big banks in Gujarat and Bombay.[105] As the representatives of English and Indian firms in Aden and Bombay, Indian merchants were able to purchase bulk goods that reached Massawa's markets and extend credit to local producers, who in turn extracted goods uniquely for their creditors and loaned money to European, Levantine, and Arab merchants who needed capital to finance their commercial operations in the port. Paraphrasing Alamanni's detailed account of the complex role of Indians as intermediaries between Indian and European trading firms in international commerce in the 1880s, Pankhurst described the use of bills of exchange as follows:

> A European trading concern desirous of obtaining capital to finance its operations at Massawa would request a corresponding firm in London which had relations with a trading house in Bombay, to authorise the latter to open a credit for a certain amount with an agent or correspondent at Massawa. The London house would request this credit in Sterling and the Bombay house would grant the equivalent in rupees by supplying the agent at Massawa with a book of cheques or assignat for the amount of credit allowed. The dealer at Massawa when in need of money had only to detach the cheques and hand them, or the *assignat,* over to the local Banyans who would pay him in Maria Theresa Dollars, the money current at the port. The Banyans would then send the cheques or *assignat* to Bombay where they would be refunded, in rupees, by the house which had originally issued them. Meanwhile with the object of repaying the amount which had thus been made available for him the agent at Massawa would make out a bill of exchange payable by the London house which had originally acted as surety for the credit, in favour of the Bombay house which had actually furnished it. When this bill was honoured by the London house the latter would inform the European house which had originally asked for the credit, and would debit its account accordingly. In this way, with the assistance of three intermediaries, and with the balancing of three different currencies, the credit operation was completed, the Banyans and the Indian trading houses having played a vitally important role in the financing of European commercial enterprise.[106]

Clearly, in Massawa's capacity as an international entrepôt, a large bulk of its trade was for long periods in the hands of the Indians. From mid-century Massawa played a distinctive role as a regional entrepôt in regional commerce, mostly with the Tihāma and Hijazi ports. The dominant networks in those commercial spheres were operated by Hijazi and Hadrami, merchants and entrepreneurs.

The two decades of Egyptian occupation (1865–85) had a paradoxical effect on the Indian community in Massawa. On the one hand they were able to prosper from the general commercial boom in the area in the 1860s and 1870s, yet on the other hand, they now had to operate under an administration that made efforts to control and regulate the port's activities, that levied duties and landing fees on commercial operations, and whose cultural affinities (Muslim and Arab) with the Hadrami traders undoubtedly led to preferential treatment (for example, in the local law court and in other urban institutions). Their preoccupations were voiced to the Egyptian governors. Seeking to maximize the commercial potential of their new colony, the Italians too were wary of the growing Indian business community, which operated for its own benefit and whose profits were sent back to India. In October 1887 the town's leading Indian merchants presented a petition to the colonial administration, outlining their grievances and demanding the presence of a British consul who would protect their interests. The Indian merchants stressed that under Ottoman and Egyptian rule their conditions were good and that those governments often offered assistance to the Indians in their commercial endeavors. They argued that since the Italian occupation, their situation has deteriorated.[107]

Indian merchants in Massawa continued to thrive in their businesses, mostly in the wholesale and retail trades and in extending credit to local and foreign entrepreneurs. In the 1870s and 1880s they probably held an almost absolute monopoly over the money-lending business in the port-town. Paolo Matteucci noted that "the Abyssinians who came with their products [to Massawa], went directly to the Indians since they had much cash."[108] In 1892 a list of the creditors of the Egyptian merchant Ḥasan Mūssa al-ᶜAqqād—recently condemned for treason and imprisoned—revealed that out of forty-five creditors who presented themselves to the court to claim their parts, twenty-eight were Indian merchants and agents.[109] The total sum of their funds in Italian lire comprised just over 50 percent of the total claims (about 325,000 lire), while one Italian creditor claimed 34 percent of the total claims. The list gives the full names of the creditors, the name of the business firms represented by them, their age, and their place of birth. More than half were in their twenties or very early thirties, all were noted as born in Bombay, and only two were Muslims.[110] One of the two was ᶜAlī ᶜAbd Allāh Dossal (b. 1862), a particularly prominent Indian Muslim in Massawa, who might have been a Bohra or a Khoja.[111] He was the son of ᶜAbd Allāh Dossal, whom Lejean had listed as one of the wealthiest and most enterprising merchants in the port already in the early 1860s. ᶜAlī ᶜAbd Allāh is mentioned in the sources as the protector and representative of the Indian community vis-à-vis the Italian authorities and an agent for several Anglo-Indian shipping companies. Unlike the more numerous Hindu Bania agents and representatives of the Bombay and Aden houses, ᶜAlī ᶜAbd Allāh owned his independent firm and traded in textiles, dhurra, and marine products, especially mother-of-pearl. Together with Minahim Missa, he presented the Italian authorities with the above-mentioned petition of October 1887. In his well-known account of the recently established colony, the Tuscan member of parliament and future enterprising governor of Eritrea, Ferdinando Martini (1841–1928), called ʿAlī ʿAbd Allāh Dossal the "Muslim Rothschild of Massawa," suggesting also his role in banking and financing.[112] In 1892 the Italian administration granted ʿAlī ʿAbd Allāh a concession to export 3,000 tons of salt from the island of Ghabbi-hu to India.

During the Egyptian and the Italian periods non-Muslim Indians in Massawa presented themselves on a regular basis to local Islamic court to legalize real estate transactions. Between 1868 and 1889 the court registers record real estate transactions in which Indians bought or sold immovable property such as water cisterns, land, and shops in the main market area, the *sūq al-Sulṭān.* In most cases transactions took place between Indians and local folk, but two cases record transactions between two Indians, and in one case an Indian bought a water cistern from the French Catholic bishop in the port. In some cases the Indian appears in the record as *al-khawāja min ahālī Bombay al-tājjir alʾān bi-Maṣawwaʿ* (Ar., the foreigner/trader from Bombay who is at present trading in Massawa); in other cases the *nisba al-Banyānī* (Ar., the Banyan) was simply added to the name. In one case from 1883 two merchants who bought a shop in the market added their signatures in Gujarati at the bottom of the manuscript detailing the case in the *qāḍī*'s register.[113]

Socially and culturally Hindu Banyans do not seem to have made efforts to integrate into Massawan society. In the 1870s they were described as coming for three years or so as agents of foreign merchant houses. As in other parts of the Indian Ocean—for example, in Zanzibar—most Banyans never came with wives or families, and they hoped to return to India after having accumulated some capital or acquired trading skills.[114] The objective of such entrepreneurs was, in the words of historian Claude Markovits, "to improve the situation of their family at home, not because they were hoping to make a better life elsewhere."[115] They were devout Hindus, strict vegetarians eating neither fish nor meat; they adored cows and were great friends of the island's animal life.[116] They mostly kept to themselves in their domestic and social life and lived and operated in a special quarter near the bazaar in Massawa.[117] Two maps of Massawa from 1863–64 and 1880 clearly indicate the *fariq al-Banyan* and the *Quartiere Baniano,* or the Indian quarter/neighborhood in the northern part of the island-port.[118] There they occupied a street with distinctly red-door shops where they sold ivory, hides, ivory boxes and drawers, Persian rugs, fans, lamps, gold dust, and silver bracelets. In the early 1970s Abdu Ali Habib noted that there was still a place referred to as *sūq Banyān,* or the Banyan market, in town. I have also heard references to the *sūq al-Hunūd,* located in the street where one still finds today the jewelers and goldsmiths of Massawa.[119] Toward the end of March the Hindu Indians celebrated the holy festival (or festival of colors, or "Holy Day of the Sun") with great ceremonies, involving special dances.[120] In the 1890s Victor Buchs noted that they celebrated the beginning of their New Year in the month of September, lavishly decorated their shops, and organized celebrations to which Europeans were also invited.[121]

But the great visibility of Hindu Indians as a socioculturally distinct group, their prominence in finance, and their profuse appearance in nineteenth-century travel literature has overshadowed the existence of other families in Massawa that settled at some point in the early to mid-nineteenth century in the port. Indian Muslim Daudi Boḥra merchants and artisans from Kutch had migrated to settlements all along the eastern coasts of Africa.[122] Unlike the Hindu Banias, the Muslim Boḥras and the Khojas migrated with wives and children and sometimes assimilated into host communities. For Massawa we are unable to identify with any precision the origin of such families and individuals. But not all settled durably. Some, such as Noorbhali Hassan Ali Kapasi (b. 1862 in Rajula), spent a couple of decades in Massawa (1890–1910), before moving on to other destinations in the Indian Ocean, such as Java and Mauritius.[123] However, several Muslim families such as the Bayt Hindī, the Bayt Mīyā, and the Bayt Khayyr ad-Dīn, one of the several Bayt Ṣāiʾghs in the Massawa region and possibly Bayt Ḥijjī, claim—or are designated by others—to be the descendants of ancestors who came from the Indian region in the first half of the nineteenth century.[124] Descendants of the Khayr ad-Dīn family, connected in kin to the Mīyā family, relate that their ancestors came to Massawa from India some two hundred years ago. They were always goldsmiths and jewelers.[125] Members of the Hindī and Ḥijjī families, who have been carpenters, claim origin from the Pakistani region. Muḥammad Hindī, undoubtedly the head of the household in the early 1880s, was referred to in the court records as the *shaykh al-najjār,* or the head of the carpenters' corporation.[126] The Hindīs relate that their ancestor, ʿAbd al-Qādir Hindī al-Jiddāwī, came to Massawa from Jiddah, suggesting that—much like other Hadramis and Egyptians—some Indians had moved to the port from other Red Sea locations and not directly from India.[127]

Unlike Hindu Indians, some Muslims originating in the Indian region made Massawa their home. They integrated into the port's Muslim urban community and intermarried with non-Indian families of local coastal patrician origins or assimilated Hadramis, as the strong kinship link between the Mīyā and Ḥayūtī families illustrates.[128] In other words, they "became Massawan," by assimilating the town's defining social, cultural, and communal characteristics. Massawa's Islamic court register records several marriages between families such as Mīyā and Hindī with high-status families such as Faqīh, Makkaᶜalī, Ṣaḥay, and others in the mid to late 1860s.[129] They joined the port's urban-mercantile elite, and some rose to a level of prominence in urban communal and religious affairs in the nineteenth and twentieth centuries, serving, for example as court-appointed witnesses in the *sharīᶜa* tribunal. According to the court records, they were never among the families who accumulated the greatest amount of wealth, for example, in real estate or movable property. The records also show how between the 1860s and the late 1880s these families were involved, albeit on a relatively small scale, in transactions of property, primarily shops and parcels of land. Women were also active in these transactions. In 1873 Khadīja b. Mīyā Khayr ad-Dīn bought a parcel of land for residential purposes in the port from Sayyid ᶜAbd Allāh al-Nimr for 40 riyals. Some three years later Amna b. Ṣāliḥ b. Muḥammad ᶜAbd al-Wasīᶜ Mīyā, represented in court by her *wakīl,* ᶜAbd Allāh ᶜUmar ᶜAlī ᶜAdūlāy, sold a shop in the port's main bazaar area, the *sūq al-Sulṭān,* for two hundred riyals to Shaykh Muḥammad ᶜAbd Allāh Aḥmad ᶜAbbāsī.[130] From the beginning of the twentieth century Hindu Indian agents and merchants for Indian trading firms were still prominent in Massawa. They were, however, coming under increasing pressure from the Italian colonial authorities, who saw them as competitors to Italian commercial activities and the agents of Britain and Indian businessmen. They also came under pressure from other merchants in Massawa, including Italians and other Mediterranean entrepreneurs. However, Indian merchants continued to flourish under Italian colonial rule, and entrepreneurs continued to arrive from Gujarat well into the 1930s. One example among many others was Narsidas Kalidas (b. 1885 in Mangrol), who settled in Eritrea in 1907 as an accountant for an Indian import/export company. At some point he established his own business firm in Massawa with a cousin. Another example was Harjivan Lalji Shah (b. 1919 in Porbandar), who settled in Eritrea as a young boy in 1929 and entered the import/export business, eventually becoming the head of the Indian community of Eritrea in 1944.[131]

Straw to Stone, Offshore Island to Coastal Town: Ordering Massawa's Urban Landscape in the Egyptian and Early Italian Eras, 1860s–90s

> When there were palaces in Massawa, Asmara was just a bunch of *tukuls*.
> —Sayyid Ibrāhīm Muḥammad Ibrāhīm al-Sayyid, April 2000[132]

> The built-up area of Massawa resembles an Arab quarter of Alexandria or Cairo.
> —Giovanni Salvadei, 1907[133]

> One would say a small town in southern Italy, blended with an Arab town.
> —Idelfonso Stanga, 1913[134]

In the early decades of the nineteenth century the built-up area of Massawa was mainly concentrated on the western half of the island. The other half was covered with old water cisterns and a Muslim cemetery.[135] In the late eighteenth century the Scottish explorer James Bruce had already remarked that "one third [of the island] is occupied by houses, one by cisterns, and the last is reserved for burying the dead."[136] In the 1840s Ferret and Galinier, members of a French scientific mission, had famously concluded that "half the island belonged to the dead, and the other half to the living."[137] The built-up area was densely packed with rectangular and circular thatched huts placed irregularly, spilling over the town's narrow alleys. Reminiscent of Sawākin, which was built on a rather limited oval-shaped island, the general street layout of Massawa Island was more or less radial. The narrow streets funneled cooling sea breezes into town and also provided direct and convenient access to the coast from the town center. Most houses were constructed of straw, reeds, and matting from date palm stretched on poles made of wood. They usually served a single or an extended family, and were enclosed by reed fencing and included a small courtyard. A few two-story stone buildings were reported in the late 1830s: the house of the Turkish governor, his harem, and the house of the chief scribe.[138] By the early 1850s, Osgood had noted that "many two-storey houses made of coral, with flat roofs" were scattered around town.[139] In January 1880 ʿAlī Riḍā Pasha noted in an Egyptian report the existence of two and three-story houses resembling those of Sawākin.[140] In between the thatched straw huts were single-story stone houses that belonged to the wealthier merchants and brokers of the port-town and its oldest families.[141] These houses often had large courtyards where caravan traders loaded and unloaded goods. The courtyard contained one or two small stone buildings serving as warehouses for storing the merchandise.[142] Stores in the bazaar were mostly constructed in coral stone, which reduced the risk of potential losses caused by the frequent fires that ravaged the island.[143] Mosques, foreign consulates, and warehouses were also among the stone edifices on the island. The basic pattern that characterized the second half of the nineteenth century was one of a gradual transition from straw huts to coral stone houses. At the end of the Ottoman period, in the middle decades of the century, new stone houses, shops, and other public buildings were constantly built on the island. Suggesting a gradual change from the earlier descriptions of the 1830s, Lejean noted in the early 1860s that from afar Massawa seemed white; the white of the houses masked and hid the poor huts of the "proletarian" classes that were still present in town.[144]

Massawa's urban landscape was already somewhat developed by the mid-1860s. When the Egyptians took over the town in 1865, they found approximately 100 stone houses, 200 wood huts, 20 mosques and *zāwiyas*, 200 shops and warehouses, and one church on Massawa Island, with a population of about 2,000. In Hetumlo, on the mainland the Egyptian report counted 507 stone and wood hut constructions (including religious edifices), four water wells, and 30 *faddān* (about 120 sq. kms) of agricultural land. In Hergigo there were 20 stone houses, 500 huts, 24 mosques and *zāwiyas*, a fortress, and 20 *faddān* (about 85 sq. kms) of agricultural land.[145] Twenty years later, a detailed map of Massawa drawn in 1885, following the Italian occupation, noted the doubling of the town's stone houses to 216. In addition, the map recorded 233 huts, 3 mosques with minarets, 10 secondary mosques, and 22 Arab and 5 European coffee houses.[146]

The Building Boom

Under the Egyptians a far-reaching transformation in Massawa's urban landscape occurred. Highly determined to boost up the port's commercial operation, the Egyptians carried out massive projects of public works and urban development resulting in the transfiguration of the town's skyline.[147] A few years after the Egyptian takeover observers noted the gradually reversing proportion between the number of stone houses and straw huts as more stone edifices increasingly replaced huts.[148] The architectural style of coral stone houses, observers noted, resembled a "more or less corrupted Arab style." The most elegant, modern, and luxurious belonged to the rich merchants, boasting beautifully carved wooden doors and, covered balconies ornate with carved wood that were sometimes painted in vivid colors.[149] Massawa houses boasted attractive woodworked casement windows, known as *rawshāns* in Jiddah, Sawākin, and Massawa, or *mashrabiyyas* in Egypt, whose function was principally to catch the slightest passing breeze while protecting from the sun.[150] One enthusiastic observer remarked that Massawa's merchants build attractive houses that surpassed in elegance those of Aden.[151] Architectural style was indeed one of the most important cultural markers reflecting regional continuity and cohesiveness in parts of the Red Sea, especially between Jiddah, Sawākin, Massawa, and perhaps Ḥudayda in some respects. Stone edifices were usually constructed with sub-fossil polyps extracted from the island itself and in the opposite peninsula of Ras Gherar.[152] But the need for a massive amount of materials in the Egyptian building boom era required greater provisions, which were extracted and brought from the bay of Nukhra in the largest island (Dahlak al-Kabīr) in the Dahlak Archipelago.[153] The building boom also necessitated a workforce whose composition and origin (free or unfree) the available evidence does not reveal. Around 1880, observers wrote—inaccurately, as the maps attest—that almost all houses were in stone, while their style was "Moorish."[154] In this context, a systematic comparative study of the architectural styles and urban form of several Red Sea towns, especially Jiddah, Sawākin, Massawa, and the Yemeni ports, would be an important project to pursue. Even a cursory visual comparison of the available documentary evidence makes it clear that there were strong similarities between the architectural styles of Sawākin, Massawa, and Jiddah.[155]

Straw huts were not entirely eradicated from the island, at least not until the early Italian colonial period. In the mid-1880s writers reported the acutely destitute living conditions of the hut dwellers, becoming increasingly a source of concern to the Italian authorities.[156] Filth, fires, and the rapid spreading of illnesses due to unhygienic conditions were commonplace and increasingly a preoccupation for local residents and the colonial authorities. The turning point occurred following the cholera outbreak of 1889–90 and a major fire that erupted in the square opposite the Ḥanafī mosque, thereafter named by the Italians as Piazza degli Incendi (Square of

Figure 3.6. Shaykh Saʿīd islet viewed from Massawa, late 1880s. Photographer: Luigi Naretti. Biblioteca Reale, Torino.

the Fires). These two events led the Italian colonial authorities to transfer a large part of the hut-dweller population to the mainland areas known to this day as ʿEdaga Beʿray (lit., ox market in Tigre and Tigrinya), ʿAd Aflanda, and ʿAd Habab.[157]

The rapid rise in the price of land also reflects the effects of the building boom.[158] In a report written following an inspection tour in the Red Sea in 1871, Aḥmad Mumtāz Pasha, governor of the eastern Sudan, recommended that land be granted free of charge by the administration to those entrepreneurs who wished to engage in construction.[159] The results of these recommendations are, however, unclear. The recording of land sales in the *sharīʿa* court throughout the 1860s, 1870s, and 1880s gives a certain sense of the building and real estate boom during the period. Of the 187 cases that I have identified in the court records between 1865 and 1888 involving either the sale or lease of land and the issuance of title deeds, several patterns appear. The records identify Massawa families owning land and real estate in this period. Most transactions were carried out among Massawans, especially in the first half of the period. A notable proportion was transactions involving the division and selling of inherited property following the death of a family head.[160] Another identifiable pattern is the purchase of parcels of land by entrepreneurs—mostly Hadramis and

Egyptians—of relatively recent establishment at Massawa. Bā Junayd, Bā Zarᶜa, and al-Ghūl bought much land, on which they consequently constructed shops and residential houses. Ownership of real estate both provided a direct source of income from rents and represented a source of political capital, securing and fostering the expansion of patronage networks.[161] From around 1875 there were also some Mediterranean merchants and entrepreneurs—many Greek and Levantine—who bought parcels of land. In 1886, for example, there were fifty-one Greeks, twenty-five Turks, fifteen Armenians, eleven French, two Maltese, and one German resident on Massawa Island.[162] Indians too were involved in land transactions.[163] The purchase of land by mostly non-Muslim foreigners accelerated and intensified from 1885, coinciding with the Italian occupation of Massawa.[164] At that stage Italian business firms such as Tagliabue purchased parcels of land.[165] From the early 1870s Egyptian officers and officials stationed in Massawa appear to have been involved in a considerable number of transactions, both as buyers and as sellers. Entrepreneurs, such as ᶜAbd Allāh Bey al-Ghūl, bought several parcels of land and a water well from the government. In addition to transactions of land there was also a great amount of buying and selling of shops and residential houses. It is interesting to note that some transactions also involved women, especially from among Massawa's elite families.

Egyptian public works in the 1860s and 1870s transformed Massawa's urban geography and its spatial organization. During these two decades the Egyptians carried out major projects improving health conditions, extending and modernizing communications, ameliorating the harbor facilities, and constructing and renovating a variety of public buildings. They all aimed at modernizing the port-town's infrastructures in accordance with Khedive Ismāᶜīl's grandiose economic aspirations for his Red Sea possessions. They might also be understood as having the objective of inscribing Egyptian rule and authority in Massawa's urban space, to observers from both within and without. Khedival Egypt aspired to display its modernizing spirit, particularly in the context of its contestations and competition with the Ottomans. Both Egyptian and European engineers were sent to Massawa to plan, supervise, and implement these major projects.[166] The project that had the most far-reaching effect on the port-town's structure was unquestionably the construction of the two causeways linking the island of Massawa to the small island of Tewalet (150 meters) and from there to the mainland (480 meters) in the early 1870s.[167] The project, undertaken under Werner Munzinger's tenure as governor (1871–73), ended Massawa's centuries-old position as a naturally protected offshore island. It physically connected the harbor part of the conurbation with its other mainland units. The construction of the causeways transfigured the spatial organization of the conurbation and deeply impacted the function of and interactions among its various elements. It led to the more dynamic and free movement of peoples and goods across the conurbation. Crossing over to Massawa Island was no longer exclusively conducted with boats; camels laden with goods could gain access to Massawa town directly by way of the causeways.[168] Among other consequences, these transformations opened up the space on the island of Tewalet for residential, administrative, and commercial purposes, including the spectacular government palace constructed under ʿArākil Bey's governorship, as well as an Egyptian prison at the other end of Tewalet. From 1874 the Egyptian government began selling parcels of land in Tewalet to Egyptian officials and wealthy Massawan entrepreneurs.[169] Urban expansion to Tewalet was welcomed by the Muslim population, who preferred not to build on the old sacred cemeteries in Massawa Island.[170] Closely related to the construction of the causeways—and almost equally revolutionary—was the piping of water from Emkullo to Tewalet, the small island, by now linked by causeways to both Massawa and the mainland.

As capital of the Italian colony between 1885 and 1899 (when Governor Ferdinando Martini transferred the capital to Asmara), Massawa underwent further projects of urban development, some building on, or improving, projects initiated by the Egyptians. In 1888 the colonial authorities issued several decrees aiming at modernizing the town, including the development of a European quarter; the regularization of urban sanitary services; the demolition of "irregular" constructions not in stone; the reconstruction of the two Egyptian causeways and the improvement of the roads on them; the casting in pipes of the brick aqueducts that brought water from Hetumlo to the Piazza degli Incendi near the bazaar; the covering of the bazaar street with a wooden roof; and a project for the construction of a port dock in the northern part of Massawa Island. In addition, the authorities built edifices for all government offices, the military and civil law courts, the port office, a hospital, the colonial treasury, customs warehouses, and various shipping and business agencies.[171] Two panoramic views of Massawa from the 1890s—a photograph and an illustration—attest quite neatly how the town was densely packed with Ottoman and Egyptian-era stone buildings and edifices as well as newer colonial constructions dating from the early years of Italian rule.[172] Unfortunately,

Figure 3.7. General view of Tewalet, 1880s. Photographer: Luigi Naretti. Biblioteca Reale, Torino.

many of the town's old buildings have not survived the devastating wave of earthquakes that hit the port beginning in August 1921.[173] It is interesting to note that the urban development of Massawa constituted a model for Ottoman officials who were promoting a particular "modern" vision of constructing and ordering space in the port of Ḥudayda on the other shores of the Red Sea. In his *Yemen Hāṭırası* (Memoirs of Yemen) published in 1909, for example, Rüşdī Pasha expressed his astonishment at Massawa's government buildings, which, he wrote, were "of a kind that caused amazement."[174]

Porters, Peddlers, and Prostitutes: Urbanization and the Making of Massawa's Underclass, 1860s–90s

The modernization of the port, the general demographic growth of the urban conglomerate, and the enhancement of commercial activities reshaped the conurbation and redefined its features. Urban transformation was characterized by the emergence of a class of laborers and service providers who settled mainly in new mainland suburbs and on Tewalet, and came to Massawa on a daily basis to make a living in various sectors of the burgeoning urban economy. Massawa's climate has always been famously unwelcoming; living conditions have been harsh in the port-town, keeping its population relatively low. In periods of economic growth and urban development the town tended to draw peoples from the inland who came to work and earn cash for a host of menial services. In the 1890s Yemeni laborers came to work as porters and dockworkers. Interestingly, the same was true a century later in post-Independence Eritrea, when the Eritrean government contracted Yemeni fishermen to boost up the nascent fishing industry in the late 1990s.

Following the Italian occupation of Massawa in 1885 the satellite villages procured an even wider array of labor, brokerage, peddling, and porterage services required by a burgeoning port-town and its bustling harbor. In 1886, shortly after Italian colonial imposition, one Italian observer recognized the organization of Massawa's urban space along occupational-ethnic lines. One segment was composed of those merchants in goods that were exchanged between the African and Arabian coasts or with Syria and Egypt. These merchants owned the houses in Massawa. The other segment, the "men of black race," possibly including freed slaves, was employed as manual laborers, servants, or peddlers selling goods in the interior.[175] Laborers were engaged in a myriad of activities around the harbor and the town's markets. Reports from the early colonial period noted that labor was abundant and that labor wages had doubled and even tripled in a short time.[176] Many of those who had insufficient capital to open shops or launch modest businesses worked as porters, sometimes on a daily basis, depending on the departure and arrival of boats and caravans. Porters carried large bales of animal hides, cotton, tobacco, ivory, and goods that came on board boats in the port, jugs (amphoras) full of water, and dried vegetables. Those who did not work as porters worked in shops, as servants in coffee shops and restaurants, as clerks in offices, and as sandal-makers.[177] Others were fishermen and sailors. Many were also employed by the Italian authorities, as rowers, domestic servants, nurses, day laborers, masons, and, last but not least, *askaris*, or colonial soldiers.[178]

In the early twentieth century sources describe the inhabitants of Hergigo as principally cattle merchants and wood and forage (fodder) traders, but also porters, caulkers, boatmen, fishermen, and water carriers.[179] Colonial officials distinguished between the well off and those who were of more modest means. In the first category were the merchants, the transportation brokers, and all those who were engaged in the import-export trade. In the second category they found those who engaged in small-scale commerce, boatmen, laborers and sailors on steamships, laborers

Figure 3.8. Market Place at Massawa, 1884. *Illustrated London News,* 1884, author's collection.

in the nascent local industries and public works, and those employed by the wealthier boat owners in the pearl and mother-of-pearl fishing enterprises.[180] But workers and laborers were not only from the Massawa mainland; there were also Sudanese, highland Habeshas, and Yemenis who came intermittently to the port for a myriad of menial jobs.[181] Alas, the data does not allow for any solid insight as to the terms of employment of slaves and freed slaves in various sectors of the urban, local, and regional economy.

This brings us to a group about which little is known—the liberated slaves, who were manumitted by owners for a host of economic, social, and religious motivations. The court records include a large number of manumission acts from the second decade of Egyptian rule. I have counted over two hundred manumission acts between 1873 and 1885. The manumission of slaves in Massawa was especially intensified following Werner Munzinger's appointment as governor of Massawa in 1871, more formally as a result of the Anglo-Egyptian convention for the suppression of the slave trade of 1877.[182] Most slaves originated in the Oromo-speaking southwestern Ethiopian region. In the records many were identified as *al-Qallawī* (Ar., the Galla), others as "Shanqala," "Dinka," "Abyssinian," or "Sudanese," or from specific locations such as Sibu, Liqqa, Jimma, Walata, Gomma,

Limmu, and other places. From the two hundred acts identified, 65 percent involved young girls, while 35 percent of the manumitted were males. Manumission acts included the name of manumitters—many of whom, such as Mentāy, al-Ghūl, Afandī, ʿAbbāsī, Nahārī, Bāho, Ṣāʾigh, Nāʾib, ʿAdūlāy—were members of Massawa's middle and higher classes. Yet a large number of manumitters included the Egyptian authorities.[183] Three such cases presented at court one after the other in a particular day in late April 1882 provide a sense of what manumission acts included.

In the first Ṭuranja *al-ḥabashiyya* (the Abyssinian) was manumitted by the government in accordance with the governorate's manumission directives. She thus became free, and nobody could oppose the decision in any way. The decision was passed on the authority of the governor [of Massawa]. The governorate decreed to publish the decision at Ṭuranja's request.[184] In the second case an Egyptian officer freed his slave ʿĀʾisha. The registration of the act stated:

> The honorable Shumātā Afandī ʿAlawī son of the honorable Ḥarb, second lieutenant of the Army, attached to the Governorate of Massawa, presented himself to the court and testified and attested that the slave belonging to him, ʿĀʾisha, daughter of ʿAbdū *al-Ḥabashī* is free for the sake of God. She is about eleven years old. He, the manumitter, possesses all the mental capacities required by the *sharīʿa*. And with this she has returned to be equal to the free. No one can oppose this decision in any way. This decision has been published and made known to all. The document that has been delivered to her constitutes proof of her freedom.[185]

In the third case a certain Nasīb was at the service of the government as baker. He was the slave of the late Sulṭān al-Ḥabaz (the baker). After his period of service ended he was manumitted according to the government's ordinance. From that point onward it was unlawful to buy or sell him and use him as a slave.[186]

Our knowledge of the activities and whereabouts of freed slaves following liberation is at present limited, although according to some evidence it appears that after their manumission many children (many were in their early teens) were taken in by mission schools and stations. Munzinger requested the Swedish Evangelical school mission of Emkullo to take care of recently manumitted slaves in the 1870s, resulting in the opening of a girls' school that took in freed slaves, Habesha prostitutes, and other girls in need of assistance.[187] In the 1880s Catholic schools in Massawa also accommodated freed slaves.[188]

The spatial division of the conurbation along ethnic, social, and occupational lines was further marked in the early decades of Italian rule. Giovanni Salvadei, Massawa's commissario in the early 1900s, observed that the Europeans, the local notables, and merchants "dressed in Arab clothes," and the Indian community all lived in Massawa Island. In the bazaar one found numerous caravaneers, Beduins, and local residents. On Tewalet, on the other hand, the "low indigenous population," composed of porters from Hadramawt, Beduin fishermen, Sudanese sailors, and Habesha laborers or caravaneers, was concentrated.[189] Indeed, one of the results of the colonial measures and urban transformations in the 1880s was the removal from Massawa Island of the lower classes and the poor, and their resettlement in Tewalet and ᶜEdaga Beᶜray. The inhabitants of Tewalet included many Habesha highlanders who came to Massawa in search of work or food, especially following the great drought and famine (Amh. *Kefu Qen,* the cruel days) that hit the northern Ethiopian area in 1888–92. There were also *askaris* (colonial soldiers), sailors, water porters, and laborers who worked in Massawa. One group drawing much attention was the prostitutes, concentrated in approximately one hundred huts arranged in a large semicircle in the northwestern part of Tewalet. Their presence there was reported as early as 1886, suggesting that it might have dated back to pre-Italian times. Census data from the early twentieth century might indeed allude to Massawa's population of prostitutes when signaling the vast outnumbering of females (141) over males (87) and the relatively low number of children (33), all under the category "Ethiopian subjects," possibly mostly from the highland province of Tigray.[190]

Prior to the construction of the causeways and the water pipelines connecting the island-port with the mainland in the early 1870s, providing the daily supply of fresh water to Massawa Island was a commonplace occupation. Young girls were employed in this harsh labor, carrying once or twice daily—under the scorching sun—large goatskins full of water from Emkullo to Massawa. They sold it for very little (about one piaster, in the early 1860s), either in the market or directly to the houses of the town dwellers.[191] Contemporary European observers did not shy away from the physical description of these "beautiful and charming" girls, who appeared quite lax in their clothing. Some alluded to the girls giving themselves to prostitution.[192] One anecdotal account from the late 1860s suggests flat-out the "cultural" clash between town and countryside customs and practices in a rapidly changing social environment:

> When I arrived [to Massawa] I found this town in revolution. The caste of pretty water carriers from Monkullo [Emkullo] was stifled as a result of the Governor's decision. It appears that several brawls on their account have occurred and some rows have resulted. There were complaints. Morality and religion have been offended. Some have said that their [young] age prohibited any rowdy pleasures. The *qāʾim maqām* decided to stop the evil-doing by impairing its cause. He sent to his divan all the sinners, from first to last. . . . Hola, what do I hear? All Massawa is talking about the scandal that your disordered behavior has caused! Your behavior is both an offense to the Prophet's religion and to the laws of the Sublime Porte, of which I am here the keeper. I order this to end . . . I will therefore marry you! . . . The Governor turned towards his soldiers: You, Sa'id Effendi, he said, you will take Madina to be your wife; you Ibrahim, you'll take Fatma and Abdallah, you'll take Maryam.[193]

Even after water was regularly piped from the mainland, the water porters did not disappear from the landscape of the conurbation. An account from the late 1890s noted that now instead of going all the way to Emkullo, the girls went to fetch water from the water reservoir in Tewalet, before carrying it from there to Massawa.[194]

Other mainland neighborhoods developed as a result of urban transformation in the early Italian period. Urban space was increasingly divided on the basis of ethnicity and economic occupation. ʿEdaga Beʿray, established in 1889, was located around the area where the causeway from Tewalet reached the mainland. The southern part of ʿEdaga was called Khatmiyya (or Khutmiyya) since a group of Sudanese families from Kassala settled there in the 1890s under the protection of Sayyid Hāshim al-Mīrghanī (1849/50–1901), son of the founder of the Khatmiyya *ṭarīqa* based in Hetumlo. Together with the suburbs' other inhabitants, ʿEdaga had a population of roughly 1,000. To the west of ʿEdaga inland one came across some one hundred other huts with an approximate population of 600 in a suburb called *Elà* Ghūl. Many there were Arabs, probably from among the Rashayda Beduins. It was named after the well-known Egyptian ʿAbd Allāh Bey al-Ghūl, who had bought there—as a charitable gesture—a water well (*elà* in Tigre) in February 1880, for the use of the local population.[195] Several well-to-do merchant families had wells dug for a

Figure 3.9. Water porters, 1885. Photographer: Mauro Ledru. Biblioteca Reale, Torino.

particular community as an act of *zakāt* (almsgiving). Another example is the *Elà* Hāshim, built by the ᶜAd Hāshim in Emkullo.[196] Finally, a suburb known as ᶜAd Aflanda (or ᶜAd Habab), commemorating by its name the origins of its first settlers, was located between ᶜEdaga and Gherar. It consisted of about one hundred huts with 350 people from Habab, Aflanda, and the northern coastal port of ᶜAqīq, who provided Massawa with milk and worked either in the port or in the salt fields in Gherar.[197]

The growth of the port throughout the nineteenth century spurred the urbanization of pastoralists and semi-pastoralists who came from the Eritrean inland. As early as the 1860s Guillaume Lejean, the French consul at Massawa, had identified a certain process of urbanization among the Semhar pastoralist and semi-pastoralist groups who gradually settled in the conurbation. He noted that Emkullo was inhabited by Beduins and "that the proximity of a mercantile town has impelled them to abandon their nomadic practices in favor of the thousands of small jobs that the inhabitants of the suburbs live on."[198] Plowden too pointed to this same phenomenon, albeit with some factual errors. He wrote that "the people of Dohona on the mainland, style themselves the tribe of Hergigo, and are by origins Hababs, though they now mixed with all the other tribes, having abandoned in a great degree their wandering and nomadic habits for the sweets of commerce and the profits of a town life."[199] Several decades later, Dante Odorizzi, an Italian colonial official, further noted the change in Massawa's human landscape and described aspects of the process of how non-settled peoples were "liberated" from their nomadic social groupings by "becoming urban":

> Concerning the transformation of the nomadic population into a settled one, it must be noted that Massawa, Hergigo, Hetumlo and Emkullo, even though they are not large settlements, constituted for the pastoralists significant centers where a process of *urbanization* took place. A pastoralist of the region north of the Lebka or of the lower Asaorta who, for example, lost his animals or was involved in litigations with the chiefs of his tribe, went to Massawa and found there work as a servant for the Europeans or the wealthy (powerful) locals or as a manual laborer. He often does not wish to return to his native tribe and live there under the authority of the ruling classes, if his tribe follows an aristocratic regime such as those of the Sahel, or under the authority of the elders in case his tribe is under a patriarchal or democratic regime, such as the Saho. Therefore, he ends up remaining in Semhar where he lives in the settled [urban] centers.[200]

Odorizzi continued by observing that other "nomads" who had served as *askari* and laborers also became "urbanized." He suggested that these experiences had changed these individuals, who had no interest in going back to their previous ways of life. To this detribalized underclass Odorizzi added the slaves who stayed in the urban region following their manumission.[201] The urbanization of Massawa's mainland spaces made the otherwise sharp divide between town and countryside fade into the blurred locus where citizenship was produced and struggled over. It was where the lower strata of a growingly stratified urban environment made their entry into town society. New forms of poverty emerged in this setting. One Italian report of 1891 observed that in contrast with some improvement of economic conditions in the Semhar countryside, "around Massawa a mob of unhappy people deprived of the means of subsistence has gathered."[202] Alberto Pascale wrote with empathy and compassion about the desolate and desperately poor roving Massawa's alleys who needed to beg for their existence.[203] Observers shocked by conjunctural poverty in Massawa from the 1860s through the 1890s witnessed the results of rapidly changing economic conditions and some of its radical social effects.[204]

On the Outskirts of Town, on the Edge of the Countryside: Linking the Port with the Interior

Massawa Island, Hetumlo, Emkullo, Zaga, Hergigo, and, to a lesser extent, the neighborhoods and peninsulas in between them, all composed a single urban system, centered on Massawa. Massawa's centrality in this urban configuration was founded on its international deep-water harbor, its vast bazaar, markets, and shop areas, and its being the political and administrative center of those who governed the region. It was the business and political center where both foreign and local Massawan merchants operated simultaneously vis-à-vis seaward trade networks, with Hijazi, Yemeni, and Indian ports on the one hand, and inland traders and producers—or their brokers—on the other. The other settlements of the conurbation were crucial to the functioning and servicing of the port, making all its units interdependent. The mainland elements of the conurbation—principally the villages of Hetumlo, Emkullo, and Hergigo, had several traditional functions.

Water was a crucial factor in Massawa Island's dependence on the mainland settlements, accounting for the principal reason for their foundation in the past. Deprived of any source of water, Massawa received daily provisions from the wells of Emkullo, Hetumlo, and Hergigo. Remarking on Hetumlo and Emkullo, Henry Blanc noted in the late 1860s that "the wells are the wealth of the villages—their very existence. . . . The wells number about twenty. Many old ones are closed, but new ones are frequently dug, so as to keep up a constant supply of water."[205]

Another vital function of the satellite villages on the outskirts of the conurbation was their role as caravan stations. The provisioning of water for incoming and outgoing caravans was crucial in this respect. Caravans bound to and from Massawa often stopped in Emkullo, Hetumlo, and Zaga, where they unloaded part of their cargoes and procured animals, water, wood, and all other provisions required for a long journey—including guides for the first part of the trip through the lowlands. Observers explicitly identified Zaga as a settlement of Beduins who provided traders and caravans with water, wood, and the means of transportation.[206] Emkullo had always been an important caravan station in the gates of Massawa and a power stronghold of the Nāʾib family section who resided there. The French traveler Denis de Rivoyre provided a vivid description of his stay at the house of the chief of cameleers in Emkullo, who boasted two old rugs brought on his pilgrimage to Mecca in the 1840s.[207]

The suburbs also provided Massawa with a variety of foodstuffs: fruit, vegetables, poultry, eggs, milk, meat, and other foods that were consumed in town on a daily basis. Hergigo, Hetumlo, and Emkullo all possessed some agricultural lands and gardens, in which a variety of fruits and vegetables were grown in order to "feed the port." Women ground dhurra, prepared bread, and made mats from palm leaves, which were all taken to be sold in Massawa. From Hetumlo too, a daily inflow of people came into Massawa to sell their produce and procure whatever they needed in the town's markets.[208] Saho girls from Hergigo came to Massawa to sell lemons and bread, and every morning a *sanbūq* left Hergigo for Massawa with people, wood, coal, vegetables, eggs, hens, sheep, goats, pigeons, and more on board.[209] During the rainy seasons Hetumlo and Amatere provided the town with vegetables, melons, tobacco, dhurra, maize, cucumbers, and bultuc (bulrush millet), which were grown there.[210]

As the population of the conurbation grew, Emkullo and then Hetumlo provided extra space for residence, with a slightly milder climate than the island's unbearable heat throughout long months of the year. Some Massawans also had their camels, cows, goats, and donkeys in the more spacious outer villages of the conurbation. Since early in the nineteenth century numerous observers had noted that some of Massawa's wealthier merchants moved—seasonally or daily—to Emkullo or Hetumlo, where they had their primary or secondary residences.[211] Guillaume Lejean called Emkullo the "Batignolles of Massawa," and Denis de Rivoyre dubbed it "a kind of Bougival or Asnières," all references to residential quarters on the outskirts of Paris.[212] In the Italian period Hetumlo was referred to in relation to its two parts, Hetumlo *maʿdei* (Tigre, further away, beyond the stream) and Hetumlo proper. Many of the Beduins from Nakfa, Afᶜabet, and Keren, mostly Habab, lived in straw huts in the first moiety, which was the locus of the markets to which the pastoralists brought their animals and produce. In contrast, many Massawan families, including the rich and the prosperous, resided in large stone houses in Hetumlo *inferiore,* as it was called in the Italian era (in contrast to *superiore*). The spatial division thus also corresponded to a social and cultural division between the Massawa merchants and the *qabāʾil* (Ar., tribes), the dwellers of the northern part of Hetumlo, whom the urban merchants tended to write off as less sophisticated and refined.[213] In the early years of the twentieth century two large markets operated in Hergigo and Hetumlo/Emkullo. On Mondays people from all over the Semhar, the eastern escarpments of Akkele Guzay, the Afar coast, the Habab regions, and the lower escarpments of Hamasen came to the Hergigo cattle market to sell all types of animals. Odorizzi referred to this market as among the most important in Eritrea. In Hetumlo and Emkullo a market was held on Thursdays in the Obel torrent, where camels, cattle, sheep, butter, hides, and sesame—all destined to be exported from Massawa—were sold.[214]

Facing the Town, Facing the Countryside: Conjoining Networks and Cementing Patronage Relations

On a more conceptual level the Massawa conurbation was the site of multiple brokering and mediating relationships, or networks that tied the wider world of the Red Sea and the northwestern Indian Ocean with the inland regions of the Ethio-Eritrean region. The outer settlements of the conurbation—Hergigo, Hetumlo, and Emkullo—were the sites where inland producing, trading, and transportation networks and the sea-facing Massawa networks were linked to each other through a dense web of bonds. It was the site where the town met the countryside, where the urban merchant met the inland trader, and where overland and seaborne networks connected. It embodied a somewhat fuzzy zone in which urban merchants extended their patron-client networks deep inland, and countryside folk could penetrate deep into the urban mercantile structures of the port. They had one foot in town and another in the countryside. Describing the features of the typical Swahili coastal conurbation, Middleton and Horton wrote that it constitutes a micro urban economic system of complementary production by exchange between different categories of settlement and is "tied together into a single unit by various bonds of neighborhood, kinship, political and religious authority, and by some expression of shared or complementary ethnicities."[215] This definition is valid for Massawa, where a host of micro economic, commercial, and social activities and relations took place throughout the conurbation, but were all at the same time geared toward serving the essential role and function of Massawa as a port dispatching goods for exportation and receiving imports for marketing locally and regionally. The structure and operation of the Massawa conurbation reveals an exchange network and an organization that was well adapted to local geographic, economic, commercial, and social conditions. The conurbation may be seen as a space delimited by the various types of bonds and interrelations that linked its inhabitants. The relationships could be based on ethnic or family connections, on patron-client or brokerage ties, or all together combined.

The spatial and human organization of the mainland elements of the conurbation suggests their socially porous character. The settled populations of Hergigo, Hetumlo, and Emkullo were mixed ones. On the one hand, they comprised settled nomadic pastoralist traders, producers, and others who provided services to caravan transportation, brokerage, and trade and who had originated from the respective inland regions facing them: the different Tigre- and Saho-speaking regions of the eastern Eritrean area. With the years, some of those who had settled in Massawa and the urban area "became urban" and acted as brokers between the port and their original homelands in Akkele Guzay, Semhar, Sahel, and the western Eritrean lowlands. On the other hand, these settlements included families, or branches of families, that are identified as Massawa's patrician classes, mainly the wealthier and more dominant urban families. They held their residences in these villages and promoted their business interests on the mainland by building on the historical domination of the inland regions by the leaders and merchants of the coast, essentially the Balaws and their associates, and the wealthy Massawa merchants. Families belonging to the urban elite, such as al-Nātī, Mentāy, and Ṣāʾigh, had branches that were dynamically involved in a dense web of networks that penetrated deep into the countryside. Historically, these families rose to their high urban status thanks to their pivotal role as mediators between town and countryside. Brokers gradually developed solid connections with both urban merchants from Massawa and pastoralists and farmers from their respective regions of origin. To the town merchants they could offer access to countryside networks, while to inland traders and producers they could offer the "keys to the city."

The formation of these villages was closely related to the operation and vitality of the caravan routes from Massawa inland and to brokerage between town and countryside. In order to gain control over the port's gates of entry and exit, the powerful coastal mercantile families established their power bases also in Emkullo and Hetumlo. Accounting for the formation and role of Emkullo, Salvadei wrote that "in a short time rich merchants had settled there." They collected cattle, butter, and hides from the adjacent tribes and ivory, gold, civet, and slaves from the Abyssinian caravans, loading all at Massawa to be shipped to the Arabian coast.[216] In the later middle decades of the century, the construction of the causeway, the relative safety provided by the Egyptian forces against possible attacks by highland Habesha warlords, and the availability of fresh water and land on the mainland all provided an impetus for extending urban mercantile structures to the close mainland. Massawa families who set base in the mainland settlements usually built homes with large compounds (*darets*) that came to be known in association with the family who owned it, such as *daret* ᶜAd ᶜAbbāsī, *daret* ᶜAd Makkaᶜalī, or *daret* ᶜAd Afandī. These compounds served as rest areas, supplying stations, and trading centers.[217] Families such as the ᶜAd Ḥāmidūy, ᶜAd Ṣāʾigh, ᶜAd Yūsuf ᶜObde, ᶜAd Yāqūt, ᶜAd Agāba, and ᶜAd Mentāy in Hetumlo, and ᶜAd Hāshim in Emkullo, have all been identified as important brokers during the Egyptian era.[218] Some of them, such as Mentāy, Yāqūt, Ḥāmidūy, and Ṣāiʾgh, were brokers and merchants with strong power bases in Massawa Island itself. In 1883 the records of the Islamic court identified ᶜUthmān b. Saᶜīd Ḥāmidūy as a *khalīfa,* which links him as an office holder to one of the active *ṭuruq* in the region.[219] The records also identified his brother, Shaykh Aḥmad b. Saᶜīd Ḥāmidūy, as "*min aᶜyān Maṣawwaᶜ,*" or one of Massawa's notables, situating the family well within the town's urban elite.[220] The Ḥāmidūys epitomize a segment of the Massawa elite whose solid power bases within both sea-facing and inland-looking webs of networks actually linked the sea and the land.

Family lists clearly show the stronghold of locally powerful families in the outward settlements of the conurbation. In addition, some of these families had built or financed mosques in these settlements. Notable examples include the Adam Barkūy, the Aḥmad Shalāl, and the Muḥammad ᶜUmar Yāqūt mosques in Hetumlo, the Shaykh ᶜUthmān Ḥābūna mosque in Amatere, and the Shaykh Muḥammad Jābir mosque and numerous others in Hergigo.[221] These mosques served as influential power bases on the non-settled and recently settled pastoralists in Hetumlo and

Hergigo, and were important in binding new patron-client relationships. The charitable endowment of water wells was also symbolically important in creating patronage networks binding urban merchants with inland-facing brokers, suppliers, and carriage providers. Early-twentieth-century lists of merchants and brokers show how both grain merchants and brokers, of whom many had firmly established urban bases (e.g., Bā ᶜĪssa, al-Nātī, Sālim, Ḥayūtī, Sharīf, Hilāl, Masāwa, and many others), operated from the outskirts of the conurbation, in Hergigo and Hetumlo. Urban coastal families' networks and connections went even further inland to a second circle comprising villages such as Weqiro to the north and ᶜAylet at the foot of the escarpment. For example, the presence of members of well-known Massawa families, such as Aḥmad ᶜAbdu Seror and Muḥammad Nūr Mentāy in Weqiro, Aḥmad ᶜUbayd Bā Zarᶜa in Emberemi, Saᶜīd Bakrī Ṣāʾigh in Harena, and Muḥammad ᶜUmar Shāwish and Muḥammad Saᶜīd Ḥābūna in Mai Atal, all clearly attest to these connections inland.[222]

Two noteworthy and suggestive observations may be made from the list mentioned above. First, the Shīnītī family, of Balaw origins and undoubtedly one of an exclusive circle of prominently wealthy and influential families, owning significant real estate property and having a central role in Massawa's urban institutions, is noted as having strongholds in all three settlements (in addition to Massawa). The Shīnītīs were but an example among other families who epitomized Massawa's urban mercantile elite, holding strong power bases in the outskirts of the conurbation and far beyond, and capitalizing on Balaw hegemony and control in the wider region. Several members of this family, such as Muḥammad ᶜUthmān b. Muḥammad b. Saᶜīd Shīnītī, Muḥammad Nūr b. ᶜĀmir b. Ḥamad Shīnītī, and Muḥammad Ṭāhir b. ᶜUthmān Shīnītī (b. ca. 1860), were referred to as among the port's most prominent notables in the last quarter of the century. The first, Muḥammad ᶜUthmān Shīnītī, the most prominent of them, was the firstborn of Muḥammad b. Saᶜīd Shīnītī, who was already considered a notable at the time of his death sometime in the early 1860s. The wealth he had accumulated and left to his sons Muḥammad ᶜUthmān and ᶜAbd Allāh enabled them to invest together in urban real estate, land, shops, and water cisterns. The court records referred to Muḥammad ᶜUthmān, the most prominent Shīnītī during the 1870s and 1880s, as "the pride of the noble merchants," a prestigious and honorable appellation that only a handful in the port could attain. He was also referred to as a *khalīfa* (like his late father), suggesting his intimate association with one of the Sufi orders, most probably the Khatmiyya.[223] Muḥammad Ṭāhir b.

ᶜUthmān Shīnītī was a foremost merchant in textiles, civet, and ivory. He was well connected in the lowland interior as far as the Beni ᶜAmer regions through Balaw networks. In the early twentieth century he registered two of his boats with the Italian authorities, attesting again to the family's relative wealth in property, with both sea- and land-facing connections and interests.[224]

Another observation concerns cultural dynamics in the conurbation. Interestingly, the al-Nātī, Mentāy, and Yāqūt families were identified as being of "Arab" origins when their origins clearly pointed to the Eritrean interior. The Mentāy were originally from the western Eritrean lowlands, and the al-Nātī family was from the Tigre-speaking Tsaura tribe and had family branches in Nakfa, Afᶜabet, Keren, and Massawa.[225] This might suggest contemporary urban cultural dynamics that had identified Massawa's rich urban families with "Arab" origins and culture, also mirroring a process of cultural "Arabization." The use and manipulation of cultural markers often epitomized struggles for citizenship. The increased urbanization of the outer circles of the conurbation prompted a process of heightened competition over the various forms of capital—social, economic, but also symbolic—necessary for joining urban sociocommercial structures to maximize one's opportunities to benefit from the port's resources. In the lesser elements and on the fringes of the conurbation, in the markets and huts of Hergigo, Emkullo, and Hetumlo, the social, economic, and cultural dynamics involved in the process of the integration into urban-dominated commercial networks could at times offer the key to membership in urban society. The villages on the periphery of the conurbation—or on the outskirts of town and the edge of the countryside—were the locus of multilayered social interactions among their dwellers and between them and the nomads and pastoralists who often settled on the fringes of the satellite settlements. These were the sites where struggles and competition over the port's resources and lucrative networks took place. The markets and caravan stations, the central sites of brokerage, were where clientship relationships and business alliances were negotiated.

4

"A Sacred Muslim Island"

Sufis, Holy Men, and Town Islam in Massawa and the Interior

We Massawans have accepted Islam even before the Meccans.
—Informant in Massawa, March 2000

Muḥammad, Lord of the Two Worlds,
and of Man and the Jinn,
Lord also of the Arabs and
non Arabs and their Kin.
—Al-Būṣīrī; inscription on door lintel of the Shīnītī family house in Massawa[1]

For when God's Prophet comes
to one's assistance and one's aid,
Were one to meet in thickets, lions
they'd be cowed and afraid.
—Al-Būṣīrī; inscription on a wooden door lintel in Massawa[2]

If both a commerce-oriented disposition and a strong sense of urban distinction were pivotal markers to individual and society in Massawa, a staunch devotion to Islam, the expression of Muslim identity, and the identification of Massawa as a distinctly Muslim space was another foundational pillar characterizing the community. An anecdotal yet revealing story epitomizing the conception of Massawa as a sacred Muslim space occurred in the 1860s. Approximately a decade after the opening of the French consulate in the port in 1841, a *firman* issued by the Ottoman Porte granted the French the right to establish a Roman Catholic mission and a church on Massawa Island. The inhabitants of Massawa responded with such indignation that the governor delayed the execution of the order for some years.[3] The *muftī* of Massawa, ʿAlī Abū ʿIlāmā Muḥammad Nūr, protested vehemently against the execution of the order, arguing that Massawa was a "Muslim island" and a sacred space for its Muslim community since it was the point of landing of the Prophet's companions (Ar. *saḥāba*), in AD 615. The island could therefore not tolerate the existence of a Christian church.[4] Some time later, as he realized that his protests had borne no fruits and the authorities had indeed approved the beginning of construction, the *muftī* left town and exiled himself to the island of Deset in the Dahlak Archipelago, where "his ears would not hear the bells of the church."[5] After some years he returned from his insular *hijra* and settled in Hetumlo on the mainland, before his death in 1866. His remains were later transferred to the family tomb in the Dhahab mosque on Massawa Island. The French had built their church, but opposition by the Muslims in subsequent years did not die out.[6]

From an Islamic historical perspective, Massawa was in a somewhat odd position. On the one hand, its geographic proximity to Mecca and the Hijaz brought it in close contact with the historical Arab-Islamic heartlands and the most sacred places of the Islamic *umma* since the very first days of the Islamic revelation. On the other hand, its relationship with and historical dependence on Christian Ethiopia and its peripheries placed it on the fringes of the Islamic world, with an ancient and hegemonic non-Muslim political entity in its hinterlands and societies practicing different forms of Christianity in the adjacent lowland areas. Massawa was thus a "Muslim island" in more than one sense, at least until the so-called Islamic revival of the nineteenth century, during which almost all lowland societies in its hinterland either converted to Islam or witnessed a strengthening of Muslim practices and belief. On a discursive level, in periods when identity and culture have been subject to politicization, Muslims in Massawa and in Eritrea at large have tended to highlight their close affinities with Islamic history and their special place within the *umma* since the very first days of Islam. As the story with the *muftī* suggests, such discourses put particular emphasis on the story of the Prophet's companions and their flight to Abyssinia in AD 615.[7] Persecuted by the Meccan Qurayshi nobility, the Prophet's companions crossed the Red Sea, landed on the Eritrean coast, and sought refuge in al-Ḥabasha, where they were welcomed by the Axumite ruler, known in Islamic tradition as al-Najāshī. The episode, known in Islamic history as the *hijra al-ūla* (Ar., the first emigration), is viewed by many northeast African Muslims (but more so Eritreans and northern

Ethiopians) as the cornerstone of a unique cross–Red Sea Islamic relationship.[8] This seminal historical event is proof to the profound attachment of Massawa's Muslims since—according to such rhetoric—they had accepted the Prophet Muḥammad's message prior to its establishment in important centers in the Islamic heartlands such as Mecca, Damascus, Baghdad, or Cairo.[9] Again, as the *muftī*'s story suggests, the alleged landing of the Prophet's companions in Ras Medr on Massawa Island also contributed to the notion of the town as a "Muslim island" possessing some type of sacred quality.

On one level and from a broader regional perspective, this chapter examines the effects of the so-called Islamic revival on the eastern Eritrean region, characterized by the emergence and operation of new Sufi brotherhoods, the revitalization of older brotherhoods, and the indefatigable activities of several holy families in the region. Massawa was situated in a pivotal location in relation to cross–Red Sea and northeast African Islamic networks that were much reinvigorated as a result of the mid-nineteenth-century commercial boom. Traders and holy men circulated between the Arabian Peninsula and the eastern Sudanese region with greater ease. It is unsurprising that from early mid-century the two most influential partisan holy families in the history of Islam in the area, the Khatmiyya and the ʿAd Shaykh holy family, had intensified their interaction with the port-town, eventually establishing their centers in its close environs (Hetumlo and Emberemi). There, they gained much success among newcomers settling in and around town and were also able to spread their influence over inland societies interacting with the conurbation. In the mid-1880s, as imperialist Italy moved into the region, it faced the task of controlling its newly conquered territories—an especially complex chore in the context of the Mahdist successes in neighboring Sudan and the new regional political and military dynamics that it triggered in northern Ethiopia and the territory that would become Eritrea. The perceived Mahdist threat shaped early Italian attitudes to Islam in the area, and led them to interfere with regional Muslim dynamics.

Moving on to a more town-focused perspective, the chapter examines the religious institutions, shared ideals, and distinctive features of urban Muslims in Massawa. In general, Islam flourished in the port-town in the second half of the nineteenth century. Muslim dynamics in town radiated throughout the region, which looked up to it as an important regional Islamic center of law, learning, and piety, and as a gateway to important Islamic centers such as the Hijazi holy towns but also Zabīd, which has played a particularly important role vis-à-vis Massawa as a center of Islamic education and scholarship. The chapter explores the relationship between Islam and the formation of an urban identity. The town's religious and cultural prestige rested in part on the existence of its more than sixty mosques (in 1910), its holy saints' tombs and shrines, its yearly celebrations and visitation sites, several Qurʾānic schools, the *sharīʿa* court, and the location of several Sufi centers. The case of Massawa shows how the local veneration of saints, the participation in local pilgrimages, and the affiliation with Sufi orders could transcend particularistic sectarian loyalties in favor of a more localized sense of a unified Muslim community, deeply identified with the town's historical trajectory and its sacred geography.

Islam in the Eritrean Region before 1800

From both a spatial and a political perspective, the Eritrean region may be perceived as an historical meeting point of several "frontiers" situated between the Red Sea and the facing Arabian Peninsula, the Sudanese Nile valley, and the northern Ethio-Eritrean highlands over which it partly extends. Accordingly, the history of Islam in the area has been markedly shaped by political, economic, migratory, and religious developments in all these spheres and by their impact on the region and its inhabitants.

In a very real sense Eritrea's heterogeneous Muslim societies reflect this kaleidoscopic historical configuration: they belong to different ethnic groups; speak a variety of Semitic, Cushitic, and Nilo-Saharan languages; practice various modes of production; and are socially and politically organized in diverse ways. More importantly for our purposes here, Muslim societies in Eritrea have adopted Islam in distinctive periods and in different ways, and have appropriated Islamic beliefs and practices in varying modes and intensities. For example, from one specific angle, the historical layering of these influences is quite neatly exemplified by the regional distribution of the *madhāhib* in Eritrea. The Shāfiʿī school was introduced by traders and holy men from the Yemeni region and adopted mostly by the Afar and some highland Jeberti.[10] The Mālikī legal rite, predominant in the pre-Turkiyya Sudan, is still influential with groups in the western lowlands and the northern Eritrean area, and the Ḥanafī *madhhab,* introduced officially by the Ottomans (but possibly present earlier), gained the adherence of the Semhar groups and other Tigre- and Saho-speaking groups of the eastern lowlands and northern highlands.[11] Clearly, the historical trajectories of Islam in the region must be imagined and examined from within a broader, transregional perspective that transcends the borders of the modern Eritrean state. Influences from Egypt and the Nile Valley, from the Arabian Peninsula, and from the historical Ethiopian polity, whose rulers and elites perceived it as inherently "Christian," have all been instrumental in shaping the development and experiences of Muslim societies and their institutions in the Eritrean region.

The early seventh century AD episode of the Prophet's companions' flight from the Hijaz to Ethiopia is more symbolic than anything. Its actual reflection of the diffusion and establishment of Islam in northeastern Africa at that early stage was nevertheless insignificant. Muslim influence in the region was more conspicuous beginning in the eighth century AD, when recently Islamized Arabs under the Umayyad Caliphate (AD 661–750) occupied the Dahlak islands off the Massawa coast and were thus one of the first East African areas to come under the influence of Islam. Approximately one century later several Arab tribes transplanted from the Arabian Peninsula and gradually assimilated into Beja Hamitic groups introduced Islam to the Beja tribes inhabiting the plains between the Red Sea and the Nile (covering also areas in northern and western present-day Eritrea).[12] In the twelfth and thirteenth centuries the Dahlak Archipelago was the seat of an independent emirate ruled by a line of sultans, serving as a lucrative transit station in the trade between Egypt and India, but also in cross–Red Sea trade between Ethiopia and Yemen. The commercial revival and relative stability in the Red Sea area resulting from Fāṭimid predominance boosted the role of Islam in the wider region. Trade and the circulation of holy men from the Arabian Peninsula enhanced the diffusion of Islam on the southern Red Sea coasts, and by the thirteenth century many of the Afar- and Saho-speaking peoples of the eastern Eritrean region had become Muslims.

Most oral and historical traditions of Eritrean Muslim groups emphasize the role of Arabian holy men in the process of their adoption of Islam and, sometimes, the foundation of their lineages. Such traditions should be taken with caution since some of those adopting them include groups who converted to Islam only in the nineteenth century. They usually adopted and adapted such traditions to both shape and accommodate their newly acquired religious and social identities. Be that as it may, some eastern Eritrean Muslim traditions recall (and still venerate) *faqīh* Muḥammad, the Hijazi cleric who sparked the spread of Islam among their societies. According to these traditions *faqīh* Muḥammad crossed the Red Sea into the coastal region known as Dankalia (or the Afar coastlands) in the eleventh century AD. There he converted many Afar-speaking communities, most often by marrying the daughters of local leaders. From there he moved inland to the eastern highland escarpments (Akkele Guzay region), where he converted the largest and most prominent Saho-speaking clans, the Asaorta and the Minifire.[13] His sons, Shaykh Sālim and Shaykh Ṣāliḥ, continued their father's holy enterprises and are regarded as the ancestors of several important holy clans and families in the region—present as far as the Barka in the west and the Sahel in the north. One of the most noteworthy of these holy clans is undoubtedly the Bayt Shaykh Maḥmūd, originally from Zula and having a solid presence in numerous settlements throughout Semhar. It was well networked in the urban setting, principally through prominent families such as Faras, Bādūrī, Mentāy, Saᶜdūy, Ḥabīb, and Khaydara.[14] Other notable Tigre- and Saho-speaking holy clans or lineages that developed are the ᶜAd Darqī, ᶜAd Muᶜallim, ᶜAd Zubayr, al-Kabīrī, and others. Some of these became "religious clans" catering to their wider social groupings or clan confederations with religious services such as providing *qāḍīs* and teachers. Most drew their legitimacy from claims of prestigious descent originating in the Hijaz or the Arabian Peninsula at large. During the nineteenth-century religious revival most were actively engaged in spreading Islam in various Eritrean regions, often by marrying into non-Muslim communities.[15]

A new identifiable phase of Islamic diffusion and activity began in the fifteenth century and culminated in the sixteenth century.[16] The politicization of Islam in northeast Africa, sparked by the rise to prominence of the sultanate of Adal, attained its climax with the *jihād* of Aḥmad b. Ibrāhīm al-Ghāzī (nicknamed in Amharic Grañ, the left-handed). One result of the Muslim victories over "Christian" Ethiopia between 1527 and 1543 was to foster the diffusion of Islam in the Ethio-Eritrean region, prompting a more elaborate formation of Jeberti communities in the highlands. Furthermore, the conflict between Christians and Muslims rallied external imperialist forces in the Red Sea area and culminated in the Ottoman occupation of Massawa in 1557, an occupation that lasted until 1865. In general, Ottoman control of the Red Sea basin revitalized transregional commerce and provided a degree of relative stability in the area. One result was the migration of Arabs from the Hijaz, Yemen, and Hadramawt to the African coastal urban centers, notably Massawa and Hergigo. In terms of religious influence, the construction of several mosques and tombs/shrines (*qubba*), most notably the Shaykh Ḥammāl al-Anṣārī religious complex and what became known as the Ḥanafī mosque, was characteristic of the

Ottoman era in Massawa. The Ottomans introduced the Ḥanafī *madhhab* as the official legal rite and sent to Massawa Ḥanafī *qāḍīs* from the Hijaz or from Egypt in the late sixteenth and early seventeenth centuries.[17] The prolonged incorporation of Massawa and its close hinterlands into the Ottoman administrative and commercial setup in the Red Sea area positioned it firmly within a political, religious, and cultural sphere of Muslim influence.

Saints and Sufis: Revival and Expansion in the Nineteenth Century

A pivotal phase in the development of Islam in the region occurred throughout the nineteenth century. It was interwoven with the wave of religious renewal and reform movement throughout the Muslim world and with Egyptian imperialism in northeast Africa. It also coincided with and was generated by the transformation of the political economy of the region, resulting from the Red Sea trade revival and the increasing integration of the broader region to the world economy. The set of movements frequently referred to as the "Islamic Revival" emerged in the late eighteenth and developed throughout the nineteenth century. They were in part a response to the increasing economic penetration of Europe into the Muslim world and the resulting weakening and decentralization of the Ottoman Empire. The stagnation and perceived "degeneration" of Islam generated what John Voll called a "spirit of socio-moral reconstruction," inspiring Muslim thinkers to reinvigorate the role of Islam in Muslim societies.[18] The period witnessed a fervent development of revivalist movements such as the Wahhābiyya, the appearance of millenarian Mahdist movements, the emergence of new Sufi brotherhoods, and the revival of the older orders.[19] On the frontiers of the Islamic world—as in many parts of Africa—the upsurge manifested itself in the missionary activities of Sufi brotherhoods, aiming at spreading Islam among non-Muslims and deepening Islamic practices and piety among those Muslim societies whom they perceived as morally and religiously adrift. This process resulted in the integration of frontier areas—such as the Eritrean region—more closely into the wider Islamic world and tied them to cross-regional, in some ways "global," Islamic networks.

In northeast Africa the Islamic revival was especially marked by the emergence of influential holy families and new Sufi orders and the revitalization of the older established orders.[20] The Qādiriyya had already attracted followers in the Eritrean area prior to the Sufi revival, especially in Massawa, where Qādirī Sufis erected a *mazār* (Ar., visitation shrine) in commemoration of ʿAbd al-Qādir al-Jīlānī.[21] In the nineteenth century groups such as the ʿAd Shaykh family revivified the Qādiriyya presence in the area and brought it further into the interior, especially to the northern and western lowland regions.[22] Other older orders such as the Shādhiliyya have also attracted some followers in Massawa, mainly among high-status families, many of whom had distant or more recent origins in the Arabian Peninsula.[23] Unsubstantiated evidence for the most part, which at this point does not establish dates of introduction or the extent of influence with any precision, also suggests that the Aḥmadiyya, Sammāniyya, Majdhūbiyya, and Tijāniyya had been introduced to some lowland and highland areas of Eritrea.[24] The most far-reaching and significant development in term of Sufi brotherhood presence and activity in the nineteenth century was the emergence of the Khatmiyya, the "seal of the orders," drawing its inspiration from the teachings of Aḥmad b. Idrīs (1749/50–1837).[25] Scholars such as O'Fahey and Radtke have argued that the new orders (often called "neo-Sufi" orders) were less innovative in terms of their intellectual dimension than in their new organizational features.[26] If prior to the eighteenth century most Sufi affiliations with the Qādiriyya and Shādhiliyya were lineage or family-based, the new orders tended to transcend lineage, "tribal," and social boundaries. They perceived themselves as organizations, were more hierarchical, and were often centered on the families of their founders.[27]

From the 1820s onward, Egyptian expansion into the Sudan and the revitalization of the commercial routes connecting the Red Sea and the Nile Valley both fueled and accompanied the spectacular process of Islamic diffusion among the largely Tigre-speaking societies of the lowland Eritrean region. The relationship between Egyptian imperialist expansion and the diffusion of Islam in the Horn of Africa in the mid to later decades of the nineteenth century is a subject worthy of more profound research. Ghada Hashim Talhami has interestingly noted the paradox between Khedive Ismāʿīl's westernizing and secularizing tendencies ("religion is a personal matter that concerns the individual alone"), on the one hand, and his shrewd and pragmatic employment of Islam in the service of the state in the context of Egypt's "civilizing mission" and imperialist agenda in northeast Africa, on the other.[28]

The political decentralization of the Ethiopian state during the period known as the *Zemene Mesefint* and the vulnerability of predominantly pastoralist societies on its northern fringes were also conducive to the success of the spread of Islam in the area. Northern Ethiopian Christian chiefs tended to raid these societies intermittently and persistently in attempting to extend their rule over them and exploit them economically. Conversion to Islam in this context vested these communities with a new identity and a powerful counter-hegemonic force and ideology, endowing them with a source of authority and political legitimacy. Several holy families played a pivotal role in the transmission and propagation of Islamic religious practice, law, and culture in the areas extending between the Red Sea and the Nile Valley during the period of Islamic revival. Their "holiness" usually derived from their claim to *sharīf* descent and from the possession of *baraka,* a heritable beneficent force of divine origin.[29] One of the most significant holy families to play a role in the history of Islam in the Eritrean area in the nineteenth century was the ʿAd Shaykh.

The ʿAd Shaykh Holy Family

Between the 1820s and 1860s the ʿAd Shaykh family was instrumental in converting all the Bet Asgede subgroups (Habab, ʿAd Tekles, and ʿAd Temaryam), the Mensaʿ, the Marya, the Bet Juk, and segments of the Bilin from various local forms of Christian practice to Islam. By the 1880s all lowland groups but the Kunama and part of the Bilin had adopted Islam. Tracing descent to *sharīf* Ḥusayn from Mecca, the ʿAd Shaykh family began gaining widespread influence in the Sahel region in the early nineteenth century, especially through the preaching and miracle working of Shaykh al-Amīn b. Ḥāmid b. Nafʿūtāy.[30] The ʿAd Shaykh operated in tandem with the Hergigo-based potent *nāʾib* family, to whom many of these societies were tributary. It also appears that it worked hard at initiating these groups into the Qādiriyya Sufi brotherhood. The ʿAd Shaykh attracted entire families of *tigre* vassals to join their ranks by undermining the master/serf structure of Tigre-speaking pastoralist and agro-pastoralist societies. Increased pressures on the more vulnerable Tigre class prompted by the ramifications of commercial transformation in the broader area might in part explain the success of this process. The unsettling of the prevailing social structure constituted a form of social revolution, culminating in the emancipation of the *tigre* serfs. It also posed a threat and a serious challenge to the traditional chiefs, such as in the case of the Beni ʿAmer.

In the course of time, the newly converted joined the holy family, which was rapidly enlarged, developing gradually into a widely influential and wealthy independent "tribe."[31] At some point the family split and

Figure 4.1. Annual *ziyāra* to ᶜAd Shaykh shrine in Emberemi, 2000. Photographer: author.

began to spread throughout the western, northern, and eastern regions of the Eritrean lowlands. Several of Shaykh al-Amīn b. Ḥāmid b. Nafᶜūtāy's sons settled in the ᶜAnseba and Barka valleys, while others stayed in the Sahel, and yet others emigrated to the north, as far as Tokar in the Sudan. This process broadened the family's influence and networks, and considerably increased its wealth. Shaykh al-Amīn's grandson, Shaykh Muḥammad b. ᶜAlī b. al-Amīn (b. Nakhra [?] ca. 1210/1795—d. Emberemi, 14 Ṣafar 1297/27 February 1877) moved to Hergigo, where he spent twelve years before moving and settling in Emberemi in about 1840, establishing there the Semhar branch of the ᶜAd Shaykh.[32] Shaykh Muḥammad gained such widespread reputation as a holy man (Ar. *walī*) possessed with *baraka* that in the early 1860s Guillaume Lejean described Emberemi as a pilgrimage site to which people from all over Semhar and Sahel came.

> Beraimi (Emberemi) has become a little Mecca. Muḥammad, today in his seventies, sends his two sons on propaganda tours in Semhar, Barka, Bet Juk and Bogos (Bilin). They cannot resist their preachings. There are no recently married couples in Massawa, or traders going to Gash who consider themselves safe against any type of ordeal without first going to Emberemi and asking for all sorts of prayers and talismans from the holy man.[33]

Shaykh Muḥammad b. ʿAlī b. al-Amīn of Emberemi was one of the more influential religious figures of the coastal region from the 1840s to his death in 1877. In the middle years of the 1860s Henry Blanc remarked that the Habab "were converted to Mohammedanism by an old Sheikh, still alive, who resides near Moncullou, and is an object of great veneration all over Semhar."[34] Shaykh Muḥammad b. ʿAlī b. al-Amīn was also successful in converting part of the Mensaʿ group. One source tells the suggestive story of Hasama Hishal, member of a leading Mensaʿ family, who was invited to Emberemi by the *shaykh,* who told him the following: "I have seen your seat awaiting you in Paradise, but you cannot gain it unless you embrace Islam. It is my duty to tell you what I know, but it is for you to take advantage of this opportunity or otherwise." Hasama Hishal, who was already old and eager to reserve his place in Heaven, converted shortly thereafter to Islam.[35] The *shaykh*'s association with the *nāʾib* family, the wealthy and powerful merchants of Massawa, and his good rapport with the Ottoman, and later the Egyptian administration, all contributed to his success, enabling him to tap into the prevailing regional networks.[36] Shortly following his death in 1877, a *qubba* was erected over his grave, with the financial assistance of the Egyptian administration in Massawa.[37] A yearly visitation (on 13 Ṣafar) to the tomb, drawing worshippers from throughout the Muslim-majority regions of Eritrea, developed shortly thereafter. As early as the 1880s Wylde remarked that Emberemi was "the burial place of an old sheikh who died many years ago, and whose tomb is greatly venerated, and at one time of the year many people visit it and bring offerings to the priest in charge."[38] Other European observers witnessed the atmosphere of religious transformation and the influence of Muslim holy men during this period. In the early 1860s Munzinger remarked that the recently converted nomadic communities adopted Islam in a superficial way. He wrote that Islam changed very little in their daily lives and that many of their "ancient Christian" customs remained intact. He also noted, with typical irony and moralistic bias, how superstitious phenomena were on the rise:

> There are here many *shaykhs* who perform miracles. They are able to cure the sick with two verses from the Qurʾān, chase away demons, and inflame the cold heart of a little girl. Naturally, in order for them to perform these miracles one has to pay them generously. There are women here who seem to get visitations from heaven from time to time. The evil spirits are abundant.[39]

Henry Blanc's sarcasm was even more blatant:

> The Bedouins of the Semhar, like all bigoted and ignorant savages, have great confidence in charms. The "medicine man" is generally an old, venerable-looking Sheikh—a great rascal, for all his sanctified looks. His most usual prescription is to write a few lines of the Koran upon a piece of parchment, wash off the ink with water, and hand it over to the patient to drink. At other times the writing is enclosed in small squares of red leather, and applied to the seat of the disease. The Mullah is no contemptible rival of his, and though he also applies the all-efficacious words of the revealed "cow," he effects more rapid cures by spitting several times upon the sick person, muttering between each ejection appropriate prayers which no evil spirit could withstand, should his already sanctified spittle not have been sufficient to cast them off.[40]

Slightly earlier, the Italian Catholic missionary Giuseppe Sapeto also described the spirit of the times, without withholding his personal views. Describing the activities of holy men among the Bilin, he noted:

> Islamic propaganda has put its hand on this work of sacrilege. Islam is making progress in all the villages and ruining the [Christian] faith. These men [the *faqīrs*, propagating Islam] . . . give amulets to the sick and are the source of moral disorder. They preach apostasy, promising Gennat (Paradise). The chief town of their mission is Keren, the meeting place of the traders from Gash and Massawa, from where they monopolize both commodities and souls (consciences).[41]

The Mīrghanī Family and the Khatmiyya ṭarīqa

Several intermittent missionary tours undertaken between about 1810 and probably some point in the late 1820s by the founder of the Khatmiyya *ṭarīqa,* Muḥammad ᶜUthmān al-Mīrghanī (1793/94–1852), propelled the influence of the order in the Eritrean region. Cursory evidence found in Sudanese Khatmi sources and an Italian colonial report written in the late 1920s suggest that Muḥammad ᶜUthmān conducted several tours in the Eritrean area, including several passages through Massawa on his way back to the Hijaz. Muḥammad ᶜUthmān's earliest contact with the Eritrean region occurred during a visit to a place referred to as Baqla, possibly the Rora Baqla located southwest of Nakfa, in ca. 1813. In the early to mid-1820s

Muḥammad ʿUthmān visited the western parts of modern Eritrea, where he met some success in initiating followers from among the Ḥalanqa, Sabderat, Algheden, Beni ʿAmer, Barya, and Marya (both branches) groups. He also toured the Semhar and Sahel regions.[42] The success of Khatmiyya influence in the Sudanese and Eritrean regions went hand in hand with the Turco-Egyptian occupation of the Sudan beginning in 1820. The Khatmiyya's broad-based organization was well adjusted to the new political order of the Turkiyya in the Sudan, contributing to its success.[43] The Khatmiyya's method of expansion was by the incorporation of preexisting religious formations (notables and holy lineages) into a supra-community brotherhood network.[44] In practice this was achieved by what the historian Knut Vikør called the "grafting" model, by which *khalīfa*s and *khalīfat al-khulafāʾ* were initiated, appointed, and linked into a broad-based transethnic and cross-regional organization covering a wide area.[45] *Ashrāf* descent and the possession of *baraka* were primordial factors in claiming holiness.[46]

The Khatmiyya relied on local *faqīh*s and religious leaders—who continued to perform their religious role locally—in order to link between commoners and the Sufi brotherhood. Explaining the success of such a flexible and assimilationist method in the Sudan, John Voll has noted that "there was no distinction drawn between the functions of the *faki* as a Khatmiyya *khalīfa* and his other local functions. It all soon came to be looked upon as the actions of a Khatmiyya representative. In this way many old forms and customs were incorporated in what came to be seen as Khatmiyya practice."[47] In stark contrast with the methods of the ʿAd Shaykh, communities coming under the influence of the supra-ethnic Khatmiyya were able to preserve their preexisting social and political structures, contributing a sense of stability and continuity. The intensification of Turco-Egyptian encroachments, especially following the conquest of Kassala in 1840, facilitated the entrenchment of the brotherhood in the eastern Sudanese and Eritrean region. Around the same year, Muḥammad al-Ḥasan al-Mīrghanī (1819–69), known also as al-Sayyid al-Ḥasan, and son of the founder of the Khatmiyya, had settled in al-Saniyya, at the foot of Kassala mountain, and established there the order's headquarters.[48] The Khatmiyya capitalized on the Turco-Egyptian imperialist drive in the region by maintaining a good relationship with its military-administrative organs, thereby extending the group's spheres of influence in territories coming under direct or indirect Turkiyya rule.[49] After Muḥammad ʿUthmān al-Mīrghanī's death in 1852 the Khatmiyya split into regional branches, each with its own *shaykh*. Sayyid al-Ḥasan became de facto the head and consolidator of the northern and eastern Sudan branches of the order. It was also under Sayyid al-Ḥasan's leadership that groups such as the Ḥalanqa and the Habab came under greater Khatmi influence. It was in this period that the Khatmiyya won the loyalty of the Habab ruling class.[50]

An important detail about the establishment of the Khatmiyya in the Massawa area requires some revision. There is still some confusion in the genealogy of the Mīrghaniyya family, at least in its eastern Sudanese and Eritrean branches. Most writers follow Trimingham's assertion that "the Mīrghaniyya was established in the Massawa district by Sayyid Hāshim al-Mīrghanī who first came there in 1860 when it was under Ottoman rule."[51] Secondary sources note that Hāshim actually settled in the port and made it his home.[52] However, on the basis of Italian colonial archival materials it appears that Hāshim settled in Massawa only in mid-April 1885, after fleeing from Kassala during the Mahdiyya together with his nephew Muḥammad ᶜUthmān b. Muḥammad Sirr al-Khatm (also known as Muḥammad ᶜUthmān Tājj al-Sirr, 1849/50–1903).[53] In the pre-Italian era Muḥammad ᶜUthmān b. Muḥammad Sirr al-Khatm interacted intensively with the eastern Eritrean region, especially with the Habab, among whom he lived in the 1860s, but also with Saho-speaking societies of the eastern highland escarpments in the 1870s. Of the Mīrghanī family members touring, visiting, and settling in the wider region between the Red Sea and the Nile Valley before 1885, Muḥammad ᶜUthmān Sirr al-Khatm's role was greatest in consolidating the Khatmiyya's influence and gaining adherence in Sahel, Semhar, and Akkele Guzay and in Massawa's burgeoning suburbs and satellite villages.[54]

In general, the Khatmiyya enjoyed great success among migrants to the conurbation, some of whom had been only recently converted as a result of the brotherhood's activities in the region. The newly converted preserved and developed their links with the Khatmiyya even after moving into the conurbation. The egalitarian flavor characteristic of many brotherhoods appealed greatly to recent converts and newcomers, eager to prove their piety and devotion, hoping thus to be better welcomed in a strong Muslim environment. The brotherhood's method of expansion by absorbing and integrating prevailing social structures was often tolerant of local practices, which were preserved by new adepts. Some scholars have labeled this type of syncretism as characteristic of "popular Islam." But following a brotherhood such as the Khatmiyya could also open the door to a wide web of networks that were useful not only in a spiritual sense but also in the very real material world of labor, commerce, and transportation, crucial to every newcomer in town.

A relatively important number of mosques in the outer neighborhoods and villages of the conurbation were associated in one way or another to the Khatmiyya. Such sites of confluence were privileged places of networking and weaving connections.[55] The success of the Khatmiyya among newcomers and "Massawans of the periphery" is also attested by several *khalīfa* appointments made by Sayyid Hāshim al-Mīrghanī in the Massawa area in the early years of the Italian period. Most were prominent figures of power, influence, and connections in the mainland neighborhoods and villages.[56] All in all, the two dominant religious formations in the Eritrean area, the ᶜAd Shaykh and the Khatmiyya, developed contrasting methods in spreading and reviving Islam among Tigre-, Saho-, and Bilin-speaking societies in the region.[57] In general, their activities were conducive to a veritable socioreligious revolution among societies coming under their influence. Some societies, such as the Marya, were at some point disrupted in the process—the *tigre* class having been converted by the ᶜAd Shaykh, which some subsequently joined, while part of the ruling/aristocratic class was converted by the Khatmiyya *shaykhs* and yet another part subsequently by the ᶜAd Shaykh.[58] All in all, on a regional level, the energetic *ṭuruq* and holy families fostered widespread spatial networks, or webs of connections, straddling the area between the Red Sea coasts and the inland regions in the eastern Sudan, with wider connections across the sea, on the one hand, and further west toward the Nile and beyond it, on the other.

Sorting Out Muslims: the Mahdist Revolution, Early Italian Colonial Rule, and Holy Families, 1880s–1900s

The advent of European imperialism, the success of the Mahdist movement in the Sudan and the responses of highland Habesha rulers to these new external challenges, especially in the 1880s, had far-reaching consequences for the history of Islam in the region.[59] Plowden's mid-century reference to the region's (Muslim) lowlanders, who as "flying-fish . . . are preyed on by all," could not be more true in the new complex configuration of international and regional struggles in the Massawa-Adwa-Kassala triangle. The host of powers involved—Abyssinians, Sudanese Mahdists, Egyptians, British, and Italians—all competed for influence over the Eritrean region's Muslim lowland ethnic groups, ultimately leading to the politicization of religion in the area and to deep internal divisions within these societies. An Italian observer went even further in evaluating Muslim lowlanders' lack of consistency and stability, adding a colonialist-minded twist to his observations. Referring to Eritrea's Muslim "tribes," Beniamino Melli wrote that "although each one [of these tribes] boasts legends about the glorious feats of their founders and ancestors, they have no history. Had it not been to the Italian occupation they would have been absorbed either by Ethiopian or Mahdist elements."[60]

Before continuing, a caveat is in order. It should be noted that the sections of this chapter dealing with the relationship between the Italian colonial authorities, the Khatmiyya, and the ᶜAd Shaykh are mostly based on Italian colonial archival sources. The "side" of the Sufi order and the holy clan is therefore either largely absent or represented by interested external sources. It is for this reason that the analytical angle taken is more significantly grounded in the shaping, development, and consequences of Italian policies and practice.

The Mahdist rebellion against the Egyptian administration in the Sudan was triggered by Muḥammad Aḥmad b. ᶜAbd Allāh's letters informing the notables of the Sudan of his *mahdi*ship in June 1881.[61] In the course of the following few years the Muslim groups inhabiting the region between Kassala and Massawa found themselves in a delicate situation, increasingly caught and divided in between pro-Mahdist and anti-Mahdist positions and loyalties. Mahdist pressure and influence over groups loyal to the *khedive* and to the anti-Mahdiyya Khatmiyya *ṭarīqa* proved effective, especially against the background of continuous northern Habesha encroachments, raids, and imposition of tribute payment on societies in these regions, in the context of Egyptian-Ethiopian struggles and trials of power in the 1870s and early 1880s.[62] Furthermore, Emperor Yohannes's nationalistic anti-Muslim policies politicized Christian-Muslim relations and increased the sense of alienation from the Christian polity. It directly contributed to the success of Mahdist propaganda and influence among these societies. Consequently, Anglo-Egyptian attempts at forming an anti-Mahdist Muslim front between Massawa and Kassala under the spiritual leadership of the Khatmiyya produced little results.[63] It seems that dominant elements of the ᶜAd Shaykh holy family took a pro-Mahdist stance, sided with ᶜUthmān Diqna's envoys, and perhaps even took on a leadership role in rallying pro-Mahdist support among the Tigre-speaking groups in the area. After the fall of Kassala to the Mahdists in late July 1885, these struggles continued, often through propaganda. Ethiopian victory at the battle of Kufit (23 September 1885) put an end to Mahdist aspirations to conquer the coastal zone north of and around Massawa, but the loyalties of the lowland groups still oscillated between the Mahdi and the *khedive.* The sudden appearance of a new force in the arena—imperialist Italy—spelt both continuity and change, at least in the short term.

European imperialism articulated by Italian colonial imposition and the creation of the politically defined territory of "Eritrea" in 1890 played a critical role in shaping the history of Islam in the region. On a broad level it confined societies that were different in terms of language, mode of production, social structure, culture, and, last but not least, religion within limited boundaries extending over the lowlands and the northern tip of the Eritrean highlands. The Muslims, comprising approximately 60 percent of the population in the early colonial period, inhabited about four-fifths of the territory, mostly in the lowlands, while the Tigrinya-speaking Christians, constituting 40 percent of the inhabitants, lived on one-fifth of the colony, exclusively on the highland plateau. Italian colonialism formed the infrastructure within which a diverse grouping of Muslim societies would gradually develop a set of shared experiences (and institutions) as Muslims in colonial Eritrea. This process was shaped by Italian attitudes toward Islam and by the incorporation of Muslims into an entity almost evenly divided between Muslims and Christians.

Italian colonial attitudes toward Islam did not amount to a clear, linear, and coherent set of policies; they were shaped throughout the period by a host of factors, both internal and external to the colony proper. Chronologically we can distinguish roughly three phases: a period characterized by the politics of conquest, the response to the Mahdist threat, and Governor Martini's "Muslim policies" (1885–ca. 1910); the phase following the conquest of Libya and the elaboration of Italy's attitudes toward Islam (1910s–20s); and the period of overt pro-Muslim policies under the fascists and the more pronounced articulation of Italy as a "Muslim power" (1920s–1941). At the outset of their occupation of Massawa in 1885, the Italian colonial authorities proclaimed that the customs and religion of the town's inhabitants would be "scrupulously respected."[64] But early policies went even beyond the mere "respect" of Islam. The authorities continued, as the Egyptians did beforehand, to grant subventions to mosques and monthly stipends to Muslim community leaders and granted the *sharīʿa* court autonomy in matters of personal status, family, and inheritance. In some contradiction with the official liberal policy of equally respecting all religions in the colony, urban Muslims and their institutions in Massawa were privileged by the authorities, at least in the first two decades of colonial rule.[65] The inhabitants of Massawa and its region were perceived by colonial officials as the most "evolved," "civilized," and "westernized" among the societies of the colony.[66]

The foundations of early Italian colonial attitudes were shaped by the need to maintain stability among the "tribes" and, inseparably, by the need to respond to the divided Mahdist and anti-Mahdist loyalties of the Khatmiyya and the ʿAd Shaykh. The Italian authorities were deeply concerned by the spilling over of the Mahdist rebellion from the Sudan into the colony and feared the destabilization of their control over occupied territories. In the lowland regions, the politics of conquest and "pacification" sought the cooperation of responsive elements in assisting the authorities to control and secure the stability of their conquered territories and mobilize local forces against the Mahdists and their supporters within the colony and on its borders.[67] The Beni ʿAmer, under the influence of the Khatmi *shaykh* in Kassala, fought the Mahdist coalition in the eastern Sudan with zeal in 1884.[68] In contrast, sections of the Habab, possibly under the influence of the ʿAd Shaykh, displayed pro-Mahdist tendencies and collaborated with the eastern Sudanese Mahdist leader, ʿUthmān Diqna.[69] The Italians therefore developed a relationship with the anti-Mahdist Khatmiyya Sufi order, to the detriment of the ʿAd Shaykh holy family, who was believed to take an active pro-Mahdist stance and therefore constituted a destabilizing element in the region.

The Italian authorities persuaded Sayyid Hāshim al-Mīrghanī to stay in Massawa—where he had arrived several months earlier in 1885—and assist them. They paid him a monthly stipend and offered him the post of *muftī* of Massawa, which he declined.[70] Sayyid Hāshim attempted to "milk" the administration as much as he could, while the Italians in turn were determined to maximize their profits from the collaboration. The colonial authorities expected Sayyid Hāshim to exercise his influence over the lowland Muslim "tribes" and also provide intelligence on the Mahdists and the Ethiopians gathered through Khatmi networks. To little avail: relations often turned sour, mutual accusations followed, and governors were often frustrated with what they perceived as Sayyid Hāshim's unresponsiveness.[71]

Distinguishing the Khatmiyya, Demoting the ʿAd Shaykh: Martini's "Islamic Practice"

The energetic and able governor of Eritrea, Ferdinando Martini (gov. 1897–1907), elaborated the strategy coopting the Khatmiyya. In 1898 he exerted considerable pressure on Sayyid Hāshim, attempting to convince him to transfer his seat from Massawa to Keren, where his authority over Eritrea's Muslim lowlanders would, it was hoped, deflect Kassala's influence from beyond the colony's borders. The return of Khatmi leaders to Kassala following the fall of the Mahdist state in the same year created a problem with "tribes," notably groups of the Beni ʿAmer, who sought to follow them into the Sudan. Nevertheless, Martini's pressure on Sayyid Hāshim bore no fruits.[72] In one entry in his copious diary, Martini's strategy is clearly revealed:

> If this Morgani [Mīrghanī] from Massawa came to Keren it would be of great service to us. But he refuses. The British in Kassala have there his nephew Sidi ʿAlī, who is greatly venerated. It is important to help in any way in the construction of a mosque in Keren. I will give another 1000 thalers and more if needed. Another more modest one should be built in Dega or in Agordat.[73]

Sayyid Hāshim died in 1901, and the authorities sought calculatingly to transport his remains to Keren, where they promised to build a shrine in his honor. This initiative was met with vigorous opposition by the Muslim community in Massawa and was eventually abandoned.[74] However, with the critical assistance of ʿAlī Yaḥyā Afandī from Massawa and the *nāʾib* of Emkullo, the colonial authorities were more successful with his nephew's son, Sayyid Jaʿfar b. Bakrī b. Jaʿfar b. Muḥammad ʿUthmān al-Mīrghanī (1871–1943).[75] Sayyid Jaʿfar was discreetly persuaded to move into the colony from Kassala and establish his seat in Keren in 1903.[76] Consequently, the colonial administration financed the construction of the tomb of Hāshim al-Mīrghanī in Hetumlo and a mosque in Keren.[77] All in all, Martini's workings were conducive to the formation of an Islamic sphere within the confines of the colony by mobilizing a large number of Muslims around an "official" representative of the Khatmiyya branch in Eritrea—a process that was to ultimately benefit both parties.

The cooption of the Khatmiyya was accompanied by a virulent campaign of discrediting and denigrating of the ʿAd Shaykh. Governor Martini worked at undermining the legitimacy and influence of what colonial officials perceived as the "tribalizing" and "exploitative" ʿAd Shaykh. Colonial officials were highly suspicious of the expanding "tribe," believed to sympathize with the Mahdists and perceived as a dangerous and potentially destabilizing element among lowland Muslims. Governor Martini

Figure 4.2. Sayyid Jaʿfar al-Mīrghanī and the *khalīfas*, ca. 1920s. Private collection, Pavoni Social Centre, Asmara.

did not make secret his wish that once the Khatmis set their stronghold in Keren they would be able to fight off the "potentially preoccupying" influence of the ʿAd Shaykh and maintain the integrity of the tribes in a period of upheaval and instability.[78] Comments he inscribed in his diary in 1902 stated bluntly and clearly his mindset and the operational conclusions to be drawn:

> The ʿAd Shaykh, a tribe of holy men who came to Sahel from Jiddah, or in any case from Arabia, and which has grown in roughly six generations to more than 2000 people, exercises great religious authority over both the Habab and the Beni ʿAmer. With time, this influence (I mean to say in roughly ten–twenty years), might become dangerous, in the context of a general upsurge of Islamism, especially if the chief of the ʿAd Shaykh is as fanatical and scheming as the current chief, Shaykh ʿĀmir, but less timid than he is.
>
> It is necessary to contrast this religious authority with another one of equal or greater influence. Of the many Morgani [*sic*] [Mīrghanī] who live in Africa we need to find one who will come

> and settle in Keren. As for the dead Morgani [Sayyid Hāshim b. Muḥammad ʿUthmān al-Mīrghanī, d. 1901], I accepted the wishes of the Muslim community of Massawa. I agreed to the inhumation in Hetumlo and to cover the expenses of the construction of the shrine. But Hetumlo is too far away, and in this case one must act energetically, even though the religious authority of the Morgani is superior to that of the ʿAd Shaykh. I am thinking of Jaʿfar Morgani [Sayyid Jaʿfar b. Bakrī b. Jaʿfar b. Muḥammad ʿUthmān al-Mīrghanī], son of Sidi Abū Bakr al-Mīrghanī who passed away in Mecca. Now he lives in Kassala. I am told that ʿAbd Allāh Sharīf of the Sabderat and *nāʾib* Idrīs of Emkullo have great ascendancy over him.[79]

The question of tribute exemption was also at the heart of the relentless criticism and accusations of conspiracy and "fanaticism" pointed at the ʿAd Shaykh. Italian colonial officials doubted their gratuitous piety. They believed, as they wrote, that "their enterprise was not only limited to religious propaganda but principally aimed at cultivating their political authority, and attaining an economic position at the expense of the tribes, stripping them from their human capital and their riches."[80] In this context colonial officials employed freely terms such as "subversion" and "plundering" in demonizing the methods and effects of the ʿAd Shaykh over the societies that came under their influence. They described the process of the extension of ʿAd Shaykh influence over the Tigre-vassal classes, expressing their deep concerns as to the breakdown of preexisting social structures, leading to "disorderly" migrations within the colony, the splitting of entire groups, and general instability. Accordingly, the colonial authorities—under Governor Martini—devised a number of measures aimed at curtailing ʿAd Shaykh influence and authority. Their traditional exemption from tribute was ended in 1904–1905. In addition, Martini deliberately severed the group, placing the Barka and Sahel/Semhar branches under distinct *commissariati* (1903). He also mustered all the dispersed elements of the family inhabiting Sahel and ʿAnseba into one group under one chief. In that way Khatmiyya influence was bound to be more effective.[81] Anti–ʿAd Shaykh colonial measures seem to have achieved their goals; the settlement of Sayyid Jaʿfar in Keren accelerated even further the decline of ʿAd Shaykh political and religious influence.[82]

All in all, policies setting apart "useful" and "potentially dangerous" Muslim elements in the colony consolidated the Khatmiyya's influence and enhanced the decline of the ʿAd Shaykh. Indeed, in the 1920s the latter

Figure 4.3. Sharīfa ʿAlawiyya Hāshim al-Mīrghanī and her entourage, ca. 1920s. Private collection, Pavoni Social Centre, Asmara.

exercised but very little authority, limited mainly to the Habab. But there too, the influence of the Khatmiyya had already spread significantly and was still making progress in the 1920s.[83] By that period the ʿAd Temaryam were under greater Khatmi than ʿAd Shaykh influence; the ʿAd Tekles were all initiated to the Khatmiyya; and the Marya too had changed their allegiance from the ʿAd Shaykh and Qādiriyya to the Khatmiyya.[84] During the 1900s and 1910s the Khatmiyya became increasingly ingrained in the colony, and its status was further formalized. In the early years of the twentieth century, the *qāḍī* of Massawa was appointed by the government and was then immediately appointed as *khalīfat al-khulafāʾ* by the head of the Khatmiyya in the colony.

Navigating Massawa's Sacred Spaces: Islam and Communal Identity

Moving from the regional to a more urban-centered perspective: piety and a strong attachment to Islamic history and culture have always been central markers in articulating Massawans' sense of citizenship. Islam has represented a defining marker and a basis for ethics for Massawans' sense of their place in the world. The proximity and historical contact with the sacred heartlands of Islam in the Hijaz, and the centuries-long participation within Muslim political, commercial, and religious networks and circuits in the Red Sea and northwestern Indian Ocean regions, have shaped this disposition. Massawans have always felt a sense of belonging to their town and perceived it as the home of an ideal and morally superior Muslim community, modeled on the concept of *umma,* or the virtuous community of Muslims. According to the Qurʾān the Muslim community *is* Islam: "Ye are the best community that hath been raised up for mankind. Ye enjoin right conduct and forbid indecency; and ye believe in Allāh" (Q. 3:110). The community of Muslims is expected to follow the Qurʾānic prescriptions that codify for individual and society how to be Muslim and the ways to lead a proper Muslim life. The social and collective character of some of the sacred pillars and duties of Islam—common prayer on Fridays, almsgiving (*zakāt*), fasting during the month of Ramaḍān (*ṣawm*), the pilgrimage to Mecca (*ḥājj*), are all pivotal in defining and maintaining the sense of sacred community.[85]

In Massawa, mosques and open-air prayer esplanades, saints' tombs (Ar. sing. *ḍarīḥ*) and sites of yearly visitations (*mazār*) and celebrations (*ḥawliyya*), as well as other locally distinct religious ceremonies and rituals, articulated the notion of the town as a sacred space. As in other settings, there were, however, sometimes gaps between ideal concepts of the Muslim community and the social, cultural, and religious realities on the ground. The coexistence of so-called orthodox Islamic practice with localized traditional or popular religious practices and rituals translated into tensions, struggles, and ultimately some accommodation in the process of defining the Muslim community. In that context, historian of East African "Swahili Islam" Randall Pouwels, referred to the "split personality" of coastal town Islam.[86] In Massawa in the second half of the nineteenth century, the meeting of pious *sādah* and *ashrāf* from the Arabian Peninsula with recently converted Tigre-speaking peoples or other inland Muslims, who were accommodating Islam with local cultural practices, created such tensions and struggles.

As suggested by the story of the *muftī* of Massawa earlier in this chapter, the association of the episode of the *hijra al-ūla* with the port-town was a highly symbolic determinant in arguing for the profoundly sacred nature of Massawa Island. The physical materialization of this tradition was institutionalized in the open-air esplanade mosque called Ras Medr, which some still believe to be the original landing place of the Prophet's companions, and which serves as the site of important religious celebrations and community-wide praying sessions to this day.[87] Of equal if not greater importance, Massawa's physical sacredness emanated largely from its particular geography as a small-scale island providing all life-cycle necessities to the community that inhabited it, including—most importantly—burial grounds. The burial of family members in the courts of family mosques, or other mosques associated with the family, contributed in an important way to the notion of Massawa as a sacred island. This was at least the case until Massawa was more closely attached with the mainland in the second half of the nineteenth century, leading to the establishment of a new cemetery on the mainland. The significance of the well-known mid-nineteenth-century European observation that "half the island belonged to the dead, and the other half to the living" went beyond the mere question of Massawa's urban spatial layout—it inadvertently implied the sacred nature of the port-town as a physical space.

Visitations to Saints' Tombs and Shrines

As common in other settings in the Muslim world, a number of tombs and shrines stood as focal points of Muslim life in Massawa's urban landscape. The veneration of holy men was expressed in periodical (often annual) visitation ceremonies to their tombs and shrines. Holy men's tombs appealed to people since it was common belief that the soul of a saint lingered around the tomb and that the saint's *baraka*—even after death—had the power to aid people seeking saintly intervention through prayers, the performing of rituals, and offerings.[88] Interestingly, as in the case of stories of origin, foundation, and primacy, holy men in Massawa too are situated within a dichotomic logic with those whose origins lay across the sea and those originally from the land. The importance of holy religious figures to urban semiotics was also reflected in the local toponymy. For example, the ᶜAbd al-Qādir peninsula was named after the *mazār* erected in commemoration of ᶜAbd al-Qādir al-Jīlānī (1077–1166), founder of the Qādiriyya *ṭarīqa*. In the past, it was the site of the yearly *ziyārat al-Jīlānī*, performed on 11 Rabīᶜ awwal and attracting worshippers from Massawa and its burgeoning mainland areas. The shrine was usually administered by the ᶜAd Shaykh family of Emberemi, but also by other Qādirīs from Massawa, such as members of the Abū ᶜIlāmā family (e.g., Abū Ḥāmid Abū ᶜIlāmā).[89] The small island called Shaykh Saᶜīd, known today as "Green Island," referred to the local mosque named after Shaykh Saᶜīd b. ᶜĪsā al-ᶜAmūdī

(d. 1272 in Wādī Dawʿan), a Sufi saint of the Hadrami *mashāʾikh* stratum, who was especially venerated by local fishermen, or the *ahl al-samak*, the "fish people," as my informant put it.[90]

The most notable *ḍarīḥ* on Massawa Island was that of Shaykh Ḥammāl ʿUmar b. Ṣādiq al-Anṣārī who, according to the inscription on his tomb, had died at the beginning of the tenth century of the Muslim calendar (ca. AD 1500). The plate notes that a new *tābūt* (Ar., coffin), prepared in Zabīd in Yemen, was placed on 7 Jumāda I 1010 (2 November 1601).[91] The first mention of the mosque in literary sources is made by the famous seventeenth-century Ottoman traveler Evliya Çelebi, who mentioned the existence of a certain tomb and mosque of Shaykh Gemali [*sic*].[92] According to the text on the plate reproduced by Ibrāhīm al-Mukhtār, almost three centuries later, the tomb was renovated and enlarged in 1878 under Muḥammad ʿIzzat, *wakīl* of the Egyptian Governorate of Massawa.[93] The Shaykh Ḥammāli religious complex consists of the mausoleum of the *shaykh* and a mosque consisting of a prayer room and an external covered prayer area.[94] Little is known about the identity of Shaykh Ḥammālī. Dante Odorizzi noted that he was born in Ḥudayda in Yemen and was considered the "protector" of Massawa after he settled in the port-town. The Italian *commissario* of Massawa further noted that he was buried in Massawa in ca. 1550.[95]

Another notable tomb is that of Shaykh Muḥammad Darwīsh b. Ibrāhīm b. Jaʿfar b. Ḥasan b. Barakāt, who was identified either as a *shaykh* of the ʿAd Darwīsh family from Hergigo or as the ancestor of a certain *sharīf* named al-Bāqir, from the same coastal village.[96] According to Ibrāhīm al-Mukhtār, Shaykh Muḥammad Darwīsh had also died in the tenth century after the *hijra*. He was at first buried in Ras Medr, where the Italians found and excavated several other *maqāms* in 1900. Some, like the Shaykh Darwīsh tomb, were transferred to more convenient sites in the proximity of newer residential neighborhoods. The other tombs and commemorating shrines found in Ras Medr, about which little is known, were Jaʿfar al-Ṭayyār, *maqām* ʿIkāsha (?), *maqām* Shaykh Abū Bakr *al-Sihāwī* ("The Saho"), *maqām* Shaykh Ḥāmid, and *maqām* al-Najāshī. This last shrine was of great importance in the context of the *ṣaḥāba* story, since according to Islamic tradition al-Najāshī was the Ethiopian emperor who had allegedly converted to Islam following his contact with the exiled companions of the Prophet. It is not clear when the visitation of the *mazār* had begun, but the *ziyārat al-Najāshī* used to take place on a yearly basis on 10 Muḥarram.[97] Evidence also suggests that a visitation to the tomb of a certain

Figure 4.4. Shaykh Ḥammāl mosque in Massawa, 2000. Photographer: Author.

Shaykh Aḥmad al-Najāsh (d. 1872), a Jeberti holy man, was performed in Hetumlo on the first day of the Muslim New Year.[98] It was performed together with the visitation to the tomb of Shaykh Muḥammad ʿUthmān b. Muḥammad ʿAlī, son of the great ʿAd Shaykh holy man of Emberemi, who had died in Hetumlo some two decades following his father, in 1898.[99] Both shrines still stand in Hetumlo. In 1877 and in about 1902–1903, coastal Muslims erected two important shrines in Emberemi (ʿAd Shaykh) and Hetumlo (Khatmiyya), around which widespread regional pilgrimages and commemorative ceremonies developed rapidly. While the ʿAd Shaykh shrine is referred to earlier in this chapter, the *ḥawliyya* at the shrine of Sayyid Hāshim al-Mīrghanī in Hetumlo (2 Jumāda II) developed following his death in 1901, attracting an even more wide-ranging following both locally and from the broader region.

Local and regional pilgrimages were significant in at least two respects. From a local perspective, tomb visitations were crucial religious and cultural markers contributing to the development and preservation of a sense of Muslim community and identity among Massawa's Muslims. At some point in time, both shrines, as well as others, came to attract *all* Muslim Massawans regardless of particular sectarian affiliations. The "communalization" of originally sectarian visitation sites contributed to create a sense of unified community in Massawa, reminiscent of the function of the *ḥājj* in relation to the Muslim *umma* at large.[100] The same process was true of *ṭarīqa* affiliation in Massawa. Oral evidence clearly points to the flexibility and fluidity of Sufi affiliation, conditioned more by local social and, without a doubt, political determinants than on the basis of variations in Sufi doctrine and practice. People switched membership, mostly between the Qādiriyya, Khatmiyya, Shādhiliyya, and Aḥmadiyya orders, in several directions. Sometimes members of the same family belonged to different orders. On the basis of oral data, quite a few Massawan notables and leading citizens had switched from the Qādiriyya to the Khatmiyya as the latter *ṭarīqa* became dominant, and especially since the late nineteenth century, when it was closely associated with the Italian authorities.[101] Visitation sites also contributed to the cementing of Massawa's role and status as a religious center radiating throughout the broader region, epitomizing urban coastal dominance over inland Tigre- and Saho-speaking Muslims. From a more regional perspective, pilgrimage sites in Massawa were instrumental in creating spaces of religious and social confluence over a large area in the Eritrean region, bringing together Muslims from Sahel, Akkele Guzay, Semhar, Hamasen, and other both highland and lowland regions. In the twentieth century these circuits were important in developing and crystallizing a sense of *imagined* "Eritrean Muslim-ness."[102]

Coral Stone and Straw Hut Mosques

As the home of a Muslim community and a notable Muslim urban center, Massawa has always had several Friday mosques (Ar. sing. *jāmiᶜ*), smaller sectarian or neighborhood mosques, and private family mosques and praying rooms. All were essential focal points of Muslim communal life in town. People gathered in mosques essentially for prayer and other religious rituals, but mosques were also places where family, social, and business relationships were tied and cultivated. Some mosques also served as Qur'ānic schools where children were educated. Their open-air courts sometimes served as meeting sites for the performance of Sufi ceremonies.[103] The religious edifices seen by Evliya Çelebi in 1673 were six *zaviye* (Tur.; in Ar. *zāwiya,* usually Sufi lodge, but can also signify small minaret-less mosques used during the week), the *oratorio* of Qara Dey, and the mosque of Shaykh Gemali [*sic*].[104]

In the mid-1830s the two French Saint-Simonian envoys, Combes and Tamisier, counted four mosques in Massawa; Rüppell counted five. Significant growth of the number of religious edifices began in mid-century, through the Egyptian and early Italian colonial period. Already in the early 1860s Lejean had counted about twelve religious edifices on Massawa Island, probably including tombs and shrines.[105] In 1885 Pennazzi counted about a dozen mosques and De Robilant identified three main mosques (Ar. sing. *jāmiᶜ*) and ten secondary mosques on Massawa Island.[106] By 1910 Odorizzi had counted sixteen mosques in Massawa, including the islet of Shaykh Saᶜīd and ᶜAbd al-Qādir peninsula. In Hergigo he counted twenty-six mosques, in Hetumlo seventeen, in Emkullo five—a total of sixty-four mosques excluding, Emberemi.[107] This impressive number of mosques for a total population that rarely exceeded 20,000 is mainly explained by urban growth. Some merchant-entrepreneurs had attained a degree of prosperity by the early decades of the twentieth century, which enabled them to fund and endow property for the benefit of Islamic institutions and causes such as mosques, religious schools, and the town cemetery. The Egyptian building drive in the 1860s and 1870s, the renovation of older "Turkish"-era mosques and shrines, and their funding of mosque administrations unquestionably also explain the reinvigoration of the town's religious edifices and institutions.

As with other crucial questions about the foundation and early history of the port-town, we possess limited information pertaining to the history of its mosques. This is so at least until some construction, reconstruction, and renovation of buildings—including mosques—occurred in the second half of the sixteenth century, following the establishment of Ottoman power.[108] Since some old mosques have been totally reconstructed from their foundation—and most often newly styled by the constructors or renovators—it is difficult to learn much from deconstructing their architectural features and design. Oral traditions collected by Odorizzi in the early twentieth century do not appear reliable in terms of dating. According to some of these the Ḥanafī and Shāfiᶜī mosques were the oldest, dating eight hundred years back from 1910.[109] But through the gathering of oral data it appears that the Shāfiᶜī mosque was older than the Ḥanafī, and in essence the oldest in Massawa. This seems plausible since pre-Ottoman Islamic influences on the Eritrean coast originated in the Yemeni region of the southern Arabian Peninsula—an area in which the Shāfiʿī legal rite is by large the predominant *madhhab.*[110]

At the present state of our knowledge it is impossible to trace with any accuracy or certainty the early diffusion of the Islamic legal schools from the Arabian Peninsula to the Eritrean coasts. Several secondary sources seem to suggest that the Ḥanafī *madhhab* was the first to make its mark in the region, yet other evidence might point to early Shāfiʿī influence in Massawa. A more accurate picture pertaining to the development and history of the legal schools in the Yemen might prove crucial in illuminating early influences on the Eritrean coasts.[111] This question might or might not be crucial in determining which of the two mosques was the oldest in town. Nonetheless, the Ḥanafī school, which was either introduced or reinforced by the Ottomans in the sixteenth century, unquestionably endowed the Ḥanafī Friday mosque with greater importance on the local scene. The Ḥanafī mosque provides an excellent example of the multi-layered development resulting from several waves of building and renovation drives. According to information collected by Ibrāhīm al-Mukhtār in 1953, the Ḥanafī mosque was first constructed in the tenth century after the *hijra.* According to some, the Ottoman government built it following the conquest of Massawa in 1557.[112] In the following centuries the mosque had been renovated several times, most importantly under the Egyptians (1865–85) during their extensive enterprises of construction and renovation of the town and its edifices. In 1901 the mosque was partly renovated under the Italians—partly explaining its exceptional resistance to the great 1921 earthquake that destroyed most of old Massawa's houses. In 1948, in the period under the British Administration in Eritrea, it was again renovated, and an adjacent open esplanade was regularized for prayer on hot days. In the early period of Eritrea's federation with Ethiopia, in early 1953, Haile Sellassie's manipulative attempts to coopt Muslim leaders throughout the territory led him to propose financing the renovation and enlargement of the Ḥanafī mosque, an initiative that stirred some controversy among Massawa's Muslim community leaders.[113]

In addition to the three Friday mosques on Massawa Island (Shaykh Ḥammāl, the Ḥanafī, and the Shāfiʿī), there were other Friday mosques and smaller mosques and praying rooms throughout the conurbation. Commercial growth and prosperity in the second half of the nineteenth century translated into the growing construction of private houses and public edifices, including mosques. The Egyptian (1865–85) and early Italian (from 1885 to 1900s) periods were characterized by intensive urban expansion and construction. Entrepreneurs built new mosques to accommodate the growing number of people living in the mainland elements of the conurbation, in Hergigo, Hetumlo, Amatere, and ᶜEdaga Beᶜray, while others were renovated and expanded to adjust to the town's changing needs. Some lived on the mainland and came to work in the port and bazaar area on a daily basis, making extra praying spaces on the port island a practical necessity. The Egyptian administration had built or supported financially the construction of mosques and other religious edifices such as schools and shrines in the 1870s.[114] The historian Marongiu-Buonaiuti noted that the early Italian colonial administration continued—as the Egyptians had done before—to support Muslim institutions in Massawa, granting them various subventions and contributing generously to the construction of new ones.[115] Mosque lists dating to the Italian colonial period also identify the association or affiliation of mosques with specific legal rites (Ar. *madhhab*) or Sufi brotherhoods. As noted above, in Massawa Island there was one Ḥanafī and one Shāfiᶜī Friday mosque. But there were other ones undoubtedly following Ḥanafī rites (Ḥusayn Bāsha, Mīrghanī), one that we know of following the Mālikī rite (Shaykh Ḥāmid ᶜĀbid),[116] and possibly several other Shāfiᶜī affiliations of mosques named after Yemeni holy men (Saᶜīd al-ᶜAmūdī, ᶜAbd Allāh Saᶜad al-Yāfiᶜī, and others).

As suggested earlier, the question of *madhhab* affiliation in Massawa is one that deserves further research. The coexistence of followers of several *madhhabs* in town might have been the source of tensions in the community. The Ḥanafī *madhhab* was predominant since it was possibly introduced by the Ottomans and followed by the Egyptians and the Khatmiyya *ṭarīqa*. However, a great majority of migrants who settled in Massawa in the nineteenth century were from the Hadrami region, and most of them followed the Shāfiᶜī *madhhab*. Moreover, the re-dynamization of exchanges between Massawa and the Sudanese region brought to the port followers of the Mālikī legal school, some of whom settled on the coast more durably.

An incident that epitomizes the results of such tensions occurred in the 1880s in Hetumlo, where a group of prominent merchants and notables, followers of the Shāfiᶜī *madhhab* and the Shādhilī *ṭarīqa*, promoted the initiative to begin conducting Friday prayers in Hetumlo instead of going to the congregation mosques on Massawa Island as had been the custom up to then. This event might reflect a Hadrami missionary drive geared toward the diffusion and consolidation of the Shāfiᶜī *madhhab* in localities across the Indian Ocean.[117] ᶜAbd Allāh Bā Junayd, a Massawa merchant of Hadrami origins and a patron of the Muslim community who was also the head of the *waqf* committee in 1882, led the Hetumlo merchants' initiative.[118] But since the Shāfiᶜīs and Shādhilīs were in a minority in Hetumlo, it appears that their project met significant resistance. While Ibrāhīm al-Mukhtār's account of the incident (in his words *fitna*,. Ar., discord in the Islamic community) reveals nothing about the identity of the opponents, it may well be the case that opposition was expressed by the majority—Ḥanafīs and Khatmīs—who thought that a Friday mosque should not be sectarian-oriented, definitely not by a minority, be it as dominant as it may be. Bā Junayd was able to "pull strings" and have a *firman* (decree) from the Ottoman Sultan issued, authorizing Friday prayers in Hetumlo. Consequently, the opposition party was determined to take its revenge on Bā Junayd; they were successful in bringing the matter to the administration, accusing him of having supplied the Ethiopians with weapons in their conflict with the government in Massawa. As a result, Bā Junayd was expelled from Massawa and left for Jiddah, where other members of his family operated as merchants and shippers.[119] The date when the expulsion took place is unclear; Ibrāhīm al-Mukhtār noted 1887, yet other sources refer to Bā Junayd as present in Massawa until the late 1890s. Bā Junayd left behind him a great deal of real estate and endowed properties. A note written by Muftī ᶜAbd Allāh Sirāj Abū ᶜIlāmā was added to all recordings of properties bought by ᶜAbd Allāh Bā Junayd, certifying that all his property was now transferred to Muḥammad Sālim Bā Ṭūq. It might well be the case that Bā Ṭūq continued to administer Bā Junayd's real estate, sending him the profits across the sea.[120]

Mosques associated with Sufi brotherhoods were also common in the Massawa area. In the early twentieth century most mosques in this category were linked to the Khatmiyya: one in Massawa Island, three in Hergigo, two in Emkullo, and two in Hetumlo, giving a total of eight mosques named after various members of the Mīrghanī family. According to an 1885 map of Massawa, the Shaykh Muḥammad ᶜUthmān al-Mīrghanī mosque (known "*masjid* as al-Mīrghanī") on Massawa Island was the third mosque to have a minaret, pointing to its considerable importance in the contemporary pious landscape.[121] There was also a Shādhilī mosque in Hergigo, a Shādhilī Friday mosque in Hetumlo, and several Qādirī-associated mosques throughout the conurbation. In the Italian period, Sayyid Jaᶜfar Saᶜīd al-Nātī, who had spent a decade in Medina and Zabīd before returning to Massawa, introduced the Aḥmadiyya order and established a *zāwiya* and a mosque in Amatere in Massawa's suburbs. A yearly visitation commemorating Sayyid Aḥmad b. Idrīs was performed there on the 22nd of *Rajab*.[122] Some prominent Massawa families enjoying high religious status had their own small mosques, usually attached to a house or a group of houses, where members of the family and others prayed during weekdays and where ancestors were sometimes buried in an adjacent court.[123]

The configuration of mosques in Massawa also reflected the spectacular success of the Sufi brotherhoods in the mainland elements of the conurbation, where large groups of Saho- and Tigre-speaking laborers, peddlers, and brokers had settled since mid-century. Hergigo, for example, had many mosques associated with local holy men, families, and lineages, such as those founded by or named after Sayyid Dirhāwī, Bayt Zubayr, Shaykh Muḥammad Jābir, Bayt Shaykh Maḥmūd, Shaykh Muḥammad Ḥāmid Minifīrāwī, and others. In Emkullo one mosque was named after Nāʾib Idrīs ʿUthmān. In Hetumlo important elite families involved in commerce, brokerage, and transportation services, such as Shalāl, Mentāy, Ṣāʾigh, and Shaykh Adam Barkūy, had mosques where their religious capital could be pivotal in establishing patronage (patron-client) networks with producers, brokers, and service providers from, or connected to, the interior. In Hetumlo we also find two ʿAd Darqī mosques, associated with the ʿAd Darqī holy clan, whose function it was to provide religious services to the Habab. The existence of two ʿAd Darqī mosques reflects the important presence of the Habab in Massawa's mainland, where they were active in brokerage and trade throughout this period.

Verses and Houses: Urban Space and Islamic Identity

A feature that particularly catches the eye in Massawa's streets—even by visitors today—are the Arabic inscriptions, carved in wood or in stone, decorating numerous door lintels or the lower parts of stone door-hoods of local houses and buildings.[124] One strolls through the streets and narrow alleys of the port-town, moving from one house to another, from door to door, constantly exposed to the powerful visual symbolism of the sacred script. Calligraphy and inscriptions are used extensively in Islamic art, architecture, and design throughout the Muslim world. In many cases, calligraphic designs transmit a powerful message that goes beyond the meaning of the inscription—the calligraphic design, or lettering, rather, is experienced as the message itself. Inscriptions in Arabic, the sacred language of the Qurʾān, are not used exclusively in religious contexts—they can also be utilized to transfer a sacred dimension into the secular sphere.[125] The

Figure 4.5. Carved door lintel (Shīnītī house) Massawa, 2006.
Photographer: Author.

placing of inscriptions on religious, public, and private buildings in Massawa makes, in a way, the entire town a space of piety and faith—home of a *sacred community.* Buildings radiate piety and religiosity and link the local community to the universal *umma.*

In the early 1960s the Italian scholar Gino Cerbella surveyed some of the Arabic inscriptions, copying, identifying, translating, and publishing them in various periodicals.[126] Cerbella found that most of the inscriptions were verses from the Qurʾān, some were verses written by classical Arab poets, and yet others were shorter phrases of praise to the Prophet or Allāh, usually reproducing one, two, or more of Allāh's ninety-nine attributes. A very small number were proverbs, or fragments of proverbs, of secular nature. Of the two dozen inscriptions collected, only three included the dates in which they were made. Two inscriptions date from the period of the Egyptian building boom: one from Rabīʿ I 1286 (ca. June 1869) and the other from 1295 (1877–78). One inscription was made in Ramaḍān 1341 (1922), pointing to the intensive period of reconstruction following the destructive earthquake of the previous year. A very popular inscription reproduced on many door lintels to this day is "Oh you who enter this door seek the mercy of the Chosen Prophet!"

The following are inscriptions found in Massawa:[127]

a) In the name of God, the Compassionate, the Merciful
We have given you a glorious victory, so that God may forgive you your past and future sins.
Rabīᶜ I 1286 [ca. June 1869].
(Qurʾān 48:1–2)

b) In the name of God, the Compassionate, the Merciful
'Peace!' shall be the word spoken by a merciful God!
(Q. 36: 58)

c) In the name of God, the Compassionate, the Merciful
This is a favour from my Lord.
Ramaḍān 1341 [1922]
(Q. 27:40)

d) In the name of God, the Compassionate, the Merciful
Blessed be God, the noblest of Creators.
(Q. 23:14)

e) (*Was read on a mill in Shaykh al-Amīn street*)
Happiness Recreated Every Day,
Contrary to the Desire of the Envious!

f) (*On door of the Shāfiᶜī Friday mosque*)
In the name of God, the Compassionate, the Merciful
Praise be to God, Lord of the Universe!
(Q. 1: 1–2)

g) In the name of God, the Compassionate, the Merciful
None should visit the mosques of God and the Last Day
1295 [1877–8]
(Q. 9: 18)

h) And as he stood praying in the Shrine, the Angels called out to Him.
(Q. 3:39)

i) In the name of God, the Compassionate, the Merciful
'Peace!' shall be the word spoken by a merciful God.
(Q. 36: 58)

j) Nor can I succeed without God's help.
In Him I have put my trust and to Him I turn in repentance
(Q. 11: 90)

k) Blessed be Allāh—in Whatever Allāh wills
Oh You Who enter this door seek the mercy of the Chosen Prophet.
l) And My Success Depends but on Allāh
m) (*Principal door of the house of Sharīfa ʿAlawiyya, daughter of Sayyid Hāshim Muḥammad ʿUthmān al-Mīrghanī [Khatmiyya]*)
Oh Allāh, oh Benefactor (of his creations), oh Rightful!
n) (*Back door of the house of Sharīfa ʿAlawiyya, daughter of Sayyid Hāshim Muḥammad ʿUthmān al-Mīrghanī [Khatmiyya]*)
Oh Vivacious, oh Protector!
o) Oh Helper, Help the Interests of the Muslims!
p) Oh, Opener, oh All-Knowing, oh Provider (of bread, of well-being), oh Generous!
q) Enter in Peace and Security!
r) Have Faith in Allāh and Confine Yourself to the Master's Secret Grace!
s) Patience is the Key to Success!

"*Sharia* in the Sea, Law in Gondar": *Qāḍīs* and Courts in Massawa[128]

As in other cities and towns of the Ottoman Empire, no other local institution has been as central to both individual and society in Massawa as the Islamic court (also *sharīʿa* court, Ar. *al-maḥkama al-sharʿiyya*) and its judges (Ar. sing. *qāḍī*).[129] Describing the historical and pivotal role of the *qāḍī* in Massawa, Ibrāhīm al-Mukhtār wrote in the 1950s as follows:

> The *qāḍī* in the court of Bāḍiʿ (Massawa) was the only authoritative person applying the *sharīʿa* from the dawn of Islam, from the time the first Muslim delegation came from Mecca and landed in the island of Bāḍiʿ. . . . Since ancient times, the *qāḍī* of Bāḍiʿ was the only official authority for Eritrean Muslims. He solved their legal and religious problems and was the only person to adjudicate. He ruled in all sorts of cases that occurred in the island of Bāḍiʿ, and for different peoples from different legal schools. He was the only authoritative person in the island dealing with issues of land and other real estate property.[130]

Nowadays too, Massawans in particular, but also Eritrean Muslims at large, attach great importance to and take pride in the town's long and rich Islamic legal tradition. Such voices emphasize the centrality of the court as an institution that organized urban and communal life, and highlight the prominent role of *qāḍīs* as leaders enjoying a position of prestige and authority, exercising an influential role on the local public scene.[131] Up to the last quarter of the nineteenth century, the court was instrumental in administering most aspects of civil, religious, communal, and family life in town. Islamic law provided the framework for regulating and controlling social and economic practices and relationships among Massawa's citizens—both Muslim and non-Muslim. During the last quarter of the nineteenth century, Egyptian judicial reform leading to the reorganization of Massawa's judicial system and the advent of Italian colonial rule had gradually and increasingly led to a restriction of the Islamic court to matters of personal status and public notary functions.

The paramount position of *qāḍīs* is rooted in the context of the judicial structure in the Ottoman Empire in the sixteenth century, where *qāḍīs* derived their authority directly from the sultan and were responsible only to him. Among several factors, this too unquestionably served as the basis for Max Weber's orientalist and stereotypical notion of "*qāḍī*-justice" (*Kadijustiz*), which described the process of justice administration in Muslim societies as erratic, emotional, and subjective, most often dependent on extralegal considerations, as opposed to the legal formalism and "rationality" of Western legal systems.[132]

Qāḍīs could attain a high level of autonomy in certain contexts, especially so where governmental presence was weak, such as over long stretches of time in Massawa's history, up to the middle of the nineteenth century. In this context a question that deserves further reflection is whether and to what extent has Massawa's Islamic legal tradition—its *sharīʿa* court, its local *qāḍīs* and *muftīs*—played a role and constituted a factor in shaping local notions of communal identity.[133]

The earliest mention of the Islamic court in Massawa in the available sources does not predate the Ottoman period (beginning in 1557), and the few traces dating from the sixteenth through the eighteenth centuries are scarce and unsubstantial. Suleyman I, sultan of the Ottoman Empire (r. 1520–66), had ordered that all courts in the Ottoman dominions be administered according to the Ḥanafī *madhhab*. On the basis of both written sources and family traditions it is reasonable to conclude that following their occupation of Massawa in 1557 and the creation of the province of Habesh, the Ottomans appointed a *qāḍī* in Massawa and made the Ḥanafī *madhhab* the official legal school.[134] Even if incomplete and in some cases approximative at best, a list of *qāḍīs* in office in Massawa since 1012/1603 prepared by Muftī Ibrāhīm al-Mukhtār with the assistance of *qāḍī* ᶜUthmān Ḥasan Muḥammad Idrīs is useful in providing some information on the history of the court.[135]

A first observation was that the first six *qāḍī*s (up to the late eighteenth century) were noted as locals—either *al-Ḥarqīqāwī* or *al-Maṣawwiᶜī* was added to their names. Of the first six on the list, four were members of the ᶜAbbāsī family. The first *qāḍī* brought by the Ottomans is believed to be an ᶜAbbāsī. The other two judges were from the Badīr family of Hergigo, perhaps suggesting a reflection of *nāʾib* power at the time of their tenure.[136] If we include the nineteenth century it thus appears that several families specialized in providing *qāḍī*s. The ᶜAbbāsī, Bā ᶜAlawī, and Abū ᶜIlāmā families exemplify this trend, which might suggest that their ancestors (who all originated from abroad) originally came to Massawa to serve as *qāḍī*s.[137] A second observation suggests that radical change occurred during the Egyptian period (1860s–80s), when a series of judicial reforms (discussed below) were passed in Egypt. The appointment of Egyptian, Sudanese, and Hijazi judges and *muftī*s in Massawa reflects a return to the Ottoman norm of not appointing judges from among local religious notables. These legal officials served in Massawa for relatively short periods of time, usually a year.[138]

We have little information about the administration of justice in Massawa prior to the establishment of the Egyptian khedival administration in the port. An early colonial Italian report reproduced typical orientalist colonial perceptions of corrupt judicial administration in Muslim societies, and especially in the dominions of the Ottoman Empire. Such discourses were obviously useful in legitimizing the colonial project, which took upon itself the ungrateful task of bringing justice and enlightenment to colonized societies. A sample of such reasoning that strongly mirrors the *Kadijustiz* paradigm goes as follows:

> In Massawa, until 1289 (1872), there was no real court as one would find in a civilized state. A Turkish governor ruled there, dealing with all affairs. In matters of justice he acted more by savviness than by reason and law. He judged as he pleased, according to the customs of those who had ruled the country. This rugged method was perhaps practical and useful in that period, but it was certainly not appropriate for an advanced civilization.[139]

The description is unquestionably inaccurate and exaggerated (partly, as court records prior to 1872 suggest), even if it points to a fairly rudimentary state of organized judicial administration. Only after the establishment of the Egyptian khedival administration in the port in 1865 were its judicial institutions restructured and modernized. This corresponded to major reforms in the judicial system in Egypt under Khedive Ismāʿīl (r. 1863–79) and his successors, which, in general, tended to restrict the power of *sharīʿa* courts in favor of a larger distribution of jurisdiction among several judicial institutions.[140] Judicial reform in Egypt obviously affected all the territorial dominions of the *khedive*—the Red Sea provinces and the Sudan included. Shortly after the takeover of Massawa in 1865 the Egyptian authorities instituted several structural and organizational reforms in the judicial field. The administration under Ḥasan Rifʿat Bey delegated an official to the market with the power to adjudicate any case of civil or commercial litigation on sums not exceeding 500 Egyptian piasters. For adjudicating on other infractions the governor established and headed a council with four to six members, who were among the town's leading notables and merchants. The office of *qāḍī* was maintained with jurisdiction over matters pertaining to the family, marriage, divorce, maintenance, *waqf*, slave manumission, gifts, succession, and other issues of personal status.

A year after taking up his post as governor of Massawa, Werner Munzinger initiated a second significant organizational reform in 1872.[141] He instituted a regular court for civil and penal affairs, headed by a president and three government-appointed and remunerated judges. The court's jurisdiction went beyond the Massawa conurbation and extended over a large population in the eastern Eritrean area: in Semhar, the northern Afar coast, the Habab areas in Sahel, the Keren region, and the Dahlak islands. The court had competence over civil cases of any sum and penal cases of any nature; it continued to follow the Ottoman legal code (*Qānūn*), and it had the right of appeal to Kassala, where a *muftī* at government service resided.[142] Commercial cases were handled by the *sarrtujjār*, who judged either alone or assisted by four individuals, depending on the importance of the cases. It was a commercial court attached to and ultimately dependent upon the civil and penal court. Notwithstanding these changes, the authorities maintained the office of *qāḍī* for all matters related to family and personal status.[143]

Several *muftī*s had been in office from the 1860s to the turn of the century, although in a rather intermittent fashion. The Mahdist revolt and the British occupation of Egypt in 1882 added to the tortuous state of administrative instability that had prevailed even beforehand. In his judge and *muftī* list, Ibrāhīm al-Mukhtār makes note of four *muftī*s, of whom two

Figure 4.6. ᶜAbd Allāh Sirāj Abū ᶜIlāmā, *muftī* of Massawa, ca. 1898. Postcard. Photographer: Errardo di Aichelburg. Author's collection.

had been sent from Egypt and the two others came from the Abū ᶜIlāmā family. The fourth *muftī* on the list was Muftī ᶜAbd Allāh Sirāj Abū ᶜIlāmā (1845–1900) who was described as the descendant of a Tunisian family of notables. His father, ᶜAlī Abū ᶜIlāmā Muḥammad Nūr—referred to in relation to the incident with the French Catholic mission—had been appointed as *muftī* by the Ottomans, who passed the office from father to son. Like other *muftī*s in Massawa, he followed the Ḥanafī *madhhab* but issued *fatwa*s in cases involving Ḥanafīs, Mālikīs, and Shāfiᶜīs. ᶜAbd Allāh Sirāj served initially as a *qāḍī* with the authority of a *muftī,* but following the Egyptian appointment of a *qāḍī* brought from Khartoum, he was appointed to the office of *muftī* in 1884. This arrangement continued until 1895–96, when ᶜAbd Allāh Sirāj held both offices of *qāḍī* and *muftī*.[144]

The advent of Italian colonial rule also generated a set of administrative and structural changes, at times somewhat paradoxical and contradictory, in relation to the status of *qāḍī*s and the administration of Islamic law. Already in 1882 after the acquisition of Assab the Italian government opted for a fairly liberal attitude in matters of judicial administration. Italian law was applied to Italian subjects of the realm, while the religious practices and customs of the "natives" were respected and administered according to local practices, by a Muslim *qāḍī*. At the outset of their occupation of Massawa in February 1885, the Italian colonial authorities proclaimed that the customs and religion of the town's inhabitants would be "scrupulously respected."[145] The Italian colonial administration reorganized the judicial system in Massawa. The Egyptian Court for Civil and Penal Affairs was converted into a Local Civil and Commercial Tribunal with jurisdiction on all types of cases, maintaining the principle of legislative and jurisdictional duality, hence a separate administration of justice to Italians and "natives." But this state of uncertain ambiguous balance and nebulousness was short lived. It ended in August 1886 with what became known as the "Regolamento giudiziario Celli," which introduced a single jurisdiction and abolished the "Natives Tribunal." The "natives," Celli's report stated, "had to submit themselves to the methods and precepts of justice administered by the conqueror," who, however, seeks to avoid offending too radically "the judicial and religious conscience" of the locals.[146]

In practice, the *qāḍī* was left to deal with all matters of personal status, as well as cases of voluntary adjudicating—all under the control of the Tribunal's president. Now that Massawans were obliged to turn to a non-Muslim colonial court, this new arrangement was indeed somewhat contradictory to the approach of full respect to the religious customs and practices of the local inhabitants. But General Genè was aware of the potential risk of stripping all their judicial powers from local Muslim leaders. Indeed, he constantly called for leaving some judicial powers in the hands of *shaykhs*, *nāʾibs*, and *qāḍīs*. In late 1886 during the ceremony of the installment in office of the president of the tribunal, to which the *qāḍī* of Massawa was aptly invited, Genè solemnly appointed a *muftī*, who became de facto leader of the Muslim community of Massawa until the turn of the century.[147] The authority of the *muftī* of Massawa extended to the entire area of the Commissariato. Villages or "tribes" had their own *qāḍīs*, who had a right of appeal to the port city's *muftī*, the supreme religious authority in the district.[148]

The process of "colonial pacification" of interior highland and lowland societies in the 1890s and the early development of elements of an Islamic policy nevertheless generated new colonial perceptions and constructions of culture and civilization, placing Muslim urban and coastal people at the top of the ladder. This approach indeed reflected the colonial authorities' favorable attitude that the Muslim inhabitants of the Massawa conurbation enjoyed, at least in relation to highland societies and until another ju-

Figure 4.7. Members of the Civil and Correctional Tribunal in Massawa, ca. 1885–88. Photographer: Luigi Fiorillo. Biblioteca Reale, Torino.

dicial reform was promulgated in 1908.[149] The following Italian report from 1893 recommended that Massawa and its region be given a distinct, more "advanced" and "refined," legislation and jurisdiction separating it from that of the highlanders. The language is revealing:

> Regarding the condition of its inhabitants, the Eritrean territory is divided into two distinct regions. Massawa and its surroundings, where the European element predominates, constitute the main commercial hub. Even the natives lose here their purely "tribal" features. With time, they have adopted customs and practices that were imported from civilized regions. . . . This zone . . . may be given the legislation of a civilized nation. In contrast, the interior has conserved its primitive character, inhabited by native tribes to whom European customs have not yet reached, and even if so, in a very imperfect manner. European legislation, with all its details

> necessary for the refinements of civilization and all its pedantic formal processes, will be adopted there with great difficulty.[150]

The significance of these comments is pertinent to our reflection on the notion advanced throughout this study, namely of Massawa as a community, whose members (or some of them) shared notions of a communal identity. Clearly, the self-designations of group identity in Massawa had several different sources, yet external designations, and moreover, the establishment of a separate juridical status, in theory or in practice, is crucial in this regard.

Dancing, Chanting, and Protesting: Orthodox versus Popular Muslim Practice

> Barth, the famous German explorer, wrote that in Africa people dance all night long; for Massawa he would have said that people dance day and night. . . . Dancing in Massawa is on the boundary between the savageness of central Africa and the refinement of the customs of the [ancient] Egyptians.
> —Paolo Matteucci, 1880[151]

> [In Massawa people] dance to chase away the Devil (*Afrit*) from the sick. The Massawans believe that the Devil is the cause for all the misfortunes that oppress humanity. They dance when one gets married; they dance when a child is born; they continue to dance when he is circumcised. They dance and sing and cry together when a friend dies.
> —Luigi Negri, 1887[152]

The effects of the Islamic revival and the growing mobility of people between the African and Arabian shores of the Red Sea—for commerce, pilgrimage, or education—influenced and shaped the animated dynamics of Islam in the region. The drastic social, political, and religious transformations of coastal society in the latter decades of the nineteenth century—added to which was the imposition of a new non-Muslim colonial power—led to a state of some degree of social, cultural, and moral perplexity and bemusement. The reconstruction of the sociomoral landscape was manifested principally in struggles and competition over power, authority, leadership, and access to various forms of capital. Some of these struggles played out in the arena of cultural, customary, and ritual practices. Since Islam constituted perhaps the most cardinal source of symbolic capital, struggles over what constituted "proper" Islamic practice and what defined the Muslim community were pervasive in such a setting.

The confluence of migrants from the Arabian Peninsula—some of whom claimed descent from the Prophet (*sādah* and *ashrāf*), as well as perhaps being learned to some extent—and newcomers from the recently Islamized (or religiously revivified) interior in only a few decades spurred religious and cultural tensions in a rapidly transforming urban community. Tensions generated complex negotiations and struggles over religious authority and leadership, expressed through rhetoric addressing notions of citizenship and conceptions of the Muslim community. Contention over Islamic purity and impurity, over *ḥalāl* (permissible) and *ḥarām* (forbidden) practices, were especially reflected in various religious, social, and cultural rituals. As the two quotes opening this section suggest, public rituals involving dances and dancing were highly popular in mid- to late-nineteenth-century Massawa. Before attempting to identify such dances it is useful to provide several of the many descriptions that characterize early Italian colonial journalistic and travel accounts. One example is Gian Pietro Porro's vivid description:

> In the native villages of Massawa and its environs there are four or five daily "fantasie" (small celebrations). A death, a sick person, a birth, a circumcision, may account for the performance of such ceremonies. The natives' drums make much noise for twenty-four hours. . . . One evening we went to see one of these "fantasie." It was performed for a sick woman who would—one of her doctors told us—either die or get better in the following morning as a result of the ceremony. The poor woman was lying down in a big hut with about thirty people around her. Two or three beat their drums, the others were dancing, hopping from one leg to another, chanting an eternally repetitive refrain.[153]

Pippo Vigoni described in detail his observations from a ceremony aiming to cure another sick woman by exorcising the spirits that had taken over her:

> Among the thousands of cries that continually vibrate the atmosphere, one very strong and continuous mix of voices and sounds attracted our attention an entire day and the best part of the night. . . . [In the morning] we entered into the hut . . . where eight young black women were sitting on two beds. They were covered

> in a sort of white cloth with silver bracelets and nose rings, the ears and on their fingers in a way that they almost covered all of them up to their red-tainted nails. The poor sick young woman lied on the ground . . . on her sides two persons were beating drums while all the sitting women chanted in a very high voice, interrupted by a very acute trill. The public, including about twenty other people accompanied with a regular clapping of hands. From time to time they poured perfumed oils on the forehead of the patient. . . . This savage and original scene aimed at chasing the devil away from the illness that took over the poor woman.[154]

The description of such ritual and festive dancing does not make their identification always simple. It appears, however, quite certain that most such descriptions refer to particular local or regional variants of the *zār* cult, which has been in practice in northeast Africa (including Egypt), the Arabian Peninsula, and as far as southwest Iran, where it is believed to have been introduced by slaves originating in Ethiopia sometime in the nineteenth century. The aim of the cult is to cure illnesses and misfortunes caused by possession of so-called *zār* spirits through a process of coming to terms with these spirits. Some scholarship on *zār* in the Sudan and Egypt interprets and places the ritual within particular social and cultural contexts, arguing that the performance of the ritual may also function to release certain family and community tensions in the individual.[155] However scanty and external the data from Massawa, it does seem the case that dances were more popular among newcomers from the inland, in the mainland villages of the conurbation, and in Tewalet. As the descriptions clearly note, it also appears that at least those kinds of variations of *zār* were mostly performed by and for women. Some dances were perceived negatively by those practicing what they thought of as a more orthodox Islam. Such voices scorned and downplayed aspects of local culture such as spirit possession and ritual dances that were associated with what they perceived as less "civilized" and less "Muslim" tribes of the interior and the non-urban coast. Differences between orthodox and local-customary practices of religious and cultural rituals generated tensions between those who stressed a more sophisticated or "civilized" behavior, associated with the Arabian holy lands of Islam, and the more numerous populace, who flowed into the port and defended their right to practice their local cultural traditions. It appears that the Khatmiyya order was more inclined to tolerate certain local customary and cultural practices of its ever-numerous

Figure 4.8. Waiting for the Arab "fantasia" at the Sharīfa ʿAlawiyya's house, ca. 1920s. Private collection, Pavoni Social Centre, Asmara.

members throughout the conurbation, including various types of dances. Two early-twentieth-century photographs showing the sharīfa ʿAlawiyya and a group of women before and during the performance of some sort of ritual dancing provide little clues but raise many fascinating questions, including whether a relationship between *zār* and *dhikr* existed in that setting. Working in the northern Sudan, Janice Boddy found a resemblance between *zār* rituals and *dhikr* performances among members of the Khatmiyya and the Qādiriyya.[156]

Other dances are more difficult to recognize and might refer to local Tigre, Afar, or Saho rituals. Hormuzd Rassam's observations from a wedding that he had attended in the 1860s reveal the dynamics of religion, culture, and tradition in a rapidly changing town. Rassam recounted how while the bride was conducted to the house of her new husband, the father of the groom danced before the procession with a drawn sword in his hand. Rassam noted that when the undoubtedly high-status Arab or "Arabized" groom's father had noticed that Rassam was observing the ceremony

> he apologized for having made himself ridiculous, alleging as an excuse the tyranny of a national custom which had been bequeathed to the true believers by the dark ages. It was his pious belief, indeed, that this and all other vain ceremonies which pre-

Figure 4.9. "Arab" dance at the Sharīfa ᶜAlawiyya's house, ca. 1920s. Private collection, Pavoni Social Centre, Asmara.

> vailed among the faithful had been handed over to them by the heathen, and that consequently in the day of judgment the sins, which had thus been inherited by the followers of the Prophet would be laid to the charge of the unbelievers.[157]

As elsewhere, antagonism between orthodox and popular practices in Massawa was also articulated in the critique of Sufism and Sufi practices. On the basis of flimsy oral data it appears that in the late nineteenth century (1890s?) the Hadrami jurist and *muftī* from the al-ᶜAmūdī tribe in Wādī Dawᶜan, ᶜAlī b. Aḥmad b. Saᶜīd Bā Ṣabrayn, had spent some time in Massawa teaching in the Shaykh Ḥammāl mosque. Bā Ṣabrayn, who was educated in Zabīd and who had composed a treatise in 1877 denouncing a number of un-Islamic practices in Hadramawt, openly criticized the Khatmiyya and Sayyid Hāshim al-Mīrghanī, who led the *ṭarīqa* in Massawa and the wider region. The anecdotal oral data suggests that some antagonistic exchange between the two had occurred. Sayyid Hāshim responded to Bā Ṣabrayn's attacks by sending him a text that he had written and that—according to my informant—had proved to Bā Ṣabrayn that the Sufi leader was a "learned man of the world," which eventually opened the door to reconciliation. This rather simplistic description leaves much to be desired but nevertheless indicates the kinds of tensions that operated on the scene as well as the role of itinerant Muslim reformers in the period of intensified mobility in the northwestern Indian Ocean region. At some point Bā Ṣabrayn left Massawa for Jiddah, where in 1917 he was noted as being about eighty years old and "of good repute and popular."[158]

Ḥāmidūy versus Bādūrī: Conflict in Hergigo, 1909

In the early twentieth century Hergigo was the site of several conflicts over ritual and religious practice. One such conflict was referred to by the inhabitants of the region as the "to pray or not to pray" dispute. Around 1903 (AH 1322) a succession of disputes occurred involving the local leaders of the Khatmiyya. According to oral history collected by Ibrāhīm al-Mukhtār, as Khalīfa ʿUthmān b. ʿAbd al-Raḥmān, the *imām* (prayer leader) and *khatīb* (preacher) in the Kekiyā ʿUmar Friday mosque in Hergigo,[159] became old, some inhabitants demanded that he be replaced by his younger cousin, Khalīfa Ḥasan b. Khalīfa Ṭāhā. The demand sparked a dispute over the issue and prompted the *qāḍī* of Massawa, Muḥammad Nūr ʿAbd Allāh Sirāj Abū ʿIlāmā, to send a delegation to investigate the matter. The delegation included the three members of the Massawa *waqf* council, Aḥmad Afandī ʿAbd Allāh Bey al-Ghūl, Muḥammad Sālim Bā Ṭūq, and Muḥammad Sālim Afandī. They asked the inhabitants one by one whether they agreed or disagreed to pray behind the old *imām*. Most agreed, and Khalīfa ʿUthmān remained in his position. Other concurrent disputes involved the same two protagonists. Some of Hergigo's inhabitants sent a letter to the head of the Khatmiyya order asking to appoint Khalīfa Ḥasan as the *khalīfat al-khulafāʾ* of the *ṭarīqa* since he was more competent—and probably more orthodox, as the story below might suggest—than his elderly cousin. Intimately connected was the dispute over the right to lead the Khatmi recitation of the *mawlid al-nabawī al-Mīrghanī* in religious celebrations. But all conflicts did not alter the status quo, thanks to Khalīfa ʿUthmān's seniority. Ibrāhīm al-Mukhtār's account remains obscure as to the deeper reasons for and roots of the contention.[160]

But the most salient conflict over customary and ritual practice in the Massawa area in the early twentieth century opposed families of the Hergigo Balaw with families of the Bayt Shaykh Maḥmūd, whose main seat was at Zula but who lived in great numbers in Hergigo, Massawa, and their neighborhoods. The Bayt Shaykh Maḥmūd was an important local holy family who attained prominence as the migration of Saho-speaking pastoralists into the conurbation intensified in the second half of the century, and also thanks to their close association with the *nāʾibs*. In the early years of the twentieth century observers such as Ilario Capomazza noted the preeminence of Bayt Shaykh Maḥmūd authority in religious rituals in the Massawa area. Yet such writers took the exercise of Bayt Shaykh Maḥmūd religious authority for granted; they were unaware of the internal conflicts and the struggles between the group and their opponents, who attempted to discredit and undermine their authority by "forbidding wrong," following the well-known Qurʾānic injunction, and arguing that their ritualistic traditions were "improper" and "inappropriate."[161]

The main source of contention was the use of drums and hand clapping in religious ceremonies. The Bayt Shaykh Maḥmūd were the custodians of a sacred drum, the *coborò;* they had the exclusive privilege to use the drum in all ceremonies such as birth, weddings, and burials, and were compensated for the special services they provided on these occasions. But elements of the Balaw, through the principal *nāʾib* family, had as well privileged usage of the *tasat,* another type of drum, which was beaten with two sticks called *cidad.*[162] Evidence suggests that the factions—in conflict over local religious leadership for a long time, some sources say four centuries—struggled over the monopoly of religious offices and religious authority in a town rapidly transformed by commerce, migration, and religion.

In May 1909 the conflict between the Bayt Shaykh Maḥmūd and families of the Balaw Yūsuf Ḥassab Allāh re-erupted in a legal controversy involving defamation and slander, brought before the Italian judicial authorities in the colony. The case opposed Ḥasan Ḥāmid Ḥāmidūy of the Balaw, accompanied by the same Khalīfa Ḥasan Khalīfa Ṭāhā from the "to pray or not to pray" incident, on the one hand, and ʿUmar Muḥammad Bādūrī of the Bayt Shaykh Maḥmūd, on the other. Ḥāmidūy accused Bādūrī of practicing rituals in weddings, burial ceremonies, and other religious occasions that were not in conformity with any legal school, especially not the Ḥanafī *madhhab.* The Ḥāmidūy claimed that hand clapping (*cufuf*) and drum beating (*duf uf* and *eidan*) were inappropriate practices, condemned in the Qurʾān, and ought therefore to be considered *ḥarām.* The Bayt Shaykh Maḥmūd argued, on the other hand, that whatever is not specifically prohibited by the Qurʾān or the four *madhāhib* was therefore legitimate and acceptable (Ar. *mustaḥab*).[163] The conflict re-erupted after several incidents opposing the two parties. On 13 May 1909, at a funeral administered by the Bayt Shaykh Maḥmūd, Ḥasan Ḥāmid Ḥāmidūy and his relative Yaḥyā ʿĀmir announced to the ceremony's participants that the beating of the drum was *ḥarām.* Shortly thereafter, Ḥāmidūy and his uncle, a certain ʿAbd al-Razzāq, went to ʿUthmān Ṣāʿigh and tried to persuade him not to ask the Bayt Shaykh Maḥmūd to administer their relative's funeral. In another incident, sometime later in the month of *Rajab,* when the Bayt Shaykh Maḥmūd celebrated the ceremony of the Prophet's birthday (Ar. *Mawlid al-Nabī*) in a private mosque, Ḥasan Ḥāmidūy and ʿAbd al-Razzāq told the owner of the mosque to throw away the mats and cloth in the praying area since they were "contaminated" by the presence of the Bayt Shaykh Maḥmūd.[164]

The Italian legal authorities sought recourse to Islamic legal interpretations, notably three *fatwa*s issued by Yemeni *muftī*s. A first *fatwa* that they referred to was issued by a Ḥanafī *muftī* in Zabid in 1822 (1245). Muftī Sulaymān ruled as follows:

> The *cufuf,* the *dufuf* and the *eidan,* have always been practiced in the four *madhhāhib.* Therefore they are not *ḥarām.* Since the scholars of the four schools Ḥanafī, Ḥanbalī, Mālikī and Shāfiʿī have not declared these practices *ḥarām,* they are to be considered *mustaḥab* (legitimate and acceptable). Such ceremonies have also been practiced in the time of the Prophet and he remained silent, which should be understood as his consent. Even Sulaymān, Ḥammār and Abder who were among the Prophet's companions, practiced such ceremonies.

Muftī Sulaymān's *fatwa* concluded by reminding that the Qurayshis asked the Prophet to stop such practices as hand clapping and drum beating. But the Prophet replied with what became Sūra 6 verse 52 in the Qurʾān:

> Do not drive away those that call on their Lord morning and evening, seeking only to gain His favor. You are in no way accountable for them, nor are they in any way accountable for you. If you dismiss them, you shall yourself become an evil-doer.[165]

A second *fatwa* upon which the Italian judges relied in making their decision in the case was decreed in 1908 (1326) by the Shāfiʿī Shaykh ʿAbd Allāh Yaḥyā Mukaram of Ḥudayda and by the Ḥanafī Shaykh Aḥmad Muḥammad Shihrī from the same Yemeni port-town. Issuing a collective *fatwa,* they declared that "those who condemn as *ḥarām* the followers of the Sufi brotherhoods who adopt local rituals, are *jāhil,* or in other words ignorant people." The third and last *fatwa* was issued in 1908 by *qāḍī* Muḥammad Ṣāliḥ Atih of the Shāfiʿī *madhhab* in Luḥayya. In his *fatwa* he said that the Prophet assisted and accepted a ceremony with hand clapping and drum beating by a slave. He said that "no one should condemn this custom."[166] On the basis of these three *fatwas*—as well as, one could argue, the pragmatic calculation of avoiding to inflame a potentially disquieted majority—the Italian *commissario* of the Massawa administrative region, Dante Odorizzi, concluded as inadmissible the exclusion of the Bayt Shaykh Maḥmūd from the Muslim community. Ḥasan Ḥāmid Ḥāmidūy and Ḥasan Khalīfa Ṭāhā were consequently convicted and sent to six months in prison in Assab.[167]

The conflict over customary practice and religious ritual opposing the two Hergigo-based families and their followers epitomizes clearly the struggle over power, authority, and legitimacy in a setting experiencing profound political, economic, and religious transformations. The conflictual cleavage between orthodox and popular versions of Muslim ritual practice reflects opposing visions in the process of negotiating a new moral order in the Muslim community of the conurbation, but also, more prosaically, a competition for local power, *tout court.*

Massawa's paradigmatic Islamic character—as it is manifested in its mosques, saints' tombs, local communal rituals, and religious notables—is part and parcel of the unique sense of identity and ethos of its citizens. Massawans and other Muslim inhabitants of the region have perceived Massawa as a "Muslim town," serving as a gateway to the wider Islamic world and solidly linking them to the worldwide *umma.* Yet external influences—chiefly from the Middle East—were not absolute, one-sided, and imposed. They were appropriated and negotiated locally in different contexts throughout the town's history, gradually leading to the development of notions of a local-regional Islamic culture.

In the nineteenth century, intensified migrations to Massawa greatly affected religious dynamics in the town and its hinterlands. The simultaneous influx of Arab and Muslim merchants from the Arabian Peninsula and the Islamic world and Tigre- and Saho-speaking pastoralists from the interior transformed the town's social landscape. It generated several arenas of struggle and agitation over the reconfiguration of Muslim society, involving competition over religious leadership, the control of the town's religious institutions, and the establishment of a new communal moral order.

Early Italian colonial attitudes to the Muslims in Eritrea also contributed to the thriving of Islam in Massawa. After the occupation of Massawa in 1885, Italian officials manipulated religion in their search for effective colonial domination and control. In the process they interfered with local and regional Muslim dynamics, preferring to develop a relationship with the anti-Mahdist Khatmiyya Sufi brotherhood, which they raised to the role of formally representing Eritrea's Muslims. Early Italian colonial officials perceived Muslim Massawans as the most evolved and civilized subjects in their colony. As a result they privileged urban Muslims and their institutions by bestowing subventions to mosques, paying monthly stipends to Muslim leaders, and granting Muslims a special juridical status permitting them to preserve the autonomy of the Islamic court in matters related to family and personal status. This attitude was not unaccompanied by some degree of contradiction, considering the inherent racially prejudiced basis of colonial rule, especially under the military administration in the early period. Thus, an anecdotal story tells that when in 1895 Aḥmad Afandī al-Ghūl, one of Massawa's most prominent citizens and a chief member of several urban institutions and legal courts, attempted to board the train to Saʿati, he was stopped by the overzealous train master, who did not admit the "native notable" to the first-class compartment that was reserved for Europeans only.[168]

5

"Being Massawan"

Citizenship, Family, and Urban Authority

> Many of the natives of Massawa boast their Arab origins—but their dark skin discloses a mixed race.
> —Arnauld d'Abbadie, 1838[1]

> Due to the refinement of their customs, the inhabitants of Massawa think of themselves as markedly superior to those who inhabit the countryside. An inhabitant of Massawa is profoundly insulted if treated as a Beduin. Family pride is so great that, only in recent times, impoverishment could force a member of an old family to work for a salary. In the past, the entire town would have acted as his creditors.
> —Werner Munzinger, 1858[2]

> The customs of the natives of Massawa are neither Abyssinian nor Arab. There is too much mixing of races and habits to discern a clear conception of their customs.
> —Pellegrino Matteucci, 1880[3]

> Thanks to its peaceful habits, its commercial relations with Arabia, India, and Egypt, as well as its frequent and continuous contact with Europeans, the population of Massawa and its environs is undoubtedly the most civilized and the one which has assimilated most to Western civilization among all the colony's peoples.
> —Ilario Capomazza, 1910[4]

Because Massawa is a town with a mixed population originating from both land and sea, and a site where access to inland and overseas trade networks was subject to competition that could be determined on the basis of social and cultural markers, constructions of identity and culture articulated by Massawans have always been multifarious. Above all, the above quotations express representations made by European observers who interpreted what they saw in Massawa within their own mindset, often marred by racial and ethnic-based prejudice stemming from a qualitatively hierarchical view of civilizations. Yet they also mirror a complex "objective" reality of cultural *métissage* and multidirectional cross-cultural influences, as well as the various self-designations, discourses, and cultural politics of nineteenth-century Massawans. They clearly unveil the predominance and valuing of "Arab" constructions of identity in the middle decades of the nineteenth century and display the preeminence of Massawa's upper classes over the control of cultural dynamics and discourses.

Several factors account for the enhancement of a particular "Arab" construction of cultural superiority characterizing Massawa's leading stratum in this period. The social and cultural impact of Egyptian hegemony in the region from the middle decades of the century, the intensified wave of merchant-entrepreneur migration from the Arab-Islamic world, the Islamic revival that witnessed the energetic activities of holy families and *ṭuruq* in propagating Islam, and, last but not least, Italian colonial attitudes toward Islam and what they perceived as a more "civilized" society in urban Massawa, all reinforced Islam and what may be identified a process of Arabization in the second half of the nineteenth century. Yet there were also more local factors. The constant flow of non-urban dwellers into the conurbation led those who viewed themselves as Massawa's lofty citizens to sharpen the distinctions between themselves and the newcomers by erecting boundaries articulated in discourses of cultural and moral distinctiveness.

This chapter investigates several aspects of these dynamics primarily by exploring the social world of Massawa's urban elite. It is therefore mostly concerned with a highly mobile group of potent families whose authority was based on their high social or religious status, their wealth, and their privileged access to political power. From the middle decades of the century Massawa's elite was able to exercise significant power, set much of the agenda in terms of urban social dynamics, and impose its own conception of what it meant "to be Massawan." Members of the elite did so in order to protect and maintain a sense of group cohesion. I would also argue that, in general, the reinvestment of commercial profits in the construction or acquisition of local urban real estate properties might have been pivotal in granting Massawan "citizenship" to only recently settled entrepreneurs, many of whom rose strikingly quickly to major positions in local urban institutions. This chapter analyzes the social and economic sources and bases of power of Massawa's elite families and the various connections that allowed them to share a set of common values and objectives and develop a distinctive sense of urban identity.

The institution of the family was fundamental to the experience of the town's elite and the articulation of its social and cultural constructions of identity. Indeed, the most striking feature in Massawa's urban social structure is the existence and centrality of the patrilineages and households (*bayt*). This feature did not resemble the social structure of the Tigre-, Saho-, and Afar-speaking populations who inhabit its environs and hinterlands and whose categories of kinship and descent were based on either various clusters of cognatic kin or the clanic structure common to pastoralists.[5] The records of Massawa's Islamic court open windows on important aspects of family and household structure, size, and dynamics in this period. This includes marriage patterns and strategies that reveal the webs of connections that both tied elite families together and linked them to the African inland and the Red Sea world.

Citizenship, Communal Cohesion, and "Arabness": Invoking a Coastal Urban Identity

The historical making and development of what Dante Odorizzi termed in the early twentieth century the "aristocratic class of Massawa" involve complex long-term processes of migration, social and cultural mixing, and cultural representations that are impossible to unravel in a neat and immaculate fashion. However, the esprit de corps and sense of group identity shared by the urban elite—in the past and the present—point to the unique position and role of this mercantile community, as well as to a sense of self-awareness of its position vis-à-vis others. Studying the coastal towns of Benaadir in southern Somalia, Scott Reese argued that as a community of cross-cultural brokers, Benaadiri merchants managed their identity by performing a delicate balancing act in which they could maintain social and cultural links with both local and overseas trade partners while at the same time remaining separate from each. The result of such cultural juggling was the creation of a local, coastal, or Benaadiri sense of identity, which, while closely linked to the cultures of the African interior, also shared close sociocultural affinities with Muslim merchants overseas.[6]

The specific makeup of Massawa's mercantile population was the result of a mixture of local coastal elites and overseas traders and entrepreneurs. Such a society was ideally able to function as a community of culture brokers, able to develop the commercial, social, and cultural mechanisms tying them to both inland and overseas trading partners. Historically, it has developed—to various degrees and at different moments—certain shared traits and ideals of a local yet worldly identity, namely a sophisticated and refined urban culture, a strong sense of Muslim identity, a link to the wider *umma* of Muslim believers, and a sense of connectedness to Arab history, Arabic literacy, and Arab culture. Urban dwellers saw the town as standing for a set of worthy ideals, primarily civilty, urbanity, culture, and religious piety. But it must be stressed that the cultural traits epitomizing this coastal, urban identity were the ideal values of the elite class in Massawa. In other words, in this context "being Massawan"—with the disposition (orientation) of identity and culture that this implied—meant being part of its elite stratum, sharing its values, its interests and goals, and "playing the same game," as anthropologist Fredrik Barth put it in a groundbreaking text on ethnic groups and boundaries.[7]

A sense of urban superiority reflected the ideal values, self-perceptions, and images of the elite town dwellers or those who aspired to become part of the urban elite. Political and economic change in the second half of the century rapidly transformed social realities in the town and its immediate environment. The increasingly heterogeneous nature of the town's population explains in part the importance of defining and maintaining social boundaries in an increasingly blurred and complex social environment. The town's traditional elite saw itself vastly outnumbered by the flow of non-urbanites into the conurbation. Struggles for citizenship and leadership—both entering the town's higher classes and preserving high status—entailed various cultural strategies, of which some of these identitary and cultural discourses were part.[8] Accordingly, for example, references in late-nineteenth-century Italian colonial reports to the Mentāy and al-Nātī families in Hetumlo as of "Arab origins," while it is known—even by their own account—that they originated in the inland and were among the port-town's first settlers, mirrors the dialectics of contemporary cultural politics. Interestingly, in the context of independent Eritrea, in the late 1990s such families told the story of their origins with strong emphases to inland provenance, as if to strengthen their connection to the contemporary Eritrean nation.[9]

In responding to oral data collection, Massawans convey a strong sense of group identity—even if partly anecdotal and to some extent reflecting more recent constructions of identity and culture. Self-designations of the citizens of Massawa—past and present—such as *Maṣawwiʿīn* (Ar., the Massawans) and *ahl Maṣawwaʿ* (Ar., the Massawa family), or expressions such as *nazionalità di Massawa* (Ita., Massawa nationality) and *shaʿab Maṣawwaʿ* (Ar., the people, nation of Massawa), constantly come up as self-designations.[10] One informant from a family of *sayyids*, whose ancestors came from Wādī Fāṭma on the outskirts of Mecca, characterized Massawa as a "big chain" whose families are all related to one another.[11] Comparing Massawa to Harar in Ethiopia, he reflected that "Harar is like Massawa. Some people are light-skinned. In Harar they also have doors that they close at night. At midnight they close the door like a family."[12] Whereas the city of Harar is physically separated from the outside by a wall that surrounds it, Massawa, as an island, was separated from the mainland by water, at least until the 1870s, when it was linked to the mainland by two causeways.

Portraying Massawa Island as a distinctly organized social space and utilizing this image as a sociocultural marker to distinguish between town and "outside" the gate in this informant's account refers to the *Bāb ʿAshara* (also *Bawābat al-ʿAsharāt*). It was initially built some time during the Ottoman era by the customs authorities and rebuilt or renovated by the Egyptians in 1879, after two causeways linked Massawa to the mainland and access to it was greatly facilitated. Imposing a fee of 10 *fiḍḍa* (hence *ʿashara*, ten) on any person entering Massawa and closing the gate every night undoubtedly aimed to control and limit the increasing flow of people entering the port island, the *Badauini di fuori* (Ita., Beduins from outside), as my informant put it.[13] The *Bāb ʿAshara* is still visible in illustrations dating from the first couple of years of colonial Massawa, but it seems to have disappeared shortly thereafter. Another expression of the urban elite used to distinguish between urban and non-urban is *seb bar* in the Tigre language, meaning "people from outside," "country folk." The self-designated *seb medinat* (townspeople) perceived themselves as the extreme opposite of what they believed were the "disorganized" and "backward" (*seb bar*).[14]

The insistence on traditions of foreign origins and a sense of cosmopolitanism have also taken a central position in the ways by which Massawans express their distinctiveness. Origins from the Arab Middle East and the Muslim world have been fundamental in cultivating and maintaining the sense of identity of those who perceived themselves as Massawans. "Here everybody is of Arab origins; we all came from outside;

Figure 5.1. Gate of Massawa (*Bāb ʿAshara*), 1885. Photographer: Luigi Naretti. Biblioteca Reale, Torino.

there are people here from Yemen, Saudi Arabia, Turkey, etc.," exemplifies the clearly one-sided message that I heard on many occasions during interviews.[15] Many families—but more so the *ashrāf* and *sayyids*—have jealously preserved family genealogies attesting to religiously prestigious origins. Elaborate family histories have always been central to the cultural dynamics of Massawa's "big" families, to the affirmation and confirmation of prestige and high social standing.[16] Unfortunately the recent turbulent decades in the history of Eritrea have made it difficult to keep documentation; much was lost and destroyed during the long nationalist struggle, and other papers were taken with family members into exile, where they are securely kept.[17]

Another marker of the sense of group connectedness cultivated by Massawans is rooted in the town's distinct historical trajectory. Urban dwellers take pride in the port's unique history of multiple occupiers, perceiving this as proof to the town's historical strategic importance and its connection to great world empires, especially Arab and Islamic polities, from the Umayyads, through the Ottomans, to khedival Egypt. The association with these empires linked Massawa to the wider world of the *umma* and connected it with other predominantly Muslim Red Sea port-towns. The flexibility necessary to adapt to new political conditions and the need to organize commercial activities and civic life in periods of loose occupation—much as the period of Ottoman indirect rule—contributed to a sense of shared destiny and a tight-knit, albeit flexible and ever-changing, urban community. Massawa was not exactly a city-state, but in some periods of its history some of its main features strongly resembled one.

Reminiscent to some extent of the situation on the East African coasts, Massawans still insist on pointing to distant origins mostly in the Middle East. It is, however, obvious that most of those who insist on distant origins descend from families who have been in the northeast African region for centuries, having no memory of migrations, unlike the more recent nineteenth-century migrants from the Arabian Peninsula and Egypt. As in other settings where family origins and history have been of much importance, in Massawa too some appear to construct convenient stories mixing elements of authentic with idealized origins.

In various sources, the Ṣāʾigh family is given a variety of origins from the "Yemen" to the "Arabian Coast," "Hergigo" (often referring to Balaw origins), and "India." One elderly member of the family claimed that seven grandfathers back, a certain Bakrī Muḥammad Ṣāʾigh came to Massawa from Baghdad. According to his account, once in Eritrea the family spread across the Eritrean lowlands as far as Keren and Aqurdat, and married into the various tribes. The Ṣāʾighs had been initially goldsmiths (Ar. sing. *ṣāʾigh*) but then they became merchants and farmers. But it appears that there are two Ṣāʾigh families in the region, one from Nakfa and the other from Massawa, to which my informant belonged. Although it is difficult to establish with any solidity the precise origins of the family, it is interesting to note how in the context of late-twentieth-century Eritrean nationalism, a member of the Massawa Ṣāʾighs appears to have mixed his family story with that of the interior and seemingly more "Eritrean" Ṣāʾighs.[18] This anecdote is, however, quite exceptional (from goldsmiths and merchants to farmers); the opposite pattern (countryside to urban) is more frequent among Massawans.

The Eritrean region's proximity to the Hijaz and the historical migration of Muslim holy men from the Arabian peninsula to the African shores of the Red Sea renders the claims of various inland societies to putative Arab/Islamic origins more complex than elsewhere. Some Saho- and Tigre-speaking groups such as the different ʿAd Shaykh branches and some of the Bet Asgede among others, have adopted the *nisbas*, or pedigrees, of *shaykhs* or holy families who had converted them to Islam in more recent times, mostly in the nineteenth century. Thus, the phenomenon of nineteenth-century-converted inlanders claiming distant Arabian origins was in general not uncommon.[19] In Massawa, in a period of competition over the town's symbolic and material resources, such claims could be even more vital. Finally, it is interesting to note that on one or two occasions more fully educated informants have themselves expressed skepticism about the authenticity of their own claimed or designated family origins, published in the family lists provided in Dante Odorizzi (1911) and Muḥammad ʿUthmān Abū Bakr's (1994) books.

Images of Race, Class, and Town versus Countryside in Nineteenth-Century European Accounts

Elaborate expressions of identity are more difficult to unveil when one examines nineteenth-century European written sources. They are cursory and often reveal more about European prejudice and constructions of race and culture during the heyday of imperialism than anything else.[20] Notwithstanding, some of these accounts do offer valuable insights on the differences between town and countryside, on customary varieties, and on the discourses of contemporary informants. Throughout the period observers noted the variety of clothes worn by Massawa's inhabitants, making clear distinctions between the wealthy notables and merchants and poorer laborers, porters, fishermen, and the like. The wealthy often wore lavishly ornate and colorful long-sleeved robes (caftans) and sandals in public rituals of supremacy that mirrored consumption habits as social markers, while members of lower-status groups were often minimally covered by a *fūta* around the waist and a simple shirt.[21] Alluding to the "Arab" character of women of high status, Combes and Tamisier noted that they were "dressed like those [women] of Ghonfouda."[22] Pascale called high-class women the "invisible princesses," who were almost always withdrawn, at home in reclusion ("in some *harem*"), and who when they went out were fully covered in colorful cloths in a way that only their eyes were exposed.[23]

The differences between Massawa's urban dwellers and the Beduins of the surrounding Semhar region have also drawn observers' attention. They are revealing and significant in terms of the construction of identities in the region. Werner Munzinger, who lived in the region for long years between the 1850s and the 1870s, provides ethnographic data on the cultural, customary, and religious distinctions between townsmen and nomads. First, he noted a physical difference: the urban dwellers were lighter-skinned than the Beduins of the interior. In terms of dress and clothing, he remarked that the Beduins did not wear the Turkish-style headgear, the *tarbūsh,* or the turban as the dwellers of Massawa and its environs used to. He also noted that Beduin dwellers of the conurbation tended to give their children Muslim names, while the more recently converted Tigre-speaking groups were not yet accustomed to this practice. In daily life, Munzinger observed, Beduin boys tended to follow their fathers to the markets of Massawa, learning rapidly to ride a camel, while in contrast, urban boys were initiated into business early and tended to learn how to read and write. He also remarked a difference in moral strictness between Beduins and townsmen, especially in what concerns young girls and women. In town, women were almost unseen, strictly covered from head to toe; they were deeply religious—"they pray a lot and are a bit fanatical." All in all, Munzinger's description reflects the different development of town vis-à-vis countryside; urban mercantile society appeared more "refined," pious, and prosperous.[24]

During the three decades following Munzinger's observations a further process of external influences made a significant impact on society and culture in Massawa. Despite its brevity in this region, an important component in Khedive Ismāᶜīl's "civilizing mission" was a cultural revolution in which Arabic and Arabization had a central role.[25] Perhaps more importantly, I would argue, the Egyptian occupation of Massawa from 1865 to 1885 marked a strong process of Arabization mainly through the establishment or reform of institutions such as the *sharīᶜa* court or the local council (*majlis maḥalī*) in which Arabic was the formal language. The close administrative and commercial contact with Egypt, the Sudan, and other Red Sea ports such as Sawākin, Jiddah, and the Yemeni ports also contributed to the new wave of Arab influences on the port. The more dynamic flow of peoples across the Red Sea, especially the migration of Hadramis, Yemenis, and Egyptians into the port, their rapid success in business, and their usually swift integration into the town's leading strata and urban leadership enhanced these processes.

All in all, one or more Arabic schools operated in the port, several new mosques and *zawāya* were constructed, and more and more Arabs—including migrants from earlier parts of the century—were able to access the upper echelons of local society, most often following success in business. Material wealth enabled intellectual activities, and some members of Massawa's prominent families were able to devote themselves to literary interests ranging from the writing of history and poetry to the collection of books. In the twentieth century, members of the Ḥayūtī, Bā Ṭūq, and Mīyā families, among others, have produced literary and historical writings. A certain Muḥammad Sālim Afandī, head of the Massawa customs, was said to have owned a library rich in Arabic, Islamic, and historical books during the Egyptian period in Massawa.[26]

This should not, however, overshadow the role of the Tigre language in the greater Massawa area and its co-practice alongside Arabic, as well as other languages. As much as Arabic was the literary and religious language in Massawa, most of the inhabitants of the conurbation used Tigre in day-to-day life, in the household, on the streets, and in the markets. The Tigre language was thus also one of the vehicles integrating migrants both from abroad and from the hinterland into the original cultural community that developed in Massawa. As in other settings, it exemplified the inherently paradoxical situation of coastal urban elites, who while scorning the "inland outsiders" had adopted their language. Some evidence, awaiting further scrutiny, points to a distinct Massawa Tigre dialect.[27] Several informants told me that Massawa Tigre is different from inland Tigre because it mixes much more Arabic into it (or, as one informant put it, "Tigre language in Massawa is not considered 'pure'"). Illustrating this statement, one informant, whose family has dwelled in Massawa for centuries, said that sometimes while speaking with friends, he might encounter a word that he does not understand, to which his friends good-humoredly react: "What do you know about Tigre? You are from Massawa!" Yet, following the dichotomic character of such discourses, the other side of this story as expressed by high-status Massawans claims that the Arabic spoken in Massawa is "pure" and resembles that spoken by "other Arab peoples."

When European observers remarked on the "Arab" character and manners of Massawans in the second half of the century, they most often witnessed a society in transformation, heavily influenced by the Red Sea world with which it had interacted with greater intensity since the early nineteenth century. The use of the term "Arab" in early colonial literature is often confused and incoherent, aptly reflecting both a bewildered colonial disposition that vacillated between racial prejudice and romanticizing assumptions and the indeed complex sociocultural realities on the ground.[28] One revealing example is Leopoldo Traversi's article, titled in translation "African Customs and Practices in Massawa," suggesting, in a way, that African culture was not inherent to his perception of Massawa; one would not expect to find articles titled "African Customs in Kano, Kassala, or Kampala."[29] Gatta, to take another example, noted in 1885 that "the inhabitants of Massawa tend to follow Arab customs"; others indistinctly qualified Massawa's upper social echelons as "Arabs." Italian photographers of the early colonial period also captioned their photographs accordingly: they photographed "Arab houses," "Arab villages," "Arab restaurants and cafes," "Arab mosques," "Arab dances," "Arab notables" and "Arab women."[30] But early European observers were undoubtedly unaware that a new vigorous flow of Arab cultural influences was relatively recent and that many whom they qualified as "Arabs" were in fact wealthy or prominent notables of local and regional origins—the coastal elite.[31] In addition, among the "Arabs" who migrated to Massawa—from the Yemen, for example—some porters, peddlers, and fishermen were extremely poor and of low social status. European ideas about the superiority of Arabs fell into some contradiction when juxtaposing ethnicity with social class and culture in late-nineteenth-century Massawa. Europeans were similarly unaware of the struggles and competition over citizenship represented in various public rituals and habits in a burgeoning town in which social and economic gaps between people widened considerably. Freed slaves and poor nomads in search of labor and opportunities, on the one hand, and very wealthy merchants and entrepreneurs, on the other, were the extremes of a social spectrum sharing—and struggling over—an urban social space in a period of accelerated transformation. Seemingly clear-cut dichotomies and binary oppositions were therefore idealized and instrumental in that context.

Elite and Notable Families: Status, Wealth, and Urban Authority

One of the outcomes of the transformation of the second half of the nineteenth century was the gradual emergence of a more pronounced and hierarchical order in Massawa's social landscape. The upper stratum of urban society consisted of a group of families, or patrilineages, that provided a sense of identity to their members and conferred social status upon them. This section discusses the social bases of elite status and explores the various attributes, or status markers, that determined social stratification and defined the class of elite and notable families. By identifying the social, economic, and religious networks, connections, and alliances of specific families, it shows the ways by which these families were connected, as well as the inherent functional coherence of this socially porous but discursively tight-knit group of families.

If in the previous sections it has been argued that the ideal of "being

Massawan" was largely based on attributes of urban refinement and "civilization" and a particular appropriation of Islamic and Arab identity, this section shows that it also meant having a family name and belonging to one of the town's potent patrilineages. That said, the concept of "elite families" should be understood in a dynamic way since status and social relations were to some extent flexible and were not always determined by fixed attributes. Kenneth Brown wrote in a study of the urban communities of Salé that social relations in the Moroccan town were "characterized by a pattern of shifting coalitions, of networks of patrons and clients," based on common interests that were "sometimes strengthened (but not determined) by descent, marriage, or friendship." The elite, Brown remarked, "dominated cross-cutting social networks" more determined by the control of "clientele groups held together by mutual interests, not ties of consanguity."[32]

In a seminal article published in 1968, historian Albert Hourani analyzed the distinctive role of the notables (Ar. *aʿyān*) in the Arab provinces of the Ottoman Empire. Departing from Max Weber's term "patriciate"—a class of urban notables *governing* a city—Hourani noted that in Islamic history the urban notables were more commonly a group *external* to formal authority and were able to exercise some type of influence and impose limits on the government in place.[33] The notables, according to Hourani, were "those who can play a certain political role as intermediaries between government and people, and—within certain limits—as leaders of the urban population."[34] But as a group that was not dependent on government, the notables had to possess some social power of their own, giving them a position of accepted leadership in the community. Hourani claimed that in different circumstances, different people with different types of social power played this role. In the Arab provinces of the Ottoman Empire there were three such groups: (1) the *ʿulamāʾ*, whose power was rooted in their religious position, (2) the leaders of the local garrisons, and (3) the "secular notables," who were individuals or families whose power derived from some military or political tradition, or the memory of some prestigious ancestor or predecessor, or their control of land and supervision of *waqf*s. The secular notables had independent bases of power and were connected to other notable families, *ʿulamāʾ*, *shaykh*s, and also potent chieftains outside the city.[35]

Differences persist among historians as to who should be labeled a notable, what precise role they played, and whether or not they formed a cohesive group. Historians of different regions and periods of the Middle

East have come up with different definitions and restrictive uses of the term to designate this amorphous category.[36] Some, like Margaret Meriwether, have used the term "notable" in a more general sense than in the historiography of Ottoman notable politics, referring to those in Ottoman urban society "whose role and importance in the city were determined by high social status and wealth, rather than their political role. The elite occupied the top layer of the social hierarchy. While there was considerable overlap between the political elite and the social elite, they were not identical."[37] In general, the foundations of high status were quite similar throughout the Ottoman Middle East in this period, but the relative weight given to specific social markers could differ in time and space and was after all localized. This meant that the composition of the higher urban echelons and the degree of integration varied widely.

In Massawa the situation is also complex, first and foremost since the port was ruled by different governments in the nineteenth century. But furthermore, even within the framework of each power, the structure of relationships between government and notables varied significantly. As a relatively marginal, distant, and isolated outpost in an unstable period of dwindling Ottoman, and forceful but erratic khedival, authority, Massawa had experience with government between the beginning of the century and 1885 that vacillated between times of a firm grip of government and more loose periods granting greater autonomy and effective control to the local political, economic, and religious elite. The imposition of Italian colonialism in 1885 also witnessed the shaping of a relationship between the port's elite and the colonial administration, largely in response to Italian policies and practice. As I have argued above, a certain degree of economic and political collaboration even led to the strengthening of Massawa's elite. In general, the special position and role of the town's mercantile community, and its unique historical trajectory since the Ottoman occupation in the sixteenth century, left considerable autonomy to local rulers and elites. Together with the port's leading merchants, the locally and regionally potent Balaw lineages were able to develop a privileged position vis-à-vis the government and were recognized as leaders of the urban community, even if their traditional political roles in the broader region were transformed and diminished. This heterogeneous yet in many respects tight-knit and cohesive group, wielding its social power and authority from various sources, constituted Massawa's urban elite.

In Massawa I have identified four loose categories of elite status groups, or notables, whose bases of power differed from one another but

Figure 5.2. Merchants of Massawa, 1887–88. Photographer: Nicotra brothers. Biblioteca Reale, Torino.

who, in practice, were in many ways connected. Social boundaries were never entirely fixed, and where to draw the boundaries between the "elite" and others is never entirely conclusive. Social markers and attributes could intersect—certain individuals could indeed be prominent in several social arenas. Marriage ties and other types of alliances among different groups of the elite could blur the lines between them. It is therefore important to note that the categorization that follows is more heuristic than reflective of clear-cut differences. First were those potent families deriving their social power from their position, role, and influence in the close and more distant interior. A second category consisted of those who were associated in some way—mainly as office-holders or militia leaders—with the Ottoman and Egyptian authorities. A third group were those whose power was founded on religious prestige and office. The last, but perhaps most porous and amorphous group category, included rich merchants and—in the context of the second half of the nineteenth century—the nouveaux riches. In a way, material wealth could cut across these status groups. It was central in determining social stratification, and there are several examples of impoverished traditional notables, on the one hand, and newly enriched individuals of relatively low social background who were able to join the elite strata thanks to their success in business, on the other. Sometimes status mobility could even be determined by the tenacious and staunch character of an individual. These caveats explain why the extent to which these traditional status groups represented meaningful social groups was after all limited.[38] A rather stunning group portrait photograph that probably would have never have been shot in the absence of colonialism was taken at the foot of the Governor's Palace in 1887 (Fig. 5.2). It was captioned "Arab merchants greeting General Genè," and shows a group of some two dozen men (visibly including Europeans) who embodied Massawa's patrician class.

NOTABLES WITH STRONG MAINLAND POWER BASES

A first category of the urban elite comprised some of the oldest families in the port, many of whom had solid bases of power in Hergigo and among the neighboring Saho-, Afar-, and Tigre-speaking pastoralist and nomad groups of the inland. This category may be qualified as the traditional coastal elite, which included families from the various Balaw branches, of whom *nāʾib*s were descended in the past. Those associated with or linked to the Nāʾib family and other powerful Balaw families from the Balaw ᶜĀmir and the Balaw Yūsuf Ḥassab Allāh branches were also among this group. One of the most characteristic examples of notable families originally belonging to the Balaw Yūsuf Ḥassab Allāh was the Shīnītī family, briefly discussed in a previous chapter. But there were others, such as the Ḥāmidūy family. ᶜUthmān b. Saᶜīd Ḥāmidūy and his brother, Shaykh Aḥmad b. Saᶜīd Ḥāmidūy, both sons of Shaykh Saᶜīd b. Muḥammad Ḥāmidūy (d. 1870s) attained high status in Massawan society as merchants and owners of urban real estate in the 1870s and 1880s. Primarily based in Hergigo, the Ḥāmidūy family exemplifies a family with high status and strong bases both in town and in the surrounding countryside. Aḥmad Saᶜīd was referred to as a "notable" (*min aᶜyān Maṣawwaᶜ*) in the Islamic court records, while his brother ᶜUthmān Saᶜīd was a *khalīfa* of the Khatmiyya *ṭarīqa*.[39] Other Balaw families of importance in this category were the Danbar, Ḥilū, and Minnī families.

Another large cluster within the category of the old coastal elite derived from the Saho-speaking clans who originated in the Zula area and moved up north to settle in Hergigo and Massawa during the Ottoman period. The two most important branches, descendant from Faqīh Muḥammad al-Zubayr, were the Bayt Shaykh Maḥmūd and the branch of ᶜAd Ṣāliḥ al-Zubayr. Both branches gained religious prestige from their descendance and were considered holy clans.[40] Families such as Faras, Bādūrī, Sirāj, Saᶜdūy, Ḥabīb, Khaydara belonged to this category and were powerful in their bases in Hergigo and Massawa. Shaykh ᶜUmar b. Maḥmūd b. Shaykh ᶜUmar Bādūrī (from Hergigo), for example, served as *qāḍī* of Massawa sometime in the 1840s or 1850s.[41]

Other leading families descended from the Asaorta and other Saho-speaking clans were Zakarī, Jabīra and ᶜAdūlāy. A large family of particularly high status in Massawa's social landscape (as eminent as the Shīnītīs and Mentāys) was the al-Nātī family, originally from the ᶜAd Tsaura. Members of this family figure prominently in the court proceedings in this period. They bought and sold parcels of land and shops, they gave and received power of attorney (*tawkīl*) to and from other elite families, and they liberated domestic slaves and inherited property in real estate.[42]

A last example representing a high-status family of Afar origins was the Dankalī family. They too were involved in a variety of real estate transactions throughout the 1860s to the late 1880s, purchasing land and shops and dividing estates by selling parts of properties. They leased several parcels of land to a foreign merchant named Stefan, they went to court to obtain title deeds for their properties and endowments (Ar. sing. *waqf*, pl. *awqāf*), and were tied in marriage bonds with several families, among which was ᶜAbd Allāh b. Muḥammad b. Saᶜīd Shīnītī, mentioned above.[43] However, much as for the al-Nātīs and several other families in this category, it might be the case that in the 1880s and 1890s some loss in wealth occurred. A new class of entrepreneurs—many of whom were Hadramis, Yemenis, and Egyptians (often better connected in the Red Sea and the port's forelands)—were able to purchase much real estate property in the port. In many cases, as the court registers attest, the new class of entrepreneurs bought property precisely from these families, who usually divided estates following the death of a household head.

AT GOVERNMENT SERVICE

A second class of families belonging to Massawa's upper echelons derived its high status from its formal association with or service to the authorities in Massawa. Association with Ottoman and Egyptian rule could elevate the social status of a family. One part of this group undoubtedly comes closest to Hourani's basic definition of the notables as a group playing some political role in the capacity of mediators between government and people. The *nāʾib*s and their families were the foremost in this group, basing their legitimacy and power on the role they played in regional politics since the Ottomans appointed them as the de facto rulers of Massawa and the coastlands. Families, specifically from Hergigo, who derived some type of status as a result of their association with the Ottomans were those who adopted family names in relation to their functions and services for the "Turks." We have noted previously families such as the Kekiyā, Sardāl, ᶜAsker, Kurdī, Basnāk, Shāwish and others whose family names are intimately linked to the experience of the Ottoman period in Massawa.[44] But in the second half of the century the status of these families was most notably limited to Hergigo. Few, if any (perhaps to some extent members of the Kāḥya and Kurdī[45] families), had made it into big commerce and were consequently wealthy and influential enough to break through into Massawa's leading elite.[46] Clearly, in this period the reconfiguration of trading structures and networks in the northwestern Indian Ocean region meant that entrepreneurs with connections in the Red Sea area fared better than the traditional coastal elite.

The political hegemony of the *nāʾibs* was curtailed as khedival Egypt took a more direct and active policy of expansion in the region and effective control in the mid-nineteenth century. But the *nāʾibs*' power and authority did not disappear altogether. They continued to wield power, first and foremost, through the domination of a widespread web of networks in commerce connecting Massawa with the Nile Valley in a period of intense commercial vitality. To some extent they also maintained the bases of their regional authority and power since the Egyptians under Khedive Ismāᶜīl—who attempted to develop the port and link it with their other possessions in the Nile Valley—were eager to develop a certain working relationship with the *nāʾibs*, a relationship of accommodation that was to benefit both parties.

The Egyptian administration made efforts to hold a tighter grip on the populations of their dominions in Massawa's hinterlands and in the process coopted the *nāʾibs*, whose political, economic, and social networks in the region were deemed instrumental for mobilizing local populations and securing their loyalty to the government. This is perhaps best exemplified by the career of Nāʾib Idrīs Ḥasan (ca. 1825–1905), who began his tenure as *nāʾib* of Hetumlo and Emkullo in the early 1850s, when rebelling and taking up arms against the Ottoman government over the question of tribute collection in the Habab region. But the revolts were followed by accommodation and cooperation, and by the mid-1860s when Ismāᶜīl's Egypt took formal control of the region, Nāʾib Idrīs began to work closely with the Massawa administration, which was astute enough to play on the division within the Nāʾib family. Idrīs was especially instrumental in securing the control of Zula and Obock on the Afar and Somali coasts. In the early 1870s he was decorated by the Egyptian army; he was awarded the honorary military title of major (*sagh qol aghāsī*), and appointed *nāẓir* of Semhar.[47] The cooperation with government continued into the early Italian colonial era.

Much as in the eighteenth century under the Ottomans, both the Egyptians and the Italians (from 1885) capitalized on the historic rivalry between two factions of the Nāʾib family, the Bayt Ḥasan and the Bayt ʿUthmān, and manipulated contesting holders to the office of the *nāʾib* and its privileges, employing "divide and rule" tactics. In the Italian colonial period, the *nāʾib*s worked with the administration in various capacities, received government subventions, and maintained but some minimal administrative autonomy in their villages in Massawa's suburbs (especially Hergigo and Emkullo). Accommodation to Italian colonial rule was instrumental in promoting local municipal and economic interests, but the *nāʾibs*' formerly politically powerful position remained a symbolic vestige of the past. In 1888 the Italian authorities formally divided the now diminished office of the *nāʾib* between the two family lines. The Bayt Ḥasan preserved Hergigo under ʿAbd al-Karīm ʿAbd al-Raḥīm and the Bayt ʿUthmān took charge of Emkullo and Hetumlo under Idrīs Ḥasan.[48] Indeed, Nāʾib Idrīs was appointed to several positions by the Italians while he and members of his family fought (and died) alongside the Italian forces in Amba Alagi, Saganeiti, and ʿAdwa in the campaigns of 1895–96.[49] It is also interesting to note that Nāʾib Idrīs Ḥasan was the chief source of information for Teobaldo Folchi, who in 1898 compiled an invaluable unpublished report on the various populations of Semhar, which served the basis of much of Dante Odorizzi's well-known published monograph of 1911.

Other individuals also worked closely with the Egyptian administration in Massawa and acquired considerable capital, both material and nonmaterial, as a result of the framework and workings of Egyptian rule. ʿAbd Allāh Bey al-Ghūl (and later his son Aḥmad Afandī al-Ghūl)—Egyptians who made Massawa their home—were without a doubt central pillars of the community in terms of wealth, connections to government, and their role in urban communal affairs and institutions from the 1860s deep into the Italian era. Entrepreneurs such as the al-Ghūls in Massawa—and Muṣṭafā Shināwī Bey in Sawākin—spearheaded the economic objectives of Egyptian imperialism in northeast Africa and the Red Sea area. Even after the Egyptian evacuation and the establishment of the Eritrean colony, figures such as al-Ghūl continued to serve as privileged intermediaries between the government authorities and local merchants, which they had by now

Figure 5.3. Nāʾib Idrīs Ḥasan, ca. 1898. Postcard. Photographer: Errardo di Aichelburg. Private collection, Pavoni Social Centre, Asmara.

joined themselves. A case in point, which also reveals the dynamics and relationship between authorities and elites in Massawa, occurred in early 1900 when, in light of the decline in Massawa's commercial competitiveness due to Djibouti's rising role in serving Ethiopia, al-Ghūl, Bā Ṭūq, and Shīnītī approached Governor Martini with specific requests to respond to the crisis by improving conditions for commerce. The three asked Martini to lower the customs duties on wool from 15 percent to 8 percent and on silk and cotton from 10 percent to 8 percent and to establish a free zone in Massawa.[50]

Merchant, Communal Leader, and Go Between: ʿAlī Afandī Yaḥyā

Another prominent example is that of ʿAlī Afandī b. Shaykh Yaḥyā b. ʿAlī Afandī, born sometime around mid-century. It is difficult to determine the origins of the family since his grandfather, ʿAlī, had already taken the title *afandī* as the family name probably in the early nineteenth century. Even though various sources note the family's origins as "Constantinople," members of the family nowadays are highly skeptical of this claim. But they are unable to provide any further clue beyond claiming that the family is "Tigre," originating in the mainland Tigre-speaking groups. ʿAlī Yaḥyā was one of the best-networked merchants in Massawa in the 1870s and 1880s, having solid influence and connections on local-regional commercial, religious, and political arenas. He served as *sartujjār* (head of the merchants) at least from the late 1870s, under the Egyptians; owing to this position, he was the most closely associated person (perhaps together with the al-Ghūls) with the Egyptian authorities. ʿAlī Afandī was able to accumulate considerable wealth and invest in real estate. According to transactions recorded in the Islamic court, between 1873 and 1889 he purchased at least five shops in the town's bazaar, the *sūq al-Sulṭān,* several parcels of urban land and part of a residential house.[51] In a court case opposing Sayyid Muḥammad Bakrī al-Mīrghanī and Maḥbūb al-Ṣāfī in 1886, ʿAlī Yaḥyā, as Sayyid Muḥammad's agent and representative, was obliged to pay Ṣāfī a considerable amount of money, almost ruining him financially.[52] On the religious scene he was also a man of influence, and as the judicial affair noted attests, he was closely related to the Mīrghanīs in Massawa. In the late 1880s he acted as go-between between the Italian authorities and Sayyid Muḥammad ʿUthmān Tājj al-Sirr (1849/50–1903) in the latter's attempts to offer his services to the Italians and settle in Massawa.[53] In the first years of the twentieth century ʿAlī Yaḥyā was noted as a *khalīfa* of the Khatmiyya in Massawa.[54] The family, according to his descendants, was always very pious. He was married to ʿĀʾisha Ḥammūda, who was from a foremost family of local notables. The Afandīs, as the family came to be known, were further linked in marriage with leading families (among whom were *sayyids* and *ashrāf*) such as Shīnītī, Ṣāfī, ʿAbbāsī, Mīyā, and others.[55]

Making use of his widespread connections and influence in politics and commerce, ʿAlī Yaḥyā continued to provide services to the colonial authorities after the Italian takeover in 1885. In 1889 he successfully conducted negotiations leading to the submission of Diglāl al-Ḥusayn and Maḥmūd Sharīf of the Beni ʿAmer. He was also instrumental in establishing and maintaining solid and secure commercial connections with the Sudanese region, and he helped supply Keren with dhurra during the devastating period of famine known in Amharic as the *kefu qen.* In 1890 he was charged with establishing commercial links with the Dervish of Ṭahar

Figure 5.4. ʿAlī Afandī Yaḥyā, Massawa, ca. 1898. Postcard. Photographer: Errardo di Aichelburg. Author's personal collection.

(name is unclear) and was appointed assistant judge in court in addition to his functions as municipal councilor. An Italian colonial report qualified ʿAlī Yaḥyā as "serious" and "extremely competent" in always providing the authorities with valuable information about commerce, caravan traffic, the salt works, and the notable class of Massawa.[56] In 1903, under Martini's enterprising "Islamic policy," ʿAlī Yaḥyā and the *nāʾib* of Emkullo were instrumental in convincing Sayyid Jaʿfar al Mīrghanī, a Khatmi leader, to move his seat from Kassala to Keren, within the confines of the colony.[57]

SAYYIDS AND *SHAYKHS*: THE MUSLIM RELIGIOUS ELITE

The third category of notables derived its status from religious prestige, as the *ʿulamāʾ* (learned men) serving in several religious offices, most notably those of *qāḍī* and *muftī*. Others were *khalīfas*, *muqqadams*, and *shaykhs* of Sufi orders active in the conurbation. While the first category of notables consisted of lineages whose origins were traced to the coastal-mainland elite and was ethno-linguistically bounded to originally Afar-, Tigre-, and Saho-speaking clans, the religious elite crossed ethnic boundaries and drew its members both from abroad and from the African inland.

The first cluster included the *sayyids* and *ashrāf,* who claimed direct descent from the Prophet Muhammad. Theoretically, they were a caste, a closed group, into which one was born. But as in other places in the Muslim world, those who claimed sacred descent already possessed other foundations for their high social position, deriving from one or more of the following: wealth, religious/legal erudition, office-holding, *ṭarīqa* leadership, or political power. In Islamic history some individuals claimed *ashrāf* status only after their success, enabling them to consolidate their position in society. In the records of Massawa's Islamic court, individuals who were recognized as members of the *sādah* had their name preceded by the title *Sayyid.* The most prominent were Ṣāfī, Hāshim, Bā ᶜAlawī, Jaᶜfar, Abū Shaᶜrayn, Masāwa, al-ᶜAṭṭās, Nahārī—all of whom were originally from either Hadramawt or other parts of the Arabian Peninsula. Yet there were also *ashrāf* families such as ᶜAlī Salam (from Hergigo), Shalabī, Ṭurkī, Maghribī, Bāqir, Adam Barkūy, Barakāt, Shakhrāy (Shagarāy), Ramaḍān, and others whose origins were either from the region or from abroad. Others who are not mentioned in the court registers used in this study are the Ḥayūtī family (descended from the al-Ḥibshī), whose members are proud to possess a minutely detailed family tree tracing direct descent from al-*muqaddam* Muḥammad (d. 1255), who is believed to have introduced Sufism to Hadramawt and who headed the *ṭarīqa* ᶜAlawiyya.[58]

Some *qāḍīs* were themselves *sayyids* (Masāwa, Bā ᶜAlawī, and Nahārī) while others were *ashrāf* from Medina (ᶜAbbāsī), and still others came from Saho-speaking holy clans in the interior (Bādūrī, Nāṣir). Members of the ᶜAbbāsī family served in religious offices—as *qāḍīs* and *waqf* administrators—for over three centuries. But even if the cultivation of religious prestige by the well-to-do was common practice, prestige derived from religious status did not automatically lead to prosperity and translate into material wealth. One elderly informant originally from Hetumlo, Sayyid Ibrāhīm Muḥammad Ibrāhīm al-Sayyid, recounted that his family was quite poor. His grandfather was a laborer working with coal on steamships, and his father had a "kiosque and a shop here and there [on the Massawa mainland]." But *sayyid* status was still pivotal for maintaining social status; indeed the family was linked in marriage with other *sayyid* families of greater prominence, such as Ṣāfī and Masāwa.[59] The combination of high religious status and modest material means was not uncommon. In 1901, following the passing of Shaykh ʿAbd Allāh Sirāj Abū ʿIlāmā, previously *muftī* and *qāḍī*, the community in Massawa presented the *commissario regionale* with a petition. In it they requested the appointment as *qāḍī* of the late *shaykh*'s son, Muḥammad Nūr, so that the family would be able to continue to support itself and avoid falling into destitution.[60]

Religious lineages based in Hergigo were the ʿAd Sayyid ʿUthmān, ʿAd Sayyid ʿUmar Barka, ʿAd Sayyid Daʾūd, ʿAd Sayyid Madanī, ʿAd Shāwish, ʿAd Sayyid Darwīsh, ʿAd Sayyid Brūj, and ʿAd Sayyid Hāshim.[61] Still, other individual families from Tigre- and Saho-speaking holy clans in Semhar and Sahel such as the Bayt Shaykh Maḥmūd (Bādūrī), the Bayt Khalīfa, Bayt Qāḍī, Bayt Tawakkal, the ʿAd Muʿallim, ʿAd Shaykh Darqī, and the ʿAd Shaykh could wield social power from their religious prestige. Many appear in the court registers with the title *ḥājj*—individuals who have made the pilgrimage to Mecca, but even if many of them indeed belonged to the ranks of Massawa's social elite, their status was not directly derived from this attribute.[62] Some of Massawa's notables' power was founded on their role in the Sufi orders. Sayyid Hāshim al-Mīrghanī (d. 1901), the Khatmi leader in Hetumlo—even if somewhat socially distanced from the local urban elite—was one example. In the court registers Shaykh Aḥmad Shalāl (Saho—Bayt Shaykh Maḥmūd) was noted as "the *khalīfa* of the Khatmi order" in 1881 in Hetumlo, where a straw hut mosque was erected and named after him.[63] A member of the Shalāl family, Ibrāhīm, was appointed *khalīfa* by Hāshim al-Mīrghanī in the late nineteenth century.[64]

The Ḥābūna family of Asaorta origins also wielded prestige in the religious sphere. Ismāʿīl Idrīs Ḥābūna was mentioned as the *wakīl* of the *nāẓir* (Ar., comptroller) of the Dhahab mosque in 1873, and in 1886 Muḥammad Saʿīd Idrīs Ḥābūna was noted as "the *khalīfa* of the Shādhiliyya order in Massawa." Ismāʿīl Idrīs Ḥābūna's daughter married Sayyid Muḥammad Yaʿqūb Jaʿfar, a noted *sayyid* of Hadrami origins, in 1872.[65] Marrying into *sayyid* families required either *sayyid* status or another form of appropriate religious prestige. It is precisely at this point of contact—via a religious attribute—that a family with strong mainland influence (Ḥābūna) and another family, possibly with some connections in the Yemeni region (Jaʿfar), were linked, thus creating what may be called the archetype model of the Massawan merchant-mediator family.

Commerce and religion were intimately intertwined in a setting such as Massawa. Religious prestige often represented the cultural capital required to maintain, expand, and glue business connections and networks. It was often done by the accumulation and cultivation of religious status, by marriage into other pious families, services in mosques, or charity, or by being a respectable member in one of the *ṭuruq* (Sufi orders). As Beshara Doumani noted when discussing merchants in nineteenth-century Nablus in Palestine, "combining a religious career with a business career was the norm rather than the exception and had an aura of a time-honored tradition."[66] In the last quarter of the nineteenth century, practically all the well-off merchants in Massawa were, in one way or another, intimately involved in the town's religious vitality.

THE VERY WEALTHY AND THE NOUVEAUX RICHES

In Massawa's merchant milieu, success in accumulating wealth was pivotal in determining social standing. The last third of the nineteenth century witnessed the emergence of a new class of entrepreneurs in Massawa—mostly from Hadramawt, the Arabian Peninsula, and Egypt—who became by far more prosperous than any family of local origins. Commercial expansion spurred the growth of the port-town, prompting a period of vast urban construction and presenting promising opportunities for investors in real estate. In the mid-1880s sources noted that the "Arabs of Massawa" dominated the trade in hides, ivory, and mother-of-pearl. They owned the most beautiful coral stone houses and controlled almost all porterage and transportation services to and from the port.[67] Hadrami traders and entrepreneurs settled in Massawa—sometimes without their families, sometimes for a decade or two—and capitalized on their webs of connections, flexible networks, and a high degree of mobility in and between the Red Sea ports (Luḥayya, Ḥudayda, Aden, Jiddah, Sawākin, etc.) and beyond, in the Indian Ocean.

Big-Money-Making Hadramis: Bā Zarᶜa and Bā Junayd

Members of the Hadrami Bā Zarᶜa and Bā Junayd families in Massawa stood out as wealthy individuals who had ridden the wave of the real estate boom, at least since the 1860s. The Bā Zarᶜa were members of the lowest stratum of Hadrami society, the *haḍar* (town dwellers) subdivision of the *masākin* (poor).[68] They thus exemplify the opportunities that the commercial boom of the second half of the nineteenth century could offer to hardworking and enterprising individuals of any social background. To judge from evidence in the records of the Islamic court, they more often came without women and children since they figure only in real estate transactions and cases involving the attribution of power of attorney (*tawkīl*), with no record whatsoever in cases regarding family issues. Indeed, as was the case on the East African coast, some Hadramis came to Massawa either alone or with male relatives such as brothers, sons, or cousins.[69] In a period of over twenty years, between 1868 and 1889, only two individuals from the Bā Zarᶜa family, Shaykh ᶜUmar b. Aḥmad Bā Zarᶜa and his son Muḥammad b. ᶜUmar Bā Zarᶜa, are mentioned in cases in the court registers, almost all in real estate purchases. Usually, members of Massawa families who had their household in town were described in the registers as *min ahālī Maṣawwaᶜ* (of the local families ["natives"] of Massawa). However, Muḥammad ᶜUmar Bā Zarᶜa was described as late as 1885—his father having conducted business in the port for almost twenty years by then—only as *al-tājir bi-Maṣawwaᶜ* (Ar., who is a merchant, or who is conducting commerce, in Massawa). This description was more commonly attributed to merchants who were not settled with their families in the port-town, such as the Greeks, Levantines, Indians, and Italians. Perhaps one explanation for maintaining a somewhat transient status was that neither one married and established a family in Massawa. Bā Zarᶜa, father and son, were involved more than others in real estate transactions and purchased shops, half shops, rooms, houses, and parcels of land in the 1870s and throughout the 1880s.[70] A careful examination of the transactions suggests that they often purchased real estate property following the division of the estate of a deceased individual among heirs.[71] Yet in some cases property was purchased from merchants whose fortunes were in decline.

Muḥammad ᶜUmar Bā Zarᶜa was also one of several merchants in Massawa who could muster enough capital to organize a considerable shipment of goods for exportation from the port. For example, on 12 October 1886 one of his boats was requisitioned by the Egyptian navy near Taklāy, between Massawa and Sawākin, since it was suspected of carrying provisions to the Mahdists south of Sawākin. The boat carried 300 kilograms of cotton textiles, 190 kilograms of fish claws, 200 kilograms of medical resin, 450 kilograms of rice, 450 kilograms of dates, 18 kilograms of Abyssinian myrrh, 18 kilograms of cloves, 450 kilograms of flour, 180 kilograms of gum and incense, and 322 kilograms of sandalwood, and 213 thalers in cash. The total value of the merchandise amounted to 3,766.25 lire (about 890 thalers).[72] Muḥammad's prominence in trade as well as the acquisition of local real estate opened the door to a more formal and active role in Massawa's urban institutions in the early Italian period. It placed him in a position of influence on the local urban scene. In 1893 he served as assistant judge, municipal commissioner, and member of Massawa's chamber of commerce. Some evidence also points to control deep in the countryside through patronage relationships. In the early twentieth century, a wealthy merchant in Keren told Governor Martini how Bā Zarᶜa (it is not clear which individual precisely), had provided him with capital for purchasing cattle and land. But after Bā Zarᶜa's departure to Aden, all his business with the Sudan was terribly affected, eventually reaching a halt.[73] Even though it seems as if the Bā Zarᶜas left Massawa in favor of Aden around the turn of the century, some merchant lists from the 1910s still mention their presence on the local scene. Yet, very much like today, with Massawans in exile in Jiddah still owning cash-producing real estate properties in town, physical absence did not automatically translate into disappearance from the local business scene. This is precisely where transregional and cross-maritime networks of agents and brokers played a crucial role.

Another even more prominent example was that of ᶜAbd Allāh b. ᶜUmar b. Saᶜīd Bā Junayd, his two sons Muḥammad b. ᶜAbd Allāh and ᶜUmar b. ᶜAbd Allāh, as well as two individuals who seem to be ᶜAbd Allāh's cousins, ᶜUmar b. Aḥmad Bā Junayd and ᶜAlī b. Aḥmad Bā Junayd. The Bā Junayd family was one of the Hadrami families who had spread across the Indian Ocean world in the early nineteenth century, from Jiddah to Singapore and Java, where they formed part of the Arab elite.[74] They did not belong to the *sādah* elite, yet it appears that some members of the family attained positions of influence in various arenas, such as for example ᶜUmar b. Abī Bakr Bā Junayd, who was a noted scholar in Mecca in the late nineteenth and early twentieth centuries.[75] The precise date of their establishment in Massawa is impossible to recover with the available sources, but we know that in 1858 an ᶜAlī Bā Junayd acted as agent for the Indian Farah Yusur, who was described at the time as the "first merchant at Jiddah." ᶜAlī was involved in shipping slaves to his brother Muḥammad Bā Junayd in Jiddah.[76] ᶜAbd Allāh Bā Junayd bought a truly impressive amount of real estate between the late 1860s and the 1880s. ᶜAbd Allāh and his relatives bought buildings, shops, land (including land on Tewalet), houses, rooms, *rawshāns* (Ar., projecting oriel window with wooden latticework, known also as *mashrabiyah*), and sailing boats. Between 1868 and 1888, ᶜAbd Allāh Bā Junayd alone bought 2 buildings, 19.5 shops, 6 parcels of land, and 4 sailing boats.[77] The Bā Junayds constructed buildings and shops on purchased or leased land. Some property was bought from families who divided property after the death of the head of a household, other property was purchased in public auctions (Ar. *mazād*), and yet another part was sold to the up and coming Bā Junayds—especially in the late 1860s and early 1870s—by merchants, from the traditional local urban elite, such as the ᶜAdūlāy, Ḥammūda Mentāy, Shīnītī, Manṣūr, Ṣāʾigh, and others.[78]

As was the case with the Bā Zarᶜas, much property was bought as a consequence of the division of family property. Since in accordance with Islamic law estates were divided equitably among the remaining members of the family, it was not uncommon that following the settling of an estate, heirs sold property that became equally owned by several of them together.[79] ᶜAbd Allāh ᶜUmar Saᶜīd Bā Junayd's wealth placed him in a prominent position in the institutions of the urban community. Indeed, he co-headed, with the Egyptian Ḥasan b. Mūsā al-ᶜAqqād, the first *lajnat al-awqāf* (pious endowments committee), which began formal operation in 1882–83.[80] ᶜAbd Allāh Bā Junayd was noted by the Italians as a "notable" and held the role of assistant judge in the local court in 1893. His son, ᶜUmar ᶜAbd Allāh, was involved in the importation of textiles and the exportation of coffee and ivory. In 1898 he was considered by Governor Martini to be the second richest merchant in Massawa after Aḥmad Afandī al-Ghūl.[81]

The cases of Bā Zarᶜa and Bā Junayd are examples of merchants who were able to accumulate much wealth in a period of commercial vitality and diversify their capital. They were able to adjust to a "modernized" Red Sea commercial system and capitalize on extensive Hadrami networks in many Red Sea ports and beyond. Their acquisition of wealth in Massawa elevated their social standing considerably. Their acquisition of local urban real estate properties might have been pivotal in granting them citizenship. In early Italian Massawa both held seats in the town's leading municipal, judicial, and commercial institutions.

There were others who attained impressive wealth during the period. The wealth of families such as al-Ghūl and Nahārī did not fall from that of the two Hadrami cases described. Still, in the early Italian era other Hadrami merchants moved to the port to conduct successful business enterprises and establish families. The ownership of boats is an important marker of wealth, but also of access to various cross–Red Sea commercial and labor networks. In 1901 there were 255 boats registered in Massawa, the Dahlak Archipelago, and Hergigo, of which the principal owners were the leading members of the al-Ghūl, ᶜAbbāsī, Bā Junayd, Ḥammoda, Shīnītī, Bā Ṭūq, Nahārī, Bā ᶜAlawī, and Hilāl families.[82] In 1908 in Massawa (excluding other localities) as much as seventeen boats were owned by the al-Ghūls, seven by the Ṣāfīs, five by Bā Ṭūq, four by Nahārī, two by

ʿAdūlāy, two by Shīnītī, and one each by Ḥayūtī, Hilāl, ʿAbbāsī, Bā Ḥamdūn and several others.[83]

Waqf and the Construction of Urban Authority

Records of the Islamic court of Massawa dating from the 1860s and 1870s confirm the use of the Islamic institution of *waqf* (Ar., pious endowment) in the port in the nineteenth century. The institution of *waqf* was undoubtedly used well before that in Massawa. One day in 1942 an individual presented himself to the Islamic court of Massawa and sued the local *waqf* committee for failing to legally ascertain properties endowed to his family by a distant forefather. He claimed that his ancestor came to Massawa from the town of Farasān in Yemen in the year AH 750 (AD 1349). He settled in the port, built there a mosque, and endowed to it forty buildings, including their vestibules and gardens. The remainder of his holdings was bequeathed as *waqf* to his offspring, including this claimant, who had attempted—with no apparent success—to gain recognition of his claimed properties for the previous forty years. The *qāḍī* of Massawa passed the case to the Grand Muftī of Eritrea, Shaykh Ibrāhīm al-Mukhtār, who eventually rejected it on the grounds of the claimant's inability to produce the proper evidence proving his family relationship with the assumed ancestor.[84]

The Islamic religious endowment institution, or *waqf,* has been central to the religious, social, economic, and political experiences of Muslim societies since the early days of Islam. A *waqf* is a gift to God for the benefit of a charitable purpose. In principle, all *waqf* are considered *khayrī,* or charitable, but modern Islamic legislation distinguishes between *waqf khayrī,* which is dedicated to pious causes and *waqf ahlī* or *dhurrī* (family), that is, endowments that benefit one's children or family. Since no distinction between the two types of *waqf* has ever been made in classical Islamic legal doctrine, the two have been administered according to the same rules. In what concerns *waqf khayrī,* the person intending to commit a pious deed declares part of his or her property to be unalienable, not subject to business transactions in perpetuity, and designates persons or public utilities such as a mosque, a cemetery, a Sufi lodge (Ar. *zāwiya*), a hospital, a water well or a fountain, or a religious school (Ar. *madrasa*) as beneficiaries of its proceeds.[85]

In many places across the Islamic world a *waqf* beneficiary could also be a person, such as a reciter of the Qurʾān, the official who calls to prayer (*muʾadhdhin*), a religious scholar, or a Sufi holy man. Prior to the twentieth century most public services such as welfare, education, religious services, hospitals, or urban infrastructures were set up and maintained almost exclusively by endowments. The external underlying ethical principle at the basis of the foundation of pious endowments was above all motivated by a will to perform an act of piety and religious devotion. Yet in many cases property was endowed by rulers, governors, or wealthy merchants and notables who used it as a strategy to spread and secure their influence and authority over local populations. In the provinces of the Ottoman Empire, rulers and high officials often endowed villages, agricultural land, and commercial establishments for the benefit of religious institutions and public works enterprises. The use of the institution of *waqf* in these cases consolidated their authority and legitimacy, fostered economic development, and provided for generous sources of income for *waqf* administrators and other officials. Furthermore, by choosing to transmit proceeds to support an institution (a particular mosque, Sufi lodge, school), founders could also promote particular ideological orientations and tendencies and thus exercise significant influence in their communities. In many settings, these strategies were also used by both provincial and urban notables and families, especially in the eighteenth and nineteenth centuries.[86]

The other type of endowment, the *waqf ahlī*, has been mainly employed as one of several strategies to devolve property to descendants and family relatives. In the absence of the freedom to dispose of property by testament or will, the family *waqf* has been one way to circumvent the law of succession in Muslim societies. Historian Beshara Doumani has distinguished several sets of social uses of family *waqf*. First, *waqf* could be used to safeguard significant family properties by protecting them from confiscation and by preserving their unity as viable economic or residential units that would maintain the family's economic resources as well as its status, stability, and solidarity. Second, *waqf* could protect vulnerable family members by securing them a source of income and stability in case of the death of a primary provider. A third use of family *waqf* was to provide the formation and enhancement of a family as a spatially bounded and symbolically distinctive corporate unit, serving to enhance a family's status and prestige in society. Usually, individuals who endowed many properties boosted their visibility and reputation in their communities, which could promote their family's status.[87]

In this section I present a cross-section of *waqf*-related cases and situate them within Massawa's particular historical conjuncture in this period. The records shed light on the strategies employed by entrepreneurs who settled in Massawa and developed their power and authority on the urban arena by converting economic capital to symbolic and, later, political capital through the institution of *waqf.* Historians of the Ottoman Empire and its provinces have identified the relationship between the establishment of *waqf*s and the gaining of control of existing endowments on one hand, and the rise of notables and newly prominent families on the other.[88]

In the case of Massawa, in the 1860s and 1870s we find records directly involving or indirectly referring to both charitable and family endowments. Most founders, trustees, and beneficiaries of *waqf*s were members of one of the branches of the mercantile religious, political and social elite. Up and coming entrepreneurs employed several mechanisms in the interrelated processes of gaining access to local and regional trading, brokering, and patronage networks, accumulating local power, establishing urban authority, and integrating into the town's social, political, and economic elite. One important strategy was through their utilization of the *waqf* institution. Acquiring real estate property, endowing part of it for the public good, and gaining control over existing *waqf* property was a way for recently settled entrepreneurs to establish their standing and authority and develop and cement social and economic networks; it basically offered the keys to high-status citizenship. Endowing property for the public good served as a strategy for establishing one's standing and authority in the community, as demonstrated by the examples of Bā Ḥubayshī, al-Ghūl, and Bā Junayd in regard to the water wells and a cemetery in mainland Massawa, which they bequeathed as charitable endowments. A related facet of this process reveals a shift in the composition of the elite, with the newly empowered and enriched entrepreneurs (in some cases, the "nouveaux riches")—mostly migrants from Hadramawt and Egypt—joining the extant urban elite, but in addition, overpowering it by their overwhelming sources and bases of power.

After having rescued the remaining twenty-nine volumes of court recordings from Massawa's Islamic tribunal in 1959, Muftī Ibrāhīm al-Mukhtār carefully studied the various types of registrations included in them. He found that in the early to mid-1860s some people had presented to the court *ḥujjāj* (Ar., legal deeds) registering or certifying endowments that were delivered to them by judges such as Muḥammad Masāwa, Maḥmūd Nāṣir, and Ādam Ismāʿīl.[89] On the basis of my own reading, Muftī ʿAlī Abū ʿIlāmā could be added to that list.[90] In general, references to *waqf* properties in the court records are relatively flimsy. Notwithstanding, they do provide some information about endowers, endowed properties, property devolution, and endowed mosques and other public utilities. For example, on the basis of the records we know that the ten following mosques, in Massawa Island and Hergigo, all had a certain number of pieces of land and shops endowed to them: Ḥusayn Bāshā mosque, the Hergigo Friday mosque, the Ḥanafī Friday mosque, ᶜAbd Allāh b. Saᶜd al-Yāfiᶜī mosque, the Shāfiᶜī Friday mosque, the Dhahab mosque, ᶜAbd Allāh al-Mahdī mosque, Adūbāsh mosque, Khawājat Ṣafar al-Rūmī mosque, and ᶜAbdu ᶜIlwān mosque.

Some of the earliest references to endowed properties available to us in the court register date from 1285/1868. In that year, for example, ᶜUthmān b. Aḥmad Ḥarak came to court to certify the endowment of eight of his shops to the mosque named ᶜAbd Allāh al-Mahdī.[91] A couple of years later, on 14 Ṣafar 1287/1870, three cases involving *waqf* properties were brought to court. In the first *Sayyid* ᶜUmar b. Sayyid Aḥmad Abū Shaᶜrayn, a prominent local notable of the *sādah,* certified that he had three pieces of land. The first had three stone shops built on it, the second had one shop belonging to ᶜAlī Yamānī, and the third had a straw hut serving as a café. Sayyid ᶜUmar Abū Shaᶜrayn declared that all the pieces of land were *waqf* that had been initially endowed by his grandfather, Ḥasan Abū Shaᶜrayn, to the Adūbāsh mosque.[92] A second case involved Muḥammad Ṣāliḥ b. Aḥmad Ṣāliḥ ᶜAdūlāy, another member of one of Massawa's most prominent families, who certified his properties at the court. He declared having three pieces of land: one was inherited by him and his brothers from their father, one he bought, and one was *waqf* of ᶜAbd Allāh Saᶜd al-Yāfiᶜī mosque.[93] In the third case, Bakr b. ᶜAlī, the legal representative (*wakīl*) of Zaᶜfrān, wife of the late ᶜAbd al-Nabī al-Maghribī, and of Amna b. Surūr, presented himself at court. Surūr was ᶜAbd al-Nabī's liberated slave. After Surūr's death, ᶜAbd al-Nabī married Zaᶜfrān (Surūr's wife) and gave her and her daughter Amna a stone house with a wooden *rawshān* as *waqf.* It was given to them and their descendants until the end of their lineage. After that it was to become *waqf* of the Shāfiᶜī Friday mosque.[94] ᶜAbd al-Nabī's aim was undoubtedly to secure Zaᶜfrān's and Amna's future. Interestingly, this case exemplifies a combined *waqf ahlī* and *khayrī.* In a similar case whereby the socioeconomic security of designated beneficiaries might have been a main motivation, land endowed by Aḥmad Qashmīr to his now late son Mūsā Aḥmad Qashmīr was devolved to Mūsā's four daughters: Fāṭima, Fāṭou, Khadīja, and Bakhīta.[95]

A more elaborate case of *waqf* foundation was recorded in the month of Shaᶜbān 1296 [1879]. The prominent and wealthy ᶜAbd Allāh Bey b. Aḥmad b. Yūsuf al-Ghūl bought a parcel of land for 25 French *riyāls* (thalers) from Bakhīta b. ᶜAbd Allāh and Fāṭma Hindī b. ᶜAbd Allāh, who were the liberated slaves of Aḥmad Hindī b. Ṣādiq al-Qashmīrī. Two days later he endowed the land to the Shāfiᶜī Friday mosque. The endowment record reproduces the elaborate references and quotations from the *Ḥadīth,* presenting the great merits of the *waqf* and its founder. The *waqfiyya* reproduces the famous *ḥadīth* transmitted by Abū Ḥurayra and often quoted when legitimizing *waqf:* "The Messenger of God said: 'when a man dies, only three deeds will survive him: continuing alms, profitable knowledge, and a child praying for him.'" Another *ḥadīth* transmitted by ᶜUqbah b. Āmir and included in the *waqf* deed narrated that the Prophet said: "The believer will be shadowed by his charity in the hereafter" and "the charity [*ṣadaqa*] extinguished God's wrath." Showcasing his deep sense of piety before the court, al-Ghūl added that God says in the Qurʾān that "you shall never be truly righteous until you give in alms what you dearly cherish. The alms you give are known to God" (Qurʾān 3:92). The piece of land, the endowment deed continued, is inalienable and irrevocable—it cannot be sold, pawned, or given as a gift "until the end of the world."[96] It was not uncommon for a prominent member of the town's leading elite to endow property to religious establishments and public utilities in developing power and cementing authority and prominence on the urban scene—acquiring symbolic capital, in other words. In another case the following year the same ᶜAbd Allāh Bey al-Ghūl presented his wish to the court to endow some land to the government on the condition that it be exclusively used for public utility (not construction). The *qāḍī* did not accept the request and explained that one cannot put conditions on *waqf.*[97]

Similarly, another prominent merchant and energetic entrepreneur in Massawa, ᶜAlī Aḥmad Bā Junayd, was involved in several *waqf khayrī* cases. In one dating from 1871, he endowed one of his shops to a water well near Hetumlo that was initially made a *waqf* by a previous family member (the well was called *bʾir* Bā Junayd).[98] He also rented some land that was *waqf* of ᶜAbd Allāh al-Mahdī mosque, while his family relative, ᶜAbd Allāh ᶜUmar Bā Junayd, bought several shops from Muḥammad b. Ḥāmid Ṣāʾigh located on land that was *waqf* of the Dhahab mosque.[99] In addition, it is very possible that one member of the Bā Junayd family had endowed some property to Massawa's old cemetery, which is known to this day as *maqbarat* Bā Junayd.[100] Similarly, Shaykh ᶜAbd Allāh Khalīl

Mentāy, a member of a locally prominent family, rented land endowed to the Ḥusayn Bāshā mosque and built two shops over it.[101] By taking over those endowed properties—some of which had not produced much usufruct for long periods of time—such entrepreneurs were able to secure a steadier flow of funds for the administration and renovation of religious institutions. As in other parts of the Middle East, this flexibility in transferring *waqf* properties in order to maximize income was not uncommon.[102] An excellent example of that occurred when ᶜAbd Allāh ᶜUmar Bā Junayd, the owner of seven shops located on land endowed to the Khawājat Ṣafar al-Rūmī mosque, paid a seven-year advance of his dues to ᶜAbd Allāh Rajab Rubāᶜī, the administrator of the mosque. Bā Junayd had to pay 1 *riyāl* per shop per year, amounting to 7 *riyāls*. The advance payment (*salf*) gave him a substantial amount of 49 *riyāls* in order to perform renovation and repair works in the mosque.[103] The registration is not crystal-clear, but this advance payment might have corresponded to the device called *murṣad*, which is a loan designated to cover repair or restoration expenses for the mosque in question. In a second example, Aḥmad Ṭahā, administrator (*nāẓir*) of the Ḥusayn Bāshā mosque took the initiative to materialize the mosque's endowed lands in order to generate income for his establishment. Aḥmad Ṭahā argued before the *qāḍī* that the piece of land in question had been empty for years, and had, as a result, failed to yield any income whatsoever. He therefore rented out the land to Shaykh Ādam Shaykh Muḥammad Barkūy, who intended to build a store on it. The store would pay a rental fee of 1 *riyāl* per month, part of which would go to the mosque.[104]

There are also some references to the use of family endowments (Ar. *waqf ahlī*) in the second half of the nineteenth century. Family endowments were instrumental in serving certain social and economic functions such as protecting against the fragmentation of viable economic or residential units, cementing the material foundations of families as corporate units, circumventing the rules of succession, securing an income to family members and protecting them from poverty, or preserving and enhancing a family's place in society.[105] Ibrāhīm al-Mukhtār noted three that he had found in deeds and court records that he had examined: the *waqf* of Mūsā Qashmīr, the *waqf* of Aḥmad ᶜAlī al-Fayrūzī, and the *waqf* of Muḥammad Adāla.[106] There were also cases where family and pious endowments were combined. In several cases a father devolved *waqf* property to his sons and their descendants until the end of the lineage, after which the *waqf* was to be transferred to such and such a mosque. In one case retrieved from the records Muḥammad Shaqrāy endowed a piece of land and designated his two sons, Muḥammad Ismāʿīl and Muḥammad ʿUthmān, as beneficiaries. The land was to remain theirs until the end of their lineage, after which it was to be devolved to the Dhahab mosque. The case was unusual since Shaqrāy wanted to replace the land with two shops. This device is known as *istibdāl,* or the exchange of one *waqf* property for another. The request was opposed by Ismāʿīl Idrīs Ḥābūna, the legal representative of the administrator (*nāzir*) of that mosque since, as he argued, the *muftī* of Mecca, ʿAbd al-Raḥmān Sirāj, had issued a *fatwa* ruling that a *waqf* cannot be replaced according to their *madhhab.* The replacement was thus rejected.[107] In another case, in 1874, ʿAbd Allāh ʿUmar Bā Junayd (encountered above) bought half of a store from Ḥājjī b. Mūsā Shīnītī (who had the store in partnership with Muḥammad Maqbūl Nāṣir). The price was 100 *riyāls* and a purse of *qurūsh* (least precious coins) of an undetermined sum. The store was built on land that was a Shīnītī family *waqf.*[108]

In 1882–83 the Muslim notables of Massawa set up a special committee that regularized and centralized *waqf* administration in the port town. The committee was placed under the jurisdiction of the town's *qāḍī.* The first committee was co-headed by Sayyid Ḥasan b. Mūsā al-ʿAqqād and Shaykh ʿAbd Allāh b. ʿUmar b. Saʿīd Bā Junayd. The second committee was headed by Shaykh Muḥammad ʿAbbāsī (d. 1899); the third, established in 1896, was headed by Shaykh Aḥmad Afandī b. ʿAbd Allāh Bey al-Ghūl (1854–1919); and the fourth was headed by Muḥammad Sālim Bā Ṭūq. In 1916, under the Italians, new regulations concerning *waqf* were decreed, and the *waqf* committee was placed under the governor of the Colony.[109]

Family, Household, and Marriage

> The town [of Massawa] does not allow one to observe the customs of the inhabitants because, with the exception of the commercial aspects, everything else is hidden within the houses [*palazzi*] of the *signori.* . . . The huts are so sheltered and the houses so closed, that beyond life on the streets, everything is mysterious in the homes of these compatriots of ours in the Red Sea.
>
> —Leopoldo Traversi, 1889[110]

Family Names and Family Structure

Several nineteenth-century writers noted the contrast between the social organization of Massawa's urban community in families and the "tribal" or clanic organization of the pastoralists and nomads of the countryside. In the late twentieth century the anecdote about identity card applications in post-independence Eritrea and Massawans' insistence on inscribing their family names as their "ethnic affiliation" reveals much about the centrality of the institution of the family in Massawa's urban mercantile society. A strong sense of family was central to a notion of urban identity and to the perpetuation of social power on the local scene. The anecdote also signals the importance of family names as markers of one's affiliation to the urban community. A family name in such a merchant milieu was a type of trademark, an identifying marker that was supposed to convey a message of prestige, respectability, reliability, and trustworthiness—all essential for success in business relationships. Family names have been in use in Massawa since a process of urbanization—most probably during the Ottoman period—was set in motion. Many town dwellers—either from the African inland or from abroad—adopted family names, most often referring to their claimed regions/cities of origin, a feature that distinguished them from non-urban nomads and pastoralists, who were usually referred to as *x* son of *y;* his son, as *z* son of *x;* and so forth.

This characteristic is also visible in the records of the Islamic court. Individuals with no family name usually designated nomads, pastoralists, agriculturalists, caravaneers, or slaves, originally not from Massawa, or not from its high-ranking families. With the process of accelerated urbanization in the last decades of the nineteenth century—and well into the twentieth—more individuals who had joined the conurbation began using surnames.[111] For example, surnames such as Wariāy (Wariā) and Ḥababāy (Habab), to name two examples that visibly refer to inland pastoralist Tigre-speaking groups, were adopted by individuals and families who became more established in the urban setting, in this case in Hetumlo. They were neither wealthy nor among the high classes, and they did not reside in stone houses, or on Massawa Island. Adopting a family name was functional in brokerage and local networks. It was a form of cultural capital that could provide access to the town's mercantile elite, on the one hand, and made them appear as respectable and powerful town dwellers in the eyes of clients in the countryside whose understanding of the subtleties of urban social dynamics was limited, on the other. In his study of merchants and peasants in eighteenth- and nineteenth-century Palestine, Beshara Doumani noted that family names were "in a sense, a form of property whose value depended on the intimate connections between physical space, economic fortune, social standing, and cultural practices of the household."[112]

In the second half of the century, individuals who migrated to Massawa or its environment usually adopted a family name. As noted in a previous chapter, a Saho-speaking convert who came to the Dahlak islands took the Kḥayl family name from his Yemeni employer. ʿAlī Saʿīd Ṣūrī, who came to the Dahlak islands to engage in the marine products trade and transportation in the 1880s, also attached the name of his town of origin (or its vicinities) in Oman, Ṣūr, to his name. Aḥmad Ḥayūtī, head of a Hadrami family of *sādah,* also changed its name from Ḥibshī to Ḥayūtī in the second half of the century, perhaps as a consequence of a household/lineage division among the Ḥibshīs. Family names could also come and go with the growing or fading fortunes of families. Other Hadrami families in Massawa, such as ʿAydarūs and Bā ʿAlawī, were noted to be "of the Ḥibshīs" in the past, strengthening a lineage division hypothesis.[113] The fragmentation of a lineage might also account for the link between the Mīyā and Khayr ad-Dīn families—sometimes unseparated and referred to as Mīyā Khayr ad-Dīn.

Another phenomenon that might be a result of the cultural capital with which a surname is charged is the utilization of one family name by two separate families, usually one tracing origins from abroad and another from the countryside. Several possible examples include Ṣāʾigh, Khaydara, Mīyā, Mentāy, and Ḥamdān. Observing that "some are 'real' and others not," one informant explained that some families added/adopted the family name of an originally foreign family, for whom they sometimes worked, or with whom they were tied in marriage alliances, in order to add to their prestige. Providing an example from contemporary Asmara, the informant argued that for example the Bā Saʿd family, whose name structure is unequivocally Hadrami, are in fact highland Tigrinya-speaking Jeberti Muslims who might have worked for the original Bā Saʿd and at some point took his name and subsequently became rich on their own account.

The words in Arabic designating "family" are quite ambiguous, much as their meanings. They vary from one location to another (even within a relatively limited space), from one period to another, and leave room for individual interpretation. Similarities, variations, and a range of levels of inclusivity in the terms *ʿāʾila* (nuclear or extended family, lineage), *bayt* (nuclear family or extended group, physical house), *dār* (household, physicalhouse), and *ahl* (family, large group of kin, lineage) exist throughout the Arabic-speaking world. In Massawa the term employed for designating a family was usually *bayt,* sometimes *ahl.* Most of those who had family names in Massawa—even more so the notable and wealthy families—are referred to as *bayt* such and such.[114] In Egyptian terminology, but also in the Fertile Crescent, *bayt* means literally "house," implying a strong association between a family and its residential space. It could therefore designate both the house and the group of people living under the same roof or in the same compound. This group could be either a nuclear family (simple household) or an extended basic family including a widowed parent, an unmarried aunt, and so on. But it could also mean an extended family (multiple households or joint family households), living under a patriarch and including father, mother, unmarried children, and married sons and their families, all living together in a compound divided into rooms (or small "flats"). In the context of elite households in eighteenth-century Egypt, for example, *bayt* could also refer to a "political household" or faction coming under a leader or the "lineage" of a political household.[115] *Ahl* is another term for family that can mean anything from immediate family to larger groups of kin.[116] Members of Massawa's leading families were sometimes referred to in the court registers (1860s–80s) as *z* the son of *y*, the son of *x*, the son of *w* + his family name, thus recalling father, grandfather, and great-grandfather, approximately to the beginning of the nineteenth century. In some cases it could perhaps refer to the first patriarch adopting a family name. But the practice of recalling a father and one grandfather was more common in the records.

In order to reveal with greater precision the process of household formation and household size, a systematic study of inheritance cases in the Massawa court records must be carried out. Counting the number of children alive at the time of a father's death allows estimating the size of households. Until such study is carried out, less precise impressions in reading through inheritance cases, divisions of family property (including estates), the appointment of legal tutors, and real estate transactions among family members reveal that in the last quarter of the century many typical Massawa households included two to four non-minor children and sometimes several other smaller children.[117] A prudent estimate would put the average household size at between four and six children. But this varied from family to family, depending on wealth, the length of stay in Massawa, and other variants. The wealthier the family, the larger it was. In the late nineteenth century, ultra-rich Massawans—all of whom were of Arab origins—such as Aḥmad Afandī al-Ghūl, ᶜAlī al-Nahārī, Muḥammad Sālim Bā Ṭūq, and Muḥammad ᶜUmar al-Ṣāfī had a large number of children, between eight and as much as seventeen—most often with several wives. Large and medium-sized households usually owned a large house, or a compound, divided into rooms or flats where married sons could live with their wives. Families of more modest means were smaller, but could grow with the accumulation of wealth.

The ability to marry several wives and support a large family required considerable material means, yet having a large family also secured the perpetuation of a family's capital by avoiding the breaking up and division of property that household divisions usually entailed. When the head of a household died and his estate was divided between his heirs, a process of redistribution of property usually followed.[118] In Massawa's economic climate many heirs substantiated property inherited from a father, as the many cases in which heirs sold property outside the family shows. Sometimes this process entailed the division of households; in other cases a process of buying and selling of property (parts of houses and land) among heirs secured the integrity of the family's assets.[119] Non-kin members of a household included servants and domestic slaves, who were owned by the household head or his wife and were part and parcel of their own private property. But the relationship with slaves could be quite close; some even adopted the household family name and could thus climb the social ladder and access urban citizenship. One example was that of Faraj b. ᶜAbd Allāh "al-Ḥabashī" ("the Abyssinian") and his sister Fāṭma, who were both manumitted by their owner, Aḥmad Hindī b. al-Ṣadīq al-Qashmīrī and who were referred to after manumission as Faraj Hindī b. ᶜAbd Allāh and Fāṭma Hindī b. ᶜAbd Allāh.[120] It was also the case of Serūr, a slave belonging to ᶜAbd al-Nabī al-Maghribī, whose daughter was referred to in the *sharīᶜa* court as Amna b. Serūr ᶜAbd al-Nabī al-Maghribī.[121]

The situation in the outer elements of the conurbation, in Hetumlo and Emkullo, seems more complex since in some cases several family structures must have coexisted and since the process of urbanization entailed a transition from a nomadic clanic kinship structure to a more individuated family.[122] In Hergigo the situation was also complex, straddling the urban family type and several types of nomadic and pastoralist clanic and kinship structures. The Balaw and the various Saho-speaking groups were organized in clusters of cognatic kin, in turn divided into branches and, further down, separate families. The Tigre-language term to designate a family was *ᶜad,* whose meaning had a wide range of alternatives: tribe, clan, people, family, village, country, home. For example, members of the ᶜAd Qūlāy family were part of the Bayt Ḥasan Nāᵓib ᶜĀmir, which was descended from the Balaw ᶜĀmir lineage, referring to the founder of the branch. Or a member of the ᶜAd Bādūrī family descended from the *faraᶜ* (Ar., branch) Bayt Shaykh Maḥmūd (which was descended from Shaykh

Sālim b. Faqīh Muḥammad), from yet the larger cognatic descent group of a lineage founder, Faqīh Muḥammad al-Zubayr.[123] On the other hand there were separate families in Hergigo that were not tied to the larger structures of the Balaw branches and the Saho clans. As in Massawa, they were autonomous families that settled in Hergigo, either from abroad or from the interior.

Houses and Families: Spatial and Domestic Arrangements

Massawans take great pride in the architectural legacy of their town.[124] Living in coral stone houses—more or less elegant, depending on a family's wealth and social standing—is another pivotal ingredient of the idealized sense of cultural superiority and urban identity that elite Massawans have often projected both inward and outward. The style and structure of residential houses is closely connected to ideal values about the institution of the family, its structure, and its domestic arrangements, on the one hand, and to the centrality of Arab and Islamic influences on self-generated cultural constructions, on the other.[125] Massawa's architectural style is of a unique and original composite and multilayered character that is not simple to unravel and identify with accuracy. Colonial urban development, earthquakes (and consequent reconstruction in an Islamic/Red Sea–inspired Italian colonial style), and the devastating effects of wars have all contributed to create a fascinating mixed pot of styles and influences. A systematic and rigorous study of the genealogy of Massawa's buildings and architectural styles is eagerly awaited.

"Jealously closed vast and mysterious Arab houses" was how one writer described the increasing number of handsome houses emerging in town at the height of the late-nineteenth-century building boom.[126] Prosperous merchants built and owned residential houses on the port island. Several houses were large, elegant, and luxurious. In the late 1880s one observer remarked that the house of ʿAbd Allāh Bey al-Ghūl, head of the Massawa local council, was the largest in town; it had a very large reception room, luxurious furniture (including European), sofas, carpets, mirrors, and a wall clock.[127] To some extent at least, ʿAbd Allāh Bey al-Ghūl's house was probably comparable to some of the larger and more luxurious mansions owned by Sawākin's business and political elite. One example would be the house of Sawākin's head of the local council, Muṣṭafā Shināwī Bey, illustrated in detail by Jean-Pierre Greenlaw in his book.[128] The same Muṣṭafā Shināwī had purchased a residential house in Massawa in 1882.[129] Another example of a large and lavish upper-scale house was that owned by another ultra-wealthy Egyptian, Ḥasan Mūsā al-ʿAqqād.[130]

But the majority of Massawa's upper classes lived in smaller coral stone houses. The basic-type Turkish house (pre-1860s) was a single-story dwelling unit of two or three rooms, divided into a small family room and a larger guest room for males, known in Arabic as *maqʿad* (in the larger and more sophisticated houses it was known as the *salāmlik*, from the Turkish). These small houses were perhaps the most common in Massawa. They reflected the basic structure of edifices other than residential dwellings; the basic prayer room of the Shaykh Ḥammāl religious complex (less the large windows for ventilation/airing) fits this model very well.[131] However, when households grew and families accumulated enough wealth, basic-type houses could grow into more elaborate compounds. These consisted of adjacent houses, a courtyard (Ar. *ḥush*), and a kitchen-room, and floors could be built over the original dwelling unit, sometimes with open terrace roofs where members of the family slept on the hot summer nights.[132] Large households dwelled in sizable compounds consisting of three, four, or five separate housing units organized around the paternal unit, surrounded by a wall, and connecting to each other by bridging corridors. In this way several married children could live in the same compound.[133] Non-kin members of the household such as slaves and servants slept in the courtyard or in specific quarters within the compound. Sometimes the ground floor was transformed into shops facing the street and warehouses for storing goods.[134] When material means permitted, beautiful wooden carved *rawshāns*, or casement windows jutting out into the street, were constructed on the second or third floors, to catch breezes and ensure privacy.[135]

The higher the status of the family and the wealthier it was, the closer it could attain the ideal domestic arrangement of the Muslim household, with a clear distinction between public and private spaces, and separation between men and women's entrances to the house and living quarters within it.[136] In the 1920s and 1930s some houses of rich Massawa merchants were so well known that they became named urban landmarks, as if they were highly charged public monuments in the town's topography, embodying the urban community. Colonial tourist guides produced in the Fascist period identify the houses (Ar. *bayt* such and such; It. *casa* such and such) of the Bā Ṭūq, al-Ghūl, Bā Ḥamdūn, Bā Mushmūsh, Bā Zarʿa, Hilāl, Ṣāfī and Shīnītī families.[137]

Figure 5.5. Shīnītī family house (prev. house of Mūsā al-ʿAqqād), ca. 1895. Photographer: Giuseppe Quattrociocchi. Istituto Italiano per l'Africa e l'Oriente, Rome.

ONE BIG FAMILY? MARRIAGE PATTERNS

The success or failure of families dedicated to commerce usually depended on their ability to reproduce and expand networks that connected them with brokers in the port's vicinities, producers, caravan operators, small retailers, influential political, religious, and other merchant families in Massawa, and also merchants from abroad. In practice it was often done through various alliances, patronage, and networks of marriage. My informants' expressions such as "Massawa is one big family" or that it is "like a big chain" are not only a figure of speech. Such statements reflect the social homogeneity of those mercantile urban dwellers who had family names, who possessed some form of religious prestige, and who shared a sense of common destiny as a culturally superior group positioned in between the sea and the "inferior" mainland. It was a "big family on an island," in more than one sense—a family integrated through family ties, marriage connections, and shared economic interests.

Marriage in Muslim societies is a central religious and social institution. It is an important strategy for achieving family aims. In her study of family in Ottoman Aleppo, Margaret Meriwether noted that "the importance of marriage as a social strategy was particularly true for the elite. Marriage was fundamentally a relationship between families rather than between individuals. Considerations of property, status, and honor meant that much was at stake in contracting a marriage and creating a relationship between families."[138] As in other such settings in the Muslim world, this was also valid in the case of Massawa, where a considerable degree of family control was exercised over marriage choices among high-status families.

From the examination of several dozen marriage contracts registered in the second half of the 1860s, a first visible pattern is the frequency of cousin marriages. Eight cases—that is, 21 percent—are recordings of in-family unions.[139] Marriage among *sādah* and families of high religious status was also unsurprisingly frequent. Examples include unions between ᶜAydarūs and Ṣāfī (both Hadrami), Ṣāfī and Masāwa (both Hadrami), and Ḥābūna and Jaᶜfar.[140] The last example is particularly interesting in that both families were linked by their high religious status even if from distinctively different origins (Saho-Asaorta and Hadrami). Other cases also followed this pattern. An alliance was recorded between the *sādah* Ṭurkī family and a girl from the Dankalī family, and a similar type between Sayyid Abū Bakr Jaᶜfar and Maryam b. ᶜUmar Nāṣir.[141] Marrying with non-*sādah* or *ashrāf* required careful scrutiny. One informant of a *sādah* family remarked that before giving one's daughter, a father had to enquire thoroughly about the other family's origins: "One had to make sure that they are 'clean' (no slaves). The rule was three 'clean' grandfathers in order to give one's daughter."[142] High-status families who wanted to acquire religious prestige were sometimes able to marry into religiously prestigious families. The daughter of the politically powerful ᶜAlī Afandī Yaḥyā thus married a *khalīfa* of the holy ᶜAd Shaykh family based in Emberemi. An informant of the Afandīs candidly observed that by forming the alliance his family became directly related to the Prophet.[143] A similar case illustrating this type of alliance is the marriage between Shaykh Muḥammad al-Amīn, of the ᶜAd Shaykh too, and the daughter of Aḥmad Afandī al-Ghūl on 24 July 1903; it was celebrated with pomp at the Shāfiᶜī mosque in Massawa.[144]

There is also a trend of families who claim or are designated by others as sharing the same origins to create family unions through marriage. Endogamous marriage was common practice among several families of Hadrami origins, particularly the *sādah* discussed above. Yet as was the case in other parts of the East African coast, the rigorous endogamy practiced in Hadramawt loosened up with time and gradually embraced Hadramis of different social strata in new places of settlement in Africa.[145] The capacity to adjust to local conditions—for example, in their matrimonial strategies—in many ways accounts for Hadrami success in East Africa and other locations in the Indian Ocean world. The registers also points to a union between the Mīyā and Hindī families, who are believed to originate in India, and the union between the Fāris and Saᶜdūy families, both of the Bayt Shaykh Maḥmūd and primarily based in Hergigo.[146] These cases reveal a certain inclusivity that would gradually dissipate in the following decades and into the twentieth century.

Yet another significant pattern that can be identified is marriage connections among the elite regardless of origins and/or religious status. In these cases one pivotal attribute of high status, or common business interests, was sufficient to favor the alliance among the families. Hypergamy or endogamy is particularly significant in revealing linkages between families who originally came from beyond the area (e.g., Hadramawt and Hijaz) with families whose origins were from the inland coastal and lowland regions. In other words, it may unveil another mechanism of social integration and assimilation, or the process of "becoming Massawan." A marriage between two such families could almost automatically offer access to a new web of connections and networks (land or seaborne), and could also confer social and cultural capital through the association with a family having high religious status. Examples include Mentāy and ᶜAbbāsī, Ṭurkī and Dankalī, and Mentāy and Masāwa.[147]

Marriage alliances extracted from the court registers together with data drawn from interviews and family genealogies confirm some of these patterns and their transformation over a longer term.[148] Evidence from the court records clearly shows the dense web of interconnections among Massawa's high-status families. The interweaving of families with different bases of prestige, social power, and authority straddling commercial and religious networks from the inland, through the urban arena, and abroad, epitomizes the social grounding of the group cohesion characterizing Massawa's urban community. On the basis of the records it appears that most Yemenis and Hadramis preferred marrying with other families of similar origins. The ᶜAydarūs, Ṣāfī, Ḥayūtī, and Nahārī families were always closely linked in marriages. Sometimes several siblings from one family were married to opposite siblings in another family (e.g., Nahārī and Ṣāfī). It also seems that newly arrived Hadrami migrants benefited from a sense of solidarity among Hadrami families who have already been in Massawa for several decades or more. Examples include Bā Ṭūq and Bā Ḥubayshī, and Bā Ṭūq and Bā Zaham.

Hadrami and Yemeni families also married out of their own families or other Hadrami families, permitting them to extend their networks into the inland (or throughout the archipelago). The first Nahārī to settle in Massawa in mid-century, ʿAbd al-Raḥīm, married Fāṭima ʿUmar Danbar of a potent Balaw lineage, enabling direct access to regional networks. Interviews confirm that in the twentieth century exogamous marriages became much more common. To some extent in a paradoxical way, they also show that in the colonial period some merchants, entrepreneurs, or sailors, usually (but not always) of Arab origins, who had settled in Massawa, sometimes went back to the Arabian Peninsula to select and take wives from Yemen or the Hijaz. Aḥmad Afandī al-Ghūl brought a woman from the Hijaz; the father of ʿAbd Allāh Sharīf (a sailor) brought a woman from Yemen on one of his trips; Aḥmad ʿAlī Afandī took a woman from Taʿizz; Ṣāliḥ Muḥammad Bā Ṭūq married ʿĀʾisha Saʿīd from the Hijaz; and ʿAlī Nahārī took a Yemeni wife, among many other examples. The "Eritreanization" of Massawa might have been perceived by some of the town's Arab or assimilated elite as a threat on their ways of life. Taking women from the other shore of the Red Sea was one way of responding to sociocultural change.

Marriage and Divorce Involving Lower-Status Individuals

Marriage and divorce cases from the first half of the 1880s also provide information on matrimonial practices among lower-status individuals and non-Massawans in the port in the heyday of the Egyptian period. A first observation reveals a relatively frequent occurrence of marriage between Egyptian officials, officers and soldiers with women most often of low status, including recently manumitted slaves. One example among others was that of Aḥmad Afandī Aḥmad, *mulāzim awwal* (1st lieutenant) of the Egyptian army in Massawa, and Ṭuranjā *al-ḥabashiyya,* who was a slave liberated six days prior to her marriage in early AH 1299 (1882) by Sayyid Muḥammad Ibrāhīm from Massawa. Another fairly similar union took place later that year between Maḥmūd Rizq, engineer on board the steamship *Kharṭūm,* docked at the port of Massawa, and ʿAjmī b. ʿAbd Allāh *al-ḥabashī.* She was a slave only recently manumitted (Ar. *maʿtūqa*) by Sayyid Ḥasan b. al-Sayyid Aḥmad Abū Shaʿrayn. He gave the bride a dowry (Ar. *mahr*) of 10 *riyāls.* Muḥammad Sulaymān, a simple sailor on

Table 3. Sample of Marriage Linkages among Families in Massawa, ca. 1850s–1950s

*(Sources: MICR and interviews 1999–2000. The list is representative, not comprehensive.) Names with a * denote sādāh.*

ᶜAbbāsī -	Dankalī, Ḥilū, Abū ᶜIlāmā, Burj, Mīyā, Nātī, Sharafāy, Muḥajjab, Shīnītī, Ḥamdān, Ṣāʾigh, Mentāy, Mensāy, Doḥolī, Makkaᶜalī
Adam Burkūy* -	Makkaᶜalī, Dankalī, al-Ghūl
ᶜAdūlāy -	Mentāy, Maghribī*, Ḥamdān
Afandī-	Ḥammūda, Shīnītī, ᶜAbbāsī, Mīyā, Nātī, ᶜAd Shaykh family
Bā ᶜAlawī* -	ᶜAydarūs*, Ṣāfī*, Damrīk
Bā Ḥamdūn -	ᶜAd Shaykh
Bā Ṭūq -	Bā Ḥubayshī, Qābūlī, Hilāl, Masāwa, Ṣāfī*, Nahārī*, Bā Zaham, Idrīs ᶜAlī (Tig.), Jeberti man
Bā Zaham -	Bā Ṭūq, Bā Ḥubayshī, Bā Ṣamad, al-ᶜAmūdī
Dankalī -	Ṭurkī*, Shīnītī, ᶜAbbāsī, Adam Barkūy*
Al-Ghūl -	Kurdī, Sanūsī, Ḥanbūlī, Sakīra, ᶜAntablī, Salīm, ᶜAdūlāy
Ḥayūtī*-	Ṣāfī*, Mīyā, Nahārī*
Hindī -	Faqīh, Ṣaḥāy, Mīyā
Jaᶜfar* -	Ḥābūna, Nāṣir
Khayr al-Dīn -	Nātī, Bayt Shaykh Maḥmūd (henceforth BSM), ᶜAdūlāy, Mihrī
Makkaᶜalī -	Adam Barkūy*, Yāqūt, Miyā, ᶜAbbāsī, Hāshim*, Minnī
Mentāy-	Balaw, Masāwa, ᶜAbbāsī, ᶜAdūlāy, ᶜAlī Salām*
Nahārī* -	Danbar, Maknūn (Dah.), Zaynab Ḥasan (Yem.), Khaḍr (Yem.), Ṣāfī*, Ṣāʾigh, Shīnītī, Bā ᶜAlawī*, Ḥayūtī*, Nahārī*, Bā Ṭūq, BSM, ᶜAdūlāy
Nātī -	Afandī, Ḥamdān, Khayr ad-Dīn, ᶜAbbāsī, Hindī, Ṣāʾigh, BSM, Ṣefāf (Ghindaᶜ)
Qūlāy -	Turkī*, Mentāy
Ṣāfī* -	Bānibala, Nahārī*, Ḥayūtī*, Masāwa, Shalabī* ᶜAydarūs*, Bayt Qāḍī (Zūlā), Bā Ṭūq, Ramaḍān (Ark.)*, Ḥamdān
Shīnītī -	Afandī, ᶜAbbāsī, Nahārī*, Dankalī
Turkī* -	Abū Shaᶜrayn*, Dankalī, Qūlāy
Wahhāb al-Bārrī -	Ṣūrī, Bā Ḥamdūn, Hilāl, Nakhrāy, Nabāb (Tigre)

board the *Kharṭūm,* married Fāṭma b. Ḥusayn b. Aḥmad Falawī a month earlier.[149] Several other marriages that reflected the more or less similar patterns appear in the court registers.[150]

But there were also marriage links between Egyptian appointed officials and Massawans of both high and low status. Ibrāhīm ᶜAbd al-Samīḥ, *muftī* of Massawa, married two women of low status in 1883 and 1884: Salāma b. ᶜAbd Allāh, who was formerly a slave liberated by ᶜAlī b. Abū Bakr Nakhrāy, and Khadīja b. Khiyyār *al-ḥabashī* (the Abyssinian).[151] Some Egyptian officers were linked in marriage to women from the Saho-speaking groups inhabiting the port's vicinities. In 1881 Shams al-Shāmī, the carpenter of the irrigation canals employed by the Egyptian administration at Massawa, divorced Saᶜīda b. Adam Muḥammad *al-Sihāwī* (Ar., the Saho); Aḥmad al-Afandī Wazan divorced Fāṭma b. Muḥammad Ḥāmid from Zula, and Diyāb ᶜAbd al-ᶜAzīz divorced Amna Ḥasan *al-Sihāwī* (the Saho).[152] Divorce cases also signal marriage alliances between non-urban dwellers of the Massawa region or with town dwellers—and often of low status, as the lack of family names might suggest. Couples came to the town's court to register marriage and divorce. Thus, for example Ṭāhir b. ᶜUmar Adhanna al-Galab from the village of Zaga divorced his wife Fāṭma b. ᶜAlī Wāriāy (Wariā group); Ibrāhīm ᶜAlī Ḥamad from Zaga divorced Zaynab b. ᶜUmar Adam from Emkullo; Muḥammad b. *ḥājj* Ḥabīb from Massawa divorced Jumᶜa b. Ḥarzāwī of the ᶜAd Temaryam; ᶜAbd Allāh from Zula divorced Khadīja b. Sulaymān, and Aḥmad Ṭalūl of the Bayt Khalīfa divorced Masᶜūda b. Muḥammad Limūnat of the Asaorta.[153] There were also links between low-status individuals, some of whom were manumitted slaves or servants from the Ethiopian or Sudanese regions. Examples include Faraj Jād al-Sūdānī, who divorced Khadra b. Aḥmad Maḥmūd Babīl; Muḥammad Nūr *al-ḥabashī,* who divorced Fāṭma Negasī; and Muḥammad b. ᶜUthmān from Kassala, who divorced Sarah b. Aḥmad from Shandī.[154]

The law court records shed light on female domestic slaves who were concubines. Concubinage was a legal institution in Muslim society, and men had sexual access to female slaves who were part of their property. But such women had clearly defined rights within the framework of the institution of concubinage. The most important was that their children were considered free and equal to the other offspring of her owner. Once she had a child she was granted the status of *umm al-walad* (Ar., mother of the child) protecting her from being sold, pawned, or given away. On the death of her master she was to be freed automatically.[155] An example from

Massawa involves Dawa, who had a daughter, Saʿīda, with her owner, ʿAlī Faqīh; on his death in 1881, she was freed by the court in accordance with Islamic law.[156] It is interesting to note that the *qāḍī* of Massawa, Shaykh ʿAlī ʿAbd al-Karīm *al-maṣrī* (Ar., the Egyptian) married the daughter in question, Saʿīda b. ʿAlī al-Faqīh, twelve days after her mother's manumission. The *mahr* (dower) that was agreed upon was 10 *riyāls,* 8 to be paid immediately and 2 *riyāls* remaining at her credit.[157] It is customary in the Ḥanafī legal school to pay part of the *mahr* immediately (*muqaddam*) and defer payment of the rest. The remaining part of the dower (*mūʾakhkhar*) is thus held to the credit of the wife and should be paid to her in case of death of one of the spouses or in the case of repudiation (after consummation).[158] But the marriage held only over a year, and they appeared back in court for their divorce in early Shawwāl 1300 (1883).[159]

An interesting case presented to the court in May 1882 involved a woman's conversion to Islam—an act that immediately canceled the validity of her marriage to a Christian husband in the eyes of the Islamic court. This case might point to a strategy with such an objective. The registration in the court records was as follows (in free translation):

> The adult and conscious woman Zaynab *al-ḥabashiyya* ["the Abyssinian"] presented herself to the *majlis al-shariʿī* [Islamic law council] and pronounced the two professions of faith of her own will in their clear and natural form in Arabic without any constraint or obligation. And on this basis she became a member of the Muslim community. This was in the presence of the witnesses Muṣṭafā Jawīsh and Ḥasan Ḥabīb from Massawa and ʿAbdullāhi Muṣṭafā Onbash (?). And the woman has claimed she was married to Kidane, and she came to the court and chose Islam. Therefore the marriage is canceled. No waiting period [*ʿidda*] is required of her according to the *sharīʿa,* unless she is pregnant. She came in the company of ʿAlī Yūsuf Balūk (?) who is the secretary of the neighborhood (?).[160]

Marriage patterns in Massawa in the second half of the nineteenth century demonstrate the centrality of the institution of the family in an urban trade-oriented society. Marriage among Massawa's commercial elite was a carefully calculated and regulated social strategy aimed at preserving, cementing, and expanding business and services networks. As such, marriage strategies offer valuable insights into the mechanisms of creating communal cohesion, solidarity, and boundaries. They also show the ways by which migrants coming from across the sea and local potent families linked their networks through marriage alliances, enabling them to perform commercial mediation between the African interior and business partners across the seas.

WEDDING CUSTOMS: IN TOWN AND OUT OF TOWN

The diversity of peoples and customs in the Semhar region—nomads, pastoralists, townsmen—was also reflected in their wedding customs. Most ethnographic accounts of marriage ceremonies in the nineteenth century describe the customs of Saho and Tigre peoples, the nomads, or Beduins. Descriptions of urban elite family weddings are more rare; Europeans had easier access to Saho- and Tigre-speaking non-urban communities outside Massawa. Observers often generalized what they witnessed as the common and most widespread practices, not always aware of variations founded on locality, culture, and status.

In the 1830s Combes and Tamisier suggested that the inhabitants of Massawa did not fully follow orthodox Islamic customs in matters of marriage. They wrote that unlike in Arabia and in Turkey, Massawan men insisted upon meeting their fiancées prior to the wedding celebration.[161] The statement undoubtedly reflects the state of religious and cultural syncretism of the region's inhabitants. Clearly, even after the process of Islamization (very recent in that context), local cultural practices were deeply ingrained among pastoralist and nomadic communities. In the 1850s Munzinger provided a detailed ethnographic account of marriage customs among the non-urban Beduins, with some useful comments as to the differences between town and countryside practices. Marriages, he observed, were pre-arranged by parents or legal guardians, aiming at forming family or clan alliances. First, a marriage pledge was made by the young man to the young woman's father, after which a decision had to be taken as to the nature and amount of the engagement gift to be given by the pledger. The young man also had to offer gifts and nice clothes to the young woman. Following the marriage all was given back to the man in cows. If for any reason the marriage did not take place, the young woman's family was required to return all gifts.[162]

In the villages, Munzinger's descriptions add, no union could be made without prior consultation of the village sorceress. If she predicted troubles, a marriage could be canceled on that basis. Weddings usually took place a year after the marriage pledge (always in winter), but in Massawa, where according to Munzinger "old customs are fading away," weddings were celebrated at any time of the year. Among the nomads boys could marry at the age of 16, girls at 12, but in town usually later. As the wedding day approached young men usually went to see the *muftī*, who talked to them about the responsibilities of marriage. On the day of the wedding guests were welcomed to the groom's parents' house; they were offered hydromel, coffee, cooked rice, meat, and sweets. Singing and dancing went on throughout the day; the entire wedding celebration lasted three days. Guests offered gifts: silver ear and nose rings, silver wrist and ankle bracelets, hair combs, and other jewelry. Married women of a certain wealth in Massawa sometimes wore 200 thalers worth of jewels, while Beduin married women often had much less—as low as 10 thalers worth. Clearly, in town marriage was an expensive business, and young men often had to wait long years before they accumulated enough capital to enable them to get married.[163]

In the late 1860s Hormuzd Rassam provided useful observations on a wedding celebration that he attended in Massawa. Most interesting was the notable difference in the meanings of money in the specific period and in the urban setting. This was a setting subject to more widespread and enhanced monetization and commodification. Money, wealth, and power gained new meanings in the urban mercantile environment of business and consumption in the heyday of the commercial boom. Rassam describes how money gifts were given to the groom and how donors' names were carefully registered. He describes a system in which marriage gifts were taken almost as loans. Money gifts were placed to the credit of donors, and on their own marriage, the same amount given by them was repaid by those first married. This provided young married men a small capital to launch business enterprises. Furthermore, Rassam added that "sometimes, when a man is in prosperous circumstances, he not only repays the sum he had received, but advances something more to be repaid at a future time to himself or to his son." Collections among the wealthier classes often exceeded 1,000 thalers; Rassam once witnessed a total gift amount of 3,000 thalers.[164] Attending a marriage among notable families in late nineteenth-century Emkullo, Victor Buchs also witnessed this system.[165] In the atmosphere of commercial intensification and the struggles over wealth and power, competition for giving large sums was current among the elite and the wealthy. Giving generously could also foster patronage ties, useful in cementing or extending business networks.

In the 1880s Traversi attended a middle-level elite family's wedding. The young groom was beautifully dressed, and hosts arranged *angarebs* (a type of cord-strung bed common in Northeast Africa) covered with elegant textiles in the courtyard for the guests. The women were separated from the men in another room, where they chanted. There was also a performance by two women dancers. The men sang too—undoubtedly performing a *dhikr* or another Sufi ritual: "They do not only emit a voice and clap their hands, but they clap their feet according to the rhythm, they move their head and are all agitated up to rapture (ecstasy), until exhaustion."[166] Ecstatic Sufi dances and ceremonies were also described by Buchs in *fin de siècle* Emkullo. After the procession had made its way to the mosque and the two witnesses sent by the *qāḍī* to the bride's home to confirm her virginity returned with the crucial and much-awaited "yes," all congratulated the young groom. In the evening, back in the groom's parents' house, more festive dances, chanting, and *dhikr* ceremonies continued into the night.

> There follows endless chanting and the ceremony ends with a singular prayer. Those present stand and continuously and with increasing rapidity repeat the word "Allah," God, in a guttural and raucous voice, that soon enough, becomes inhuman, until one of them exhausts himself and falls unconscious. It is obviously a sign that the prayer was pleasing to God; it is certain that since it came not from the lips but from inside the man, from his stomach, it is a real expression of the believer's faith.[167]

Ilario Capomazza, undoubtedly one of the more informed Italian colonial officials in matters of Islam and Eritrea's Muslim populations, published a monograph in 1910 devoted to Islamic customary practice in Massawa.[168] Capomazza's detailed account takes the reader step by step from the first moments of engagement until the birth of offspring well after the marriage. But once again, as in all the above descriptions, the crucial question remained: "who exactly was getting married?" Which culture (status) is the description depicting? Did practices diverge from community to community? Central to the administering of wedding ceremonies in Capomazza's account is the Saho-speaking holy clan Bayt Shaykh Maḥmūd. The question remains who exactly was served by them, who they represented (other Saho-speaking groups), and, perhaps more importantly and interestingly, who contested their religious authority.[169]

Between roughly the 1850s and the 1880s several broad political, commercial, and migratory processes were critical to the development of the social and cultural constructions of identity of Massawa's leading strata. Those processes formed, enhanced, and revitalized a sense of urban and urbane, Arabized and Islamic, identity that Massawans pride themselves with to this day. To be Massawan meant to be part of an urban culture that perceived the town as an idealized and superior site of refined civilization, culture, and religious piety. Such conceptions translated into owning a family name, residing in a coral stone house, holding Arabic and Arab culture in high esteem, and cultivating a strong sense of connection to the wider Muslim *umma*. In other words, in this period "being Massawan" meant being urban and being "Arab."

The spectacular waves of migration to the port of a number of merchants and entrepreneurs—especially from the Arabian Peninsula and the Middle East—was another process that contributed to the development of specific sociocultural constructions of identity in Massawa during this period. Some newly settled entrepreneurs employed several strategies in integrating into Massawa's social structures and in developing their power on the urban arena. Those who were able to rapidly accumulate impressive wealth often reinvested in local urban real estate. They sometimes endowed part of their properties as *waqf* for the benefit of the community. Marriage and business alliances with the local coastal elite offered access into commercial webs of networks in the hinterland and across the seas, enabling them to penetrate local and regional structures of commercial mediation. The most successful entrepreneurs subsequently became the town's leading elite, controlled some of its urban institutions, and enjoyed privileged relations with the authorities.

Conclusion

Constructing and Deconstructing a Red Sea Society

The economic, political, and social consequences of the ongoing conflict between Eritrea and Ethiopia (since 1998) have not been easy on Eritreans. Always hopeful to see better days soon, women and men continue to struggle in their daily lives with courage, creativity, and the captivating grace that anyone who knows Eritreans recognizes instantly. A recent trip to Massawa—eight years after I visited the town for the first time—left the impression of a ghost town, deserted and lifeless, at least in comparison with what I have previously experienced. It is also no secret that the context of economic hardships has led some Eritreans to seek better opportunities for themselves and their families, including the option of leaving the country—against the stout will of the government. It is in this context that during my most recent visit, one of my old Massawan acquaintances told me about the case of several individuals from Massawa and Hergigo who have been able to apply successfully for Saudi and Sudanese citizenships, enabling them to leave Eritrea and relocate to those countries. Since citizenship was granted to them on the basis of their family origins, he asked me whether I have uncovered documents or any "hard evidence" about his own family's well-known and established origins in the Arabian Peninsula—something that would support an application for citizenship. Saddened by the general context yet quite surprised by the potential ramifications of my research and my power as a historian, I said that, somewhat ironically, the prestige of the older families, like his, is hardly beneficial in this context, since the more recently migrated families have an easier time proving origins abroad! This anecdote epitomizes in many ways the cosmopolitanism of the people whom this study has focused upon—people who belonged to one place and many others at the same time, and who creatively used their special positionality in responding to the realities of their day.

My initial interest in Massawa's history was triggered by representations of the port-town and its inhabitants in nineteenth-century accounts, Italian colonial manuals, and more recently published books, newspaper articles, and even tourist travel guides. Descriptions characteristically represented Massawa as the epitome of an "Oriental," that is, Arab, Muslim, or Ottoman, town, that in many ways, observers wrote or suggested, seemed quite exotic, separate, in some cases "alien" to its "African" environment. Massawa was, and still is, described as a town sui generis, bearing a singular cachet, which is perhaps nowadays best characterized by its unique mixture of Ottoman, Egyptian, and colonial Italian architectural styles. Such representations reminded me in many ways of the situation on the East African Swahili coasts, where—for a host of motley reasons and mirroring different political, social, racial, and cultural positionalities—very complex societies were categorically classified and stereotyped by both coastal East Africans and those who observed them.

Added to that was the new political context of the early 1990s. Eritrean independence in 1993 generated a host of nationalist and cultural discourses expressed by Massawans and Eritreans about Massawa's history and its particular cultural features. These expressions appeared in the nascent Eritrean press and in local publications. Their importance was in opening windows onto particular constructions of identity that somewhat paradoxically portrayed Massawa as the "product" of a distinct historical trajectory, having its own particular culture and identity, yet at the same time naturally "Eritrean" from times immemorial. It seemed very clear that both external and internal designations and images revealed complex constructions of race, culture, and identity that not only mirrored a dynamic reality of local cultural *métissage,* but also reflected the ideological backgrounds and political agendas of the observers as well as the various self-designations, discourses, and cultural politics of Massawans themselves. It appeared obvious that Massawa's social and cultural makeup—including the production of various discourses—hid complex processes of social, cultural, and identity formation and transformation that needed to be historically situated and contextualized.

Yet the consequences of Massawa's unique situation as a distinctive historical space were not restricted to images and representations alone. They could, indeed, translate into real political claims and action on the ground that undoubtedly left a mark on internal and external conceptions and perceptions of the port-town and its dwellers. A somewhat anecdotal but revealing example occurred at the turn of the twentieth century, when Italo-Ottoman rivalry over sovereignty, maritime boundaries, and the policing of navigation in the southern Red Sea area, between Massawa and the Yemen coasts, attained a climax. In March 1900 the Ottoman navy seized near the Tihāma coasts three Massawa-registered "Eritrean" sailing boats that they suspected of engaging in smuggling and that they subsequently conducted to Ḥudayda. As tensions mounted, the following month the Ottoman authorities, who had never formally recognized the substitution of Ottoman by Italian sovereignty over Eritrea, took the drastic step of declaring the "natives" (It. *indigeni*) of Massawa as Ottoman subjects. In practice this meant that the Eritrean merchants and boat crew could not benefit from Italian consular protection and were to be accountable solely to the Ottoman authorities, who had the right to inspect their vessel and its cargo. Seen from a particular angle, the issue seemed even more convoluted, bearing in mind what one Italian colonial official termed "the delicate issue of Massawa's Arabs," whereby many of the port's merchants and boat owners—as this study has shown—had recently moved into the colony from parts of the Red Sea littorals that were under Ottoman sovereignty. This state of affairs often made their legal situation rather equivocal.[1] In a sense, one could say that this legal ambiguity was paralleled in the cultural or symbolic arena, which was the site of rivalry, competition, and the production of contesting and, at times, contrasting discourses about "what is Massawa," "who are the Massawans," and "what is it specifically that makes one a Massawan?"

In this study I have focused on several critical decades in the making of a complex Red Sea urban coastal society. I examined how a specific configuration of interregional interactions and connections shaped a Red Sea coastal urban locality. In a very central sense my study focused precisely on how a particular new *conjoncture* of political, commercial, and migratory factors in the wider Red Sea and western Indian Ocean area in the middle and latter decades of the century transformed Massawa, "re-created" or "re-invented" it. These decades represented a relatively brief and intense period during which the world of the Red Sea and the western Indian Ocean left a strong mark on Massawa's social and cultural orientation. More specifically, I have shown that beginning roughly in the 1830s, the introduction of steamship navigation to the Red Sea area, commercial intensification and expansion, the reconfiguration of port hierarchies and trading networks, and accentuated Egyptian, Ottoman, and European imperialist activities in the region reorganized the structure of Massawa's commercial relationships. One of the salient aspects of this process involved the adjustment and rearrangement of Arab and Indian commercial networks to the new mercantile landscape of the region. These networks dominated the trade of particular commodities, specific navigation routes, the means of transportation, and the organization of credit relations by establishing sociocommercial webs linking ports ranging from the Indian region to the eastern Mediterranean Sea. The process spurred the rearrangement of the Red Sea city system and the intensification of migratory waves across the Red Sea and the western Indian Ocean region. Massawa became an attractive destination for merchants and entrepreneurs, who settled in the port and eventually connected and reconnected to business networks. This process was not new in essence, but it was intensified, and it altered a previous configuration of trading, brokering, and shipping networks relatively rapidly in the latter part of the nineteenth century. Indeed, at some point in the late nineteenth century, Massawa could seem as a town overtaken, appropriated, "hijacked" by migrants—mostly "Arabs"—from a host of locations beyond the Eritrean coasts.

From mid-century a group of individuals and families—some of whom only recently had migrated to Massawa from the Arabian Peninsula and other regions of the Middle East, others of whom were potent families of local origin constituting the traditional coastal elite—were able to accumulate much power on the local urban scene. The new Hadrami, Hijazi, Egyptian, and Indian migrant-entrepreneurs replaced the prominence of the local-regional "Eritrean" coastal elites. They also replaced the dominance of those international-oriented merchants/agents originating from beyond the Red Sea realm who had operated in the old system prevalent in the western Indian Ocean area prior to the mid-nineteenth century. Nevertheless, the new wave of entrepreneurs continued to collaborate with the prominent families of the local coastal elite in order to tap into regional brokerage networks and resources. In other words, one can discern an alliance, or a process of mutual incorporation, of the traditional coastal political, economic, and religious elite with the dynamic migrants who had adjusted to the new Red Sea system. In this way, sea-oriented migrants gained access to local-regional circuits and networks, while the coastal elite gained access to transregional and transnational networks in the Red Sea area.

A central aspect of the study has precisely examined the social and cultural consequences and manifestations of the formation of the new urban elite, which was mainly composed of the local notables, the leading merchants, brokers, and entrepreneurs, and the religious dignitaries. I have examined the commercial, social, religious, and cultural institutions and strategies through which the town's inhabitants shaped and defined their community and the ways by which they came to develop a distinct sense of citizenship, of "being Massawan." Many elite-status individuals and families in Massawa enjoyed privileged relations with the Ottoman, then Egyptian, then Italian authorities and were able to hold central positions and control key urban institutions such as the Islamic court, the professional corporations, and Massawa's other Islamic institutions. It seems clear that in one sense, the various long-standing—even if transforming—brokerage institutions were the kernel of a sense of solidarity, common interest, and connectedness in Massawa's merchant community.

This group of families shared certain material, political, social, and religious bases of power and authority, granting its members high status and convertible social capital. The Massawa elite developed ideal values such as a keen sense of urban sophistication and superiority, a strong sense of Muslim identity, a sense of connectedness to the wider *umma* of believers, and a distinctly "Arab" cultural orientation. Even though Massawa has always been connected to the Arab and Islamic world to one degree or another, both the Egyptian occupation between 1865 and 1885 and the effects of the Islamic revival had a tenacious impact on their manifestations and significance in our period. This particular sense of identity defined Massawan citizenship and prescribed porous yet protective communal boundaries.

Massawa's rapidly transforming social scene raised several major questions, such as what were the strategies of social integration, as well as what were the sources of urban authority and social communal cohesion? One effective way to integrate "from the top," acquire social standing, and develop urban power was through the accumulation of capital and through investments in local real estate. In other words, Massawa's richest merchants were able—through various strategies—to convert their economic capital into symbolic, cultural, and social capital. These strategies often involved the acquisition of much real estate property in town, which made them, in a certain sense, the "owners" of a great deal of the urban landscape. Closely connected was their use of the institution of *waqf* as a way to build power and legitimacy on the social scene. Merchant-entrepreneur magnates such as Bā Junayd and al-Ghūl endowed properties designating specific public services (water wells) and religious institutions (mosques) as beneficiaries—which benefited the urban society at large. They also rented unexploited *waqf* land that failed to yield income for beneficiary institutions and built houses or shops that ultimately led to their economic profitability, which, again, was propitious to the urban community.

A major source of urban authority was founded on family politics and on the access that it enabled into transregional networks. Marriage and business alliances between newcomers and the local coastal elite offered both parties access into commercial webs of networks in the hinterland and overseas. The result was the creation of a tight-knit community that defined itself and protected its privileged role in the mercantile milieu through the construction of an idealized communal moral order. The patrilineal family was the fundamental institution in embodying and articulating the town's elite social and cultural constructions of identity. The family was the primary carrier and producer of the town's ideals and ethos. Families were organized in patrilineal households, and, within that commercial milieu, family names served as a type of trademark, an identifying marker emitting prestige, respectability, and, most importantly, trustworthiness. Families resided in coral stone homes, in marked contrast with non-urban surrounding societies, who carried no family names and usually lived in quite desolate thatched-roof huts. Only those who became urban, or "became Massawan," and had the financial means and the right connections enabling them to enter the citizenry had gradually adopted these features.

Marriage patterns also demonstrate the centrality of the institution of the family in a society dedicated to trade and brokerage. Marriage among Massawa's commercial elite was a carefully calculated and regulated social strategy aimed at preserving, reproducing, and expanding business networks both in the hinterland and across the seas. Initially, higher-status families of Hadrami, Hijazi, or Egyptian origins, for example, maintained their sociocultural distinction through endogamous marriage choices, by taking women in Arabia, Yemen, and Red Sea ports, and by marrying into established families of Arab descent in Massawa. However, they also married into locally prestigious Muslim families among the Tigre-

and Saho-speaking clans. These alliances enabled them to reproduce their high status and deal with family relatives, who were also business associates, in other Red Sea ports such as Jiddah, Sawākin, Luḥayya, Ḥudayda, and Qunfudha, and at the same time with kin-related groups of the African interior. Massawa families constituted the link between these worlds. The discernment of marriage strategies offered valuable insights into the mechanisms of creating communal cohesion and solidarity, clearly showing the ways by which migrants coming from across the sea and local potent families linked their networks between the African interior and business partners across the seas.

I have insisted that the features that made Massawa a distinctively Red Sea town, deeply influenced by Islamic and Middle Eastern Arab culture, as well as the various cultural discourses and self-designations of its inhabitants in the era of my concern, do not invalidate in any way its growth and development out of and within its own "African" environment. I have argued that it was the interaction of inland peoples and peoples from abroad that met on the coast and made what I am calling a "Red Sea society." Accordingly, I have also argued how in Massawa local traditions and documentary evidence demonstrate the pivotal role of inland Tigre- and Saho-speaking peoples in the development of local notions of society and culture in Massawa. Neither processes of Arabization nor specific religious influences were ever totally pervasive, and in this context one could still creatively and pragmatically manage and juggle different identities in different situations and contexts or in different localities within the broader regional sphere.

On a broader level, following the end of Italian colonial rule in 1941 and during the middle decades of the twentieth century, the sense of Arabism—which in many ways developed and crystallized in the period of this study—was politicized in the process of the development of Eritrean nationalism and different ideologies of identity. The establishment of a local cultural association in Massawa as well as a political party—the National Moslem Party of Massawa—in the 1940s reflects the embodiment of a sense of consciousness with which the community, or parts thereof, was imbued.[2] It also comes as little surprise that some of the champions of the idea of Eritrea's Arab identity during the early part of the Eritrean national struggle were from Massawa and Hergigo; the best example is undoubtedly ʿUthmān Ṣāliḥ Sabī.[3] These issues, which might complete, in a way, my long nineteenth-century story, are among several other questions that deserve to be further researched.

The significance of this study operates on several different levels and in different arenas: the historiographies of Eritrea and northeast Africa; the historical connections and relationships between the Horn of Africa and the broader Red Sea area, the Arabian Peninsula, and the northwestern Indian Ocean; and the conceptualization of the Red Sea as an interregional arena and as a historical space. Although it goes without saying that carrying out the research for this book would not have been possible without the independence of Eritrea in 1993, I have, perhaps in an unpopular fashion, somewhat against the grain, conceptualized my subject—for reasons that are grounded in my historiographic vision—in a way that did not focus on categories such as the nation, the state, or even ethnicity. My work has therefore avoided espousing an outright nationalist ideological outlook that might attempt to "redress the picture" by offering a counter-hegemonic meta-narrative—this time imposed from an Eritrean nationalist perspective and written "backwards," from present to past. While to the superficial eye sympathetic to the "Eritrean cause" my work may appear as of little service, I do hope to have contributed modestly to the reconstruction of the historical experiences of some of the peoples of Eritrea and the regions that they inhabit. The book might not tell the story of Eritrea, but it certainly tells the story of the forebears of individuals and families who identify themselves today as Eritreans.

The study indeed joins a revisionist effort in the historiography of the Horn of Africa that attempts to write into the historical record societies and regions that have hitherto been perceived as somewhat marginal, peripheral, or simply nonexistent in relation to the state-, highland-, Semitic-, and Christian-centric historiography that has prevailed in the field until recently. It also attempts to cross ethnic and national analytical boundaries and favors a regional approach that understands space, connections, and movement as more useful in thinking about history and reconstructing histories in the Horn of Africa.[4] The book has shed light on historical processes occurring in the nineteenth century (and beforehand) that have made significant impact on the societies that inhabit present-day Eritrea. The state of political instability in the northern Ethiopian provinces during the *Zemene Mesefint* (the Era of the Princes), Ottoman indirect rule, and the pivotal role of the *nāʾib*s in shaping a historical space in parts of eastern and northern Eritrea are essential in understanding the spread and appropriation of Islam in the region, migratory patterns of Tigre- and

Saho-speaking people, the relationship between inland and coast, and the role of these societies in the commercial and transportation networks and circuits between the Red Sea coast and the Nile Valley.

The study of Massawa's history also contributes to aspects of the economic, urban, and social history of the Eritrean region. It reconstructs aspects of the history of the most important urban center in the area prior to the colonial era and the subsequent gradual shift inland, much as was the case of some of the towns of the East African coast in the same period. With the establishment of Eritrea, Massawa served as capital of the colony from 1890 to 1899. Major urban works were conducted during the period, but soon enough the Italians transferred the impetus of urban growth and development to the new capital, Asmara, in the highlands.[5] Massawa became the port of a colony, integrated into its territorial boundaries and confined by an artificial space with limited hinterland markets. The construction of the railroad, which reached Asmara in 1911, and the growth of the city as the economic and political capital of the colony were crucial in that respect. As Italian economic investment and development in Eritrea increased from the 1920s onward, the process of integration was further enhanced and consolidated. One aspect of integration that had a significant effect on Massawa was the gradual migration of Christian Tigrinya-speaking highlanders to the port-town. This process eventually led to a shift in the population structure of Massawa, leaving the "Massauini," or "*Maṣawwiʿīn*," as a minority in their hometown. Regarding "facing the land, facing the sea," the story by now seems to be tending toward attributing the "facing the land" part a greater role, reflecting the increasing impact of inland influences from the latter half of the Italian colonial period (ca. 1920s onward).

The study also contributes to the reconstruction of interregional interactions in the Red Sea area by telling the stories of merchants and entrepreneurs who came to Massawa from abroad in a period when the port was deeply influenced by the sea and who made it their home. Some merchant-entrepreneurs in Massawa were rapidly and spectacularly enriched. The limited degree of Italian economic investment in early colonial Eritrea (1885 onward) and the supremacy of Arab and Indian transregional trading, labor, and finance networks in the Red Sea area provided entrepreneurs in Massawa opportunities in various lucrative business ventures such as the wholesale trade, the pearling economy, transportation services, agricultural concessions, salt mining, banking services, construction and real estate investments, and the provisioning of the Italian military forces.

Entrepreneurs and other actors in the economic arena adjusted to the colonial framework, operated within it, and were in some instances able to shape its orientation. The pearling business, for example, shows how colonial intervention and the imposition of a new order of production, taxing, and marketing proved ultimately unsuccessful because of the resistance mounted by pearlers who found the new system unfavorable to them. With the accession of the enterprising Ferdinando Martini to the position of governor of Eritrea, colonial economic policy went as far as favoring the cooperation with local merchants, who were themselves tied to wider Red Sea commercial networks. On the whole, colonial intervention did not shatter local and regional networks—it reconfigured them and generated processes of adjustment, in many cases enhancing them.

The success of the merchants-entrepreneurs whose trajectories I have sketched in the book refutes previously perceived sharp breaks in terms of "indigenous" trading and entrepreneurial networks' resilience, vitality, and effectiveness after the growing penetration of Europe to the area. Common wisdom has perceived a sharp disruption in the assumed unity of the Indian Ocean in the age of European imperialism and colonialism. Yet the study of smaller-scale interregional arenas—such as the Red Sea area—reveals that transformation came with continuity, adaptation, and adjustment. In Massawa, local and regional entrepreneurs were able to adjust to the new Red Sea system and take advantage of new opportunities. They adapted and diversified their business ventures while preserving and promoting their interests. On the whole, Italian commercial operators were not able to effectively compete with the more flexible and solidly rooted Arab and Indian networks in the southern Red Sea area and beyond. Some of the descendants of Massawa's mercantile families became prominent members of the Muslim community and its institutions and important protagonists in the formation and development of Eritrean nationalism. This is in addition to their overall contribution to the economic, commercial, and urban development of the country in the first half of the twentieth century. Indeed, once Asmara became the capital of the Colonia Eritrea in 1900, many Massawa merchants and entrepreneurs moved up to the highlands or opened businesses and commercial branches and agencies there. They had a pivotal role in its development; one informant proudly told me that "half of the buildings" of Asmara were built by rich Massawan merchants in the early Italian colonial period. Later on, in the 1930s and beyond, some entrepreneurs expanded their inland business operations to Ethiopia and the Sudan.

In the broader Red Sea arena, the turn of the century also marked a renewed reconfiguration of port hierarchies and interport competition, mainly due to the new requirements of larger shipping vessels and the inadequacy of some harbors after the opening of the Suez Canal in 1869. Sawākin was abandoned in favor of the newly built Port Sudan, and the creation of Djibouti in 1896 replaced Zaylaᶜ and Tajūra in the Gulf of Aden. The foundation of Addis Ababa by Emperor Menelik II and the construction of the Addis Ababa–Djibouti railroad between 1897 and 1917 made Djibouti the shortest way to the sea for central, western, and southern Ethiopia. The formation and development of these new Red Sea port-towns—including the port of Aseb—is thus inscribed within the histories and roles of European colonial powers in the area.

This book also aspires to make a contribution toward conceptualizing the Red Sea area as a historical space shaped by various political, economic, religious, and cultural factors. Cross–Red Sea interactions in the period under study contributed to shape the societies inhabiting both shores of the Red Sea. As I have shown, Ottoman and Egyptian imperialism in the area created cross–Red Sea political, economic, and cultural spaces that linked northeastern Africa with the Arabian Peninsula in conspicuous ways. Perhaps the most salient phenomenon spurred by transforming economic conditions involved the circulation, migration, and settlement of merchants, entrepreneurs, agents, financiers, brokers, and laborers in Massawa and other localities. An example of meaningful cross–Red Sea circulation drawn from the religious field is the trajectory of the Khatmiyya order, whose influence straddled the entire area, including the Hijaz, Sudan, the Eritrean region, and Yemen. The various missionary trips of the founder of the *ṭarīqa,* Muḥammad ᶜUthmān al-Mīrghanī, mapped the contours of this space within which members of the Mīrghanī family and different itinerant *shaykh*s and *khalīfa*s associated with the order operated circuits and transmitted authority, knowledge, and religious practice. Yet reformist ideas also crossed the Red Sea, as in the case of the Zabīd-educated Hadrami ᶜAlī b Aḥmad b. Saᶜīd Bā Ṣabrayn, who criticized the Khatmiyya for practices perceived as deviating from Islamic orthodox practice. Legal learning and practices joined Sufism and reformist ideas in crisscrossing the Red Sea, as several references to *fatwa*s issued by *muftī*s in Mecca and Zabīd and provided as supporting materials in court deliberations reveal.

Another topic of interest would be a comparative study of the architectural history and styles of several Red Sea ports. Even a cursory exploration of the subject reveals strong commonalities between port-towns that came under Ottoman and Egyptian rule, such as Sawākin, Jiddah, and Massawa. A subject of interest requiring further research is the political economy of "illegal" navigation, piracy, and smuggling in the southern Red Sea area in the context of the extension of Italian hegemonic aspirations in the region, on the one hand, and Ottoman efforts to maintain their presence and control in the area, on the other. In the last two decades of the nineteenth century the major competing imperial powers in the area—especially Britain, Italy, and the Ottoman Empire—often contested each other's maritime borders, sovereignties, and jurisdictions. In one specific arena, tensions and conflict opposing the Italians and Ottomans revolved chiefly in the areas between Massawa and the Tihāma coasts, and especially in the nebulous insular regions between the Dahlak Archipelago and the Farasān islands, where smugglers were able to ingeniously shun and dodge the authorities. Outlaws devised imaginative strategies, including the switching of vessel flags (Italian and Ottoman) during hot pursuits and co-ownership of sailboats by members of the same family, for example, one residing in Massawa as a subject of Italy while the other resided on the Yemeni or Arabian coasts as an Ottoman subject.[6]

I hope that this book will stimulate further comparative research into other subjects that would provide a clearer picture of the Red Sea area as a historical space in this period. Such research should shed more light on the resourcefulness, creativity, and agency of other Red Sea citizens.

Glossary

The abbreviations—(Ar.) for Arabic, (Amh.) for Amharic, (Tgn.) for Tigrinya, (Tgr.) for Tigre, and (Tur.) for Turkish—indicate the language in which the term is used.

ʿaawlet (Tgr.)	highland areas
abun (Amh.)	title of metropolitan bishop or head of the Ethiopian Orthodox Church
ʿad (Tgr.)	family, people, village, country
adar/adari (Tgr.)	a term used to refer to a broker, guide, representative in the context of cross-regional trade; roughly the same meaning as *nazīl*
afandī (Ar.)	in general Mister, Mr., as well as an honorary appellation given to members of learned professions; same as *efendī* (Tur.)
aghā (Tur.)	officer below the rank of *bey*
ahl (Ar.)	family, people; *ahā lī* is "the natives," "the native population"
al-ḥājj (Ar.)	title given to one who has performed the pilgrimage (*ḥājj*) to Mecca
bahr negash (Amh.)	"Ruler of the Sea"; until eighteenth century, title and office of the governor of the Red Sea coastal provinces; *Bahri Negasi* in Tgn.
baraka (Ar.)	heritable beneficent force of divine origin; divine benediction or grace
bāshā	Arabic form of *pasha* (Tur.)
bayt (Ar.)/*bet* (Tgr.)	house, also family
bey (Tur.)	civil and military title below *pasha*
daga (Amh. /Tgn.)	temperate areas of 2,000 meters and more above sea level
daret (Tgr.)	fenced house forming a compound or enclosure
ḍarīḥ (Ar.)	a tomb, usually of a holy man
dejazmatch (Amh.)	commander of the gate; Ethiopian political-military title below *ras;* a general second only to *ras*
dhikr (Ar.)	remembrance, invocation of God; for Sufis the ceremony in which a litany of a brotherhood is recited
efendī (Turk.)	same as *afandī* (Ar.)
faqīh (Ar.)	a jurist, one versed in Islamic jurisprudence
fatwa (Ar.)	non-binding legal opinion issued by a *muftī*
firman	decree, order (from *ferman* in Tur.)
gult (Amh.)	non-hereditary right to collect tribute and rent held by the historic Ethiopian nobility and clergy

Habesha	"Abyssinian," a common appellation of the Semitic-speaking people inhabiting the highlands of Ethiopia or Eritrea
Ḥadīth (Ar.)	"tradition," the recorded actions and sayings of the Prophet Muhammad
ḥājj (Ar.)	pilgrimage
ḥalāl (Ar.)	permissible
ḥarām (Ar.)	forbidden
ḥawliyya (Ar.)	from *ḥawla*, "year," the yearly commemoration of the death of a holy man or woman
ḥujja (Ar.)	deed, proof, record (legal)
ḥukmdār (Ar.)	commissioner; Egyptian governor-general of the Sudan to 1885
jallāba (Ar.)	itinerant merchant; used in the Sudan
Jeberti	Amharic and Tigrinya-speaking Muslims inhabiting the highlands of Ethiopia and Eritrea
kāhia (Tur.)	an Ottoman title; lieutenant-commander, superintendent, major-domo, or quartermaster
kantebay (Tgr.)	a title referring to tribe, clan, or district chief, used by Tigre-speaking groups such as the Habab, Mensaᶜ, ᶜAd Temaryam, ᶜAd Tekles; the position is hereditary but not strictly so; the term *kantiba* is used in Amh. and Tgn. for town/city mayor
kebessa (Tgn.)	the highlands of the central plateau
khalīfa (Ar.)	"successor"; representative of the head of a Sufi brotherhood in a particular region or country
*khalīfat al-khulāfā*ᵓ (Ar.)	head of the *khalīfas*
Khatmiyya	Sufi brotherhood established by Muḥammad ᶜUthmān al-Mīrghanī (1793–1852)
khedive	derived from Persian term for "lord" or "ruler"; title used by the governor of Egypt informally since ca. 1850 and officially since 1867.
madhhab (Ar.)	school, applied to the four schools of Islamic jurisprudence; pl. *madhāhib*
mahdī (Ar.)	"the divinely guided one" who will appear before the end of time to re-establish justice on earth
maḥkama sharᶜiyya (Ar.)	Islamic court
majlis maḥalī (Ar.)	local council, usually established in localities administered by the Egyptians in northeast Africa in the nineteenth century
mawlid (Ar.)	the celebration of the Prophet's birthday on 12 Rabīᶜ I (*mawlid al-nabī*)
mazād (Ar.)	public auction
metahit (Tgn.)	the dry lowlands of the coastal and western plains of Eritrea
midun (Tgr.)	towns, cities; sing. *medinat;* the Mensaᶜ refer to Massawa as *midun*
muftī (Ar.)	Muslim legal specialist qualified to expound and interpret the law
muḥāfaẓa (Ar.)	province, governorate
muqqadam (Ar.)	one who represents a prominent Sufi *shaykh;* in the Sudanese region, head of a local branch in the Qādiriyya, or assistant to the *khalīfa* in the Khatmiyya
mushīr (Ar.)	one who directs; rank of marshal
mutaḥaḍḍir (Ar.)	settled, urban, but also "civilized"

nāʾib (Ar.)	deputy; title given by the Ottomans to the Balaw chief based in Hergigo
nakhūda (Ar.)	boat captain
nazīl (Ar.)	broker who lodges a trader, protects him, and represents him in business transactions
nāẓir (Ar.)	an appointed notable in charge of a tribe or an area; also a *waqf* administrator
neggadras (Amh.)	head of merchants; leader of caravan; later, government official in charge of collecting customs
negus (Amh.)	king
nisba (Ar.)	genealogical origin, reference to one's descent or origin
pasha (Tur.)	highest title in the Ottoman and Egyptian court hierarchy; rendered in Arabic as *bāshā*
qabīla (Ar.)	tribe
qāḍī (Ar.)	judge
Qādiriyya	a Sufi brotherhood named after ʿAbd al-Qādir al-Jīlānī (1077–1166)
qāʾim maqām (Ar.)	"he who replaces"; lieutenant; sub-governor; also rank in the Egyptian army equivalent to lieutenant-colonel or colonel
qalaaqil (Tgr.)	lowland areas
qawm/ qawmiyya (Ar.)	tribe, ethnic group, nation
qolla (Amh. /Tgn.)	hot lowland areas below 700 meters above sea level
qubba (Ar.)	domed tomb of a holy man; shrine
ras (Amh.)	"head," highest traditional title below *negus;* in Tgn. *ra'si*
Ṣaḥāba (Ar.)	"companions"; the Prophet Muhammad's companions, some of whom crossed the Red Sea to Abyssinia in AD 615
sanbūq (Ar.)	a sailing boat, usually recognized by its transom stern and spoon-shaped bow
sanjak (Tur.)	Ottoman sub-province, administrative district
sartujjār (Ar.)	prominent merchant chosen to represent the merchant community in a town
sayyid (Ar.)	a person tracing descent of the Prophet Muhammad; pl. *sādah*
seb bar (Tgr.)	people of the mainland, villagers; appellation used by urban dwellers to refer to those living outside town
seb medinat (Tgr.)	townspeople, urban dwellers
Shādhiliyya	a Sufi brotherhood named after Abū al-Ḥasan al-Shādhilī (d. 1258)
sharīʿa (Ar.)	sacred, revealed law in Islam
sharīf (Ar.)	a person tracing descent to the Prophet Muhammad; pl. *ashrāf*
shaykh (Ar.)	"old man"; tribal chief, religious leader, or head of a Sufi brotherhood
shum (Amh./ Tgn./Tgr.)	appointee, chief; a term used in a variety of configurations among communities in Ethiopia and Eritrea; the title/office is not strictly hereditary
sirdār (Ar.)	supreme commander, commander-in-chief
tājir (Ar.)	merchant; pl. *tujjār*
ṭarīqa (Ar.)	way, path; Sufi (mystic) brotherhood; pl. *ṭuruq*
Tigray	Province in northern Ethiopia
tigre	The serf class in some Tigre-speaking societies
Tigre	A Semitic language and ethnic group inhabiting northern and western Eritrea

ʿulamāʾ (Ar.)	learned men, scholars; sing. *ʿalīm*
umma (Ar.)	the worldwide community of Muslim believers
wakīl (Ar.)	legal proxy, legal representative
walī (Ar.)	"friend"; friend of God; holy man blessed with *baraka*
waqf (Ar.)	pious endowment; foundation in favour of a religious or charitable institution
wayna daga (Amh./Tgn.)	sub-tropical climate areas between 700 and 2000 meters above sea level
zāwiya (Ar.)	"corner"; a religious center often associated with a Sufi brotherhood; may also refer to a small minaret-less mosque
Zemene Mesefint (Amh.)	"Era of the Princes," 1769–1855
ziyāra (Ar.)	"visit"; visitation to the tomb of a holy man

Notes

Introduction

1. Rassam, *Narrative of the British Mission to Theodore,* 10.

2. Blanc, *A Narrative of Captivity in Abyssinia,* 66.

3. Plowden, *Travels in Abyssinia and the Galla Country,* 3. It goes without saying that the above statements say much about the mode of thought of those who had made them; unsurprisingly all British or associated with its empire.

4. Speakers of the Barka and Sahel dialects of Tigre call the town Bāṭe^{c}.

5. The following articles adopt the position that assumes that Bāḍi^{c} was early Massawa: Lusini, "Bāḍi^{c}," in *Encyclopaedia Aethiopica* (hereafter *EA*), 1:430–31; van Donzel, "Maṣawwa^{c}," in *Encyclopaedia of Islam,* new ed., 6:641–44; Smidt, "Massawa," in *EA,* 3:849. A different interpretation situating Bāḍi^{c} to the north of Massawa at the site of al-Rīḥ is argued by Crowfoot, "Some Red Sea ports in the Anglo-Egyptian Sudan," 523–50; Tedeschi, "La questione di Bāḍi^{c}," 179–99. I tend to find Tedeschi's study and conclusions convincing. I also tend to think that the positionality of scholars working from within the traditions of Ethiopian, Islamic, and Sudanese studies have influenced their interpretations and conclusions on the matter.

6. For overarching treatments of Italian colonialism in Eritrea, see Taddia, *L'Eritrea colonia 1890–1952;* Negash, *Italian Colonialism in Eritrea, 1882–1941;* and Mesghenna, *Italian Colonialism.* Since the publication of these studies, significant and sophisticated research has been published on the subject.

7. Bloss, "The Story of Suakin," 20, no. 2, 247.

8. Clarence-Smith, "The Rise and Fall of Hadrami Shipping," 249. Kenneth McPherson offers a more sober definition of cosmopolitanism in the context of Indian Ocean port towns as denoting "the presence of a variety of confessional, cultural, and racial groups within a single urban setting." McPherson, "Port Cities as Nodal Points of Change," 83.

9. Simpson and Kresse, "Introduction," in *Struggling with History,* 2–3.

10. See pertinent comments in the context of Swahili towns in Middleton, *The World of the Swahili,* 103–104.

11. Cohen, "Cultural Strategies," 267.

12. The Red Sea is approximately 1,200 miles (1,900 km) long, and on average, 170 miles (280 km) wide. At Massawa and Sawākin it is roughly 220 miles (350 km) from shore to shore.

13. See judicious comments on the affinities shared by littorals and ports in the Red Sea space in Lavergne, "Les relations yéméno-érythréennes à l'épreuve du conflit des

Hanish," 79–86. On the historical relations between the African and Arabian shores of the Red Sea see remarks in Lenci, *Eritrea e Yemen,* 13–18.

14. See, for example, most recently Wigen, "AHR Forum: Oceans of History," 717–21; Horden and Purcell, "The Mediterranean and 'the New Thalassology,'" 722–40.

15. For example, Toussaint, *History of the Indian Ocean;* Chaudhuri, *Trade and Civilisation in the Indian Ocean;* McPherson, *The Indian Ocean: A History of People and the Sea;* Pearson, *The Indian Ocean;* Bose, *A Hundred Horizons.*

16. Among these are three articles in Fawaz and Bayly, *Modernity and Culture;* Lunde and Porter, *Trade and Travel in the Red Sea Region;* Starkey, *People of the Red Sea;* Starkey, Starkey, and Wilkinson, *Natural Resources and Cultural Connections of the Red Sea.* One earlier provocative and thought-provoking short text, even if idiosyncratic and ideologically driven (Afro-centric), raised some fundamental questions about the Red Sea as a geographical, cultural, and political boundary: Mazrui, "Towards abolishing the Red Sea and re-Africanizing the Arabian Peninsula."

17. One recent study is a forthcoming book on Mukhā by Nancy Um.

18. See especially the stimulating contributions by Fuccaro and Onley in al-Rasheed, *Transnational Connections and the Arab Gulf.* For an earlier study of this area see also Fattah, *The Politics of Regional Trade in Iraq, Arabia and the Gulf.*

19. Cooper, "What Is the Concept of Globalization Good For?" 208–11.

20. Lewis and Wigen, *The Myth of Continents.* I found Principles 9 ("contextual specificity") and 10 ("a creative cartographic vision") particularly pertinent in this context (199–200).

21. De Monfreid, *Les secrets de la mer Rouge.* The book was translated into English and published as *Secrets of the Red Sea* (London, 1934).

22. Bose, *A Hundred Horizons,* 78–79.

23. See remarks along this line in Taddia, "Modern Ethiopia and Colonial Eritrea," 133–38, and "Ethiopian and African Studies," 255–64. For a sensitive approach to regional and comparative perspectives see also Lee Cassanelli, "New Directions in Southern Somali History."

24. A pioneering study "from the periphery" whose historiographic vision and methodology has been a source of inspiration is Triulzi, *Salt, Gold and Legitimacy.*

25. See Reid, "The Challenge of the Past," 246–47.

26. Examples may be drawn from numerous studies of Ethiopian history. One good example is the book by Franz Amadeus Dombrowski, *Ethiopia's Access to the Sea.* Historically deterministic views tend to perceive periods in which Massawa was not directly under Ethiopian sovereignty as almost "historical anomalies."

27. An example reflected in the historiography is Ghada H. Talhami's study, which examined the Egyptian occupation of Sawākin and Massawa, placing the expansionist Egyptian polity under Khedive Ismāʿīl at the center of the account and perceiving the ports as forming part of a temporally and spatially distinct historical unit shaped by Egyptian expansionism in the Red Sea. Talhami wrote the study as a student of Middle Eastern and Egyptian history and based it largely on Egyptian published archival documents. Talhami, *Suakin and Massawa under Egyptian Rule.* See also Triulzi's review of Talhami in the *IJAHS* 14, no. 4 (1981): 764–66.

28. Hanssen, Philipp, and Weber, "Introduction: Towards a New Urban Paradigm."

29. For the roots and foundations of such dynamics in the colonial period see Uoldelul Chelati Dirar, "Colonialism and the Construction of National Identities."

30. For the 1940s and 1950s see the writings of Shaykh Ibrāhīm al-Mukhtār Aḥmad ʿUmar, Grand Muftī of Eritrea. On his life and career see my "Grand mufti, érudit et nationaliste érythréen."

31. For the literature since the 1960s–70s see especially the writings of ᶜUthmān Ṣāliḥ Sabī. See also texts by Muḥammad ᶜUthmān Abū Bakr and Muḥammad Saᶜīd Nāwad. For this type of representation see also Kurdi, *L'Erythrée,* especially the first four chapters. With the exception of Muhammad Saᶜīd Nāwad, the authors mentioned here are originally from Hergigo.

32. See his massively documented biography written by his friend and comrade in struggle (and fellow native of Hergigo). Abū Bakr, *ᶜUthmān Ṣāliḥ Sabī wa-l-thawra al-iritriyya.* Sabī wrote a general history of Eritrea in Arabic, later translated into English: *Taʾrīkh Iritrīyā.*

33. Reid, "The Challenge of the Past." See Reid's disillusioned observations several years later in his "War and Remembrance." See also remarks on the inherent problematic in this process in Taddia, "Modern Ethiopia and Colonial Eritrea," 125–38. On the historiography of Eritrea, see also and Cayla-Vardhan, *Les enjeux de l'historiographie érythréenne.*

34. For the growing interest in Massawa's past and its cultural, religious, and architectural heritage since the independence of Eritrea, see press articles and publications containing strong historical dimensions: Jacky Sutton, "Dateline Massawa: A Desert Pearl Revives," *Eritrea Profile* 1, no. 49 (18 February 1995); Marianne Scott, "Magical Massawa," *Eritrea Profile* 5, no. 47 (30 January 1999): 4; Tedros Abraham, "Cara Massaua . . . ," *Eritrea Profile* 6 (15 April 2000): 6; Daniel Tekeste, "Massawa Reflections," *EriTempo,* May 2000, 31; Hermon Berhane, "Massawa on my mind," *Eritrea Profile* 7, no. 43 (30 December 2000); (unsigned), [English] "The Shaykh Hammal Mosque: A Three-Hundred-Year-Old Building," *Hadas Ertra* 9, no. 113 (20 Genbot 2000): 5; Hāshim Bashīr, "Sirr al-Maṣawwiᶜīn . . . wa fiḍa wāḥad yujmaᶜ mudun al-baḥr al-aḥmar," *Iritrīyā al-Ḥadītha* 11, no. 33 (17 October 2001): 5. And two official pamphlets: *Risālat Maṣawwaᶜ* (in Arabic; published by the Massawa city administration on the occasion of the commemoration of the 4th year of its liberation), 4 February 1994, and *The Pearl of the Red Sea,* (in English, Tigrinya, Arabic; published by the Massawa city administration on the occasion of the commemoration of the 10th year of its liberation), 10 February 2000. A booklet in Tigrinya on Eritrea's coastal history is: Abba Yshaq Ghebre Iyasus, *Gemagem Bahr Ertra* (Asmara, n.d. [1998–99?]). A more recent publication surveying Massawa's built form and architecture is *Massawa: A Guide to the Built Environment* (Asmara, 2005).

35. Although largely concerned with dominant interior polities of northeast Africa, the work of historians Jay Spaulding and Donald Crummey has been among the rare examples of social history loosely inspired by the *Annales* School tradition, working from within a framework that addressed the concerns of historians of Africa at large. See, for example, Spaulding, *The Heroic Age in Sinnar;* Crummey, *Land and Society in the Christian Kingdom of Ethiopia.*

36. Ralph Austen, "The Nineteenth Century Islamic Slave Trade from East Africa," 33. The figures for Massawa are more or less equal to those for Sawākin, while those for the Gulf of Aden are estimated at 250,000 slaves exported during the entire century.

37. Among studies that have dealt with the Red Sea slave trade, for some offering data on the question of slave traffic to and from Massawa see Abir (1985), Ahmad (1988), Austen (1978, 1988), Ewald (1988, 1992, 2000), Pankhurst (1964, 1968), Toledano (1982, 2007).

38. For an essay on the state of the field, see Spear, "Early Swahili History Reconsidered." See also Nurse and Spear *The Swahili;* Pouwels, *Horn and Crescent;* Allen, *Swahili Origins.* Two specific historical studies that have shaped my understanding of the dynamics of Swahili societies in the nineteenth century are Ylvisaker, *Lamu in the Nineteenth Century;* Glassman, *Feasts and Riot.* For other studies on Swahili identity construction see the work of A. H. J. Prins, Carol Eastman, David Parkin, Alamin Mazrui and Ibrahim

Noor Shariff, James de Vere Allen, Ahmed Salim, Farouk Topan, Justin Willis and others. Two important studies in the context of the Benaadir coast of southern Somalia are Cassanelli, *The Shaping of Somali Society,* and Reese, "Patricians of the Benaadir." See also Alpers, "Muqdisho in the Nineteenth Century," Molon and Vianello, "Brava, città dimenticata," and Cresti, "Città e società urbane a sud del Sahara."

39. Middleton, *The World of the Swahili,* and Horton and Middleton, *The Swahili.*

40. Talhami, *Suakin and Massawa,* 38, 55.

41. Warburg, *Historical Discord in the Nile Valley,* 5.

42. Jedrej, "The Red Sea and the Eastern Sudan in the Early 19th Century," 108.

43. Cohen, "Cultural Strategies," 267. See also Cohen's *Custom and Politics in Urban Africa,* 3–4, and Curtin, *Cross-Cultural Trade in World History.*

44. For an example of the role of the court in group cohesion see Swartz, "Religious Courts, Community, and Ethnicity among the Swahili of Mombasa." Other historians refined Cohen's understanding of "trade diaspora," suggesting that they were not necessarily exclusively composed of foreign and alien members but could include individuals belonging to local communities who had come to adopt distinct identities in order to perform the role of cultural mediators between local and overseas partners. See especially Wink, *Al-Hind,* 66–67. For a criticism of Curtin's model of "trade diaspora" see Chaudhuri, *Trade and Civilisation in the Indian Ocean,* 223–28.

45. Cohen, "Cultural Strategies," 267.

46. See illuminating insights on "commonality," "connectedness," "groupness" in Brubaker and Cooper, "Beyond 'Identity,'" 19–21.

47. For studies of Hadrami migrants' assimilation into host societies (especially in Southeast Asia) and the resulting creation of creole senses of identity, see the studies of Engseng Ho: "Hadhramis Abroad in Hadhramaut," and "Names beyond Nations," "Before Parochialization," and specific comments in "Empire through Diasporic Eyes," 215–16.

48. Interview with Ḥāmid ʿAbd al-Bāqī ʿAbbāsī, Massawa, 18 March 2000. Letter from Fouad Makki, 30 July 2004, and interview with Muḥammad Ṣāliḥ Afandī, Asmara, 3 July 2006. On ethnicity and politics in contemporary Eritrea see Tekle M. Woldemikael, "The Cultural Construction of Eritrean Nationalist Movements," 179–99; Bariagaber, "The Politics of Cultural Pluralism in Ethiopia and Eritrea," 1056–73; and Tronvoll, "Borders of Violence," 1037–60.

49. I have also seen some of these terms and their variants, for example in articles from the late 1940s in *Ṣawṭ al-Rābiṭa al-Islāmiyya al-Iritriyya,* the newspaper of the Muslim League in the late 1940s and early 1950s.

50. Interview with ʿAlī Yūsuf ʿAlī al-Ghūl, Massawa, 26 February 2000.

51. This sense of solidarity exists also on a practical level. For example Sayyid Ṣādiq Muḥsin al-Ṣāfī (b. 1921), who currently resides in Massawa, is the *wakīl* (Ar. legal representative) in matters of real estate to members of the Bā Ḥamdūn, Bā Zaham, ʿAdūlāy, Bā Ḥubayshī, Sardāl, and Nahārī families who fled the country in the 1960s and 1970s. Many of them reside in Jiddah, Saudi Arabia.

52. Interview with Muhammad ʿAbdu Bakrī Ḥijjī, Massawa, 5 May 2000.

53. Conversations with Fouad Makki, Asmara, 27 July 2001, and Ḥāmid ʿAbd al-Bāqī ʿAbbāsī, Massawa, 3 October 2007. In Arabic the word *bar* refers to the land, as opposed to the sea. So in some contexts *seb bar* designates "people of the mainland" as opposed to those of the islands. Saleh Mahmud Idris, personal communication, 15 March 2008.

54. Of the many studies on Swahili identity politics, a recent useful article that includes discussion of the positionality of authors and informants is Pat Caplan, "'But the Coast, of Course, Is Quite Different.'" See also Caplan and Topan, *Swahili Modernities,*

and Loimeier and Seesemann. *The Global Worlds of the Swahili,* for a critique of what the editors see as essentialist dichotomies between constructions of the "universal" and the "local" in analyzing the structure of Swahili culture.

55. Interestingly, it appears that the term *ṭarashat al-baḥr* is also used on the other shores of the Red Sea, in the context of cultural competition between the inhabitants of Jiddah and those of the Arabian inland. According to one version, the expression *ṭarsh al-baḥr* has its origins in the way Hijazis used to refer to non-Arabic-speaking Muslim pilgrims who landed in Jiddah. They were thus referred to as the "deaf of/from the sea." I thank Alessandro Gori for this information.

56. Indeed, one person who intimately knows Massawan society and who has read the entire study made the criticism that I overemphasize the discussion of origins while not stressing enough the social and cultural unity of the community. I would argue that it is precisely the tension between these two tendencies ("we are one, but we come from many places") that is an integral and central part of the story that is told here.

57. Bruce's account made an important impact, alas all too often negative, on the perceptions of subsequent nineteenth-century travelers in Massawa and Hergigo. In some cases, even late-nineteenth-century accounts seem to have been directly inspired by Bruce's exaggerated remarks on the *nā'ibs,* for example. Bruce's impact on the formation of preconceptions of nineteenth-century travelers to Ethiopia deserves a short study on its own. On Munzinger, see Peck, "A Swiss Pasha at Massawa."

58. The book was published in Schaffhausen in 1864. In this study I have used the Italian translation titled *Studi sull'Africa orientale* (Rome, 1890).

59. Pennazzi, *Dal Po ai due Nili,* 29. Another expression that was often cited was British: "Pondichery is a warm bath, Aden is an oven, and Massawa hell."

60. Saint-Yves, "A travers l'Erythrée italienne," 148.

61. Odorizzi, *Il Commissariato Regionale di Massaua;* Folchi, "Commissariato Regionale di Massaua."

62. Muḥammad ʿUthmān Ḥayūtī, untitled ms. (Ḥayūtī family, Asmara).

63. A copy of the entire translated manuscript (of Odorizzi) is with the Ḥayūtī family in Asmara. Some sources, however, attribute to Bā Ṭūq the translation of this text. Interviews with Ḥasan Muḥammad ʿUthmān Ḥayūtī, Asmara, 27 November 1999, Asmara, 11–12 July 2006, and Muḥammad Yāsīn Bā Ṭūq, Massawa, 17 March 2000. Both were also the editors of *Ṣawṭ al-Rābiṭa al-Islāmiyya al-Iritriyya,* newspaper of the Muslim League. The Bā Ṭūq ms. title is found in http://www.mukhtar.ca (under "tarājim").

64. Ibrāhīm al-Mukhtār Aḥmad ʿUmar, *Al-Jāmiʿ li-akhbār jazīrat Bāḍiʿ,* ms. completed in 1378 H/1958, 122 pp., and Id. *al-Rāwiya fī taʾrīkh mudun Iritrīyā,* ms. completed in 1372 H./1953, 146 pp.

65. Abū Bakr, *Taʾrīkh Iritrīyā al-muʿāṣir: arḍan wa-shaʿban,* chapter 35 on Semhar, 279–353.

66. Credit for drawing my attention to this source goes to Tom Killion, who indicated its existence in his *Historical Dictionary of Eritrea,* 456. This is without overlooking the fact that Abdu Ali Habib was the first to find and make use of several registers in his thesis, "History of Massawa from Early Nineteenth Century to the Coming of the Italians." See also my "Islamic Court Records."

67. Vianello and Kassim, with Kapteijns, *Servants of the Sharia.*

68. A more variegated division of climatic gradations as highland Amharic and Tigrinya speakers define it includes the *qolla* (hot lowlands: areas below 700 m.), the *wayna daga* (subtropical climate: 700–2000 m.), and the *daga* (temperate: 2000 m. and more above sea level). In Tigre the word for lowland is *qalaaqil,* while the word for highland is *ʿaawlet.*

69. Killion, *Historical Dictionary of Eritrea,* 1–8; Ullendorff, *The Ethiopians,* 23–37; Young, "Rašayda" and "From Many, One."

1. Making a Region between the Sea and the Mountain

1. Letter from Nāʾib Idrīs ʿUthmān to Lord Valentia, [July 1805]. Document no. 1, in Rubenson, *Correspondence and Treaties 1800–1854,* 3. Also, Valentia, *Voyages and Travels to India,* 3:252

2. Nāʾib Ḥasan to the Ottoman governor of Massawa; Munzinger, "Les contrées limitrophes de l'Habesch," 15; Lejean, *Voyage aux Deux Nils,* 169.

3. The intellectual roots of this outlook can be traced even further back to the popular medieval legend of the Christian Kingdom of Prester John.

4. Some travelers were probably directly inspired by James Bruce's late-eighteenth-century negative account. For a sample of anti-*nāʾib* slant in the literature see Combes and Tamisier, *Voyage en Abyssinie,* 92–93; Munzinger, "Les contrées limitrophes de l'Habesch," 8–9; Douin, *Histoire du règne de Khédive Ismail,* vol. 3, part 1, 235. See also Abir, "Ethiopia and the Horn of Africa," 550, 563, 567–58, and *Ethiopia: The Era of the Princes,* 8.

5. On the uses of the past in constructing legitimacy in the present see Reid, "The Challenge of the Past."

6. Cooper, "Africa's Pasts and Africa's Historians," 318.

7. See my "Constructing and Deconstructing the 'Tigre Frontier.'"

8. See Faroqhi, "Coping with the Central State, Coping with Local Power." See also Khoury, "The Ottoman Centre versus Provincial Power-Holders."

9. "Baláwi" means "Arab" in Beja. For the most detailed analysis of Balaw etymology, origins, and migrations see Morin, *Poésie traditionnelle des afars,* 2–7, and *Le texte légitime,* 15–17. Also very useful for name etymologies and toponyms, especially Afar, is Morin, *Dictionnaire historique Afar.* Paul, *A History of the Beja Tribes of the Sudan,* chapter 8, 80–90; Conti Rossini, "Schizzo etnico e storico delle popolazioni eritree," 61–90.

10. According to Odorizzi, Zaga was founded about two centuries before Emkullo, hence in the sixteenth century. The Balaw ʿAd Jamīl are recognized as important elements in its population. Odorizzi, *Il commissariato,* 186; Munzinger, *Studi sull'Africa orientale,* 111, 113, 129; Abū Bakr, *Taʾrīkh Iritrīyā,* 282, 305, and Abdu Ali Habib, "History of Massawa," 1.

11. According to traditions collected by Salvadei, Sayyid ʿĀmir Qunnu traced his descent from ʿAbd Allāh b. ʿAbbās, the Prophet's uncle. Giovanni Salvadei, "Massaua" (Allegato N. 110), in Ferdinando Martini, *Relazione sulla Colonia Eritrea.* "Dakano" means "elephant" in Saho and "Dakanu" in Afar. Its preeminently Tigre-speaking inhabitants call their town Hergigo. In its Arabized form it is also referred to as Ḥarqīqū, subsequently Italianized to Archico. On Hergigo toponomy see Odorizzi, *Il commissariato,* 126–27.

12. See descriptions and versions of this tradition in Munzinger, *Studi,* 130, Odorizzi, *Il commissariato,* 132. Obviously, there are certain discrepancies regarding dates and persons stemming from the use/misuse of the term *nāʾib* as the leader of the family in its earlier stages in Semhar. Clearly, the *nāʾib* was appointed by the Ottomans only later, but nineteenth-century traditions were unsurprisingly inclined to establish a *nāʾib* as the founder of the Balaw dynasty in Semhar. Some versions place Ḥummād's father, Sayyid ʿĀmir Qunnu as the founder of the dynasty. See the genealogical tree of the *nāʾibs* in Odorizzi, *Il commissariato,* 150–52.

13. For details on Hergigo prior to the nineteenth century see Pankhurst, "Some Notes on the Historical and Economic Geography of the Mesewa Area," and *History of Ethiopian Towns,* 82–83.

14. Odorizzi, *Il commissariato,* 127, 159, and interviews with Ṣāliḥ ʿAbd Allāh Zubayr, Hergigo, 7 March 2000, and Nāfiʿ ʿAlī Khaydar, Hergigo, 7 March 2000, both from the Bayt Shaykh Maḥmūd. On the Bayt Shaykh Maḥmūd see also Abū Bakr, *Taʾrīkh Iritrīyā,* 312–16.

15. Examples of the Balaw Yūsuf Ḥassab Allāh include the Shīnītī and Ḥāmidūy families, and examples of the Bayt Shaykh Maḥmūd include the Faras and Mentāy families.

16. See detailed family lists with origins in Odorizzi, *Il commissariato,* 112–15, 159–60, and Abū Bakr, *Taʾrīkh Iritrīyā,* 294–97, 304–11.

17. For a detailed study of the Ottoman province of Habesh based on Ottoman archives see Orhonlu, *Habeş Eyaleti* (in Turkish). The study includes a reproduction of 96 official Ottoman documents pertaining to Ethiopia and covering the years 1553–1897 (181–291). See also Orhonlu, "Turkish Archival Sources on Ethiopia"; Smidt, "Habeš"; Gori, "L'Etiopia nei testi ottomani"; and Özbaran, *The Ottoman Response to European Expansion.*

18. The appearance of firearms in the Red Sea area in the sixteenth century significantly strengthened the *Bahr Negash.* Some, like Bahr Negash Ishaq, had sought to gain more independence from the Ethiopian king. For more about Ottoman-Abyssinian struggles between the 1560s and 1590s, see Orhonlu, *Habesh Eyaleti,* 48–68.

19. Hourani, *A History of the Arab Peoples,* 226; Faroqhi, *The Ottoman Empire and the World around It,* 75–97.

20. See Çelebi's description of Massawa, Hergigo, and the Dahlak islands under the Ottomans in Bombaci, "Il viaggio in Abissinia di Evliya Çelebi (1673)," 263–70.

21. Dombrowski, *Ethiopia's Access to the Sea,* 21–23, 32–34; Guérinot, "L'islam et l'Abyssinie," 20–21; Donzel, "Maṣawwaʿ," 642; and Pankhurst, *History of Ethiopian Towns,* 86–91.

22. Khoury, "The Ottoman Centre versus Provincial Power-Holders," 138–39.

23. Some versions relate that Ḥummād was the first appointed *nāʾib.*

24. Pollera, *Le popolazioni indigene dell'Eritrea,* 217–18, Odorizzi, *Il commissariato,* 132–34; Salvadei, "Massaua," 1831; Conti Rossini, *Tradizioni storiche dei Mensa,* 43. Odorizzi estimated that this had taken place around 1690. Salvadei put it around 1680. Lejean reports that the Balaws of Hergigo comprised 600 families. Lejean, *Voyage en Abyssinie,* 56.

25. Odorizzi, *Il commissariato,* 137–38; Munzinger, *Studi,* 130; Salvadei, "Massaua," 1831–32. Full accounts of *nāʾib* dynastic history are given in Odorizzi, *Il commissariato,* 132–52, and Munzinger, *Studi,* 130–40. See a general note on the *nāʾib*s and their history with excerpts by travelers in Perini, *Di qua dal Marèb,* 226–31.

26. Historically, in some cases when a strong emperor acceded to the throne he renewed territorial claims over the peripheral regions, including the coastal area.

27. Faroqhi, "Coping with the Central State," 366.

28. Dombrowski, *Ethiopia's Access,* 38–39; Pankhurst, *History of Ethiopian Towns,* 91–92; Trimingham, *Islam in Ethiopia,* 105.

29. Bruce, *Travels to Discover the Source of the Nile,* 5–6.

30. Consul Plowden to the Earl of Clarendon (No. 184), Massowah, July 9, 1854, Report, in Great Britain, Parliamentary Papers, 124.

31. Munzinger, *Studi,* 109.

32. Bloss, "The Story of Suakin," (1936) 296. Bloss relies on Henry Salt's account (1814).

33. Douin, *Histoire du règne,* vol. 3, part 1, 234. On the Bet Taqwe—*nāʾib* link see Munzinger, *Studi,* 160.

34. Douin, *Histoire du règne,* vol. 3, part 1, 235; Munzinger, *Studi,* 139; Munzinger, *Les contrées limitrophes,* 9–10; Lejean, *Voyage aux deux Nils,* 171; Valentia, *Voyages,* 1:31–32.

35. Odorizzi, *Il commissariato,* 134; Pollera, *Le popolazioni,* 218–19; Lejean, *Voyage en*

Abyssinie, 56. According to Odorizzi this had occurred during the period of Nāʾib ʿĀmir's rule (r. 1690–1720, the year of his death).

36. Valentia, *Voyages,* 1:54.

37. Folchi, "Commissariato Regionale di Massaua," 120 (189).

38. They are often referred to as the "Arnauts" (irregular infantry serving in the Ottoman army and especially composed of Albanians). Munzinger, *Studi,* 130; Habib, "History of Massawa," 3.

39. Hourani, *History of the Arab Peoples,* 227. See also Hathaway, *The Politics of Households in Ottoman Egypt.* On the mixing of Ottoman officials/soldiers and locals in the process of forming and incorporating "Ottoman-local elites" see Toledano, "The Emergence of Ottoman-Local Elites," 155.

40. On notable members of the Kekiyā family see Puglisi, *Chi è? dell'Eritrea,* 169, 262, and Killion, *Historical Dictionary of Eritrea,* 282–83.

41. Munzinger, *Studi,* 139. Traditions from Hamasen collected by Kolmodin suggest that in some military campaigns in the highlands the *nāʾib* was aided by the Ottomans ("le naib revint, ayant reçu des renforts du Turc"). It would be reasonable to assume that the reference is to those coast-based militias initially formed by the Ottomans. Kolmodin, *Traditions de Tsazzega et Hazzega,* 2:76.

42. Odorizzi, *Il commissariato,* 136.

43. Munzinger, *Studi,* 139, Lejean; *Voyage aux deux Nils,* 171.

44. Munzinger, *Studi,* 137, Lejean; *Voyage en Abyssinie,* 61–62; and Ferret and Galinier, *Voyage en Abyssinie,* 389.

45. *Gult* is a bundle of income rights associated with highland peasant agriculture. Unlike in Europe, where fiefs entailed ownership of land, *gult* granted "sovereignty," or tributary rights that derived from a position of political overlordship. See more in Donham, "Old Abyssinia and the New Ethiopian Empire," 5–11.

46. Odorizzi, *Il commissariato,* 136.

47. Kolmodin, *Traditions de Tsazzega et Hazzega,* 2:75–76 and 3:xiii. According to these traditions the *nāʾib* in question was Yaḥyā Aḥmad (r. 1831–38 and 1841–44). All dates should be taken with utmost caution.

48. Lejean, *Théodore II,* 145; Pollera, *Le popolazioni,* 48; D'Avray, *Lords of the Red Sea,* 5–6; Rüppell, *Reise in Abyssinien,* 1:310; Lejean, *Voyage aux deux Nils,* 168–69. Pennazzi put the number at 17 villages. Pennazzi, "Massauah (Mar Rosso), " 329. The following is Abir's rendering of the circumstances of the handing over of *gults*: "Taking advantage of the disorder in Ethiopia . . . the *nāʾib* of Hergigo forced the weak *bahr negash* who ruled some of the provinces north of the Marèb to cede him a number of districts in Hamasen and Akkele Guzay," Abir, "Ethiopia and the Horn of Africa," 567.

49. Bose, *A Hundred Horizons,* 52.

50. Abbadie, *Géographie de l'Éthiopie,* 51.

51. On Emkullo see Odorizzi, *Il commissariato,* 164–67.

52. Abbadie, *Douze ans de séjour dans la Haute-Éthiopie* (1980), 1:10.

53. Abbadie, *Géographie de l'Éthiopie,* 41.

54. Odorizzi, *Il commissariato,* 175–80; Folchi, "Commissariato Regionale di Massaua," 203–204 (219–20). For a description of ʿAylet's inhabitants, their customs and Islamic practices see Parkyns, *Life in Abyssinia,* 34–38. ʿĀmir Nūrāy was chief of ʿAylet in the mid 1880s. He was originally from Hergigo and a descendant of the Nāʾib family. Archivio storico diplomatico del Ministero affari esteri, Rome (hereafter ASDMAE), *Archivio Eritrea* (hereafter *AE*), b. 53 (17) memo: "Amer Nurai," Massaua, 2.5.1888.

55. Odorizzi, *Il commissariato,* 194–95; Pollera, *Le popolazioni,* 220; Salvadei, "Massaua," 1836; Folchi, "Commissariato Regionale di Massaua," 243 (235). On the ʿAd Asker

see ASDMAE, *AE*, b. 178, "Notabili e capi indigeni dipendenti dal Commissariato Regionale di Massaua" (1902–1903), entry: "Scium Idris Zaccari (Ad Ascar)," 20. The Ghedem Sikta clan also served in this function, see Odorizzi, *Il commissariato*, 208–11.

56. On Gumhod and ᶜAsus see Odorizzi, *Il commissariato*, 180–85. See also Salvadei, "Massaua," 1835.

57. Munzinger, *Studi*, 137; Douin, *Histoire du règne*, vol. 3, part 1, 234.

58. Odorizzi, *Il commissariato*, 141.

59. Combes and Tamisier, *Voyage*, 113; Ferret and Galinier, *Voyage*, 375; Nott, "Report," 34. Nott estimated the annual sum paid by the *nāʾib* to the government at 1,600–1,700 thalers.

60. Lejean, *Voyage en Abyssinie*, 56.

61. Valentia, *Voyages*, 1:57.

62. Nott, "Report," 32–34.

63. D'Avray, *The Nakfa Documents*, Document 81, Captain Boari to the Gov. Civile e Militare della Colonia Eritrea (Massaua), Asmara, 11 March 1891, "Tributi nel Semhar e paesi limitrofi," 274. Plowden notes that a *koba* is 2.5 lbs.

64. Valentia, *Voyages*, 1:449; Munzinger, "Les contrées limitrophes," 15.

65. Abbadie, *Douze ans de séjour dans la Haute-Éthiopie* (1980), 1:548.

66. Valentia, *Voyages*, 1:55.

67. Munzinger, *Studi*, 111.

68. D'Avray, *The Nakfa Documents*, Document 81, Captain Boari to the Gov. Civile e Militare della Colonia Eritrea (Massaua), Asmara, 11 March 1891, 273–74.

69. Ibid., 274–75.

70. Munzinger, "Les contrées limitrophes," 9.

71. See a detailed account of the legend in Folchi, "Commissariato Regionale di Massaua," 235–36 (231); interview with Muḥammad Saᶜīd Shūmāy, Asmara, 30 November 1999.

72. Interview with "Captain" Aḥmad Shaykh Ibrāhīm Faras, Massawa, 3 March 2000; Folchi, "Commissariato Regionale di Massaua," 390 (301). For an example of further evidence of marriage alliances between the *nāʾib* family and Saho-speaking peoples, see de Rivoyre, *Au pays du Soudan*, 253–54.

73. The *sādah* (sing. *sayyid*) claim direct descent from the Prophet Muḥammad.

74. Odorizzi, *Il commissariato*, 164; Folchi, "Commissariato Regionale di Massaua," 177–78 (209).

75. Munzinger, "Les contrées limitrophes,"14.

76. Odorizzi, *Il commissariato*, 177.

77. Munzinger, *Studi*, 124, 138.

78. Trimingham, *Islam in Ethiopia*, 162.

79. Rodén, *Le tribù dei Mensa,*, 49, 60. See also Conti Rossini, *Tradizioni.*

80. On Nāʾib Ḥasan Idrīs, see Odorizzi, *Il commissariato*, 138.

81. Since Tedros's father, Idrīs, had died before his father, Tesfamikael.

82. Rodén, *Le tribù dei Mensa*, 96–98.

83. *Midun* (sing. *madinat*) in Tigre means "towns," "cities," or "urban settings." This was how the Mensaᶜ referred to the urban centers on the coast, especially Massawa. See more on this word in Rodén, *Le tribù dei Mensa*, 76; Munzinger, *Studi*, 106; and Conti Rossini, *Tradizioni*, 55. Some sources claim that the term *midun* designated the Semhar region. Odorizzi, *Il commissariato*, 108, and Gatta, "Massaua e le regioni circostanti," 476.

84. Rodén, *Le tribù dei Mensa*, 102–104. Guillaume Lejean sees the episode as part of Nāʾib Ḥasan's efforts to convert the Mensaᶜ to Islam; *Voyage en Abyssinie*, 59.

85. See a more detailed account of the diffusion of Islam in the Eritrean region in

the nineteenth century in Jonathan Miran, "A Historical Overview of Islam in Eritrea," 183–94.

86. See, for example, an account of the socially devastating Abyssinian and Egyptian raids against the Bilin in the 1850s. Ghaber, *The Blin of Boghos,* 12–22.

87. Sapeto tells of the numerous *faqīrs* who travel throughout the region (Keren and Bogos area, in this case) preaching Islam, giving talismans to the sick, and "generating moral disorder." Sapeto, *Viaggio e missione cattolica,* 156–57. The book contains useful descriptions of the recently converted Tigre-speaking societies in the northern Abyssinian region. See especially 145–262.

88. Odorizzi, *Il commissariato,* 159, 167, 178, 181.

89. Interviews with "Captain" Aḥmad Shaykh Ibrāhīm Faras, Massawa, 3 March 2000, and ᶜUsman Ḥājjī Maḥmūd, Massawa, 5 May 2000. The families of both interviewees are linked to the Kekiyās by marriage.

90. The Ghedem Sikta asked the *nāʾib* to send them a religious chief. Salvadei, "Massaua," 1837. Their chiefs were also appointed by the *nāʾib:* Folchi, "Commissariato Regionale di Massaua," 281–22 (252); ASDMAE, *AE,* b. 178, "Notabili e capi indigeni dipendenti dal Commissariato Regionale di Massaua" (1902–1903), entry: "Scium Ali Ghenenai," 35. The composition of the clan as noted in the early twentieth century includes important elements of the Bayt Shaykh Maḥmūd. So as the other clans mentioned. See Odorizzi, *Il commissariato,* 210 (Ghedem Sikta), 189–91 (ᶜAd Ha), 194–97 (ᶜAd Asker).

91. Abū Bakr, *Taʾrīkh Iritrīyā,* 312–16.

92. On the Bet Asgede and Habab adoption of Islam estimated at ca. 1820 see Munzinger, "Les contrées limitrophes," 10; Munzinger, *Studi,* 112; Trimingham, *Islam in Ethiopia,* 113, 160–61; Pollera, *Le popolazioni,* 200.

93. See d'Avray, *Lords of the Red Sea,* 63.

94. For more sources and a detailed discussion of the ᶜAd Shaykh see chapter 4.

95. Lejean, *Voyage aux deux Nils,* 142.

96. On the Marya's adoption of Islam see Trimingham, *Islam in Ethiopia,* 113, 168; Pollera, *Le popolazioni,* 185. On the adoption of Islam by the Mensaᶜ, see Munzinger, "Les contrées limitrophes," 11; Trimingham, *Islam in Ethiopia,* 162; Pollera, *Le popolazioni,* 176. On the propagation of Islam by the ᶜAd Shaykh among specific groups in the region see Pollera, *Le popolazioni,* 200; Trimingham, *Islam in Ethiopia,* 113, 161–62; d'Avray, *Lords of the Red Sea,* 63.

97. Salvadei, "Massaua," 1830.

98. Trimingham, *Islam in Ethiopia,* 232.

99. Abir, "Origins of the Ethio-Egyptian Border Problem," 443–61.

100. For example *1808–1809:* Habib, "History of Massawa," 4; *1813–14:* Pankhurst, "L'Ethiopie et la Somalie," 423; *1847–49:* Abir, *Ethiopia,* 132, Dombrowski, *Ethiopia's Access to the Sea,* 48, Rubenson, *Survival of Ethiopian Independence,* 117; *1865–66:* Perini, *Di qua dal Marèb,* 231.

101. Abir, *Ethiopia,* 6; Rubenson, *Survival of Ethiopian Independence,* 44.

102. Habib, "History of Massawa," 4; d'Avray, *The Nakfa Documents,* Document 81, Captain Boari to the Gov. Civile e Militare della Colonia Eritrea (Massaua), Asmara, 11 March 1891, "Tributi nel Semhar e paesi limitrofi," 274.

103. Rüppell, *Reise in Abyssinien,* 1:188.

104. Abir, *Ethiopia,* 6; Rubenson, *Survival of Ethiopian Independence,* 57; Habib, "History of Massawa," 4.

105. Habib, "History of Massawa," 4–5; Pankhurst, *History of Ethiopian Towns,* 243–44. Events in the mid-1820s would benefit from further clarification. See supplementary details in Smidt, "Habeš," 951.

106. Rüppell, *Reise in Abyssinien*, 1:189.

107. Abir, *Ethiopia*, 33–37; Abir, "Origins of the Ethio-Egyptian Border Problem," 443–44; Rubenson, *Survival of Ethiopian Independence*, 66–8.

108. For an analysis of the concept of borders in the Ethiopian region in the nineteenth century see Abir, "Origins of the Ethio-Egyptian Border Problem," 459.

109. Ibid, 449.

110. Bayyūmī, *Siyāsat Miṣr fī al-Baḥr al-Aḥmar*, 141–42; Abir, *Ethiopia*, 119.

111. Douin, *Histoire du règne*, vol. 3, part 1, 235, Rubenson, *Survival of Ethiopian Independence*, 104–106.

112. Rubenson, *Survival of Ethiopian Independence*, 108.

113. Odorizzi, *Il commissariato*, 138; Abir, *Ethiopia*, 121.

114. On the French role in the region, see Malécot, *Les voyageurs français*.

115. Douin, *Histoire du règne*, vol. 3, part 1, 236–37; Abir, *Ethiopia*, 122–23.

116. Douin, *Histoire du règne*, vol. 3, part 1, 238–39, Abir, *Ethiopia*, 132.

117. Douin, *Histoire du règne*, vol. 3, part 1, 240–41. See the description of Webe's raid in Léon des Avanchers, "Notes historiques et géographiques sur l'Abyssinie," 370, and Lejean, *Voyage en Abyssinie*, 56.

118. Plowden to Addington, August 28, 1847, Memorandum, in Great Britain, Parliamentary Papers, 8A.

119. The Ottoman "push" in the southern Red Sea area is in some ways paralleled in Yemen, where after an absence of nearly two centuries, the Ottomans returned to the Tihāma in 1849. There too, the Ottoman reconquest eroded the power of lowland tribal chiefs who had previously served as power brokers. See Farah, *The Sultan's Yemen*, chapter 4.

120. Odorizzi, *Il commissariato*, 138–39, 154–55; Douin, *Histoire du règne*, vol. 3, part 1, 238–43; Habib, "History of Massawa," 5–14.

121. See for example the convoluted career of Nāʾib Ḥasan Idrīs. ASDMAE, *AE*, b. 178 "Notabili e capi indigeni dipendenti dal Commissariato Regionale di Massaua (1902–3)," 11. Also Odorizzi, *Il commissariato*, 140–43.

122. Munzinger, "Les contrées limitrophes," 22; Lejean, *Voyage aux deux Nils*, 168–69.

123. Plowden to Clarendon, July 9, 1854, Report, in Great Britain, Parliamentary Papers, 129, and Douin, *Histoire du règne*, vol. 3, part 1, 243.

124. Ibid.

125. Douin, *Histoire du règne*, vol. 3, part 1, 244.

126. Munzinger, "Les contrées limitrophes," 17–18.

127. Ibid., 19; Douin, *Histoire du règne*, vol. 3, part 1, 247; Lejean, *Voyage en Abyssinie*, 57.

128. Habib, "History of Massawa," 8–9. See also d'Avray, *The Nakfa Documents*, Document 81, Captain Boari to the Gov. Civile e militare della Colonia Eritrea (Massaua), Asmara, 11 March 1891, "Tributi nel Semhar e paesi limitrofi," 274–76.

129. For example, various Balaw families settled among the Marya. It appears that after the Italian occupation of Massawa (1885), many of these families returned to Hergigo. *Trevaskis Papers*, Box 1, File 2, "The Tribes and Peoples of Northern Eritrea. A Survey of the Keren Division," 25–26.

130. Munzinger, *Studi*, 140; Douin, *Histoire du règne*, vol. 3, part 1, 255 and 258 ("Commerce is in the hands of the people of Hergigo. They only pay their hosts small gifts *en route*. Their hosts, in turn, provide them with safe passage from one tribe to another."). Following the burning of Hergigo, approximately 80 Balaws settled among the Marya. Munzinger, *Studi*, 190.

131. For this idea as exemplified in the wider Indian Ocean world see Bose, *A Hundred Horizons*, 36–55.

132. This period is covered, albeit from a very Egyptian-centered perspective, by G. H. Talhami, *Suakin and Massawa under Egyptian Rule.*

133. See for example Farah, *The Sultan's Yemen,* 68.

2. On Camels and Boats

1. On Braudel's use of the term 'conjuncture,' see Fernand Braudel, *On History* (Chicago, 1980).

2. André Raymond, "A Divided Sea: The Cairo Coffee Trade in the Red Sea Area during the Seventeenth and Eighteenth Centuries," in Fawaz and Bayly, (eds.) *Modernity and Culture,* 53–56.

3. Ennio Alamanni, *La colonia Eritrea e i suoi commerci* (Torino, 1891), 682 and William Facey, "The Red Sea: the wind regime and location of ports," in Paul Lunde and Alexandra Porter, (eds.) *Trade and Travel in the Red Sea Region* (Oxford, 2004), 7–17. See also Pearson, *The Indian Ocean,* 19–23.

4. Georges Malécot, "Quelques aspects de la vie maritime en Mer Rouge dans la première moitié du XIXe siècle," *L'Afrique et l'Asie modernes,* 164, Printemps 1990, 35. See also Colette Dubois, "The Red Sea Ports during the Revolution in Transportation, 1800–1914" in Fawaz and Bayly, (eds.) *Modernity and Culture,* 58–74 and Colette Dubois, "Changements dans la continuité ou dans la rupture. Les implantations portuaires égyptiennes et européennes en mer Rouge, dans la deuxième moitié du XIXe siècle," In Abdeljelil Temimi (ed.), *Les Villes Arabes, la Démographie Historique et la Mer Rouge à l'Epoque Ottomane, Actes du Ve symposium International d'Etudes Ottomanes,* Ceromdi—Zaghouan (Tunisia) 1994, 43–65 [also published in the *Arab Historical Review for Ottoman Studies,* 9–10 (1994)].

5. See detailed accounts for both ports in R. J. Gavin, *Aden under British Rule 1839–1967* (London, 1975) and William Ochsenwald, *Religion, Society and the State in Arabia: The Hijaz Under Ottoman Control, 1840–1908* (Columbus, OH., 1984) and idem, "The Commercial History of the Hijaz Vilayet 1840–1908," *Arabian Studies* 6 (1982), 57–77. For Britain's role in the Red Sea region see Thomas E. Marston, *Britain's Imperial Role in the Red Sea Area (1800–1878)* (Hamden, CT., 1961).

6. On Sawākin's history see Bloss, "The Story of Suakin," (1936) 271–300, and (1937) 247–80; Hofheinz, "Sawākin"; Massimo Zaccaria, "Sawakin nel ricordo degli italiani residenti (1880–1905)," *Storia urbana* 74 (1996): 5–21, and Muḥammad Ṣāliḥ Dirār, *Taʾrīkh Sawākin wa-ʿl-baḥr al-aḥmar* (Khartūm, 1991); Spaulding, "Suakin," 39–53.

7. Ewald, "Crossers of the Sea," 79

8. Miège, "Djeddah, port d'entrepôt au XIXe siècle," 94–102 ; Tuchscherer, "Coffee in the Red Sea Area," 62–63.

9. Maltzan, *Reisen nach Südarabien,* 83 (in Tuchscherer, "Coffee in the Red Sea Area from the Sixteenth to the Nineteenth Century," 63).

10. See Bayly, "'Archaic and 'Modern' Globalization," 47–73.

11. Several examples of the launching of new steamship lines: In 1829: the East India Company; 1842: Peninsular and Oriental; 1856: the Australian Navigation Company; 1862: Messageries Impériales; 1869: Austrian Lloyd's. See Miège, "Djeddah," 93, and Malécot, "Quelques aspects," 35.

12. Miège, "Djeddah," 97–98.

13. Pearson, *The Indian Ocean,* 211.

14. See descriptions of these vessels with their special characteristics and functions in Malécot, "Quelques aspects," 30–31. See also Villiers, "Some Aspects of the Arab Dhow

Trade," 399–416; Rouaud, "Boats," 599–600; Prados, "Indian Ocean Littoral Maritime Evolution," 185–98; and Tibbetts, "Arab Navigation in the Red Sea."

15. On maritime dualism in the Indian Ocean see Pearson, *The Indian Ocean,* 208.

16. Salvadei, "La pesca e il commercio delle perle," 1158–59.

17. Atti Parlamentari, Camera dei Deputati, *Relazione sulla Colonia Eritrea del R. Commissario Civilie straordinario onorevole Ferdinando Martini (anni 1898–1899),* 31–32.

18. Tuchscherer, "Coffee in the Red Sea Area," 63.

19. Hill, *Egypt in the Sudan,* 123. Already in 1857, the Majidiyah Steamship Company had linked different Red Sea ports, especially transporting Muslim pilgrims. But the company went bankrupt after several years. Talhami, *Suakin and Massawa,* 4, 24.

20. On the Indians in Massawa see Pankhurst, "The 'Banyan' or Indian Presence at Massawa," *JES* 12, no. 1 (January 1974): 185–212, and "Indian Trade with Ethiopia," 453–81.

21. Ewald, "The Nile Valley System," 82.

22. Miège, "Djeddah," 100–101.

23. Zaccaria, "Early Italian Approaches to Economic Resources in the Red Sea region." For a detailed account see chapter 2 in Podestà, *Sviluppo industriale e colonialismo,* 65–182.

24. On the presence of Jews in Massawa, see, for example, Cavallarin, *Juifs en Erythrée.* 25. Puglisi, *Chi è? dell'Eritrea,* 49; Bonati, "Rolph Bienenfeld."

26. See details on quantities, values, and directions of imports and exportations in nineteenth-century Massawa in Pankhurst, "The Trade of Northern Ethiopia," 49–159.

27. Ministère des Affaires Etrangères (hereafter MAE), Paris. *Correspondance Consulaire et Commerciale, Massaouah,* t.1 (1840–59), Rapport commercial, Degoutin to Guizot, 20 April 1841.

28. Lefebvre, *Voyage en Abyssinie,* 1:35.

29. Abbadie, "Les causes actuelles de l'esclavage en Ethiopie," 20. Three years earlier, in 1838, "Moosa Maffairah" was reported by Commander Nott as Massawa's principal merchant and banker, who used to loan money to the governor of Massawa when the income of the authorities could not cover its expenses. Nott, "Report," 34.

30. MAE, *Correspondance Consulaire et Commerciale, Massaouah,* t.1, Rochet d'Héricourt to Minister of Foreign Affairs, 1 February 1848.

31. Report by Vice-Consul Walker on the Commerce, etc. of Abyssinia for the Year 1863, No 353, Great Britain, Parliamentary Papers, *Correspondence Respecting Abyssinia, 1846–1868,* 230.

32. Munzinger, *Studi,* 84–86; Douin, *Histoire du règne,* vol. 3, part 1, 254.

33. Douin, *Histoire du règne,* vol. 3, part 1, 260. See also Pankhurst, "The Trade of Northern Ethiopia," 130–31.

34. See Malécot, "Quelques aspects," 29.

35. Combes and Tamisier, *Voyage en Abyssinie,* 101; Lefebvre, *Voyage en Abyssinie,* 1:39.

36. Ferret and Galinier, *Voyage en Abyssinie,* 372.

37. Munzinger, "Les contrées limitrophes," 29.

38. See an essay on caravan trade and history in the wider region. Mordechai Abir, "Caravan Trade and History in the Northern Parts of East Africa," *Paideuma* 14 (1968): 103–20. For maritime and caravan trade in Eritrea in the first quarter of the 20th century see Michel Perret, "Commerce maritime et commerce caravanier de l'Erythrée au début du XXe s.," In *Minorités et gens de mer en océan indien, XIXe–XXe siècles,* IHPOM, Université de Provence, Etudes et Documents No 12, (Aix, 1979), 147–56.

39. Jean-Louis Miège, "Le commerce trans-saharien au XIXe siècle: essai de quantification," *Revue de l'Occident Musulman et de la Mediterranée* 32 (1981–82): 93–119.

40. See for example Abir's map of the main trade routes in nineteenth century Ethiopia, *Ethiopia: the Era of the Princes,* 45. The indication to the westerly route seems to be somewhat abstract. This is typical to past approaches that tried exclusively to contain historic processes in the present borders of the Ethiopian state without fully appreciating broader regional dimensions.

41. See for example the last two chapters of Mohammed Hassen's *The Oromo of Ethiopia: A History 1570–1860* (Cambridge, 1990) and also Triulzi, *Salt, Gold and Legitimacy.*

42. See Haar, 'Long-Distance Trade, Political Economy and National Reunification,' chapters 1 and 2. On the impact of monetization and taxation on the political and economic dominance of central Ethiopian polities in relation to long-distance trade see also Richard Pankhurst, "The advent of the Maria Theresa dollar in Ethiopia, its effects on taxation and wealth accumulation, and other economic, political and cultural implications," *Northeast African Studies* 1, no. 3 (1979–80): 27–28.

43. Abir, *Ethiopia: The Era of the Princes,* 50.

44. On the Jeberti see Trimingham, *Islam in Ethiopia,* 150–53.

45. See a useful map of the southwestern region with trade routes and regional markets in Hassen, *The Oromo of Ethiopia,* 137.

46. Combes and Tamisier, *Voyage en Abyssinie,* IV, 117.

47. Munzinger, "Les contrées limitrophes," 43; Lejean, *Theodore II,* 281.

48. On the role of the *neggadras* in Ethiopia see Peter Garretson, "The Naggadras, Trade, and Selected Towns in Nineteenth and Early Twentieth Century Ethiopia," *IJAHS* 12, no. 3 (1979): 416–39.

49. Consul Plowden to the Earl of Clarendon, Massowah, July 9, 1854, enclosure in No.184, Report, Great Britain Parliamentary Papers, *Correspondence Respecting Abyssinia, 1846–1868,* 112; Combes and Tamisier, *Voyage en Abyssinie,* IV, 116–17, Lefebvre, *Voyage en Abyssinie,* 2:26.

50. Abdussamad H. Ahmad, "Darita, Bagemdir: An Historic Town and its Muslim Population, 1830–1889," *IJAHS* 22, no. 3 (1989): 439–51; Alamanni, *La Colonia Eritrea e i suoi commerci,* 779–91.

51. Combes and Tamisier, *Voyage en Abyssinie,* IV, 92.

52. Consul Plowden to the Earl of Clarendon, Massowah, July 9, 1854, enclosure in No.184, Report, Great Britain Parliamentary Papers, *Correspondence Respecting Abyssinia, 1846–1868,* 113.

53. Alamanni, *La Colonia Eritrea e i suoi commerci,* 770–75.

54. Combes and Tamisier, *Voyage en Abyssinie,* IV 94.

55. Abbadie, *Géographie de l'Ethiopie,* 51.

56. Combes and Tamisier, *Voyage en Abyssinie,* IV, 94. E. A. De Cosson, *The Cradle of the Blue Nile, A Visit to the Court of King John of Ethiopia* (London, 1877), I, 31–2.

57. Report by Vice-Consul Walker on the Commerce, etc. of Abyssinia for the Year 1863, No 353, Great Britain, Parliamentary Papers, *Correspondence Respecting Abyssinia, 1846–1868,* 229.

58. Munzinger, "Les contrées limitrophes," 37; Rassam, *Narrative of the British Mission to Theodore,* 12.

59. Pankhurst, "The Trade of Northern Ethiopia," 86–87.

60. Munzinger, "Les contrées limitrophes," 40.

61. Habib, "History of Massawa," footnotes section, ix (chapter 2, footnote 20). In Tigre: *wasrgohan dahab-tu minken matsi' min Sinnar.* I am indebted to Mr. Saleh Mahmud Idris for correcting the transliteration (in simplified form) of the Tigre.

62. Estimates are made by Rüppell, Blondeel, Christopher, Plowden, and Heuglin. See

Pankhurst, "The Trade of Northern Ethiopia," 104. Writing from Massawa in 1860, von Beurmann observed that the slave trade was disappearing and that the annual exportation stood at seldom more than 1000 individuals. Beurmann, *Voyages et explorations,* 39. Janet Ewald also pointed to a decline in slave exports from Sawākin in the 1840s and 1850s. Ewald, "The Nile Valley System," 73.

63. Austen, "The Nineteenth Century Islamic Slave Trade." See also contributions by Abdussamad H. Ahmad, Timothy Fernyhough, and Janet Ewald. See Abir, *Ethiopia,* 53–70, and Toledano, *The Ottoman Slave Trade and Its Suppression.*

64. Lefebvre, *Voyage en Abyssinie,* 2:29; Consul Plowden to Earl of Malmesbury, Massowah, March 24, 1853, enclosure 1 in No. 132, "'Produce of Abyssinia Exported from Massowah," Great Britain, Parliamentary Papers, *Correspondence Respecting Abyssinia, 1846–1868,* 73; Pankhurst, "The Trade of Northern Ethiopia," 105–108 and for all exported commodities: 102–31; Haar, "Long Distance Trade," 20–31.

65. Lefebvre, *Voyage en Abyssinie,* 1:39.

66. On the Takrūrīs (or Takārīr) in northeast Africa see Ellero, "I Tacruri in Eritrea," 189–99; Birks, *Across the Savannas to Mecca;* Yamba, *Permanent Pilgrims;* Shun'ya Hino, "Pilgrimage and Migration of the West African Muslims: A Case Study of the Fellata People in the Sudan," in *Sudan Sahel Studies II,* ed. Morimichi Tomikawa (Tokyo: Institute for the Study of the Languages and Cultures of Asia and Africa [ILCAA], 1986), 15–109; A. Robinson, "The Tekruri Sheikhs of Gallabat"; Naqar, "The Takarir of Gallabat."

67. Miège, "Le commerce trans-saharien," 93–119.

68. On the history of Kassala see Cumming, "The History of Kassala and the Province of Taka."

69. The center of the northern appendages and a vital point on the Massawa–Kassala axis in the region called Bogos by Tigrinya speakers and Senhit by Tigre speakers. It is a mountainous region that stands about 700 meters above the Barka and 800 meters below the Hamasen. Its average altitude is of approximately 1,200 meters. It is split into two by the ᶜAnseba valley. In the eastern side live the Habab and the Mensaᶜ, while on the western side live the Marya and the Bilin.

70. Douin, *Histoire du règne,* vol. 3, part 1, 258.

71. Munzinger, *Studi,* 162.

72. The Habab cameleers dominated caravan activities in Semhar and Sahel, to the west and north of Massawa. The Saho cameleers covered the southwestern regions of Semhar, principally from Hergigo to the slopes of Akkele Guzay. See also Buchs, "Voyages en Abyssinie," 40.

73. Gatta, "Da Massaua a Cheren," 477–78. Gatta provides information on the various camel types of the region and their advantages and limitations. The camels of the Habab, according to him, were much better suited for the mountainous journey than the Semhar camels, and far better from the Afar camels. The quality of camels improved "as one advanced towards the Gash region and Sennar." His observations are mostly based on Munzinger's comments, *Studi,* 121–22.

74. A second route, more difficult and therefore less utilized route by large caravans, passed through ᶜAylet and ᶜAsus. A detailed description of the route is provided in Gatta, "Da Massaua a Cheren," 489–98.

75. Sapeto, *Viaggio e missione,* 207–208.

76. Douin, *Histoire du règne,* vol. 3, part 1, 258.

77. Alamanni, *La Colonia Eritrea.* Description of itineraries: 625–26, 647–68, 671ff. For the 1850s, see Munzinger, "Les contrées limitrophes," 53–55.

78. For the Egyptian occupation of the Bilin in the Keren area, see Ghaber, *The Blin of*

Bogos, chapters 2, 3, and 4 (pp. 12–44). See also Talhami, *Suakin and Massawa,* chapters 3 and 4 (35–66 and 143 for Bogos/Keren occupation), and Rubenson, *Survival of Ethiopian Independence,* chapter 5.

79. Gatta, "Da Massaua a Chartum per Keren e Cassala," 405. See also Dubois, "Miel et sucre en Afrique orientale," 453–72; Munzinger, "Les contrées limitrophes," 52–53, 55; Abbadie, *Géographie de l'Ethiopie,* 33.

80. Douin, *Histoire du règne,* vol. 3, part 1, 253.

81. To take but a few examples from two registers see: Massawa Islamic Court Record (hereafter MICR) 8/44b, 8/44c, 8/54a, 8/69b, 8/76a, 8/86a, 14/10d, 14/11a, 14/11b, 14/12c, 14/19b, 14/20a, 14/20e, 14/21a, 14/21c, 14/23a, 14/23b, 14/23f.

82. Douin, *Histoire du règne,* vol. 3, part 1, 258; Wylde *'83 to '87 in the Soudan,* 84; Adhana Mengisteab, "The Strategic Position of Karan in the Metsewa-Kassala Trade Route," unpublished paper submitted to the African History Conference, Nazareth, Ethiopia, 15–20 December 1982, 20.

83. Munzinger, "Les contrées limitrophes," 55.

84. Munzinger, *Studi,* 110.

85. Observers mention that coastal merchants traveled far inland, to the Gash region and Kassala. See Lejean, *Voyage aux deux Nils,* 142.

86. Munzinger, *Studi,* 140, and Douin, *Histoire du règne,* vol. 3, part 1, 255, 258.

87. Munzinger, *Studi,* 172–74.

88. Ibid, 190.

89. Habib, "History of Massawa," 16.

90. ASDMAE, *AE,* Pacco 21, ("Inchiesti su ricorsi contro il tribunale di Massaua, 1888"), "Relazione sui ricorsi presentati da Said Omar El Nahari e da Ali Afandi Iahia," 12. The Ṣāfīs in Massawa also had family relatives in Sawākin. Interview with Sayyid Ṣādiq Muḥsin al-Ṣāfī, Massawa, 3 October 2007.

91. Abbadie, *Géographie de l'Ethiopie,* 46; Sapeto, *Viaggio e missione,* 159.

92. Abbadie, *Géographie de l'Ethiopie,* 36.

93. Douin, *Histoire du règne,* vol. 3, part 1, 258; Lejean, *Voyage aux Deux Nils,* 158–61; Hotten, *Abyssinia and Its People,* 216.

94. MAE, Massawa 3, Munzinger to MAE, 22 December 1865 (quoted in Zewde Gabre-Sellassie, *Yohannes IV of Ethiopia,* 37.

95. Munzinger, "Les contrées limitrophes," 51–52.

96. Douin, *Histoire du règne,* vol. 3, part 1, 255.

97. Ismāʿīl's plans included, at some point, the construction of a railway line connecting Massawa to Kassala and beyond. Later, in 1894, an Italian initiative to construct such a railway line was abandoned in favor of a more modest project linking Massawa and the highlands of Hamasen. Talhami, *Suakin and Massawa,* chapter 6; Podestà, *Il mito dell'impero,* 20.

98. Talhami, *Suakin and Massawa,* 69–77.

99. For a comparable process of monetization in 18th-century Sinnār see Spaulding, *The Heroic Age,* 142–49; For 19th-century East Africa, see Koponen, *People and Production in Late Precolonial Tanzania,* 109, 117.

100. Toledano, *The Ottoman Slave Trade,* 203–12 and 219–23.

101. On export estimates see Pankhurst, "The Trade of Northern Ethiopia," 119–31.

102. Alamanni, *La Colonia Eritrea,* 710.

103. On the evolution of tribute payment in the Semhar throughout the nineteenth century see *The Nakfa Documents,* Document 81, Capitano Boari to the Governatore Civile e Militare della Colonia Eritrea, Asmara, 11 marzo 1891, 'Tributi nel Semhar e paesi limi-

trofi'. Reproduced in d'Avray, *The Nakfa Documents,* 272–85. On Egyptian "modernization" of taxation see Talhami, *Suakin and Massawa,* 80, 91.

104. Combes and Tamisier, *Voyage en Abyssinie,* 1:104 and 4:203; Ferret and Galinier, *Voyage en Abyssinie,* 2:390; Abbadie, *Géographie de l'Ethiopie,* 46.

105. Munzinger, "Les contrées limitrophes," 51.

106. In 1840 Zula was reported to have 214 huts. Abbadie, *L'Abyssinie et le roi Théodore,* 8 and 14; Munzinger, "Les contrées limitrophes," 51.

107. Roberti, "Gli Habab," 12.

108. Ibid., and Munzinger, "Narrative of a Journey through the Afar Country," 217. See also Odorizzi, "La Dancalia italiana del nord," 171, and *Il commissariato,* 222–28.

109. Consul Plowden to the Earl of Clarendon, Massowah, July 9, 1854, enclosure in No. 184, Report, Great Britain, Parliamentary Papers. *Correspondence Respecting Abyssinia, 1846–1868,* 123.

110. Munzinger, "Narrative of a Journey," 191, 219.

111. ᶜAbdin Archives (Cairo) (hereafter AA), box 38, document 143, Report from Ismāᶜīl Ṣādiq Bāshā, 12 June 1866. In Douin, *Histoire du règne,* vol. 3, part 1, 283.

112. Munzinger, *Studi,* 108; Lejean, *Voyage aux Deux Nils,* 163 and map in the annexed "Atlas."

113. AA (Cairo), Khedival order to the Governor of Massawa, *Daftar* (Notebook) Maᶜiya Turkish 558, Translation of document 3, page 3, section 2, 23 Shawwāl 1283 (28 February 1867). Reproduced in al-Jamal, *al-Wathāʾiq al-taʾrīkhiyya,* 87–89; Talhami, *Suakin and Massawa,* 229.

114. AA (Cairo), Order to the *Muḥāfiẓa* of Massawa, *Daftar* no. 1936, v 2, p 21, order no. 142, 24 Rabīᶜ II 1288 (12 July 1871). In al-Jamal, *al-Wathāʾiq al-taʾrīkhiyya,* 119. See also Talhami, *Suakin and Massawa,* 76

115. Talhami, *Suakin and Massawa,* 101; Hill, *A Biographical Dictionary of the Sudan,* 37–38.

116. Salvadei, "Massaua," 1823; Wylde, *'83 to '87 in the Soudan,* 1:101–102.

117. ACS, *Carte Martini,* s.12, f. 59, "Massaua-possesso e godimento dei terreni," Copia di rapporto no.1760, diretto dal Commissariato regionale di Massaua (G. Salvadei) al Governo della Colonia, 5 gennaio 1905.

118. Munzinger, "Les contrées limitrophes," 35.

119. ACS, *Carte Martini,* s.12, f. 59, "Sahel-Regime delle terre per le tribù del Sahel," Copia di rapporto no. 38, diretto dal Residente del Sahel (Marazzani Visconti Terzi) al Governo della Colonia, 23 gennaio 1905.

120. ACS, *Carte Martini,* s.12, f. 59, "Cheren-Regime delle terre," Copia di rapporto no. 858, diretto dal Commissario Regionale di Cheren (V. Fioccardi) al Governo della Colonia, 5 maggio 1905.

121. Podestà, *Il mito dell'impero,* 42; Puglisi, *Chi è? dell'Eritrea,* 163, 210.

122. ASDMAE, *AE,* Pacco 154, "Letter from Aly Dossal to the Governor of the Colony" (16 January 1892); "Circa la concessione al Sig. Aly Dossal" (29 gennaio 1892); "Concession Contract between Aly Dossal and Giacomo Console, Director of the Massawa Customs" (10 February 1892).

123. Zaccaria, "Early Italian approaches"; Podestà, *Il mito dell'impero,* 32–35, 186–90.

124. Glassman, *Feasts and Riot,* 52–54. For Glassman the urbanization of the countryside not only was an economic process but included a political and ideological dimension. See also the volume edited by Jane I. Guyer, *Feeding African Cities.*

125. See information about these villages in Salvadei, "Massaua," 1833–40. According to Salvadei both ᶜAsus and Zaga were founded in association with the arrival from Mecca

of a certain Shaykh Muʿallim, founder of the ʿAd Muʿallim group. This seems like traditions produced following settlement for more material purposes, such as the servicing of the caravan route.

126. Munzinger, *Studi*, 110–11.

127. Gatta, "Massaua e le regioni circostanti," 479. Zaga provided merchants with water, wood, and the means of transportation. Douin, *Histoire du règne*, vol. 3, part 1, 255.

128. Salvadei, "Massaua," 1835, and Abū Bakr, *Taʾrīkh Iritrīyā*, 332.

129. Folchi, "Commissariato Regionale di Massaua," 99 (182).

130. Abbadie, *Géographie de l'Ethiopie*, 41.

131. Sapeto, *Viaggio e missione*, 166.

132. Gabrawold, "Origin and Early Development," 17. The first mission of the Evangeliska Fosterlands Stiftelsen (EFS) arrived to Massawa on 15 March 1866.

133. De Cosson, *The Cradle of the Blue Nile*, I, 31–32.

134. Parkyns, *Life in Abyssinia*, 34–38.

135. Ibid., 33.

136. On the presence of the *nāʾib* at ʿAylet see de Rivoyre, *Mer Rouge et Abyssinie*, 277; Pennazzi, "Massauah," 329.

137. Interviews with ʿUsmān Ḥājjī Maḥmūd, Massawa, 25 April 2000, and his brother Ismāʿīl Ḥājjī Maḥmūd, Asmara, 2 May 2000.

138. Gatta, "Da Massaua a Cheren," 494.

139. Salvadei, "La pesca e il commercio delle perle," 1157 (my translation is a paraphrased version). On pearls, in general, see the handsome book by G. F. Kunz and C. H. Stevenson, *The Book of the Pearl: The History, Art, Science and Industry of the Queen of Gems;* on the Red Sea area, 139–44. See also Millward, "Oysters, Pearls and Pearling in Sudan Waters," 203–12. On pearling in the Gulf see Carter, "The History and Prehistory of Pearling in the Persian Gulf," 139–209, and Hopper, "The African Presence in Arabia, chapter 4.

140. Salvadei, "Massaua," 1841.

141. On Indian financing of pearling activities see Clarence-Smith, "Indian Business Communities in the Western Indian Ocean in the Nineteenth Century," 20.

142. Interview with Ḥasan Muḥammad ʿUthmān Ḥayūtī, Asmara, 11 July 2006. Other, slightly different, traditions also grounded in the Arabic root *ḥ l k* and its meaning have been recently collected in the Archipelago. Saleh Mahmud Idris, Naples, 9 February 2008.

143. Donzel and Kon, "Dahlak Islands," 65–69; Longrigg, "Dahlak." Of the several studies on the history of the Dahlak islands see especially: Schneider, *Stèles funéraires musulmanes des îles Dahlak;* Tedeschi, "Note storiche sulle isole Dahlac"; Basset, "Les inscriptions de l'île de Dahlak"; and works by Giovanni Oman. See a detailed overview of the islands of the archipelago in Odorizzi, *Il commissariato*, 252–63

144. R. H. Major, *India in the Fifteenth Century* (London, 1857). Cited in Pankhurst, "The 'Banyan' or Indian Presence at Massawa," 197.

145. Bombaci, "Il viaggio in Abissinia,," 266, 268.

146. See Jedrej, "The Red Sea and the Eastern Sudan in the Early 19th Century," 109.

147. Odorizzi, *Il commissariato*, 253.

148. Issel, *Viaggio nel Mar Rosso e tra i Bogos*, 76–81.

149. Munzinger, *Studi*, 79–82.

150. See a detailed biographical note on Arturo Issel in Puglisi, *Chi è? dell'Eritrea*, 172.

151. Issel, *Viaggio*, 70.

152. Reclus, *The Earth and Its Inhabitants*, 180, and Munzinger, *Studi*, 80. Given in its Italian version: "Le lacrime del cielo."

153. Buchs, "Voyages en Abyssinie," 37.

154. Monfreid, *Les secrets,* 50.

155. Vigoni, "Massaua e il nord dell'Abissinia," 1; "La pesca delle perle e della madreperla nel Mar Rosso," 179. For the sake of comparison and scale, Dubai's pearl boat fleet in 1844 numbered 90, while in 1907 it rose to 335. The number of boats in Qatar's in 1907 was 817. Carter, "The History and Prehistory of Pearling," 160. The number of boats in the Gulf in general stands at 3,000–4,000 in the early twentieth century.

156. ASDMAE, *AE,* Pacco 16, "Promemoria rimesso al Sig. Ammiraglio Noce (da Ferdinando Filosa)," 26 Giugno 1885. In 1898 the number of sailing boats owned by Dahlakis in the archipelago was put at 84. Folchi, "Commissariato Regionale di Massaua," 305 (262).

157. Salvadei, "La pesca e il commercio delle perle," 1158, 1171–72. Parazzoli, "La pesca nel Mar Rosso," 187, and Alamanni, *La Colonia Eritrea,* 266.

158. Alamanni, *La Colonia Eritrea,* 267.

159. For interesting remarks on credit and debt ties between divers and financiers see Monfreid, *Les secrets,* 47–48, 62.

160. Salvadei, "La pesca e il commercio delle perle," 1171.

161. Alamanni, *La Colonia Eritrea,* 267.

162. Mantegazza, *Da Massaua a Saati,* 29.

163. Monfreid, *Les secrets,* 79–81.

164. Clarence-Smith. "The Economics of the Indian Ocean and Red Sea Slave Trades," 8.

165. Salvadei, "La pesca e il commercio delle perle," 1158–59, 1172.

166. *Elenco dei commercianti, industriali, negozianti, imprenditori, appaltatori o fornitori, e degli esercenti professioni, arti e mestieri inscritti nel ruolo dei contribuenti della Colonia Eritrea (Esercizio 1912–13),* Colonia Eritrea N. 58, Asmara 1913, 40–47; Baratieri, "Il commercio della madreperla," 373.

167. Buchs, "Voyages en Abyssinie," 37.

168. Parazzoli, "La pesca nel Mar Rosso," 186.

169. Salvadei, "La pesca e il commercio delle perle," 1181.

170. Salvadei, "Massaua," 1841.

171. Podestà, *Sviluppo industriale e colonialismo,* 198.

172. Baratieri, "Il commercio della madreperla," 372–73; Stefanelli, "Madreperla," 158–59; Salvadei, "La pesca e il commercio delle perle," 1157 and 1173.

173. Baratieri, "Il commercio della madreperla"; a reproduction of Baratieri's letter to the *Società veneta per la pesca e l'acquicoltura.* See also Podestà, *Sviluppo industriale e colonialismo,* 211–16.

174. Parazzoli, "La pesca nel Mar Rosso," 177–81, 187–90, and see comments by Vigoni, "Massaua e il nord dell'Abissinia," 1.

175. Martini, *Relazione sulla Colonia Eritrea (anni 1898–1899).* See the twenty-article agreement: Doc. VII, Allegato I, 69–72. See also Odorizzi, *Il commissariato,* 253. See later modifications to the initial agreement in Salvadei, "La pesca e il commercio delle perle," 1182–92.

176. Zaccaria, "Early Italian approaches"; Podestà, *Il mito dell'impero,* 57.

177. Salvadei, "La pesca e il commercio delle perle," 1175.

178. Martini, *Relazione sulla Colonia Eritrea (anni 1898–1899),* 42.

179. Pearson, *The Indian Ocean,* 271.

180. Dei Gaslini, *L'Italia nel Mar Rosso,* 158; Podestà, *Il mito dell'impero,* 185–86.

181. Pearson, *The Indian Ocean,* 272.

182. For suggestive descriptions of the intertwined nature of legal and illegal commerce in the Red Sea area in the early twentieth century see Monfreid, *Les secrets.*

183. Douin, *Histoire du règne,* vol. 3, part 1, 255. On illegal activities around Harat Island, opposite the coastal plain between the Lebka and Weqiro rivers, see Wylde, *'83 to '87 in the Sudan.* For a stimulating study that includes an examination of smuggling and piracy against the backdrop of colonial contestations between Italian and Ottomans in the southern Red Sea area in the late nineteenth and early twentieth centuries, see Lenci, *Eritrea e Yemen.*

184. De Rivoyre, *Aux pays du Soudan,* 22.

185. See Ewald, "The Nile Valley System," 80–81.

3. Connecting Sea and Land

1. De Cosson, *The Cradle of the Blue Nile,* 17.

2. Horton and Middleton, *The Swahili,* 136–37.

3. Stoianovich, *French Historical Method,* 86. For reflections on the concept of "littoral society," see Pearson, "Littoral Society," 1–8.

4. Sources for these estimates are: Henry Salt, *A Voyage to Abyssinia* (London, 1814), lxx; Munzinger, "Les contrées limitrophes," 31; Mantegazza, *Da Massaua a Saati,* 20; Martini, *Nell'Affrica italiana,* 12. For more 19th-century estimates of Massawa's population see Pankhurst, "Notes on the Demographic History of Ethiopian Towns and Villages," 66–67. Folchi, "Commissariato Regionale di Massaua," 109 (186).

5. Mordechai Abir, "Brokerage and Brokers," 1–5. On the Somali institutions of *abbaan* (host, patron, protector) and *dillaal* (commercial broker) see Cassanelli, *The Shaping of Somali Society,* 156–59, and Reese, "'Patricians of the Benaadir," 90–94. On the *adhari* in the Sudanese context (pre-nineteenth century) see Spaulding, *The Heroic Age,* 108–10.

6. It should be noted that variations in specific temporal and geographical settings did exist. Many references, including Ibn Battutah, the 14th-century North African traveler, describe such practices. For the Swahili coast see Middleton, *The World of the Swahili,* 21–22, 75; For Mukhā see Um, "Spatial Negotiations in a Commercial City," 178–93.

7. *Nazīl* (pl. *nuzalā*) means in Arabic guest, stranger, lodger, boarder, tenant. *Nāzil* means resident.

8. Lejean, *Théodore II,* 283.

9. Abir, "Brokerage and Brokers in Ethiopia," 1; Nott, "Report," 32; Lefebvre, *Voyage sur la côte orientale de la mer Rouge,* 39; Munzinger, "Les contrées limitrophes," 30.

10. Abir, "Brokerage and Brokers in Ethiopia," 2.

11. Abbadie, *Douze ans de séjour dans la Haute-Éthiopie* (1980), 1:7.

12. Abir, "Brokerage and Brokers in Ethiopia," 1.

13. Munzinger, "Les contrées limitrophes," 38–39 and 44. See also Munzinger, *Studi,* 96–97.

14. Abir, "Brokerage and Brokers in Ethiopia," 2.

15. MAE, *Correspondance Consulaire et Commerciale, Massaouah,* t.1, Rochet d'Héricourt to Minister of Foreign Affairs, 1 February 1848.

16. Munzinger, "Les contrées limitrophes," 39. The same principle of exchange was also reported in the mid-1880s. Simon, *L'Ethiopie,* 15.

17. Lejean, *Théodore II,* 282–83.

18. For the various stages and measures regarding administrative and judicial change in the Egyptian period see Talhami, *Suakin and Massawa,* chapter 5 (67–96). The *majlis maḥalī* was a local court of first instance with a president and eight members. In the Egyptian Sudan it had competences in commercial and financial matters where the sum did not exceed 15 pounds. Hill, *Egypt in the Sudan,* 42–43.

19. See Odorizzi, *Il commissariato,* 112–15 and 159–60; Abū Bakr, *Taʾrīkh Iritrīyā,* 304–11.

20. Another example that is not included in the mentioned list is Bayt Hāshim Ramaḍān, who claim that they came to Massawa/Hergigo from Jordan. Letter from Fouad Makki, 30 July 2004.

21. Odorizzi, *Il commissariato,* 135, 159–60, and Abū Bakr, *Taʾrīkh Iritrīyā,* 308.

22. Vikør, *Between God and the Sultan,* 209.

23. Interviews with Muḥammad Aḥmad ʿUmar Aḥmad ʿAbbāsī and Ḥāmid ʿAbd al-Bāqī ʿAbbāsī, Massawa, 18 and 20 March 2000 and with ʿAbd al-Bāqī Muḥammad ʿAbdu ʿAbbāsī, Massawa, 24 June 2006. Members of the family claimed that the first ʿAbbāsī came to Massawa in 1090/1679. All these dates should be taken very cautiously. See also Ibrāhīm al-Mukhtār, *al-Jāmiʿ,* 77.

24. On Hadrami and Yemeni migrations to the Horn of Africa see Rouaud, "L'émigration yéménite," 227–37. On Hadrami migration in general see also Serjeant, "The Hadrami Network," 145–53. See also Pearson, "The Indian Ocean and the Red Sea," 37–59; On migrations in that period in the broader western Indian Ocean region, see Martin, "Arab Migrations to East Africa in Medieval Times," 367–90, and Pouwels, "East Africa and the Indian Ocean to 1800," 385–425.

25. Pedigree (*shajarat nisb al-ashrāf*) of the Ḥayūtī family and interview with Ḥasan Muḥammad ʿUthmān Ḥayūtī and Aḥmad Muḥammad ʿUthmān Ḥayūtī, Asmara, 31 July 2001. The *shajara* goes back to al-*Muqaddam* Muḥammad (d. 1255), who is believed to have introduced Sufism to Hadramawt and who headed the *ṭarīqa* ʿAlawiyya. More scattered information on the Ḥibshīs is found in Hadrami genealogies in al-Mashhūr and in Bā Maṭraf (see bibliography). On the wave of Hadrami migration to the eastern parts of the Horn of Africa between ca. 1490 and the 1540s, see Martin, "Migrations from the Hadramawt to East Africa and Indonesia, c. 1200 to 1900," 3–5.

26. According to oral data the Adam Barkūy family is descended from the Prophet's companions, known as the *Ṣahāba.* One informant related that the Makkaʿalī family descends from the Adam Barkūy family. It was a leading family in Massawa in the second half of the 19th century, well connected in both foreland and inland sociocommercial networks. In one instance in the early 1880s, Muḥammad Bey b. Muṣṭafā al-Shināwī, the head of *majlis Sawākin* and the chief of Sawākin's merchants (Ar. *sarrtujjār*), gave power of attorney to ʿAbd al-Qādir b. Adam b. Muḥammad b. Ādam Barkūy, to represent his interests in Massawa. MICR 4/16b (1 Rabīʿ I 1299).

27. *Meṣewwaʿ* is derived from an Arabized form of Tigre *ṣawweʿa* (to call). Massawa is the place where people call each other.

28. Donzel, "Maṣawwaʿ," 641; Salvadei, "La pesca e il commercio delle perle," 1172; Salvadei, "Massaua," 1816.

29. Pennazzi, "Massauah," 325. Also Habib, "History of Massawa," ii and http://www.mukhtar.ca ("al-sayyid Muḥammad Masāwa," under "Tarājim"). It must be noted that the *qāḍī*'s name is spelt differently, with an Arabic 'sīn' and not with a 'ṣād'; the second alīf is a long vowel. The Masāwa family is well known in Massawa. One of the town's old mosques (not in function at present) is called *masjid* Masāwa. It is located behind the Ḥanafī mosque. In the 1860s some people came to the Islamic court and presented legal deeds signed by the *qāḍī.* For example MICR 16/2b (23 Shaʿbān 1283) and 16/17b (11 Jumāda II 1285).

30. Salvadei, "Massaua," 1817. See also Odorizzi, *Il commissariato,* 112.

31. In September 1769 James Bruce sought the services of a certain "Mahomet Adulai" who was, according to the Scottish traveler, "a person kept by Ras Michael as a spy upon the Naybe, and in the same character by Metical Aga." Bruce, *Travels to Discover the Source of the Nile,* 23–24.

32. Interview with Ibrāhīm Ḥusayn Mentāy, Massawa, 7 May 2000. Odorizzi's family list associates the Mentāys with "Hadendoa" origins.

33. From data drawn from the records it seems almost positive to conclude that "Moosa Maffarah" was of the Mentāy family. MICR 9/25a (23 Jumāda I 1296/1879). Ḥalīl b. Mūsā b. Muffaraḥ Mentāy is mentioned as the seller of a water cistern to Shaykh Muḥammad b. al-Ḥājj ᶜAbdu b. Aḥmad Ḥammūda.

34. Nott, "Report," 34. Around 1840 Antoine d'Abbadie too mentioned the Mentāys as dominant in trade. The same "Moosa Maffarah" was said to be one of the four principal boat owners in Massawa, and Aḥmad ᶜAnja ᶜUmar Mentāy was considered as one of the town's wealthiest merchants. Abbadie, *Les causes actuelles de l'esclavage en Ethiopie,* 19–20.

35. Odorizzi, *Il commissariato,* 145; Talhami, *Suakin and Massawa,* 92.

36. MICR vol. 16 (1866–77), 16/1a, 16/5b, 16/6a, 16/7a, 16/7b, 16/8b, 16/12c, 16/13a, 16/18a, 16/33c, 16/43a, 16/45a, 16/61c, 16/67a, 16/71a, 16/73a, 16/73b, 16/76a, 16/77b, 16/78a, 16/78b, 16/78c, 16/83a, 16/84b, 16/98a, 16/100b, 16/112b, 16/113a, 16/116c. The Bā Junayd family was originally from Dawᶜan. See also Serjeant, "The Hadhrami Network," 151.

37. Combes and Tamisier, *Voyage en Abyssinie,* 1:102.

38. Lefebvre, *Voyage sur la côte orientale de la mer Rouge,* 38–39.

39. Munzinger, "Les contrées limitrophes," 28.

40. There was a community of Somalis on Baka Island, south of Massawa. In the town itself, Aḥmad Muḥammad Abū Bakr al-Sūmālī, who died in 1867, was the head of a family of some importance and wealth. See cases involving family members in regard to the division of his inheritance among his heirs, legal guardianship, slave manumission, and real estate transactions in the late 1860s and 1870s. MICR 11/6a (1867), 11/7a (1867), 11/7b (1867), 11/8a (1867), 11/22a (1870), 14/11c (1872), 14/11d (1872), 16/10a (1867), 16/10b (1867), 16/40b (1868), 16/108b (1875).

41. For example MICR 16 (1866–77): Dankalī (case 16/5a), Diḥlī (16/7a), Sūmālī (16/10b), Yamānī (16/11b, 16/65b) [According to Odorizzi's list this family is from Zabīd in Yemen], Qashmīr (16/13b), ᶜIrāqī (16/13c), Jiddāwī (16/36c), Ṭurkī (16/38c, 16/59b, 16/74a), al-Maghribī (16/57a,b), Kurdī (16/79c), al-Izmīrī (16/115a).

42. Bayly, "'Archaic and 'Modern' Globalization in the Eurasian and African Arena," 61.

43. On North African commercial entrepreneurs in late eighteenth-century Cairo, see Raymond, "Tunisiens et Maghrébins au Caire au XVIIIe siècle," and "Deux familles de commerçants Fasi au Caire à la fin du XVIIe siècle."

44. Combes and Tamisier, *Voyage en Abyssinie,* 105.

45. Munzinger, "Les contrées limitrophes," 28. An important slave trader in Sawākin in the 1870s was named "Mughraby." Ewald, "The Nile Valley System," 81.

46. Abū Bakr, *Taʾrīkh Iritrīyā,* 307, and Odorizzi, *Il commissariato,* 161.

47. The term "entrepreneur" is referred to in the Schumpeterian sense. Entrepreneur is understood as "innovative entrepreneur" in terms of introducing new commodities, new methods of production, new markets, and a new type of commercial organization. Schumpeter, *The Theory of Economic Development,* 65–66.

48. For the role of prominent *tujjār* (merchants) in the Middle East, see Gilbar, "The Muslim Big Merchant-Entrepreneurs of the Middle East," 1–36.

49. Odorizzi, *Il commissariato,* 125.

50. Martini, *Il diario eritreo,* 1:51 (Massaua, 7 February 1898). Another source refers to the ᶜAbd al-Nabī al-Qābūlī family as coming from India, while Odorizzi refers to a "Capili" [*sic*] family from Bukhara.

51. Martini, *Il diario eritreo,* 2:105 (Massaua, 28 March 1900); Lenci, *Eritrea e Yemen,* 54–55.

52. ASDMAE, *AE*, b. 178, 'Notabili e Capi Indigeni Dipendenti dal Commissariato Regionale di Massaua' (1903), 3, 5; interview with Muḥammad Yāsīn Bā Ṭūq, Massawa, 17 March 2000. Puglisi, *Chi è? dell'Eritrea*, 210.

53. A certain ᶜAbd Allāh Afandī is mentioned as an important trader in Massawa in ca. 1864–65. Lejean, *Théodore II*, 284. It is very probable that he is the very well known ᶜAbd Allāh Afandī al-Ghūl.

54. Terry Walz, personal communication.

55. *Bey* (Tur.), *Bik* (Ar.), is a civil and military title immediately below *Pasha*. Hill, *A Biographical Dictionary*, x.

56. Martini, *Il diario eritreo*, 2:468–69 (Senafe, 26 May 1901).

57. Interview with ᶜAlī Yūsuf al-Ghūl, Massawa, 26 February 2000; Puglisi, *Chi è? dell'Eritrea*, 2.

58. Mantegazza, *Da Massaua a Saati*, 92–93. Mantegazza estimated ᶜAbd Allāh al-Ghūl's age at seventy in 1887. He also reported that ᶜAbd Allāh had lived several years in Cairo. In the second half of the 18th century Giovanni Raimondo Torlonia, son of a French cloth merchant, founded his bank, which during the French occupation of Rome at the beginning of the nineteenth century grew in importance and made the Torlonia one of the wealthiest families of Rome.

59. Bloss, "The Story of Suakin," (1937) 253.

60. Real estate transactions of ᶜAbd Allāh and Aḥmad Bey al-Ghūl. *Land:* MICR 16/83b (1290), 16/85a (1290), 16/101b (1291), 9/27b (1296), 9/41a (1297), 9/42a (1297), 9/43a (1297), 9/44a (1297), 8/36a (1299), 8/100a (1301), 10/35b (1303), 12/53b (1305), 12/59a (1306). *Shops:* 16/76a (1289), 16/85a (1290), 9/15a (1295), 9/26a (1296), 9/27a (1296), 9/40a (1297), 8/5b (1298), 8/10d (1298), 8/75b (1301), 12/4b (1303), 12/5a (1303), 12/6a (1303). *Residential houses:* 9/45a (1297), 8/10d (1298), 12/44b (1306).

61. Martini, *Il diario eritreo*, 1:51 (7 February 1898). Ḥamīda, one of Muḥammad Sālim Bā Ṭūq's daughters, was also known for her piety. She was the first to endow some of her properties in real estate to the *maᶜhad al-dīnī al-islāmī* (the Islamic religious institute) of Massawa in 1948. Ibrāhīm al-Mukhtār, *al-Jāmiᶜ*, 55–56. The *maᶜhad* was built by Aḥmad ᶜAbd al-Raḥmān Hilāl. Maḥmūd Muḥammad Bā Ṭūq's son, Yāsīn (1914–67), was a journalist and local and nationalist activist who was appointed deputy-mayor of Massawa in August 1958. In the same year, he also became *naqīb* of the Shādhiliyya *ṭarīqa*, replacing in that position Ḥājj Ṣāliḥ Muḥammad Bashīr Bā Saᶜad (http://www.mukhtar.ca under "tarajim").

62. Puglisi, *Chi è? dell'Eritrea*, 277.

63. ASDMAE, *AE*, b. 16, "Stato degli impiegati esistenti negli uffici del Governo Egiziano in Massaua" (1885).

64. Abū Bakr, *Taᵓrīkh Iritrīyā*, 296. Interview with ᶜAlī Yūsuf al-Ghūl, Massawa, 26 February 2000. According to this informant the Bayt Sanūsī [al-Ghūl] and Bayt Sakīra were in fact sections of the al-Ghūl family. Conversation with Muḥammad al-Rifāᶜī, Massawa, 3 July 2006.

65. Ewald and Clarence-Smith, "The Economic Role of the Hadhrami Diaspora," 284.

66. Douin, *Histoire du règne*, vol. 3, part 1, 257.

67. MICR vol. 16 (1866–77), ᶜAydarūs: 16/21b, Bā ᶜAlawī: 16/20a, 16/20b, 16/21b, 16/21c, 16/22a, 16/47b, 16/79a, Bā Ḥamdūn: 16/12b, 16/110a, 16/116b, Bā Junayd: 16/40b, 16/41a, 16/41b, 16/42a, 16/42b, 16/43a, 16/43b, 16/43c, 16/53b, 16/58a, 16/58b, 16/64a, 16/67b, 16/69c, 16/70a, 16/70b, 16/70c, 16/71b, 16/77a, 16/80a, 16/82b, 16/85b, 16/95a, 16/100a, 16/103a, 16/103b, 16/107a, 16/107c, 16/109b, 16/117b, Bā Mushmūsh: 16/5a, 16/11b, 16/36a, Bā Zarᶜa: 16/34a, 16/59c, Hāshim: 16/4b, 16/12a, 16/25b, 16/30c, 16/82a, 16/104a, Ṣāfī: 16/51b, 16/52a, 16/53a, 16/62b, 16/73c, 16/82b, 16/83a, 16/89b, 16/93a, 16/99a, 16/106b, 16/111b. The Bā ᶜAlawī and ᶜAydarūs lineages, for example, attained prominent political and/or economic sta-

tus in other regions of the Indian Ocean. See both names in the index of Freitag and Clarence-Smith, *Hadhrami Traders, Scholars and Statesmen*, 368–70. I might be mistaken in considering the Hāshims as Hadramis. Some sources assert that they are from the Hijaz. But again, many Hadramis came to Massawa via Jiddah. Letter from Fouad Makki, 30 July 2004.

68. ASDMAE, *AE*, b. 210, From Gov. Civile e Militare della Col. Eritrea (Dogana, Massaua) to Sig. Capo dell'Ufficio affari Civili (Massaua), "Gestione facchinaggio durante l'anno 1894," 15 gennaio 1895.

69. Puglisi, *Chi è? dell'Eritrea*, 223. Interview with Ḥasan Muḥammad ʿUthmān Ḥayūtī, Asmara, 11 July 2006. Today, the heirs of Bā Zaḥam, who died in Jiddah in 2006, are perhaps the most prominent owners of real estate property in Massawa, with approximately 300 rented rooms. They do not reside in Eritrea.

70. MICR 16/5a (1284), 16/11b (14 Rabīʿ I 1285) and 16/36a (13 Jumāda II 1285).

71. MICR 8/72a (15 Ṣafar 1301). This case, from 1884, records the purchase of a shop in Massawa by ʿAbd Allāh and Muḥammad, sons of Shaykh Ḥasan Bā Mushmūsh.

72. Puglisi, *Chi è? dell'Eritrea*, 165. On page 162 Puglisi includes an entry of another member of the family, Ḥasan ʿAbd Allāh Bā Mushmūsh, who was born in Dawʿan in 1874 and came to Massawa in 1890.

73. On patterns of Hadrami migration and their social integration in East Africa see Le Guennec-Coppens, "Social and Cultural Integration," 185–95, and "Changing Patterns of Hadhrami Migration and Social Integration in East Africa," 157–74.

74. Odorizzi, *Il commissariato*, 125.

75. They had eight children together: five boys and three girls. According to the family tree of the Bā Ḥubayshīs, the eight children engendered not less than 82 children!

76. After Asmara became the colonial capital at the turn of the century, Aḥmad ʿUbayd and some of his brothers moved to Asmara to expand their trade and opened import/export offices. He was a wealthy merchant and owner of property in real estate in Massawa and Asmara who funded schools in Eritrea during the 1940s, most notably the Arabic Community School (*al-madrasa al-jāliyya*) in Asmara. He served from 1951 until his death in 1959 as president of the Arab community in Asmara. Interviews with Anīs ʿUbayd Bā Ḥubayshī and Aḥmad Muḥammad Bā Ḥubayshī, Asmara, 10 March 2000; Puglisi, *Chi è? dell'Eritrea*, 8, 223, 290. Today the Bā Ḥubayshīs claim that the family ("a real *qabīla*," [tribe] in their words) consists of several hundred members (about 500–700) scattered around the globe in Germany, New York City, Cairo, Jiddah, Yemen, Eritrea, and other places.

77. An interesting treatment of labor in the wider region is offered in Ewald, "Crossers of the Sea," 69–91.

78. But the movement included also sailors and fishermen from the African coasts, mainly Afaris, working on the Yemeni littorals. See for example Odorizzi, "La Dancalia italiana del nord," 171.

79. Odorizzi, *Il commissariato*, 115; Abū Bakr, *Taʾrīkh Iritrīyā*, 294–97. It does not, however, automatically mean that those families were originally from the mentioned ports and could disguise origins inland, for example in Hadramawt.

80. Interview with Sayyid Ibrāhīm ʿAbd Allāh Sharīf, Massawa, 2 March 2000.

81. Massawa Council Records (hereafter MCR), Register of Sentences/Judgements. [*Daftar li qayd al-muḍābiṭ al-muḥarrara min majlis Maṣawwaʿ (1882)*], 1. Sentence given on 25 Shawwāl 1299 (14 June 1882).

82. For a detailed pedigree of ʿAlī al-Nahārī's descendance from his four wives, see Miran, "Facing the Land, Facing the Sea," appendix 12, 357–58.

83. Odorizzi, *Il commissariato*, 253–58.

84. Martini, *Il diario eritreo,* 4:585 (on board the *Vespucci,* 11 September 1906); de Monfreid, *Journal de Bord,* 36; Grandclément, *L'incroyable Henry de Monfreid,* 154; interview with Maryam ᶜUmar al-Nahārī, Asmara, 26 March 2000 and additional details by Sayyid Ḥasan Muḥammad ᶜUthmān Ḥayūtī from Asmara. It was not uncommon that European-based dealers traveled directly to pearl producing regions, largely in order to cut out Indian middlemen. Victor Rosenthal, for example, operated in the Gulf early in the twentieth century. Bose, *A Hundred Horizons,* 86. Usually they had agents in the region. Rosenthal, for example, employed a certain Jacques Schouchana, a French Jew of Tunisian origins based in Alexandria. Around 1915, Schouchana offered de Monfreid to act as his agent in Massawa. Monfreid rejected the offer.

85. Monfreid, *Les secrets,* 68, 80, 82, 84, 107–29.

86. Interview with Sayyid Ḥasan Muḥammad ᶜUthmān Ḥayūtī, Asmara, 11 July 2006. Another source notes that the Italian authorities borrowed funds from ᶜAlī al-Nahārī (apparently in 1928) and on payment of the debt, the family invested it in Paris in real-estate property and placed it in banks. Puglisi, *Chi è? dell'Eritrea,* 11. See more details that shed light on the context of major Parisian pearl dealers' business ventures in Hopper, "The African Presence in Arabia," 202–13. Hopper's account is mainly based on the autobiography of Léonard Rosenthal, *The Pearl Hunter.*

87. Interviews with ᶜĀdil Muḥammad ᶜAlī Saᶜīd Ṣūrī al-Ṭāhirī, Massawa, 22 March 2000 and ᶜAbdu ᶜAlī Saᶜīd Ṣūrī al-Ṭāhirī, Massawa, 27 April 2000.

88. On religion and society in Ethiopia in the era of emperor Yohannes IV see Caulk, "Religion and State in Nineteenth Century Ethiopia," 23–42.

89. The phenomenon of name appropriation is signaled, for example, in 18th-century Nablus (Palestine). See Doumani, *Rediscovering Palestine,* 64.

90. Interviews with Jamāl Wahhāb al-Bārrī, Asmara, 11 March 2000, and ᶜUmar Wahhāb al-Bārrī, Massawa, 17 March 2000.

91. Saint-Yves, "A travers l'Erythrée italienne," 142.

92. Pankhurst, "The 'Banyan' or Indian Presence at Massawa," 185–212, "Indian Trade with Ethiopia," 453–97, and "La presenza e il declino dei Baniani a Massaua e Dahlac," 13–36. See also by the same author "The History of Ethiopia's Relations with India prior to the Nineteenth Century." For a study of the commercial links between India and East Africa see Alpers, "Gujerat and the Trade of East Africa, 1500–1800."

93. Originating in the Gujarati word *vâniyo,* Banyan, Banias, banians, *bâniyâns* means "trader" or "shopkeeper." The term seems to have developed to refer to all traders, brokers and middlemen regardless of religious origin or social stance. See also Pankhurst, "Banyan," 1:467.

94. Markovits, *The Global World of Indian Merchants,* 11. See also Prakash, "The Indian Maritime Merchant," 435–57.

95. Pankhurst, "The 'Banyan' or Indian presence," 188–89.

96. On Indian entrepreneurs in the western Indian Ocean in this period, see Clarence-Smith, "Indian Business Communities," 18–21. See also Markovits, "Indian Merchant Networks," 883–911.

97. Bose, *A Hundred Horizons,* 75

98. Pankhurst, "The 'Banyan' or Indian presence," 190, 198.

99. Bonnenfant, "La marque de l'Inde à Zabîd."

100. See examples of individuals in Puglisi, *Chi è? dell'Eritrea,* 160–61, 217, 221.

101. MAE, *Correspondance Consulaire et Commerciale, Massaouah,* t.1, Rapport commercial, Degoutin to Guizot, 20 April 1841, and MAE, *Correspondance Consulaire et Commerciale, Massaouah,* t.1, Rochet d'Héricourt to Minister of Foreign Affairs, 1 February 1848.

102. Lejean, *Théodore II,* 282.

103. Pankhurst, "The 'Banyan' or Indian presence," 204–10; Odorizzi, *Il commissariato,* 125.

104. Miège, "Djeddah: port d'entrepôt," 100–102.

105. Clarence-Smith, "Indian Business Communities," 19.

106. Pankhurst, "The 'Banyan' or Indian presence," 210–11. Based on Alamanni, *La colonia Eritrea,* 284–85.

107. Pankhurst, "The 'Banyan' or Indian presence," 203–209; F.O. 403/90 "Petition," enclosure in No. 96, Sir E. Baring to the Marquis of Salisbury, Cairo, October 20, 1887. I am indebted to Wolbert Smidt for providing me a copy of this document.

108. Matteucci, *In Abissinia,* 35.

109. Ḥasan Mūsā al-ʿAqqād was a member of a leading Egyptian trading family that played an important role in commerce in the Sudan under the Turkiyya. He was a man of considerable wealth. He was banished to the Sudan twice. He supported the ʿUrābī revolt of 1882, was tried and banished to Massawa. There the Italians sentenced him to death on account of his alleged "conspiratory" activities together with [Ḥasan Ḥāmid] Kantibāy in favor of the Mahdists. Hill, *A Biographical Dictionary,* 158. G. M., "I traditori di Massaua," 21–24. See also Ewald, "The Nile Valley System," 79.

110. ASDMAE, *AE,* Pacco 153, "Repertorio No. 210—No. 843 Registro Atti Notabili" (1892).

111. Daudi Bohras, a Mustaʿlī sub-sect of the Ismāʿīlīs, principally live in western India and Pakistan, in Gujarat (including Kutch) and Sind. The Khojas also live in Gujarat, Sindh, Rajastan, and Maharasstra. They are subdivided into Nizārī Ismāʿīlī Khojas, Ḥanafī Khojas, and Twelver Shīʿa Khojas.

112. Martini, *Nell'Affrica italiana,* 31.

113. See a sample of cases involving non-Muslim Indians (in chronological order): MICR 16/14c (1868), 16/65a (1870), 16/67a (1871), 16/74c (1871), 16/76c (1872), 16/118b (1877), 9/1c (1877), 9/12a (1878), 8/1d (1881), 8/63a (1883), 12/1a (1885), 12/3b (1885), 12/60b (1889).

114. Bose, *A Hundred Horizons,* 101.

115. Markovits, *The Global World of Indian Merchants,* 6.

116. Pankhurst, "The 'Banyan' or Indian Presence," 206–207.

117. Gatta, "Massaua e le regioni circostanti," 474.

118. Lejean, *Voyage aux deux Nils* (or *Voyage en Abyssinie*), Atlas. And "Pianta dell'isola e città di Massauah ridotta dal. Luogo Tenente G.A. Bessone," in Pennazzi, *Dal Po ai due Nili.* For a verbal reference to an Indian quarter see Mah Bey, *Massauah,* 24.

119. Habib, "History of Massawa," footnote section, xii (chapter 2, footnote 56). Interview with Muḥammad Aḥmad ʿAbbāsī, Massawa, 15 May 2000.

120. Pascale, *Massaua,* 50, and Mantegazza, *Da Massaua a Saati,* 236.

121. Buchs, "Voyages en Abyssinie," 38.

122. Bonnenfant, "La marque de l'Inde à Zabîd."

123. Puglisi, *Chi è? dell'Eritrea,* 221.

124. See also Habib, "History of Massawa," footnote section xiii (chapter 2, footnote 61). He includes the Ḥabīb family in this group.

125. In 1912 ʿUthmān Khayyr ad-Dīn and ʿUthmān Ṣāʾigh are both mentioned as goldsmiths in Hetumlo. *Elenco dei commercianti, etc.,* 45–46.

126. MICR 8/27a (21 Rajab 1299).

127. Interviews with Muḥammad Zubūy Ṣāliḥ Mīyā Khayr ad-Dīn, ʿAbd al-Qādir Hindī, and ʿAbd al-Laṭīf Aḥmad Hindī, Massawa, 20 March 2000, and interview with Sulaymān ʿAbdu Hindī and Muḥammad ʿAbdu Bakrī Ḥijjī, Massawa, 16 May 2000.

128. Interview with Ḥasan Muḥammad ᶜUthmān Ḥayūtī, Asmara, 27 November 1999.

129. MICR 14/3i (1866) Hindī with Faqīh; 14/4b (1867) Mīyā with Sayyid Bakrī; 14/6a (1868) Mīyā with Hindī; 14/6b (1868) Ṣaḥay with Hindī; 14/7a (1868) Hindī with Saᶜīd; 14/9d (1868) Mīyā with Makkaᶜalī.

130. MICR 16/63c (Muḥarram 1290/1873) and 16/109a (5 Muḥarram 1293/1876).

131. Puglisi, *Chi è? dell'Eritrea,* 161, 217.

132. Interview with Sayyid Ibrāhīm Muḥammad Ibrāhīm al-Sayyid, Massawa, 26 April 2000.

133. Salvadei, "Massaua."

134. Stanga, *Una gita in Eritrea,* 36.

135. Another burial place was located on Shaykh Saᶜīd Island. Al-Jamal, *Siyāsat Miṣr fī al-baḥr al-aḥmar,* 79.

136. Bruce, *Travels to Discover the Source of the Nile,* 3:2.

137. Ferret and Galinier, *Voyage en Abyssinie,* 369.

138. Combes and Tamisier, *Voyage en Abyssinie,* I, 101. Parkyns provides a description of the house of Ḥusayn Afandī, the chief scribe. Parkyns, *Life in Abyssinia,* 20.

139. Osgood, *Notes of Travel,* 246.

140. Report by ᶜAlī Riḍā Pāshā, governor of the Red Sea Coasts, to the *khedive.* Report no. 4 on Massawa, 9 Ṣafar 1297. In al-Jamal, *al-Wathāᵓiq al-taᵓrīkhiyya,* 162.

141. Munzinger, "Les contrées limitrophes" 28.

142. Abbadie, *Douze ans de séjour dans la Haute-Éthiopie* (1980), 1:7–8.

143. See descriptions of the Massawa bazaar in Combes and Tamisier, *Voyage en Abyssinie,* 1:99; Lefebvre, *Voyage en Abyssinie,* 1:39; Negri, *Massaua e dintorni,* 9; Gatta, "Da Massaua a Chartum," 400; Gatta, "Massaua e regioni circostanti," 473–74; Vigoni, "Massaua e il nord dell'Abissinia," 20–21; Pascale, *Massaua,* 75–76.

144. Lejean, *Voyage aux deux Nils,* 164.

145. Douin, *Histoire du règne,* vol. 3, part 1, 281 (AA Maᶜiya Saniyah, box 38, piece 143, report by Ismāᶜīl Ṣādiq Pacha, 5 June 1866). One *faddān* equals 4200.833 square meters. Wehr, *Arabic-English Dictionary,* 700.

146. See eight useful maps (but quite imprecise, for the earlier period) demonstrating Massawa's urban development from the pre-1870 period to 1962 and a population chart from 1885 to 1961; Ferronato, "La città di Massaua," annexes.

147. On Egyptian efforts at the development of Massawa under Khedive Ismāᶜīl (1863–79), see Talhami, *Suakin and Massawa,* especially chapter 6 (97–124); Talhami, "Massawa under Khedive Ismail, 1865–1879," 481–93. See also Pankhurst, *History of Ethiopian Towns,* 135–38.

148. A similar building drive in this period was observed in Sawākin; Bloss, "The Story of Suakin," (1937) 247.

149. See examples of such doors in Cerbella, *Aspetti etnografici della casa in Etiopia,* 13, 21, 41. See also Issel, *Viaggio nel Mar Rosso* (1872), 46, 50; Issel,*Viaggio nel Mar Rosso* (1885) 63; Porro, "Notizie da Massaua," 97. For doors in Sawākin—some strongly resembling the style of Massawa's doors—see Greenlaw, *The Coral Buildings of Suakin,* 112–15.

150. Greenlaw, *The Coral Buildings,* 21. For remarks on the distinctive features of a Red Sea style see also Matthews, "The Red Sea Style," 60–86.

151. Douin, *Histoire du règne,* vol. 3, part 2, 530.

152. The word Gherar means "rocky madreporic blocs," refelcting the nature of the peninsula's land. Odorizzi, *Il commissariato,* 108. On building forms and construction methods see Pulver and Goujon, *A Preliminary Conservation and Development Scheme for Old Massawa,* 3–4

153. Issel, *Viaggio nel Mar Rosso* (1885), 63.

154. Matteucci, *In Abissinia,* 31–32; Negri, *Massaua e dintorni,* 8.

155. For Sawākin see Greenlaw, *The Coral Buildings.* For Jiddah see Pesce, *Jiddah,* and Buchan, *Jeddah Old and New.* For Massawa see Gebremedhin, Denison, and Abraham, *Massawa.* On architectural similarities between Sawākin, Jiddah, and Massawa see also comments in Bloss, "The Story of Suakin," (1936) 272.

156. Mantegazza, *Da Massaua a Saati,* 21–23; Pascale, *Massaua,* 59–61; Vigoni,"Massaua e il nord," 2.

157. Buchs, "Voyages en Abyssinie," 33; Odorizzi, *Il commissariato,* 121; Ferronato, "La città di Massaua," 197–98.

158. Blanc, *A Narrative of Captivity,* 59.

159. Talhami, *Suakin and Massawa,* 100.

160. MICR 16/1b, 6/38b, 16/41c, 16/53b, 16/56a, 16/59b, 16/61c, 16/72b, 16/74a, 16/102b, 16/103c and many other examples.

161. Real estate transactions of ʿAbd Allāh and Aḥmad Bey al-Ghūl. *Land:* MICR 16/83b (1290), 16/85a (1290), 16/101b (1291), 9/27b (1296), 9/41a (1297), 9/42a (1297), 9/43a (1297), 9/44a [water-well and land in Hetumlo] (1297), 8/36a (1299), 8/100a (1301), 10/35b (1303), 12/53b (1305), 12/59a (1306). *Shops:* 16/76a (1289), 16/85a (1290), 9/15a (1295), 9/26a (1296), 9/27a (1296), 9/40a (1297), 8/5b (1298), 8/10d (1298), 8/75b (1301), 12/4b (1303), 12/5a (1303), 12/6a (1303). *Residential houses:* 9/45a (1297), 8/10d (1298), 12/44b (1306).

162. *L'Esplorazione Commerciale,* Fasc. II, Feb. 1886, 38 (survey conducted by Lt. Brengola).

163. MICR 16/14c, 16/74c, 12/66a.

164. MICR 16/105c, 8/34c, 8/101a, 8/106b, 8/113a, 10/14a, 10/18a, 10/21a, 10/25b, 10/26a, 10/26b, 10/27b, 10/33a, 12/40a, 12/56a, 12/58a, 12/62a, 12/64a, 12/66a.

165. MICR 12/1b (1303), 12/38b (1303). The following two texts were published by the Italian businessman Enrico Tagliabue: "Massaua e i suoi abitanti" and *Dieci anni a Massaua.*

166. Talhami, "Massawa under Khedive Ismaʿil, 1865–1879," 482; Pankhurst, "Some Notes on the Historical and Economic Geography of the Meṣewa Area," 112–16; al-Jamal, *al-Wathāʾiq al-taʾrīkhiyya,* 119; Douin, *Histoire du règne,* vol. 3, part 2, 508ff.

167. According to an oral tradition Tewalet derives from the name of a Sudanese woman who used to sell drinks in the area. *Luʾluʾ al-baḥr al-aḥmar,* 32.

168. Saint-Yves, "A travers l'Érythrée italienne," 139.

169. The Islamic court recorded the selling and purchasing of land on Tewalet. The land belonged to the government, and Governor Arākil Bey [Dabroyan] (gov. 1873–75) sold individual parcels to Egyptian officials and local entrepreneurs. See examples in MICR 16/99b (1874: Sold to Fayrūz Afandī [Egy. Off.]); 16/100b (1874: Sold to Shaykh ʿAbd Allāh Khalīl Mentāy); 16/100c (1874: Sold to Shaykh Ḥusayn Muḥammad Khaṭīb); 16/100d (1874: Sold to Ṭāhā Ibrāhīm [Egy. Off.].), 16/100e (1874: Sold to Kafal Bey [Egy. Off.]); 16/101a (1874: Sold to Shaykh Muḥammad b. ʿAbd Allāh ʿAbbāsī); 16/101b (1874: Sold to Shaykh ʿAbd Allāh b. Aḥmad al-Ghūl); 16/102a (1875: Sold to ʿIrāqi Afandī Muḥammad [Egy. Off.]); 16/103a (1875: Sold to Shaykh ʿAbd Allāh b. ʿUmar b. Saʿīd Bā Junayd) and other cases in the same register.

170. See similar comments in the early Italian era in Di Robilant, "Presidi e domini dell'Italia nel Mar Rosso," 15.

171. For more details see Ferronato, "La città di Massaua," 200–208.

172. Photographer Luigi Naretti's panorama of Massawa (1895) is reproduced in Palma, *L'Italia coloniale,* 10–11. The illustration is printed in Bizzoni, *L'Eritrea nel passato e nel presente,* 4–5.

173. The most damaged area was the old commercial center—the bazaar and the al-

leys around it. But it also ruined the Shāfiʿī mosque—believed to have been the oldest in town. Following the earthquake the Italians launched a massive project of reconstruction whose results may be seen up to this day (less those edifices destroyed by Ethiopian air strikes in 1990). Interestingly, Italian architects and construction engineers repaired, designed, and built by maintaining and improvising on features of the traditional "Turkish" and "Egyptian" styles, using local coral stone. Reviglio, "Ricordi e riflessioni sui terremoti di Massaua," 87–91. Paolo Reviglio was chief engineer in the Department of Public Works of the *Governorato Generale* of Eritrea in the colonial period. He was among several engineers participating in the reconstruction of Massawa following the earthquakes. See also a "visitor's guide" with numerous post-reconstruction photographs. Mario Moretto, *Guida della città di Massaua,* and Ferronato, "La città di Massaua," 212–16.

174. Kühn, "Ordering Urban Space in Ottoman Yemen," 341–42.

175. Porro, "Notizie da Massaua," 134.

176. Di Robilant, "Presidi e domini dell'Italia nel Mar Rosso," 15.

177. According to Munzinger, sandal-making was a much valued and elaborate profession in town. *Studi,* 121.

178. Pascale, *Massaua,* 76–77, and Mantegazza, *Da Massaua a Saati,* 24 and 230.

179. Salvadei, "Massaua," 1832.

180. Odorizzi, *Il commissariato,* 94.

181. For a report on Yemeni porters see ASDMAE, *AE,* b. 210, From Gov. Civile e Militare della Col. Eritrea (Dogana, Massaua) to Sig. Capo dell'Ufficio affari Civili (Massaua), "Gestione facchinaggio durante l'anno 1894," 15 gennaio 1895.

182. Toledano, *The Ottoman Slave Trade,* 224–27; Gabrawold, "Origin and Early Development," 15–21.

183. For a sample of several dozen manumission registrations (date, name of manumitter, and manumitted) from MICR Registers 8, 10, 11 and 14 (1868–85), see Miran, "Facing the Land," appendix 21, 371–72.

184. MICR 8/23a (11 Jumāda II 1299/29 April 1882).

185. MICR 8/23b (11 Jumāda II 1299/29 April 1882).

186. MICR 8/23c (11 Jumāda II 1299/29 April 1882).

187. *Missions-Tidning,* Letters from Lundahl, 23 March 1873 and 4 July 1873. Cited in Gabrawold, "Origin and Early Development," 21–22. See also Tron and Jwarson, *Notizie storiche e varie sulla missione evangelica svedese in Eritrea,* and Arén, *Evangelical Pioneers in Ethiopia.*

188. Gabrawold, "Origin and Early Development," 22.

189. Salvadei, "Massaua," 1817.

190. Porro, "Notizie da Massaua," 102; Buchs, "Voyages en Abyssinie," 36; Saint-Yves, "A travers l'Erythrée italienne," 139–41, 147. In 1908 there were 322 straw and wood huts in Tewalet; Odorizzi, *Il commissariato,* 121 and 125.

191. Lejean, *Voyage aux deux Nils,* 164.

192. Blanc, *A Narrative of Captivity,* 67–68; Issel, *Viaggio nel Mar Rosso* (1872), 59, 62; Negri, *Massaua e dintorni,* 13.

193. De Rivoyre, *Mer Rouge et Abyssinie,* 268–69. See also Guillot, "La mer Rouge et l'Abyssinie," 197.

194. Saint-Yves, "A travers l'Érythrée italienne," 147.

195. The real estate transaction recorded in the court registers includes the purchasing of a parcel of land; MICR 9/44a (23 Ṣafar 1297).

196. I thank Fouad Makki for providing these details. Letter of 30 July 2004.

197. Odorizzi, *Il commissariato,* 120–22; Ferronato, "La città di Massaua," 198.

198. Lejean, *Voyage aux deux Nils,* 163.

199. Plowden, *Travels in Abyssinia*, 3.

200. See Odorizzi, *Il commissariato*, 92–93.

201. Ibid. The fate of liberated slaves in urban colonial Sudan and their transformation into wage laborers is the subject of the interesting study *Slaves into Workers: Emancipation and Labor in Colonial Sudan*, by Ahmad Alawad Sikainga.

202. D'Avray, *The Nakfa Documents*, Document 81, Captain Boari to the Gov. Civile e Militare della Colonia Eritrea (Massaua), Asmara, 11 Marzo 1891, "Tributi nel Semhar e paesi limitrofi," 279.

203. Pascale, *Massaua*, 74–75.

204. On the difference between "structural" and "conjunctural" poverty see Iliffe, *The African Poor*, 4. Iliffe even gives a quotation from Rüppell on poverty in Massawa on page 18. In the early 1840s Antoine d'Abbadie remarked that many poor people come to Massawa during funerary processions, where in exchange for prayers for the deceased they received a meal. Abbadie, *Géographie de l'Ethiopie*, 20.

205. Blanc, *A Narrative of Captivity*, 63–66.

206. Lejean, *Voyage en Abyssinie*, 60–61; Hotten, *Abyssinia and its Peoples*, 212; Issel, *Viaggio* (1872), 61; Douin, *Histoire du règne*, vol. 3, part 1, 255; Gatta, "Da Massaua a Chartum," 404; Gatta, "Massaua e regioni circostanti," 479; Vigoni, "Massaua e il nord dell'Abissinia," 4.

207. De Rivoyre, *Au pays du Soudan*, 16. See also De Cosson, *The Cradle of the Blue Nile*, 31–32.

208. Gatta, "Da Massaua a Chartum per Cheren e Kassala," 404–405.

209. Matteucci, *In Abissinia*, 54; Negri *Massaua e dintorni*, 18; Pippo Vigoni, "Massaua e il nord dell'Abissinia," 5.

210. Wylde, *'83 to '87 in the Soudan*, 61; Salvadei, "Massaua," 1833.

211. Combes and Tamisier, *Voyage en Abyssinie*, 1:113; Munzinger, *Les contrées limitrophes*, 34; Issel, *Viaggio nel mar Rosso* (1872), 61; De Rivoyre, *Mer Rouge et Abyssinie*, 63; Gatta, "Massaua e regioni," 478; Vigoni, "Massaua e il nord dell'Abissinia," 4; Salvadei, "Massaua," 1833.

212. Lejean, *Voyage aux deux Nils*, 164; De Rivoyre, *Mer Rouge et Abyssinie*, 64.

213. Interviews with Sayyid Ibrāhīm Muḥammad Ibrāhīm al-Sayyid, Massawa, 26 April 2000, Muḥammad Aḥmad ʿUmar Aḥmad ʿAbbāsī, Massawa, 29 April 2000, and Muḥammad Abū Bakr al-Nātī, Massawa, 16 May 2000.

214. Salvadei, "Massaua," 1832–33, and Odorizzi, *Il commissariato*, 163, 170. According to Salvadei a modest cattle market took place on Tuesday in Hetumlo.

215. Horton and Middleton, *The Swahili*, 136–37.

216. Salvadei, "Massaua," 1833.

217. Letter from Fouad Makki, 30 July 2004.

218. Habib, "History of Massawa," 21.

219. MICR 8/61c (6 Dhū ʾl-ḥijja 1300) also 2/46a.

220. MICR 8/94d (10 Rajab 1301).

221. Ibrāhīm al-Mukhtār, *al-Jāmiʿ*, 59–61, and Odorizzi, *Il commissariato*, 160–61.

222. *Elenco dei commercianti, industriali, negozianti, imprenditori, appaltatori o fornitori, e degli esercenti professioni, arti e mestieri inscritti nel ruolo dei contribuenti della Colonia Eritrea (Esercizio 1912–13)*, Colonia Eritrea N. 58 (Asmara, 1913), 40–47. One could add to this list Shūm ʿAbd Allāh Mentāy in Zaga. Folchi, "Commissariato Regionale di Massaua," 187 (213).

223. MICR 16/4a, 14/3b [1866]; 16/8a [1867]; 16/18b, 16/28b, 16/31b, 16/32c, 1637b, 16/40a, 16/46a, 14/7h [1868]; 16/95a, 16/96a, 16/96b, 16/98a [1873]; 16/100a [1874]; 16/112a,

16/113b [1876]; 11/31a, 9/9a, 9/13a [1878], 9/50a, 9/55a [1880], 8/4b, 8/5b [1881]; 8/43a, 8/56b [1883]; 12/9a [1886]; 12/51a [1888].

224. ASDMAE, *AE*, b. 178, "Elenco dei Notabili di Massaua" (1893), and ASDMAE, *AE* 193 "R. Capitaneria di porto di Massaua": Matricola dei Sambuchi, 1 gennaio 1908.

225. Interview with Muḥammad Abū Bakr al-Nātī, Massawa, 8 May 2000.

4. "A Sacred Muslim Island"

1. Al-Būṣīrī, *Al-Busiri's Burda*, verse 34, p. 56. Translated also as "Muhammad, the Prince of the two universes [material and spiritual], of the two ponderable classes [men and demons], and of the two sections [of mankind], of the Arabians and the Non-Arabians." "Poem of the Cloak" in Clouston, *Arabian Poetry for English Readers*, "al-Burdah," trans. J. W. Redhouse, 326. Inscription in Cerbella, *Aspetti etnografici*, 12.

2. Al-Būṣīrī, *Al-Busiri's Burda*, verse 135, p. 128. Translated also as "For whoso hath his stay in the Apostle of God, if lions meet him in their thickets, they are struck mute and motionless." Clouston, *Arabian Poetry*, 338. Inscription in Cerbella, *Aspetti etnografici*, 11.

3. F.O. 24, Plowden—F.O. 11/5/52. Cited in Marston, *Britain's Imperial Role*, 192.

4. Ibrāhīm al-Mukhtār, *al-Jāmiᶜ*, 70 and 119. There is some inconsistency in the sources regarding the name. It might be ᶜAlī Muḥammad Nūr Abū ᶜIlāmā.

5. *Hijra* (migration) is an Islamic concept modeled on the experience of the Prophet Muḥammad and the early Muslim community's migration from Mecca to Medina. *Hijra* was defined by Eickelman and Piscatori as "the obligation to migrate from lands where the practice of Islam is constrained to those where in principle no such constraint exists." Eickelman and Piscatori, *Muslim Travellers*, 5. *Hijra* has been applied by both individuals and communities in particular historical contexts, for example in northern Nigeria in the early colonial period. See Muhammad Khalid Masud's chapter in the same volume: "The Obligation to Migrate: The Doctrine of *Hijra* in Islamic Law," 29–49.

6. Ibrāhīm al-Mukhtār, *al-Jāmiᶜ*, 120. For various transactions involving the French bishop in the early 1880s see MICR 8/1d (10 Rajab 1298), 8/10d (29 Dhū l-ḥijja 1298), 12/47a (8 Shawwāl 1305). At some point the mission was moved to Emkullo and the Massawa hospital constructed by the Italians where the mission was previously located. In the 1950s there was a small church inside the hospital building, but Ibrāhīm al-Mukhtār observes in his account that it was not in stone.

7. Such expressions had already been recorded in the politically liberal, but communally (and religiously) politicized 1940s under the British Military Administration. Eritrean Muslim intellectuals attempted to rally Eritrean Muslims and define the specificity of Eritrean Islam, finding inspiration in Massawa's history and its links to Islamic history. Grand Muftī Ibrāhīm al-Mukhtār (1909–69) had been particularly active in this respect, publishing (anonymously) articles in the Muslim League's journal *Ṣawṭ al-Rābiṭa al-Islāmiyya al-Iritriyya* and composing a lengthy unpublished study on Massawa from a pronounced Islamic perspective, titled *al-Jāmiᶜ li-akhbār jazīrat Bāḍiᶜ*, completed in Asmara in 1958.

8. On the *ṣaḥāba* and Ethiopia see Erlich, *Ethiopia and the Middle East*, 5–19. See also Guérinot, "L'islam et l'Abyssinie," 6–8; Pollera, *Le popolazioni*, 43–44; Trimingham, *Islam in Ethiopia*, 44–46; Cuoq, *L'islam en Ethiopie*, 28–35, and Odorizzi, *Note storiche sulla religione mussulmana*, 15–18. A most recent text written by an Eritrean highlighting the *ṣaḥāba* episode is Muḥammad Saᶜīd Nāwad's *Iritrīyā*, 41–51.

9. Nāwad, *Iritrīyā*, 37 and 50. Other Muslims in the Horn of Africa, such as the So-

malis, have also expressed similar ideas attesting to their strong attachment to their faith. See for example Mokhtar, "Islam in Somali History," 1.

10. The Jeberti are Muslims inhabiting the Ethiopian and Eritrean highlands. They are mostly urban and are engaged in commerce and artisanal work. See Abdulkader Saleh, "Ǧäbärti."

11. An Italian census of 1931 gave the following proportions: Mālikīs 65%, Ḥanafīs 26%, and Shāfiᶜīs 9%. Pollera doubted these figures and presumed that the Ḥanafīs were nevertheless the majority. Both of Eritrea's grand muftīs, originally from eastern Eritrea and educated in Egypt, have followed the Ḥanafī school. Bertola, *Il regime dei culti nell'Africa italiana,* 163; Pollera, *Le popolazioni,* 285–86; Trimingham, *Islam in Ethiopia,* 232–33; Gori, "Soggiorno di studi in Eritrea ed Etiopia," 94–97. Folchi noted in 1898 that *qāḍīs* in northern Eritrea used the Khalīl al-Mukhtaṣar, copies of which (printed in Egypt and Syria) were distributed by the Egyptians. This compendium of Mālikī law was composed by the Egyptian jurisprudent Khalīl b. Isḥāq al-Jundī (d. 1374 A.D.). Folchi, "Commissariato Regionale di Massaua," 59 (168), and Miran, "Mālikism," 696–98.

12. Trimingham, *Islam in the Sudan,* 10; Guérinot, "L'islam et l'Abyssinie," 9.

13. His descendants from his marriage within the Minifire founded the pious subclan Faqīh Ḥarak, of whom descended Eritrea's most important scholar in the 20th century, Grand Muftī Shaykh Ibrāhīm al-Mukhtār. Faqīh Muḥammad is buried in a place called ᶜAla off the mountain chain of Nefasit and on the road to Dekemhare.

14. In his early twentieth-century description of marriage, divorce, and funerary customs in Massawa, Capomazza placed families and members of the Bayt Shaykh Maḥmūd in a prominent position as communal religious leaders. Capomazza, *Usanze islamiche hanafite di Massaua e dintorni.*

15. In most Arabic sources they are identified as *qabāʾil shaykha.* For more detailed information, including their role in diffusing Islam among communities in the region, see Abū Bakr, *Taʾrīkh Iritrīyā,* 97–98, 312–16; Nāwad, *Iritrīyā,* 52–53 and id. *ᶜUmq al-ᶜalāqāt al-ᶜarabiyya al-iritriyya* (Kuwait 2004), 129–33. On the ᶜAd Darqī see D'Avray, *Lords of the Sea,* 35–36.

16. Broadly, the identification of these phases follows Hussein Ahmed's reasoning in relation to Ethiopia at large. It attempts to balance between external and internal dynamics. Ahmed, *Islam in Nineteenth-Century Wallo,* 74–75. As noted above, Balaw traditions also place their migration from the Barca region eastward towards the Red Sea coast (and ultimately to Hergigo) some time in the fifteenth century. The head of the lineage was said to be a *sayyid* descendant of ᶜAbd Allāh b. ᶜAbbās, the Prophet's uncle. Salvadei, "Massaua," 1831.

17. Members of the ᶜAbbāsī family still recall the reason for their ancestors' emigration from the Hijaz to Massawa. Their family traditions converge with *qāḍī* lists that mention several *qāḍīs* from the family in the 17th and 18th centuries. See Ibrāhīm al-Mukhtār, *al-Jāmiᶜ,* 77.

18. See Voll, *Islam,* 34–39.

19. Levtzion and Voll, "Introduction," 3–20.

20. For a short overview of *ṭarīqa* presence in northeast Africa see Grandin, "Le nord-est et l'est de l'Afrique," 428–41.

21. The Qādiriyya is the most popular and widespread *ṭarīqa* in the Muslim world. The teachings of the Persian Sufi ᶜAbd al-Qādir al-Jīlānī (1077–1166) have served as the basis for its foundation.

22. Trimingham, *Islam in Ethiopia,* 239–40; Grandin, "Le nord-est et l'est de l'Afrique," 430–31.

23. The foundation of the Shādhiliyya is ascribed to Shaykh Abū al-Ḥasan al-Shādhilī (1196–1258). In Massawa, members of the ᶜAbbāsī family claim a long-term historical af-

filiation with the Shādhiliyya. The family has been associated with the office of *qāḍī* and other religious institutions for several centuries to this day. Interviews with ᶜAbd al-Bāqī Muḥammad ᶜAbdu ᶜAbbāsī, Massawa, 27 September 1999 and 24 June 2006. See also Trimingham, *Islam in Ethiopia*, 236, and, for the Shādhiliyya in the Sudan, Karrar, *The Sufi Brotherhoods in the Sudan*, 35.

24. Nāwad, *ᶜUmq al-ᶜalāqāt*, 130, 169, and Trimingham, *Islam in Ethiopia*, 236, 247. The names of those *shaykhs* who had introduced the orders is provided in Nāwad.

25. See O'Fahey, *Enigmatic Saint*.

26. See O'Fahey and Radtke, "Neo-Sufism Reconsidered."

27. O'Fahey, "Ṭarīḳa [in Northeastern and Eastern Africa]," 248. See also O'Fahey, *Enigmatic Saint*, 4–7.

28. Talhami, *Suakin and Massawa*, 227–28

29. Holt, "Holy Families and Islam in the Sudan," 121–22.

30. A copy of the *nisba* (Ar., pedigree) of Shaykh Ḥāmid b. Nafᶜūtāy was given to me during the *ziyāra* to the tomb of Shaykh Muḥammad b. ᶜAlī (d. 1877) at Emberemi in May 2000. It is assumed that the *nisba* was given to Abū Bakr b. Ibrāhīm b. Ḥāmid b. Nafᶜūtāy in AH 999. (1590) at Mecca. Twenty-seven generations are traced from Shaykh Ḥāmid to ᶜAlī. (See also a *nisba* in Abū Bakr, *Taʾrīkh Iritrīyā*, 317). Other typed and manuscript documents were given to me on the same occasion, some of which provide details in the account that follows. See a simplified genealogical table also in Pollera, *Le popolazioni*, 205. The first member of the lineage who came from the Hijaz to the eastern Sudanese region (via Sawākin) was ᶜUthmān b. Muḥammad. He had a son (ᶜĀmir) with a woman of the Aliyab. ᶜĀmir's son, Maḥmūd, settled in Kassala, where he had Nafᶜūtāy with a woman of the ᶜAd Qayiᶜ. Nafᶜūtay, and later his son Ḥāmid, moved eastward to the Eritrean Sahel. There, in the early nineteenth century, Shaykh al-Amīn b. Ḥāmid b. Nafᶜūtāy gradually gained widespread reputation as a holy man through his preaching and miracle working among Christian *tigre*-serfs of the Bet Asgede confederacy who approached him to seek his *baraka*. Shaykh al-Amīn married the daughter of the Bet Asgede *kantebay* (Tig., chief) and thus began a process of marriages with Bet Asgede women that eventually resulted in the conversion of part of that group to Islam. A saintly cult developed around the person of Shaykh al-Amīn, and after his death a visitation to his tomb was begun in the vicinity of Afᶜabet. See Höfner, "Überlieferungen bei Tigre-stämmen (I) Ad Sek." The Tigre-language text translated (into German) and annotated by Höfner is titled "Fagret Ad Shekh" ("Origins of the Ad Shaykh").

31. On the role and methods of the ᶜAd Shaykh in converting these specific societies see Trimingham, *Islam in Ethiopia*, 154–55, 159–69; Pollera, *Le popolazioni*, 204–10. See also Nadel, *Races and Tribes of Eritrea*, 42–43; Killion, *Historical Dictionary of Eritrea*, 30; Guérinot, "L'islam et l'Abyssinie," 31–57; Abū Bakr, *Taʾrīkh Iritrīyā*, 316. See also ACS, *MAI*, Gov. dell'Eritrea b. 1066. Allegato no 9. Amerio Liberati, "Note sul commissariato regionale di Cheren," Cheren, July 1928, 53–57, and *Trevaskis Papers*, Box 1, File 2, "The Tribes and Peoples of Northern Eritrea. A Survey of the Keren Division," 19–20.

32. Ibrāhīm al-Mukhtār, *al-Jāmiᶜ*, 65. Two of Shaykh al-Amīn's sons settled among the Garabit and the Faydab and lived under the patronage of the Beni ᶜAmer.

33. Lejean, *Voyage aux deux Nils*, 142. See also Miran, "Embärämi," 272.

34. Blanc, *A Narrative of Captivity*, 88.

35. Raka, *Future Life and Occult Beings*, 27–28. Another source noted that in the 1870s Be'emnat, a Mensaᶜ chief, came to Shaykh Muḥammad in Emberemi and converted there to Islam. Roden, *Le tribù dei Mensa*, 115.

36. Pollera suggested that one of the factors in ᶜAd Shaykh success was their association with "Ottoman prestige." Pollera, *Le popolazioni*, 200.

37. Ibrāhīm al-Mukhtār, *al-Jāmiʿ,* 65.

38. Wylde, *'83 to '87 in the Soudan,* 61. See also Salvadei, "Massaua," 1833.

39. Munzinger, *Studi,* 125–26.

40. Blanc, *A Narrative of Captivity,* 71–72.

41. Sapeto, *Viaggio e missione,* II, 156–57.

42. On Muḥammad ʿUthmān al-Mīrghanī and his writings see Hunwick and O'Fahey, *Arabic Literature of Africa* (hereafter *ALA*),1:187–98, 208–209. For a short and outdated treatment of the Khatmiyya in Eritrea see Trimingham, *Islam in Ethiopia,* 244–45. On Muḥammad ʿUthmān's travels in the Sudan see Karrar, *The Sufi Brotherhoods,* 57–64; For the Eritrean region see O'Fahey, "Sudanese (and Some Other) Sources for Eritrean History," 135–37; ACS, *MAI,* Governo dell'Eritrea, b. 1066, Allegato no. 9, Liberati, Note sul commissariato, 69–70; al-Rubāṭābī, *al-Ibāna al-Nūriyya fī sha'n ṣāḥib al-ṭarīqa al-Khatmiyya,* 66ff. See also Miran, "Muḥammad ʿUthmān al-Mīrghanī," 1060–61.

43. Voll, "A History of the Khatmiyyah Tariqa in the Sudan," 178–81.

44. O'Fahey and Radtke, "Neo-Sufism," 79.

45. Vikør, "Sufi Brotherhoods in Africa," 463.

46. According to Voll *baraka* was hereditary in the Mīrghanī family. Voll, "A History of the Khatmiyyah Tariqa,"158.

47. Ibid., 189–90.

48. Karrar, *The Sufi Brotherhoods,* 76.

49. On the ambiguous Khatmi-Egyptian relationship, see O'Fahey and Radtke, "Neo-Sufism," 82–83.

50. Voll, "A History of the Khatmiyyah Tariqa," 224–25.

51. Trimingham, *Islam in Ethiopia,* 245.

52. On Hāshim al-Mīrghanī see *ALA* 1:208–209; Trimingham, *Islam in Ethiopia,* 245, 252; Hofheinz, "Sons of a Hidden Imam," 25.

53. The sources are: ASDMAE, *Archivio storico del Ministero dell'Africa italiana,* (hereafter *ASMAI*), Pos 3 / 4, fasc 23, "Copia della lettera dello scek Saied Mohamed Hascem El Morgani a S. M. il Re d'Italia, d'Africa e dell'Eritrea Vittorio Emanuele III," Massaua, 7 Shaʿbān 1318 / 29 November 1900; ACS, *MAI,* b.1066, Allegato no. 9, Liberati, "Note sul commissariato," 72–73. Puglisi, whose sources are not entirely reliable, noted that Hāshim's daughters, Maryam and ʿAlawiyya, were both born in Algheden (Sabderat) in 1862 and 1863 respectively, reinforcing the argument that Hāshim did not settle in Massawa in 1860. Puglisi, *Chi è? dell'Eritrea,* 213; also ASDMAE, *ASMAI,* Pos 3 / 4, fasc 23, Genè to Minister of Foreign Affairs, 28 December 1886. On Muḥammad ʿUthmān Tājj al-Sir see *ALA,* 1:201.

54. In 1875 Shaykh Aḥmad b. ʿUmar Kūrī (d. 1924), father of the Eritrean Grand Muftī Ibrāhīm al-Mukhtār and head of the Saho-speaking holy Faqīh Ḥarak clan (of the Minifire), had met Muḥammad ʿUthmān Tājj al-Sirr—a meeting that had profoundly marked him. In one of his unpublished manuscripts Ibrāhīm al-Mukhtār noted that Muḥammad ʿUthmān Tājj al-Sirr came to Massawa in 1876. The Italian documents note the extent to which, upon his arrival in Massawa in 1885, he was venerated and respected by the local population, leaving a strong impression that he was already known and influential in the region. In 1889, from his seat in Sawākin, Muḥammad ʿUthmān Tājj al-Sirr negotiated his return to Massawa with the Italian authorities. In this exchange of messages he remarked that he had family among the Habab and that he considered Massawa his "homeland" (It. *patria*). Eventually, the plan for his transferal did not materialize. Miran, "Grand Mufti," 36; Ibrāhīm al-Mukhtār, *al-Bidāya fī ta'rīkh Iritrīyā,* 166. Odorizzi seemed to have confused the names of members of the family. In one place he states that "Muhammad Osman El Morgani" came to Massawa in 1860 and remained there when the town passed over to

the Egyptians in 1865. Odorizzi, *Note storiche sulla religione mussulmana,* 20; ASDMAE, *ASMAI,* Pos 3 / 4, fasc 23, serie politica no. 184, From Genè to Minister of Foreign Affairs, Massaua, 21 June 1886; ASDMAE, *ASMAI,* Pos. 3 / 4, fasc 23, From Baldissera to Ministro della Guerra (Roma), Massaua, 13 June 1889.

55. One part of a neighborhood, the southern part of ᶜEdaga Beᶜray, was known as "Khatmiyya" (or "Khutmiyya") shortly after its establishment in the 1890s, and is known by that name to this very day. Odorizzi, *Il commissariato,* 121.

56. One example was Sayyid ᶜUthmān Abū Shaᶜrayn, a *sharīf* from Massawa with a strong power base in Hetumlo, where he actually resided. A second *khalīfa* was ᶜUthmān Shimo from Hetumlo and originally from the Saho-speaking Taroᶜa group. A third was Khalīfa Ibrāhīm Shalāl, who represented the most prominent Bayt Shaykh Maḥmūd family in Hetumlo and had a mosque there. Another *khalīfa* was Muḥammad ᶜEgel from the Aflanda group, which saw many of its members migrate to the Massawa mainland. A last appointment was that of a certain al-Tom Makkī, a Sudanese identified in the Italian document as originally from the "tribe of Shaghi" [*sic*]; ASDMAE, *AE,* 43, Nr. 3277 di protocolo. From Dante Odorizzi (Commissario Regionale of Massawa) to the governor (Affari Civili) in Asmara. Massawa, 24 August 1910. For Shalāl see also Capomazza, *Usanze islamiche hanafite,* 35.

57. For the ramifications of this process on nationalist politics since the 1940s see Pool, *From Guerrillas to Government,* 20–24, 44–49.

58. On the Marya and Islam see *Trevaskis Papers,* Box 1, File 2: "The Tribes and Peoples of Northern Eritrea. A Survey of the Keren Division," 19; Trimingham, *Islam in Ethiopia,* 167–68 and Guérinot, "L'islam et l'Abyssinie," 53–57.

59. For the relationship between Italian colonial authorities and *ṭuruq* in the Somali region see Battera, "Le confraternite islamiche somale."

60. Melli, *La Colonia Eritrea dalle sue origini fino al 1° marzo 1899.*

61. The *mahdi* is the "Awaited One." A divinely guided leader who is supposed to come some time in the future to restore the original purity of the Islamic faith and God's rule on earth. For the best treatment of the Mahdiyya in the Sudan see Holt, *The Mahdist State in the Sudan 1881–1898.*

62. For the tortuous political, diplomatic, and military struggles in the region in the 1880s involving Ethiopians, Egyptians, Sudanese Mahdists, and Italians, see Gabre-Sellassie, *Yohannes IV of Ethiopia;* Rubenson, *Survival of Ethiopian Independence;* and Erlich, *Ras Alula and the Scramble for Africa.* The main Abyssinian (Tigrayan) figure in this context was Ras Alula Engeda (ca. 1847–97), who was Emperor Yohannes IV's (r. 1872–89) military commander in northern Abyssinia. For references to Alula's collisions with the Tigre- and Saho-speaking groups see Erlich, *Ras Alula,* 35, 51–54, 58–64, 71–72, 85, 90–94, 100, 112, and more. In general, the Beni ᶜAmer maintained an anti-Mahdist position throughout the period, while segments of the Habab and the ᶜAd Temaryam strongly supported the Mahdist cause and cooperated with ᶜUthmān Diqna's envoys in the region.

63. Erlich, *Ras Alula and the Scramble for Africa,* 54–55.

64. ASDMAE, *AE,* Pacco 16, "Proclama agli abitanti di Massaua," by Rear Admiral Caimi, 5 February 1885.

65. Marongiu-Buonaiuti, *Politica e religioni nel colonialismo italiano,* 41–45, 103–107, and interview with Ḥasan Ibrāhīm Muḥammad Sālim, Massawa, 20 March 2000. For a study of the complex relationship between French colonial authority and Muslim Sufi leaders in West Africa, see Robinson, *Paths of Accommodation.*

66. See such explicit comments in Capomazza, *Usanze islamiche hanafite,* 9.

67. In this process surveillance and information gathering was part and parcel of colonial practices. The authorities collected detailed genealogies and biographical notices

on all groups in the colony. See for example ACS, *Carte F. Martini,* box 8, "Biografie dei capi indigeni della colonia Eritrea," (Asmara 1903). See also Irma Taddia, "Constructing Colonial Power and Political Collaboration in Italian Eritrea."

68. Talhami, *Suakin and Massawa,* 234–35.

69. One British report stated that the principal chief of the Habab, Shaykh ʿUmar b. Muḥammad, had claimed to have joined the Mahdist holy war. Ibid., 187–88. An Italian report from the 1920s remarked how the ʿAd Shaykh had secretly allied with the Mahdists (to fight the Khatmiyya) through a certain Shaykh Ḥājj Yaʿqūb Muḥammad ʿAlī who occupied an eminent position with the forces of ʿUthmān Diqna, *amīr* of the Hadendoa. ACS, *MAI,* b. 1066, Allegato no. 9, Liberati, "Note sul commissariato," 55.

70. The exact balance of power between the *muftī* and Sayyid Hāshim, and their relationship vis-à-vis the authorities, awaits further scrutiny. For public purposes such as the New Year reception it was the *muftī* who took the role of representative of the Muslim community. But on the other hand Sayyid Hāshim's influence across the wider area put him in a rather higher and more important position in the eyes of colonial officials. One letter from General Genè to the Italian Foreign Minister in late 1886 explicitly opens by stating that "Hāshim al-Mīrghanī is not the religious chief of the Muslim community of Massawa but since he is a descendant of the Prophet, he is venerated by the Muslims here who give him gifts." Furthermore, at some point Sayyid Hāshim had appointed Muftī ʿAbd Allāh Sirāj Abū ʿIlāmā as *khalīfat al-khulafāʾ,* the highest-ranking Khatmi representative in Massawa. Italian colonial material from 1910 suggests that the representative of the Mīrghanī family in Eritrea began at some stage in the early colonial period to appoint as *khalīfat al-khulafāʾ* whoever was appointed by the colonial government as *muftī,* or in the absence of this position, *qāḍī* of Massawa. ASDMAE, *ASMAI,* Pos. 3 / 4 fasc. 23, Genè to Minister of Foreign Affairs, Massaua, 28 December 1886. On the *muftī*'s delivery of the 1887 New Year speech see Porro, "Notizie da Massaua," 52, and the full Arabic text in ASDMAE, *ASMAI,* 34 / 1 fasc. 3. On Muftī ʿAbd Allāh Sirāj's appointment as *khalīfat al-khulafāʾ* of the Khatmiyya see ASDMAE, *AE,* 43, Commissario Regionale di Massaua to Governatore, Massaua, 24 August 1910.

71. On the early contacts between the Khatmī leader in Hetumlo and the colonial authorities see especially ASDMAE, *ASMAI,* pos. 3 / 4, fasc. 23, "Famiglia Morgani," Genè to Ministro Aff. Esteri, (Massaua, 21 January 1886 and 28 December 1886) and Baldissera to Ministro della Guerra (Massaua, 13 June 1889); ASDMAE, *AE,* Pacco 43, Ministro Aff. Esteri, Robilant to Genè (Rome, 6 December 1886). Martini wrote in his diary that Sayyid Hāshim was half "imbeciled" since his wife and sisters were raped by the Dervishes. Martini, *Il diario eritreo,* 1:30 (Massaua, 22 January 1898).

72. See correspondence and reports during 1898 in ACS, *Carte F. Martini,* s. 16, fasc. 54–55 and ASDMAE, *ASMAI,* Pos 3 / 4, fasc 23, Martini to Ministro Affari Esteri, Asmara, 3 May 1901. See also Martini, *Il diario eritreo,* 1:43–45 (Massaua, 2–3 February 1898). See also Martini, *Il diario eritreo,* 1:52 (7 February 1898).

73. Martini, *Il diario eritreo,* 1:63 (Keren, 20 May 1898).

74. See correspondence 1902–1903 in ACS, *Carte F. Martini,* b. 16, fasc, 54–55, "Morgani." See also Martini, *Il diario eritreo,* 2:15 (4 June 1902).

75. The dates are based on Puglisi, *Chi è? dell'Eritrea,* 213.

76. ASDMAE, *AE,* 43, (Il direttore ?) to the Commissario regionale di Massaua, Asmara, 28 December 1902 ("Oggetto: Sidi Giafer el Morgani'". For Sayyid Jaʿfar's agreement to transfer to Keren see ASDMAE, *AE,* 43, Salvadei to Governor in Asmara (Massaua, 8 January 1903).

77. Romandini, "Politica musulmana in Eritrea durante il governorato Martini," 127–31, and Atti Parlamentari, Legislazione XXIII-sessione 1909–13, Camera dei Deputati, *Alle-*

gati alla Relazione sulla Colonia Eritrea, 32–33. The *ḥawliyya* that was until then performed at the mosque of Jaᶜfar al-Ṣadīq b. Muḥammad ᶜUthmān al-Mīrghanī (1822/23–1860/61) in Emkullo was now combined with that commemorating Sayyid Hāshim al-Mīrghanī on 2 Jumāda II, attracting followers from the wider region. A *ḥawliyya* (Ar.) is a commemorative ceremony in which the tour of the *qubba,* the chanting of *mawlids,* and usually a *dhikr* are performed. On Jaᶜfar al-Ṣadīq b. Muḥammad ᶜUthmān al-Mīrghanī (1822/23–1860/61), see *ALA,* 1:207. ASDMAE, *AE,* 43, Dante Odorizzi (Massaua) a Regente del Governo (Asmara), 3 November 1910 ("circa la festa del Holl di Morghani"). On the *qubba* see Ibrāhīm al-Mukhtār, *al-Jāmiᶜ,* 65.

78. Atti Parlamentari, Legislazione XXIII-sessione 1909–13, Camera dei Deputati, *Allegati alla Relazione sulla Colonia Eritrea,* 33. See also ACS, *MAI,* b. 1066, Allegato no. 9, Liberati, "Note sul commissariato," 75–77.

79. Martini, *Il diario eritreo,* 3:63 (25 July 1902). Martini was preoccupied by the potentially dangerous influence of the ᶜAd Shaykh on the Habab. See ibid., 63–64 (26 July 1902). Colonial officials went as far as discrediting the religious legitimacy and genealogical authenticity of the ᶜAd Shaykh while giving full credence to that of the Khatmiyya: "The ᶜAd Shaykh came from the Hijaz and claim to be linked to the Prophet. But even though this ancestry has not been proven the ᶜAd Shaykh dare to boast it in front of authentic Meccan sharifs (such as the Morgani), whose Arab origins have been proved beyond any doubt. It is more probable that they are Sahos who have adopted the descent of some Arab element who had migrated from Mecca and settled among them with the aim of spreading religious propaganda." ACS, *MAI,* b. 1066, Allegato no. 9, Liberati, "Note sul commissariato,"' 53.

80. ACS, *MAI,* b. 1066, Allegato no. 9, Liberati, "Note sul commissariato," 53.

81. Ibid., 54, 75–77. *Atti parlamentari,* 33–34.

82. Anti–ᶜAd Shaykh discourses were pervasive in colonial literature throughout the period of Italian rule in Eritrea. Pollera's handbook on the populations of Eritrea reproduces the same arguments (and tone) typical of the beginning of the century. Pollera, *Le popolazioni,* 204–209 and 286–87.

83. ACS, *MAI,* b. 1066, Allegato no. 9, Liberati, "Note sul commissariato," 55.

84. Ibid., 26–27, 48.

85. Gardet, *L'islam,* 274–76, and *La cité musulmane,* part 3. On the *umma* see also Voll, *Islam,* 2–12; Martin, *Islamic Studies,* 77ff, and Denny, "Umma."

86. Pouwels, *Horn and Crescent,* 64–65.

87. On the edge of the esplanade there is a *minbār* (Ar., pulpit) and a *miḥrāb* (Ar., prayer niche) in stone. The name of the site is also sometimes pronounced "Midri" or "Mudur." Some local traditions link it with the Ethiopic root *m d r,* "signifying "land." Others say "midri" is a deformation of a word from the Arabic (perhaps *mudun*) with the root *m d n,* signifying "town" or "urban settlement." Interview with Muḥammad Ṣāliḥ Aḥmad Afandī, Massawa, 13 March 2000. In his official correspondence Ibrāhīm al-Mukhtār noted that both ᶜĪd al-Fiṭr and ᶜĪd al-Aḍḥā celebrations were performed in Ras Medr in commemoration of the Prophet's companions' landing at the site. See *al-Jāmiᶜ,* 85–87.

88. Insoll, *The Archaeology of Islam,* 183–84.

89. Odorizzi, *Note storiche sulla religione mussulmana,* 35–36, and interview with ᶜAbd al-Bāqī Muḥammad ᶜAbdu ᶜAbbāsī, Massawa, 24 June 2006.

90. Odorizzi, *Il commissariato,* 108. Interview with ᶜAbd al-Bāqī Muḥammad ᶜAbdu ᶜAbbāsī, Massawa, 24 June 2006. Knysh, "The Cult of Saints and Religious Reformism in Hadhramaut," 209. One source based on Egyptian military correspondence from the 1860s–'70s also noted that Shaykh Saᶜīd Island served as a cemetery. Al-Jamal, *Siyāsat Miṣr fī al-baḥr al-aḥmar,* 79. Some sources have referred to the non-ᶜAlawī Shaykh Saᶜīd as hav-

ing been introduced to Sufism in Hadramawt very early on. See Freitag, *Indian Ocean Migrants and State Formation in Hadhramaut,* 91.

91. Ibrāhīm al-Mukhtār, *al-Jāmiʿ,* 62–63. It is not clear which plate Ibrāhīm al-Mukhtār is transcribing. perhaps the two stone plates located immediately before the entrance to the mausoleum. Cresti, "Alcune note storiche su Massaua," 418–19 and table 3. A second text drawing on the same research is Cresti, "La mosquée du Sayh Hammali à Massaoua," 1:303–15.

92. Bombaci, "Il viaggio in Abissinia," 263. In his two articles Cresti surveys 19th- and 20th-century literary and iconographic sources pertaining to the religious complex in question.

93. Ibrāhīm al-Mukhtār, *al-Jāmiʿ,* 63.

94. See a detailed plan of the religious complex in Cresti, "Alcune note storiche," 416. According to oral data a special visitation and celebration day at the tomb took place in the past. Visit to the Shaykh Ḥammāl religious complex with ʿUmar Wahhāb al-Bārrī on ʿĪd al-Aḍḥā day, 16 March 2000.

95. Odorizzi, *Il commissariato,* 119. He dates the foundation of the tomb in AD 1550.

96. Ibrāhīm al-Mukhtār, *al-Jāmiʿ,* 63. The tomb is commonly known as Shaykh Darwīsh (but also ʿShaykh Darbūsh). Abū Bakr, *Taʾrīkh Iritrīyā,* 291. Odorizzi wrote that Shaykh Darwīsh was originally from Mecca; *Il commissariato,* 120. Another source identifies a Sayyid Barakāt family, who were originally members of the Meccan *ashrāf.* It is also interesting to note the existence of a Shaykh Darwīsh shrine on the island of Nukhra. Ibrāhīm al-Mukhtār, *al-Jāmiʿ,* 38.

97. Ibrāhīm al-Mukhtār Aḥmad ʿUmar, *al-Jāmiʿ,* 62–63. Interview with Ṣādiq Muḥsin al-Ṣāfī and ʿUsmān Ḥājjī Maḥmūd, Massawa, 14 March 2000, and interview with Muḥammad Aḥmad ʿUmar Aḥmad ʿAbbāsī, Massawa, 15 May 2000. The tomb believed to be that of Najāshī Aṣḥama is located in Negāsh in northern Ethiopia. Jaʿfar al-Ṭayyār was Afar (Ankala). Abū Bakr, *Taʾrīkh Iritrīyā,* 360.

98. Pollera, *Le popolazioni indigene dell'Eritrea,* 150.

99. Muḥammad ʿUthmān lived in Hetumlo and had much cattle in Saati, Sabarguma, and Ghinda and among the ʿAd Temaryam. Perini, *Di qua dal Marèb,* 287; Odorizzi, *Il commissariato,* 169–70.

100. See more on pilgrimage sites in Eritrea dedicated to Muslim holy men in "Maqāmāt al-awliyāʾ fī Iritrīyā wa-ḥawliyātihum al-sanawiyya." Another "small" Mīrghanī *ziyāra* commemorated the *sharīfa* ʿAlawiyya (b. 1892/93? d. 1940?) on 22 Shawwāl. For insights about pilgrimage and identity see relevant parts in Anderson, *Imagined Communities.* Insoll, *The Archaeology of Islam,* 114. For Muslim pilgrimages in northeast Africa see Scott Reese, "*Ziyāra* [in the Horn of Africa]."

101. Examples include members of the Afandī family (Qādiriyya to Khatmiyya); Ṣāfī (Qādiriyya to Khatmiyya to Aḥmadiyya); ʿAbbāsī (Qādiriyya to Shādhiliyya) and others.

102. As other religious communities, Muslim communities may be thought of as *imagined,* following Benedict Anderson's term; *Imagined Communities,* 14–16.

103. Traversi, "Usi e costumi africani di Massaua," 378.

104. For such *zāwiyas* in the Red Sea region see Greenlaw, *The Coral Buildings of Suakin,* 62ff. Bombaci, "Il viaggio in Abissinia," 259–75.

105. Lejean, *Voyage aux Deux Nils,* 166. On mosques in Massawa in that period see also Issel, *Viaggio nel Mar Rosso,* 63, and Blanc, *A Narrative of Captivity in Abyssinia,* 59. Blanc noted that a "big mosque" was being rebuilt in 1864–65. This would refer to either the Ḥanafī or the Shāfiʿī mosque.

106. Pennazzi, "Massauah (Mar Rosso)," 326; Di Robilant, "Presidi e domini dell'Italia nel Mar Rosso," 16.

107. Odorizzi, *Il commissariato*, 119–20, 160–61, 168–70. For a comprehensive list of mosques with additional information mostly drawn from Odorizzi and Ibrāhīm al-Mukhtār see Miran, "Facing the Land," appendix 18, 366–68.

108. A building drive following the Ottoman takeover in the early sixteenth century is similarly noted in Sawākin; Bloss, "The Story of Suakin," (1936) 289.

109. Odorizzi, *Il commissariato*, 119–20.

110. The Afar on the Red Sea coasts follow the Shāfiʿī *madhhab*.

111. On the distribution of the *madhhāhib* in the Eritrean region see Trimingham, *Islam in Ethiopia*, 231–33 and Odorizzi, *Note storiche sulla religione mussulmana*, 29. See a discussion on the early distribution of the legal schools in Gori, "Lo Yemen e l'islam in Africa orientale," 203–209.

112. Others said it was built by Shaykh Adam b. Muḥammad Barkūy, whose father, Muḥammad (d. 981/1573), was a Turkish religious scholar and author of many books, among which was the *Kitāb al-muḥammadiyya bi-bayān al-ṣīra al-Aḥmadiyya*. Shaykh Adam had stores and shops and he built the Ḥanafī mosque as a second floor on top of his shops. Following his passing the shops were divided among his inheritors and sold; the mosque was subsequently moved to the place where it currently stands. Ibrāhīm al-Mukhtār, *al-Rāwiya*, 53–57. The location of the old Ḥanafī mosque is shown in the map of Massawa in this book. It was located in the northern part of the island and slightly west of the Shāfiʿī mosque.

113. Ibid.

114. As noted above, the Shaykh Ḥammāli tomb was renovated in 1878 under the Egyptians. See also al-Jamal, *al-Wathāʾiq al-taʾrīkhiyya*, 139 (document no. 59). Ḥasan Rifʿat, Massawa's first Egyptian governor, requested funds to build a religious school in Massawa that would serve students from Ethiopia, who usually sought further religious education in the Hijaz and Yemen. Douin, *Histoire du règne*, vol. 3, part 1, 324.

115. Marongiu-Buonaiuti, *Politica e religioni nel colonialismo italiano*, 103.

116. Interview with Nāfiʿ ʿAlī Khaydar, Hergigo, 7 March 2000.

117. See Bang, *Sufis and Scholars of the Sea*, 23.

118. Ibrāhīm al-Mukhtār, *al-Jāmiʿ*, 51. He co-chaired the *waqf* committee with the Egyptian merchant Sayyid Ḥasan b. Mūsā al-ʿAqqād.

119. Ibrāhīm al-Mukhtār, *al-Jāmiʿ*, 114. Salvadei too noted the departure of Bā Junayd and Bā Zarʿa "back to their countries" in the early twentieth century. Salvadei, "Massaua," 1817. For example, in the 1910s ʿAbd al-Raḥmān Bā Junayd of Jiddah was a merchant and a shipper running arms-cargoes. Hogarth, *Hejaz before World War I*, 58.

120. In 1898 a note attesting to this, and signed by the *muftī*, was added to all acts recording ʿAbd Allāh Bā Junayd's real estate acquisitions. See MICR 16. For details on the incident see Ibrāhīm al-Mukhtār, *al-Jāmiʿ*, 114.

121. Second Lieutenant Giuseppe Brengola, *Pianta di Massaua (1:2000), 24 Settembre 1885*, Istituto geografico militare. Nowadays the Mīrghanī mosque has no minaret.

122. Sayyid Jaʿfar al-Nātī was from the Tsaora (Almada) group. He died in 1965 and was replaced in his function as responsible for the Aḥmadiyya in the area by Shaykh Ṣāliḥ Muḥammad ʿAlī Abū Bakr (from Barka). Interview with Muḥammad Abū Bakr al-Nātī, Massawa, 16 May 2000; ʿAbd al-Bāqī Muḥammad ʿAbdu ʿAbbāsī, Massawa, 24 June 2006, and Muḥammad Ṣāliḥ Aḥmad Afandī, personal communication, 13 November 2006.

123. In Massawa Island examples include the Makkaʿalī, Adūbāsh (ʿAdūlāy), Masāwa, and Dhahab li-Abū ʿIlāmā mosques—the latter two being families of notable *qāḍīs*. There

is also a Sayyid Masāwa mosque in Hetumlo, revealing a certain pattern of duplication in mosque names throughout the elements of the conurbation.

124. A door lintel is a horizontal support made of wood (or stone) across the top of a door. Stone door-hoods are very common in Massawa. They are called *ʿaqd mawshah* in Arabic. On building techniques and designs see Greenlaw, *The Coral Buildings of Suakin,* 94–5.

125. Insoll, *The Archaeology of Islam,* 139–40. See also Blair, *Islamic Inscriptions.*

126. Cerbella, *Aspetti etnografici della casa in Etiopia.* The book reproduces, with some additional editing, the following Cerbella articles: "Il fascino e l'attrattività di Massaua alla luce di un ricordo d'arte"; "Il Waldebit dei notabili eritrei, e qualche cenno ancora sulle iscrizioni delle abitazioni musulmane in Eritrea"; Cerbella, "La diffusione in Eritrea della casa musulmana tipica."

127. Cerbella, *Aspetti etnografici,* 5–16. See photographs of inscriptions in other parts of the same book.

128. *"Sharīʿa ab bahari, seriʿat ab Gwonder."* A saying in Tigrinya quoted in Habib, "History of Massawa," 46.

129. This seems to have been also the case in Sawākin—in many ways Massawa's sister town in that period. See a detailed chapter on the Islamic court of Sawākin in Ḍirār, *Taʾrīkh Sawākin wa al-baḥr al-aḥmar,* 131–46.

130. Ibrāhīm al-Mukhtār, *al-Jāmiʿ,* 73.

131. As noted in a previous chapter, one unfounded, yet revealing, tradition collected in the early 1970s attributed the town's name, "Massawa," to a well-known *qāḍī,* Sayyid Muḥammad Masāwa b. Aḥmad al-ʿAlawī, who was in office in the middle of the nineteenth century. His reputation as a judge was so great throughout the region that people coming to see him said "they had gone to Masawa," gradually interchanging it with the town's name.

132. Halil Inalcik, *"Maḥkama."* On the notion of *"qāḍī*-justice" see also Agmon, *Family and Court,* 169.

133. See a thought-provoking study on the role of the *qāḍī*s court in preserving the distinct character of the Swahili of Mombasa. Swartz, "Religious Courts, Community, and Ethnicity," 29–41.

134. Inalcik, *"Maḥkama."*

135. *Qāḍī* ʿUthmān Ḥasan (from Hergigo and a Ḥanafī) is very well remembered for his strong personality and his sense of leadership during his period in office in the Italian era. He was also a *khalīfa* of the Khatmiyya *ṭarīqa.* In June 1943 Muftī Ibrāhīm al-Mukhtār had formally requested *qāḍī* ʿUthmān Ḥasan to collect any piece of information he could find about Massawa's past *qāḍī*s. Following his investigating among the town notables and sifting through old court registers, *qāḍī* ʿUthmān sent Muftī Ibrāhīm a list, augmented and completed by the *muftī.* See Ibrāhīm al-Mukhtār, *al-Jāmiʿ,* 75–76.

136. According to one source, the origins of the Badīr family is Baghdad, from the descent of Shaykh ʿAbd al-Qādir al-Jīlānī (d. 1166), founder of the Qādiriyya Sufi order. Muḥammad ʿUthmān Abū Bakr, *Taʾrīkh Iritrīyā,* 309.

137. Examples of prominent ʿAbbāsīs include Shaykh Muḥammad ʿAbd Allāh Aḥmad ʿAbbāsī (d. 1899), who was a successful merchant and the second head of the *waqf* committee in Massawa in the late nineteenth century. Still in the early twenty-first century the *waqf* council of the town of Massawa was headed by a member of the ʿAbbāsī family and administered by two ʿAbbāsīs.

138. A similar trend is also noted since the mid-nineteenth century in Ottoman areas such as Palestine. See Agmon, *Family and Court,* 64–65.

139. Mellana, *L'Italia in Africa,* 288. Also ASDMAE, *ASMAI,* 12 / 1, fasc. 1.

140. Schacht, *"Maḥkama."* See more on Egyptian judicial reform in the last quarter

of the nineteenth century in N. J. Brown, *The Rule of Law in the Arab World,* 23–40. See also Hunter, *Egypt under the Khedives,* 44–45.

141. Mellana, *L'Italia in Africa,* 288–90.

142. Due to the interruption of communications between Massawa, Kassala, and Khartoum during the Mahdist revolt, the court of appeal for Massawa's tribunal was designated as the Supreme Court of Appeal in Cairo.

143. Useful sources providing clues about recording procedures, aspects of court bureaucracy, and *qāḍīs* in the Islamic court of Massawa from the 1860s through the 1880s are the registers of the *maḥkama.* In the 1940s, the first Grand Muftī of Eritrea, Shaykh Ibrāhīm al-Mukhtār (1909–69), made great efforts to uncover and preserve the religious, legal, and cultural heritage of Eritrean Muslims. His investigations led him to the court in Massawa, where he had discovered one hundred and two bound volumes of court registers, of which sixty-three corresponded to the Egyptian era (1865–85), and the rest to the Italian period (ca. 1885/90 to 1941). Unfortunately, the Ethiopian army destroyed most registers in the 1950s. While visiting the court in 1959 Ibrāhīm al-Mukhtār was able to salvage only about 30 volumes from the Egyptian era, which he subsequently transferred to Asmara. Ibrāhīm al-Mukhtār, *al-Jāmiᶜ,* 80–84.

144. ASDMAE, *AE,* Pacco 349 fascicolo 37. "Foglietto di servizio dello Scech ᶜAbd Allah Seraj ben Ali Abū Alama," Massaua, December 1900. In 1898 the Italians awarded him the honorific title *Cavaliere della Corona d'Italia.*

145. ASDMAE, *AE,* Pacco 16, "Proclama agli abitanti di Massaua," by Rear Admiral Caimi, 5 February 1885. Marongiu-Buonaiuti, *Politica e religioni nel colonialismo italiano,* 40–41.

146. Marongiu-Buonaiuti, *Politica e religioni nel colonialismo italiano,* 43.

147. Ibid., 43–44. A vivid and somewhat anecdotal description of a court session held at the beginning of 1888 is provided in Mantegazza, *Da Massaua a Saati,* 239–40.

148. Folchi, "Commissariato Regionale di Massaua," 11 (149–50), 370 (287), 381 (295).

149. Marongiu-Buonaiuti, *Politica e religioni nel colonialismo italiano,* 103.

150. Tribunale Civile e Penale di Massaua, *Relazione statistica deo lavori compiuti nell'anno 1892 dal Tribunale Civile e Penale di Massaua (Dal Pres. Avv. Luigi Scotti),* Massaua, 1893, 3 (in ASDMAE, *AE,* 156).

151. Matteucci, *In Abissinia,* 38–39.

152. Negri, *Massaua e dintorni,* 12–13.

153. Porro, "Notizie da Massaua," 101–102.

154. Vigoni, *Abissinia,* 24–5. Other elaborate descriptions include Pascale, *Massaua,* 78–80 and Traversi, "Usi e costumi africani di Massaua," 367–9, 372–4.

155. There is an extensive literature on zar. See Natvig, "Oromos, Slaves, and Zar Spirits," 669–89; Boddy, *Wombs and Alien Spirits;* Lewis, al-Safi, and Hurreiz, *Women's Medicine.* See also Ehud Toledano, *As If Silent and Absent,* chapter 5. See also Alpers, "Dance and Society in Nineteenth Century Mogadishu," 127–44.

156. In Toledano, *As if Silent,* 217–18. Such resemblances were also found in other settings such as Iran and northern Africa. One of the photographs (I assume from the 1920s) is captioned: "Arab 'fantasia' in the house of the Sharīfa." On the Sharīfa, see Caniglia, *La Sceriffa di Massaua.*

157. Rassam, *Narrative of the British Mission,* 16.

158. Interview with ᶜAbd al-Bāqī Muḥammad ᶜAbdu ᶜAbbāsī, Massawa, 24 June 2006. Hogarth, *Hejaz before World War I,* 63; Knysh, "The Cult of Saints," 212, 295; Serjeant, "Materials for South Arabian History," 593.

159. The mosque was destroyed and rebuilt by Aḥmad Afandī ᶜAbd Allāh Bey al-Ghūl in 1912. It was again destroyed by the earthquake of 1921.

160. Ibrāhīm al-Mukhtār, *al-Jāmiʿ*, 115–16.

161. The reference is to "Let there be one community (*umma*) of you, calling to good, and commanding right and forbidding wrong; those are the prosperers" (Qurʾān 3:104). See also Qurʾān 3:110 and Qurʾān 9:71.

162. Capomazza, *Usanze islamiche hanafite*, 34–37. Remarks on their role in funerary ceremonies: 69–74. Transcriptions are undoubtedly inaccurate. They follow Capomazza's Italianized transliteration.

163. Colonia Eritrea. *Giurisprudenza Coloniale.* (N. 23). Sentenza 18 maggio 1909 del Commissario Regionale di Massaua—*usanze rituali del Semhar*, (Asmara, 1909), 3–4.

164. Ibid., 5–6.

165. Ibid., 7.

166. Ibid., 7–8.

167. Ibid., 9.

168. Labanca, *In marcia verso Adua*, 186–87. With the institution of rigid racial laws in the fascist period (1920s and 1930s), such contradictions became even more significant. Thus, one of my informants, a respected elderly Massawan of *sādah* Hadrami origins, revealingly remarked: "Can you imagine, the fascists called *us* 'indigeni' [natives], *us*!!! And we couldn't even get into the Savoia Hotel!!!" The most interesting question raised by my informants' comments would be his notion of "us." Who are the "us" in this case? All Massawans? Elite/notable Massawans? Massawans of Arab origins? Interview with Sayyid Ṣādiq b. Muḥsin al-Ṣāfī, Massawa, 14 March 2000.

5. "Being Massawan"

1. Abbadie, *Douze ans de séjour dans la Haute-Éthiopie* (1980), 1:9.

2. Munzinger, *Studi*, 92, and "Les contrées limitrophes de l'Habesch," 28–29.

3. Matteucci, *In Abissinia*, 38.

4. Capomazza, *Usanze islamiche hanafite di Massaua e dintorni*, 9.

5. On the originality of Massawa's social structure see Abū Bakr, *Taʾrīkh Iritrīyā*, 293. The author also uses the term *usra* to designate family.

6. Reese, "Patricians of the Benaadir," 11.

7. Barth, "Introduction," 15.

8. For the Swahili coast see the judicious analysis of Glassman in part 2 of *Feasts and Riot* (especially 117–20, introducing the relevant section).

9. Folchi, "Commissariato Regionale di Massaua," 167 (207).

10. I have also seen some of these terms and their variants in articles from the late 1940s (under the British Military Administration) in *Ṣawṭ al-Rābiṭa al-Islāmiyya al-Iritriyya.*

11. This sense of solidarity exists also on a practical level. For example Sayyid Ṣādiq b. Muḥsin al-Ṣāfī (b. 1921), who curently resides in Massawa, is the *wakīl* (Ar., legal representative) in matters of real estate to members of the Bā Ḥamdūn, Bā Zaḥam, ʿAdūlāy, Bā Ḥubayshī, Sardāl, and Nahārī families who have fled the country in the 1960s and 1970s as a result of Ethiopian oppression. Many of them reside in Jiddah, Saudi Arabia. Sayyid Ṣādiq collects the rent from their properties and administers them.

12. Interview with Sayyid Ibrāhīm Muḥammad Ibrāhīm al-Sayyid, Massawa, 26 April 2000.

13. Ibid. and al-Jamal, *Siyāsat Miṣr fī al-baḥr al-aḥmar*, 78; Blanc, *A Narrative of Captivity in Abyssinia*, 59. Interviews with Muḥammad Qaʿaṣ, Massawa, 10 April 2000, and ʿUsmān Ḥājjī Maḥmūd, Massawa, 28 April 2000.

14. Conversation with Fouad Makki, Asmara, 27 July 2001.

15. Interview with Muḥammad ʿAbdu Bakrī Ḥijjī, Massawa, 5 May 2000.

16. Muḥammad ʿUthmān Ḥasan Ḥayūtī (1901–96), perhaps Massawa's most prominent intellectual and activist in the twentieth century, was known to possess an exceptional knowledge of the town's family histories. Puglisi, *Chi è? dell'Eritrea,* 209.

17. Many interviewees talked about the importance of genealogies and family trees. Some have also kept family records pertaining to property and inheritance, especially the *ḥujjāj* (Ar., deeds, sing. *ḥujja*) issued to their ancestors by the *sharīʿa* court.

18. Extracted from family lists in Abū Bakr, *Taʾrīkh Iritrīyā,* and in Odorizzi, *Il commissariato.* Interview with ʿAbd Allāh Yūsuf Ṣāʾigh, Massawa, 5 and 6 May 2000.

19. This is also true today. Ḥāmid Gūlāy's article, with its revealing contradictory title, is a typical example: "We Are 'Non-Arabic-Speaking' Arabs." Posted on http://www.awate.com and dated May 1, 2001.

20. The following quote from Combes and Tamisier's account from the late 1830s exemplifies this type of judgemental characterization: "The astuteness of the Arabs, the notorious bad will of the Chohos (Sahos), the ridiculous pretentions of the Abyssinian Muslims, the savagery of the Gallas (Oromo) and the pride of the Turks, all combined together, constitute the character of the man of Massawa." Combes and Tamisier, *Voyage en Abyssinie,* 1:102. For similar characterizations see also Gatta, "Massaua e le regioni circostanti," 1885, 482.

21. Abbadie, *Douze ans de séjour dans la Haute-Éthiopie* (1980), 1:9; Munzinger, *Studi,* 94; Rassam, *Narrative of the British Mission,* 10; Blanc, *A Narrative of Captivity,* 67; Issel, *Viaggio nel Mar Rosso* (1885), 61; Salvadei, "Massaua," 1819. Describing Muftī ʿAbd Allāh Sirāj Abū ʿIlāmā's appearance, Ferdinando Martini noted that "except for the color of his skin, he looks like a Turk from an engraving." Martini, *Nell'Affrica italiana,* 19. For the East African coast, Jonathon Glassman has analyzed the political power of the Swahili urban patricians in terms of their conspicuous consumption serving to establish and maintain their position of supremacy. These rituals were constantly imitated, challenged, and struggled over by outsiders who aspired to citizenship; Glassman, *Feasts and Riot.*

22. Combes and Tamisier, *Voyage en Abyssinie,* 1:103. Al-Qunfudha is a port town located south of Jiddah and opposite Sawākin.

23. Pascale, *Massaua,* 54–56; Traversi, "Usi e costumi africani in Massaua," 5:372.

24. Munzinger, *Studi,* 114–28.

25. Talhami, *Suakin and Massawa,* 228.

26. Ibrāhīm al-Mukhtār, *al-Bidāya,* 144. See also the collection of Arabic manuscripts discovered in the Italian colonial archives and catalogued by Albrecht Hofheinz. See his "A Yemeni Library in Eritrea," 98–136, and Blumi, "The Consequences of Empire in the Balkans and the Red Sea," 474–80.

27. Some sources have noted how the "Tigre dialect of Massawa" incorporates much Arabic. See for example Conti Rossini, *Tradizioni,* 41.

28. The whole subject of nineteenth-century European racial designations is interesting, yet might be truly disorienting. In 1880s Durban, for example, Indian Gujarati Muslims were locally known as "Arabs." Markovits, "Indian Merchant Networks," 892.

29. Traversi, "Usi e costumi africani di Massaua," 365–82. The first two sentences of this article are also revealing of early constructions of race and identity: "The town of Massawa is inhabited by real Arabs, some from Jiddah. However, there are Somali families mixed with Arab blood and one encounters a variety of colors due to the presence of black Sudanese, and Abyssinians, and white Egyptians."

30. See the following photographic collection catalogue: Palma, *L'Africa nella collezione fotografica dell'IsIAO.* For example, pages 50, 84–85,102, 183, 324, and elsewhere.

31. Gatta, "Da Massaua a Cheren," 486.

32. Kenneth L. Brown, *People of Salé,* 6, 56, 60, 224. Cited in Eickelman, *The Middle East,* 119–20.

33. On Weber's "Patrician City" see Weber, *The City,* 121–56.

34. Hourani, "Ottoman Reform and the Politics of the Notables," 48. On the "politics of the notables" see also Toledano, "The Emergence of Ottoman-Local Elites." See also a snapshot of the debates around the "notables" in Ottoman historiography in Khoury, "The Ottoman Centre versus Provincial Power-Holders," 152–55.

35. Hourani, "Ottoman Reform," 48–49.

36. In the context of Ottoman North Africa, Julia Clancy-Smith differentiates between "elites" who "drew some, although not all, of their political authority from relationships with the state" and "religious notables" who "tapped deep into other sources—sharifian descent, special piety, erudition, charity. . . . They thus wielded sociospiritual and moral authority"; Clancy-Smith, *Rebel and Saint,* 269–270n4.

37. Meriwether, *The Kin Who Count,* 34.

38. One technical method in identifying individuals of a somewhat high, or notable, status is the use of personal seals in the records of the Islamic court. See for example Agmon, *Family and Court,* 86.

39. MICR 2/46a, 8/61c, 8/62c [1883]; 8/94d [1884]; 12/64b [1889].

40. Abū Bakr, *Taʾrīkh Iritrīyā,* 99.

41. MICR 9/27b (18 Shaʿbān 1296). In this land sale act, a *ḥujja* delivered by *qāḍī* ʿUmar Bādūrī in 1264/1847 was presented at the court as proof of ownership. See also Ibrāhīm al-Mukhtār, *al-Jāmiʿ,* 77.

42. MICR 14/2g, 14/2i [1866]; 16/59c [1870]; 16/72b [1871]; 9/35a, 9/47a, 9/48a, 9/49a [1880]; 8/31c, 8/42b, 8/45b, 8/49b [1883]; 8/89a, 8/97a, 8/102a [1884]; 12/4a, 12/6a [1886]; 12/42a [1888]; 12/65a, 12/66a [1889].

43. MICR 14/2e, 14/2f, [1866]; 16/5a [1867]; 14/7h, 16/24a, 16/24b [1868]; 16/62a [1870]; 8/21a, 8/33a [1882]; 8/59a [1883]; 8/65a [1884]; 8/114a, 10/25b, 10/26a, 10/27b [1885]; 10/37a [1886].

44. Odorizzi, *Il commissariato,* 135.

45. Much the same as several other families, the Kurdīs prospered during the Italian era. In 1901 Idrīs ʿUthmān Kurdī and his son Ḥasan Idrīs Kurdī (1884–1950), opened a commercial firm in Massawa dealing principally in marine products, coffee, and textiles. Ḥasan Idrīs was a prominent merchant who was also active in various political and religious matters. Puglisi, *Chi è? dell'Eritrea,* 162. One member of the family published in France a book on Eritrea and its history: Kurdi, *L'Erythrée.*

46. ASDMAE, *ASMAI,* 34 / 1 fasc. 2, Letter from the leading members of Hergigo to the Superior Commander of the Italian forces in the Red Sea, 10 June 1887.

47. *Nāẓir al-khuṭṭ* is a notable in charge of a subdivision of an administrative district; Hill, *A Biographical Dictionary of the Sudan,* xiii.

48. Odorizzi, *Il commissariato,* 142–50. Another figure who exemplified such a trajectory to some degree was Nāʾib Muḥammad ʿAbd al-Raḥīm (Bayt Ḥasan line, d. 1904), whose loyalty to the Italian authorities was more ambiguous than that of Idrīs Ḥasan. Suspected of collaborating with Ras Alula, he was tried and sent to imprisonment in Assab for a short period of time in 1887–88.

49. ASDMAE, *AE,* b. 178, "Notabili e capi indigeni dipendenti dal Commissariato Regionale di Massaua" (1902–3), entry: "Nāʾib Idris Hassan (Moncullo)," 11. Puglisi, *Chi è? dell'Eritrea,* 168–69.

50. Martini, *Il diario eritreo,* 2:85 (Massaua, 4 March 1900).

51. MICR 14/6e [1867]; 16/38b [1868]; 16/88b [1873]; 16/113a [1876]; 9/3b, 9/3d, 9/4a

[1877]; 9/30a [1879]; 9/46a [1880]; 8/3a [1881]; 8/32b [1882]; 8/50b [1883]; 10/10a [1885]; 12/70a, 12/71a [1889]. See an illustration of ʿAlī Yaḥyā's main residential home in Martini, *Nell'Affrica italiana,* 18.

52. ASDMAE, *AE,* b. 21, "Incartamento reelativo ai ricorsi Naharo [*sic*] e Aly Afandi Iahia, Annesso XI," 1886. Also ASDMAE, *AE,* b. 178, "Notabili e Capi indigeni dipendenti dal Commissariato Regionale di Massaua (1902–3)," Entry: "Ali Afandi Iehia," 6.

53. ASDMAE, *ASMAI,* Pos. 3 / 4, fasc. 23., No. 2031/95 del protocolo. Baldissera to War Minister, Massaua, 13 June 1889.

54. His son Aḥmad ʿAlī [1892–1962] was also a Khatmi *khalīfa.*

55. Interview with Muḥammad Ṣāliḥ Aḥmad Afandī, Massawa, 13 March 2000.

56. ASDMAE, *AE,* b. 43, From the Commissario di Massaua G. Salvadei to the Governor's office in Asmara. Oggetto: "Ali *Afandi* Yehia," 9 March 1903.

57. ASDMAE, *AE,* b. 43, From the Commissario di Massaua G. Salvadei to the Governor's office in Asmara. Oggetto: "Sidi Giafer Morgani," 8 January 1903.

58. Sayyid Ḥasan Aḥmad Ḥayūtī Sayyid (b. Massawa ca. 1850), son of a merchant, was employed by the Egyptian authorities as an envoy to Ras Alula in Asmara in 1884 to coordinate the liberation of Egyptians held in Kassala by the Mahdists in accordance with the Hewett accords. Puglisi, *Chi è? dell'Eritrea,* 163.

59. Interview with Sayyid Ibrāhīm Muḥammad Ibrāhīm al-Sayyid, Massawa, 26 April 2000. Interestingly, the family has no family name, something uncommon in the landscape of Massawa's elite stratum.

60. ASDMAE, *AE,* Pacco 349 fasc. 37, "Petition from 62 members of the Muslim community to the Commissario Regionale di Massaua" (12 Ramaḍān 1318 / 3 January 1901).

61. Abū Bakr, *Taʾrīkh Iritrīyā,* 307.

62. Between the 1860s and 1880s individuals from the following families were designated as Ḥājj: Ṭalūl, ʿAdūlāy, Madanī, Sarūr, Ḥabīb, Dankalī, Daʾūd, Ḥammūda, Minnī, Karrār, Mentāy, Ḥalīl, Manṣūr, Yāqūt, Ḥamdān.

63. MICR 8/8b, 8/66b [1881]. Odorizzi, *Il commissariato,* 169. Capomazza, *Usanze islamiche hanafite,* 35. The term in Arabic used in the records was *khalīfat al-sādah al-Mīrghaniyya.*

64. ASDMAE, *AE,* 43, Nr. 3277 di protocolo. From Dante Odorizzi (Commissario Regionale of Massawa) to the governor (Affari Civili) in Asmara. Massawa, 24 August 1910.

65. MICR 14/9b [1872]; 16/90a [1873]; 10/37b [1886].

66. Doumani, *Rediscovering Palestine,* 66.

67. Negri, *Massaua e dintorni,* 12.

68. Freitag, *Indian Ocean Migrants,* 44. Freitag noted that the Bā Zarʿa also ran business operations in Djibouti.

69. Le Guennec-Coppens, "Changing Patterns of Hadhrami migration," 161.

70. MICR 16/34a [1868]; 16/59c [1870]; 9/23a [1879]; 9/36a, 9/47a, 9/48a, 9/49a [1880]; 10/4b, 10/10c, 10/23a [1885]; 10/38a, 10/39a, 12/2a, 12/3a [1886]; 12/54a, 12/55a [1888]; 12/60a, 12/67a [1889].

71. MICR 9/48a [al-Nātī family]; 9/49a [al-Nātī family]; 10/4b [heirs of Ḥamad Aḥmad Aia]; 10/38a [heirs of ʿAlī b. ʿUmar Shaqrāy]; 10/39a, 12/54a [daughter of Ṣafāf Bāqī].

72. ASDMAE, *AE,* Pacco 151, "Nota delle merci facenti parte di quelle sequestrate dal piroscafo El-Gafarieh nel porto di Taklai," 2 August 1887.

73. Martini, *Il diario eritreo,* 3:169 (Keren, 23 April 1903). The grandsons of ʿUmar Bā Zarʿa seem to have been still active in import/export activities in Aden in the 1950s and 1960s. Mercier, *Aden,* 114, 122.

74. See, for example, Mandal, "Natural Leaders of Native Muslims," 189–90, 195. See

more details on members of the Bā Junayds in Southeast Asia in Ho, "Empire through Diasporic Eyes," 139, and Clarence-Smith, "Hadhrami Entrepreneurs," 307, in the same volume. See also Freitag, *Indian Ocean Migrants.*

75. Bang, *Sufis and Scholars,* 115

76. Ewald and Clarence-Smith, "The Economic Role of the Hadhrami Diaspora," 290; Ewald, "The Nile Valley System," 83.

77. See transactions of the Bā Junayds between 1868 and 1888 in MICR 16. Cases 40b, 41a, 41b, 42a, 42b, 43a, 43b, 43c, 53b, 58a, 58b, 64a, 67b, 69c, 70a, 70b, 70c, 71b, 77a, 80a, 82b, 85b, 95a, 100a, 103a, 103b, 107a, 107c, 109b, 117b and MICR 9/36a, 9/53a, 8/59a, 8/107b, 10/7a, 10/20a, 12/49a. For more details (dates, seller, property sold) see Miran, "Facing the Land," appendix 22, 373–74.

78. ᶜAbd Allāh Bā Junayd bought three shops in an auction disposing of the property of Sayyid Muḥammad Masāwa, who had been a prominent *qāḍī.* MICR 16/41a and 16/41b (Jumāda II 1286/1869).

79. A sample is MICR 16/53b [heirs of ᶜUthmān b. Mūsā ᶜAdūlāy]; 16/77a [heirs of Jābir Yamanī]; 16/80a [heirs of Ibrāhīm Ḥamdān]; 16/117b [heirs of ᶜAlī ᶜAdūlāy]; 8/59a [heirs of Dankalī]; 10/7a [heirs of Maḥmūd Nāṣir].

80. Ibrāhīm al-Mukhtār, *al-Jāmiᶜ,* 51.

81. Martini, *Il diario eritreo,* 1:50 (Massaua, 7 February 1898).

82. ASDMAE, *AE,* Pacco 349, From Capitaneria di Porto (Massaua) al Ufficio del Governo (Asmara), No. 554, Oggetto: "Sambucchi italiani di Massaua," 2 November 1901.

83. ASDMAE, *AE,* 193 (Categoria XIII), R. Capitaneria di Porto di Massaua. Matricola dei Sambucchi (1 January 1908). The Nahārīs, it must be noted, owned many other boats registered in the Dahlak islands.

84. Ibrāhīm al-Mukhtār, *al-Jāmiᶜ,* 108. Apparently, an account of the case under the title "613 year-old [court] case" was published in the *al-Jarīda al-usbūᶜiyya al-ᶜarabiyya* (Arabic Weekly News) in Asmara in the 1940s.

85. Peters, "Waḳf, In Classical Islamic Law," *EI.*

86. Hoexter, "*Waqf* Studies in the Twentieth Century," 481; Doumani, "Endowing Family," 10.

87. Doumani, "Endowing Family," 12–17.

88. See, for example, the cases of Aleppo and Jerusalem. Roded, "The *Waqf* and the Social Elite of Aleppo," 71–91, and Baer, "Jerusalem's Families of Notables," 109–22; Baer, "The Waqf as a Prop for the Social System," 264–97.

89. Ibrāhīm al-Mukhtār, *al-Jāmiᶜ,* 46.

90. MICR 16/90a (1290).

91. MICR 16/39a (17 Jumāda II 1285), 16/39b (17 Jumada II 1285), 16/39c (17 Jumāda II 1285). Ibrāhīm al-Mukhtār noted that before the mosque was destroyed in the 1921 earthquake, it had eight shops and eleven pieces of land as *waqf.* In 1922 ᶜAbd al-Raḥmān Hilāl built the *maᶜhad* (Islamic Institute) at that same location; *al-Jāmiᶜ,* 55.

92. MICR 16/54b (14 Ṣafar 1287).

93. MICR 16/55a (14 Ṣafar 1287).

94. MICR16/56b (14 Ṣafar 1287). Other references to *waqf khayrī* are found in: MICR 16/60b (17 Rabi' I 1287); MICR 16/91a (1290); MICR 16/105a (1 Rajab 1292).

95. MICR 16/13b (3 Jumāda II 1285).

96. *MICR* 9/27b (18 Shaᶜbān 1296/7 August 1879), 9/28a (20 Shaᶜbān 1296/9 August 1879). The *ḥadīth* transmitted by Abū Ḥurayra can be found in Ṣaḥīḥ Muslim, Book 13.

97. MICR 2/33e (20 Dhū al-Ḥijja 1297).

98. MICR 16/69c (? Shaᶜbān 1287).

99. MICR 16/70a (5 Jumāda II 1288) and 16/70c (? Jumāda 1288)

100. Interview with Muḥammad Ṣāliḥ Afandī, Asmara, 3 July 2006.

101. MICR 16/73b (? Dhū al-ḥijja 1288).

102. See, for example, Roded, "The *Waqf* and the Social Elite of Aleppo," 89–90.

103. MICR 16/71b (? Rajab 1288). On *murṣad,* see Deguilhem, "Waqf Documents," 76.

104. MICR 16/68c (1 Muḥarram 1287).

105. On the social uses of family *waqf* endowments see Doumani, "Endowing Family," 12–17.

106. Ibrāhīm al-Mukhtār, *al-Jāmiʿ,* 47. The *waqf* of Muḥammad Adāla is also mentioned in MICR 16/61b (15 Rabīʿ II 1287). Another record made note of a *waqf* owned by the Shīnītī family. MICR 16/100a (Jumāda II 1291).

107. MICR 16/90a (1290). On the device of *istibdāl,* see Leeuwen, *Waqfs and Urban Structures,* 159–62.

108. MICR 16/100a (Jumāda II 1291).

109. Ibrāhīm al-Mukhtār, *al-Jāmiʿ,* 50–53; Aberra, "Muslim Institutions in Ethiopia: the Asmara Awqaf," 206.

110. Traversi, "Usi e costumi africani in Massaua," 365.

111. In the twentieth-century this process was also due to the break-up of clans, the individuation of the family, and the transition to a record-keeping administration. In Eritrea, leading clan families also adopted their titles as family names. Examples are Kantebāy (*Kantebay*—Habab) and Shūmāy (*Shūm*—ʿAd Shuma). Members of the Kantebāy family, who were still referred to as *min ahālī Ḥabāb* (Ar., from the Habab), appear in the court records several times in the 1880s; MICR 8/3b [1881], 8/94b [1884], 12/44b [1888], 12/49b [1888].

112. Doumani, *Rediscovering Palestine,* 63.

113. Interview with the brothers Ḥasan Muḥammad ʿUthmān Ḥayūtī and Aḥmad Muḥammad ʿUthmān Ḥayūtī, Asmara, 31 July 2001, and Asmara, 11 July 2006 (with Ḥasan).

114. Fouad Makki has informed me that the terms *bayt* and *ʿad* were, and continue to be, used interchangeably by Massawans.

115. Cuno, "The Reproduction of Elite Households," 240–42.

116. Rugh, *Family in Contemporary Egypt,* 54–55; Meriwether, *The Kin Who Count,* 17–18; Hildred Geertz, "The Meaning of Family Ties," 341–55.

117. Several examples between 1867 and 1888 include MICR 2/62b (Adam Barkūy), 4/36b (ʿAdūlāy), 4/41b (Ḥaṭam), 8/56b (Bādūrī), 8/72b (Ḥijjī), 8/110a (Shaykh), 10/25a (Mihrī), 10/38b (ʿAlī Faqīh), 16/8a (Shīnītī), 16/59b (Ṭurkī).

118. See among many examples of this strategy MICR 16/106b (3 Dhū ʿl-qaʿda 1292). Sayyid Muḥammad b. ʿUmar b. ʿAbd Allāh al-Ṣāfī bought parts in real estate inherited by his brothers and sisters, Sayyid Shaykh, Sharīfa Shūfa, Sharīfa Nūr, and Sharīfa Ṭayiba.

119. On inheritance in Islamic law see Schacht, *An Introduction to Islamic Law,* 169–74. On inheritance and family structure see also Meriwether, *The Kin Who Count,* 153–77.

120. MICR 9/27b (18 Shaʿbān 1296) and 9/28a (20 Shaʿbān 1296).

121. MICR 16/56b (14 Ṣafar 1287). The same case was mentioned in an earlier chapter concerning slaves belonging to the Ṣāfī household.

122. See comments on this matter in Ferronato, "La città di Massaua," 282.

123. Abū Bakr, *Taʾrīkh Iritrīyā,* 304–306.

124. Even though al-Mukhtar was not from Massawa, his remarks and the tone of his account reflect the relationship between the town's prestige and its old stone edifices. See Ibrāhīm al-Mukhtār, *al-Jāmiʿ,* 18–19.

125. See the stimulating chapter on the structures, meanings, and diversity of the domestic environment in Muslim societies in Insoll, *The Archaeology of Islam,* 60–92.

126. Buchs, "Voyages en Abyssinie," 33.

127. Mantegazza, *Da Massaua a Saati,* 92.

128. Greenlaw, *The Coral Buildings of Suakin,* 29–35. The origin of this style most probably leads to Ottoman Cairo (but also very common in places such as Jiddah). See Pauty, *Les palais et les maisons d'époque musulmane.* For a detailed study of a house built by a merchant in Luḥayya, opposite Massawa on the Tihāma coast, see Bonnenfant and Gentilleau, "Une maison de commerçant-armateur sur la mer Rouge, 125–88.

129. MICR 4/24b (and 8/26a) 20 Rajab 1299.

130. See two illustrations of this house in Bizzoni, *L'Eritrea nel passato e nel presente,* 201, 233. The photograph of this exact house, identifying it as the Shīnītī family house, is printed in *L'illustrazione coloniale* 3, No. 9 (September 1921): 341.

131. Cresti, "La mosquée du Sayh Hammali à Massaoua," 303–15.

132. Ferronato, "La città di Massaua," 220–21; Greenlaw, *The Coral Buildings of Suakin,* 22–23.

133. Ferronato, "La città di Massaua," 222.

134. Matthews, "The Red Sea Style," 62. On this point see also Um, "Spatial Negotiations in a Commercial City."

135. On the *rawshāns* see Greenlaw, *The Coral Buildings of Suakin,* 21, and Matthews, "The Red Sea Style," 64–66. In the court records the existence and positioning of *rawshāns* were often clearly specified in house or shop transactions.

136. Greenlaw, *The Coral Buildings of Suakin,* 17–20. See also Cerbella, "La diffusione in Eritrea," 292–93.

137. Bertarelli, *Guida d'Italia del Touring Club Italiano,* map between 600 and 601, 604–605; *Guida dell'Africa Orientale, Italiana, Consociazione Turistica Italiana,* 178–79.

138. Meriwether, *The Kin Who Count,* 112.

139. Examples include: Diḥlī: MICR 14/3g, 14/4k; Ṣāʾigh: 14/7f, Jaᶜfar: 14/9a; ᶜAdūlāy: 14/4f, Nātī: 14/2i, Karanī: 14/4i; Dankalī: 14/7i.

140. ᶜAydarūs and Ṣāfī: MICR 14/8f; Ṣāfī and Masāwa: 14/8d; Ḥābūna and Jaᶜfar 14/9b.

141. MICR 14/2f, 14/3j.

142. Interview with Sayyid Ibrāhīm Muḥammad Ibrāhīm al-Sayyid, Massawa, 26 April 2000.

143. Interview with Muḥammad Sālim Afandī, Asmara, 31 July 2001.

144. *Bulletino Ufficiale della Colonia Eritrea* 12, no. 31 (Asmara, 1–8–1903).

145. Le Guennec-Coppens, "Changing Patterns of Hadhrami migration," 163.

146. MICR 14/6a, 14/4j.

147. MICR 14/1f, 14/2f, 14/7d.

148. In the twentieth century marriage alliances became more inclusive. As they became increasingly assimilated, the second and third generations of certain Hadrami and Egyptian families married more easily into "Eritrean" families. If this practice was also pervasive in the late nineteenth century among families sharing high religious status, the circle of families slightly expanded throughout the twentieth century. The geographical integration of Eritrea also influenced these patterns.

149. MICR 8/13b (28 Muḥarram 1299), 8/37d (27 Dhū al-ḥijja 1299), 8/34a (15 Dhū ᶜl-qaᶜda 1299).

150. MICR 8/11b (2 Muḥarram 1299), 8/21b (16 Jumāda I 1299), 8/42a (9 Rabīᶜ I 1300), 8/90b (19 Jumāda II 1301), 8/115a (4 Ṣafar 1302), 8/117a (20 Ṣafar 1302).

151. MICR 8/53a (7 Rajab 1300), 8/83a (22 Jumāda I 1301).

152. MICR 8/1c (3 Rajab 1298), 8/9b (17 Dhū l'qaᶜda 1298), 10/13b (14 Jumāda II 1302).

153. MICR 8/1a (1 Rajab 1298), 8/20d (29 Rabīᶜ II 1299), 8/94a (4 Rajab 1301), 10/31b (26 Shawwāl 1302), 10/34b (23 Dhū ᶜl-ḥijja 1302).

154. MICR 8/22e (9 Jumāda II 1299), 8/31a (27 Shaʿbān 1299), 10/35a (14 Muḥarram 1303).

155. Marmon, "Concubinage, Islamic," 527–29; Schacht, *An Introduction to Islamic Law,* 127.

156. MICR 8/1b (2 Rajab 1298).

157. MICR 8/2a (14 Rajab 1298).

158. Schacht, *An Introduction to Islamic Law,* 167; Esposito and DeLong-Bas, *Women in Muslim Family Law,* 24.

159. MICR 8/58b (4 Shawwāl 1300).

160. MICR 8/23d (14 Jumāda II 1299). Interestingly, she already appeared in court with a Muslim name, Zaynab.

161. Combes and Tamisier, *Voyage en Abyssinie,* 1:102.

162. Munzinger, *Studi,* 116.

163. Ibid., 117–18.

164. Rassam, *Narrative of the British Mission,* 15.

165. Buchs, "Voyages en Abyssinie," 41–42.

166. Traversi, "Usi e costumi africani in Massaua," 372–74.

167. Buchs, "Voyages en Abyssinie," 42.

168. In early colonial Eritrea several colonial officials stand out as "specialists" of Islam and Eritrea's Muslim societies: Teobaldo Folchi (b. 1846), Dante Odorizzi (Mantova 1867–Mersa Fatma Heri [Eritrea] 1917), and Ilario Capomazza (Pozzuoli 1875–Merca [Somalia] 1932). Odorizzi, the highest ranking of the three, served as *commissario regionale* of Massawa from 1908 to 1915. Both Odorizzi and Capomazza published valuable monographs and dictionaries related to Islam, customary law, and the Tigre-, Afar-, and Saho-speaking peoples of the colony. Puglisi, *Chi è? dell'Eritrea,* 67, 222.

169. Capomazza, *Usanze islamiche hanafite,* 34ff.

Conclusion

1. Lenci, *Eritrea e Yemen,* 54ff.

2. As mentioned in the introductory chapter, Sayyid Muḥammad ʿUthmān Ḥayūtī (1901–1996) and Yāsīn Maḥmūd Bā Ṭūq (1914–67), served as editors of *Ṣawt al-Rābiṭah al-Islāmiyya al-Iritriya,* newspaper of the Muslim League, in the 1940s.

3. In the 1940s this was also true with others from Hergigo, such as members of the Kurdī and Kekiyā families, who emphasized their Arab identity and their attachment to Arab culture. Ṣāliḥ Aḥmad Kekiyā opened an Arabic school in Hergigo in 1944, while the prominent businessman Ḥasan Idrīs Kurdī—I recall while sifting through the British Military Administration's archives in Asmara—constantly referred to himself in official correspondence as an "Arabian merchant."

4. See insightful comments in Clapham, "Rewriting Ethiopian History," 37–54.

5. A recent social history of colonial Asmara is Locatelli, "Asmara during the Italian Period: Order, Disorder and Urban Identities, 1890–1941."

6. Lenci, *Eritrea e Yemen,* 59. Lenci's study is a pioneering attempt to examine cross–Red Sea relations, including contraband and "illegal" sailing in the area in the late nineteenth–early twentieth centuries. While his approach is mainly from a political and diplomatic historical perspective, a study of the ramifications of these dynamics on the political economy of the southern Red Sea area would be of great interest and also a contribution to the study of the various colonial states in the region. There is an abundance of relevant materials in ASDMAE, *ASMAI.* For a study based on Ottoman sources see Farah, *The Sultan's Yemen,* 192–211. For a stimulating study on Southeast Asia see Eric Tagliacozzo, *Secret Trades, Porous Borders.*

Bibliography

Informants

Massawa

ᶜAbd al-Bāqī Muḥammad ᶜAbdu ᶜAbbāsī (27 September 1999, 24 June 2006).
ᶜAbd al-Laṭīf Aḥmad Hindī (20 March 2000).
ᶜAbd al-Qādir Hindī (20 March 2000).
ᶜAbd al-Wahhāb Muḥammad Ṣāliḥ ᶜAbdu (22 March, 27 March 2000).
ᶜAbd Allāh Yūsuf Ṣāʾigh (5 May, 6 May 2000).
ᶜAbdu ᶜAlī Saᶜīd Ṣūrī al-Ṭāhirī (27 April 2000).
ᶜĀdil Muḥammad ᶜAlī Saᶜīd Ṣūrī al-Ṭāhirī (22 March 2000).
Aḥmad Shaykh Ibrāhīm Faras (3 March 2000).
ᶜAlī Yūsuf al-Ghūl (26 February, 4 March, 8 March 2000).
ᶜEgebet Negassi G'awg' Ezaz (28 March 2000).
Ḥāmid ᶜAbd al-Bāqī Muḥammad ᶜAbdu ᶜAbbāsī (18 March, 20 March 2000, 2–3 October 2007).
Ḥasan Ibrāhīm Muḥammad Sālim (27 September 1999, 20 March, 8 May 2000).
Sayyid Ibrāhīm ᶜAbd Allāh Sharīf (2 March 2000).
Ibrāhīm Ḥusayn Mentāy (7 May 2000).
Sayyid Ibrāhīm Muḥammad Ibrāhīm (26 April 2000).
Ibrāhīm Muḥammad Nūr Mentāy (7 May 2000).
Muḥammad ᶜAbdu Bakrī Ḥijjī (5 May, 16 May 2000).
Muḥammad Abū Bakr al-Nātī (8 May, 16 May 2000).
Muḥammad Aḥmad ᶜUmar Aḥmad ᶜAbbāsī (20 March, 29 April, 15 May 2000).
Muḥammad al-Rifāᶜī (3 July 2006).
Muḥammad Qaᶜaṣ (21 February, 25 February, 10 April 2000).
Muḥammad Ṣāliḥ Aḥmad Afandī (13 March 2000, [Asm.] 31 July 2001, [Asm.] 3 July 2006).
Muḥammad Yāsīn Bā Ṭūq (17 March 2000).
Muḥammad Zubūy Ṣāliḥ Mīyā Khayr ad-Dīn ᶜAbd al-Qādir Hindī (20 March, 3 April, 7 May 2000).
Qāḍī Sulaymān Muḥammad Aḥmad al-Ḥanafī (20 March 2000).
Sayyid Ṣādiq Muḥsin al-Ṣāfī (8 March, 14 March, 16 March, 18 March, 19 March, 2 April, 15 May, 19 May 2000, 24 June 2006).
Sulaymān ᶜAbdu Hindī (16 May 2000).
Ṭāhā Jaᶜfar Dankalī (16 May 2000).

ᶜUmar Wahhāb al-Bārrī (16–17 March 2000).
ᶜUsmān Ḥājjī Maḥmūd (16 March, 19 March, 25 April, 28 April, 5 May 2000).
ᶜUthmān Ibrāhīm Egal (17 March 2000).

Asmara

Aḥmad Muḥammad Bā Ḥubayshī (10 March 2000).
Sayyid Aḥmad Muḥammad ᶜUthmān Ḥayūtī (31 July 2001).
Anis ᶜUbayd Bā Ḥubayshī (10 March 2000).
Fouad Makki (27 July 2001).
Sayyid Ḥasan Muḥammad ᶜUthmān Ḥayūtī (9 October, 27 November 1999, 31 July 2001, 11–12 July 2006).
Ismāᶜīl Ḥājjī Maḥmūd (2 May 2000).
Jamāl Muḥammad ᶜUmar Bā Bikhayr (24 March 2000).
Jamāl Wahhāb al-Bārrī (11 March 2000).
Maryam ᶜUmar al-Nahārī (26 March 2000).
Muḥammad Saᶜīd Shūmāy (30 November 1999).
Salma Ṣāliḥ Bā Ṭūq (25 March 2000).
Ustādh Muḥammad ᶜUmar (12 June 2000).

Emberemi

ᶜAbd al-Qādir ᶜAlī al-Amīn (24 April 2000).
ᶜAbd al-Qādir Yūsuf ᶜAlī Aḥmad al-Ghūl (17 May 2000).
Shaykh al-Amīn ᶜUthmān al-Amīn, Asmara and Emberemi (22 September 1999, 17 May 2000).
Khalīfa Shaykh Ḥasan Shaykh al-Amīn (ᶜAd Shaykh *khalīfa*) (17 May 2000).
Ibrāhīm Shaykh Ḥusayn Shaykh al-Amīn (17 May 2000).
Muḥammad Saᶜīd Nāwad, founder of the Eritrean Liberation Movement (ELM).
Muḥammad Shaykh Muḥammad ᶜAlī Shaykh al-Amīn (17 May 2000).

Hetumlo

Khalīfa ᶜUthmān Khalīfa Ṭāhā, head of the Khatmiyya center (14 April 2000).

Ghinda

Shaykh Maḥmūd Ḥummād Ḍarīr (4 May 2000).

Hergigo

Nāfiᶜ ᶜAlī Khaydar (7 March 2000).
Ṣāliḥ ᶜAbd Allāh Zubayr (6 March, 7 March 2000).

Archives

Eritrea

Majlis al-Awqāf Office, Asmara.
Massawa Islamic Court Records (*maḥkama al-sharᶜiyya*) (MICR): vol. 2 (1880–81); vol. 3 (1880–81); vol. 4 (1881–85); vol. 8 (1881–85); vol. 9 (1877–80); vol. 10 (1885–86); vol. 11 (1866–77); vol. 12 (1886–90); vol. 14 (1866–80); vol. 16 (1866–77).
[Note: The numbering of the volumes follows the order established by Shaykh Ibrāhīm al-Mukhtār in the early 1960s].

Italy

Archivio Centrale dello Stato, Rome (ACS).
Ministero dell'Africa italiana, Governo dell'Eritrea (MAI): 1066.
Carte Ferdinando Martini: 8, 12, 16, 21.
Archivio storico diplomatico del Ministero affari esteri, Rome (ASDMAE).
Archivio storico del Ministero dell'Africa italiana (ASMAI): Pos. 3 / 4, 34 / 1.
Archivio Eritrea (AE): 16, 21, 43, 53, 151, 153, 154, 178, 193, 210, 349.
Biblioteca Reale, Torino
Photographic collections (Luigi Naretti, Roberto Gentile, Fratelli Nicotra, Mauro Ledru, Luigi Fiorillo, and other photographers)

United Kingdom

Rhodes House Library, Oxford.
Trevaskis Papers: Box 1.

France

Ministère des Affaires Etrangères (MAE), Paris
Correspondance Consulaire et Commerciale, Massaouah, t.1 (1840–59)
Correspondance Consulaire et Commerciale, Massaouah, t.2 (1860–85)

Published Archival Materials

d'Avray, Anthony, ed. *The Nakfa Documents. The Despatches, Memoranda, Reports and Correspondence Describing and Explaining the Stories of the Feudal Societies of the Red Sea Littoral from the Christian-Muslim Wars of the Sixteenth Century to the Establishment 1885–1901 of the Italian Colony of Eritrea.* Wiesbaden, Germany: Harrassowitz Verlag, 2000.

Folchi, Teobaldo. "Commissariato Regionale di Massaua. Brevi Cenni storico-amministrativi sulle popolazioni dal suddetto Commissariato Regionale dipendenti," 1898 (conserved at the Guglielmo Pecori Girardi Archive, Vicenza). Edited by Massimo Zaccaria and published in *Ethnorêma* 3 (2007): 143–383 (available online www.ethnorema.it).

Jamal, Shawqī ʿAtāʾ Allāh al-. *al-Wathāʾiq al-taʾrīkhiyya li-siyāsat miṣr fī al-baḥr al-aḥmar, 1863–1879.* Cairo: Maṭbaʿat lajnat al-bayān al-ʿarabī, 1959.

Rubenson, Sven, ed. *Acta Aethiopica.* Vol. 1: *Correspondence and Treaties 1800–1854.* Evanston, Ill.: Northwestern University Press, 1987.

Official Publications

Atti Parlamentari. Camera dei Deputati. *Relazione sulla Colonia Eritrea del R. Commissario Civilie straordinario onorevole Ferdinando Martini (anni 1898–1899).* Rome, 1900.

Atti Parlamentari. Legislazione XXIII-sessione 1909–13, Camera dei Deputati. *Allegati alla Relazione sulla Colonia Eritrea, Dal R. Commissario Ferdinando Martini per gli esercizi 1902–1907 presentato dal ministro delle colonie (Bertolini) nella seduta del 14 giugno 1913.* 4 Vols. Rome, 1913.

Colonia Eritrea. *Giurisprudenza coloniale. No. 23. Sentenza 18 maggio 1909 del commissario di Massaua—usanzi rituali del Semhar.* Asmara, 1909.

Colonia Eritrea. No 58. *Elenco dei commercianti, industriali. Negozianti, imprenditori, appaltatori o fornitori, e degli esercenti professioni, arti e mestieri inscritti nel ruolo dei contribuenti della Colonia Eritrea (Esercizio 1912–1913).* Asmara, 1913.

Great Britain, House of Commons. Parliamentary Papers. *Correspondence Respecting Abyssinia 1846–1868*. London, 1868.

Salvadei, Giovanni. "La pesca e il commercio delle perle e della madreperla in Eritrea." Allegato N. 91, 3:1157–81. In *Relazione sulla Colonia Eritrea del Commissario Civile Ferdinando Martini per gli esercizi 1902–07*. Rome, 1913.

———. "Massaua." Allegato N. 110, 3:1813–43. In *Relazione sulla Colonia Eritrea del Commissario Civile Ferdinando Martini per gli esercizi 1902–07*. Rome, 1913.

Tribunale Civile e Penale di Massaua. *Relazione statistica deo lavori compiuti nell'anno 1892 dal Tribunale Civile e Penale di Massaua. (Dal Pres. Avv. Luigi Scotti)*. Massaua, 1893.

Unpublished Arabic Manuscripts

Ibrāhīm al-Mukhtār Aḥmad ʿUmar. *al-Jāmiʿ li-akhbār jazīrat Bāḍiʿ*. Completed in Asmara, 1378/1958.

———. *al-Rāwiya fī taʾrīkh mudun Iritrīyā*. Completed in Asmara, 1372/1953.

Nisbat al-shaykh Ḥāmid b. Nafʿūtāy.

Taʾrīkh li-minṭaqat Zūlā wa-madīnat Maṣawwaʿ.

Theses and Conference Papers

Blumi, Isa. "The Consequences of Empire in the Balkans and the Red Sea: Reading Possibilities in the Transformations of the Modern World." Ph.D. diss., New York University, 2005.

Ferronato, A. "La città di Massaua." Tesi di Laurea, Istituto Universitario Maria SS. Assunta. Rome, 1961–62.

Gabrawold, Joseph. "The Origin and Early Development of the Evangelical Church of Eritrea, 1866–1917." B.A. thesis, Addis Ababa University, 1972.

Haar, Stephen G. "Long-Distance Trade, Political Economy and National Reunification in the Christian Kingdoms of Ethiopia, c. 1800–1900." Ph.D. dissertation, UCLA, 1990.

Habib, Abdu Ali. "History of Massawa from the Early 19th Century to the Coming of the Italians." B.A. thesis submitted to Haile Sellassie I University, Addis Ababa, 1973.

Hopper, Matthew S. "The African Presence in Arabia: Slavery, the World Economy, and the African Diaspora in Eastern Africa, 1840–1940." Ph.D. diss., UCLA, 2006.

Locatelli, Francesca. "Asmara during the Italian Period: Order, Disorder and Urban Identities, 1890–1941." Ph.D. diss., School of Oriental and African Studies, University of London, 2005.

Mengisteab, Adhana. "The Strategic Position of Karan in the Metsewa-Kassala Trade Route." Unpublished paper presented to the African History Conference, Nazareth (Ethiopia), 15–20 December 1982.

Miran, Jonathan. "Constructing and Deconstructing the 'Tigre Frontier' in the Long Nineteenth Century." Presented at the workshop History and Language of the Tigre-Speaking Peoples, University of Naples, ""L'Orientale," 8 February 2008.

———. "Facing the Land, Facing the Sea: Commercial Transformation and Urban Dynamics in the Red Sea Port of Massawa, 1840s–1900s." Ph.D. dissertation, Michigan State University, 2004.

———. "Islamic Court Records: A Source for the Social and Economic History of Massawa in the Nineteenth Century." Presented at the First International Conference of Eritrean Studies "Independent Eritrea: Lessons and Prospects," Asmara, Eritrea, July 2001.

Reese, Scott. "Patricians of the Benaadir: Islamic Learning, Commerce and Somali Urban

Identity in the Nineteenth Century." Ph.D. dissertation, University of Pennsylvania, 1996.

Voll, John. "A History of the Khatmiyyah Tariqa in the Sudan." Ph.D. dissertation, Harvard University, 1969.

Published Sources

Abbadie, Arnauld d'. *Douze ans de séjour dans la Haute-Éthiopie (Abyssinie).* Paris, 1868. Vatican City: Biblioteca apostolica vaticana, 1980.

Abbadie, Antoine d'. "Les causes actuelles de l'esclavage en Ethiopie," extrait de *La Revue des Questions Scientifiques.* Louvain, 1877.

———. *Géographie de l'Éthiopie.* Vol. 1. Paris: G. Mesnil, 1890.

Abdulkader Saleh. "Ǧäbärti." In *Encyclopaedia Aethiopica,* ed. Siegbert Uhlig, 2:597–98. Wiesbaden, Germany: Harrassowitz, 2005.

Aberra, Yassin M. "Muslim Institutions in Ethiopia: The Asmara Awqaf." *Journal of the Institute of Muslim Minority Affairs* 5 (1983–84): 203–23.

Abir, Mordechai. "Brokerage and Brokers in Ethiopia in the First Half of the Nineteenth Century." *Journal of Ethiopian Studies* 3, no. 1 (1965): 1–5.

———. "Caravan Trade and History in the Northern Parts of East Africa." *Paideuma* 14 (1968): 103–20.

———. *Ethiopia: The Era of the Princes.* London: Longman, 1968.

———. "Ethiopia and the Horn of Africa." In *Cambridge History of Africa,* ed. R. Gray, 4:537–77. New York: Cambridge University Press, 1975.

———. "The Ethiopian Slave Trade and Its Relation to the Islamic World." In *Slaves and Slavery in Muslim Africa.* Vol. 2: *The Servile Estate,* ed. John Ralph Willis, 123–36. London: Frank Cass, 1985.

———. "The Origins of the Ethio-Egyptian Border Problem in the Nineteenth Century." *Journal of African History* 8, no. 3 (1967): 443–61.

Abū Bakr, Muḥammad ʿUthmān. *Taʾrīkh Iritrīyā al-muʿāṣir: arḍan wa-shaʿban.* Cairo, 1994.

———. *ʿUthmān Ṣāliḥ Sabī wa-l thawra al-iritriyya.* Cairo: al-Maktab al-Miṣri li-Tawzīʿ al-Maṭbūʿāt, 1998.

Agmon, Iris, *Family and Court: Legal Culture and Modernity in Late Ottoman Palestine.* Syracuse, N.Y.: Syracuse University Press, 2006.

Ahmad, Abdussamad H. "Darita, Bagemdir: An Historic Town and Its Muslim Population, 1830–1889." *International Journal of African Historical Studies* 22, no. 3 (1989): 439–51.

———. "Ethiopian Slave Exports at Matamma, Massawa and Tajura, c. 1830–1885." *The Economics of the Indian Ocean Slave Trade in the Nineteenth Century,* ed. W. G. Clarence-Smith. Special issue of *Slavery and Abolition* 9, no. 3 (December 1988): 93–102.

———. "Trade and Islam: Relations of the Muslims with the court in Gondar, 1864–1941." In *Papers of the Thirteenth International Conference of Ethiopian Studies, Kyoto, 12–17 December 1997,* ed. Katsuyoshi Fukui, Eisei Kurimoto, and Masayoshi Shigeta, 1:128–37. Kyoto, Japan: Shokado Book Sellers, 1997.

Ahmed, Hussein. *The Historiography of Islam in Ethiopia.* London: Ethio-International Press (for the) Centre of Ethiopian Studies, 1992.

———. *Islam in Nineteenth-Century Wallo, Ethiopia: Revival, Reform and Reaction.* Leiden, Neth.: Brill, 2001.

Ahmed, Hussein, and Jonathan Miran. "Islamic Brotherhoods." In *Encyclopaedia Aethiopica,* ed. Siegbert Uhlig, 3:212–16. Wiesbaden, Germany: Harrassowitz, 2007.

Alamanni, Ennio Quirino Mario. *La colonia Eritrea e i suoi commerci.* Turin: Flli. Bocca, 1891.

Allen, James de Vere. *Swahili Origins, Swahili Culture and the Shungwaya Phenomenon.* Athens: Ohio University Press, 1993.

Alpers, Edward A. "Dance and Society in Nineteenth Century Mogadishu." *Proceedings of the Second International Congress of Somali Studies, University of Hamburg, August 1–6 1983*, ed. Thomas Labahn, 2:127–44. Hamburg: H. Buske, 1984.

———. "Gujerat and the Trade of East Africa, 1500–1800." *International Journal of African Historical Studies* 9, no. 1 (1976): 22–44.

———. "Muqdisho in the Nineteenth Century: A Regional Perspective." *Journal of African History* 24 (1983): 441–59.

Anderson, Benedict. *Imagined Communities.* London: Verso, 1983.

Antinori, Orazio. "Viaggio nei Bogos." *Bolletino della Società Geografica Italiana* 24 (1877): 468–81, 511–50, 614–40, 668–94.

Arén, Gustav. *Evangelical Pioneers in Ethiopia: Origin of the Evangelical Church Mekane Yesus.* Stockholm: EFS-förl., 1978.

Austen, Ralph. "The Islamic Red Sea Slave Trade: An Effort at Quantification." In *Proceedings of the Fifth International Conference of Ethiopian Studies,* ed. R. L. Hess, 433–68. Chicago: Office of Publication Services, University of Illinois at Chicago Circle, 1979.

———. "The Nineteenth Century Islamic Slave Trade from East Africa (Swahili and Red Sea Coasts): A Tentative Census." In *The Economics of the Indian Ocean Slave Trade in the Nineteenth Century,* ed. W. G. Clarence-Smith. Special issue of *Slavery and Abolition* 9, no. 3 (1988): 21–44.

Baer, Gabriel. "Jerusalem's Families of Notables and the Wakf in the Early 19th Century." In *Palestine in the Late Ottoman Period: Political, Social and Economic Transformation,* ed. David Kushner, 109–22. Leiden, Neth.: Brill, 1986.

———. "The Waqf as a Prop for the Social System (Sixteenth–Twentieth Centuries)." *Islamic Law and Society* 4, no. 3 (1997): 264–97.

Baldinetti, Anna. *Orientalismo e colonialismo: La ricerca di consenso in Egitto per l'impresa di Libia.* Rome: Istituto per l'Oriente C. A. Nallino, 1997.

Bā Maṭraf, Muḥammad ʿAbd al-Qādir. *Al-Jāmi: Jāmiʿ shamal aʿlām al-muhājirīn al-muntasibīn ilā al-Yaman wa qabāʾilihim.* Aden, Yemen: Dār al-Hamadānī, 1984.

Bang, Anne. *Sufis and Scholars of the Sea: Family Networks in East Africa, 1860–1925.* London: Routledge, 2003.

Baratieri, Oreste. "Il commercio della madreperla." *L'Esplorazione commerciale,* no. 12 (1894): 372–73.

Bariagaber, Assefaw. "The Politics of Cultural Pluralism in Ethiopia and Eritrea: Trajectories of Ethnicity and Constitutional Experiments." *Ethnic and Racial Studies* 21, no. 6 (November 1998): 1056–73.

Barth, Fredrik. Introduction to *Ethnic Groups and Boundaries: The Social Organization of Culture Difference,* ed. Fredrik Barth. Bergen: Universitetsforlaget; London: Allen and Unwin, 1969.

Basset, René. "Les inscriptions de l'île de Dahlak." *Journal Asiatique* (Paris) 1, 9th series (1893): 77–111.

Basu, Dilip K., ed. *The Rise and Growth of Port Cities in Asia.* Santa Cruz: Center for South Pacific Studies, University of California, 1979.

Battera, Federico. "Il 'risveglio islamico' e le confraternite (*turuq*) somale dagli inizi del XIX secolo al XX: diffusione, modalità di insediamento e impatto sul contesto sociale." *Africana* (Pisa) (1997): 15–29.

———. "Le confraternite islamiche somale di fronte al colonialismo (1890–1920): Tra contrapposizione e collaborazione." *Africa* (Rome) 53, no. 2 (1998): 155–85.

Bayly, C. A. "'Archaic and 'Modern' Globalization in the Eurasian and African Arena, c. 1750–1850." In *Globalization in World History,* ed. A. G. Hopkins, 47–73. London: Pimlico, 2002.

———. *The Birth of the Modern World, 1780–1914.* Malden, Mass.: Blackwell, 2004.

Bayyūmī, Ṭāriq ᶜAbd al-ᶜĀṭī Ghunaym, *Siyāsat Miṣr fī al-Bahr al-Aḥmar fī al-niṣf al-awwal min al-qarn al-tāsiᶜ ᶜashar, 1226–1265 H (1811–1848).* Cairo: al-Hayʾa al-Miṣriyya al-ᶜĀmma lil-kitāb, 1999.

Bertarelli, L. V. *Guida d'Italia del Touring Club Italiano: Possedimenti e colonie, isole Egee, Tripolitania, Cirenaica, Eritrea, Somalia.* Milan: Touring Club Italiano, 1929.

Bertola, Arnaldo. *Il regime dei culti nell'Africa italiana.* Bologna: L. Cappelli, 1939.

Beurmann, Moriz von. *Voyages et explorations 1860–1863. Nubie, Soudan, Libye, Fezzan, Lac Tchad, Bornou.* St. Illide Le Gibanel, 1973.

Birks, J. S. *Across the Savannas to Mecca: The Overland Pilgrimage Route from West Africa.* London: Frank Cass, 1978.

Bizzoni, Achille. *L'Eritrea nel passato e nel presente.* Milan: Società Editrice Sonzogno, 1897.

Bjørkelo, Anders. *Prelude to the Mahdiyya: Peasants and Traders in the Shendi Region, 1821–1885.* Cambridge: Cambridge University Press, 1989.

Blair, Sheila. *Islamic Inscriptions.* Edinburgh: Edinburgh University Press, 1998.

Blanc, Henry. *A Narrative of Captivity in Abyssinia.* London: Smith, Elder, 1868.

Bloch, Marc. *Apologie pour l'histoire, ou, Métier d'historien.* Paris: A. Colin, 1952.

Bloss, J. F. E. "The Story of Suakin." *Sudan Notes and Records* 19, no. 2 (1936): 271–300; 20, no. 2 (1937): 247–80.

Boddy, Janice. *Wombs and Alien Spirits: Women, Men and the Zar Cult in Northern Sudan.* Madison: University of Wisconsin Press, 1989.

Bombaci, Alessio. "Il viaggio in Abissinia di Evliya Çelebi (1673)." *Annali dell'Istituto Universitario Orientale di Napoli* (Rome), new series 2 (1943): 259–75.

———. "Notizie sull'Abissinia in fonti turche." *Rassegna di studi etiopici,* 3, no. 1 (January–April 1943): 79–86.

Bonacucina, A. *Due anni in Massaua.* Fabriano, Italy, 1887.

Bonati, Manlio. "Rolph Bienenfeld." In *Encyclopaedia Aethiopica,* ed. Siegbert Uhlig. Vo. 4. Wiesbaden, Germany: Harrassowitz, forthcoming.

Bonnenfant, Paul. "La marque de l'Inde à Zabîd." *Chroniques yéménites,* 2000 (http://cy.revues.org/document7.html).

Bonnenfant, Paul, and Jean-Marie Gentilleau. "Une maison de commerçant-armateur sur la mer Rouge: Bayt ᶜAbd al-Udûd à al-Luhayya (Yémen)." In *Les villes dans l'empire ottoman: activités et sociétés,* ed. Daniel Panzac, 2:125–88. Paris: Editions du CNRS, 1994.

Bono, Salvatore. "Islam et politique coloniale en Libye." *Maghreb Review* 13, no. 1–2 (1988): 70–76.

Bose, Sugata. *A Hundred Horizons: The Indian Ocean in the Age of Global Empire.* Cambridge, Mass.: Harvard University Press, 2006.

———. "Space and Time on the Indian Ocean Rim." In *Modernity and Culture from the Mediterranean to the Indian Ocean, 1890–1920,* ed. L. Fawaz and C. A. Bayly, 365–88. New York: Columbia University Press, 2002.

Bourdieu, Pierre. *An Outline of a Theory of Practice.* Cambridge: Cambridge University Press, 1977.

Braudel, Fernand. *On History.* Chicago: University of Chicago Press, 1980.

Broeze, Frank. "Brides of the Sea Revisited." In *Gateways of Asia: Port Cities of Asia in the 13th–20th Centuries,* ed. F. Broeze, 1–16. New York: Kegan Paul International, 1997.
Broeze, Frank, Peter Reeves, and Kenneth McPherson. "Imperial Ports and the Modern World Economy: The Case of the Indian Ocean." *Journal of Transport History* 7, no. 2 (1986): 2–20.
———. "Studying the Asian Port City." In *Brides of the Sea: Port Cities of Asia from the 16th–20th Centuries,* ed. F. Broeze, 29–53. Honolulu: University of Hawaii Press, 1989.
Brown, Kenneth L. *People of Salé: Tradition and Change in a Moroccan City, 1830–1930.* Manchester, UK: Manchester University Press, 1976.
Brown, N. J. *The Rule of Law in the Arab World: Courts in Egypt and the Gulf.* Cambridge: Cambridge University Press, 1997.
Bruce, James. *Travels to Discover the Source of the Nile.* Edinburgh: J. Ruthven, for G. G. J. and J. Robinson, 1790.
———. *Travels to Discover the Source of the Nile,* selected and ed. with introd. by C. F. Beckingham. Edinburgh: Edinburgh University Press, 1964.
Brubaker, Rogers, and Frederick Cooper. "Beyond Identity." *Theory and Society* 29, no. 1 (2000): 1–47.
Buchan, John. *Jeddah Old and New.* London: Stacey International, 1980.
Buchs, Victor. "Voyages en Abyssinie, 1889–1895." *Bulletin de la Société Neuchateloise de Géographie* 9 (1896–97): 32–56; 11 (1899): 137ff; 13 (1901): 58–83.
Buṣīrī, Muḥammad b. Saʿīd al-. *Al-Busiri's Burda, The Prophet's Mantle.* Trans. Thoraya Mahdi Allam. Cairo: General Egyptian Book Organization Press, 1987.
Caniglia, Giuseppe. *La Sceriffa di Massaua. (La tarica Katmia).* Rome: Cremonese, 1940.
Caplan, Pat. "'But the Coast, of Course, Is Quite Different': Academic and Local Ideas about the East African Littoral." *Journal of Eastern African Studies* 1, no. 2 (July 2007): 305–20.
Caplan, Pat, and Farouk Topan, eds. *Swahili Modernities: Culture, Politics and Identity on the East Coast of Africa.* Trenton, N.J.: Africa World Press, 2004.
Capomazza, Ilario. *Usanze islamiche hanafite di Massaua e dintorni.* Macerata, Italy: Giorgetti, 1910.
Carter, Robert. "The History and Prehistory of Pearling in the Persian Gulf." *Journal of the Economic and Social History of the Orient* 48, no. 2 (2005): 139–209.
Cassanelli, Lee. "New Directions in Southern Somali History: An Agenda For the Next Decade." In *Mending Rips in the Sky: Options for Somali Communities in the 21st Century,* ed. Hussein M. Adam and Richard Ford, 99–103. Lawrenceville, N.J.: Red Sea Press, 1997.
———. *The Shaping of Somali Society: Reconstructing the History of a Pastoral People, 1600–1900.* Philadelphia: University of Pennsylvania Press, 1982.
Caulk, Richard. "Religion and State in Nineteenth Century Ethiopia." *Journal of Ethiopian Studies* 10, no. 1 (1972): 23–42.
Cavallarin, Marco. *Juifs en Erythrée* (Photographies de Marco Mensa). Asmara, Eritrea: Alliance Française, 2003.
Cayla-Vardhan, Fabienne. *Les enjeux de l'historiographie érythréenne.* Travaux et Documents, 66–67, CEAN. Pessac, France: Centre d'étude d'Afrique noire—IEP Bordeaux, 2000.
Cerbella, Gino. *Aspetti etnografici della casa in Etiopia.* Rome: Istituto Italiano per l'Africa, 1963.
———. "Il fascino e l'attrattivita di Massaua alla luce di un ricordo d'arte." In *Il Quotidiano eritreo,* 11 February 1962.

———. "Il Waldebit dei notabili eritrei, e qualche cenno ancora sulle iscrizioni delle abitazioni musulmane in Eritrea." *Africa* (Rome) 18, no. 2 (1963): 78–88.

———. "La diffusione in Eritrea della casa musulmana tipica." *Africa* (Rome) 17, no. 6 (1962): 291–300.

Chaudhuri, K. N. *Trade and Civilisation in the Indian Ocean: An Economic History from the Rise of Islam to 1750*. Cambridge: Cambridge University Press, 1985.

Clancy-Smith, Julia. *Rebel and Saint: Muslim Notables, Populist Protest, Colonial Encounters (Algeria and Tunisia, 1800–1914)*. Berkeley and Los Angeles: University of California Press, 1994.

Clapham, Christopher. "The Price of Land." *Times Literary Supplement*, 23 November 2001, 20–21.

———. "Rewriting Ethiopian History." *Annales d'Ethiopie* 18 (2002): 37–54.

Clarence-Smith, William Gervase. "The Economics of the Indian Ocean and Red Sea Slave Trades in the 19th Century: An Overview." *The Economics of the Indian Ocean Slave Trade in the Nineteenth Century*, ed. W. G. Clarence-Smith. Special issue of *Slavery and Abolition* 9, no. 3 (December 1988): 1–20.

———, ed. *The Economics of the Indian Ocean Slave Trade in the Nineteenth Century*. Special issue of *Slavery and Abolition* 9, no. 3 (December 1988).

———. "Hadhrami Entrepreneurs in the Malay World, c. 1750 to 1940." In *Hadhrami Traders, Scholars and Statesmen in the Indian Ocean, 1750s–1960s*, ed. Ulrike Freitag and William G. Clarence-Smith, 297–314. Leiden, Neth.: Brill, 1997.

———. "Indian and Arab Entrepreneurs in Eastern Africa, 1800–1914." In *Négoce blanc en Afrique Noire; l'évolution du commerce à longue distance en Afrique Noire, du 18e au 20e siècles*, ed. H. Bonin and M. Cahen, 335–49. Paris: Société Française d'Histoire d'Outremer, 2001.

———. "Indian Business Communities in the Western Indian Ocean in the Nineteenth Century." *Indian Ocean Review* 2, no. 4 (December 1989): 18–21.

———. "The Rise and Fall of Hadhrami Shipping in the Indian Ocean, c. 1750–c. 1940." In *Ships and the Development of Maritime Technology in the Indian Ocean*, ed. D. Parkin and R. Barnes, 227–58. London: RoutledgeCurzon, 2002.

Clouston, W. A. *Arabian Poetry for English Readers*. Glasgow: privately printed, 1881.

Cohen, Abner. "Cultural Strategies in the Organization of Trading Diasporas." In *The Development of Indigenous Trade and Markets in West Africa*, ed. Claude Meillassoux, 266–81. London: Oxford University Press, 1971.

———. *Custom and Politics in Urban Africa: A Study of Hausa Migrants in Yoruba Towns*. Berkeley and Los Angeles: University of California Press, 1969.

Combes, Edmond, and Maurice Tamisier. *Voyage en Abyssinie*. Paris: L. Deséssart, 1838.

Conti Rossini, Carlo. "Schizzo etnico e storico delle popolazioni eritree." In *L'Eritrea Economica*, ed. F. Martini, 61–90. Novara-Rome: Istituto Geografico de Agostini, 1913.

———. *Storia d'Etiopia* Milan: Officina d'Arte Grafica A. Lucini, 1928.

———. "Studi su popolazioni dell'Etiopia (iii-Note sul Sahel Eritreo)." *Rivista degli studi orientali* 6 (1914): 365–425.

———. *Tradizioni storiche dei Mensa*. Rome: Tipografia della Casa Edit. Italiana, 1901. Estratto dal *Giornale della Società Asiatica Italiana* 14 (1901): 41–99.

Cooper, Frederick. "Africa's Pasts and Africa's Historians." *Canadian Journal of African Studies* 34, no. 2 (2000): 298–336.

———. "What Is the Concept of Globalization Good For? An African Historian's Perspective." *African Affairs* 100 (2001): 189–213.

Crawford, O. G. S. *The Fung Kingdom of Sennar* Gloucester: J. Bellows, 1951.

———. "The Habab Tribe." *Sudan Notes and Records* 36 (1955): 183–87.

Cresti, Federico. "Alcune note storiche su Massaua, con particolare riferimento ad un complesso religioso islamico: la moschea dello Sayh Hammali." *Africa* (Rome) 45, no. 3 (1990): 410–31.

———. "Città e società urbane a sud del Sahara: studi fonti e documenti d'archivio italiani." In *Islam e città nell'Africa a sud del Sahara. Tra sufismo e fondamentalismo*, ed. A. Piga, 95–113. Naples: Liguori, 2001.

———. "La mosquée du Sayh Hammali à Massaoua." In *Études Éthiopiennes. Actes de la Xe Conférence Internationale des Études Éthiopiennes, Paris 24–28 aout 1988*, ed. C. Lepage et al, 1:303–15. Paris: Société Française pour les Études Éthiopiennes, 1994.

Crowfoot, J. W. "Some Red Sea Ports in the Anglo-Egyptian Sudan." *Geographical Journal* 37 (1911): 523–50.

Crummey, Donald. *Land and Society in the Christian Kingdom of Ethiopia: From the Thirteenth to the Twentieth Century.* Urbana: University of Illinois Press, 2000.

———. "Society, State and Nationality in the Recent Historiography of Ethiopia" (review article). *Journal of African History* 31 (1990): 103–19.

Cufino, Luigi. *Nel Mar Rosso.* Naples: Società Africana d'Italia, 1914.

Cumming, D. C. "The History of Kassala and the Province of Taka." *Sudan Notes and Records* 20, part 1 (1937): 1–45.

Cuno, Kenneth. *The Pasha's Peasants: Land, Society, and Economy in Lower Egypt, 1740–1858.* Cambridge: Cambridge University Press, 1992.

———. "The Reproduction of Elite Households in Eighteenth-Century Egypt: Two Examples from al-Manṣūra." In *Études sur les Villes du Proche-Orient, XVIe–XIXe Siècle: Hommage à André Raymond*, ed. Brigitte Marino, 237–61. Damascus: Institut Français d'Études Arabes de Damas, 2001.

Cuoq, Joseph. *L'Islam en Ethiopie dés origines au XVIIe siècle.* Paris: Nouvelles Éditions Latines, 1981).

Curtin, Philip. *Cross-Cultural Trade in World History.* Cambridge: Cambridge University Press, 1984.

D'Avray, Anthony. *Lords of the Red Sea: The History of a Red Sea Society from the 16th to the 19th centuries.* Wiesbaden, Germany: Harrassowitz, 1996.

De Cosson, E. A. *The Cradle of the Blue Nile.* London: J. Murray, 1877.

Deguilhem, Randi. "Waqf Documents: A Multi-Purpose Historical Source—the Case of 19th Century Damscus." In *Les villes dans l'Empire Ottoman: Activités et Sociétes*, ed. Daniel Panzac, 1:67–95. Paris: Editions du CNRS.

Dei Gaslini, Mario. *L'Italia sul Mar Rosso.* Milan: "La Prora," 1938.

De Leone, Enrico. "Il 'waqf' nel diritto coloniale italiano." *Rivista delle colonie italiane* 4, no. 8 (August 1930): 651–70 (1st part); no. 9 (September 1930): 770–87 (2nd part).

De Monfreid, Henry, *Journal de Bord.* Paris: Arthaud, 1984.

———. *Les Secrets de la mer Rouge.* Paris: Grasset, 1932.

Denny, Frederick M. "Umma." *Encyclopaedia of Islam.* 2nd ed. 10:859–63.

De Rivoyre, Denis. *Aux pays du Soudan.* Paris: E. Plon, 1885.

———. *Mer Rouge et Abyssinie.* Paris: E. Plon, 1880.

Des Avanchers, Léon. "Notes historiques et géographiques sur l'Abyssinie; tirées d'une lettre du R. P. Léon des Avanchers, Missionnaire, datée de Massouah, 12 mars 1850." *Nouvelles annales des voyages* 132 (1851): 362–81.

Ḍirār, Muḥammad Ṣāliḥ. *Taʾrīkh qabāʾil al-Ḥabāb wal-Ḥamasien bil-Sudān wa Iritrīyā.* Khartoum, 1991.

———. *Taʾrīkh Sawākin wa al-baḥr al-aḥmar.* Khartoum, 1991.

Dirar, Uoldelul Chelati. "Colonialism and the Construction of National Identities: the Case of Eritrea." *Journal of Eastern African Studies* 1, no. 2 (2007): 256–76.

Di Robilant, Carlo Felice Nicolis, conte. "Presidi e domini dell'Italia nel Mar Rosso." *Bolletino della Società Geografica Italiana* 2, no. 12 (1887): 8–24.

Dombrowski, Franz Amadeus. *Ethiopia's Access to the Sea.* Leiden, Neth.: E. J. Brill, 1985.

———. "Some Ideas about the Historical Role of Ethiopia's Access to the Sea." *Northeast African Studies*, 6, nos. 1–2 (1984): 171–77.

Donham, Donald L. "Old Abyssinia and the New Ethiopian Empire: Themes in Social History." In *The Southern Marches of Imperial Ethiopia: Essays in History and Social Anthropology*, ed. Wendy James and Donald Donham, 3–48. Cambridge: Cambridge University Press, 1986.

Donzel, Emeri van. "Maṣawwaᶜ." *Encyclopaedia of Islam.* 2nd ed. 6:641–44.

Donzel, Emeri van, and Ronald E. Kon. "Dahlak Islands." In *Encyclopaedia Aethiopica*, ed. Siegbert Uhlig, 2:65–69. Wiesbaden, Germany: Harrassowitz, 2005.

Douin, Georges. *Histoire du règne du Khédive Ismail.* 3 vols. Cairo: Impr. de l'Inst. Français d'Archéologie Orientale du Caire, pour la Société Royale de Géographie d'Égypte, 1936–41.

Doumani, Beshara. "Endowing Family: *Waqf*, Property Devolution, and Gender in Greater Syria, 1800 to 1860." *Comparative Studies in Society and History* 40, no. 1 (1998): 3–41.

———. *Rediscovering Palestine: Merchants and Peasants in Jabal Nablus, 1700–1900.* Berkeley and Los Angeles: University of California Press, 1995.

Dubois, Colette. "Changements dans la continuité ou dans la rupture. Les implantations portuaires égyptiennes et européennes en mer Rouge dans la deuxième moitié du XIXe siècle." In *Actes du Ve symposium international d'études ottomanes sur les villes Arabes, la démographie historique et la mer Rouge à l'époque ottomane*, ed. A. Temimi. Zaghouan, Tunisia: Ceromdi, 1994, 43–65. (Also *Arab Historical Review for Ottoman Studies* 9–10 [1994]: 43–65).

———. "Miel et sucre en Afrique orientale, 1830–1870: complémentarité ou concurrence?" *International Journal of African Historical Studies* 22, no. 3 (1989): 453–72.

———. "The Red Sea Ports during the Revolution in Transportation, 1800–1914." In *Modernity and Culture from the Mediterranean to the Indian Ocean, 1890–1920*, ed. L. Fawaz and C. A. Bayly, 58–74. New York: Columbia University Press, 2002.

Eickelman, Dale. *The Middle East: An Anthropological Approach.* Englewood Cliffs, N.J.: Prentice Hall, 1989; 1st ed. 1981.

Eickelman, Dale, and Piscatori, James. eds. *Muslim Travellers: Pilgrimage, Migration, and the Religious Imagination.* London: Routledge, 1990.

Ellero, Giovanni. "I Tacruri in Eritrea." *Rassegna di Studi Etiopici* 6 (1947): 189–99.

Erlich, Haggai. "1885 in Eritrea: 'The Year in Which the Dervishes Were Cut Down." *Asian and African Studies* 10, no. 3 (1975): 282–322.

———. *Ethiopia and the Middle East.* Boulder: Lynne Rienner, 1994.

———. *Ras Alula and the Scramble for Africa. A Political Biography: Ethiopia and Eritrea 1875–1897.* Lawrenceville, N.J.: Red Sea Press, 1996.

Esposito, John, and N. J. DeLong-Bas. *Women in Muslim Family Law.* Syracuse, N.Y.: Syracuse University Press, 2001; 1st ed. 1982.

Ewald, Janet. "Crossers of the Sea: Slaves, Freedmen, and Other Migrants in the Northwestern Indian Ocean, c.1750–1914." *American Historical Review* 105, no. 1 (February 2000): 69–91.

———. "The Nile Valley System and the Red Sea Slave Trade 1820–1880." *The Economics of the Indian Ocean Slave Trade in the Nineteenth Century*, ed. W. G. Clarence-Smith. Special issue of *Slavery and Abolition* 9, no. 3 (December 1988): 71–92.

———. "Slavery in Africa and the Slave Trades from Africa" (review article). *American Historical Review* 97, no. 2 (April 1992): 465–85.

Ewald, Janet, and William Clarence-Smith. "The Economic Role of the Hadhrami Diaspora in the Red Sea and Gulf of Aden, 1820s to 1930s." In *Hadhrami Traders, Scholars, and Statesmen in the Indian Ocean, 1750s–1960s*, ed. Ulrike Freitag and William G. Clarence-Smith, 281–96. Leiden, Neth.: Brill, 1997.

Facey, William. "The Red Sea: The Wind Regime and Location of Ports." In *Trade and Travel in the Red Sea Region*, ed. Paul Lunde and Alexandra Porter, 7–17. Oxford: Archaeopress, 2004.

Farah, Caesar E. *The Sultan's Yemen: Nineteenth-Century Challenges to Ottoman Rule*. London: I. B. Tauris, 2002.

Faroqhi, Suraiya "Coping with the Central State, Coping with Local Power: Ottoman Regions and Notables from the Sixteenth to the Early Nineteenth Century." In *The Ottomans and the Balkans: A Discussion of Historiography*, ed. Fikret Adanir and Suraiya Faroqhi, 351–81. Leiden, Neth.: Brill, 2002.

———. *The Ottoman Empire and the World Around It*. London: I. B. Tauris, 2004.

Fattah, Hala. *The Politics of Regional Trade in Iraq, Arabia and the Gulf, 1745–1900*. Albany: State University of New York Press, 1997.

Fawaz, Leila, and Chris A. Bayly, eds. *Modernity and Culture from the Mediterranean to the Indian Ocean, 1890–1920*. New York: Columbia University Press, 2002.

Febvre, Lucien. *Combats pour l'histoire*. Paris: A. Colin, 1953.

Fernyhough, Timothy. "Slavery and the Slave Trade in Southern Ethiopia in the 19th Century." *The Economics of the Indian Ocean Slave Trade in the Nineteenth Century*, ed. W. G. Clarence-Smith. Special issue of *Slavery and Abolition* 9, no. 3 (December 1988): 103–30.

Ferret, Pierre Victor, and Joseph Germain Galinier. *Voyage en Abyssinie, dans les provinces du Tigré, Samen et de l'Amhara*. Paris: Paulin, 1847.

Freitag, Ulrike. *Indian Ocean Migrants and State Formation in Hadhramaut: Reforming the Homeland*. Leiden, Neth.: Brill, 2003.

Freitag, Ulrike, and William G. Clarence-Smith, eds. *Hadhrami Traders, Scholars, and Statesmen in the Indian Ocean, 1750s–1960s*. Leiden, Neth.: Brill, 1997.

Gabre-Sellassie, Zewde. *Yohannes IV of Ethiopia: A Political Biography*. Oxford: Clarendon Press, 1975.

Gardet, Louis. *La cité musulmane*. Paris: J. Vrin, 1961; 1st ed. 1954.

———. *L'Islam: Religion et Communauté*. Paris: Desclée De Brouwer, 1967.

Garretson, Peter. "The Naggadras, Trade, and Selected Towns in Nineteenth and Early Twentieth Century Ethiopia." *International Journal of African Historical Studies* 12, no. 3 (1979): 416–39.

Gatta, Luigi. "Da Massaua a Chartum per Keren e Cassala." *Bolletino della Società Geografica Italiana* 22 (1885): 398–406.

———. "Da Massaua a Cheren." *Nuova Antologia di scienze, lettere ed arti* 51, 2nd series, (1885): 465–98.

———. "Massaua e le regioni circostanti." *Nuova Antologia di scienze, lettere ed arti*, 2nd series, 50 (1885): 470–86.

Gavin, R. J. *Aden under British Rule, 1839–1967*. London: Hurst, 1975.

Gebremedhin, Naigzy, Edward Denison, and Mebrahtu Abraham. *Massawa: A Guide to the Built Environment*. Asmara, Eritrea: Cultural Assets Rehabilitation Project [CARP], 2005.

Geertz, Hildred. "The Meanings of Family Ties." In Clifford Geertz, Hildred Geertz, and Lawrence Rosen, *Meaning and Order in Moroccan Society*, 315–91. Cambridge: Cambridge University Press, 1979.

Ghaber, Michael. *The Blin of Bogos*. Baghdad: Sarafian, 1993.

Ghersi, Emanuele. "Di alcune questioni di politica indigena." *Rivista delle Colonie* 7, no. 10 (1936): 770–83.

Gilbar, Gad. "The Muslim Big Merchants-Entrepreneurs of the Middle East, 1860–1914." University of Haifa, 2001. Published in *Welt des Islams* 43, no. 1 (2003): 1–36.

Glassman, Jonathon. *Feasts and Riot: Revelry, Rebellion and Popular Consciousness on the Swahili Coast, 1856–1888*. Portsmouth, N.H.: Heinemann, 1995.

Gori, Alessandro *Contatti culturali nell'Oceano Indiano e nel Mar Rosso e processi di islamizzazione*. Venice: Lib. Ed. Cafoscarina, 2006.

———. "L'Etiopia nei testi ottomani." In *Turcica et Islamica. Studi in Memoria di Aldo Gallotta*, ed. Ugo Marazzi. Naples: Università degli Studi di Napoli "L'Orientale," 2003), 623–635

———. "Lo Yemen e l'Islam in Africa Orientale: Contatti, Testi, Personaggi." In *Storia e cultura dello Yemen in età islamica con particolare riferimento al periodo Rasulide*, 201–18. Accademia Nazionale dei Lincei, Fondazione Leone Caetani. Rome: Bardi Editore, 2006.

———. "Soggiorno di studi in Eritrea ed Etiopia. Brevi annotazioni bibliografiche." *Rassegna di studi etiopici* 39 (1995): 81–129.

Grandclément, Daniel. *L'incroyable Henry de Monfreid*. New ed. Paris: Grasset, 1998.

Grandin, Nicole. "Le nord-est et l'est de l"Afrique." In *Les Voies d'Allah : les ordres mystiques dans le monde musulman des origines à aujourd'hui*, ed. A. Popovic and G. Veinstein, 428–41. Paris: Fayard, 1996.

———. "Les turuq au Soudan, dans la Corne de l'Afrique et en Afrique orientale." In *Les Ordres mystique dans l'Islam. Cheminements et situation actuelle*, ed. A. Popovic and G. Veinstein, 165–204. Paris, EHESS, 1986.

Greenlaw, Jean-Pierre. *The Coral Buildings of Suakin: Islamic Architecture, Planning, Design and Domestic Arrangements in a Red Sea Port*. London: Kegan Paul, 1995; prev. publ. 1976.

Guérinot, A. "L'Islam et l'Abyssinie." *Revue du Monde Musulman* 34 (1917–1918): 1–66.

Guida dell'Africa Orientale, Italiana, Consociazione Turistica Italiana. Milan, 1938.

Guillot, Eugène. "La mer Rouge et l'Abyssinie." *Bulletin de la Société de Géographie de Lille* 12, 10th year (1889).

Guyer, Jane I., ed. *Feeding African Cities: Studies in Regional Social History*. Bloomington: Indiana University Press, 1987.

Hailu Wolde Emmanuel. "Major Ports of Ethiopia: Aseb, Jibuti, Mesewa." *Ethiopian Geographical Journal* 3, no. 1 (1965): 35–49.

Hanssen, Jens, Thomas Philipp, and Stefan Weber. "Introduction: Towards a New Urban Paradigm." In *The Empire in the City: Arab Provincial Capitals in the Late Ottoman Empire*, ed. Hanssen, Philipp, and Weber, 1–25. Würzburg, Germany: Ergon in Komission, 2002.

Hassen, Mohammed. *The Oromo of Ethiopia: A History 1570–1860*. Cambridge: Cambridge University Press, 1990.

Hathaway, Jane. *The Politics of Households in Ottoman Egypt: The Rise of the Qazdaglis*. New York: Cambridge University Press, 1997.

Henze, Paul. *Layers of Time: A History of Ethiopia*. London: C. Hurst, 2000.

Hill, Richard. *A Biographical Dictionary of the Anglo-Egyptian Sudan*. Oxford: Clarendon Press, 1951.

———. *Egypt in the Sudan, 1820–1881.* London: Oxford University Press, 1959.

Hino, Shun'ya. "Pilgrimage and Migration of the West African Muslims: A Case Study of the Fellata People in the Sudan." In *Sudan Sahel Studies II,* ed. Morimichi Tomikawa, 15–109. Tokyo: Institute for the Study of the Languages and Cultures of Asia and Africa (ILCAA), 1986.

Hirsch, Bertrand, and Michel Perret. *Notes de prosopographie éthiopienne.* Paris: ARESAE, 1992.

Ho, Engseng. "Before Parochialization: Diasporic Arabs Cast in Creole Waters." In *Transcending Borders: Arabs, Politics, Trade and Islam in Southeast Asia,* ed. Huub de Jonge and Nico Kaptein, 11–35. Leiden, Neth.: Brill, 2002.

———. "Empire through Diasporic Eyes: A View from the Other Boat." *Comparative Studies in Society and History* 46, no. 2 (2004): 210–46.

———. "Hadhramis Abroad in Hadhramaut: The Muwalladīn." In *Hadhrami Traders, Scholars and Statesmen in the Indian Ocean, 1750s–1960s,* ed. Ulrike Freitag and W. G. Clarence-Smith, 131–46. Leiden, Neth.: Brill, 1997.

———. "Names beyond Nations: The Making of Local Cosmopolitans." *Etudes rurales,* July–December 2002, 163–64, 215–32.

Hoexter, Miriam, "*Waqf* Studies in the Twentieth Century: The State of the Art." *Journal of the Economic and Social History of the Orient* 41, no. 4 (1998): 474–95.

Hofheinz, Albrecht. "Sawākin," *Encyclopaedia of Islam.* 2nd ed. 9: 87–89.

———. "Sons of a Hidden Imām: The Genealogy of the Mirghani Family." *Sudanic Africa* 3 (1992): 9–27.

———. "A Yemeni Library in Eritrea: Arabic Manuscripts in the Italian Foreign Ministry." *Der Islam. Zeitschrift für Geschichte und Kultur des islamischen Orients* 72, no. 1 (1995): 98–136.

Höfner, Maria. "Überlieferungen bei Tigre-stämmen (I) Ad Sek." *Annales d'Ethiopie* 4 (1961): 181–203.

Hogarth, David George, *Hejaz before World War I: A Handbook.* 2nd ed. (1917). Reprint, New York: Oleander, 1978.

Holt, Peter M. "Holy Families and Islam in the Sudan." In *Studies in the History of the Near East,* ed. P. M. Holt, 121–34. London: Cass, 1973.

———. *The Mahdist State in the Sudan, 1881–1898.* 2nd ed. Oxford: Clarendon Press, 1970

Holt, Peter M. and Martin W. Daly. *A History of the Sudan, from the Coming of Islam to the Present Day.* 4th ed. London: Longman, 1988.

Horden, Peregrine, and Nicholas Purcell. "The Mediterranean and 'the New Thalassology.'" *American Historical Review* 111, no. 3 (June 2006): 722–40.

Horton, Mark, and John Middleton. *The Swahili: The Social Landscape of a Mercantile Society.* Oxford: Blackwell, 2000.

Hotten, J. C. *Abyssinia and Its People, or, Life in the Land of Prester John.* London: J. C. Hotten, 1868.

Hourani, Albert. *A History of the Arab Peoples.* Cambridge, Mass.: Belknap Press of Harvard University Press, 1991.

———. "Ottoman Reform and the Politics of the Notables." In *Beginnings of Modernization in the Middle East,* ed. W. R. Polk and R. L. Chambers, 41–68. Chicago: University of Chicago Press, 1968.

Hunter, Robert F. *Egypt under the Khedives, 1805–1879: From Household Government to Modern Bureaucracy.* Pittsburgh, Pa.: University of Pittsburgh Press, 1984.

Hunwick, John and R. S. O'Fahey, eds. *Arabic Literature of Africa.* Vol. 1: *The Writings of Eastern Sudanic Africa to c. 1900.* Comp. R. S. O'Fahey. Leiden, Neth.: Brill, 1994.

———. *Arabic Literature of Africa.* Vol. 3A: *The Writings of the Muslim Peoples of Northeastern Africa.* Comp. R. S. O'Fahey. Leiden, Neth.: Brill, 2003.

Iliffe, John. *The African Poor: A History.* Cambridge: Cambridge University Press, 1987.

Inalcik, Halil. "*Maḥkama* [The Ottoman Empire. i. The earlier centuries]." *Encyclopaedia of Islam.* 2nd ed. 6:3–5.

Insoll, Timothy. *The Archaeology of Islam.* Oxford: Blackwell, 1999.

Issel, Arturo. "La pesca delle perle nel mar Rosso." *L'Esplorazione commerciale* 12 (1894): 374–82.

———. *Viaggio nel Mar Rosso e tra i Bogos.* 1st ed. Milan: E. Treves, 1872.

———. *Viaggio nel Mar Rosso e tra i Bogos.* Milan: Fratelli Treves, 1885.

Jamal, Shawqī ʿAtāʾ Allāh al-. *Siyāsat miṣr fī al-baḥr al-aḥmar fī al-niṣf al-thānī min al-qarn al-tāsiʿ ʿashar.* Cairo: al-Hayʾa al-Miṣriyya al-ʿĀmmah lil-Kitāb, 1974.

Jedrej, M. C. "The Red Sea and the Eastern Sudan in the Early 19th Century." In *Africa and the Sea: Colloquium at the University of Aberdeen* (March 1984), Proceedings, ed. J. C. Stone, 104–17. Aberdeen: Aberdeen University African Studies Group, 1985.

Kapteijns, Lidwien. "Ethiopia and the Horn of Africa." In *The History of Islam in Africa,* ed. Nehemia Levtzion and Randall L. Pouwels, 227–50. Athens: Ohio University Press, 2000.

Karrar, Ali Salih. *The Sufi Brotherhoods in the Sudan.* Evanston: Northwestern University Press, 1992.

Khallaf, ʿAbd al-ʿAlīm Ibrāhīm. *Kushūf Miṣr al-Afriqiyā fī ʿahd al-Khidīwī Ismāʿīl, 1863–1879.* Cairo: al-Hayʾa al-Miṣriyya al-ʿĀmmah lil-Kitāb, 1999.

Khoury, Dina Rizk. "The Ottoman Centre versus Provincial Power-Holders: An Analysis of the Historiography." In *The Cambridge History of Turkey,* ed. Suraiya N. Faroqhi. Vol. 3: *The Later Ottoman Empire, 1603–1839,* 135–56. Cambridge: Cambridge University Press, 2006.

Killion, Tom. "The Eritrean Economy in Historical Perspective." *Eritrean Studies Review* 1, no. 1 (Spring 1996): 91–118.

———. *Historical Dictionary of Eritrea.* Lanham, Md.: Scarecrow Press, 1998.

Knysh, Alexander. "The Cult of Saints and Religious Reformism in Hadhramaut." In *Hadhrami Traders, Scholars, and Statesmen in the Indian Ocean, 1750s–1960s,* ed. Ulrike Freitag and William G. Clarence-Smith, 199–216. Leiden, Neth.: Brill, 1997.

Kolmodin, Johannes. *Traditions de Tsazzega et Hazzega.* Vol. 2: *Traduction française.* Uppsala, Sweden: K. W. Appelberg, 1915. Vol. 3: *Annales et Documents.* Uppsala, Sweden: K. W. Appelberg, 1914.

Koponen, Juhani. *People and Production in Late Precolonial Tanzania: History and Structures.* Helsinki: Finnish Society of Development Studies, 1988.

The Koran. Trans. N. J. Dawood. London: Penguin Books, 1956.

Kühn, Thomas. "Ordering Urban Space in Ottoman Yemen, 1872–1914." In *The Empire in the City: Arab Provincial Capitals in the Late Ottoman Empire,* ed. Jens Hanssen, Thomas Philipp, and Stefan Weber, 329–47. Würzburg, Germany: Ergon in Komission, 2002.

Kunz, F., and C. H. Stevenson. *The Book of the Pearl: The History, Art, Science, and Industry of the Queen of Gems.* New York: Century, 1908.

Kurdi, Hassan Nafi. *L'Erythrée, une identité retrouvée.* Paris: Karthala, 1994.

Labanca, Nicola. *In marcia verso Adua.* Turin: Einaudi, 1993.

"La pesca delle perle e della madreperla nel Mar Rosso." *Bolletino della Sezione Fiorentina della Società Africana d'Italia* 4 (1888): 179.

Lavergne, Marc. "Les relations yéméno- érythréennes à l'épreuve du conflit des Hanish." *Maghreb-Machrek,* no. 155 (January–March 1997): 68–86.

Le Chatelier, Alfred. *Les confréries musulmanes du Hedjaz*. Paris: E. Leroux, 1887.

Leeuwen, Richard van. *Waqfs and Urban Structures: The Case of Ottoman Damascus*. Leiden, Neth.: Brill, 1999.

Lefebvre, Théophile. *Voyage en Abyssinie exécuté pendant les années 1839, 1840, 1841, 1842, 1843*. 6 vols. Paris: A. Bertrand, 1845–48.

Le Guennec-Coppens, Françoise. "Changing Patterns of Hadhrami Migration and Social Integration in East Africa." In *Hadhrami Traders, Scholars, and Statesmen in the Indian Ocean, 1750s–1960s*, ed. Ulrike Freitag and William G. Clarence-Smith, 157–74. Leiden, Neth.: Brill, 1997.

———. "Social and Cultural Integration: a Case Study of the East African Hadhramis." *Africa* 59, no. 2 (1989): 185–95.

Lejean, Guillaume. *Théodore II: Le Nouvel empire d'Abyssinie et les intérêts français dans le sud de la mer Rouge*. Paris: Amyot, 1865.

———. *Voyage aux deux Nils*. Paris: Hachette, 1865.

———. *Voyage en Abyssinie*. Paris: Hachette, 1868.

Lenci, Marco. *Eritrea e Yemen, tensioni italo-turche nel mar Rosso, 1885–1911*. Milan: Franco Angeli, 1990.

———. "Gli Habab d'Eritrea e il governorato di Ferdinando Martini: dalla defezione alla sottomissione." *Africa* 54, no. 3 (1999): 349–78.

Levtzion, Nehemia, and Voll, John O. "Introduction." In *Eighteenth-Century Renewal and Reform in Islam*, ed. N. Levtzion and J. O. Voll, 3–20. Syracuse, N.Y.: Syracuse University Press, 1987.

Lewis, Ioan M. *Peoples of the Horn of Africa: Somali, Afar and Saho*. New ed. London: HAAN, 1994; first pub. 1955.

Lewis, Ioan M., Ahmed al-Safi, and Sayyid Hurreiz, eds. *Women's Medicine: The Zar-Bori Cult in Africa and Beyond*. Edinburgh: Edinburgh University Press, 1991.

Lewis, Michael W. and Kären E. Wigen. *The Myth of Continents: A Critique of Metageography*. Berkeley and Los Angeles: University of California Press, 1997.

Loimeier, Roman, and Rüdiger Seesemann, eds. *The Global Worlds of the Swahili: Interfaces of Islam, Identity and Space in 19th and 20th Century East Africa*. (Münster, Germany: LIT, 2006).

Longrigg, Stephen H. "Dahlak." *Encyclopaedia of Islam*. 2nd ed. 2:90–91.

———. *A Short History of Eritrea*. Oxford: Clarendon Press, 1945.

Luʾluʾ al-baḥr al-aḥmar. Massawa: Massawa City Administration, 2000.

Lunde, Paul, and Alexandra Porter, eds. *Trade and Travel in the Red Sea Region: Proceedings of Red Sea Project I held in the British Museum, October 2002*. Oxford: Archaeopress, 2004.

Lusini, Gianfrancesco. "Bāḍiʿ." In *Encyclopaedia Aethiopica*, ed. Siegbert Uhlig, 1:430–31. Wiesbaden, Germany: Harrassowitz, 2003.

G.M. "I traditori di Massaua." *Bolletino della Società Africana d'Italia* 9 (1890): 21–24.

Mah-Bey. *Massauah*. Naples: Tip. Edit. dell'Indicatore Generale del Commercio E. Pietrocola, 1885.

Malécot, Georges. *Les voyageurs français et les relations entre la France et l'Abyssinie de 1835 à 1870*. Paris: Société Française d'Histoire d'Outre Mer, 1972.

———. "Quelques aspects de la vie maritime en Mer Rouge dans la première moitié du XIXe siècle." In *Minorités et gens de mer en océan Indien, XIXe–XXe siècles*, ed. Jean-Louis Miège, 85–112. Etudes et documents, n. 12. Aix-en-Provence, France: Institut d'Histoire des Pays d'Outre-Mer, Université de Provence, 1979. Published also in *L'Afrique et l'Asie Modernes* 164 (1991): 22–43.

Maltzan, H. von. *Reisen nach Südarabien und geographische Forschungen im und über den südwestlichen Theil Arabiens.* Braunschweig: Friedrich Liebeg, 1873.
Mandal, Sumit K. "Natural Leaders of Native Muslims: Arab Ethnicity and Politics in Java under Dutch Rule." In *Hadhrami Traders, Scholars, and Statesmen in the Indian Ocean, 1750s–1960s*, ed. Ulrike Freitag and William G. Clarence-Smith, 185–98. Leiden, Neth.: Brill, 1997.
Mantegazza, Vico. *Da Massaua a Saati.* Milan: Treves, 1888.
"Maqāmāt al-awliyāʾ fī Iritrīyā wa-ḥawliyātihum al-sanawiyya." *Ṣawt al-Rābiṭah al-Islāmiyya al-Iritriyya*, no. 147 (2 December 1951): 2, 8, and no. 148 (9 December 1951): 3.
Marcus, Abraham. *The Middle East on the Eve of Modernity: Aleppo in the 18th Century.* New York: Columbia University Press, 1989.
Markovits, Claude. *The Global World of Indian Merchants, 1750–1947: Traders of Sind from Bukhara to Panama.* Cambridge: Cambridge University Press, 2000.
———. "Indian Merchant Networks outside India in the Nineteenth and Twentieth Centuries: A Preliminary Survey." *Modern Asian Studies* 33, no. 4 (1999): 883–911.
Marmon, Shaun. "Concubinage, Islamic." In *Dictionary of the Middle Ages*, ed. Joseph R. Strayer et al., 3:527–29. New York: Charles Scribner's Sons, 1983.
Marongiu-Buonaiuti, Cesare. *Politica e religioni nel colonialismo italiano (1882–1941).* Milan: Giuffrè, 1982.
Marston, T. E. *Britain's Imperial Role in the Red Sea Area (1800–1878).* Camden, Conn.: Shoe String Press, 1961.
Martin, B. G. "Arab Migrations to East Africa in Medieval Times." *International Journal of African Historical Studies* 5 (1974): 367–90.
———. "Migrations from the Hadramawt to East Africa and Indonesia, c. 1200 to 1900." *Research Bulletin* (Ibadan: University of Ibadan) 7, nos. 1–2 (1971): 1–21.
Martin, Richard C. *Islamic Studies: A History of Religions Approach.* Upper Saddle River, N.J.: Prentice Hall, 1996; 1st ed. 1982.
Martini, Ferdinando, ed. *Il diario eritreo.* 4 vols. Florence: Vallecchi, 1947.
———. *L'Eritrea Economica.* Novara-Rome: Istituto Geografico de Agostini, 1913.
———. *Nell'Affrica italiana.* Milan: Fratelli Treves, 1891.
Mashhūr, ʿAbd al-Raḥmān b. Muḥammad b. Ḥusayn al-. *Shams al-ẓahīra fī nasab ahl al-bayt min Banī ʿAlawī furūʿ Fāṭima al-Zahrāʾ wa Amīr al-Muʾminīn ʿAlī raḍī Allāh ʿanhu.* Jeddah, Saudi Arabia: ʿĀlam al-Maʿrifa, 1984.
Matteucci, Paolo. *In Abissinia.* Milan: Fratelli Treves, 1880.
Matthews, D. H. "The Red Sea Style." *Kush* 1 (1953): 60–87.
Mazrui, Ali A. "Towards Abolishing the Red Sea and Re-Africanizing the Arabian Peninsula." In *Africa and the Sea: Colloquium at the University of Aberdeen* (March 1984), Proceedings, ed. J. C. Stone, 98–103. Aberdeen: Aberdeen University African Studies Group, 1985.
McPherson, Kenneth. *The Indian Ocean: A History of People and the Sea.* Delhi: Oxford University Press, 1993.
———. "Port Cities as Nodal Points of Change: The Indian Ocean, 1890s–1920s." In *Modernity and Culture from the Mediterranean to the Indian Ocean, 1890–1920*, ed. L. Fawaz and C. A. Bayly, 75–95. New York: Columbia University Press, 2002.
Mellana, Vincenze. *L'Italia in Africa*: serie giuridico-amministrativa: v. 2, t.1. L'amministrazione della giustizia in Eritrea e in Somalia (1869–1936). Testo di Vincenzo Mellana. Rome: Instituto Poligrafico dello Stato, 1971.
Melli, B., *La Colonia Eritrea dalle sue origini al 1° marzo 1899.* Parma: Luigi Battei, 1899.
Mercier, Eric. *Aden: Un parcours interrompu.* Tours: CFEY -URBAMA, 1997.

Meriwether, Margaret. *The Kin Who Count: Family and Society in Ottoman Aleppo, 1770–1840*. Austin: University of Texas Press, 1999.

Mesghenna, Yemane. *Italian Colonialism: A Case Study of Eritrea, 1869–1934, Motive, Praxis and Result*. Lund, Sweden: University of Lund, 1988.

Middleton, John. *The World of the Swahili: An African Mercantile Civilization*. New Haven, Conn.: Yale University Press, 1992.

Miège, Jean-Louis. "Djeddah, port d'entrepôt au XIXe siècle." In *Les ports de l'océan indien, XIXe et XXe s*, ed. Jean-Louis Miège. Etudes et documents, no. 15. Aix-en-Provence, France: Institut d'Histoire des Pays d'Outre-Mer, Université de Provence, 1982.

———. "Le commerce transaharien au XIXe siècle: essai de quantification." *Revue de l'Occident Musulman et de la Méditerranée*, 1981–82, no. 32: 93–119.

Millward, G. R. "Oysters, Pearls and Pearling in Sudan Waters." *Sudan Notes and Records* 27 (1946): 203–12.

Miran, Jonathan. "Embärämi." In *Encyclopaedia Aethiopica*, ed. Siegbert Uhlig, 2:272. Wiesbaden, Germany: Harrassowitz, 2005.

———. "Grand mufti, érudit et nationaliste érythréen: note sur la vie et l'oeuvre de Cheikh Ibrâhîm al-Mukhtâr (1909–1969)." *Chroniques yéménites* 10 (2002): 35–47. Online at http://cy.revues.org/document126.html.

———. "A Historical Overview of Islam in Eritrea." *Die Welt des Islams* 45, no. 2 (2005): 177–215.

———. "Mālikism." In *Encyclopaedia Aethiopica*, ed. Siegbert Uhlig, 3:696–98. Wiesbaden, Germany: Harrassowitz, 2007.

———. "Muḥammad ᶜUthmān al-Mīrghanī." In *Encyclopaedia Aethiopica*, ed. Siegbert Uhlig, 3: 1060–61. Wiesbaden, Germany: Harrassowitz, 2007.

Mokhtar, M. H. "Islam in Somali History: Fact and Fiction." In *The Invention of Somalia*, ed. Ali Jimale Ahmed, 1–27. Lawrenceville, N.J.: Red Sea Press, 1995.

Molon, M. and A. Vianello. "Brava, città dimenticata." *Storia Urbana* 14, no. 53 (1990): 199–240.

Moretto, Mario. *Guida alla città di Massaua*. Asmara, Eritrea: Tipografia Coloniale M. Fioretti, 1939.

Morin, Didier. *Dictionnaire historique Afar (1288–1982)*. Paris: Karthala, 2004.

———. *Le texte légitime. Pratiques littéraires orales traditionnelles en Afrique du nord-est*. Paris: Peeters, 1999.

———. *Poésie traditionnelle des afars*. Paris: Peeters, 1997.

Munzinger, Werner. "Die Inselstadt Massua im Rothen Meer." *Das Ausland* 37 (1864): 1079–80.

———. "Die Schohos und die Beduan bei Massaua." *Zeitschrift für allgemeine Erdkunde* 6 (1859): 89–110.

———. "Les contrées limitrophes de l'Habesch." *Nouvelles Annales des Voyages* 4, 6th series (April 1858): 5–55.

———. "Narrative of a Journey through the Afar Country." *Journal of the Royal Geographical Society* 39 (1869): 188–232.

———. *Studi sull'Africa orientale*. Rome: Voghera Carlo, 1890. Translation of *Ostafrikanische Studien*, (Schaffhausen, 1864).

Nadel, S. F. *Races and Tribes of Eritrea*. Asmara, Eritrea: British Military Administration of Eritrea, 1944.

Naqar, Umar. "The Takarir of Gallabat." In *Proceedings of the Eighth International Conference of Ethiopian Studies, Addis Ababa University, 1984*, 2:67–71. Addis Ababa: Institute of Ethiopian Studies, 1988–89.

Natvig, Richard. "Oromos, Slaves, and Zar Spirits: A Contribution to the History of the Zar Cult." *International Journal of African Historical Studies* 20, no. 4 (1987): 669–89.

Nāwad, Muḥammad Saᶜīd. *al-ᶜUrūba w-al-islām bi-l qarn al-ifrīqī.* Asmara, 199-.

———. *Iritrīyā, ṭarīq al-hijrāt wa-l-diyānāt wa-madkhal al-islām ilā Afrīqiyā.* al-Kuwait: al-Hayʾah al-Khayriyya al-Islāmiyya al-ᶜAlamiyya, 2001.

———. *ᶜUmq al-ᶜalāqāt al-ᶜarabiyya al-iritriyya.* al-Kuwait: maṭbaᶜat al-Kuwayt, 2004.

Negash, Tekeste. *Italian Colonialism in Eritrea, 1882–1941: Policies, Praxis and Impact.* Uppsala, Sweden: Uppsala University, 1987.

Negri, Luigi. *Massaua e dintorni.* Valenza, Italy: Farina, 1887.

Nott, (?). "Report from Acting Commander Nott of the Indian Navy, on the Traffic in Slaves, etc. Carried on at Massowah." *Transactions of the Bombay Geographical Society* 2 (November 1838): 32–35.

Nurse, Derek, and Thomas Spear. *The Swahili: Reconstructing the History and Language of an African Society, 800–1500.* Philadelphia: University of Pennsylvania Press, 1985.

Ochsenwald, William. "The Commercial History of the Hijaz Vilayet, 1840–1908." In *Arabian Studies,* ed. R. B. Serjeant and R. L. Bidwell, 6: 57–76. London: Scorpion 1982.

———. *Religion, Society and the State in Arabia: The Hijaz under Ottoman Control, 1840–1908.* Columbus: Ohio State University Press, 1984.

Odorizzi, Dante. "Il commercio eritreo e il mercato etiopico." *Rivista coloniale* 1, no. 1 (1906): 91–106.

———. *Il Commissariato Regionale di Massaua al 1° gennaio 1910.* Asmara, Eritrea: Tip. Fioretti e Beltrami, 1911.

———. "La Dancalia Italiana del nord." *L'Esplorazione commerciale* 24 (1909): fasc.5, 135–46 fasc.6, 164–76; fasc. 7, 206–17; fasc. 8, 235–45.

———. *Note storiche sulla religione mussulmana e sulle divisioni dell'Islam con appunti speciali relativi all'Islam in Eritrea.* Asmara, Eritrea: Stabilimento Tipografico Coloniale. M. Fioretti, 1916.

———. "Studio storico sulla provincia Arabica dello Jemen e sulle sue relazioni etniche con l'Eritrea e con l'Etiopia." Extracted from *Atti del congresso coloniale in Asmara, settembre-ottobre 1905,* ed. Carlo Rossetti. Rome: Tip. Dell'Unione Cooperativa Editrice, 1906.

O'Fahey, R. S. *Enigmatic Saint: Ahmad Ibn Idris and the Idrisi Tradition.* Evanston, Ill.: Northwestern University Press, 1990.

———. "Sudanese (and Some Other) Sources for Eritrean History: A Bibliographical Note." *Sudanic Africa* 12 (2001): 131–42.

———. "Ṭarīḳa [in Northeastern and Eastern Africa]." *Encyclopaedia of Islam.* 2nd ed. 10:248–50.

O'Fahey, R. S. and B. Radtke. "Neo-Sufism Reconsidered." *Der Islam* 70, no. 1 (1993): 52–87.

Orhonlu, Cengiz. *Habesh Eyaleti.* Istanbul: Edebiyat Fakültesi Matbaasi, 1974.

———. "Turkish Archival Sources on Ethiopia." In *IV Congresse Internazionale di Studi Etiopici (Roma, 10–15 aprile 1972),* 455–62. Rome: Accademia Nazionale dei Lincei, 1974.

Osgood, J. B. F. *Notes of Travel or Recollections of Majunga, Zanzibar, Muscat, Aden, Mocha, and other Eastern Ports.* Salem, Mass.: G. Creamer, 1854.

Özbaran, Salih. *The Ottoman Response to European Expansion: Studies on Ottoman-Portuguese Relations in the Indian Ocean and Ottoman Administration in the Arab Lands during the Sixteenth Century.* Istanbul: Isis Press, 1994.

Palma, Silvana. "Fotografia di una colonia: l'Eritrea di Luigi Naretti (1885–1900)." *Quaderni Storici,* 37, 109, no. 1 (April 2002): 83–147.

———. *L'Africa nella collezione fotografica dell'IsIAO: Il fondo Eritrea-Etiopia.* Rome: IsIAO, 2005.
———. *L'Italia coloniale.* Rome: Editori Reuniti, 1999.
Pankhurst, Richard. "The Advent of the Maria Theresa Dollar in Ethiopia, Its Effect on Taxation and Wealth Accumulation, and Other Economic, Political and Cultural Implications." *Northeast African Studies* 1, no. 3 (1979–80): 19–48.
———. "Banyan." In *Encyclopaedia Aethiopica*, ed. Siegbert Uhlig, 1:467. Wiesbaden, Germany: Harrassowitz, 2003.
———. "The 'Banyan' or Indian Presence at Massawa, the Dahlak Islands and the Horn of Africa." *Journal of Ethiopian Studies* 12, no. 1 (January 1974): 185–212.
———. *Economic History of Ethiopia, 1800–1935.* Addis Ababa: Haile Sellassie I University Press, 1968.
———. "The Ethiopian Slave Trade in the Nineteenth and Early Twentieth Centuries: A Statistical Inquiry." *Journal of Semitic Studies* 9, no. 1 (1964): 220–28.
———. *History of Ethiopian Towns from the Middle Ages to the Early Nineteenth Century.* Wiesbaden, Germany: F. Steiner Verlag, 1982.
———. "The History of Ethiopia's Relations with India prior to the Nineteenth Century." In *IV Congresso Internazionale di Studi Etiopici: (Roma, 10–15 aprile 1972)*, ed. Enrico Cerulli, 1:205–312. Rome: Accademia Nazionale dei Lincei, 1974.
———. "Indian Trade with Ethiopia, the Gulf of Aden and the Horn of Africa in the XIXth and early XXth Century." *Cahiers d'Etudes Africaines* 14, no. 55 (1974): 453–97.
———. "Notes on the Demographic History of Ethiopian Towns and Villages." *Ethiopia Observer* 9, no. 1 (1965): 60–83.
———. "Some Notes on the Historical and Economic Geography of the Mesewa Area (1520–1885)." *Journal of Ethiopian Studies* 13, no. 1 (January 1975): 89–114.
———. "The Trade of Northern Ethiopia in the Nineteenth and Early Twentieth Centuries." *Journal of Ethiopian Studies* 2, no. 1 (January 1964): 49–159.
Paoli, Renato. "Le condizioni commerciali dell'Eritrea." In *L'Eritrea Economica,* ed. F. Martini, 159–224. Novara-Rome: Istituto Geografico de Agostini, 1913.
Parazzoli, A. "La pesca nel Mar Rosso." *L'Esplorazione commerciale* 13, no. 6 (June 1898): 177–90.
Parkyns, Mansfield. *Life in Abyssinia.* New York, 1856; reprint, London: Frank Cass, 1966.
Pascale, Alberto. *Massaua: usi e costumi de'suoi indigeni.* Naples: Iride, 1887.
Paul, Andrew. *A History of the Beja Tribes of the Sudan.* Cambridge: University Press, 1954.
Pauty, Edmond. *Les palais et les maisons d'époque musulmane au Caire* t. 62. Cairo: Institut Français d'Archéologie Orientale, 1932.
Pearson, Michael N. *The Indian Ocean.* London: Routledge, 2003.
———. "The Indian Ocean and the Red Sea." In *The History of Islam in Africa*, ed. Nehemia Levtzion and Randall L. Pouwels, 37–59. London: James Currey and Ohio University Press, 2000.
———. "Littoral Society: The Case for the Coast." *Great Circle* 7, no. 1 (April 1985): 1–8.
———. *Port Cities and Intruders: The Swahili Coast, India, and Portugal in the Early Modern Era.* Baltimore, Md.: Johns Hopkins University Press, 1998.
Peck, Edward. "A Swiss Pasha at Massawa: Werner Munzinger (1832–1875)." *Eritrean Studies Review* 3, no. 1 (1999): 127–38.
Pennazzi, Luigi. *Dal Po ai Due Nili (Massaua, Keren, Kassala).* Modena: Con Tipidella Società Tipografica, 1887.
———. *Dal Po ai Due Nili. (I) A Dorso di Camello.* Milan: Fratelli Treves, 1882.
———. "Massauah (Mar Rosso), il suo suolo, la sua popolazione, i suoi dintorni." *Nuova Antologia di scienze, lettere ed arti*, 2nd ser., 22 (1880): 322–30.

Penrad, Jean-Claude "Societies of the *Ressac*: The Mainland Meets the Ocean." In *Continuity and Autonomy in Swahili Communities*, ed. David Parkin, 41–48. London: Imprint, 1994.

Perini, Rufillo. *Di qua dal Mareb*. Florence: Tipografia Cooperativa, 1905.

Perkins, Kenneth, J. *Port Sudan: the Evolution of a Colonial City*. Boulder, Colo.: Westview Press, 1993.

Perret, Michel. "Commerce maritime et commerce caravanier de l'Erythrée au début du XXe siècle." In *Minorités et gens de mer en océan Indien, XIXe–XXe siècles*, ed. Jean-Louis Miège, 147–56. Etudes et documents, no. 12. Aix-en-Provence, France: Institut d'Histoire des Pays d'Outre-Mer, Université de Provence, 1979.

Pesce, Angelo. *Jiddah: Portrait of an Arabian City*. London: Falcon Press, 1976.

Peters, Rudolph. "Waḳf [in Classical Islamic Law]." *Encyclopaedia of Islam*. 2nd ed. 11: 59–63.

Plowden, Walter. *Travels in Abyssinia and the Galla Country with an Account of a Mission to Ras Ali in 1848*. London: Longmans, Green, 1868.

Podestà, Gian Luca. *Sviluppo industriale e colonialismo. Gli investimenti italiani in Africa orientale 1869–1897*. Milan: Giuffrè 1996.

———. *Il mito dell'impero. Economia, politica e lavoro nelle colonie italiane dell'Africa orientale 1898–1941*. Turin: Giappichelli 2004.

Pollera, Alberto. *Le popolazioni indigene dell'Eritrea*. Bologna: L. Cappelli, 1935.

Pool, David. *From Guerrillas to Government: The Eritrean People's Liberation Front*. London: James Currey; Athens: Ohio University Press, 2001.

Porro, Gian Pietro. "Notizie da Massaua." *Esplorazione commerciale* 4 (April 1886).

Pouwels, Randall. *Horn and Crescent: Cultural Change and Traditional Islam on the East African Coast, 800–1900*. Cambridge: Cambridge University Press, 1987.

———. "East Africa and the Indian Ocean to 1800." *International Journal of African Historical Studies* 35, nos. 2–3 (2002): 385–425.

Prados, Edward. "Indian Ocean Littoral Maritime Evolution: The Case of the Yemeni Huri and Sanbuq." *Mariners's Mirror* 83, no. 2 (May 1997): 185–98.

Prakash, Om. "The Indian Maritime Merchant, 1500–1800." *Journal of the Economic and Social History of the Orient* 47, no. 3 (2004): 435–57.

Puglisi, Giuseppe. *Chi é? dell'Eritrea*. Asmara, Eritrea: Agenzia Regina, 1952.

Pulver, Anne, and Arnaud Goujon. *A Preliminary Conservation and Development Scheme for Old Massawa*. UNESCO Technical Report. Paris: UNESCO, 1998.

Raka, Mikael Hassama. *Future Life and Occult Beings*. New York: Vantage Press, 1984.

Rassam, Hormuzd. *Narrative of the British Mission to Theodore, King of Abyssinia*. London: J. Murray, 1869.

Rasheed, Madawi al-, ed. *Transnational Connections and the Arab Gulf*. London: Routledge, 2005.

Raymond, André. "A Divided Sea: The Cairo Coffee Trade in the Red Sea Area during the Seventeenth and Eighteenth Centuries." In *Modernity and Culture from the Mediterranean to the Indian Ocean, 1890–1920*, ed. L. Fawaz and C. A. Bayly, 46–57. New York: Columbia University Press, 2002.

———. "Tunisiens et Maghrébins au Caire au XVIIIe siècle." *Cahiers de Tunisie* 26–27 (1959): 336–71.

———. "Deux familles de commerçants Fasi au Caire à la fin du XVIIe siècle." *Revue de l'Occident musulman et de la Mediterranée* 15–16 (1974): 269–73.

Reclus, Élisée. *The Earth and Its Inhabitants: Africa*. New York, 1892.

Reese, Scott. "*Ziyāra* [in the Horn of Africa]." *Encyclopaedia of Islam*. 2nd ed. 11:538–39.

Reid, Richard. "The Challenge of the Past: The Quest for Historical Legitimacy in Independent Eritrea." *History in Africa* 28 (2001): 239–72.

———. "War and Remembrance: Orality, Literacy and Conflict in the Horn." *Journal of African Cultural Studies* 18, no. 1 (2006): 89–103.

Religious Freedom in Ethiopia. Addis Ababa: Publications of Foreign Languages Press Dept., Ministry of Information, 1965.

Reviglio, Paolo. "Ricordi e riflessioni sui terremoti di Massaua." *Sestante* 1, no. 2 (July–December 1965): 87–91.

Righini, G. *La regione fra Massaua e Cassala.* Rome, 1885.

Roberti, Ferruccio. "Gli Habab." *L'Esplorazione commerciale* 1 (January 1889): 2–14.

Robinson, A. "The Tekruri Sheikhs of Gallabat." *Journal of the Royal African Society* 26 (1926): 47–54.

Robinson, David. *Paths of Accommodation: Muslim Societies and French Colonial Authorities in Senegal and Mauritania, 1880–1920.* Athens: Ohio University Press, 2000.

Rochet d'Hericourt, C. F. X. *Voyage sur la côte orientale de la Mer Rouge dans le pays d'Adel et le Royaume du Choa.* Paris: A. Bertrand, 1841.

Roded, Ruth. "The *Waqf* and the Social Elite of Aleppo in the Eighteenth and Nineteenth Centuries." *Turcica* 20 (1988): 71–91.

Rodén, Karl Gustav. *Le tribù dei Mensa. Storia, legge e costumi.* Stockholm: Evangeliska fosterlands-stiftelsens förlags-expedition, 1913.

Romandini, Massimo. "Personaggi musulmani nelle pagine di Ferdinando Martini." *Islam, storia e civiltà* 4, no. 1 (January–March 1985): 57–62.

———. "Politica musulmana in Eritrea durante il governorato Martini." *Islam, storia e civiltà* 3, no. 2 (April–June 1984): 127–31.

Rosenthal, Léonard. *The Pearl Hunter: An Autobiography.* New York: Henry Schuman, 1952.

Rouaud, Alain. "Boats." In *Encyclopaedia Aethiopica,* ed. Siegbert Uhlig, 1:599–600. Wiesbaden, Germany: Harrassowitz, 2003.

———. "L'émigration yéménite." In *L'Arabie du Sud, Histoire et Civilisation,* ed. Joseph Chelhod. Vol. 2: *La société yéménite de l'hégire aux idéologies modernes,* 227–50. Paris: Maisonneuve et Larose, 1984.

———. "Pour une histoire des Arabes de Djibouti, 1896–1977." *Cahiers d'Etudes Africaines* 146 (1997): 319–48.

Rubāṭābī, Aḥmad b. Idrīs b. Aḥmad al-. *Al-Ibāna al-nūriyya fī sha'n ṣāḥib al-ṭarīqa al-Khatmiyya,* ed. M. I. Abu Salim. Beirut: Dār al-Jīl, 1991.

Rubenson, Sven. *The Survival of Ethiopian Independence.* Addis Ababa: Kuraz Pub. Agency, 1991; 1st ed. 1976.

Rugh, Andrea. *Family in Contemporary Egypt.* Syracuse, N.Y.: Syracuse University Press, 1984.

Rüppell, Eduard. *Reise in Abyssinien,* 2 vols. Frankfurt am Main: Gedruckt auf Kosten des Verfassers und in Commission bei S. Schmerber, 1838–40.

Sabī, ʿUthmān Ṣāliḥ. *Ta'rīkh Iritrīyā.* Beirut: Sharikat al-Nahār lil-Khidāmāt al-Ṣaḥafiyya, 1974.

Saint-Yves, G. "A travers l'Erythrée italienne." *Bulletin de la Société de Géographie de Marseille* 23 (1899): 137–60.

Salt, Henry A. *Voyage to Abyssinia and Travels into the Interior of That Country.* London: Rivington, 1814.

Sapeto, Giuseppe. *Viaggio e missione cattolica fra i Mensa i Bogos e gli Habab con un cenno geografico storico dell'Abissinia.* Rome: Propaganda Fide, 1857.

Schacht, Joseph. *An Introduction to Islamic Law.* Oxford: Oxford University Press, 1964.

———. [Layish, Aharon.] "*Maḥkama* [The Arab lands and Israel. i. Egypt]." *Encyclopaedia of Islam.* 2nd ed. 6:22–25.

Schneider, Madeleine. *Stèles funéraires musulmanes des îles Dahlak (Mer Rouge.)* Cairo: Institut Français d'Archéologie Orientale, 1983.
Schroeter, Daniel. *Merchants of Essaouira: Urban Society and Imperialism in Southwestern Morocco, 1844–1886.* Cambridge: Cambridge University Press, 1988.
Schumpeter, Joseph A. *The Theory of Economic Development.* Cambridge, Mass.: Harvard University Press, 1961; 1st ed. 1934.
Serjeant, R. B. "The Hadhrami Network." In *Asian Merchants and Businessmen in the Indian Ocean and the China Sea,* ed. J. Aubin and D. Lombard, 145–53. Oxford: Oxford University Press, 2000; 1st ed. Paris 1988.
———. "Materials for South Arabian History: Notes on New MSS from Hadramawt." *Bulletin of the School of Oriental and African Studies* 13, no. 3 (1950): 281–307, 581–60.
Sikainga, Ahmad Alawad. *Slaves into Workers: Emancipation and Labor in Colonial Sudan.* Austin: University of Texas Press, 1996.
Simon, Gabriel. *L'Ethiopie, ses moeurs, ses traditions: Voyage en Abyssinie et chez les Gallas-Raias* Paris: Challamel Aîné, 1885.
Simpson, Edward, and Kai Kresse, eds. *Struggling with History: Islam and Cosmopolitanism in the Western Indian Ocean.* London: Hurst, 2007.
Smidt, Wolbert. "Habeš." In *Encyclopaedia Aethiopica,* ed. Siegbert Uhlig, 2:950–52. Wiesbaden, Germany: Harrassowitz, 2005.
———. "Massawa." In *Encyclopaedia Aethiopica,* ed. Siegbert Uhlig, 3:849–54. Wiesbaden, Germany: Harrassowitz, 2007.
———. "Massawa Governorate." In *Encyclopaedia Aethiopica,* ed. Siegbert Uhlig, 3:855–57. Wiesbaden, Germany: Harrassowitz, 2007.
Spaulding, Jay. "The Evolution of the Islamic Judiciary in Sinnar." *International Journal of African Historical Studies* 10, no. 3 (1977): 408–26.
———. *The Heroic Age in Sinnar.* East Lansing: African Studies Center, Michigan State University, 1985.
———. "Suakin: A Port City of the Early Modern Sudan." In *Secondary Cities and Urban Networking in the Indian Ocean Realm, c. 1400–1800,* ed. Kenneth R. Hall, 39–53. Lanham, Md.: Lexington Books, 2008.
Spear, Thomas. "Early Swahili History Reconsidered." *International Journal of African Historical Studies* 33, no. 2 (2000): 257–90.
Stanga, Idelfonso. *Una gita in Eritrea.* Milan: L. F. Cogliati, 1913.
Starkey, Janet, ed. *People of the Red Sea: Proceedings of Red Sea Project II held in the British Museum, October 2004.* Oxford: Archaeopress, 2005.
Starkey, Janet, Paul Starkey, and Tony Wilkinson, eds. *Natural Resources and Cultural Connections of the Red Sea: Proceedings of Red Sea Project III held in the British Museum, October 2006.* Oxford: Archaeopress, 2007.
Stefanelli, P. "Madreperla." *Bolletino della Sezione Fiorentina della Società Africana d'Italia* 5 (1889): 158–59.
Stoianovich, T. *French Historical Method. The Annales Paradigm.* Ithaca, N.Y.: Cornell University Press, 1976.
Stone, J. C., ed. *Africa and the Sea: Colloquium at the University of Aberdeen* (March 1984), Proceedings. Aberdeen: Aberdeen University African Studies Group, 1985.
Swartz, Marc, J. "Religious Courts, Community, and Ethnicity among the Swahili of Mombasa: An Historical Study of Social Boundaries." *Africa* 49, no. 1 (1979): 29–41.
Taddia, Irma. "Constructing Colonial Power and Political Collaboration in Italian Eritrea." In *Personality and Political Culture in Modern Africa,* ed. M. Page et al., 23–36. Boston: African Studies Center, Boston University, 1998.
———. "Ethiopian and African Studies." In *Wälättä Yohanna: Ethiopian Studies in Hon-*

our of Joanna Mantel-Niecko . . ., ed. Witold Witakowski and Laura Likowska. *Rocznik Orientalistyczny* 59, no. 1 (2006): 255–64.

———. *L'Eritrea colonia 1890–1952: Paesaggi, strutture, uomini del colonialismo.* Milan: Franco Angeli, 1986.

———. "Modern Ethiopia and Colonial Eritrea." *Aethiopica* 5 (2002): 125–38

Tafla, Bairu. "Interdependence through Independence: The Challenges of Eritrean Historiography." In *New Trends in Ethiopian Studies,* ed. Harold Marcus, 497–514. Lawrenceville, N. J. : Red Sea Press, 1994.

Tagliabue, Enrico. *Dieci anni a Massaua: Considerazioni politico-coloniali.* Milan: Tip. P. B. Bellini, 1888.

———. "Massaua e i suoi abitanti." *L'Esploratore* 4 (Milan, 1880): 55–58.

Tagliacozzo, Eric. *Secret Trades, Porous Borders: Smuggling and States along a Southeast Asian Frontier, 1865–1915.* New Haven, Conn.: Yale University Press, 2005.

Talhami, Ghada Hashim. "Massawa under Khedive Ismail." In *Proceedings of the Fifth International Conference of Ethiopian Studies,* ed. R. L. Hess, 481–94. Chicago: Office of Publication Services, University of Illinois at Chicago Circle, 1979.

———. *Suakin and Massawa under Egyptian Rule, 1865–1885.* Washington D.C.: University Press of America, 1979.

Tedeschi, Salvatore. "La questione di Bāḍiʿ." *Rivista degli Studi Orientali* 58 (1987): 179–99.

———. "Note storiche sulle isole Dahlac." In *Proceedings of the International Conference of Ethiopian Studies,* 1:49–74. Addis Ababa: Institute of Ethiopian Studies, 1969.

Tibbetts, G. R. "Arab Navigation in the Red Sea." *Geographical Journal* 127 (1961): 322–34.

Toledano, Ehud. *As If Silent and Absent: Bonds of Enslavement in the Islamic Middle East.* New Haven, Conn.: Yale University Press, 2007.

———. "The Emergence of Ottoman-Local Elites (1700–1900): A Framework for Research." In *Middle Eastern Politics and Ideas: A History from Within,* ed. M. Ma'oz and I. Pappe, 145–62. London: I. B. Tauris, 1997.

———. *The Ottoman Slave Trade and Its Suppression, 1840–1890.* Princeton, N.J.: Princeton University Press,1982.

Topan, Farouk. "From Coastal to Global: The Erosion of the Swahili 'Paradox.'" In *The Global Worlds of the Swahili: Interfaces of Islam, Identity and Space in 19th and 20th-Century East Africa,* ed. Roman Loimeier and Rüdiger Seesemann, 55–66. Münster: LIT, 2006.

Toussaint, A. *History of the Indian Ocean.* Chicago: University of Chicago Press, 1966.

Traversi, Leopoldo. "Usi e costumi africani in Massaua." In *Archivio per lo studio delle tradizioni popolari,* 5:365–82. Palermo, 1889.

Trevaskis, G. K. N. *Eritrea, a Colony in Transition.* Oxford: Oxford University Press, 1960.

Trimingham, John Spencer. *Islam in Ethiopia.* London: F. Cass, 1965; 1st ed. 1952.

———. *Islam in the Sudan.* London: F. Cass, 1965; 1st ed. 1949.

Triulzi, Alessandro. Review of G. Talhami, *Suakin and Massawa under Egyptian rule, 1865–1885* (Washington D.C., 1979). *International Journal of African Historical Studies* 14, no. 4 (1981): 764–66.

———. *Salt, Gold and Legitimacy: Prelude to the History of a No-Man's Land Bela Shangul, Wallagga, Ethiopia (ca. 1800–1898).* Naples: Istituto Universitario Orientale, 1981.

Tron, A., and J. Jwarson. *Notizie storiche e varie sulla missione evangelica svedese in Eritrea, 1866–1916.* Asmara, Eritrea: Missione evangelica svedese, 1918.

Tronvoll, Kjetil. "Borders of Violence—Boundaries of Identity: Demarcating the Eritrean Nation-State." *Ethnic and Racial Studies* 22, no. 6 (November 1999): 1037–60.

Tuchscherer, Michel. "Coffee in the Red Sea Area from the Sixteenth to the Nineteenth Century." In *The Global Coffee Economy in Africa, Asia, and Latin America, 1500–1989,* ed. William Gervase Clarence-Smith and Steven Topik, 50–66. New York: Cambridge University Press, 2003.

Ullendorff, Edward. *The Ethiopians.* 2nd ed. London: Oxford University Press, 1965.

Um, Nancy. "Spatial Negotiations in a Commercial City—the Red Sea Port of Mocha, Yemen, during the First Half of the Eighteenth Century." *Journal of the Society of Architectural Historians* 62, no. 2 (June 2003): 178–93.

Valentia, George. *Voyages and Travels to India, Ceylon, the Red Sea, Abyssinia and Egypt in the Years 1802, 1803, 1804, 1805 and 1806.* 3 vols. London: Printed for W. Miller, 1809.

Vianello, Alessandra, and Mohammed M. Kassim and Lidwien Kapteijns, eds. *Servants of the Sharia: The Civil Register of the Qadis' Court of Brava, 1893–1900.* 2 vols. Leiden, Neth.: Brill, 2006.

Vigoni, Pippo. *Abissinia, giornale di un viaggio.* Milan: U. Hoepli, 1881.

———. "Massaua e il nord dell'Abissinia." *Esplorazione commerciale* 3 (suppl. to January 1888 issue): 1–18.

Vikør, Knut S. *Between God and the Sultan: A History of Islamic Law.* New York: Oxford University Press, 2005.

———. "Sufi Brotherhoods in Africa." In *The History of Islam in Africa,* ed. Nehemia Levtzion and Randall L. Pouwels, 441–76. Athens: Ohio University Press, 2000.

Villiers, Alan. "Some Aspects of the Arab Dhow Trade." *Middle East Journal* 2, no. 4 (October 1948): 399–416.

Voll, John O. *Islam: Continuity and Change in the Modern World.* Boulder, Colo.: Westview Press, 1982.

Volterra, Alessandro. "Amministrazione e giustizia alle origini della colonia Eritrea, 1882–1886." *Clio* 31, no. 2 (1995): 199–222.

———. "Verso la colonia Eritrea: la legislazione e l'amministrazione (1887–1889)." *Storia Contemporanea* 26, no. 5 (October 1995): 817–50.

Walz, Terence. "Family Archives in Egypt: New Light on Nineteenth-Century Provincial Trade." In *L'Egypte au XIXe siècle,* ed. Robert Mantran, 15–33. Paris: Editions du CNRS, 1982.

———. *Trade between Egypt and the Bilad as-Sudān 1700–1820.* Cairo: Institut Français d'Archéologie Orientale du Caire, 1978.

Warburg, Gabriel. *Historical Discord in the Nile Valley.* Evanston, Ill.: Northwestern University Press, 1992.

Weber, Max. *The City.* New York: Collier Books, 1958.

Wehr, Hans. *Arabic-English Dictionary.* Ed. J. Milton Cowan. 3rd ed. Ithaca, N.Y.: Spoken Language Services, 1976.

Wigen, Kären. "AHR Forum: Oceans of History." *American Historical Review* 111, no. 3 (June 2006): 717–21.

Wink, André. *Al-Hind: The Making of the Indo-Islamic World.* Leiden, Neth.: Brill, 1991.

Woldemikael, Tekle M. "The Cultural Construction of Eritrean Nationalist Movements." In *The Rising Tide of Cultural Pluralism: The Nation-State at Bay?* ed. Crawford Young, 179–99. Madison: University of Wisconsin Press, 1993.

Wylde, Augustus B. *'83 to '87 in the Soudan.* London: Remington, 1888.

Yamba, C. Bawa. *Permanent Pilgrims: The Role of Pilgrimage in the Lives of West African Muslims in Sudan.* Edinburgh: Edinburgh University Press, 1995.

[Abba] Yeshaq Gebre Iyasus. *Gemagem Baher Ertra: kab Seba Punt kela' le'ulan Hirgigu.* Asmara, Eritrea: Hidri, 1998.

Ylvisaker, Marguerite. *Lamu in the Nineteenth Century: Land, Trade and Politics.* Boston: African Studies Center, Boston University, 1979.

Young, William C., "From Many, One: The Social Construction of the Rashayda Tribe in Eastern Sudan." *Northeast African Studies* 4, no. 1, new series (1997): 71–108.

———. "Rašayda." In *Encyclopaedia Aethiopica*, ed. Siegbert Uhlig, vol. 4. Wiesbaden, Germany: Harrassowitz, forthcoming.

Zaborski, Andrzej. "Some Eritrean Place Names in Arabic Medieval Sources." *Folia Orientalia* 12 (1970): 327–37.

Zaccaria, Massimo. "Early Italian Approaches to Economic Resources in the Red Sea Region." *Eritrean Studies Review* 5, no. 1 (2007): 113–55.

———. "Sawakin nel ricordo degli italiani residenti (1880–1905)." *Storia Urbana* 20, no. 74 (1996): 5–21.

Zeevi, Dror. "The Use of Ottoman Shari'a Court Records as a Source for Middle Eastern Social History: A Reappraisal." *Islamic Law and Society* 5, no. 1 (1998): 35–56.

Index

Italicized page numbers indicate illustrations.

Oman, 136
orientalism, 1, 12, 201, 269
Oromo language, speakers of, 31, 121, 125, 153
Osgood, J.B.F., 145
Ostafrikanische Studien (Munzinger), 24
Ottoman Empire, 2, 3, 222, 228, 295n119; administrative reform, 40; Arab traders and, 71; architecture of port cities, 279; decentralized rule of, 18, 35–36, 38–42, 47, 63, 172, 275; governor of Massawa, 59, 60–61; Ḥanafī school and, 56, 122, 169, 172, 195, 201; Indian merchants and, 141; Islam and, 169, 171–72; Italian rivalry with, 270; judicial structure, 201; Massawa on periphery of, 12, 14, 34; Massawa's elite and, 230; militias under, 292n41; modernization under, 151; *nāʾibs* and, 38–42, 48; "Ottoman" identity, 6; port towns under control of, 60; Portuguese struggle with, 38; regional networks and, 10; renewed centralization, 56; slave trade and, 83, 92; soldiers and officials of, 20, 125; *waqf* institution in, 245, 246; weakened by European powers, 172
Özdemir Pasha, 33, 38

Pakistan, 22, 143
Palestine, 240, 251
Pankhurst, Richard, 137, 139–40
Panorama of Massawa (photo), 10
Parazzoli, Ambrogio, 106, 107
Paris, city of, 57, 100
Parkyns, Mansfield, 98, 99
Parsis, 71
Pascale, Alberto, 159, 224
pastoralists, 30, 31, 112; caravan trade and, 66, 88, 162; clan organization of, 250; Egyptian agricultural policy and, 95; family names of, 251; Islam adopted by, 54; kinship structure, 219; migration of, 109, 215; *nāʾibs* and, 42, 43, 47, 86; in production and exchange networks, 93–97; spread of Islam and, 173–74; urbanization of, 158
patrilineages, 227, 228, 273
patronage (patron-client) relations, 42–43, 114, 161–65, 197, 242, 246; alms-giving and, 265; marriage alliances and, 257; *nāʾibs* and, 88; real estate ownership and, 149
patronymic names, 120
pearling economy, 5, 11, 99–101, 133; "Arabs of Massawa" and, 240; colonial intervention and pearlers' resistance, 106–110, 277; divers and merchants, 101–106, *103, 109;* in Italian colonial period, 66; steamship navigation and, 70. *See also* mother-of-pearl
Pennazzi, Luigi, 24, 107, 193
Persian Gulf, 9, 11, 104, 105
Pescherie Italiane d'Africa Orientale (Italian Fisheries of East Africa), 110
Piazza degli Incendi (Square of the Fires), 147–48, 150
piracy, 110
Plowden, Walter, 1, 42, 94; on caravan trade, 80–81; on Muslim lowlanders, 180; on *nāʾibs'* sovereignty, 60; on nomadic tribes, 158
Porro, Gian Pietro, 208
Porte, Ottoman, 4, 57, 58, 166
porters, 5, 111, 151, 152, 227; water porters, 155, *157;* Yemeni, *132*
Portugal, 3, 38
Pouwels, Randall, 188
property, distribution of, 254
prostitutes, 154, 155

al-Qābūlī, ʿAbd al-Nabī, 128
Qābūlī family, 128
Qādiriyya order, 56, 172–73, 174, 187, 192, 316n21; *dhikr* performances, 210; founder, 189; Islamic revival and, 54
qāḍīs (judges), 56, 122, 124, 134, 171, 237; family backgrounds, 238; Islamic *(sharīʿa)* court and, 200–207, *206*
Qashmīr, Aḥmad, 247
Qashmīr, Mūsā Aḥmad, 249
al-Qashmīrī, Aḥmad Hindī b. Ṣādiq, 248
Qūlāy family, 254
Qunfudha, port of, 21
Qunnu, Nāʾib Mūsā b. ʿUmar, 39–40
Qurʾān, 45, 103, 213, 214; on alms-giving, 248; inscriptions on door lintels, 2, 197–200, *198;* on Muslim community, 188, 326n161; popular Islam of nomads

JONATHAN MIRAN is Assistant Professor of Islamic Civilization in the Department of Liberal Studies at Western Washington University.